KU-133-376

Contents

Peugeot 205 GTI

Peugeot 205 Van

Peugeot 205 Owners Workshop Manual

A K Legg T Eng MIMI

Models covered
All Peugeot 205 models, including GTI, Cabriolet,
Automatic & special/limited editions
954 cc, 1124 cc, 1360 cc, 1580 cc & 1905 cc petrol
engines

Covers mechanical features of Vans
Does not cover Diesel or T16 Turbo models

(932-5P4)

ABCDE
FGHIJ
KLI

THE
BOOK

Haynes Publishing Group
Sparkford Nr Yeovil
Somerset BA22 7JJ England

Haynes Publications, Inc
861 Lawrence Drive
Newbury Park
California 91320 USA

Acknowledgements

Thanks are due to the Champion Sparking Plug Company Limited who supplied the illustrations showing the spark plug conditions, and to Duckhams Oils, who supplied lubrication data. Certain other illustrations are the copyright of Peugeot Talbot Motor Company Limited, and are used with their permission. Thanks are also due to Sykes-Pickavant who supplied some of the workshop tools, and all the staff at Sparkford who assisted in the production of this Manual.

A book in the **Haynes Owners Workshop Manual Series**

Printed by J. H. Haynes & Co. Ltd, Sparkford, Nr Yeovil, Somerset BA22 7JJ, England

ISBN 1 85010 524 3

British Library Cataloguing in Publication Data
Legg, A. K. (Andrew K.). *1942-*
    Peugeot 205 owners workshop manual.
    1. Cars. Maintenance & repair – Amateurs' manuals
    I. Title   II. Series
    629.28'722
    ISBN 1-85010-524-3

About this manual

Its aim

The aim of this manual is to help you get the best value from your vehicle. It can do so in several ways. It can help you decide what work must be done (even should you choose to get it done by a garage), provide information on routine maintenance and servicing, and give a logical course of action and diagnosis when random faults occur. However, it is hoped that you will use the manual by tackling the work yourself. On simpler jobs it may even be quicker than booking the car into a garage and going there twice, to leave and collect it. Perhaps most important, a lot of money can be saved by avoiding the costs a garage must charge to cover its labour and overheads.

The manual has drawings and descriptions to show the function of the various components so that their layout can be understood. Then the tasks are described and photographed in a step-by-step sequence so that even a novice can do the work.

Its arrangement

The manual is divided into thirteen Chapters, each covering a logical sub-division of the vehicle. The Chapters are each divided into Sections, numbered with single figures, eg 5; and the Sections into paragraphs (or sub-sections), with decimal numbers following on from the Section they are in, eg 5.1, 5.2, 5.3 etc.

It is freely illustrated, especially in those parts where there is a detailed sequence of operations to be carried out. There are two forms of illustration: figures and photographs. The figures are numbered in sequence with decimal numbers, according to their position in the Chapter – eg Fig. 6.4 is the fourth drawing/illustration in Chapter 6. Photographs carry the same number (either individually or in related groups) as the Section or sub-section to which they relate.

There is an alphabetical index at the back of the manual as well as a contents list at the front. Each Chapter is also preceded by its own individual contents list.

References to the 'left' or 'right' of the vehicle are in the sense of a person in the driver's seat facing forwards.

Unless otherwise stated, nuts and bolts are removed by turning anti-clockwise, and tightened by turning clockwise.

Vehicle manufacturers continually make changes to specifications and recommendations, and these, when notified, are incorporated into our manuals at the earliest opportunity.

Whilst every care is taken to ensure that the information in this manual is correct, no liability can be accepted by the authors or publishers for loss, damage or injury caused by any errors in, or omissions from, the information given.

Introduction to the Peugeot 205

The Peugeot 205 was introduced in the UK in September 1983 as a five-door Hatchback with a transversely-mounted engine and transmission assembly driving the front wheels. The suspension is of front coil springs and rear transverse torsion bars.

Three engine sizes were originally available, featuring a chain driven overhead camshaft design mounted directly over the transmission. The GTI was introduced in the Spring of 1984 and was fitted with a belt-driven overhead camshaft engine with a side-mounted transmission. The GTI engine is equipped with an electronically-controlled fuel injection system.

In October 1984 three-door versions became available, with an X series designation, in addition to the three-door GTI. Van versions were introduced in June 1985, together with the limited edition Lacoste, based on the GT version. In September 1985 the XT was introduced, being a three-door version of the GT, and at the same time the 954 cc XL three-door was introduced, having a higher specification than the XE. The 1580 cc Automatic was introduced in April 1986 at the same time as the Cabriolet CTI. The XS replaced the XT in July 1986, at which time the limited edition Junior, based on the XE, became available. The 1.9 GTI was introduced in August 1986, and at the same time dim-dip headlights and rear seat belts were fitted as standard. In December 1987 the new TU engines and MA gearboxes were fitted to all except fuel injection, diesel and automatic models.

General dimensions, weights and capacities

Dimensions

Overall length	3705 mm (145.98 in)
Overall width:	
Basic, GL, GE and Van	1562 mm (61.54 in)
SR, GR, GT, XE, XL, XR, XT, XS, GTI, Lacoste, Junior and Automatic	1572 mm (61.93 in)
CTI	1589 mm (62.6 in)
Overall height:	
Basic, GL, GE, XE, XL, XR Junior and Van	1376 mm (54.21 in)
GR (1124 cc engine)	1374 mm (54.14 in)
SR, GR (1360 cc engine)	1373 mm (54.10 in)
GT, XT, XS, Lacoste and Automatic	1372 mm (54.06 in)
GTI	1355 mm (53.39 in)
CTI	1381 mm (54.40 in)
Wheelbase	2420 mm (95.35 in)

Weights

Basic, GE, XE, XL and Junior (XV8 engine models)	740 kg (1632 lb)
GL and XL (XW7 engine models)	745 kg (1643 lb)
GR and XR (XW7 engine models)	780 kg (1720 lb)
GR and XR (XY7 engine models)	785 kg (1731 lb)
GT, XT, XS and Lacoste	810 kg (1786 lb)
GTI and Automatic	850 kg (1874 lb)
CTI	935 kg (2062 lb)
Van	746 kg (1645 lb)
Maximum towing weight (braked trailer):	
XV8 and XW7 engines	800 kg (1764 lb)
All other engines	900 kg (1984 lb)
Maximum roof rack load	50 kg (110 lb)

Capacities

Engine/transmission oil:	
954 and 1124 cc engines	4.5 litres (8.0 pints)
1360 cc engines	5.0 litres (8.8 pints)
Engine oil:	
TU engines (with filter)	3.5 litres (6.2 pints)
1580 cc engine	5.0 litres (8.8 pints)
Transmission:	
BE 1/5 and MA	2.0 litres (3.5 pints)
ZF 4 HP14:	
From dry	6.2 litres (10.9 pints)
Drain and refill	2.4 litres (4.25 pints)
Cooling system:	
XV8 and XW7 engines	5.8 litres (10.2 pints)
XY7 and XY8 engines	6.0 litres (10.6 pints)
XU5J and XU5JA engines	6.6 litres (11.6 pints)
XU51C engine	6.7 litres (11.8 pints)
TU9 and TU3 engines	5.8 litres (10.2 pints)
TU1 engine	7.0 litres (12.3 pints)
Fuel tank	50.0 litres (11.0 gallons)

Jacking and towing

Jacking

The jack supplied with the car is designed for use only when changing a wheel. The jack engages in one of the two holes provided below each sill on either side of the car.

If you are going to carry out work under the car it is preferable to position the car over an inspection pit. If this is not available use a workshop trolley jack or substantial screw or bottle type hydraulic jack. *Always supplement a jack with axle stands.* The sill jacking points or their adjacent re-inforced areas should be used as jacking points for raising the car. A beam may be placed under the front subframe and the front end jacked up under that. The side-members of the front subframe should be used as axle stand support points. The rear side-members may be used in a similar way.

Towing and being towed

Front and rear anchorage points are provided for securing the car during transportation on a car transporter, boat, train and so on. These points can also be used for towing the car (all wheels on the ground) or for towing another in an emergency (photos). For permanent towing requirements a tow-bar is necessary, properly attached to the vehicle.

Do not tow BH type gearbox models with the front wheels on the ground for long distances, as the engine lubrication system also supplies pressure-fed oil to the gears and differential bearings. Unnecessary wear may occur if the car is towed with the engine stopped.

Similarly, automatic transmission models should not be towed with the front wheels on the ground for more than 30 miles, or at speeds over 30 mph. See Chapter 13, Section 12.

Front towing eye

Front jacking point

Position front part of jack (1) directly under the jacking point (2)

Rear towing eye

Buying spare parts
and vehicle identification numbers

Buying spare parts

Spare parts are available from many sources. Peugeot have many dealers throughout the UK, and other dealers, accessory stores and motor factors will also stock some spare parts suitable for Peugeot cars.

Our advice regarding spare part sources is as follows:

Officially appointed vehicle main dealers – This is the best source for parts which are peculiar to your vehicle and are otherwise not generally available (eg, complete cylinder heads, internal transmission components, badges, interior trim etc). It is also the only place you should buy parts if your vehicle is still under warranty. To be sure of obtaining the correct parts it will always be necessary to give the storeman your vehicle's engine and chassis number, and if possible, to take the 'old' part along for positive identification. Remember that many parts are available on a factory exchange scheme – any parts returned should always be clean. It obviously makes good sense to go straight to the specialists on your vehicle for this type of part, for they are best equipped to supply you.

Other dealers and auto accessory stores – These are often very good places to buy materials and components needed for the maintenance of your vehicle (eg, oil filters, spark plugs, bulbs, drivebelts, oils and greases, touch-up paint, filler paste etc.) They also sell general accessories, usually have the convenient opening hours, charge lower prices and can often be found not far from home.

Motor factors – Good factors will stock all the more important components which wear out relatively quickly (eg, clutch components, pistons, valves, exhaust systems, brake cylinders/pipes/hoses/seals/shoes and pads etc). Motor factors will often provide new or reconditioned components on a part exchange basis – this can save a considerable amount of money.

Vehicle identification numbers

Modifications are a continuing and unpublicised process in vehicle manufacture. Spare parts manuals and lists are compiled on a numerical basis, the individual vehicle numbers being essential to identify correctly the component required.

The *vehicle identification plate* is located on the right-hand front wing valance in the engine compartment (photo).

Vehicle identification plate (1) and body serial number (2)

The *body serial number* is stamped on the scuttle crossmember above the vehicle identification plate.

The *engine number* is riveted on the cylinder block at the flywheel housing flange on non-XU engine models or on the left-hand side of the cylinder block on XU engine models.

The *body colour reference plate* is located on the left-hand end of the radiator grille crossmember.

General repair procedures

Whenever servicing, repair or overhaul work is carried out on the car or its components, it is necessary to observe the following procedures and instructions. This will assist in carrying out the operation efficiently and to a professional standard of workmanship.

Joint mating faces and gaskets

Where a gasket is used between the mating faces of two components, ensure that it is renewed on reassembly, and fit it dry unless otherwise stated in the repair procedure. Make sure that the mating faces are clean and dry with all traces of old gasket removed. When cleaning a joint face, use a tool which is not likely to score or damage the face, and remove any burrs or nicks with an oilstone or fine file.

Make sure that tapped holes are cleaned with a pipe cleaner, and keep them free of jointing compound if this is being used unless specifically instructed otherwise.

Ensure that all orifices, channels or pipes are clear and blow through them, preferably using compressed air.

Oil seals

Whenever an oil seal is removed from its working location, either individually or as part of an assembly, it should be renewed.

The very fine sealing lip of the seal is easily damaged and will not seal if the surface it contacts is not completely clean and free from scratches, nicks or grooves. If the original sealing surface of the component cannot be restored, the component should be renewed.

Protect the lips of the seal from any surface which may damage them in the course of fitting. Use tape or a conical sleeve where possible. Lubricate the seal lips with oil before fitting and, on dual lipped seals, fill the space between the lips with grease.

Unless otherwise stated, oil seals must be fitted with their sealing lips toward the lubricant to be sealed.

Use a tubular drift or block of wood of the appropriate size to install the seal and, if the seal housing is shouldered, drive the seal down to the shoulder. If the seal housing is unshouldered, the seal should be fitted with its face flush with the housing top face.

Screw threads and fastenings

Always ensure that a blind tapped hole is completely free from oil, grease, water or other fluid before installing the bolt or stud. Failure to do this could cause the housing to crack due to the hydraulic action of the bolt or stud as it is screwed in.

When tightening a castellated nut to accept a split pin, tighten the nut to the specified torque, where applicable, and then tighten further to the next split pin hole. Never slacken the nut to align a split pin hole unless stated in the repair procedure.

When checking or retightening a nut or bolt to a specified torque setting, slacken the nut or bolt by a quarter of a turn, and then retighten to the specified setting.

Locknuts, locktabs and washers

Any fastening which will rotate against a component or housing in the course of tightening should always have a washer between it and the relevant component or housing.

Spring or split washers should always be renewed when they are used to lock a critical component such as a big-end bearing retaining nut or bolt.

Locktabs which are folded over to retain a nut or bolt should always be renewed.

Self-locking nuts can be reused in non-critical areas, providing resistance can be felt when the locking portion passes over the bolt or stud thread.

Split pins must always be replaced with new ones of the correct size for the hole.

Special tools

Some repair procedures in this manual entail the use of special tools such as a press, two or three-legged pullers, spring compressors etc. Wherever possible, suitable readily available alternatives to the manufacturer's special tools are described, and are shown in use. In some instances, where no alternative is possible, it has been necessary to resort to the use of a manufacturer's tool and this has been done for reasons of safety as well as the efficient completion of the repair operation. Unless you are highly skilled and have a thorough understanding of the procedure described, never attempt to bypass the use of any special tool when the procedure described specifies its use. Not only is there a very great risk of personal injury, but expensive damage could be caused to the components involved.

Tools and working facilities

Introduction

A selection of good tools is a fundamental requirement for anyone contemplating the maintenance and repair of a motor vehicle. For the owner who does not possess any, their purchase will prove a considerable expense, offsetting some of the savings made by doing-it-yourself. However, provided that the tools purchased are of good quality, they will last for many years and prove an extremely worthwhile investment.

To help the average owner to decide which tools are needed to carry out the various tasks detailed in this manual, we have compiled three lists of tools under the following headings: *Maintenance and minor repair, Repair and overhaul*, and *Special*. The newcomer to practical mechanics should start off with the *Maintenance and minor repair* tool kit and confine himself to the simpler jobs around the vehicle. Then, as his confidence and experience grow, he can undertake more difficult tasks, buying extra tools as, and when, they are needed. In this way, a *Maintenance and minor repair* tool kit can be built-up into a *Repair and overhaul* tool kit over a considerable period of time without any major cash outlays. The experienced do-it-yourselfer will have a tool kit good enough for most repair and overhaul procedures and will add tools from the *Special* category when he feels the expense is justified by the amount of use to which these tools will be put.

It is obviously not possible to cover the subject of tools fully here. For those who wish to learn more about tools and their use there is a book entitled *How to Choose and Use Car Tools* available from the publishers of this manual.

Maintenance and minor repair tool kit

The tools given in this list should be considered as a minimum requirement if routine maintenance, servicing and minor repair operations are to be undertaken. We recommend the purchase of combination spanners (ring one end, open-ended the other); although more expensive than open-ended ones, they do give the advantages of both types of spanner.

> Combination spanners - 10, 11, 12, 13, 14 & 17 mm
> Adjustable spanner - 9 inch
> Engine sump/gearbox/drain plug key
> Spark plug spanner (a deep reaching one is required)
> Spark plug gap adjustment tool
> Set of feeler gauges
> Brake bleed nipple spanner
> Screwdriver - 4 in long x ¼ in dia (flat blade)
> Screwdriver - 4 in long x ¼ in dia (cross blade)
> Combination pliers - 6 inch
> Hacksaw (junior)
> Tyre pump
> Tyre pressure gauge
> Grease gun
> Oil can
> Fine emery cloth (1 sheet)
> Wire brush (small)
> Funnel (medium size)

Repair and overhaul tool kit

These tools are virtually essential for anyone undertaking any major repairs to a motor vehicle, and are additional to those given in the *Maintenance and minor repair* list. Included in this list is a comprehensive set of sockets. Although these are expensive they will be found invaluable as they are so versatile - particularly if various drives are included in the set. We recommend the ½ in square-drive type, as this can be used with most proprietary torque wrenches. If you cannot afford a socket set, even bought piecemeal, then inexpensive tubular box spanners are a useful alternative.

The tools in this list will occasionally need to be supplemented by tools from the *Special* list.

> Sockets (or box spanners) to cover range in previous list
> Reversible ratchet drive (for use with sockets)
> Extension piece, 10 inch (for use with sockets)
> Universal joint (for use with sockets)
> Torque wrench (for use with sockets)
> 'Mole' wrench - 8 inch
> Ball pein hammer
> Soft-faced hammer, plastic or rubber
> Screwdriver - 6 in long x 56 in dia (flat blade)
> Screwdriver - 2 in long x 56 in square (flat blade)
> Screwdriver - 1½ in long x ¼ in dia (cross blade)
> Screwdriver - 3 in long x ⅛ in dia (electricians)
> Pliers - electricians side cutters
> Pliers - needle nosed
> Pliers - circlip (internal and external)
> Cold chisel - ½ inch
> Scriber
> Scraper
> Centre punch
> Pin punch
> Hacksaw
> Valve grinding tool
> Steel rule/straight-edge
> Allen keys
> Selection of files
> Wire brush (large)
> Axle-stands
> Jack (strong trolley or hydraulic type)

Special tools

The tools in this list are those which are not used regularly, are expensive to buy, or which need to be used in accordance with their manufacturers' instructions. Unless relatively difficult mechanical jobs are undertaken frequently, it will not be economic to buy many of these tools. Where this is the case, you could consider clubbing together with friends (or joining a motorists' club) to make a joint purchase, or borrowing the tools against a deposit from a local garage or tool hire specialist.

The following list contains only those tools and instruments freely available to the public, and not those special tools produced by the vehicle manufacturer specifically for its dealer network. You will find occasional references to these manufacturers' special tools in the text of this manual. Generally, an alternative method of doing the job without the vehicle manufacturers' special tool is given. However, sometimes, there is no alternative to using them. Where this is the case and the relevant tool cannot be bought or borrowed, you will have to entrust the work to a franchised garage.

Valve spring compressor
Piston ring compressor
Balljoint separator
Universal hub/bearing puller
Impact screwdriver
Micrometer and/or vernier gauge
Dial gauge
Stroboscopic timing light
Dwell angle meter/tachometer
Universal electrical multi-meter
Cylinder compression gauge
Lifting tackle
Trolley jack
Light with extension lead

Buying tools

For practically all tools, a tool factor is the best source since he will have a very comprehensive range compared with the average garage or accessory shop. Having said that, accessory shops often offer excellent quality tools at discount prices, so it pays to shop around.

Remember, you don't have to buy the most expensive items on the shelf, but it is always advisable to steer clear of the very cheap tools. There are plenty of good tools around at reasonable prices, so ask the proprietor or manager of the shop for advice before making a purchase.

Care and maintenance of tools

Having purchased a reasonable tool kit, it is necessary to keep the tools in a clean serviceable condition. After use, always wipe off any dirt, grease and metal particles using a clean, dry cloth, before putting the tools away. Never leave them lying around after they have been used. A simple tool rack on the garage or workshop wall, for items such as screwdrivers and pliers is a good idea. Store all normal wrenches and sockets in a metal box. Any measuring instruments, gauges, meters, etc, must be carefully stored where they cannot be damaged or become rusty.

Take a little care when tools are used. Hammer heads inevitably become marked and screwdrivers lose the keen edge on their blades from time to time. A little timely attention with emery cloth or a file will soon restore items like this to a good serviceable finish.

Working facilities

Not to be forgotten when discussing tools, is the workshop itself. If anything more than routine maintenance is to be carried out, some form of suitable working area becomes essential.

It is appreciated that many an owner mechanic is forced by circumstances to remove an engine or similar item, without the benefit of a garage or workshop. Having done this, any repairs should always be done under the cover of a roof.

Wherever possible, any dismantling should be done on a clean, flat workbench or table at a suitable working height.

Any workbench needs a vice: one with a jaw opening of 4 in (100 mm) is suitable for most jobs. As mentioned previously, some clean dry storage space is also required for tools, as well as for lubricants, cleaning fluids, touch-up paints and so on, which become necessary.

Another item which may be required, and which has a much more general usage, is an electric drill with a chuck capacity of at least 56 in (8 mm). This, together with a good range of twist drills, is virtually essential for fitting accessories such as mirrors and reversing lights.

Last, but not least, always keep a supply of old newspapers and clean, lint-free rags available, and try to keep any working area as clean as possible.

Spanner jaw gap comparison table

Jaw gap (in)	Spanner size
0.250	$\frac{1}{4}$ in AF
0.276	7 mm
0.313	$\frac{5}{16}$ in AF
0.315	8 mm
0.344	$\frac{11}{32}$ in AF; $\frac{1}{8}$ in Whitworth
0.354	9 mm
0.375	$\frac{3}{8}$ in AF
0.394	10 mm
0.433	11 mm
0.438	$\frac{7}{16}$ in AF
0.445	$\frac{3}{16}$ in Whitworth; $\frac{1}{4}$ in BSF
0.472	12 mm
0.500	$\frac{1}{2}$ in AF
0.512	13 mm
0.525	$\frac{1}{4}$ in Whitworth; $\frac{5}{16}$ in BSF
0.551	14 mm
0.563	$\frac{9}{16}$ in AF
0.591	15 mm
0.600	$\frac{5}{16}$ in Whitworth; $\frac{3}{8}$ in BSF
0.625	$\frac{5}{8}$ in AF
0.630	16 mm
0.669	17 mm
0.686	$\frac{11}{16}$ in AF
0.709	18 mm
0.710	$\frac{3}{8}$ in Whitworth; $\frac{7}{16}$ in BSF
0.748	19 mm
0.750	$\frac{3}{4}$ in AF
0.813	$\frac{13}{16}$ in AF
0.820	$\frac{7}{16}$ in Whitworth; $\frac{1}{2}$ in BSF
0.866	22 mm
0.875	$\frac{7}{8}$ in AF
0.920	$\frac{1}{2}$ in Whitworth; $\frac{9}{16}$ in BSF
0.938	$\frac{15}{16}$ in AF
0.945	24 mm
1.000	1 in AF
1.010	$\frac{9}{16}$ in Whitworth; $\frac{5}{8}$ in BSF
1.024	26 mm
1.063	$1\frac{1}{16}$ in AF; 27 mm
1.100	$\frac{5}{8}$ in Whitworth; $\frac{11}{16}$ in BSF
1.125	$1\frac{1}{8}$ in AF
1.181	30 mm
1.200	$\frac{11}{16}$ in Whitworth; $\frac{3}{4}$ in BSF
1.250	$1\frac{1}{4}$ in AF
1.260	32 mm
1.300	$\frac{3}{4}$ in Whitworth; $\frac{7}{8}$ in BSF
1.313	$1\frac{5}{16}$ in AF
1.390	$\frac{13}{16}$ in Whitworth; $\frac{15}{16}$ in BSF
1.417	36 mm
1.438	$1\frac{7}{16}$ in AF
1.480	$\frac{7}{8}$ in Whitworth; 1 in BSF
1.500	$1\frac{1}{2}$ in AF
1.575	40 mm; $\frac{15}{16}$ in Whitworth
1.614	41 mm
1.625	$1\frac{5}{8}$ in AF
1.670	1 in Whitworth; $1\frac{1}{8}$ in BSF
1.688	$1\frac{11}{16}$ in AF
1.811	46 mm
1.813	$1\frac{13}{16}$ in AF
1.860	$1\frac{1}{8}$ in Whitworth; $1\frac{1}{4}$ in BSF
1.875	$1\frac{7}{8}$ in AF
1.969	50 mm
2.000	2 in AF
2.050	$1\frac{1}{4}$ in Whitworth; $1\frac{3}{8}$ in BSF
2.165	55 mm
2.362	60 mm

Safety first!

Professional motor mechanics are trained in safe working procedures. However enthusiastic you may be about getting on with the job in hand, do take the time to ensure that your safety is not put at risk. A moment's lack of attention can result in an accident, as can failure to observe certain elementary precautions.

There will always be new ways of having accidents, and the following points do not pretend to be a comprehensive list of all dangers; they are intended rather to make you aware of the risks and to encourage a safety-conscious approach to all work you carry out on your vehicle.

Essential DOs and DON'Ts

DON'T rely on a single jack when working underneath the vehicle. Always use reliable additional means of support, such as axle stands, securely placed under a part of the vehicle that you know will not give way.

DON'T attempt to loosen or tighten high-torque nuts (e.g. wheel hub nuts) while the vehicle is on a jack; it may be pulled off.

DON'T start the engine without first ascertaining that the transmission is in neutral (or 'Park' where applicable) and the parking brake applied.

DON'T suddenly remove the filler cap from a hot cooling system – cover it with a cloth and release the pressure gradually first, or you may get scalded by escaping coolant.

DON'T attempt to drain oil until you are sure it has cooled sufficiently to avoid scalding you.

DON'T grasp any part of the engine, exhaust or catalytic converter without first ascertaining that it is sufficiently cool to avoid burning you.

DON'T allow brake fluid or antifreeze to contact vehicle paintwork.

DON'T syphon toxic liquids such as fuel, brake fluid or antifreeze by mouth, or allow them to remain on your skin.

DON'T inhale dust – it may be injurious to health (see *Asbestos* below).

DON'T allow any spilt oil or grease to remain on the floor – wipe it up straight away, before someone slips on it.

DON'T use ill-fitting spanners or other tools which may slip and cause injury.

DON'T attempt to lift a heavy component which may be beyond your capability – get assistance.

DON'T rush to finish a job, or take unverified short cuts.

DON'T allow children or animals in or around an unattended vehicle.

DO wear eye protection when using power tools such as drill, sander, bench grinder etc, and when working under the vehicle.

DO use a barrier cream on your hands prior to undertaking dirty jobs – it will protect your skin from infection as well as making the dirt easier to remove afterwards; but make sure your hands aren't left slippery. Note that long-term contact with used engine oil can be a health hazard.

DO keep loose clothing (cuffs, tie etc) and long hair well out of the way of moving mechanical parts.

DO remove rings, wristwatch etc, before working on the vehicle – especially the electrical system.

DO ensure that any lifting tackle used has a safe working load rating adequate for the job.

DO keep your work area tidy – it is only too easy to fall over articles left lying around.

DO get someone to check periodically that all is well, when working alone on the vehicle.

DO carry out work in a logical sequence and check that everything is correctly assembled and tightened afterwards.

DO remember that your vehicle's safety affects that of yourself and others. If in doubt on any point, get specialist advice.

IF, in spite of following these precautions, you are unfortunate enough to injure yourself, seek medical attention as soon as possible.

Asbestos

Certain friction, insulating, sealing, and other products – such as brake linings, brake bands, clutch linings, torque converters, gaskets, etc – contain asbestos. *Extreme care must be taken to avoid inhalation of dust from such products since it is hazardous to health.* If in doubt, assume that they *do* contain asbestos.

Fire

Remember at all times that petrol (gasoline) is highly flammable. Never smoke, or have any kind of naked flame around, when working on the vehicle. But the risk does not end there – a spark caused by an electrical short-circuit, by two metal surfaces contacting each other, by careless use of tools, or even by static electricity built up in your body under certain conditions, can ignite petrol vapour, which in a confined space is highly explosive.

Always disconnect the battery earth (ground) terminal before working on any part of the fuel or electrical system, and never risk spilling fuel on to a hot engine or exhaust.

It is recommended that a fire extinguisher of a type suitable for fuel and electrical fires is kept handy in the garage or workplace at all times. Never try to extinguish a fuel or electrical fire with water.

Fumes

Certain fumes are highly toxic and can quickly cause unconsciousness and even death if inhaled to any extent. Petrol (gasoline) vapour comes into this category, as do the vapours from certain solvents such as trichloroethylene. Any draining or pouring of such volatile fluids should be done in a well ventilated area.

When using cleaning fluids and solvents, read the instructions carefully. Never use materials from unmarked containers – they may give off poisonous vapours.

Never run the engine of a motor vehicle in an enclosed space such as a garage. Exhaust fumes contain carbon monoxide which is extremely poisonous; if you need to run the engine, always do so in the open air or at least have the rear of the vehicle outside the workplace.

If you are fortunate enough to have the use of an inspection pit, never drain or pour petrol, and never run the engine, while the vehicle is standing over it; the fumes, being heavier than air, will concentrate in the pit with possibly lethal results.

The battery

Never cause a spark, or allow a naked light, near the vehicle's battery. It will normally be giving off a certain amount of hydrogen gas, which is highly explosive.

Always disconnect the battery earth (ground) terminal before working on the fuel or electrical systems.

If possible, loosen the filler plugs or cover when charging the battery from an external source. Do not charge at an excessive rate or the battery may burst.

Take care when topping up and when carrying the battery. The acid electrolyte, even when diluted, is very corrosive and should not be allowed to contact the eyes or skin.

If you ever need to prepare electrolyte yourself, always add the acid slowly to the water, and never the other way round. Protect against splashes by wearing rubber gloves and goggles.

When jump starting a car using a booster battery, for negative earth (ground) vehicles, connect the jump leads in the following sequence: First connect one jump lead between the positive (+) terminals of the two batteries. Then connect the other jump lead first to the negative (–) terminal of the booster battery, and then to a good earthing (ground) point on the vehicle to be started, at least 18 in (45 cm) from the battery if possible. Ensure that hands and jump leads are clear of any moving parts, and that the two vehicles do not touch. Disconnect the leads in the reverse order.

Mains electricity

When using an electric power tool, inspection light etc, which works from the mains, always ensure that the appliance is correctly connected to its plug and that, where necessary, it is properly earthed (grounded). Do not use such appliances in damp conditions and, again, beware of creating a spark or applying excessive heat in the vicinity of fuel or fuel vapour.

Ignition HT voltage

A severe electric shock can result from touching certain parts of the ignition system, such as the HT leads, when the engine is running or being cranked, particularly if components are damp or the insulation is defective. Where an electronic ignition system is fitted, the HT voltage is much higher and could prove fatal.

Routine maintenance

For information applicable to later models, see Supplement at end of manual

Maintenance is essential for ensuring safety and is desirable for the purpose of getting the best in terms of performance and economy from the car. Over the years the need for periodic lubrication – oiling and greasing – has been drastically reduced, if not totally eliminated. This has unfortunately tended to lead some owners to think that because no such action is required the components either no longer exist or will last for ever. This is a serious delusion. If anything, there are now more places, particularly in the steering and suspension, where joints and pivots are fitted. Although you do not grease them any more you still have to look at them – and look at them just as often as you may previously have had to grease them. The largest initial element of maintenance is visual examination. This may lead to repairs or renewal.

Under-bonnet view (GT/1360 cc)

1   Right-hand front engine mounting
2   Jack
3   Drivebelt
4   Oil filter
5   Bottom hose
6   Water pump
7   Throttle cable
8   Fuel pump
9   Brake master cylinder
10 Brake fluid reservoir filler cap
11 Vehicle identification plate
12 Choke cable
13 Heater hose
14 Oil filler cap/crankcase ventilation filter
15 Windscreen wiper arm
16 Hydraulic brake lines
17 Cooling fan motor resistor
18 Front suspension shock absorber top mounting nut
19 Ignition coil cover
20 Distributor
21 Bottom hose
22 Clutch release fork
23 Clutch housing
24 Washer reservoir
25 Battery
26 Ignition timing aperture
27 Diagnostic socket
28 Radiator filler cap
29 Air cleaner
30 Bonnet lock
31 Oil pressure switch
32 Alternator
33 Cooling system expansion bottle

View of front underside of car (GT/1360 cc)

1 Bottom hose	5 Gear linkage	9 Lower suspension arm	14 Fuel feed and return pipes
2 Reverse lamp switch	6 Clutch housing and transfer	10 Anti-roll bar	15 Hydraulic brake lines
3 Engine/transmission oil drain	gear assembly	11 Track rod	16 Subframe
plug	7 Washer reservoir	12 Guide bar	17 Driveshaft
4 Radiator	8 Disc caliper	13 Exhaust front pipe	18 Front towing eye

View of rear underside of car (GT/1360 cc)

1 Exhaust front pipe	5 Brake hydraulic flexible hose	9 Exhaust rubber mounting	12 Rear towing eye
2 Handbrake cables	6 Rear shock absorber	10 Exhaust rear silencer	13 Torsion bars
3 Heatshield	7 Trailing arm	11 Spare wheel	14 Fuel tank
4 Rear suspension cross-tube	8 Side-member		

At weekly intervals

Engine
   Check the oil level. Top up if necessary (photo)

Cooling system
   Check the coolant level. Top up if necessary

Braking system
   Check the brake fluid level. Top up if necessary

General
   Check the tyres for condition and pressure
   Check all systems for operation leaks and security
   Check the washer fluid level. Top up if necessary

Topping-up the engine oil

After first 1000 to 1500 miles (1500 to 2250 km) – new cars

Engine
   Renew the oil and filter

Transmission
   Renew the oil (pre-1988 models only)

Every 5000 miles (7500 km) on models up to July 1984
Every 6000 miles (9000 km) on models from July 1984 on –
or six monthly, if sooner

In addition to the weekly maintenance

Engine
   Renew the oil
   Renew the filter (first 5000/6000 miles only)
   Clean and regap the spark plugs

Automatic transmission
   Check the fluid level. Top up if necessary

Braking system
   Check the brake pads for wear. Renew if necessary (Chapter 8, Section 3)

Electrical system
   Check the battery electrolyte level. Top up if necessary (not usually required on low maintenance type)

Every 10 000 miles (15 000 km) on models up to July 1984 only

Engine
   Renew the oil filter (every second oil change)

Every 15 000 miles (22 500 km) on models up to July 1984
Every 12 000 miles (18 000 km) on models from July 1984 on
– or annually, if sooner

In addition to the six monthly maintenance

Engine
   Renew the oil filter (models July 1984 on only)
   Renew the spark plugs

Fuel system
   Check and, if necessary, adjust the throttle cable
   Lubricate the throttle and choke cables

Clutch
   Check and, if necessary, adjust the clutch cable (Chapter 5, Section 2)

Braking system
   Check the brake shoes for wear. Renew if necessary (Chapter 8, Section 4)
   Check the operation of the handbrake. Adjust if necessary (Chapter 8, Section 14)

Bodywork
   Check the bodywork for condition. Repair as necessary

Electrical system
   Check the alternator drivebelt tension. Adjust if necessary (Chapter 12, Section 2)

Every 30 000 miles (45 000 km) on models up to July 1984
Every 24 000 miles (36 000 km) on models from July 1984 on
– or two yearly, if sooner

In addition to the annual maintenance

Cooling system
   Renew the coolant

Fuel system
   Renew the air cleaner element

Ignition system
   Check the ignition timing. Adjust if necessary (not July 1984 on models)

Manual transmission (BE 1/5 – pre-1988 models only)
   Renew the oil

Automatic transmission
   Renew the fluid

Braking system
   Renew the brake fluid (Chapter 8, Section 2)

Suspension and steering
   Check the wheel bearings for wear and damage
   Check the steering and suspension balljoints for wear and damage
   Check the shock absorbers for operation and leaks

Every 60 000 miles (90 000 km) all models – or five yearly, if sooner

Fuel system
   Renew the fuel filter (injection models only)

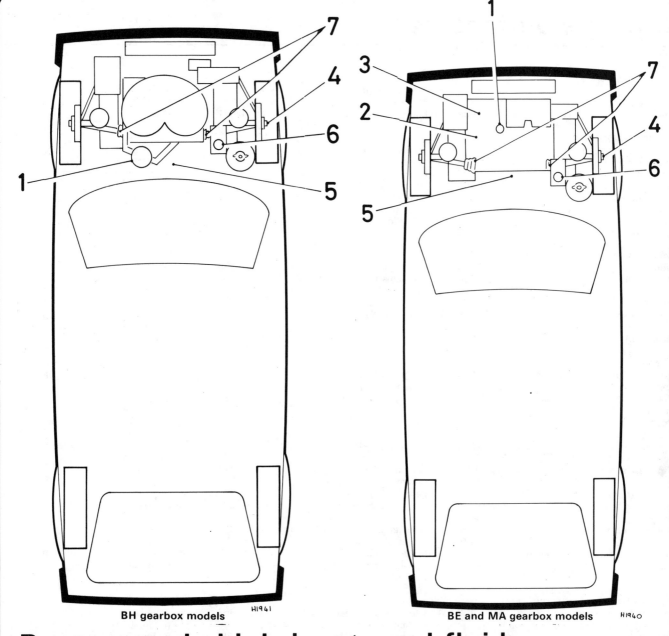

BH gearbox models   HI941

BE and MA gearbox models   HI940

Recommended lubricants and fluids

Component or system	Lubricant type/specification	Duckhams recommendation
Engine (1)	Multigrade engine oil, viscosity SAE 10W/40 or 15W/40	Duckhams QXR, Hypergrade, or 10W/40 Motor Oil
Manual gearbox:		
BH3 type (1)	As above (integral with engine)	As above
BE1 type (pre-1988 models)	Multigrade engine oil, viscosity SAE 10W/40 or 15W/40	Duckhams QXR, Hypergrade, or 10W/40 Motor Oil
BE1 and MA types (1988-on models)	Gear oil, viscosity SAE 75W/80	Duckhams Hypoid PT 75W/80
Automatic transmission (3)	Dexron II type ATF	Duckhams D-Matic
Wheel bearings (4)	Multi-purpose lithium-based grease	Duckhams LB 10
Steering rack (5)	Multi-purpose lithium-based grease with molybdenum disulphide	Duckhams LBM 10
Brake fluid reservoir (6)	Hydraulic fluid to SAE J1703 or DOT 3	Duckhams Universal Brake and Clutch Fluid
Driveshaft CV joints (7)	Special lubricant supplied in repair kit	

Conversion factors

Length (distance)
Inches (in)	X	25.4	=	Millimetres (mm)	X	0.0394	= Inches (in)
Feet (ft)	X	0.305	=	Metres (m)	X	3.281	= Feet (ft)
Miles	X	1.609	=	Kilometres (km)	X	0.621	= Miles

Volume (capacity)
Cubic inches (cu in; in³)	X	16.387	=	Cubic centimetres (cc; cm³)	X	0.061	= Cubic inches (cu in; in³)
Imperial pints (Imp pt)	X	0.568	=	Litres (l)	X	1.76	= Imperial pints (Imp pt)
Imperial quarts (Imp qt)	X	1.137	=	Litres (l)	X	0.88	= Imperial quarts (Imp qt)
Imperial quarts (Imp qt)	X	1.201	=	US quarts (US qt)	X	0.833	= Imperial quarts (Imp qt)
US quarts (US qt)	X	0.946	=	Litres (l)	X	1.057	= US quarts (US qt)
Imperial gallons (Imp gal)	X	4.546	=	Litres (l)	X	0.22	= Imperial gallons (Imp gal)
Imperial gallons (Imp gal)	X	1.201	=	US gallons (US gal)	X	0.833	= Imperial gallons (Imp gal)
US gallons (US gal)	X	3.785	=	Litres (l)	X	0.264	= US gallons (US gal)

Mass (weight)
Ounces (oz)	X	28.35	=	Grams (g)	X	0.035	= Ounces (oz)
Pounds (lb)	X	0.454	=	Kilograms (kg)	X	2.205	= Pounds (lb)

Force
Ounces-force (ozf; oz)	X	0.278	=	Newtons (N)	X	3.6	= Ounces-force (ozf; oz)
Pounds-force (lbf; lb)	X	4.448	=	Newtons (N)	X	0.225	= Pounds-force (lbf; lb)
Newtons (N)	X	0.1	=	Kilograms-force (kgf; kg)	X	9.81	= Newtons (N)

Pressure
Pounds-force per square inch (psi; lbf/in²; lb/in²)	X	0.070	=	Kilograms-force per square centimetre (kgf/cm²; kg/cm²)	X	14.223	= Pounds-force per square inch (psi; lbf/in²; lb/in²)
Pounds-force per square inch (psi; lbf/in²; lb/in²)	X	0.068	=	Atmospheres (atm)	X	14.696	= Pounds-force per square inch (psi; lbf/in²; lb/in²)
Pounds-force per square inch (psi; lbf/in²; lb/in²)	X	0.069	=	Bars	X	14.5	= Pounds-force per square inch (psi; lbf/in²; lb/in²)
Pounds-force per square inch (psi; lbf/in²; lb/in²)	X	6.895	=	Kilopascals (kPa)	X	0.145	= Pounds-force per square inch (psi; lbf/in²; lb/in²)
Kilopascals (kPa)	X	0.01	=	Kilograms-force per square centimetre (kgf/cm²; kg/cm²)	X	98.1	= Kilopascals (kPa)
Millibar (mbar)	X	100	=	Pascals (Pa)	X	0.01	= Millibar (mbar)
Millibar (mbar)	X	0.0145	=	Pounds-force per square inch (psi; lbf/in², lb/in²)	X	68.947	= Millibar (mbar)
Millibar (mbar)	X	0.75	=	Millimetres of mercury (mmHg)	X	1.333	= Millibar (mbar)
Millibar (mbar)	X	1.40	=	Inches of water (inH₂O)	X	0.714	= Millibar (mbar)
Millimetres of mercury (mmHg)	X	1.868	=	Inches of water (inH₂O)	X	0.535	= Millimetres of mercury (mmHg)
Inches of water (inH₂O)	X	27.68	=	Pounds-force per square inch (psi, lbf/in², lb/in²)	X	0.036	= Inches of water (inH₂O)

Torque (moment of force)
Pounds-force inches (lbf in; lb in)	X	1.152	=	Kilograms-force centimetre (kgf cm; kg cm)	X	0.868	= Pounds-force inches (lbf in; lb in)
Pounds-force inches (lbf in; lb in)	X	0.113	=	Newton metres (Nm)	X	8.85	= Pounds-force inches (lbf in; lb in)
Pounds-force inches (lbf in; lb in)	X	0.083	=	Pounds-force feet (lbf ft; lb ft)	X	12	= Pounds-force inches (lbf in; lb in)
Pounds-force feet (lbf ft; lb ft)	X	0.138	=	Kilograms-force metres (kgf m; kg m)	X	7.233	= Pounds-force feet (lbf ft; lb ft)
Pounds-force feet (lbf ft; lb ft)	X	1.356	=	Newton metres (Nm)	X	0.738	= Pounds-force feet (lbf ft; lb ft)
Newton metres (Nm)	X	0.102	=	Kilograms-force metres (kgf m; kg m)	X	9.804	= Newton metres (Nm)

Power
Horsepower (hp)	X	745.7	=	Watts (W)	X	0.0013	= Horsepower (hp)

Velocity (speed)
Miles per hour (miles/hr; mph)	X	1.609	=	Kilometres per hour (km/hr; kph)	X	0.621	= Miles per hour (miles/hr; mph)

Fuel consumption*
Miles per gallon, Imperial (mpg)	X	0.354	=	Kilometres per litre (km/l)	X	2.825	= Miles per gallon, Imperial (mpg)
Miles per gallon, US (mpg)	X	0.425	=	Kilometres per litre (km/l)	X	2.352	= Miles per gallon, US (mpg)

Temperature
Degrees Fahrenheit = (°C x 1.8) + 32   Degrees Celsius (Degrees Centigrade; °C) = (°F - 32) x 0.56

*It is common practice to convert from miles per gallon (mpg) to litres/100 kilometres (l/100km), where mpg (Imperial) x l/100 km = 282 and mpg (US) x l/100 km = 235

Fault diagnosis

Introduction

The vehicle owner who does his or her own maintenance according to the recommended schedules should not have to use this section of the manual very often. Modern component reliability is such that, provided those items subject to wear or deterioration are inspected or renewed at the specified intervals, sudden failure is comparatively rare. Faults do not usually just happen as a result of sudden failure, but develop over a period of time. Major mechanical failures in particular are usually preceded by characteristic symptoms over hundreds or even thousands of miles. Those components which do occasionally fail without warning are often small and easily carried in the vehicle.

With any fault finding, the first step is to decide where to begin investigations. Sometimes this is obvious, but on other occasions a little detective work will be necessary. The owner who makes half a dozen haphazard adjustments or replacements may be successful in curing a fault (or its symptoms), but he will be none the wiser if the fault recurs and he may well have spent more time and money than was necessary. A calm and logical approach will be found to be more satisfactory in the long run. Always take into account any warning signs or abnormalities that may have been noticed in the period preceding the fault – power loss, high or low gauge readings, unusual noises or smells, etc – and remember that failure of components such as fuses or spark plugs may only be pointers to some underlying fault.

The pages which follow here are intended to help in cases of failure to start or breakdown on the road. There is also a Fault Diagnosis Section at the end of each Chapter which should be consulted if the preliminary checks prove unfruitful. Whatever the fault, certain basic principles apply. These are as follows:

Verify the fault. This is simply a matter of being sure that you know what the symptoms are before starting work. This is particularly important if you are investigating a fault for someone else who may not have described it very accurately.

Don't overlook the obvious. For example, if the vehicle won't start, is there petrol in the tank? (Don't take anyone else's word on this particular point, and don't trust the fuel gauge either!) If an electrical fault is indicated, look for loose or broken wires before digging out the test gear.

Cure the disease, not the symptom. Substituting a flat battery with a fully charged one will get you off the hard shoulder, but if the underlying cause is not attended to, the new battery will go the same way. Similarly, changing oil-fouled spark plugs for a new set will get you moving again, but remember that the reason for the fouling (if it wasn't simply an incorrect grade of plug) will have to be established and corrected.

Don't take anything for granted. Particularly, don't forget that a 'new' component may itself be defective (especially if it's been rattling round in the boot for months), and don't leave components out of a fault diagnosis sequence just because they are new or recently fitted. When you do finally diagnose a difficult fault, you'll probably realise that all the evidence was there from the start.

Electrical faults

Electrical faults can be more puzzling than straightforward mechanical failures, but they are no less susceptible to logical analysis if the basic principles of operation are understood. Vehicle electrical wiring exists in extremely unfavourable conditions – heat, vibration and chemical attack – and the first things to look for are loose or corroded connections and broken or chafed wires, especially where the wires pass through holes in the bodywork or are subject to vibration.

All metal-bodied vehicles in current production have one pole of the battery 'earthed', ie connected to the vehicle bodywork, and in nearly all modern vehicles it is the negative (–) terminal. The various electrical components – motors, bulb holders etc – are also connected to earth, either by means of a lead or directly by their mountings. Electric current flows through the component and then back to the battery via the bodywork. If the component mounting is loose or corroded, or if a good path back to the battery is not available, the circuit will be incomplete and malfunction will result. The engine and/or gearbox are also earthed by means of flexible metal straps to the body or subframe; if these straps are loose or missing, starter motor, generator and ignition trouble may result.

Assuming the earth return to be satisfactory, electrical faults will be due either to component malfunction or to defects in the current supply. Individual components are dealt with in Chapter 12. If supply wires are broken or cracked internally this results in an open-circuit, and the easiest way to check for this is to bypass the suspect wire temporarily with a length of wire having a crocodile clip or suitable connector at

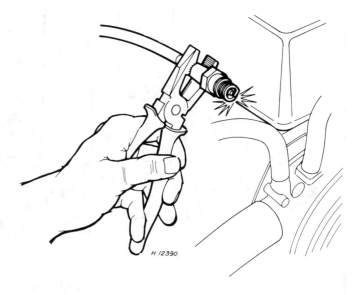

Crank engine and check for spark. Hold lead with an insulated tool

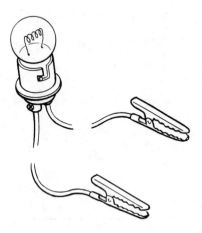

A simple test lamp is useful for checking electrical faults

each end. Alternatively, a 12V test lamp can be used to verify the presence of supply voltage at various points along the wire and the break can be thus isolated.

If a bare portion of a live wire touches the bodywork or other earthed metal part, the electricity will take the low-resistance path thus formed back to the battery: this is known as a short-circuit. Hopefully a short-circuit will blow a fuse, but otherwise it may cause burning of the insulation (and possibly further short-circuits) or even a fire. This is why it is inadvisable to bypass persistently blowing fuses with silver foil or wire.

Spares and tool kit

Most vehicles are supplied only with sufficient tools for wheel changing; the *Maintenance and minor repair* tool kit detailed in *Tools and working facilities*, with the addition of a hammer, is probably sufficient for those repairs that most motorists would consider attempting at the roadside. In addition a few items which can be fitted without too much trouble in the event of a breakdown should be carried. Experience and available space will modify the list below, but the following may save having to call on professional assistance:

Spark plugs, clean and correctly gapped
HT lead and plug cap – long enough to reach the plug furthest from the distributor
Distributor rotor
Drivebelt(s) – emergency type may suffice
Spare fuses
Set of principal light bulbs
Tin of radiator sealer and hose bandage
Exhaust bandage
Roll of insulating tape
Length of soft iron wire
Length of electrical flex
Torch or inspection lamp (can double as test lamp)
Battery jump leads
Tow-rope
Ignition waterproofing aerosol
Litre of engine oil
Sealed can of hydraulic fluid
Emergency windscreen
Worm drive clips
Tube of filler paste

If spare fuel is carried, a can designed for the purpose should be used to minimise risks of leakage and collision damage. A first aid kit and a warning triangle, whilst not at present compulsory in the UK, are obviously sensible items to carry in addition to the above.

When touring abroad it may be advisable to carry additional spares which, even if you cannot fit them yourself, could save having to wait

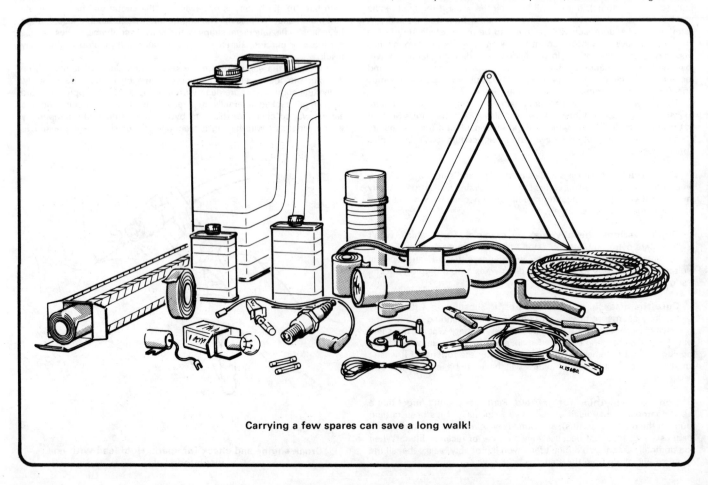

Carrying a few spares can save a long walk!

while parts are obtained. The items below may be worth considering:

Clutch and throttle cables
Cylinder head gasket
Alternator brushes
Fuel pump repair kit (if available)
Tyre valve core

One of the motoring organisations will be able to advise on availability of fuel etc in foreign countries.

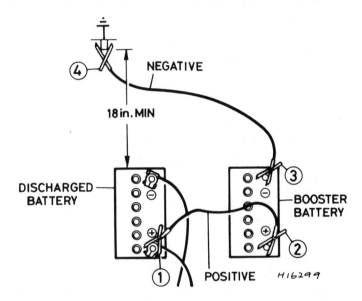

Jump start lead connections for negative earth vehicles – connect leads in order shown

---

Engine will not start

Engine fails to turn when starter operated

Flat battery (recharge, use jump leads, or push start)
Battery terminals loose or corroded
Battery earth to body defective
Engine earth strap loose or broken
Starter motor (or solenoid) wiring loose or broken
Ignition/starter switch faulty
Major mechanical failure (seizure)
Starter or solenoid internal fault (see Chapter 12)

Starter motor turns engine slowly

Partially discharged battery (recharge, use jump leads, or push start)
Battery terminals loose or corroded
Battery earth to body defective
Engine earth strap loose
Starter motor (or solenoid) wiring loose
Starter motor internal fault (see Chapter 12)

Engine turns normally but fails to start

Damp or dirty HT leads and distributor cap (crank engine and check for spark)
No fuel in tank (check for delivery at carburettor or fuel filter, as applicable)
Excessive choke (hot engine) or insufficient choke (cold engine)
Fouled or incorrectly gapped spark plugs (remove, clean and regap)

Other ignition system fault (see Chapter 4)
Other fuel system fault (see Chapter 3)
Poor compression
Major mechanical failure (eg camshaft drive)

Engine fires but will not run

Insufficient choke (cold engine)
Air leaks at carburettor or inlet manifold
Fuel starvation (see Chapter 3)
Ignition fault (see Chapter 4)

Engine cuts out and will not restart

Engine cuts out suddenly – ignition fault

Loose or disconnected LT wires
Wet HT leads or distributor cap (after traversing water splash)
Coil failure (check for spark)
Other ignition fault (see Chapter 4)

Engine misfires before cutting out – fuel fault

Fuel tank empty
Fuel pump defective or filter blocked (check for delivery)
Fuel tank filler vent blocked (suction will be evident on releasing cap)
Carburettor needle valve sticking, where applicable
Carburettor jets blocked (fuel contaminated), where applicable
Other fuel system fault (see Chapter 3)

Engine cuts out – other causes

Serious overheating
Major mechanical failure (eg camshaft drive)

Engine overheats

Ignition (no-charge) warning light illuminated

Slack or broken drivebelt – retension or renew (Chapter 12)

Ignition warning light not illuminated

Coolant loss due to internal or external leakage (see Chapter 2)
Thermostat defective
Low oil level
Brakes binding
Radiator clogged externally or internally
Electric cooling fan not operating correctly
Engine waterways clogged
Ignition timing incorrect or automatic advance malfunctioning
Mixture too weak

Note: *Do not add cold water to an overheated engine or damage may result*

Low engine oil pressure

Gauge reads low or warning light illuminated with engine running

Oil level low or incorrect grade
Defective gauge or sender unit
Wire to sender unit earthed
Engine overheating
Oil filter clogged or bypass valve defective
Oil pressure relief valve defective
Oil pick-up strainer clogged
Oil pump worn
Worn main or big-end bearings

Note: *Low oil pressure in a high-mileage engine at tickover is not necessarily a cause for concern. Sudden pressure loss at speed is far more significant. In any event, check the gauge or warning light sender before condemning the engine.*

Engine noises

Pre-ignition (pinking) on acceleration

    Incorrect grade of fuel
    Ignition timing incorrect
    Distributor faulty or worn
    Worn or maladjusted carburettor, where applicable
    Excessive carbon build-up in engine

Whistling or wheezing noises

    Leaking vacuum hose
    Leaking carburettor or manifold gasket, as applicable
    Blowing head gasket

Tapping or rattling

    Incorrect valve clearances
    Worn valve gear
    Worn timing chain or belt
    Broken piston ring (ticking noise)

Knocking or thumping

    Unintentional mechanical contact
    Peripheral component fault (alternator, water pump etc)
    Worn big-end bearings (regular heavy knocking, perhaps less under load)
    Worn main bearings (rumbling and knocking, perhaps worsening under load)
    Piston slap (most noticeable when cold)

Chapter 1 Engine

For modifications, and information applicable to later models, see Supplement at end of manual

Contents

Specifications

XV8, XW7, XY7 and XY8 engines
General

Type	Four-cylinder in-line overhead camshaft. All alloy with wet cylinder liners. Mounted transversely with transmission and inclined to rear at 72° from vertical
Code and displacement:	
XV8 (108C)	954 cc (58.2 cu in)
XW7 (109F)	1124 cc (68.5 cu in)
XY7 (150D)	1360 cc (82.9 cu in)
XY8 (150B)	1360 cc (82.9 cu in)
Bore:	
954 cc	70.0 mm
1124 cc	72.0 mm
1360 cc	75.0 mm
Stroke:	
954 cc	62.0 mm
1124 cc	69.0 mm
1360 cc	77.0 mm
Compression ratio:	
954 cc	9.3 : 1
1124 cc	9.7 : 1
1360 cc	9.7 : 1
Maximum power (DIN):	
954 cc	44.5 bhp at 6000 rpm
1124 cc	49.0 bhp at 4800 rpm
1360 cc (XY7)	59.0 bhp at 5000 rpm
1360 cc (XY8)	79.0 bhp at 5800 rpm
Maximum torque (DIN):	
954 cc	50.6 lbf ft at 2750 rpm
1124 cc	62.9 lbf ft at 2800 rpm
1360 cc (XY7)	78.8 lbf ft at 2500 rpm
1360 cc (XY8)	81.0 lbf ft at 2800 rpm
Firing order	1–3–4–2 (No 1 at clutch end)

Crankshaft

Number of main bearings	5
Journal diameter	49.965 to 49.981 mm
Regrind undersize	0.30 mm
Crankpin diameter	44.975 to 44.991 mm
Regrind undersize	0.30 mm
Endfloat	0.07 to 0.27 mm
Thrust washer thicknesses	2.30; 2.40; 2.45; 2.50 mm

Cylinder liners

Type .... Cast-iron, wet type

Grades:

Piston	**Liner**
A	One file mark
B	Two file marks
C	Three file marks

Paper type gasket seals:

Identification	**Thickness**
Blue	0.087 mm
White	0.102 mm
Red	0.122 mm
Yellow	0.147 mm

Cylinder liner projection above block:

With paper gasket	0.11 to 0.18 mm
With O-ring	0.10 to 0.17 mm

Pistons

Type .... Aluminium alloy, bulged skirt and oval cross-section. Two compression rings and one oil control ring. Gudgeon pin free in piston, interference fit in connecting rod

Running clearance .... 0.07 to 0.09 mm

Valve and valve gear

Clearance (cold):

Inlet	0.10 mm (0.004 in)
Exhaust	0.25 mm (0.010 in)

Seat angle (inclusive):

Inlet	120°
Exhaust	90°
Stem diameter	8.0 mm

Head diameter:

	XV8	**XW7, XY7 and XY8**
Inlet	34.8 mm	37.0 mm
Exhaust	27.8 mm	29.5 mm

Oil capacity (engine/transmission)

954 and 1124 cc engines	4.5 litres (8.0 pints)
1360 cc engines	5.0 litres (8.8 pints)

Oil type/specification

Oil type/specification .... Multigrade engine oil, viscosity SAE 10W/40 or 15W/40 (Duckhams QXR, Hypergrade, or 10W/40 Motor Oil)

Oil pump

Endfloat	0.02 to 0.10 mm
Maximum lobe-to-body clearance	0.064 mm

Torque wrench settings

	Nm	lbf ft
Engine mounting nuts	34	25
Main bearing bolts:		
Stage 1	36	27
Stage 2	51	38
Big-end cap nuts	36	27
Oil pump screws	7	5
Cylinder head bolts (cold):		
Stage 1	50	37
Stage 2	77	57
Chain tensioner bolts	7	5
Camshaft sprocket bolt	73	54
Oil pick-up strainer bolts	10	7
Sump plate bolts	12	9
Engine/transmission connecting bolts	9	7
Timing chain cover bolts	7	5
Crankshaft pulley nut	88	65
Coolant pump bolts	13	10
Carburettor nuts	17	13
Clutch cover bolts	9	7
Transfer gear plate bolts	9	7
Starter motor mounting nuts	12	9
Starter motor mounting bolts	16	12

25

	Nm	lbf ft
Flywheel bolts	66	49
Rocker cover bolts	7	5
Alternator pivot bolt	45	33
Alternator adjuster link bolt	17	13
Oil drain plug	27	20
Flywheel housing bolts	11	8

XU5J engine
General
Type .... Four-cylinder in-line overhead camshaft. All alloy with wet cylinder liners. Mounted transversely and inclined 30° to rear. Transmission mounted on left-hand end of engine.

Code and displacement:
XU5J (180A) .... 1580 cc (96.4 cu in)
Number of cylinders 4
Bore x stroke .... 83 x 73 mm
Compression ratio .... 9.8 : 1
Maximum power (DIN) .... 104 bhp at 6250 rpm
Maximum torque (DIN) .... 13.7 kgf m at 4000 rpm
Firing order .... 1-3-4-2 (No 1 at clutch end)

Camshaft
Drive .... Toothed belt
Action .... Directly onto bucket tappets
Endfloat (not adjustable) .... 0.07 to 0.16 mm
Lift:
Early models .... 10.4 mm
Later models .... 9.7 mm

Connecting rods
Type .... Forged steel
Big-end bore .... 48.655 to 48.671 mm
Small-end bore .... 21.959 to 21.971 mm

Crankshaft and main bearings
Number of main bearings 5
Main bearing bore in crankcase .... 63.708 to 63.727 mm
Main journal diameter:
New .... 59.981 to 60.000 mm
After regrinding .... 59.681 to 59.700 mm
Crankpin diameter:
New .... 44.971 to 44.990 mm
After regrinding .... 44.671 to 44.690 mm
Journal or crankpin out-of-round .... 0.007 mm max
Endfloat .... 0.07 to 0.27 mm
Thrust washer thicknesses available .... 2.30, 2.35, 2.40, 2.45 and 2.50 mm

Cylinder liners
Type .... Wet, removable, matched to piston
Protrusion from block (without seal) .... 0.08 to 0.15 mm
Protrusion difference between liners .... 0.05 mm max
Coding mark .... One, two or three slashes

Pistons
Type .... Aluminium alloy with three compression rings and one scraper; matched to liner

Coding marks:
For gudgeon pin .... Figure 1 (blue), 2 (white) or 3 (red)
For liner .... One, two or three slashes

Gudgeon pins
Nominal diameter .... 22 mm
Coding mark .... Coloured paint (see piston specs)
Fit .... Clearance in piston, interference in connecting rod

Cylinder head
Material .... Aluminium alloy
Warp limit .... 0.05 mm
Number of camshaft bearings 5

Valves

Head diameter:	
Inlet	40 mm
Exhaust	32 mm (early models), 32.95 mm (later models)
Stem diameter:	
Inlet	7.965 to 7.980 mm
Exhaust	7.945 to 7.960 mm
Length:	
Inlet	109.29 mm
Exhaust	108.72 mm
Valve clearances (cold):	
Inlet	0.15 to 0.25 mm (0.006 to 0.010 in)
Exhaust	0.35 to 0.45 mm (0.014 to 0.018 in)
Adjustment method	Shims between tappet and valve stem
Valve springs:	
Identification:	
Early type (high lift camshaft)	Blue marking
Later type (reduced lift camshaft)	Black marking
Valve timing:	
Notional clearance	1 mm
Inlet opens	5°5' BTDC
Inlet closes	34°3' ABDC
Exhaust opens	38°3' BBDC
Exhaust closes	0°5' ATDC

Lubrication system

Type	Wet sump, pressure feed and splash
Filter type	Full flow, disposable cartridge
Sump capacity	5.0 litres (8.8 pints)
Oil type/specification	Multigrade engine oil, viscosity SAE 10W/40 or 15W/40 (Duckhams QXR, Hypergrade, or 10W/40 Motor Oil)
Pressure	3.5 bar at 4000 rpm
Warning light sender operates at	0.44 to 0.58 bar
Oil pump drive	Chain from crankshaft

Torque wrench settings

	Nm	lbf ft
Camshaft cover bolts	10	7
Camshaft bearing caps	15	11
Camshaft sprocket bolt	78	58
Crankshaft pulley bolt	109	80
Sump bolts	20	15
Main bearing cap nuts and bolts	49	36
Main bearing cap side bolts	24	18
Big-end cap nuts	49	36
Flywheel bolts (renew bolts and use thread locking compound)	49	36
Cylinder head bolts (see text):		
Stage 1	58	43
Stage 2 (after slackening)	20	15
Stage 3	One third of a turn (120°) further	
Distributor and thermostat housing	15	11
Spark plugs	18	13
Engine mounting bracket bolts:		
M8	34	25
M10	45	33
Oil pump-to-block bolts	20	15
Oil seal carrier plate bolts	15	11
Camshaft drivebelt tensioner nuts	15	11
Coolant outlet housing bolt	20	15
Oil pressure switch	24	18
Alternator pivot bolt	39	29
Alternator strap bolt	20	15
Engine-to-transmission bolts	45	33
Starter motor bolts	34	25
Inlet manifold nuts	20	15
Exhaust manifold nuts	20	15
Coolant pump securing bolts	15	11
Engine mountings:		
RH nut	27	20
LH nut	35	26
Battery tray/bracket	18	13
Lower mounting centre bolt	34	25
Lower mounting to subframe	45	33
Driveshaft intermediate bearing bracket	23	17

PART A: GENERAL DESCRIPTION AND ROUTINE MAINTENANCE

1 General description

XV8, XW7, XY7 and XY8 engines

One of three different capacity engines may be fitted, the difference in displacement being achieved by increasing the bore and stroke. The engine, which has four cylinders and an overhead camshaft, is mounted transversely, driving the front wheels, and it is inclined to the rear at an angle of 72° from vertical.

The manual gearbox is also mounted transversely in line with and below the engine, and the final drive to the roadwheels is via the differential unit which is integral with the gearbox. Drive from the engine to the transmission is by means of transfer gears which are separately encased in the clutch housing.

The crankcase, cylinder head, gearcase and clutch housing are all manufactured from aluminium alloy. Removable wet cylinder liners are fitted; the aluminium pistons each have two compression rings and one oil control ring. The valves are operated by the single overhead camshaft

Fig. 1.1A Cutaway view from front of engine (XV8, XW7, XY7 and XY8) (Sec 1)

Fig. 1.1B Cutaway view from rear of engine (XV8, XW7, XY7 and XY8) (Sec 1)

and rocker arms. The camshaft drives the distributor at the flywheel end. The timing sprocket, located at the other end of the camshaft, incorporates a separate eccentric lobe which actuates the fuel pump. The timing chain is driven from the crankshaft sprocket. Next to the timing chain sprocket is the gearwheel which drives the oil pump. This is mounted low down against the crankcase face and is enclosed in the timing chain cover.

The crankshaft runs in five shell main bearings and the endfloat is adjustable via a pair of semi-circular thrust washers. Somewhat inconveniently, the lower half crankcase interconnects the engine with the transmission unit. The engine and transmission units share the same mountings. A forced feed lubrication system is employed. The oil pump

is attached to the crankcase in the lower section of the timing chest and it incorporates the pressure relief valve. The pump is driven by gears from the crankshaft.

Oil from the pump passes via an oilway to the oil filter, and thence to the crankshaft main bearings, connecting rod bearings and transmission components. Another oilway from the filter delivers oil to the overhead camshaft and rocker components. Oil from the cylinder head passes to the transfer gear housing and then back to the sump contained within the transmission housing.

Apart from the standard replaceable canister filter located on the outside of the crankcase there is a gauze filter incorporated in the oil pump suction intake within the transmission casing.

XU5J engine

The engine, which has four cylinders and an overhead camshaft, is mounted transversely, driving the front wheels, and it is inclined to the rear at an angle of 30° from vertical.

The manual gearbox is also mounted transversely in line with and on the left-hand end of the engine. The final drive unit is integral with the gearbox and transmits drive to the front wheels via driveshafts.

The engine has four wet liner cylinders, a five-bearing crankshaft and an overhead camshaft.

Camshaft drive is by toothed belt. The belt is tensioned by a spring loaded wheel and also drives the coolant pump. The camshaft operates directly on bucket tappets; valve clearance adjustment is by shims inserted between the tappet and the valve stem. The distributor is driven directly from the tail of the camshaft.

The oil pump is located in the sump and is chain driven from the crankshaft. A forced feed lubrication system is employed. Oil from the pump passes to the oil filter then to the oil gallery, crankshaft and camshaft. The valve stems are lubricated by oil returning from the camshaft to the sump. The oil pump chain and sprockets are lubricated by oil in the sump.

Fig. 1.2 Cutaway view of the engine (XU5J) (Sec 1)

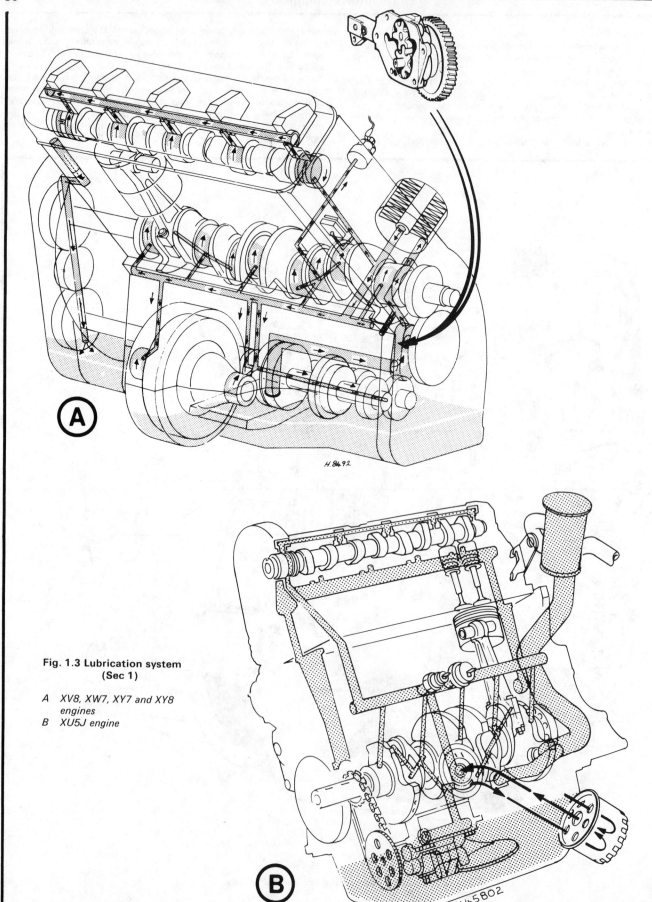

H.8492

Fig. 1.3 Lubrication system (Sec 1)

A XV8, XW7, XY7 and XY8 engines
B XU5J engine

H145802

2 Routine maintenance

Carry out the following procedures at the intervals given in Routine Maintenance at the beginning of the manual.

1 The oil level should be checked preferably when the engine is cold.

2 Withdraw the dipstick, wipe it clean, re-insert it and then withdraw it for the second time. The oil level should be between the high and low marks. If it is too low, top up through the filler cap.

3 The quantity of oil required to raise the oil level from the low to the high mark is 1.0 litre (1.75 pints).

4 To drain the engine oil it is preferable for the engine to be hot. First raise the front of the car on ramps or with a jack. Unscrew the socket-headed plug in the sump, remove the filler cap and allow the oil to drain into a suitable container (photos).

5 When the oil has drained, wipe clean the drain plug then refit and tighten it.

6 The oil filter is of disposable cartridge type. Unscrew it with an oil filter wrench, but first wrap it in cloth as some oil will run out. If a proper wrench is not available a large worm drive hose clip can be fitted to the filter and the screw used as a gripping point. If all else fails, a screwdriver can be driven right through the cartridge and this used as a lever to unscrew it (photo).

7 It is very important to purchase and fit the correct type of filter as some engines have a bypass valve incorporated in the filter mounting base of the crankcase whilst others have the valve incorporated in the filter cartridge.

8 No problem will arise if genuine Peugeot filters are used as they all incorporate a bypass valve. This will have no bearing upon the fact that a valve may already be built into the crankcase.

9 Clean the filter mounting ring on the crankcase and apply engine oil to the rubber seal on the cartridge. Do not use grease as it may make the filter difficult to unscrew.

10 Check that the threaded sleeve is tight on the crankcase, offer up the new filter and screw it on using hand pressure only.

11 Lower the car to the ground then fill the engine with the specified quantity and grade of oil.

12 Start the engine. There will be a short delay before the oil warning lamp goes out. This is normal and is caused by the new filter having to fill with oil.

13 Switch off the engine, wait ten minutes and check the oil level and top up if necessary.

14 Periodically, particularly on an engine which has covered a high mileage, remove the engine oil filler cap and check the filter mesh incorporated in the cap (photo). The filter is a breather for the crankcase ventilation system and should be cleaned or renewed if it is blocked with sludge.

2.4B Sump drain plug (GTI models)

2.6 Bottom view of the oil filter (GTI models)

2.4A Sump drain plug (non-GTI models)

2.14 Oil filler cap (non-GTI models) showing filter mesh

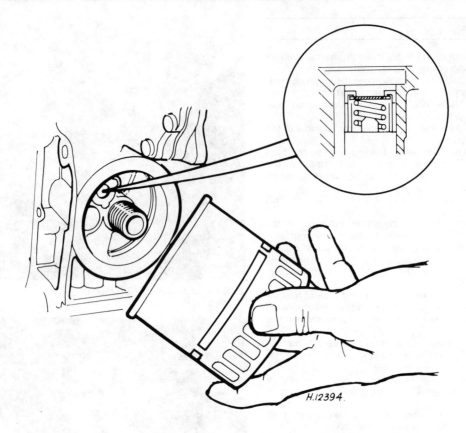

Fig. 1.4 Bypass valve built into oil filter mounting base (Sec 2)

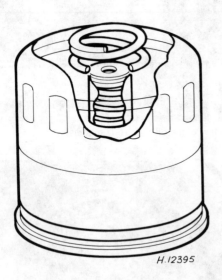

Fig. 1.5 Oil filter cartridge with integral bypass valve (Sec 2)

PART B: XV8, XW7, XY7 AND XY8 ENGINES

3   Operations possible without removing the engine from the car

The following operations can be carried out without having to remove the engine from the car:

(a) Valve clearances – adjustment
(b) Timing chain – removal and refitting
(c) Cylinder head – removal and refitting
(d) Engine mountings – renewal

4   Valve clearances – adjustment

1   Disconnect the spark plug HT leads and remove the oil filler/crankcase ventilation cap from the rocker cover.
2   The engine can be turned by using a spanner on the crankshaft pulley nut – rotation is made easier if the spark plugs are removed.
3   Remove the rocker cover (photo) and then turn the engine until the valves on No 1 cylinder are rocking (ie inlet valve opening and exhaust valve closing). The rocker arm clearances of both valves of No 4 cylinder can now be checked and, if necessary, adjusted. Remember that No 1 cylinder is at the flywheel/clutch end of the engine.
4   The feeler gauge of the correct thickness is inserted between the valve stem and rocker arm. When the clearance is correctly set the feeler gauge should be a smooth stiff sliding fit between the valve stem and rocker arm.
5   If the feeler gauge is a tight or loose fit then the clearance must be adjusted. To do this, loosen the locknut of the adjustment stud and screw the adjuster stud in or out until the feeler gauge blade can be felt to drag slightly when drawn from the gap.
6   Hold the adjuster firmly in this position and tighten the locknut. Recheck the gap on completion to ensure that it has not altered when locking the nut and stud (photo).
7   Check each valve clearance in turn in the following sequence remembering that the clearances for inlet and exhaust valves are different. The valves are numbered from the flywheel end of the engine.

Valves rocking	Valves to adjust
1 In 2 Ex	7 In 8 Ex
5 In 6 Ex	3 In 4 Ex
7 In 8 Ex	1 In 2 Ex
3 In 4 Ex	5 In 6 Ex

8   Fit the rocker cover using a new gasket, then refit the spark plugs, HT leads and oil filler/crankcase ventilation cap.

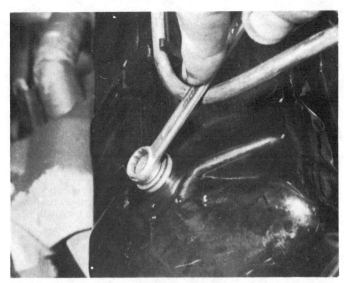

4.3 Removing the rocker cover

4.6 Adjusting a valve clearance

5 Timing chain – removal and refitting

1 Support the engine/transmission on a trolley jack with a block of wood as an insulator.
2 Release the nuts on the right-hand flexible engine mounting at the base of the timing chain cover.
3 Raise the engine just enough to clear the side-member and anti-roll bar.
4 Release the drivebelt tension, remove the belt. Remove the fuel pump.
5 Unscrew and remove the crankshaft pulley nut. To do this the crankshaft must be held against rotation by jamming the starter ring gear. Remove the starter, as described in Chapter 12. Alternatively, if an assistant is available, apply the brakes fully with a gear engaged. Withdraw the pulley.
6 Unbolt and remove the rocker cover, and disconnect the spark plug HT leads.
7 Unscrew and remove the timing chain cover bolts. Take off the cover and extract the fuel pump operating rod.

8 Turn the crankshaft either by temporarily refitting the pulley nut or by engaging a gear and turning a front wheel (raised) until the timing marks are located in the following positions. Camshaft sprocket mark between two bright links on chain. Crankshaft sprocket mark opposite centre of single bright link.
9 Remove the crankshaft oil pump drivegear and its Woodruff key.
10 Unbolt the oil pump. Some socket-headed screws are accessible through the holes in the driven gear.
11 Jam the camshaft sprocket and unscrew the sprocket retaining bolt. Take off the fuel pump operating eccentric.
12 Turn the lock on the chain tensioner anti-clockwise to lock it in its retracted state.
13 Remove the camshaft sprocket with timing chain.
14 Commence reassembly by engaging the chain around the crankshaft sprocket so that the timing mark on the sprocket is in the centre of the single bright link on the chain.
15 Now engage the upper loop of the chain over the camshaft sprocket so that the timing mark is between the two bright links on the chain.
16 Now offer the camshaft sprocket to the shaft. Adjust the position of the camshaft so that the sprocket keyway aligns with the key.
17 Push the camshaft sprocket into position. Insert and tighten its retaining bolt with the fuel pump eccentric correctly located.
18 Using a very thin screwdriver blade, turn the lock on the chain tensioner fully clockwise to release the slipper.
19 Refit the oil pump with its spacer plate.
20 Fit the oil pump drivegear to the crankshaft.
21 Bolt on the timing chain cover using a new gasket. The bolt nearest the coolant pump pulley must be located in the cover before offering it up, otherwise the pulley will prevent the bolt entering its cover hole. Do not tighten the cover bolts until the crankshaft pulley has been pushed into place to centralise the cover. Fit the coolant hose safety rod under its cover bolts. This rod prevents the coolant hose being cut by the rim of the coolant pump pulley should the hose sag.

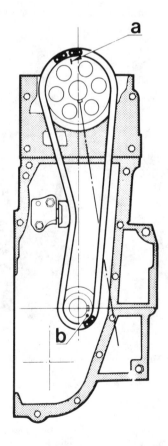

Fig. 1.6 Timing marks (Sec 5)

a   Camshaft sprocket   b   Crankshaft sprocket

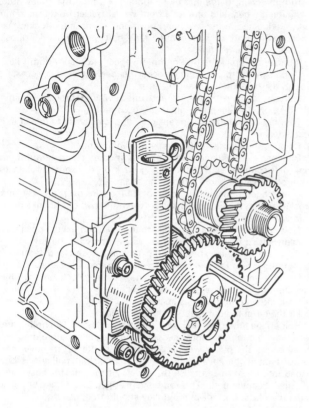

Fig. 1.7 Removing oil pump screw with Allen key (Sec 5)

Fig. 1.8 Timing chain tensioner lock (2) (Sec 5)

Turn in direction of arrow to release slipper

22 Fit the fuel pump operating rod and fuel pump.
23 Tighten the timing chain cover bolts to the specified torque and then trim the upper ends of the gasket flush. Fit the rocker cover using a new gasket. Do not overtighten the securing bolts.
24 Tighten the crankshaft pulley nut to the specified torque, again jamming the flywheel to prevent the crankshaft rotating.

25 Refit the starter, if removed.
26 Refit and tension the drivebelt.
27 Lower the engine, reconnect the mounting.

6 Cylinder head – removal and refitting

Note: *The following paragraphs describe the removal and refitting of the cylinder head with the engine in the car. If the home-made tool described in paragraph 28 is used note that it will not be possible to turn the engine for cleaning the tops of the pistons or checking bore wear. However, the engine can be turned when using the special Peugeot tool but if this is not available the timing chain and sprockets should be removed, as described in Section 5.*

1 Disconnect and remove the battery, as described in Chapter 12.
2 Remove the air cleaner, complete with mounting brackets, hot air hose and inlet hose, with reference to Chapter 3. Also remove the inlet cowl.
3 Drain the cooling system, as described in Chapter 2.
4 Remove the engine oil filler/crankcase ventilation cap and disconnect the hoses from the inlet cowl and carburettor.
5 Jack up the front of the car and support on axle stands. Apply the handbrake.
6 Disconnect the gearchange selector and engagement rods with reference to Chapter 6 (photo). Unscrew the engagement rod nut. Make sure that the gears are in neutral.

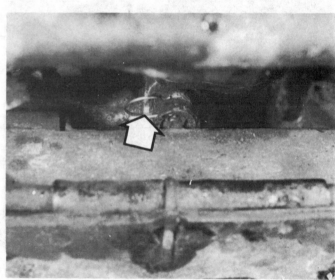

6.6 Removing a gearchange rod retaining clip (arrowed)

7 Unscrew the bolt and nuts, and disconnect the exhaust downpipe from the exhaust manifold. An Allen key will be required to unscrew the bolt.
8 Loosen the left-hand engine mounting nuts beneath the battery tray so that the mounting is lowered by approximately 4.0 mm (0.16 in).
9 Disconnect the heater hoses from the bulkhead, water pump and cylinder head outlet (photo).
10 Remove the fuel pump, as described in Chapter 3.
11 Disconnect the top hose from the thermostat housing.
12 Disconnect the temperature sender wiring.
13 Remove the distributor, as described in Chapter 4.
14 Disconnect the spark plug HT leads and remove them from the rocker cover.
15 Disconnect the throttle and choke cables, as described in Chapter 3.
16 Disconnect the brake servo vacuum hose from the inlet manifold (if applicable) and place to one side.

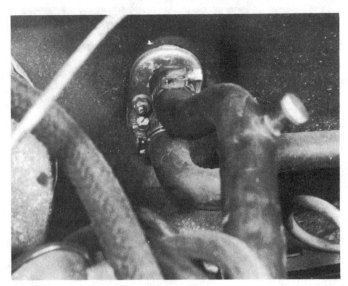

6.9 Heater hoses at the bulkhead

6.18 Lever up the engine and support with a block of wood

17 Unscrew and remove the two bolts securing the right-hand rear engine mounting to the subframe (photo).
18 Using a suitable long bar inserted through the right-hand rear engine mounting bracket, lever up the rear of the engine as far as possible, without damaging the radiator, and support with a block of wood (photo). If necessary, loosen the left-hand engine mounting to gain extra height. Make sure that the right-hand front mounting is not damaged by excessive twisting.
19 Unbolt the rocker cover and remove the gasket.
20 Turn the engine on the crankshaft pulley nut until the key slot in the camshaft is facing upwards, then remove the ignition timing aperture cover and turn the engine as necessary until the mark on the flywheel is aligned with the TDC mark on the timing plate (refer to Chapter 4 if necessary). Pistons No 2 and 3 will be at TDC.
21 Extract the fuel pump plunger from the timing cover (photo).
22 Unbolt the access plate from the top of the timing cover.
23 Unscrew and remove the camshaft sprocket retaining bolt from the end of the camshaft using an Allen key (retain the sprocket with a suitable bar) (photo).

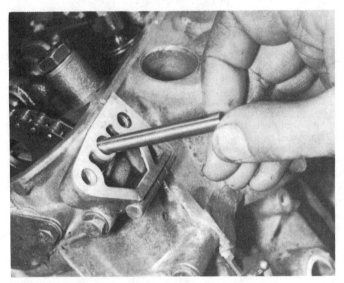

6.21 Removing the fuel pump plunger

6.17 Right-hand rear engine mounting

6.23 Removing the camshaft sprocket retaining bolt

6.24 Loosening the timing cover-to-cylinder head bolts

6.26 Removing the rocker shaft assembly

24 Loosen only the four bolts securing the timing cover to the cylinder head (photo).
25 Progressively unscrew the cylinder head bolts in the order shown in Fig. 1.9, and recover the nuts from their channels in the crankcase.
26 Remove the head bolts and lift off the rocker shaft assembly (photo). It may be necessary to leave one or two bolts in the assembly if they foul the bulkhead due to insufficient engine height.
27 Loosen the camshaft thrust plate bolt, pull out the plate and temporarily retighten the bolt (photos).
28 The camshaft sprocket must now be supported in its normal position while the cylinder head is removed. If it is allowed to drop it will be possible to lift it again without releasing the timing chain tensioner which will necessitate removal of the timing cover. Peugeot dealers use a special mandrel, tool number 70132, but as this is unlikely to be available to the home mechanic it is suggested that a plate and bolt are used, together with the access plate, as shown (photo). Tighten the bolt on the plate with a nut and use a further nut to prevent the sprocket coming off the end of the bolt.

6.27A Loosening the camshaft thrust plate bolt

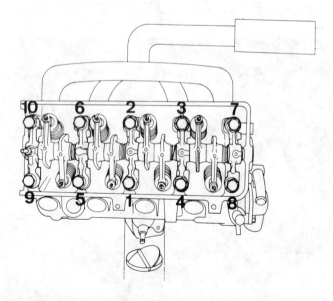

Fig. 1.9 Sequence for tightening or loosening cylinder head bolts (Sec 6)

6.27B The camshaft thrust plate and elongated hole (cylinder head removed)

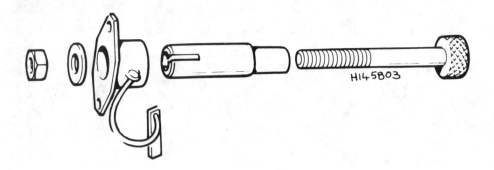

Fig. 1.10 Special Peugeot tool 70132 for use when removing the cylinder head (Sec 6)

6.28 Using a home-made plate to support the camshaft sprocket

6.29A The fuel pump eccentric (arrowed)

6.29B End of camshaft removed from sprocket

29 Slide the camshaft from the fuel pump eccentric and camshaft sprocket and let it rest in the cylinder head (photos).

30 Before removing the cylinder head the following must be noted. The cylinder head is positioned during assembly by means of two dowels. When removing the cylinder head it is most important not to lift it directly from the cylinder block; it must be twisted slightly. This action prevents the cylinder liners from sticking to the cylinder head face and being lifted with it, thus breaking their bottom seals. Before the cylinder head can be twisted, the dowel at the flywheel end must be tapped down flush with the top of the cylinder block, using a drift as shown in Fig. 1.11.

31 Remove the four timing cover-to-cylinder head bolts then move the flywheel end of the cylinder head sideways slightly to release the gasket.

32 Lift the cylinder head from the block and remove the gasket without disturbing the liners (photo). Do not turn the engine over as this also will break the liner bottom seals. If further work is to be carried out on the engine, such as cleaning the tops of the cylinder liners, they should be clamped in position using two cylinder head bolts, metal tubing, and large washers (photo).

33 Before refitting the head, the nuts must be retained in their channels. The use of rubber or plastic tubing is very effective, or wooden wedges may be used (photo).

34 Commence refitting by lifting the location dowel (paragraph 30) and retaining it by inserting a short pin in the hole provided – leaving room for the bolt to pass through (photo).

35 Locate a new cylinder head gasket on the cylinder block, making sure that all the holes are aligned (photos).

36 Apply a silicone sealing compound to the timing cover mating surface (photo).

37 Lower the cylinder head into position over the dowels.

38 Fit the four timing cover-to-cylinder head bolts finger tight.

39 Slide the camshaft into the sprocket and fuel pump eccentric.

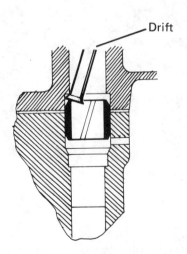

Fig. 1.11 Driving cylinder head dowel down flush with block (Sec 6)

Slight rotation of the eccentric may be necessary in order to align its key with the camshaft slot.

40 Push the thrust plate fully into the camshaft groove then tighten the bolt.

41 Unbolt and remove the sprocket retaining tool.

42 Insert the sprocket retaining bolt and tighten it with an Allen key while holding the sprocket with a bar through one of the holes resting on packing pieces (photo).

6.32A Lifting the cylinder head (complete with carburettors on GT model) from the block

6.32B One method of clamping the cylinder liners

6.33 Using rubber tubing to hold the cylinder head nuts in position

6.34 Using a pop rivet to retain the head location dowel

6.35 Cylinder head gasket located on the block

6.36 Applying sealing compound to the timing cover

6.42 Tightening the camshaft sprocket retaining bolt

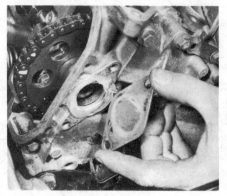

6.43 Refitting the access plate

6.45 Tightening the cylinder head bolts

43 Apply a silicone sealing compound to the access plate then refit it and tighten the bolts (photo).

44 Refit the rocker shaft assembly with the two location pegs towards the front.

45 Insert the head bolts (threads and heads oiled) and tighten them in two stages to the specified torques and in the sequence shown in Fig. 1.9 (photo). Note that washers must be fitted beneath the bolt heads on XY7 and XY8 engines.

46 Remove the nut retainers (paragraph 33) from the cylinder block.

47 Tighten the four timing cover-to-cylinder head bolts.

48 Insert the fuel pump plunger in the timing cover.

49 Adjust the valve clearances, with reference to Section 4.

50 Refit the rocker cover with a new gasket.

51 Remove the block of wood and lower the engine to its normal position.

52 Insert and tighten the right-hand rear engine mounting bolts, also tighten the left-hand mounting bolts.

53 Reconnect the brake servo vacuum hose to the inlet manifold (if applicable).

54 Reconnect the throttle and choke cables (Chapter 3).

55 Refit the distributor and spark plug HT leads (Chapter 4).

56 Reconnect the temperature sender wiring.

57 Refit the top hose to the thermostat housing.

58 Refit the fuel pump (Chapter 3).

59 Reconnect the heater hoses.

60 Refit the exhaust downpipe to the exhaust manifold.

61 Reconnect the gearchange rods (Chapter 6).
62 Lower the car to the ground.
63 Refit the oil filler/crankcase ventilation cap and hoses.
64 Refill the cooling system (Chapter 2).
65 Refit the air cleaner, inlet cowl and inlet hoses.
66 Refit the battery.
67 After the engine has been started and run to full operating temperature, it should be switched off and allowed to cool for at least two hours. Remove the rocker cover.
68 Unscrew the first cylinder head bolt one half a turn and then retighten it to the Stage 2 torque. Repeat the operation on the remaining bolts, one at a time in the sequence specified (Fig. 1.9).
69 Check the valve clearances and readjust if necessary.

7 Engine mountings – renewal

1 The engine/transmission is supported by three mountings, two at the timing chain end and one at the transfer gear end.
2 It is recommended that one mounting is renewed at a time after the weight of the unit has been taken on a jack with a block of wood as an insulator.
3 The battery and tray must be removed when renewing the left-hand mounting.
4 Tighten the bolts to the specified torque after renewing the mountings.

8 Engine/transmission – removal

1 The engine and transmission assembly is removed by lifting upwards from the engine compartment. The transmission is separated from the engine on the bench.
2 Jack up the front of the car and support on axle stands. Apply the handbrake.
3 Remove the drain plug and drain the engine/transmission oil. Clean and refit the drain plug on completion.
4 Drain the cooling system, as described in Chapter 2.
5 Unscrew the bolt and nuts, and disconnect the exhaust downpipe from the exhaust manifold. An Allen key will be required to unscrew the bolt.
6 Disconnect the gearchange selector and engagement rods, with reference to Chapter 6. Unscrew the engagement rod nut. Make sure that the gears are in neutral.
7 Unscrew the nut and detach the bonnet stay from the right-hand front suspension tower then raise the bonnet to vertical and retain by inserting two suitable U-bolts in the special holes provided in the bonnet hinges. Alternatively use welding rod or bend metal dowel rod.
8 Disconnect and remove the battery, as described in Chapter 12.
9 Remove the air cleaner, complete with mounting brackets, hot air hose and inlet hose, with reference to Chapter 3. Also remove the inlet cowl.
10 Disconnect and remove the radiator top and bottom hoses.
11 Disconnect and remove the heater hoses.
12 Disconnect and plug the fuel pump hoses.
13 Disconnect all wiring from the engine and transmission noting the correct routing for reassembly (photos).
14 Disconnect the throttle and choke cables, as described in Chapter 3.
15 Disconnect the brake servo vacuum hose from the inlet manifold (if applicable) and place to one side.
16 Disconnect the clutch cable and remove the pushrod, with reference to Chapter 5.
17 Connect a suitable hoist to the engine lifting eyes and take the weight of the assembly.
18 Unscrew and remove the right-hand engine mounting bolts and the top left-hand mounting nut.
19 Unbolt and remove the battery tray and the right-hand front and left-hand mounting brackets.
20 Lift the assembly slightly, then move to the left to disconnect the right-hand driveshaft and to the right to disconnect the left-hand driveshaft. Let the driveshafts rest on the subframe.
21 Lift the assembly from the engine compartment and also disconnect the speedometer cable from the gearbox.

8.13A Oil pressure switch and cable

8.13B Reverse lamp switch leads

9 Engine/transmission – separation

1 With the power unit out of the car, clean away external dirt using paraffin and a stiff brush, or a water soluble solvent.
2 Unscrew and remove the flywheel housing-to-engine connecting bolts and nuts.
3 There are thirteen bolts and two nuts altogether. Note that an engine lifting lug and earth strap are fitted under some of the bolts.
4 Refer to Chapter 5 and remove the clutch assembly.
5 Unbolt and remove the flywheel. Remove the starter motor (Chapter 12).
6 Unscrew and remove the two bolts and the nut close to the crankshaft oil seal.
7 Unscrew the engine-to-transmission flange connecting bolts. Unbolt the right-hand rear engine mounting.
8 Unscrew and remove the crankshaft pulley nut. In order to hold the crankshaft against rotation, temporarily screw in two bolts into the holes in the flywheel mounting flange and place a long lever between them.
9 Remove the crankshaft pulley.

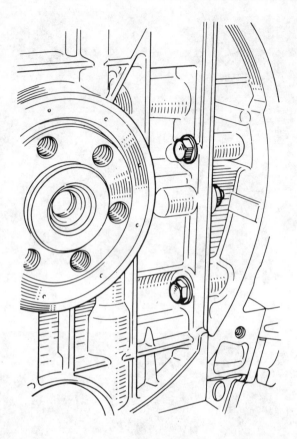

Fig. 1.12 Flange connecting bolts and nuts adjacent to crankshaft oil seal (Sec 9)

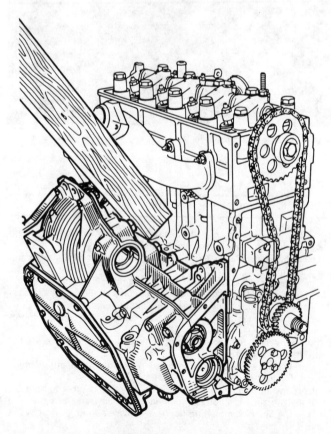

Fig. 1.13 Separating transmission from engine (Sec 9)

10 Remove the rocker cover.

11 Remove the timing chain cover and extract the fuel pump operating plunger.

12 Unscrew and remove the remaining connecting bolts and nuts which are located on the final drive casing side near the driveshaft oil seals.

13 Using a length of wood, prise the engine and transmission apart.

10 Engine dismantling – general

1 As the engine is stripped, clean each part in a bath of paraffin.

2 Never immerse parts with oilways in paraffin (eg crankshaft and rocker shaft). To clean these parts, wipe down carefully with a petrol-dampened rag. Oilways can be cleaned out with wire. If an air line is available, all parts can be blown dry and the oilways blown through as an added precaution.

3 Re-use of old gasket or oil seals is false economy. To avoid the possibility of trouble after the engine has been reassembled always use new items throughout.

4 Do not throw away the old gaskets, for sometimes it happens that an immediate replacement cannot be found and the old gasket is then very useful as a template. Hang up the gaskets as they are removed.

5 If this is the first time that you have dismantled your engine/transmission unit then special attention should be given to the location of the various components and sub-assemblies. This is especially necessary due to the slightly unconventional layout of the model.

6 Many of the component casings are manufactured in aluminium alloy and special care must therefore be taken not to knock, drop or put any unnecessary pressure on these components.

7 Whenever possible, refit nuts, bolts and washers from where they were removed in order not to mix them up. If they cannot be reinstalled lay them out in such a way that it is clear where they came from.

8 Do not remove or disturb the timing plate on the clutch housing if this can be avoided. To reset, refer to Chapter 4.

11 Engine – complete dismantling

1 Support the engine on the bench or strong table. If such facilities are not available then it will have to be dismantled on the floor, but at least cover the floor with a sheet of hardboard.

2 Unbolt and remove the exhaust manifold (three bolts and two nuts) with hot air box.

3 Unbolt the spring-loaded throttle reel (if applicable) from the cylinder head and the thermostat housing. Remove the carburettor(s).

4 Unscrew the oil pressure switch from the crankcase. Unscrew and discard the oil filter.

5 Unbolt and remove the alternator adjuster link and the water pump (Chapter 2).

6 Remove the spark plugs using the special spanner supplied with the car. Remove the distributor.

7 Retract the chain tensioner by turning the lock in an anti-clockwise direction. Unbolt the tensioner and remove it.

8 Unscrew the camshaft sprocket bolt which is of socket-headed type. The crankshaft must be held against rotation for this operation. Do this by screwing two bolts into the flange and passing a long lever between them.

9 Remove the fuel pump eccentric fan.

10 Remove the oil pump socket-headed screws. Some of these are accessible through the holes in the oil pump driven gear.

11 Remove the oil pump and backplate.

12 Remove the camshaft sprocket with the timing chain.

13 Remove the Woodruff key and take off the crankshaft oil pump gear.

14 Remove the second Woodruff key and take off the crankshaft timing chain sprocket.

15 Reposition the engine and unbolt and remove the exhaust manifold and hot air box for the air cleaner.

16 Remove the cylinder head bolts by unscrewing them in the order shown in Fig. 1.9.

17 Lift off the rocker assembly.

18 Drive down the cylinder head positioning dowel, as described in Section 6, so that the cylinder head can be swivelled rather than lifted

from the block. This is to prevent breaking the cylinder liner base seals. If the liners are to be removed then obviously this precaution is not necessary, neither is the need to fit cylinder liner clamps to hold the liners down once the cylinder head has been removed.

19 Dismantling the cylinder head and removal of the camshaft is covered in Section 14.

20 Unscrew and remove the bolts which hold the crankcase half sections together. Split the crankcase and keep the main bearing shells with their crankcase web recesses if the shells are to be used again.

21 Remove the crankshaft oil seal.

22 Mark the rim of the cylinder liners in respect of position in the block and orientation.

23 Mark the big-end caps and the connecting rods so that they can be refitted in their original sequence and the correct way round. A centre punch or hacksaw blade is useful for this purpose.

24 Unscrew the big-end nuts and remove the caps. If the bearing shells are to be used again, keep them taped to their respective cap or connecting rod.

25 Lift the crankshaft from its crankcase half section, keep the shell bearings in their original web recesses if they are to be used again and retrieve the semi-circular thrust washers from either side of Number 2 web.

26 Remove each liner/piston/connecting rod as an assembly from the crankcase. Use a plastic-faced or wooden mallet to tap the liners out if necessary. Make sure that the liners and their respective piston rod assemblies are marked as to position in the block and orientation. A spirit marker is useful for this purpose.

27 Discard the liner base seals which may be of paper or rubber O-ring type.

12 Crankcase ventilation system – description

The system is designed to extract oil, fuel and exhaust gas from the engine crankcase, the latter having passed the piston rings (blow-by gas) particularly when the rings have worn.

The system consists of an intake for fresh air in the oil filler cap with connecting hoses to the carburettor air intake.

The crankcase gases are drawn up into the rocker cover, out through the filler cap hoses and into the manifold where they are burned during the normal engine combustion process.

13 Engine components – examination and renovation

1 With the engine dismantled, all components must be thoroughly cleaned and examined for wear, as described in the following Sections.

2 If a high mileage has been covered since new or the last engine rebuild, and general wear is evident, consideration should be given to renewing the engine with a reconditioned one.

3 If a single component has malfunctioned and the rest of the engine is in good condition endeavour to find out the cause of its failure if not readily apparent. For example, if a bearing has failed, check that the adjoining oilways are clear; the new bearing will not last long if it is not being lubricated.

4 If uncertain about the condition of any components, seek a second opinion, preferably from a Peugeot Talbot dealer/mechanic who will obviously have an expert knowledge of your model and be able to advise on the best course of action.

5 Check on the availability of replacement parts before discarding the old ones. Check the new part against the old to ensure that you have the correct replacement.

6 Some of the measurements required will need the use of feeler blades or a micrometer, but in many instances wear will be visually evident or the old component can be compared with a new one.

14 Cylinder head – dismantling, decarbonising and reassembly

1 Having removed the cylinder head, place it onto a clean workbench where it can be dismantled and examined. Unbolt the retaining plate (if necessary) and withdraw the camshaft (photos).

2 Remove each valve and spring assembly using a valve spring compressor. Extract the split collets from between the spring retaining cup washer and valve stem (photo).

3 Progressively release the tension of the compressor until it can be removed, the spring and retainer withdrawn, and the valve extracted from the guide (photos).

4 As the valves are removed, keep them in order by inserting them in a card having suitable holes punched in it, numbered from 1 to 8. Discard the valve stem oil seals.

5 Wash the cylinder head clean and carefully scrape away the carbon build-up in the combustion chambers and exhaust ports, using a scraper which will not damage the surfaces to be cleaned. If a rotary wire brush and drill is available this may be used for removing the carbon. Take care to prevent foreign matter entering the inlet manifold; it is cast into the cylinder head and cleaning is difficult.

6 The valves may also be scraped and wire-brushed clean in a similar manner.

7 With the cylinder head cleaned and dry, examine it for cracks or damage. In particular inspect the valve seat areas for signs of hairline cracks, pitting or burning. Check the head mating surfaces for distortion, the maximum permissible amount being 0.05 mm (0.002 in).

8 Minor surface wear and pitting of the valve seats can probably be removed when the valves are reground. More serious wear or damage should be shown to your Peugeot Talbot dealer or a competent automotive engineer who will advise you on the action necessary.

9 Carefully inspect the valves, in particular the exhaust valves. Check the stems for distortion and signs of wear. The valve seat faces must be in reasonable condition and if they have covered a high mileage they will probably need to be refaced on a valve grinding machine; again, this is a job for your Peugeot Talbot dealer or local garage/automotive machine shop.

10 Insert each valve into its respective guide and check for excessive side play. Worn valve guides allow oil to be drained past the inlet valve stem causing a smoky exhaust, while exhaust leakage through the exhaust valve guide can overheat the valve guide and cause sticking valves.

14.1A Camshaft retaining/thrust plate

14.1B Removing camshaft

14.2 Compressing a valve spring

14.3A Valve spring cup retainer

14.3B Removing a valve spring

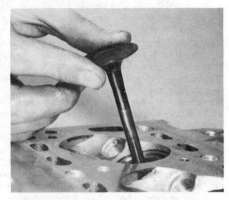

14.3C Removing a valve

14.14 Valve stem oil seal

14.15 Valve spring seating washer

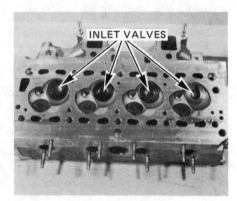

14.16 Cylinder head cleaned and reassembled

11 If the valve guides are to be renewed this is a job best left to your Peugeot Talbot agent who will have the required specialist equipment.

12 Assuming the valves and seats are in reasonable condition they should be reseated by grinding them using valve grinding carborundum paste. The grinding process must also be carried out when new valves are fitted.

13 The carborundum paste used for this job is normally supplied in a double-ended tin with coarse paste at one end and fine at the other. In addition, a suction tool for holding the valve head so that it may be rotated is also required. To grind in the valve, first smear a trace of the coarse paste onto the seat face and fit the suction grinder to the valve head. Then with a semi-rotary motion grind the valve head into its seat, lifting the valve occasionally to redistribute the grinding paste. When a dull matt continuous line is produced on both the valve seat and the valve then the paste can be wiped off. Apply a little fine paste and finish off the grinding process, then remove all traces of the paste. If a light spring is placed over the valve stem behind the head this can often be of assistance in raising the valve from time to time against the pressure of the grinding tool so as to redistribute the paste evenly round the job. The width of the line which is produced after grinding indicates the seat width, and this width should not exceed about 2 mm (0.08 in). If, after a moderate amount of grinding, it is apparent that the seating line is too wide, it probably means that the seat has already been cut back one or more times previously, or else the valve has been ground several times. Here again, specialist advice is best sought.

14 Examine all the valve springs to make sure that they are in good condition and not distorted. If the engine has covered 30 000 miles (45 000 km) then fit new springs at reassembly. Renew the valve stem oil seals. Earlier models are fitted with seals on the inlet valves only, later models have seals on all valves (photo).

15 At the same time renew the valve spring seating washers which sit directly on the cylinder head (photo). These wear fairly quickly.

16 Before reassembling the valve and springs to the cylinder head make a final check that everything is thoroughly clean and free from grit (photo), then lightly smear all the valve stems with engine oil prior to reassembly. The camshaft can now be refitted in the cylinder head and located with the retaining plate. This is then secured with its bolt and a new shakeproof washer. If the cylinder head is being refitted with the engine already in the car leave the camshaft loose in the head without fitting the retaining/thrust plate.

15 Examination and renovation of dismantled components

Crankshaft and main bearings

1 Carefully examine the crankpin and main journal surfaces for signs of scoring or scratches, and check the ovality and taper of each journal in turn. Use a dial gauge and V-blocks and check the main bearing journals for ovality. If any journals are found to be more than 0.02 mm (0.001 in) out of round then they will have to be reground. If the crankpins are scored or scratched, don't bother measuring them as they will have to be reground.

2 If a bearing has failed after a short period of operation look for the cause and rectify before reassembly.

3 If the crankshaft is to be reground this will have to be done by your Peugeot Talbot dealer or a competent automotive engineer. The regrinder will also be able to supply the new shell bearings to suit the undersize requirement. New thrust washers to control endfloat will also be supplied.

Big-end bearings

4 The main bearing shells themselves are normally a matt grey in colour all over and should have no signs of pitting or ridging or discolouration as this usually indicates that the surface bearing metal has worn away and the backing material is showing through. It is worthwhile renewing the main bearing shells anyway if you have gone to the trouble of

removing the crankshaft, but they *must*, of course, be renewed if there is any sign of damage to them or if the crankshaft has been reground.

5 If the crankshaft is not being reground, yet bearing shells are being renewed, make sure that you check whether or not the crankshaft has been reground before. This will be indicated by looking at the back of the bearing shells and will show whether it is undersize or not. The same type of shell bearing must be used when they are renewed.

6 The big-end bearings are subject to wear at a greater rate than the crankshaft journals. A sign that one or more big-end bearings are getting badly worn is a pronounced knocking noise from the engine, accompanied by a significant drop in oil pressure due to the increased clearance between the bearing and the journal permitting oil to flow more freely through the resultantly larger space. If this should happen quite suddenly and action is taken immediately, and by immediately is meant within a few miles, then it is possible that the bearing shell may be renewed without any further work needing to be done.

7 If this happens in an engine which has been neglected, and oil changes and oil filter changes have not been carried out as they should have been, it is most likely that the rest of the engine is in a pretty terrible state anyway. If it occurs in an engine which has been recently overhauled, then it is almost certainly due to a piece of grit or swarf which has got into the oil circulation system and finally come to rest in the bearing shell and scored it. In these instances renewal of the shell alone accompanied by a thorough flushing of the lubrication system may be all that is required.

Cylinder liners

8 The liner bores may be examined for wear either in or out of the engine block; the cylinder head must, of course, be removed in each case.

9 First of all examine the top of the cylinder about a quarter of an inch below the top of the liner and with a finger feel if there is any ridge running round the circumference of the bore. In a worn cylinder bore a ridge will develop at the point where the top ring on the piston comes to the uppermost limit of its stroke. An excessive ridge indicates that the bore below the ridge is worn. If there is no ridge, it is reasonable to assume that the cylinder is not badly worn. Measurement of the diameter of the cylinder bore both in line with the piston gudgeon pin and at right angles to it, at the top and bottom of the cylinder, is another check to be made. A cylinder is expected to wear at the sides where the thrust of the piston presses against it. In time this causes the cylinder to assume an oval shape. Furthermore, the top of the cylinder is likely to wear more than the bottom of the cylinder. It will be necessary to use a proper bore measuring instrument in order to measure the differences in bore diameter across the cylinder, and variations between the top and bottom ends of the cylinder. As a general guide it may be assumed that any variation more than 0.25 mm (0.010 in) indicates that the liners should be renewed. Provided all variations are less than 0.25 mm (0.010 in) it is probable that the fitting of new piston rings will cure the problem of piston-to-cylinder bore clearances. Once again it is difficult to give a firm ruling on this as so much depends on the amount of time, effort and money which the individual owner is prepared, or wishes to spend, on the task. Certainly if the cylinder bores are obviously deeply grooved or scored, the liners must be renewed, regardless of any measurement differences in the cylinder diameter.

10 If new liners are to be fitted, new pistons will be required also, as they are supplied as matched sets.

11 Examine the piston surface and look for signs of any hairline cracks especially round the gudgeon pin area. Check that the oil drain holes below the oil control ring groove are clear, and, if not, carefully clean them out using a suitably sized drill, but don't mark the piston.

12 If any of the pistons are obviously badly worn or defective they must be renewed. A badly worn top ring land may be machined to accept a wider, stepped ring, the step on the outer face of this type of ring being necessary to avoid fouling the unworn ridge at the top of the cylinder bore.

13 Providing the engine has not seized up or suffered any other severe damage, the connecting rods should not require any attention other than cleaning. If damage has occurred or the piston/s show signs of irregular wear it is advisable to have the connecting rod alignment checked. This requires the use of specialised tools and should therefore be entrusted to a Peugeot Talbot agent or a competent automotive engineer, who will be able to check and realign any defective rods.

14 New Peugeot Talbot rings are supplied with their gaps already preset, but if you intend to use other makes the gaps should be checked and adjusted if necessary. Before fitting the new rings on the pistons,

each should be inserted approximately 75 mm (3 in) down the cylinder bore and the gap measured with a feeler gauge. This should be between 0.38 mm (0.015 in) and 0.97 mm (0.038 in). It is essential that the gap should be measured at the bottom of the ring travel, as if it is measured at the top of a worn bore and gives a perfect fit, it could easily seize at the bottom. If the ring gap is too small, rub down the ends of the ring with a very fine file until the gap, when fitted, is correct. To keep the rings square in the bore for measurement, line each up in turn by inserting an old piston in the bore upside down, and use the piston to push the ring down. Remove the piston and measure the piston ring gap.

Gudgeon pins

15 The gudgeon pins float in the piston and are an interference fit in the connecting rods. This interference fit between gudgeon pin and connecting rod means that heat is required (230 to 260°/446°C to 500°F) before a pin can be satisfactorily fitted in the connecting rod. If it is necessary to renew either the piston or connecting rod, we strongly recommend that the separation and assembly of the two be entrusted to someone with experience. Misapplied heat can ruin one, or all, of the components very easily.

16 Never re-use a piston if the original gudgeon pin has been removed from it.

Connecting rod/piston

17 With the pistons removed from the liners, carefully clean them and remove the old rings, keeping them in order and the correct way up. The ring grooves will have to be cleaned out, especially the top, which will contain a burnt carbon coating that may prevent the ring from seating correctly. A broken piston ring will assist in groove cleaning. Take care not to scratch the ring lands or piston surface in any way.

18 The top ring groove is likely to have worn the most. After the groove has been cleaned out, refit the top ring and any excessive wear will be obvious by a sloppy fit. The degree of wear may be checked by using a feeler gauge.

Timing chain, sprocket and tensioner

19 Examine the teeth of both sprockets for wear. Each tooth on a sprocket is an inverted V-shape and wear is apparent when one side of the tooth becomes more concave in shape than the other. When badly worn, the teeth become hoop-shaped and the sprockets must be renewed.

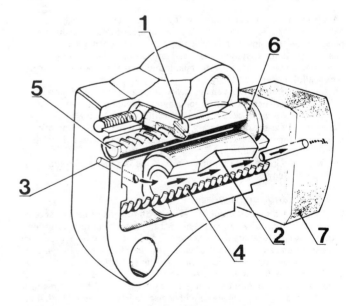

Fig. 1.14 Cutaway view of timing chain tensioner (Sec 15)

1	Ratchet screw	5	Rack
2	Piston	6	Washer
3	Oil supply	7	Slipper
4	Spring		

20 If the sprockets need to be renewed then the chain will have worn also and should also be renewed. If the sprockets are satisfactory, examine the chain and look for play between the links. When the chain is held out horizontally, it should not bend appreciably. Remember, a chain is only as strong as its weakest link and, being a relatively cheap item, it is worthwhile fitting a replacement anyway.

21 Check the condition of the tensioner slipper. If it is worn, renew it.

22 Inspect the oil pump drive gears for wear or damage and renew if necessary. Always fit a new timing cover oil seal (photo).

15.31A Rocker shaft end circlip

15.22 Timing cover oil seal

Transfer gears (refer also to Chapter 5)

23 The condition of the transfer gears, their bearings and the input and output shafts, is obviously critical as they transmit the power of the engine to the transmission unit, and are liable to be a source of noise if worn.

24 Clean the input and output shaft ball-bearings and check them for excessive play and/or signs of damage. Inspect the intermediate shaft needle roller bearings. Renew any suspect or worn bearings. If a bearing has collapsed due to general wear and fatigue, then the chances are that the other bearings are close to failure and it is therefore advisable to renew all the bearings.

25 Carefully inspect the transfer gears. If excessive transmission noise has been experienced it may be reduced by changing the transfer gears. If the teeth are worn or damaged, then the gears should be renewed. Renew the gear set rather than a single gear; it is not good practice to mesh new gears with old as the wear rate of both is increased and they will be noisy in operation.

26 Check the input and output shafts, and inspect their splines for wear or damage. Renew them if necessary.

Camshaft and rocker gear

27 The camshaft lobes should be examined for signs of flats or scoring or any other form of wear or damage. At the same time the rocker arms should also be examined, particularly on the faces where they bear against the camshaft, for signs of wear. Very slight wear may be removed by rubbing with an oilstone but maintain the original contour.

28 The camshaft bearing journals should be in good condition and show no signs of pitting or scoring as they are relatively free from stress.

29 If the bearing surfaces are scored or discoloured it is possible that the shaft is not running true, and in this case it will have to be renewed. For an accurate check get your Peugeot Talbot agent to inspect both the camshaft and cylinder head.

30 Worn camshaft bearings in the cylinder head can only be rectified by renewal of the head, an expensive business, as the bearings are machined directly in the head.

31 The rocker arm assembly can be dismantled on removing the circlip from the end of the rocker shaft (photos).

15.31B Dismantling the rocker shaft assembly

32 When removing the various rocker components from the shaft take careful note of the sequence in which they are removed. In particular note that the No 2 and No 4 rocker bearings are identical, keep the components in order as they are removed from the shaft for inspection. The final rocker bearing (timing chain end) is secured to the rocker shaft by the rocker cover stud, or an Allen screw under that stud.

33 Check the rocker shaft for signs of wear. Check it for straightness by rolling it on a flat surface. It is unlikely to be bent but if this is the case it must either be straightened or renewed. The shaft surface should be free of wear ridges caused by the rocker arms. Check the oil feed holes and clear them out if blocked or sludged-up.

34 Check each rocker arm for wear on an unworn part of the shaft. Check the end of the adjuster screw and the face of the rocker arm where it bears on the camshaft. Any signs of cracks or serious wear will necessitate renewal of the rocker arm.

Flywheel and starter ring gear

35 There are two areas in which the flywheel may have been worn or damaged. The first is on the driving face where the clutch friction plate bears against it. Should the clutch plate have been permitted to wear down beyond the level of the rivets, it is possible that the flywheel will have been scored. If this scoring is severe it may be necessary to have it refaced or even renewed.

36 Evidence of tiny cracks on the flywheel driving face will indicate that overheating has occurred.

37 The other part to examine is the teeth of the starter ring gear around the periphery of the flywheel. If several of the teeth are broken or missing, or the front edges of all teeth are obviously very badly chewed up, then it would be advisable to fit a new ring gear.

38 The old ring gear can be removed by cutting a slot with a hacksaw down between two of the teeth as far as possible, without cutting into the flywheel itself. Once the cut is made a chisel will split the ring gear which can then be drawn off. To fit a new ring gear requires it to be heated first to a temperature of 220°C (428°F), no more. This is best done in a bath of oil or an oven, but not with a naked flame. It is much more difficult to heat evenly and to the required temperature with a naked flame. Once the ring gear has attained the correct temperature it can be placed onto the flywheel; making sure that it beds down properly onto the register. It should then be allowed to cool down naturally. If by mischance, the ring gear is overheated, it should not be used. The temper will have been lost, thereby softening it, and it will wear out in a very short space of time.

39 Although not actually fitted into the flywheel itself, there is a bush in the centre of the crankshaft flange onto which the flywheel fits. Whilst more associated with gearbox and clutch, it should always be inspected when the clutch is removed. The main bearing oil seal is revealed when the flywheel is removed. This can be prised out with a screwdriver but must always be renewed once removed. The spigot bush is best removed using a suitable extractor. Another method is to fill the recess with grease and then drive in a piece of close fitting steel bar. This should force the bush out. A new bush may be pressed in, together with a new seal. Make sure that the chamfered end of the bush abuts the seal. The bush is self-lubricating.

Oil pump

40 The oil pump gears are exposed once the spacer plate is removed.

41 Side movement of the gear spindles will indicate wear in the bushes and the pump should be renewed complete.

42 Worn or chipped gearteeth must be rectified by renewal of the gear.

43 Check the endfloat of the gears using a straight-edge and feeler blades (photo).

15.43 Checking oil pump gear endfloat

44 Check the clearance between the tip of the gear lobes and the oil pump body (photo).

45 If any of these clearances exceed the specified limit, renew the pump.

46 Remove the retaining pin from the relief valve housing and withdraw the cup, spring, guide and piston. Renew any worn components (photo).

15.44 Checking oil pump lobe tip clearance

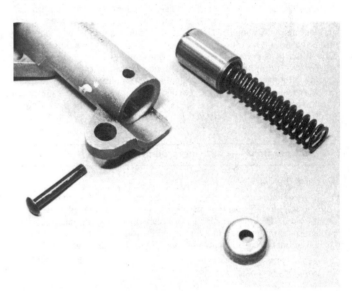

15.46 Oil pump relief valve components

16 Engine reassembly – general

1 It is during the process of engine reassembly that the job is either made a success or a failure. From the word go there are certain basic rules which is folly to ignore, namely:

   (a) Absolute cleanliness. The working area, the components of the engine and the hands of those working on the engine must be completely free of grime and grit. One small piece of carborundum dust or swarf can ruin a big-end in no time, and nullify all the time and effort you have spent.

   (b) Always, no matter what the circumstances may be, use new gaskets, locking tabs, seats, nyloc (self-locking) nuts and any other parts mentioned in the Sections in this Chapter. It is pointless to dismantle an engine, spend considerable money and time on it and then waste all this for the sake of something as small as a failed oil seal. Delay the rebuilding if necessary.

   (c) Don't rush it. The most skilled and experienced mechanic can easily make a mistake if he is rushed.

(d) Check that all nuts and bolts are clean and in good condition and ideally renew all spring washers, lockwashers and tab washers as a matter of course. A supply of clean engine oil and clean cloths (to wipe excess oil off your hands) and a torque spanner are the only things which should be required in addition to all the tools used in dismantling the engine.

(e) The torque wrench is an essential requirement when reassembling the engine (and transmission) components. This is because the various housings are manufactured from aluminium alloy and whilst this gives the advantage of less weight, it also means that the various fastenings must be accurately tightened as specified to avoid distortion and/or damage to the components.

17 Engine – preparation for reassembly

1 Assuming that the engine has been completely stripped for reconditioning and that the block is now bare, before any reassembly takes place it must be thoroughly cleaned both inside and out.
2 Clean out the oilways using a bottle brush, wire or other suitable implement, and blow through with compressed air. Squirt some clean engine oil through to check that the oilways are clear.
3 If the core plugs are defective and show signs of weeping, they must be renewed at this stage. To remove, carefully drive a punch through the centre of the plug and use the punch to lever the plug out. Clean the aperture thoroughly and prior to fitting the new plug, smear the orifice with sealant. Use a small-headed hammer and carefully drive the new core plug into position with the convex side outwards. Check that it is correctly seated on completion.
4 As the components are assembled, lubricate them with clean engine oil and use a suitable sealant where applicable.
5 Make sure that all blind tapped holes are clean, with any oil mopped out of them. This is because it is possible for a casting to fracture when a bolt is screwed in owing to hydraulic pressure.

18 Cylinder liners – checking projection

Paper type gasket seals

1 If the cylinder liners had paper type base seals, the first thing to do is to check the liner projection and select new paper seals (photo).
2 If rubber O-rings are used, no checking or measurement of liner projection is required, simply renew the O-rings.
3 Paper gaskets are available in four different thicknesses:

Blue 0.087 mm
White 0.102 mm
Red 0.122 mm
Yellow 0.147 mm

Fig. 1.15 Cylinder liner and block match marks (a) (Sec 18)

4 The correct projection for each liner above the surface of the cylinder block is between 0.13 and 0.18 mm, preferably nearer to the greater projection.
5 Fit the liners without gaskets into their original locations. If new liners are being fitted, they of course can be fitted in any order.
6 Using a dial indicator or feeler gauges and a straight-edge, measure the projection of each liner.
7 It is now a simple matter to select a paper gasket which, when its thickness is added to the recorded projection, will equal the specified projection.
8 Make sure that the difference in projection between adjacent liners does not exceed 0.04 mm. If it does, reduce the gasket thickness on the greater projecting liner.
9 If new liners are being fitted, the projection differences can be eliminated by changing the position of the liner in the block or by twisting it on its base.
10 Once selected, mark each liner's position in the block, then remove them and place with their paper gaskets ready for final assembly.

O-ring type seals

11 If the original liners are being refitted then the projection should be correct once new O-ring seals have been fitted.
12 If new liners are being fitted, then measure the projection of each

18.1 Liner with paper gasket

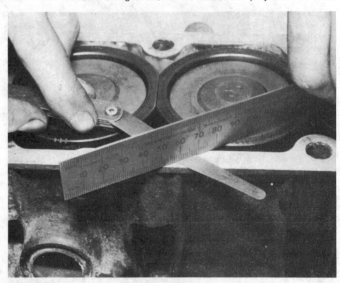

18.12 Measuring cylinder liner projection

liner without its seal. This should be between 0.10 and 0.17 mm, with a maximum difference between liners of 0.05 mm (photo).

13 If the difference between adjacent liners exceeds 0.05 mm, rotate the liners through half a turn or interchange the liner position in the block.

14 Once correctly located, mark their sequence in the block and withdraw them so that their piston/rods can be fitted.

19 Engine – complete reassembly

Pistons and liners

1 Fit the piston rings to the pistons. Always fit the rings from the piston crown end. Use three old feeler blades equally spaced behind the ring so that it will slide down to the lower grooves without dropping into the higher ones (photo).

2 Make sure that the rings are correctly located and the right way up. If genuine Peugeot Talbot piston rings are being used, refer to Fig. 1.16. If special proprietary rings are being fitted, follow the manufacturer's instructions.

3 Twist the piston rings so that the gap in the oil control ring expander aligns with the gudgeon pin and the gaps in the rails are offset from the gudgeon pin by between 20.0 and 50.0 mm (0.79 and 1.97 in). The caps in the top two compression rings should be equally spaced (120°) from the gap in the oil control expander around the piston.

4 If new piston/liner assemblies have been supplied, the identification marks on the piston and liner should be:

Piston	Liner
A	One file mark on rim
B	Two file marks on rim
C	Three file marks on rim (photo)

5 All four pistons should be of the same grading.

6 Fit the liners to the piston/connecting rod assemblies so that when installed in the cylinder block, the rim mark on the liner will be towards the oil gallery side and the arrow on the piston crown facing towards the timing chain cover end of the engine (photo). Piston-to-rod relationship is not important.

7 Oil the piston rings liberally and fit a compressor to the piston and compress the rings fully.

19.1 Method of fitting piston rings

19.4 Piston/liner grading mark

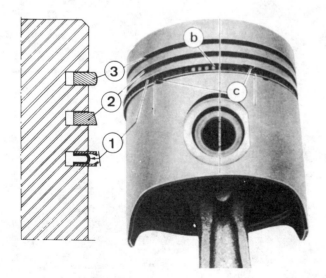

Fig. 1.16 Piston ring identification (Sec 19)

1	Oil control ring	3	Compression ring
2	Compression ring	b	Oil control expander gap
	(tapered)	c	Oil control rail gaps

19.6 Piston crown directional arrow

8   Lubricate the bore of the liner and insert the piston. As this is done, the compressor will be pushed off (photo).

9   Push the piston right into the liner.

10 Fit either the selected paper gasket seals so that their tabs are diametrically opposite to the liner rim marks or locate the O-ring seals making sure that they are not twisted (photo).

11 Remove the big-end caps, wipe the recesses in rod and cap absolutely clean and fit the bearing shells. If the original shells are being used again, make sure that they are being returned to their original locations.

12 Push the liner/rod assemblies into the block, without disturbing the seals and aligning the location marks (photo).

13 Fit clamps to hold the liners in the block.

14 Place the block so that it rests on its top face and wipe out the recesses and fit the main bearing shells (photo).

15 Fit the semi-circular thrust washers which control crankshaft endfloat. The oil grooves of the thrust washers must be against the machined face of the crankshaft (photo).

16 Oil the shell bearings and lower the crankshaft into position (photo).

17 Now check the crankshaft endfloat. Do this by first pushing the crankshaft fully in one direction and then in the other. A dial gauge or feeler blades should be used to measure the endfloat (photo). If the endfloat is outside the specified tolerance, change the thrust washers for ones of different thickness, from the four thicknesses available.

18 Fit the big-end caps complete with bearing shells, well lubricated. Make sure that the cap/rod matching marks are in alignment. This will ensure that both tongues of the shells are on the same side (photo).

19 Tighten the big-end nuts to the specified torque (photo).

20 Into the crankcase flange fit a new O-ring seal and check that the locating dowels are in position (photo).

21 Apply jointing compound to the flange.

22 Clean the recesses in the remaining crankcase housing section and fit the main bearing shells. Note that the grooved shells are located in positions 2 and 4.

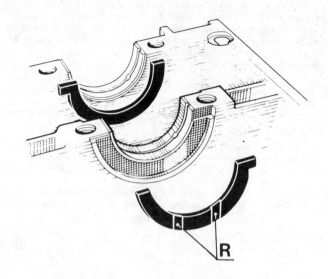

Fig. 1.17 Crankshaft thrust washers (Sec 19)

R   Oil grooves

23 Locate the housing, taking care not to displace the bearing shells (photo).

24 Screw in the ten main bearing/casing bolts with flat washers; noting that the two longer bolts are at the flywheel housing end and the very long one at the crankshaft pulley end on the oil pump side (photo).

19.8 Inserting piston in liner

19.10 Cylinder liner O-ring seal

19.12 Installing piston/liner assembly

19.14 Main bearing shells in position

19.15 Crankshaft thrust washers

19.16 Lowering crankshaft into place

19.17 Checking crankshaft endfloat

19.18 Fitting a big-end cap

19.19 Tightening a big-end cap nut

19.20 Crankcase flange O-ring seal

19.23 Fitting crankcase housing

19.24 Tightening main bearing bolts

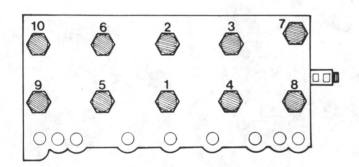

Fig. 1.18 Main bearing bolt tightening sequence (Sec 19)

19.26 Crankcase housing flange bolts

19.27 Fitting crankshaft oil seal

19.29A Chain tensioner filter

19.29B Fitting chain tensioner

25 Tighten the bolts in the sequence given in two stages to the specified torque (see Fig. 1.18).

26 Now screw in and tighten the seven housing flange bolts with their spring washers (photo).

27 Grease the lips of a new crankshaft oil seal and drive it squarely into position (photo).

28 Fit the cylinder head, as described in Section 6.

29 Fit the timing chain tensioner oil filter and the crankshaft sprocket Woodruff key. Bolt the chain tensioner into position (photos).

30 Rotate the crankshaft by temporarily screwing in two flywheel bolts and placing a bar between them until the key is in alignment with the crankcase joint (Fig. 1.19).

31 Temporarily fit the camshaft sprocket and rotate the camshaft until the keyway is positioned as shown in Fig. 1.19.

32 Fit the crankshaft sprocket (photo).

33 Loop the chain around the crankshaft sprocket so that the bright link on the chain is centred on the timing mark on the sprocket (photo).

34 Now loop the chain around the camshaft sprocket so that the two bright links are positioned one on each side of the sprocket timing mark (photo). Push the sprocket with chain onto the camshaft, if necessary move the camshaft a fraction to align the keyway.

35 Screw in the camshaft sprocket bolt with fuel pump eccentric and tighten to the specified torque (photo).

36 Turn the key in the chain tensioner fully clockwise to release the slipper (photo).

37 Check that the locating dowel is in position and fit the oil pump with spacer plate; no gasket is used (photo). If the pump driven sprocket is hard to turn, release the pump mounting bolts and turn the pump slightly on its locating dowel. Re-tighten the bolts.

38 Fit the oil pump drive sprocket and Woodruff key to the crankshaft (photo).

39 Fit the spark plugs. Do not overtighten them.

40 Fit the alternator adjuster link and coolant pump.

41 Screw in the oil pressure switch (photo).

42 Fit a new oil filter.

43 Bolt on the throttle reel with return spring (where applicable).

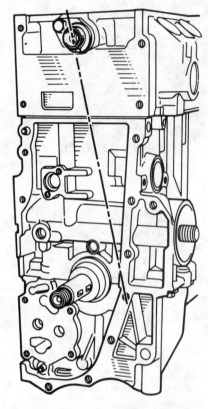

Fig. 1.19 Crankshaft and camshaft keyway positions when fitting the timing chain (Sec 19)

19.32 Crankshaft sprocket

19.33 Timing chain bright link at crankshaft sprocket (arrowed)

19.34 Timing chain bright links (arrowed) at camshaft sprocket

19.35A Fuel pump eccentric

19.35B Tightening camshaft sprocket bolt

19.36 Releasing timing chain tensioner

19.37 Fitting oil pump with spacer plate

19.38 Oil pump drive sprocket

19.41 Oil pressure switch

19.44A Fitting the exhaust manifold ...

19.44B ... and hot air box

20.6 O-ring seal on transmission casing

44 Bolt on the exhaust manifold using new gaskets. Leave the end nuts loose until the hot air collector has been fitted and then tighten them (photos).
45 Fit the fuel pump and operating rod.
46 Fit the distributor (Chapter 4).
47 Fit the carburettor(s) with a new gasket.
48 Fit the thermostat and thermostat housing cover using a new gasket.
49 The engine is now ready for connecting to the transmission, as described in the next Section.

20 Engine/transmission – reconnection

1 Check that the oil pick-up strainer is in position within the transmission casing.

2 Fit the sump cover using a new gasket.
3 Tighten the fixing bolts and drain plug to the specified torque.
4 Fit the cover plate.
5 Apply jointing compound to the mating surfaces on the engine and transmission.
6 On the transmission, locate a new O-ring seal and check that the locating dowels and the studs are in position (photo).
7 Offer the transmission to the engine, screw in the connecting bolts and nuts and tighten to the specified torque (photo).
8 Locate a new timing chain cover gasket and fit the cover.
9 Before offering the cover to the engine, put the bolt nearest the coolant pump pulley into its cover hole otherwise the pulley will prevent it from being fitted later. Do not tighten the cover bolts yet (photo).
10 Fit the coolant hose safety rod under its cover bolts (photo).
11 Use the crankshaft pulley to centralise the timing chain cover and then tighten the cover bolts.

20.7 Offering transmission to engine

20.9A Fitting timing chain cover and gasket

20.9B Timing cover bolt nearest coolant pump pulley

20.10 Coolant hose safety support rod

20.13 Tightening crankshaft pulley nut

20.14A Inserting flywheel bolts

20.14B Tightening flywheel bolts

20.16 Offering up flywheel housing

12 Cut the upper ends of the cover gasket off flush.

13 Apply grease to the crankshaft pulley oil seal contact surface and push it onto its key. Fit a new lockplate, tighten the nut to the specified torque and then bend up the lockplate (photo).

14 Fit the flywheel. Apply thread locking fluid to clean threads and screw in the flywheel bolts to the specified torque (photos). The flywheel holes are offset so it will only go onto the crankshaft flange in one position.

15 Fit the clutch and centralise the driven plate, as described in Chapter 5.

16 Fit a new gasket and offer up the flywheel housing (Chapter 5), complete with transfer gears (photo). Make sure that the engine lifting lug and earth strap are correctly located under their respective bolts (photo).

17 If they were removed, bolt the engine mountings to the flywheel housing.

18 Fit the starter motor. Tighten the bolts and nuts in the following order:

    1   Starter drive end flange to flywheel housing
    2   Brush end bracket to engine crankcase
    3   Brush end bracket to starter motor

19 Adjust the valve clearances. Use a new gasket and fit the rocker cover.

20 Fit the alternator.

21 The engine/transmission is now ready for refitting to the car.

21 Engine/transmission – refitting

1 Refitting is a reversal of the removal procedure given in Section 8 with particular attention to the following points:

    (a) To assist engagement of the driveshafts, turn the front wheels as necessary until the splines engage

    (b) Adjust the clutch cable, as described in Chapter 5

    (c) Adjust the throttle and choke cables, as described in Chapter 3

    (d) Fill the engine/transmission with oil

    (e) Fill the cooling system, as described in Chapter 2

22 Engine – initial start-up after overhaul

1 Make sure that the battery is fully charged and that all lubricants, coolant and fuel are replenished.

2 It will require several revolutions of the engine on the starter motor to pump the petrol up to the carburettor(s).

3 As soon as the engine fires and runs, keep it going at a fast tickover only (no faster) and bring it up to the normal working temperature.

4 As the engine warms up there will be odd smells and some smoke from parts getting hot and burning off oil deposits. The signs to look for are leaks of water or oil which will be obvious if serious. Check also the exhaust pipe and manifold connections, as these do not always 'find' their exact gastight position until the warmth and vibration have acted on them, and it is almost certain that they will need tightening further. This should be done with the engine stopped.

5 When normal running temperature has been reached, adjust the engine idling speed, as described in Chapter 3. Run the engine until the fan cuts in and then switch off. Check that no oil or coolant is leaking with the engine stationary.

6 Allow at least two hours for the engine to cool down and then retighten the cylinder head bolts after removing the rocker cover. Follow the bolt tightening sequence and, starting with the first, slacken the bolt and retighten it to the specified final tightening torque before loosening the second bolt. Repeat until all bolts have been retightened.

7 Check and adjust the valve clearances.

8 Check the ignition timing.

9 Road test the car to check that the timing is correct and that the

engine is giving the necessary smoothness and power. Do not race the engine – if new bearings and/or pistons have been fitted it should be treated as a new engine and run in at a reduced speed.

10 Change the engine oil at 1000 miles (1500 km) if many of the engine internal components have been renewed. At the same mileage, check the tension of the drivebelt.

PART C: XU5J engine

23 Operations possible without removing the engine from the car

The following items can be removed and refitted with the engine in the car:

(a) *Cylinder head*
(b) *Camshaft drivebelt and camshaft*
(c) *Sump and oil pump*
(d) *Clutch and flywheel (after removal of transmission)*

Since the sump and cylinder head can be removed *in situ*, it is possible to renew the pistons, liners and big-end bearings without removing the engine. Such work is not recommended, however, since it can be performed more easily with the engine on the bench.

24 Cylinder head – removal and refitting

1 Remove the camshaft drivebelt (Section 25).
2 Drain the cooling system (Chapter 2).
3 Slacken, but do not remove, the engine lower mounting rubber centre nut and bolt (photo).

24.3 Engine lower mounting

4 Remove the air cleaner, its pipes and trunking, and the crankcase breather and its pipes.
5 Remove the nut which secures the engine right-hand mounting rubber.
6 Carefully raise the engine 6 to 8 mm (say 3 inches) using a hoist or a well-protected jack. Remove the two bolts which secure the right-hand mounting bracket to the cylinder head, then lower the engine back into position.
7 Remove the airflow sensor, inlet manifold, injectors and associated components with reference to Chapter 3.
8 Disconnect all coolant and vacuum hoses.
9 Disconnect the electrical leads.

10 Disconnect the exhaust downpipes at the manifold flange.
11 Remove the coolant pipe from the pump inlet housing. Also remove the diagnostic socket from its bracket and unbolt the oil filler pipe from the inlet manifold, if applicable.
12 Remove the camshaft cover, at the same time removing the distributor cap and HT leads.
13 Slacken the cylinder head bolts in the reverse sequence to that used when tightening (Fig. 1.20). Remove the bolts.
14 Remove the cylinder head, using a couple of bars through two of the bolt holes and 'rocking' it towards the front of the car. Do not lift the head directly from the block, as this will disturb the liners. Remove the gasket and recover any loose dowels.
15 Fit cylinder liner clamps, or large washers secured with nuts and bolts, to keep the liners in position (photo). *If the liners are disturbed, the engine will have to be removed for new seals to be fitted.*

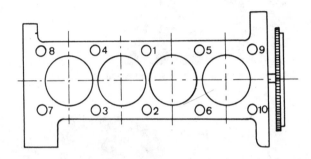

Fig. 1.20 Cylinder head bolt tightening sequence (Sec 24)

24.15 Cylinder liners clamped with washers and bolts

16 Commence refitting by fitting the dowels to the cylinder block. Keep the flywheel-end dowel raised by inserting a 5 mm punch or large nail through the hole in the front of the block (photo). Remove the liner clamps.
17 Fit the new gasket, dry, with the tab at the flywheel end. Lower the cylinder head into position, making sure that it mates with the dowels. Remove the punch or nail.
18 Fit the cylinder head bolts, their threads clean and lightly oiled. Remember to fit the spacer to the bolt above the coolant pump.
19 Progressively tighten the bolts in the order shown in Fig. 1.20 to the Stage 1 specified torque.

24.16 Dowel is kept raised by inserting a nail beneath it

24.21 Home-made disc for measuring tightening angle. Disc is fixed and pointer rotates

20 Raise the engine slightly and refit the two bolts which secure the right-hand mounting bracket to the cylinder head. Tighten these bolts and slacken the one which holds the same bracket to the engine block. Lower the engine and tighten the right-hand mounting nut and the lower mounting rubber nut and bolt.
21 Slacken cylinder head bolt No 1, then immediately retighten it to the Stage 2 specified torque. Tighten further by the angle specified for Stage 3 (photo). Repeat for all the bolts, following the tightening sequence.
22 Check the valve clearances and adjust, if necessary.
23 Refit the remaining components in the reverse order of removal.
24 Refill and bleed the cooling system (Chapter 2).
25 Start the engine and warm it up until the cooling fan cuts in, then switch off and allow it to cool for at least two hours.
26 Retighten the cylinder head bolts, as described in paragraph 21, then recheck the valve clearances.
27 If a new camshaft drivebelt has been fitted, retension it as described in Section 25.
28 Tighten the engine mounting bracket bolt.

25 Camshaft drivebelt – removal and refitting

1   Disconnect the battery earth lead.
2   Remove the alternator drivebelt.
3   Remove the inner shield from the right-hand wheel arch (photo) and wedge the radiator bottom hose under the sump.
4   Remove the shield from the camshaft sprocket.
5   Turn the crankshaft until the dowel hole in the pulley is at about 12 o'clock and the hole in the camshaft sprocket is at about 7 o'clock. In this position a 10 mm dowel should pass through each hole and into the timing recess behind. Verify this and then remove the dowels (photo).
6   Remove the clutch bottom shield. Have an assistant jam the starter ring gear while the crankshaft pulley bolt is undone. This bolt is very tight. **Do not** jam the pulley by means of the timing dowel: damage will result. Remove the bolt and washer.
7   Check that the 10 mm dowels will still enter the timing holes: adjust the crankshaft position if necessary by means of the starter ring gear. Remove the crankshaft pulley, retrieving the Woodruff key if it is loose.
8   Remove the plastic covers from the front of the camshaft drivebelt. Note the location of the various bolts.

25.3 Removing the inner shield

25.5 Timing dowels in position – engine removed for clarity

9   Slacken the two nuts on the front of the drivebelt tensioner and the single nut at the rear. Use a spanner on the square end of the tensioner cam spindle to turn the cam to the horizontal position and so compress the tensioner spring (photo). Tighten the cam locknut.
10 Remove the camshaft drivebelt, taking care not to kink it or contaminate it with oil if it is to be re-used.
11 Commence refitting by positioning the belt on the crankshaft sprocket, then refitting the pulley and verifying the correct position of the crankshaft by means of the dowel. (Observe the arrows on the belt showing the direction of rotation, and the timing lines which align with marks on the crankshaft and camshaft sprockets) (photo).
12 Fit the belt to the camshaft sprocket, round the tensioner and to the coolant pump sprocket.
13 Release the tensioner cam locknut and turn the cam downwards to release the spring. Tighten the locknut and the tensioner front nuts (photo).
14 Remove the timing dowels and turn the crankshaft through two full turns in the normal direction of rotation. Turn the crankshaft further to bring No 1 piston to TDC on the firing stroke.
15 Slacken the tensioner front nuts and the cam locknut, then retighten them.

25.13 Drivebelt tensioner front nuts

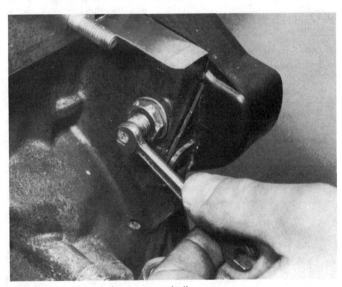

25.9 Turning the tensioner cam spindle

16 Turn the crankshaft further and make sure that the timing dowels can still be inserted. If not, remove the drivebelt and start again.
17 If a new belt has been fitted, it must be run in and retensioned, as follows.
18 Tighten the crankshaft pulley bolt to the specified torque, then refit and tension the alternator drivebelt. Temporarily refit the camshaft sprocket cover.
19 Run the engine up to operating temperature, indicated by the cooling fan operating, then stop it and allow it to cool for at least two hours.
20 Rotate the crankshaft to the TDC position, No 1 cylinder firing, then slacken and retighten the tensioner nuts once more.
21 Remove the alternator drivebelt and the crankshaft pulley. Refit and secure the plastic covers, then refit the pulley and tighten its bolts to the specified torque. Refit and tension the alternator drivebelt.
22 Check the ignition timing and adjust if necessary.

26 Camshaft – removal and refitting

1   Remove the camshaft drivebelt as previously described in Section 25.
2   Remove the camshaft cover. For ease of access, remove the distributor cap and HT leads, air cleaner and brake servo vacuum hose.
3   Remove the distributor, as described in Chapter 4.
4   Remove the camshaft lubrication manifold.
5   Lock the camshaft sprocket (eg with a timing dowel) and remove the sprocket retaining bolt. Remove the sprocket and the cover plate behind it. Remove the thrust plate (photos).
6   Progressively slacken the camshaft bearing cap securing nuts. Make identifying marks if necessary, then remove the caps. Be prepared for the camshaft to spring upwards. Remove the camshaft.
7   Commence refitting by making sure that the crankshaft is in the correct (dowelled) position – if not, move it to this position to avoid possible piston/valve contact.
8   Refit the camshaft, then oil and fit its bearing caps. Tighten the cap nuts progressively to the specified torque. Refit and secure the thrust plate.
9   Fit a new oil seal to the sprocket end of the camshaft.
10 Refit the sprocket rear cover plate, locate it correctly with a 10 mm dowel and tighten its fastenings (photo). Fit the camshaft sprocket, dowel it and tighten its securing bolt to the specified torque.
11 Refit the lubrication manifold and distributor.
12 Refit the camshaft cover, HT leads and distributor cap, air cleaner, and brake servo vacuum hose.
13 Refit the camshaft drivebelt (Section 25).

25.11 Line on belt aligns with mark on sprocket

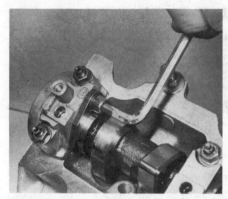
26.5A Removing the camshaft thrust plate screw

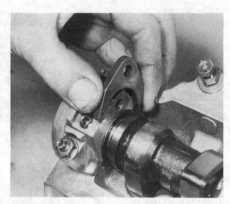
26.5B Removing the camshaft thrust plate

26.10 Locating the cover plate with a 10 mm dowel

27 Valve clearances – checking and adjustment

1   Remove the air cleaner and trunking, and the brake servo vacuum hose.

2   Remove the camshaft cover, trying not to damage the gasket.

3   Prepare to rotate the crankshaft, either by jacking up one front wheel and turning the wheel with 4th or 5th gear engaged, or with a spanner on the crankshaft pulley bolt. The crankshaft will be easier to rotate if the spark plugs are first removed.

4   Have ready a pencil and paper to record the measured clearances.

5   Turn the crankshaft until the cam lobe nearest the pulley end of the engine is pointing vertically upwards. Use feeler gauges to measure the clearance between the base of the cam and the tappet (photo). Record the clearance.

6   Repeat the measurement for the other seven valves, turning the crankshaft as necessary so that the cam lobe in question is always vertically upwards.

7   Calculate the difference between each measured clearance and the desired value (see Specifications). Note that the value for inlet valves is different from that for exhaust. Counting from either end of the engine, the valve sequence is:

Exhaust – Inlet – Inlet – Exhaust – Exhaust – Inlet – Inlet – Exhaust

8   If any clearance measured is outside the specified tolerance, adjustment must be carried out as described below. If all clearances are within tolerance, refit the camshaft cover, using a new gasket if necessary. Note the diagnostic socket and copper washer under the bolt at the timing belt end.

9   To adjust the clearances remove the camshaft as described in Section 26.

10   Lift off a tappet and its shim. Be careful that the shim does not fall out of the tappet. Clean the shim and measure its thickness with a micrometer (photos).

11   Refer to the clearance recorded for the valve concerned. If the

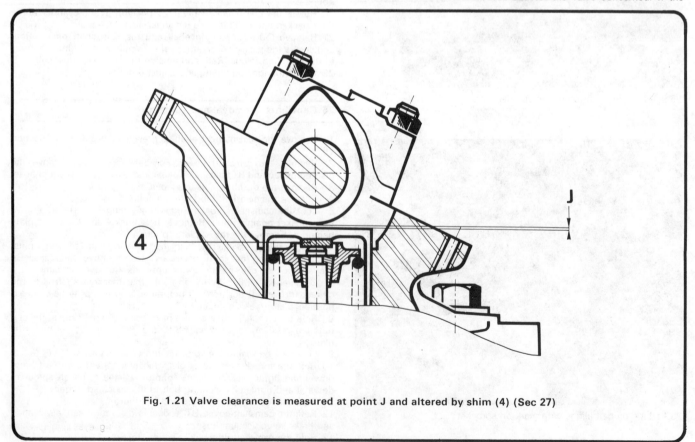
Fig. 1.21 Valve clearance is measured at point J and altered by shim (4) (Sec 27)

27.5 Measuring a valve clearance

27.10A Lift off the tappet

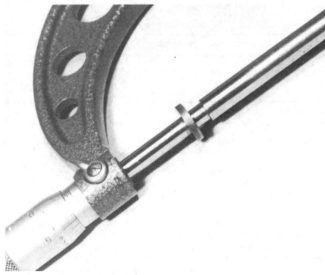

27.10B Measuring the thickness of a shim

clearance was larger than specified, a thicker shim must be fitted; if the clearance was too small, a thinner shim must be fitted.

Sample calculation – clearance too large:

Desired clearance (A) 0.20 mm
Measured clearance (B) 0.28 mm
Difference (B – A) = +0.08 mm
Original shim thickness 2.62 mm
Required shim thickness 2.62 + 0.08 = 2.70 mm

Sample calculation – clearance too small:
Desired clearance (A) 0.40 mm
Measured clearance (B) 0.23 mm
Difference (B-A) = −0.17 mm
Original shim thickness 2.86 mm
Required shim thickness 2.86 − 0.17 = 2.69 mm

12 Shims are available in thicknesses from 1.650 to 4.000 mm, in steps of 0.025 mm in the middle of the range and at the ends in steps of 0.075 mm. Clean new shims before measuring or fitting them.
13 Repeat the operations on the other tappets and shims, keeping each tappet identified so that it can be refitted in the same position.
14 When reassembling, oil the shim and fit it on the valve stem, then oil the tappet and lower it smoothly into position. If the tappet is raised at any stage the shim may be dislodged.
15 When all the tappets are in position with their shims, refit the camshaft. Check the valve clearances before refitting the camshaft drivebelt in case a mistake has been made and the camshaft has to be removed again. With the drivebelt disconnected the camshaft will not be moved by rotation of the crankshaft. Before rotating the camshaft alone, position all the pistons halfway down the bores to avoid piston-to-valve contact.

28 Engine – removal

1 The engine and transmission assembly is removed by lifting upwards from the engine compartment. The transmission is separated from the engine on the bench.
2 Unscrew the nut and detach the bonnet stay from the right-hand front suspension tower, then raise the bonnet vertical and retain by inserting two suitable U-bolts in the special holes provided in the bonnet hinges. Alternatively use welding rod or bend metal dowel rod.
3 Jack up the front of the car and support on axle stands. Apply the handbrake.
4 Remove the drain plug and drain the engine oil. Clean and refit the drain plug on completion.
5 Drain the cooling system, as described in Chapter 2.
6 Disconnect the coolant hoses by the water pump.
7 Disconnect the exhaust downpipe from the manifold.
8 Disconnect the gear linkage (Chapter 6) and speedometer cable (Chapter 12).
9 Unscrew and remove both front clamp bolts securing the hub carriers to the bottom of the front suspension struts.
10 Pull the lower suspension arms down from the hub carriers and unbolt the balljoint guard plates.
11 Pull the left-hand hub carrier outwards and at the same time withdraw the inner end of the driveshaft from the final drive unit.
12 Refer to Chapter 7 and fit the special tool to the differential side gear in order to prevent it from falling into the final drive housing.
13 Unbolt the right-hand rear engine mounting link then loosen the two nuts retaining the right-hand driveshaft intermediate bearing in the bracket bolted to the rear of the cylinder block and turn the bolt heads through 90°.
14 Pull the right-hand hub carrier outwards and at the same time withdraw the inner end of the driveshaft from the final drive unit. Unbolt the intermediate bearing bracket from the cylinder block.
15 Disconnect the wiring from the oil temperature sensor (photo).
16 Remove the air cleaner and trunking, airflow sensor, inlet manifold, injectors and associated components, with reference to Chapter 3.
17 Remove the battery (Chapter 12) and radiator (Chapter 2).
18 Disconnect all coolant and vacuum hoses.
19 Disconnect all electrical leads.
20 Disconnect the throttle cable (Chapter 3) and clutch cable (Chapter 5).
21 Connect a suitable hoist to the engine lifting eyes and take its weight.

28.15 Oil temperature sensor and wiring

29.1A Starter motor is secured by three Allen bolts ...

22 Unscrew the left-hand engine mounting upper nut in the battery
tray aperture.
23 Lower the engine slightly, then unbolt and remove the battery tray
and bracket.
24 Unscrew the right-hand engine mounting upper nut (photo).
25 Lift the assembly from the engine compartment.

29.1B ... and a mounting bracket

28.24 Right-hand engine mounting

30 Engine dismantling – general

Refer to Section 10.

31 Engine – complete dismantling

1   Remove the ancillary components still on the engine:

   (a) Alternator and drivebelt (Chapter 10)
   (b) Oil filler and breather pipes
   (c) Clutch (Chapter 5)
   (d) Oil filter
   (e) Oil pressure switch

29 Engine – separation from transmission

1   Remove the starter motor, which is secured by three Allen bolts and
a mounting bracket (photos).
2   Remove the remaining engine-to-transmission bolts.
3   Support the engine and pull the transmission away from it. Do not
allow the weight of the transmission to hang on the input shaft.
Recover any loose dowels.

2   The exhaust manifold may be removed now, or it can be left in
place to serve as a handle until the head is removed.
3   Unbolt and remove the crankshaft pulley. Jam the flywheel teeth
when undoing the pulley bolt to stop the crankshaft rotating.
4   Remove the camshaft drivebelt covers, noting the location of the
various sizes of bolt.

5   Unbolt and remove the camshaft cover.

6   Rotate the crankshaft by means of the flywheel until a 10 mm diameter rod can be passed through the hole in the camshaft sprocket and into the timing recess. The pistons are now at mid-stroke so piston/valve contact cannot occur.

7   Release the camshaft drivebelt tensioner by slackening its nuts (two at the front and one behind the front plate) and using the square end of the cam spindle to bring the cam into a horizontal position.

8   Remove the camshaft drivebelt, taking care not to kink it and noting its direction of travel if it is to be re-used.

9   Unbolt and remove the camshaft drivebelt tensioner.

10 Remove the belt side covers and the crankshaft sprocket. Recover the Woodruff key.

11 Unbolt and remove the camshaft sprocket. Restrain the sprocket from turning if necessary using the 10 mm diameter rod inserted through the timing hole in the sprocket (photo).

12 Unbolt and remove the engine mounting bracket, the camshaft sprocket backplate and the coolant pump.

13 Slacken the ten cylinder head bolts, working in the reverse sequence of that used when tightening (Fig. 1.20). Remove the bolts and washers, noting the spacer under the No 8 bolt (directly above the coolant pump) (photo).

14 Remove the cylinder head. If it seems to be stuck, use a couple of metal rods in two of the bolt holes to rock it free. Do not attempt to hammer or lever it off. Retrieve the two locating dowels if they are loose.

15 Fit liner clamps if it is not proposed to remove the pistons and liners (see Section 24). Invert the engine.

16 Unbolt and remove the flywheel. It is dowelled so it can only be refitted one way.

17 Remove the suction drain pipe (photo).

18 Unbolt and remove the sump. Note the location of the three Allen-headed bolts (photo).

31.17 Removing the suction drain pipe

31.11 Lock the sprocket with a 10 mm rod

31.13 Removing the cylinder head bolts – note spacer (arrowed)

31.18 The three Allen-headed bolts are fitted here

19 Remove the bolts which secure the oil pump, noting the special centering bolt at the rear.

20 Unbolt and remove the oil seal carrier plate.

21 Lower the oil pump into the engine so that its chain can be removed. Withdraw the pump and recover the spacer, the dowel and the chain.

22 Pull the oil pump sprocket off the crankshaft and recover the Woodruff key.

23 Unbolt the connecting rod big-end caps and push the pistons out through the tops of the liners. (If it is intended to re-use the pistons, it is prudent to remove the wear ridge at the top of the liner bores first, using a ridge reamer or scraper). Make identification marks on the pistons, rods and caps so that they can be refitted in their original positions.

24 Remove the bolts from main bearing caps, 1, 2, 4 and 5. Also remove the two nuts and the two side bolts from the centre cap. Make alignment marks on the bearing caps and remove them. Keep the bearing shells with their caps if they are to be re-used. Recover the thrust washer segments from either side of No 2 bearing cap.

25 Remove the oil seal from the flywheel end of the crankshaft.

26 Lift the crankshaft out of the crankcase. Recover the upper half main bearing shells and the other two thrust washer segments.

27 Make alignment marks on the cylinder liners if they are to be re-used, then release the liner clamps and remove the liners. Dismantling of the engine is now complete.

32 Cylinder head – dismantling, decarbonising and reassembly

1   If not already done, remove the spark plugs and exhaust manifold.

2   Unbolt and remove the coolant outlet housing. Do not overlook the recessed securing screw in the end (photo). Remove the thermostat elbow from the housing and withdraw the thermostat.

3   Lift out the camshaft lubrication manifold (photo).

4   Unbolt and remove the camshaft thrust fork.

5   Progressively slacken the camshaft bearing cap nuts. Remove the caps – be prepared for the camshaft to spring upwards. Remove the oil seal from the sprocket end, then remove the camshaft (photo).

6   Remove the tappets and shims, identifying their locations if they are to be re-used.

7   Extract the oil filter gauze from the oilway (photo).

8   Use a universal type valve spring compressor to compress a valve spring. Remove the collets, carefully release the compressor and extract the valve and spring. Repeat for the other seven valves.

9   Use long-nosed pliers, carefully remove the valve stem oil seals from their locations in the head. Dismantling of the cylinder head is now complete.

10 Decarbonise the cylinder head with reference to Section 14.

11 The makers state that no machining of the cylinder head surface is permitted. A warped head must therefore be renewed.

12 Factory exchange cylinder heads may have had 0.2 mm machined off the mating face. These heads are identified by the letter 'R' stamped on a boss at the distributor end of the head. A gasket 0.2 mm thicker than normal must be used with such a head; the thicker gasket is identified by a cut-out in the tab at the clutch end.

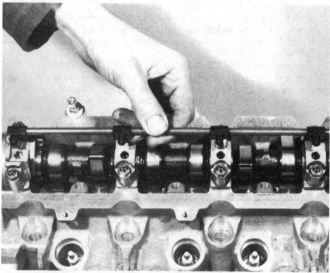

32.3 Lifting out the camshaft lubrication manifold

32.5 Removing the camshaft

32.2 Undoing the recessed securing screw in the coolant outlet housing

32.7 Oil filter gauze in the cylinder head oilway

13 Commence reassembly by fitting new valve stem oil seals, then fit the valves, springs and collets. Oil the valve stems liberally; a smear of of grease will hold the collets in position while the spring is compressed. The valve springs can be fitted either way up.

14 Lubricate the tappet bores. Secure each shim to its valve stem with a dab of grease and carefully fit the tappets. If new components have been fitted so that the valve clearances are unknown, fit the thinnest possible shims to all valves.

15 Fit the camshaft to the head and oil its lobes and journals. Fit the bearing caps, making sure that the middle ones are the right way round. Progressively tighten the bearing cap nuts to the specified torque (photo).

32.15 Tightening the camshaft bearing nuts

16 Fit the camshaft thrust plate and tighten its securing bolt.

17 Press the lubrication manifold into position.

18 Fit a new filter gauze in the oilway.

19 Fit the coolant outlet housing, using a new gasket.

20 Fit the exhaust manifold with a new gasket and tighten the bolts.

21 Fit a new oil seal to the sprocket end of the camshaft, using a piece of tube to drive it home.

22 If valve clearance adjustment is to be carried out now, temporarily fit the camshaft sprocket and stand the cylinder head on wooden blocks so that open valves do not strike the work surface.

33 Engine components – examination and renovation

Refer to Section 13.

34 Examination and renovation of dismantled components

1 Refer to Section 15 for the examination and renovation of the following components:

   (a) Crankshaft and main bearings
   (b) Big-end bearings
   (c) Cylinder liners
   (d) Gudgeon pins
   (e) Connecting rod/pistons
   (f) Flywheel and starter ring gear

Camshaft and drivebelt

2 Renew the camshaft drivebelt as a matter of course unless it is in perfect condition and is known to have covered only a nominal mileage. Renew the sprockets if they are damaged.

3 Inspect the camshaft lobes and bearing journals for wear and damage: if evident, renewal is probably necessary. Also inspect the bearing surfaces in the cylinder head and bearing caps.

4 Clean the camshaft lubrication manifold with solvent and then blow through it with compressed air. All the holes must be clear (photo).

5 Inspect the tappets for wear and scuffing; renew them as necessary. New tappets **must** be fitted if the camshaft is renewed; it is also advisable to renew the valve springs.

6 The camshaft drivebelt tensioner should be examined for roughness of the wheel bearing and wear or distortion of the spring. Renew as necessary – the wheel, bearing and backplate must be renewed as an assembly (photo).

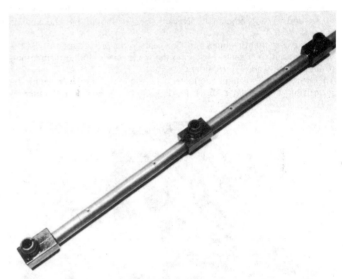

34.4 The pinholes in the lubrication manifold must be clear

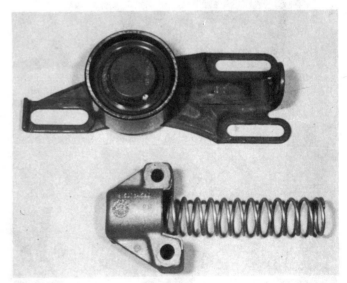

34.6 Camshaft drivebelt tensioner components

Crankshaft spigot bush

7 Later engines have no spigot bush in the crankshaft tail; the diameter of the gearbox input shaft is correspondingly increased.

8 If fitting a new style crankshaft to mate with an old style input shaft, obtain and insert a spigot bush. If the reverse situation applies (new input shaft and old crankshaft), extract the spigot bush.

Oil pump – dismantling, inspection and reassembly

9   Remove the six bolts which hold the two halves of the oil pump together. Separate the halves; being prepared for the release of the relief valve spring and plunger (photo).

10 Inspect the rotors and their housing for wear and damage. No wear limits are published for this pump; any visible wear on the moving parts suggests that renewal is necessary. With the exception of the relief valve spring and plunger, individual components are not available (photos).

11 Lubricate the pump components well before reassembly. Bolt the two halves together, being careful not to trap the spring.

12 If the pump is to be renewed it is wise to renew the chain and the crankshaft sprocket also.

Cylinder liner protrusion – checking

13 Liner protrusion is determined by the dimensions of the block and liners and is not adjustable. Nevertheless it should be checked as follows.

14 Make sure that the liners and their seats in the block are clean. Fit the liners without their seals, observing the marks made during dismantling if the old liners are being refitted.

15 Using a straight-edge and feeler blades, or a dial gauge, measure the protrusion of each liner above the block and the relative difference in

34.10B Oil pump relief valve spring and plunger

protrusion between adjacent liners. Desired values are given in the Specifications.

16 New liners can be rotated half a turn (180°), and/or fitted in a different position in the block, to bring protrusion within tolerance. Old liners which will not produce the desired results are best scrapped. Consult a Peugeot dealer for advice.

17 When the liners are correctly positioned, mark each one so that it may be refitted in the same position, then remove the liners from the block.

35 Engine reassembly – general

Refer to Sections 16 and 17.

36 Engine – complete reassembly

1   Position the block for access to the bottom end and fit the main bearing upper shells. Also fit the thrust washer segments to No 2 bearing, grooved sides outwards (photo); retain them with a smear of grease. Note that the recommended placement of grooved (G) and plain (P) bearing shells varies according to model:

Early models (up to Serial No 9 207 534)

Bearing No	1	2	3	4	5
Top	P	G	P	G	P
Bottom	P	P	P	P	P

Later models (from Serial No 9 207 535)

Bearing No	1	2	3	4	5
Top	G	P	P	P	G
Bottom	G	P	P	G	G

The arrangement of shells on the engine dismantled did not agree with either of the above schemes; no harm seemed to have resulted. Consult the supplier of the bearings if in doubt.

2   Oil the bearing shells and lower the crankshaft into position, taking care not to dislodge the thrust washer segments (photo). Inject some oil into the crankshaft oilways.

3   Fit new side seals to No 1 main bearing cap. Carefully fit the cap with its bearing shell; lubricate the shell, the sides of the cap and the locating surfaces in the block. There is a risk of displacing or distorting the side seals as the cap is fitted, so protect them with a couple of feeler blades or thin strips of tin which can be withdrawn rearwards after fitting the cap (photos).

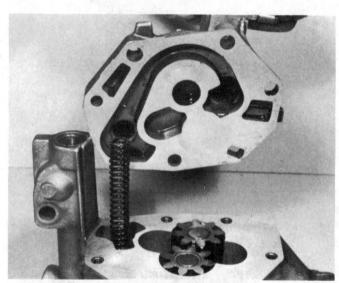

34.9 Separating the two halves of the oil pump

34.10A Inspect the pump gears for wear

36.1 Fitting the thrust washer upper segments

36.2 Fitting the crankshaft

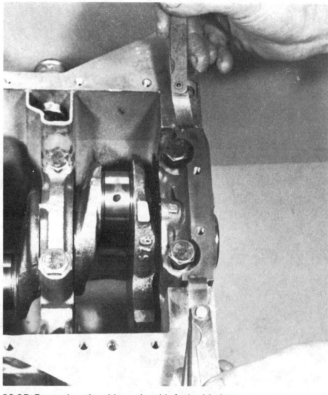

36.3B Protecting the side seals with feeler blades

4 Fit the shells to the other main bearing caps, lubricate them and fit the caps. Fit the thrust washer segments, grooved side outwards, to No 2 cap. Observe the mating marks when dismantling; the lug on each bearing cap points towards the timing sprockets.
5 Fit the main bearing cap nuts and bolts and tighten them to the specified torque. Tighten the side bolts on No 3 cap last (photo).
6 Check the protrusion of No 1 cap side seals above the sump mating face: it should be 2 mm. Trim off any excess.
7 Now check the crankshaft endfloat by first pushing it in one direction and using a feeler blade between the thrust washer and crankshaft. Alternatively a dial gauge may be used. If the endfloat is outside the specified tolerance, change the thrust washers for ones of different thicknesses.

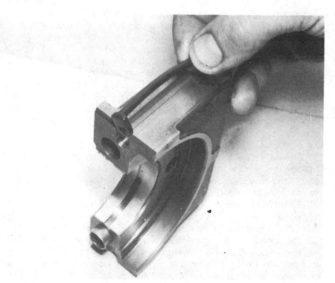

36.3A Fitting a side seal to No 1 main bearing cap

36.5 Tightening the side bolts on No 3 main bearing

36.8 Crankshaft oil seal – flywheel end

36.9 Arrow on piston crown points to camshaft sprocket end. Letter and number show liner and gudgeon pin grade

36.10A Fitting the oil pump drive sprocket – the chain must be engaged first

36.10B Oil pump drive chain

36.11A Fitting the oil pump – the chain must be engaged first

36.11B Sliding in the oil pump spacer

8   Fit a new oil seal, lips inwards and lubricated, to the flywheel end of the crankshaft (photo). Drive it into place with a piece of tube.

9   Fit new O-rings seals to the cylinder liners, then fit the pistons and liners and big-end caps, as described in Section 19, paragraphs 1 to 13, 18 and 19. The arrow on the piston crown should point to the timing belt end (photo).

10 Fit the Woodruff key and oil pump drive sprocket to the crankshaft nose. Fit the chain over the sprocket (photos).

11 Make sure that the locating dowel is in position, then engage the oil pump sprocket in the chain and offer the pump to the block (photo). Engage the pump on the dowel, then lift it up far enough to slide the L-shaped spacer in underneath it (photo).

12 Fit the oil pump securing bolts, remembering that the special centering bolt is nearest the flywheel (photo), and tighten them to the specified torque. Generously lubricate the pump and the chain.

13 Refit the pulley oil seal carrier plate, using silicone jointing compound on the block mating faces. Fit a new oil seal, lubricated lips inwards and drive it home with a piece of tube.

14 Fit the sump, using a new gasket, and tighten its securing bolts progressively to the specified torque. Remember the correct location of the three Allen-headed bolts.

15 Refit the suction drain pipe, using a new O-ring. Do not overtighten the securing nuts – 5 Nm (say 3.5 lbf ft) is the maximum allowed.

16 Fit the flywheel to the crankshaft flange and secure with new bolts, using thread locking compound. Tighten the bolts progressively to the specified torque.

17 Fit the clutch disc and pressure plate, as described in Chapter 5.

18 Position the engine for access to the cylinder head face. Rotate the crankshaft to bring the pistons to mid-stroke (none at TDC), then remove the liner clamps.

19 Check that the head mating surface is clean and that the two locating dowels are present. Place a 5 mm diameter rod in the hole beneath the

dowel at the flywheel end to stop the dowel being displaced downwards.

20 Fit a new cylinder head gasket, dry, with the protruding tab at the flywheel end (photo).

21 Lower the assembled cylinder head into position, making sure that it engages with the dowels.

22 Fit the cylinder head bolts, with their threads clean and lightly oiled. Remember to fit the spacer to the bolt above the coolant pump.

23 Tighten the cylinder head bolts progressively in the order shown in Fig. 1.20 to the Stage 1 specified torque.

24 Slacken bolt No 1 and then retighten it to the Stage 2 specified torque. Tighten the bolt further through the angle specified for Stage 3. Repeat this operation on the other bolts in sequence.

25 Fit the camshaft sprocket backplate, using a 10 mm rod through the timing hole to locate it precisely before tightening its securing bolts.

26 Fit the camshaft sprocket, washer and bolt. Use the 10 mm rod to lock the sprocket in the correct position and tighten the bolt to the specified torque. Remove the rod.

27 Fit the engine mounting bracket and tighten its bolts (photo).

28 Fit and secure the coolant pump, using a new gasket. Tighten the bolts to the specified torque.

29 Fit the covers around the coolant pump, noting the locations of the various special bolts (Fig. 1.22).

30 Fit the Woodruff key and the crankshaft sprocket.

31 Fit the camshaft drivebelt tensioner, but leave the nuts slack. Compress the spring by locking the cam in the horizontal position.

32 Temporarily fit the crankshaft pulley, its washer and bolt; lightly tighten the bolt. Carefully turn the crankshaft until a 10 mm rod will pass through the timing hole in the pulley and into the timing recess. If piston/valve contact occurs, back off and try again with the camshaft in a slightly different position. **Do not** try to force the crankshaft if a piston contacts a valve.

36.12 Special bolt fits here

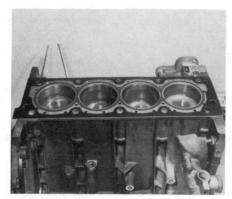

36.20 Head gasket correctly fitted

36.27 Fitting the engine mounting bracket

33 Use the 10 mm rod to position the camshaft sprocket, then remove the crankshaft pulley and fit the camshaft drivebelt. Be careful not to kink the belt as it is fitted, and observe the arrows showing the correct direction of rotation. The white stripes on the belt should align with the timing marks on the sprockets.

34 Withdraw the timing rod. Tension the belt by turning the tensioner cam so that it points downwards; secure it with its locknut. Tighten the two nuts at the front of the tensioner.

35 Turn the crankshaft through two full turns in the normal direction of rotation; rotate it further to bring Nos. 1 and 4 pistons to TDC with the valves on No 1 cylinder open.

36 Slacken the two nuts and the cam locknut on the drivebelt tensioner, then retighten them.

37 Temporarily refit the crankshaft pulley, rotate the crankshaft and check that the timing rods can be inserted simultaneously in the crankshaft pulley and camshaft sprocket holes. If not, remove the belt and try again. Remove the pulley.

38 Fit the drivebelt covers in the sequence shown in Fig. 1.23. (Note, however, that they will have to be removed to retension the drivebelt if a new one has been fitted).

39 Fit the crankshaft pulley, washer and bolt, making sure that the Woodruff key is still in position. Jam the starter ring gear teeth and tighten the bolt to the specified torque.

40 Refit the camshaft cover, noting the copper washer and diagnostic socket at the sprocket end bolt, and using a new gasket.

41 Refit the ancillary components listed below:

    (a) Oil pressure switch
    (b) New oil filter
    (c) Oil filler and breather pipes (photo)
    (d) Alternator and drivebelt

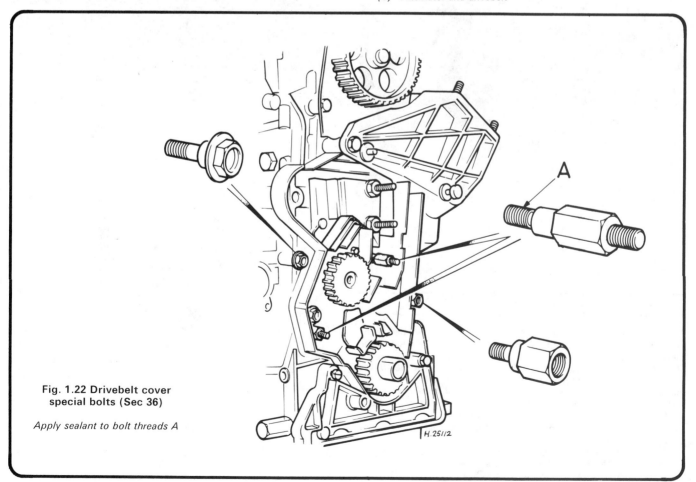

Fig. 1.22 Drivebelt cover special bolts (Sec 36)

Apply sealant to bolt threads A

H.25/12

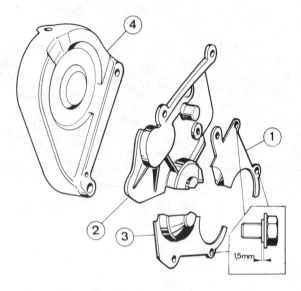

Fig. 1.23 Fit the covers in numerical sequence (Sec 36)

36.41 Oil filler and breather pipes

37 Engine – reconnection to transmission

1   Check that the clutch release components are correctly fitted in the gearbox and that the pressure plate and friction disc are fitted to the flywheel.

2   Smear a little anti-seize compound on the nose and splines of the transmission input shaft, then offer the transmission to the engine. Do not allow the weight of the transmission to hang on the input shaft. If the input shaft does not wish to pass the clutch, it is possible that the clutch disc is not centred. Check also that the transmission input shaft is compatible with the spigot recess in the crankshaft (Section 34 paragraphs 7 and 8).

3   Engage the engine-to-transmission dowels and loosely fit the bolts. Also fit the starter motor, which is secured by three Allen bolts and a bracket. Tighten the bolts to the specified torque.

38 Engine – refitting

Refitting is a reversal of the removal procedure given in Section 28 with particular attention to the following points:

(a)   Use a final drive oil seal protector (photo) when inserting the right-hand driveshaft. Remove the protector when the driveshaft is fitted

(b)   Adjust the clutch cable, with reference to Chapter 5, and the throttle cable, with reference to Chapter 3

(c)   Tighten the exhaust flange bolts, as described in Chapter 3

(d)   If necessary, adjust the right-hand engine mounting side buffers with spacers to give the clearances shown in Fig. 1.24

(e)   Fill the engine with oil

(f)   Fill the cooling system, as described in Chapter 2

(g)   Route the wiring as shown in Fig. 1.25

38.1 Right-hand driveshaft oil seal protector

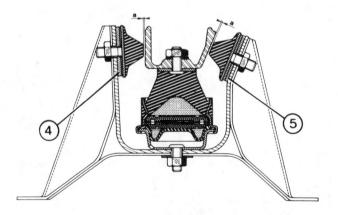

Fig. 1.24 Engine right-hand mounting (Sec 38)

a = 1.0 mm (0.04 in)   4   Spacer
                                     5   Spacer

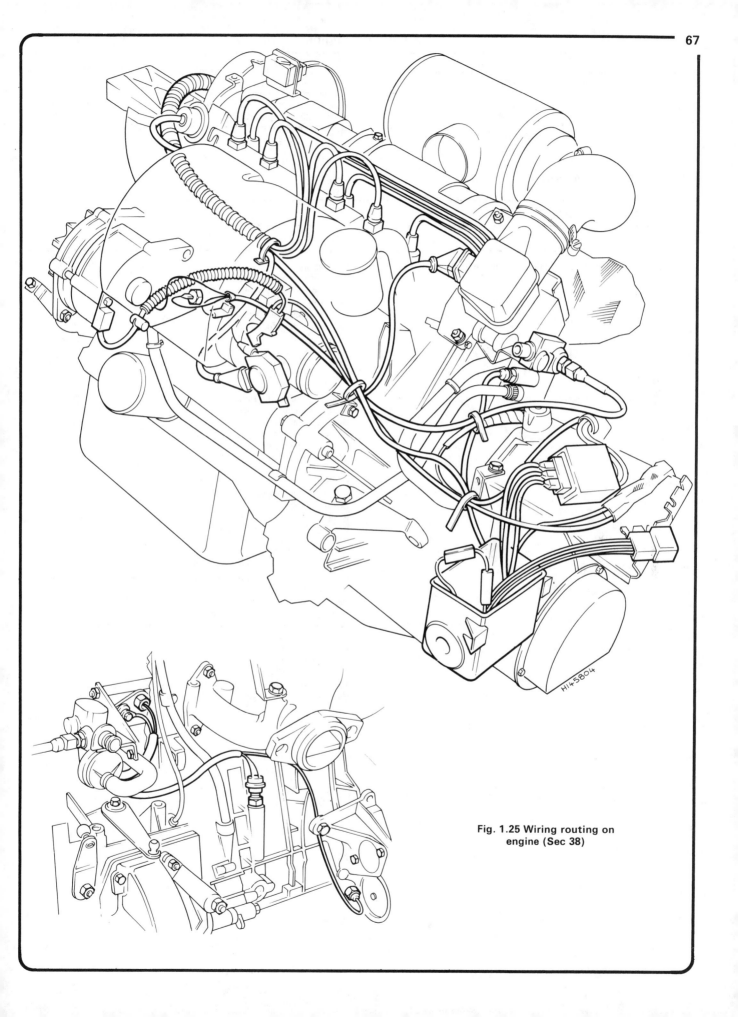

H145804

Fig. 1.25 Wiring routing on
engine (Sec 38)

39 Engine – initial start-up after overhaul

1   Refer to Section 22, paragraphs 1, 3, 4 and 5.
2   Allow the engine to cool for at least two hours. Loosen the bolt which secures the engine right-hand mounting bracket to the block then retighten the cylinder head bolts, as described in Section 36,

paragraph 24. Tighten the mounting bracket bolt on completion. No subsequent retightening is necessary.
3   Recheck the valve clearances.
4   If a new camshaft drivebelt was fitted, retension it as described in Section 25, paragraphs 20 and 21.
5   Refer to Section 22, paragraphs 8, 9, and 10.

PART D: Fault diagnosis

40 Fault diagnosis – engine

Symptom	Reason(s)
Engine will not turn over when starter switch is operated	Flat battery Bad battery connections Bad connections at solenoid switch and/or starter motor Starter motor jammed Defective solenoid Starter motor defective
Engine turns over normally but fails to fire and run	No sparks at plugs No fuel reaching engine Too much fuel reaching engine (flooding)
Engine starts but runs unevenly and misfires	Ignition and/or fuel system faults Incorrect valve clearance Burnt out valves Blown cylinder head gasket, dropped liners Worn out piston rings Worn cylinder bores
Lack of power	Ignition and/or fuel system faults Incorrect valve clearance Burnt out valves Blown cylinder head gasket Worn out piston rings Worn cylinder bores
Excessive oil consumption	Oil leaks from crankshaft oil seal, timing cover gasket and oil seal (where applicable), rocker cover gasket, crankcase or gearbox joint (where applicable) Worn piston rings or cylinder bores resulting in oil being burnt by engine (smoky exhaust is an indication) Worn valve guides and/or defective valve stem oil seals
Excessive mechanical noise from engine	Wrong valve clearance Worn crankshaft bearings Worn cylinders (piston slap) Slack or worn timing chain and sprockets (where applicable) Worn transfer gears and/or bearings (where applicable)

Chapter 2 Cooling system

For modifications, and information applicable to later models, see Supplement at end of manual

Contents

Specifications

General

System type	Pressurised with expansion tank/bottle and front-mounted radiator, electric cooling fan, water pump and thermostat

System capacity:

XV8 and XW7 engines	5.8 litres (10.2 pints)
XY7 and XY8 engines	6.0 litres (10.6 pints)
XU5J engine	6.6 litres (11.6 pints)

Pressure cap setting:

XU5J engine	1.0 bar (14.5 lbf/in²)
Except XU5J engine	0.8 bar (11.6 lbf/in²)

Thermostat:

Starts to open	79° to 82° (174° to 180°F)
Fully open (7.5 mm/0.296 in)	93°C (199°F)
Warning lamp switch cut-in temperature	102 to 108°C (216 to 226°F)

Electric coolant fan operating temperatures:

	Cut-in	Cut-out
XV8 and XW7 engines	87 to 89.5°C (189 to 193°F)	77.5 to 81°C (172 to 178°F)
XY engine (up to engine 5065000)	87 to 89.5°C (189 to 193°F)	77.5 to 81°C (172 to 178°F)
XY engine (from engine 5065001):		
1st stage	82 to 86°C (180 to 187°F)	77 to 81°C (171 to 178°F)
2nd stage	86 to 90°C 187 to 194°F)	81 to 85°C (178 to 185°F)
XU5J engine:		
1st stage	82 to 86°C (180 to 187°F)	77 to 81°C (171 to 178°F)
2nd stage	86 to 90°C (187 to 194°F)	81 to 85°C (178 to 185°F)

Temperature sensor (XU5J engine):

Resistance at 40°C (104°F)	1045 to 1215 ohm
Resistance at 95.6°C (206°F)	136 to 150 ohm
Antifreeze type/specification	Ethylene glycol based antifreeze (Duckhams Universal Antifreeze and Summer Coolant)

Antifreeze mixture:

Protection to −15°C (5°F)	27% antifreeze
Protection to −35°C (−31°F)	50% antifreeze

Torque wrench settings

	Nm	lbf ft
Water pump:		
XU5J engine	15	11
Except XU5J engine	13	10
Thermostat elbow	15	11

1 General description

The cooling system is of pressurised type incorporating an expansion bottle on non-GTI models and an expansion tank on GTI models. The system includes a front-mounted cross-flow radiator, thermoswitch controlled electric cooling fan, water pump and thermostat. The car interior heater matrix is supplied with a continuous supply of coolant since there is no water valve and the hot air supply is controlled by an air flap.

On GTI models the water pump is driven by the engine camshaft drivebelt, but on non-GTI models it is driven by the alternator drivebelt.

The cooling system functions in the following way. After a cold start the thermostat valve is shut and coolant circulation is restricted to the engine and heater matrix. When the coolant reaches the normal engine operating temperature the thermostat starts to open and coolant circulation also flows through the radiator. The engine temperature is then controlled by the thermostat and the electric cooling fan located on the front of the radiator.

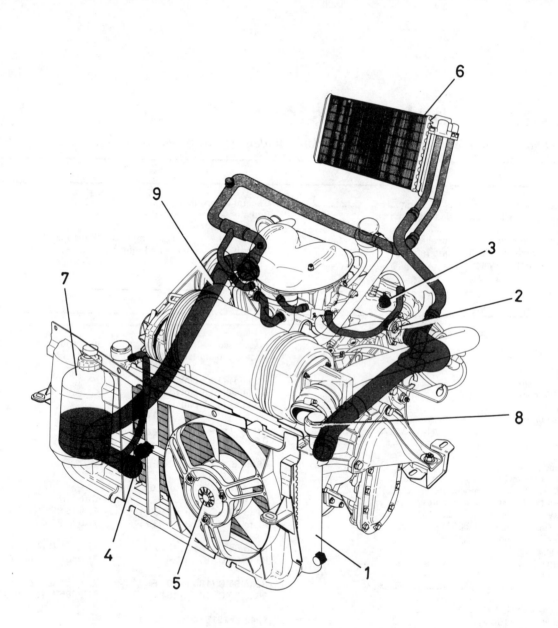

Fig. 2.1 Cooling system layout for non-GTI models (Sec 1)

1 Radiator	4 Electric cooling fan thermoswitch	7 Expansion bottle
2 Thermostat	5 Electric cooling fan and motor	8 Radiator filler plug
3 Coolant temperature switch	6 Heater matrix	9 Water pump

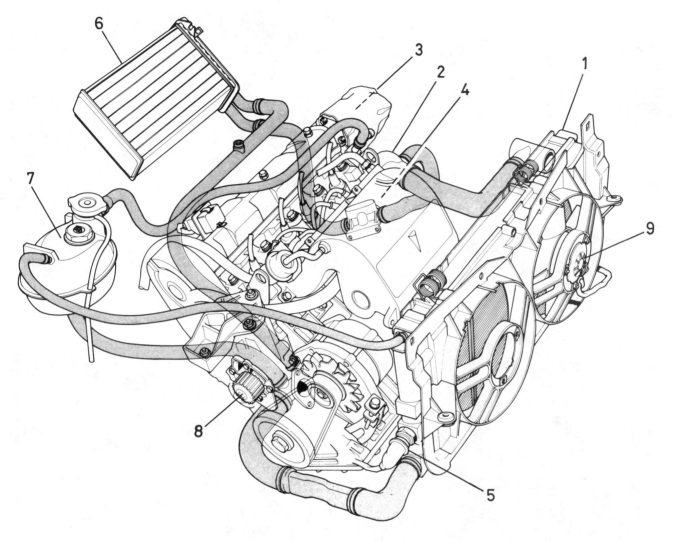

Fig. 2.2 Cooling system layout for GTI models (Sec 1)

1 Radiator	4 Temperature gauge sensor	7 Expansion tank
2 Thermostat	5 Electric cooling fan thermoswitch	8 Water pump
3 Coolant temperature switch	6 Heater matrix	9 Electric cooling fan and motor

2 Routine maintenance

Carry out the following procedures at the intervals given in Routine Maintenance at the beginning of the manual.

1 Check the level of coolant in the expansion bottle/tank with the engine cold and top up to the maximum mark if necessary (refer to Section 3, paragraph 14).

2 Check the cooling system hoses, thermostat housing and water pump for leakage and rectify as necessary.

3 Drain the coolant, flush the cooling system and fill with fresh coolant, as described in Section 3.

3 Cooling system – draining, flushing and refilling

1 Unscrew the filler cap from the expansion bottle located on the front right (non-GTI models) or rear left (GTI models) of the engine compartment (photos). **Do not** remove the cap if the engine is hot, but allow it to cool first otherwise pressurised steam and boiling water may be found out.

2 On non-GTI models unscrew and remove the filler plug fom the top left-hand side of the radiator.

3.1A Expansion bottle on non-GTI models

3.1B Expansion tank on GTI models

3.9A Cooling system bleed screw located in the heater return hose

3.3 Radiator drain plug (arrowed)

3.9B Cooling system bleed screw located in the inlet manifold coolant hose (non-GTI models)

3   Place a suitable container beneath the left-hand side of the radiator then unscrew the drain plug and drain the coolant (photo).

4   Drain the cylinder block by removing the plug located above the right-hand driveshaft (non-GT! models) or above the right-hand driveshaft intermediate bearing (GTI models).

5   On non-GTI models remove the expansion bottle and invert it to drain the remaining coolant if necessary.

6   Provided the coolant has been renewed at the specified intervals there should be no need to flush the system. If the system has been neglected and the coolant contains excessive amounts of sediment, disconnect the radiator top hose and use cold water to flush the radiator until the water runs clear from the radiator and cylinder block.

7   In severe cases, remove the radiator and reverse flush it, or alternatively use a proprietary chemical cleaner.

8   With the system clean, refit the hoses and drain plugs as necessary.

9   To refill the system, first loosen the bleed screw(s) located in the heater return hose and, on non-GTI models only, also in the inlet manifold coolant hose (photos).

10 On non-GTI models the manufacturers recommend that the expansion bottle is raised as high as possible (see Fig. 2.3) to prevent an air trap; however, in practice, the system can be refilled satisfactorily with the bottle in its normal position.

11 Fill the system with the correct quantity of coolant (photo) and close the bleed screw(s) when the water runs clear of air bubbles. On non-GTI models the radiator should be first completely filled and the filler plug retightened before the expansion bottle is refilled.

12 With the system full, refit the expansion bottle filler cap.

13 Run the engine at a fast idle speed until it reaches the normal operating temperature indicated by the electric cooling fan cutting in. Run it for several more minutes then switch off and allow to cool for approximately 2 hours.

14 Top up the coolant level in the expansion bottle and refit the cap. On non-GTI models the bottle incorporates maximum and minimum level marks visible from the outside, but on GTI models a stepped tube is fitted in the filler neck.

Fig. 2.3 Tie up the expansion bottle when refilling the cooling system (Sec 3)

3.11 Filling the expansion bottle on non-GTI models

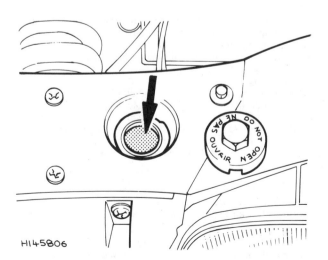

Fig. 2.4 Fill the radiator full on non-GTI models (Sec 3)

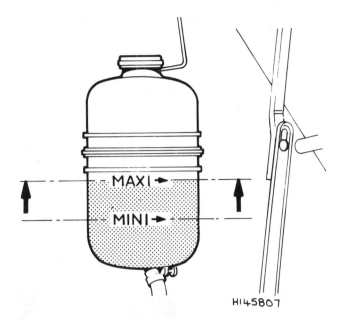

Fig. 2.5 Expansion bottle level marks on non-GTI models (Sec 3)

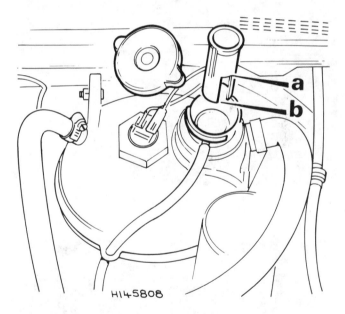

Fig. 2.6 Level indicators in the expansion tank on GTI models (Sec 3)

a   Maximum   b   Minimum

4 Coolant mixture – general

1   Plain water should never be used in the cooling system. Apart from giving protection against freezing, an antifreeze mixture protects the engine internal surfaces and components against corrosion. This is very important in an alloy engine.

2   Always use a top quality glycol-based antifreeze which is recommended for alloy engines.

3   Ideally a 50% mixture of antifreeze and soft or demineralised water should be used to maintain maximum protection against freezing and corrosion. On no account use less than 25% antifreeze.

4   Renew the coolant at the specified intervals as the inhibitors contained in the antifreeze gradually lose their effectiveness.
5   Even when operating in climates where antifreeze is not required never use plain water, but add a corrosion inhibitor to it.

5   Thermostat – removal, testing and refitting

1   The thermostat housing is located on the cylinder head adjacent to the distributor.
2   Drain the cooling system as previously described.
3   Disconnect the radiator top hose from the thermostat housing (photo). On GTI models first remove the air inlet duct from the air cleaner.
4   Unscrew and remove the two thermostat housing cover bolts and remove the cover. This may need a little persuasion with a wooden or plastic-faced hammer (photo).
5   Remove the thermostat. If it is stuck, do not lever it out under its bridge piece, but cut around its edge with a sharp knife.
6   Remove the rubber ring(s) and clean the mating faces of the housing and cover.

5.3 Thermostat housing on non-GTI models (arrowed)

5.4 Removing the thermostat housing cover on non-GTI models

7   If the thermostat is suspected of being faulty, suspend it in a container of water which is being heated. Using a thermometer, check that the thermostat starts to open at the specified temperature and is fully open also at the specified temperature.
8   Remove the thermostat from the water and allow it to cool. The valve plate should close smoothly.
9   If the unit fails to operate as described or is stuck open or shut, renew it with one of similar temperature rating (photo).

5.9 Thermostat, showing temperature rating (arrowed)

10   Fit the thermostat and new rubber ring(s). Bolt on the cover.
11   Reconnect the coolant hose and refill and bleed the system, as described in Section 3.

6   Radiator – removal, repair and refitting

1   Drain the cooling system, as described in Section 3.
2   Remove the front grille (Chapter 12) then unbolt the engine compartment front crossmember (photos).
3   Disconnect the top and bottom hoses from the radiator and, on GTI models, disconnect and unclip the vent hose for the expansion tank (photo).
4   Disconnect the wiring from the electric cooling fan, the thermo-switch and, where applicable, the low level sensor.
5   Disconnect the top mountings, as applicable, then lift the radiator, complete with cooling fan, from the car – taking care not to damage the matrix. The base of the radiator incorporates pins which locate in rubber mountings.
6   If necessary separate the cooling fan, with reference to Section 7.
7   The radiator side tanks are of plastic on non-GTI models or a copper core on GTI models. If it is leaking it must either be renewed or exchanged for a reconditioned unit. A temporary repair may be possible by adding a proprietary product to the coolant.
8   Refitting is a reversal of removal; fill the cooling system as described in Section 3.

7   Cooling fan and thermoswitch – removal and refitting

1   The electric cooling fan may be removed with the radiator, as described in the preceding Section, and then separated. Alternatively it may be unbolted or unclipped (as applicable) from the radiator after having removed the front grille and crossmember. The motor can be

6.2A Engine compartment front crossmember mounting bolts (arrowed)

6.2B View of radiator with front grille and crossmember removed (GTI models)

6.3 Vent hose for the expansion tank (GTI models)

7.1A Clip for retaining the electric cooling fan assembly to the radiator (GTI models)

7.1B Electric cooling fan motor and mounting bolts

7.1C Cooling fan motor resistor on wing valance

7.2 Electric cooling fan thermoswitch and wiring

8.1 Coolant temperature switch – arrowed (non-GTI models)

unbolted from the frame and then the fan removed from the motor (photos). No spare parts are available for the motor.

2   The thermostatically controlled switch for the cooling fan is screwed into the radiator. Before this can be removed, the system must be drained and the switch leads disconnected (photo).

3   When refitting the switch, use a new sealing ring.

8   Coolant temperature switch, gauge and level switch – general

1   The coolant temperature switch is located in the left-hand end of

the cylinder head on non-GTI models and beneath the thermostat housing on GTI models (photo).

2   It is difficult to test a temperature switch without special equipment and the best method to use if a fault develops is to substitute a new switch, but only after the wiring to the gauge has been thoroughly checked.

3   When refitting the switch, make sure that the seal is in good condition and do not overtighten it.

4   If the switch is changed and the gauge still does not register, then the gauge should be checked by a competent auto-electrician. Access to the gauge is obtained after removing the instrument panel, as described in Chapter 12.

5   On non-GTI models, the coolant level switch is located in the

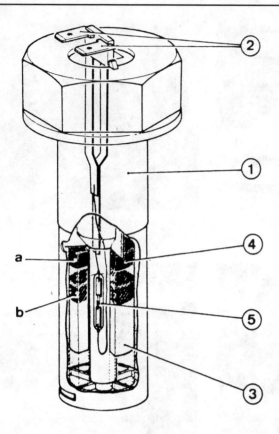

Fig. 2.7 Cutaway diagram of the coolant level switch (Sec 8)

1 Body
2 Terminal connections
3 Float
4 Magnet
5 Reed contact (inside glass
   bulb)
a Off position (float lifts magnet above reed contact)
b On position (magnetic field switches on reed contact)

radiator right-hand side tank, but on GTI models it is located in the expansion tank. The switch is float-operated and actuates a warning lamp in the event of a low coolant level. If the switch malfunctions it must be renewed as no repair is possible.

9 Water pump – removal and refitting

1 Drain the cooling system, as described in Section 3.

Non-GTI models
2 Remove the drivebelt, as described in Chapter 12.
3 Disconnect the radiator bottom hose, heater return hose, and inlet manifold return hose from the water pump (photo). For better access, remove the air cleaner and inlet cowl, with reference to Chapter 3.
4 Unscrew the mounting bolts and remove the water pump from the cylinder block. Remove the O-ring (photos).

GTI models
5 Remove the camshaft drivebelt, as described in Chapter 1, followed by the tensioner.
6 Remove the plastic shield, noting the locations of the different types of bolt.
7 Unscrew the five mounting bolts and remove the water pump from the cylinder block. Remove the gasket.

All models
8 If the water pump is worn, noisy or leaks coolant it must be renewed, as repair is not possible. However, on non-GTI models, if either of the

half casings is individually damaged it may be renewed, together with the central gasket.
9 Refitting is a reversal of removal, but clean the mating faces and always fit a new O-ring or gasket, as applicable. Fill the cooling system, as described in Section 3, and on non-GTI models tension the drivebelt, as described in Chapter 12.

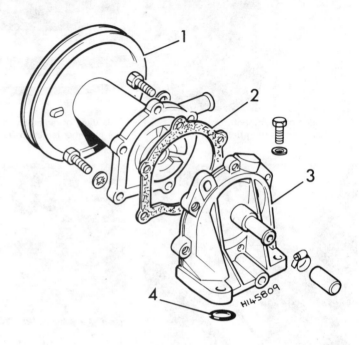

Fig. 2.8 Water pump fitted to non-GTI models (Sec 9)

1 Pulley and vane assembly   3 End casing
2 Gasket   4 O-ring

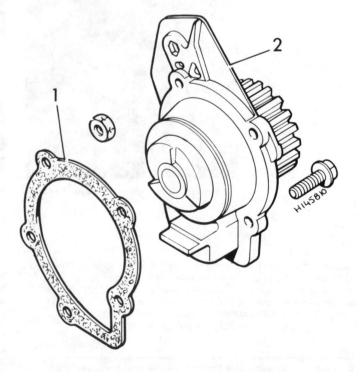

Fig. 2.9 Water pump fitted to GTI models (Sec 9)

1 Gasket   2 Water pump

9.3 Bottom hose and heater return hose locations on the water pump (non-GTI models)

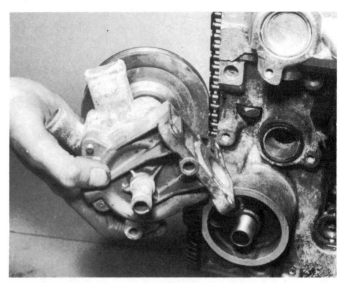

9.4B Withdrawing the water pump from the cylinder block (non-GTI models)

9.4A Removing the water pump mounting bolts (non-GTI models)

9.4C The water pump O-ring in the cylinder block (arrowed)

10 Fault diagnosis – cooling system

Symptom	Reason(s)
Overheating	Insufficient coolant in system Loose drivebelt (non-GTI models only) Radiator blocked either internally or externally Thermostat not opening Electric cooling fan or thermoswitch faulty Pressure cap faulty
Overcooling	Faulty, incorrect or missing thermostat Electric cooling fan thermoswitch not switching off
Loss of coolant	Damaged hoses or loose clips Leaking water pump O-ring or gasket, as applicable

Chapter 3 Fuel and exhaust systems

For modifications, and information applicable to later models, see Supplement at end of manual

Contents

Specifications

Carburettor engines
General

System type .... Rear-mounted fuel tank, mechanical fuel pump, single or twin carburettor

Fuel tank capacity .... 50 litres (11.0 gallons)
Fuel octane rating 97 (4-star)

Carburettor
Type .... Fixed jet, downdraught
Application:

XV8 (954 cc)	Solex 32 PBISA
XW7 (1124 cc)	Solex 32 PBISA
XY7 (1360 cc)	Solex 34 PBISA
XY8 (1360 cc)	Solex 35 PBISA 8

Calibrations and settings:	XV8	XW7	XY7	XY8
Choke	25 mm	25 mm	26 mm	28 mm
Main jet	120 ± 5	125 ± 5	130 ± 25	145 ± 10
Air correction jet	155 ± 20	175 ± 20	160 ± 20	175 ± 10
Idling fuel jet	44 ± 5	42 ± 5	45 ± 5	47 ± 5
Acceleration pump injector	35 ± 5	32 ± 5	40 ± 5	40 ± 10
Enricher calibration	55 ± 20	60 ± 20	75 ± 20	–
Needle valve	1.6 mm	1.6 mm	1.6 mm	1.5 mm*
Initial throttle opening	20°40' ± 30'	20°40' ± 30'	20°40' ± 30'	15°
Normal idling position	–	–	–	7° 45'
Choke opening after starting	–	–	–	2.5mm ± 0.3
Idling speed	650 ± 50 rpm	650 ± 50 rpm	650 ± 50 rpm	950 to 1000 rpm**
CO percentage	1.5 ± 0.5	1.5 ± 0.5	1.5 ± 0.5	2.0 ± 0.5

* 1.2 from serial number 5043526
** 850° to 900 rpm from serial number 5043526

Torque wrench settings

	Nm	lbf ft
Exhaust manifold	20	15
Inlet manifold	18	13
Carburettor nuts	18	13
Fuel pump	18	13

Fuel injection engine
General

System type	Rear-mounted fuel tank, Bosch LE2-Jetronic fuel injection system, electric fuel pump
Fuel tank capacity	50 litres (11 gallons)
Fuel octane rating	97 (4-star)
Idling speed	850 to 900 rpm
CO% at idling	1 to 2
CO_2% at idling	10 minimum
Fuel pressure	2.9 to 3.1 bar (42.1 to 45.0 lbf/in²)
Fuel pump delivery	540 cc/15 sec
Tachometric relay cut-out speed	6600 rpm
Fuel cut-off speed (decelerating)	Above 1600 rpm

Torque settings

As carburettor engines (as applicable)

PART A: GENERAL DESCRIPTION AND ROUTINE MAINTENANCE

1 General description

The fuel system comprises a rear-mounted fuel tank, single downdraught Solex carburettor on XV8, XW7 and XY7 engines, twin downdraught Solex carburettors on the XY8 engine, and a Bosch LE2-Jetronic fuel injection system on the XU5J engine.

On carburettor versions the fuel pump is mounted on the cylinder head and driven by a plunger from an eccentric on the camshaft. On the fuel injection system the electric fuel pump is located in the fuel tank.

The air cleaner incorporates a dry element and the inlet air is temperature controlled.

2 Routine maintenance

Carry out the following procedures at the intervals given in Routine Maintenance at the beginning of the manual.
1 Check all fuel lines and hoses for damage and security, including those located on the underbody.
2 Check the accelerator pedal operation and the throttle cable for correct adjustment.
3 Renew the air filter element (Section 3 or 18).
4 On carburettor engines, clean the fuel pump filter (Section 5).
5 On fuel injection engines, to renew the fuel filter first unscrew the union bolt from the top of the unit (photo) then place the bolt union and washers to one side and cover to prevent ingress of dirt. Unscrew the clamp bolt, then lift the filter and unscrew the bottom union. Fit the new filter using a reversal of the removal procedure; making sure that dust and dirt is prevented from entering the fuel lines.

2.5 Fuel filter canister on fuel injection models

PART B: CARBURETTOR ENGINES

3 Air cleaner element – renewal

1 Unscrew the wing nut on the air cleaner casing end-face (photo).
2 Withdraw the end cover with element (photo).
3 Discard the element and wipe the casing interior clean.
4 Fit the new element and the cover, tighten the wing nut.

4.2 Air cleaner rubber strap

3.1 Air cleaner and wing nut

4.4A Air cleaner bracket bolt (arrowed) also retaining diagnostic socket

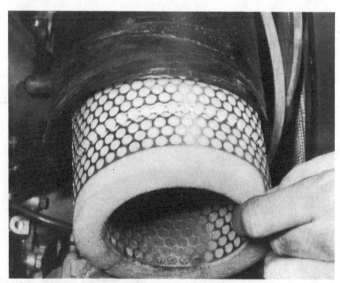

3.2 Removing the air cleaner element

4 Air cleaner – removal and refitting

1 Disconnect the intake and warm air hoses.
2 Release the rubber straps from the mounting brackets (photo).
3 Lift the air cleaner from the brackets then disconnect the outlet hose and, where fitted, the crankcase ventilation hose.
4 If necessary, unbolt the mounting brackets – noting the location of the diagnostic socket and cable retaining brackets (photos).
5 Refitting is a reversal of removal.

4.4B Cable retaining bracket on air cleaner bracket

5.1 Removing the fuel pump cover

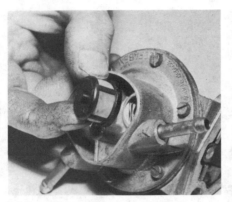

5.2 Removing the fuel pump filter

6.2 Removing the fuel pump

5 Fuel pump – cleaning

1 The fuel pump may be one of several types. On one type, the filter cover is simply unbolted and removed. On another, the pump cover is removed (two screws). With some pumps, the fuel outlet hose must be removed in order to be able to withdraw the pump cover. Inspection will determine (photo).
2 With the cover removed, take out the filter screen and wash it in fuel until it is free from fluff and dirt (photo).
3 Mop out the fuel from the pump body and wipe out any sediment.
4 Refit the filter screen and cover, making sure that the gasket is in good condition.

6 Fuel pump – removal, overhaul and refitting

1 Disconnect the fuel hoses from the pump. Plug the inlet hose.
2 Unscrew the pump mounting bolts and lift the pump away (photo).
3 Remove the gasket.
4 Once the pump is removed, the pushrod may be withdrawn.
5 If the pump is to be dismantled, remove the cover, gasket and filter screen.
6 Scribe a mark across the edges of the upper and lower body flanges and extract the flange screws.
7 Remove the upper body.
8 Drive out the operating arm pivot pin, withdraw the arm and lift out the diaphragm.
9 Obtain a repair kit which will contain a new diaphragm and the necessary gaskets.
10 If the valves are damaged, reassemble the pump and obtain a new one complete.
11 If the valves are in good condition, locate the diaphragm, push the operating arm into position so that its forked end engages with the groove in the end of the diaphragm rod, with the coil springs in position.
12 Fit the pivot pin and stake around the holes to secure both ends of the pin.
13 Fit the upper body so that the alignment marks are opposite and then fit the screws and tighten evenly.
14 Fit the filter screen and cover with gasket.
15 Refitting to the cylinder head is a reversal of removal, but fit a new gasket.

7 Fuel level transmitter – removal and refitting

1 Disconnect the battery earth lead.
2 Open the tailgate and remove the floor covering from the luggage area.

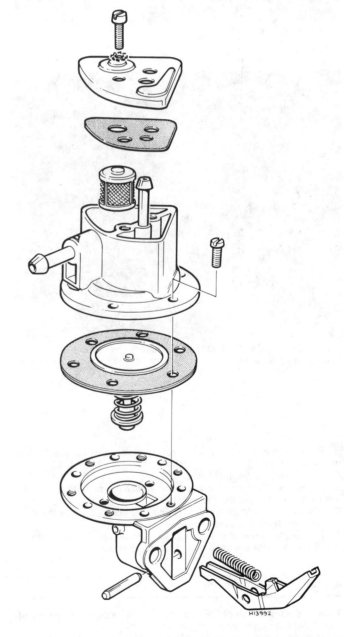

Fig. 3.1 Exploded view of the fuel pump (Sec 6)

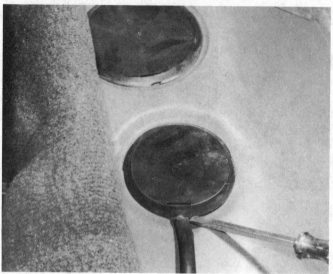

7.3A Prise up the cover ...

8.6 Fuel tank mounting bolt

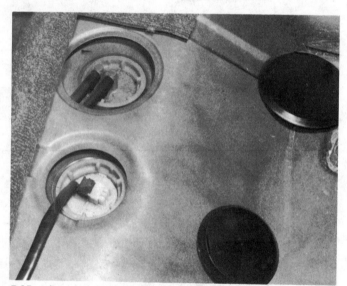

7.3B ... for access to the fuel level transmitter (fuel supply and return pipes also shown)

4   Unbolt and remove the heat shield.

5   Disconnect the wiring from the fuel level transmitter (Section 7).

6   Unscrew the mounting and safety strap bolts (photo) and nuts, then lower the tank – at the same time disconnecting the filler, breather and supply hoses.

7   If the tank is leaking or badly rusted, leave repair to a specialist. *On no account attempt to solder or weld a fuel tank as it requires a great deal of purging before every trace of explosive vapour is removed.*

8   If the tank contains sediment, pour in some paraffin, remove the fuel level transmitter and shake the tank vigorously. Repeat as necessary and finally rinse out with clean fuel.

9   Refitting is a reversal of removal.

9   Carburettors – description

A Solex carburettor is fitted to all models as listed in the Specifications, but the XY8 engine (GT) has two carburettors linked together. All carburettors are of single choke fixed jet design with a manually-operated choke. On the XY8 engine the choke is automatically opened after starting by a pneumatic device.

10   Carburettor – idle speed and mixture adjustment

Solex 32 and 34 PBISA

1   The following adjustments must be made with the ignition timing correctly adjusted, the air cleaner and filter element fitted, and the engine at normal operating temperature.

2   Connect a tachometer to the engine and where necessary remove the tamperproof cap from the mixture adjustment screw.

Without an exhaust gas analyser

3   Turn the throttle stop screw to adjust the engine speed to 650 rpm.

4   Turn the mixture adjustment screw to obtain the highest idling speed.

5   Repeat the procedure given in paragraphs 3 and 4 until the engine speed is 650 rpm (ie after adjusting the mixture screw).

6   Screw in the mixture adjustment screw slightly until the engine speed starts to decrease.

With an exhaust gas analyser

7   Turn the throttle stop screw to adjust the engine speed to 650 rpm.

8   Turn the mixture adjustment screw to obtain the specified CO reading.

9   Repeat the procedure in paragraphs 7 and 8 until the idle speed is 650 rpm.

3   Remove the circular plastic cover to expose the fuel level transmitter (photos).

4   Disconnect the electrical lead.

5   Using a suitable tool, unscrew the transmitter mounting plate to release it from the securing tabs.

6   Withdraw the transmitter unit, taking care not to damage the float as it passes through the hole in the tank.

7   Refitting is a reversal of removal, but use a new sealing ring if there is any doubt about the condition of the original one.

8   Fuel tank – removal, repair and refitting

1   As a drain plug is not fitted, the tank must be syphoned empty of fuel using a length of plastic or rubber tubing.

2   Remove the exhaust system (Section 16).

3   Remove the handbrake cables, as described in Chapter 8.

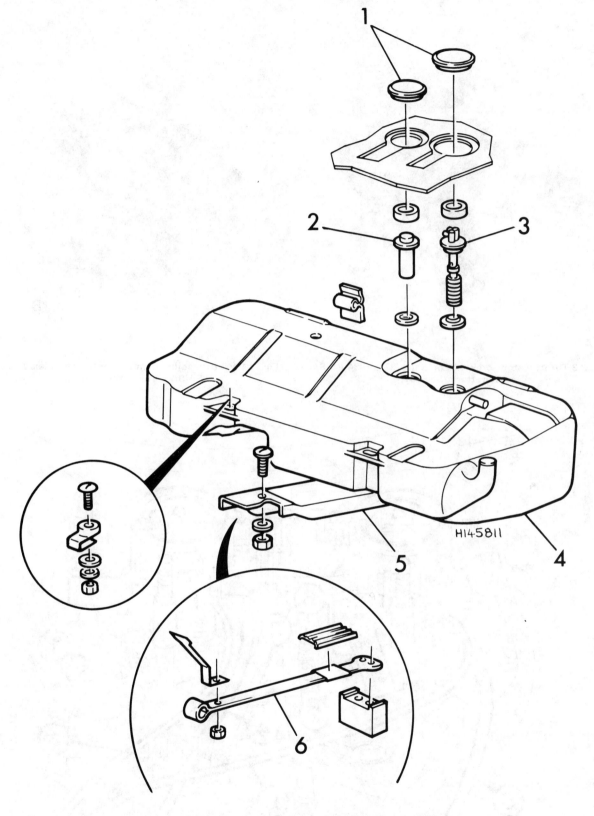

H145811

Fig. 3.2 Fuel tank components (Sec 8)

1	Access cover	3	Outlet assembly and filter	5	Heat shield
2	Fuel level transmitter	4	Fuel tank	6	Safety strap

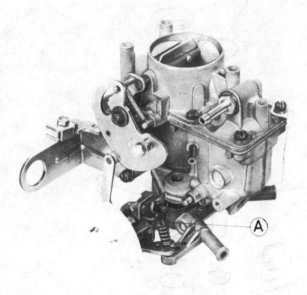

Fig. 3.3 Throttle stop screw (A) on Solex 32 and 34 PBISA carburettors (Sec 10)

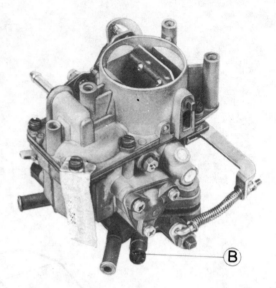

Fig. 3.4 Mixture adjustment screw (B) on Solex 32 and 34 PBISA carburettors (Sec 10)

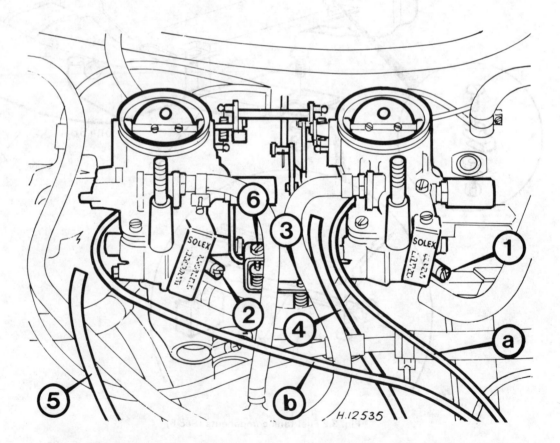

Fig. 3.5 Adjustment screw locations on the Solex 35 PBISA 8 carburettor (Sec 10)

1	Mixture screw	3	Combined idle speed screw	5	Pipe	a	Vacuum gauge pipe
2	Mixture screw	4	Pipe	6	Screw	b	Vacuum gauge pipe

Solex 35 PBISA 8

10 Before attempting to adjust the idle speed and mixture ensure that the carburettors are synchronised. Refer to Fig. 3.5 for screw locations.

Synchronising with a vacuum gauge

11 Have the engine at working temperature with the air cleaner removed.

12 Turn the mixture screws (1) and (2) in until they lightly seat and then unscrew them four complete turns.

13 With the engine running, set the idle speed screw (3) until the speed is 1000 rpm.

14 Disconnect the pipes (4) and (5) and connect the gauge pipe (a).

15 Turn the screw (3) to obtain a reading on the gauge of 100 mmHg (150 mbar).

16 Transfer the gauge pipe to (b). If the reading is not as previously recorded, turn the screw (6) in or out until it is.

17 Blip the throttle once or twice and check that both vacuum readings are as previously indicated.

Synchronising with a synchroniser

18 These are available at most motor stores and should be used as directed by the manufacturers.

19 These instruments are basically airflow meters and should show identical readings when moved from one venturi to the other. Adjust where necessary by turning screws (3) and (6).

Idle speed and mixture adjustment without an exhaust gas analyser

20 Have the engine at normal operating temperature.

21 Disconnect the twin wiring plug from the rear face of the alternator.

22 Turn the mixture screws (1) and (2) in until they lightly seat and then unscrew them four complete turns.

23 Obtain the highest idle speed by turning the mixture screws (1) and (2) by equal amounts.

24 Reset the idle speed to 1000 rpm by means of screw (3).

25 Repeat the operations with screws (1) and (2) and then reset once again by using screw (3).

26 With the engine idling at 1000 rpm reduce its speed by screwing in screws (1) and (2) equally until the engine speed drops to 970 rpm.

27 Reconnect the alternator wiring plug and, where originally fitted, fit new tamperproof caps to screws (1) and (2).

Idle speed and mixture adjustment with an exhaust gas analyser

28 Follow the procedure given in paragaphs 20 to 22.

29 Set the idle speed to 950 rpm by means of screw (3).

30 Turn the mixture screws (1) and (2) until the CO level is as specified.

31 Reset the idle speed to specified level using screw (3).

32 Reconnect the alternator wiring plug and, where originally fitted, fit new tamperproof caps to screws (1) and (2).

11 Carburettor – removal and refitting

1 Remove the air cleaner, as desribed in Section 4.

2 Unscrew the bolts or nuts and remove the air intake duct from the top of the carburettor(s).

3 Remove the short hose which runs between the oil filler cap and the carburettor. Disconnect the solenoid valve wiring, where fitted.

4 Disconnect the distributor vacuum hose from the carburettor.

5 Disconnect the fuel intake hose(s) from the carburettor(s) (photo).

6 Disconnect the balljointed throttle control rod from the carburettor(s) (photo).

7 Disconnect the choke cable (Section 15).

8 Disconnect and plug the carburettor coolant hose(s).

9 Disconnect the brake servo vacuum hose (if applicable).

10 Unscrew the mounting nuts and lift the carburettor(s) from the inlet manifold. Remove the gasket(s).

11 Refitting is a reversal of removal, but renew the gasket(s) and bleed the cooling system, as described in Chapter 2.

12 Carburettor (Solex 32 and 34 PBISA) – dismantling, reassembly and adjustment

1 Remove the screws and lift off the float chamber cover (photo).

2 Unscrew the air correction jet, followed by the main jet and idling fuel jet.

3 Unscrew the accelerator pump valve and remove the pump injector.

11.5 Hoses attached to carburettor

11.6 Throttle control rod – arrowed (XY8 engine)

12.1 Removing the float chamber cover on the Solex PBISA carburettor

4   Remove the enricher valve.
5   Unscrew the needle valve.
6   Clean the float chamber and removed components with fuel and blow through the internal channels using an air line if possible.
7   Obtain a repair kit of gaskets then reassemble the carburettor in reverse order. The float level is not adjustable.
8   The only adjustment possible is the fast idle setting of the throttle

valve. To adjust this accurately it will be necessary to measure the angular movement of the throttle valve. The use of a piece of card with the angle drawn on it will provide the necessary setting.
9   Fully close the choke valve then check that the throttle valve has opened by 20° 40′ ± 30′.
10   If necessary turn the fast idle adjustment screw as required.

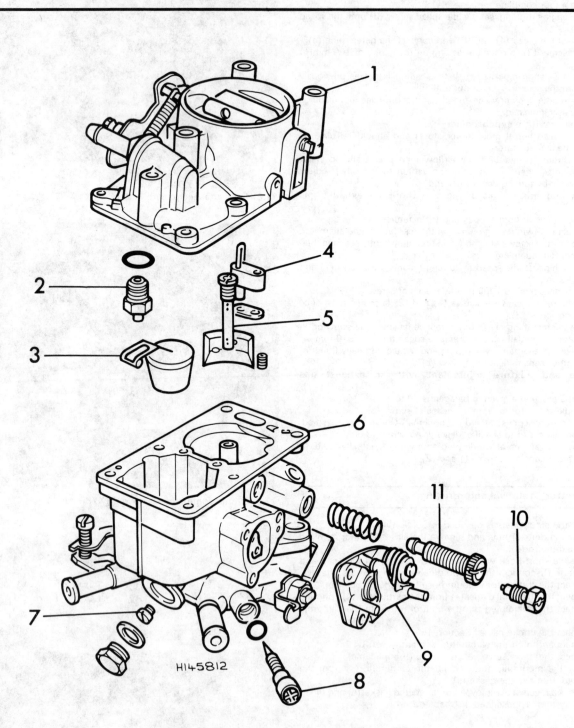

Fig. 3.6 Exploded view of the Solex 32 PBISA carburettor (Sec 12)

1 Float chamber cover	4 Accelerator pump injector	7 Main jet	10 Idling fuel jet
2 Needle valve	5 Air correction jet	8 Idle mixture screw	11 Throttle stop screw
3 Float	6 Main body	9 Enricher device	

H145812

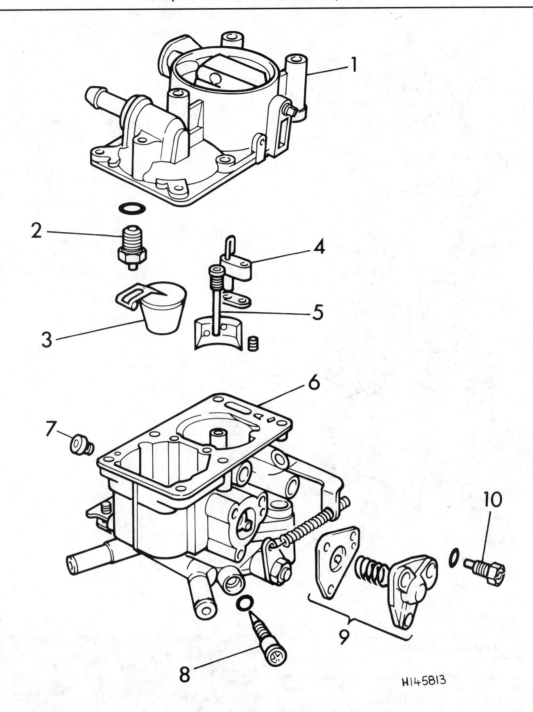

H145813

Fig. 3.7 Exploded view of the Solex 34 PBISA carburettor (Sec 12)

1	Float chamber cover	4	Accelerator pump injector	7	Main jet	9	Enricher device
2	Needle valve	5	Air correction jet	8	Idle mixture screw	10	Idling fuel jet
3	Float	6	Main body				

13 Carburettor (Solex 35 PBISA 8) – dismantling, reassembly and adjustment

1   The dismantling and reassembly procedure is identical to that for the carburettor described in Section 12, but there is no enricher valve. The adjustment procedure is as follows.

2   To adjust the initial throttle valve opening, fully unscrew the adjustment screw then, using a piece of card as described in Section 12, turn the screw until the valve is opened by 7° 45′.

3   The fast idle setting is only made on the LH carburettor with the reference number 346. First close the choke valve then check that the throttle valve has opened by 15°. If not, turn the adjustment screw as required.

4   To adjust the choke opening after starting first close the choke then pull the pneumatic opener rod and, using a suitable twist drill, check that the gap between the bottom edge of the throttle valve and the carburettor wall is 2.5 ± 0.3 mm. If not, turn the nut on the end of the pneumatic opener as required.

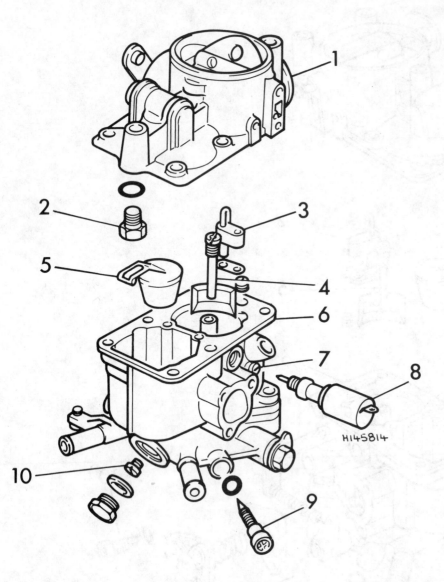

Fig. 3.8 Exploded view of the
Solex 35 PBISA 8 carburettor
(Sec 13)

1   Float chamber cover
2   Needle valve
3   Accelerator pump injector
4   Air correction jet
5   Float
6   Main body
7   Idling fuel jet
8   Idling shut-off solenoid
    (deleted from serial number
    5043526)
9   Idle mixture screw
10 Main jet

H145814

14 Throttle cable – removal and refitting

1   The throttle cable is connected to a spring-loaded reel which pivots
on the face of the cylinder head. The reel then operates the throttle
lever on the carburettor through a plastic balljointed control rod.
2   Extract the spring clip from the adjustment ferrule at the cable
bracket on the cylinder head.
3   Working inside the car, disconnect the cable end fitting from the
top of the accelerator pedal arm (photo).
4   Release the cable from the bracket on the carburettor intake cowl
(photo).
5   Withdraw the throttle cable through the bulkhead grommet.
6   Refitting is a reversal of removal, but adjust the cable at the ferrule
to remove all but the slightest amount of play. Check that full throttle
can be obtained with the accelerator pedal fully depressed.

15 Choke cable – removal and refitting

1   Remove the carburettor intake cowl.
2   Unscrew the pinch bolts and disconnect the inner and outer cables
from the lever and bracket (photo).
3   Release the cable from the clips in the engine compartment.

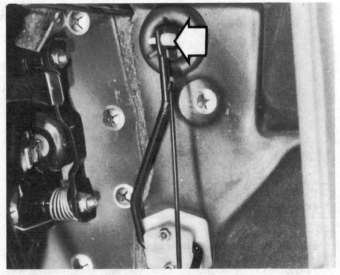

14.3 Throttle pedal and cable end fitting (arrowed)

14.4 Throttle cable bracket on the intake cowl

16.2A Removing the exhaust manifold

15.2 Choke cable connection (XY8 engine)

16.2B Exhaust manifold gaskets

4   Working inside the car, disconnect the warning lamp wiring and detach the cable from the support bracket.
5   Refitting is a reversal of removal, but adjust the cable at the carburettor end so that, when the control knob is pushed fully in, the choke valve plate is fully open.

16 Manifolds and exhaust system – general

1   The inlet and exhaust manifolds are located on opposite sides of the cylinder head.
2   The exhaust manifold is simply bolted into position with separate flange gaskets for each port (photos).
3   The inlet manifold has coolant connections and before it can be removed, the cooling system should be at least partially drained to avoid any coolant running into the cylinder bores as the manifold is removed.
4   The exhaust system is in two main sections with a short extension

16.4A Exhaust silencer front joint

16.4B Exhaust rear flexible mounting

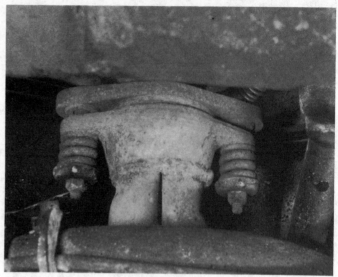

16.6 Exhaust front flange showing compression springs

connecting the exhaust manifold to the twin front section. The mountings are of flexible rubber type (photos).

5 Even if only one section of the system is to be renewed, it is recommended that the complete system is removed from under the car with the car supported on axle stands.

6 When fitting the exhaust system tighten the flange mounting nuts evenly so that the special springs are compressed equally; approximately four threads of the bolt should be visible and the springs should be compressed to 22.0 mm/0.866 in (photo) (Fig. 3.9).

PART C: FUEL INJECTION ENGINE

17 Fuel injection system – general description and precautions

The fuel injection system components are shown in Fig. 3.10. A roller type electric pump located in the fuel tank pumps fuel through

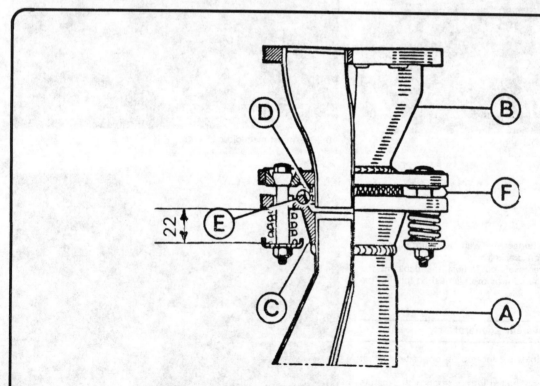

Fig. 3.9 Exhaust flange components showing spring compression dimension (Sec 16)

A Exhaust downpipe	C Collar	E Chamfered edge
B Extension	D Ring	F Parallel faces

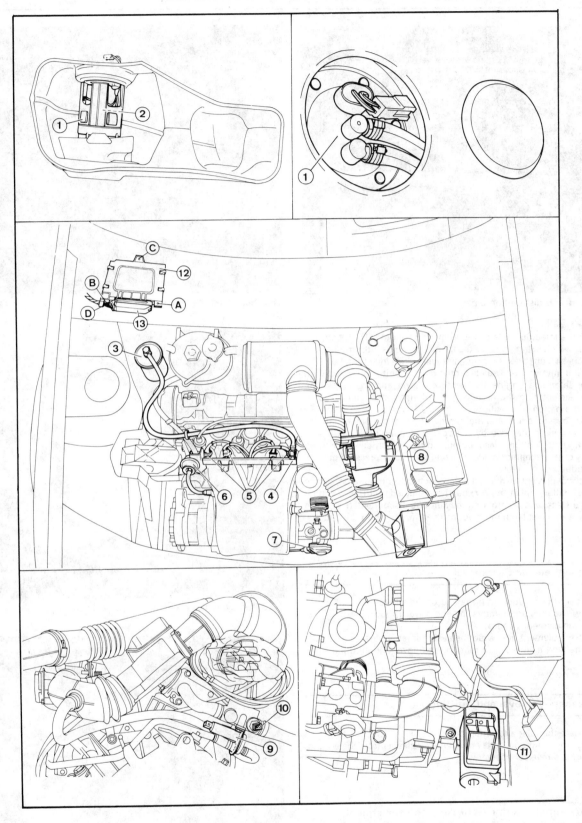

Fig. 3.10 Fuel injection system components (Sec 17)

A	Securing screw	2	Fuel pump
B	Securing screw	3	Fuel filter
C	Securing screw	4	Distribution pipe
D	ECU connector	5	Injectors
1	Fuel pump housing	6	Fuel pressure regulator

7	Throttle switch unit	11	Tachometric relay and engine speed limiter
8	Airflow sensor	12	Electric control unit (LHD model shown)
9	Supplementary air device	13	Connector
10	Temperature cover		

17.1 Injectors and distribution pipe

18.2 Removing the air cleaner end cover

the filter to the injectors via a distribution pipe (photo). The electronic control unit which is triggered by the ignition circuit sends impulses to the injectors which operate simultaneously and inject fuel in the vicinity of the inlet valves. The electronic control unit is provided with sensors to determine engine temperature, speed and load, and the quantity of air entering the engine. This information is computed to determine the period of injection.

For cold starting, additional fuel is provided and, to compensate for this, additional air is provided by a supplementary air device.

The following Sections describe procedures which can be carried out by the home mechanic. Work involving the use of pressure gauges is not included.

In order to prevent damage to the electrical components of the system the battery must **never** be disconnected with the engine running, the electronic control unit must not be disconnected with the ignition on, and a test lamp must not be used for checking the circuits.

18.3 Removing the element

18 Air cleaner element – renewal

1   Disconnect the air duct from the end of the air cleaner.
2   Unscrew the nuts and remove the end cover (photo).
3   Extract the element (photo).
4   Discard the element and wipe the casing interior clean.
5   Insert the new element then refit the end cover and air duct.

19 Air cleaner – removal and refitting

1   Disconnect the inlet and outlet ducts.
2   Unscrew the mounting bolts and lift the air cleaner from the engine.
3   Refitting is a reversal of removal.

20 Throttle initial position – checking and adjustment

1   Run the engine to normal operating temperature – indicated when the electric cooling fan has cut in and out twice. The ignition timing must be correctly adjusted, as described in Chapter 4.
2   Connect a vacuum gauge to the test point (Fig. 3.11) in the distributor vacuum advance line.
3   Check that the throttle movement is smooth.
4   With the engine stopped turn the air screw fully in (photo).
5   Prise the tamperproof cap from the throttle stop screw (photo).

20.4 Air (volume) adjustment screw

20.5 Throttle stop screw (arrowed)

rpm. Check that the vacuum reading does not exceed 50 mmHg (65 mbar) and if necessary adjust the throttle stop screw.

4   Stop the engine and adjust the throttle switch, as described in Section 22.

5   With the engine at normal operating temperature, unscrew the air screw to set the idling speed between 850 and 900 rpm.

6   Check that the CO reading is between 1 and 2% and the CO_2 reading is more than 10%.

7   If adjustment is necessary, prise out the tamperproof cap on the airflow sensor (photo) and use an Allen key to adjust the mixture. Turn the screw in to richen the mixture and out to weaken it.

8   Blip the throttle two or three times and then recheck that the idle speed and mixture is correct.

9   If the CO_2 reading is less than 10% check that the air filter is clean and that there are no leaks in the inlet or exhaust systems.

21.7 The mixture adjustment screw is located below this tamperproof cap (arrowed)

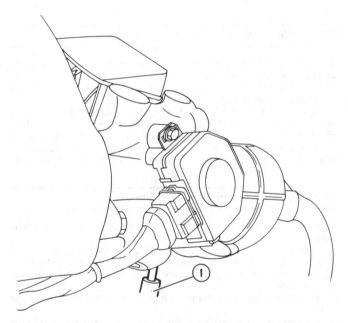

Fig. 3.11 Vacuum gauge test point (1) (Sec 20)

6   Loosen the two screws on the throttle switch unit.

7   Unscrew the throttle stop screw then retighten it until it just touches the throttle lever. Tighten the screw a further four complete turns.

8   Adjust the idling speed and mixture, as described in the following Section.

21 Idle speed and mixture – adjustment

Note: *Fine adjustment of the idle speed should be done using the air screw (photo 20.4)*

1   Connect a tachometer and an exhaust gas analyser to the engine.

2   With the throttle initial position set, as described in Section 20, run the engine at idle speed.

3   Turn the throttle stop screw to obtain an idle speed of 650

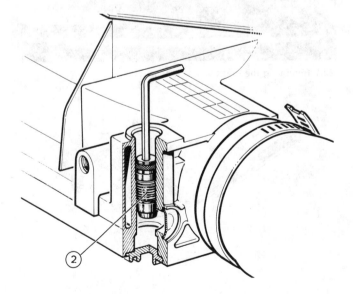

Fig. 3.12 Mixture adjustment screw (2) (Sec 21)

22 Throttle switch – checking and adjustment

1   Pull the connector from the throttle switch (photo).
2   Connect a voltmeter between the middle terminal on the connector and earth.
3   Pull the connector from the ignition control module (see Chapter 4), then operate the starter motor and check that there is a reading of at least 9 volts.
4   Disconnect the air hose from the throttle housing.
5   Position a 0.30 mm (0.012 in) feeler blade between the throttle stop screw and the throttle lever.
6   Loosen the two throttle switch screws.
7   Connect an ohmmeter between terminals 18 and 2 on the throttle switch, then rotate the switch until the internal contacts close and the reading is zero ohms. Tighten the screws with the switch in this position.
8   Remove the feeler blade and insert in its place a 0.70 mm (0.028 in) feeler blade. The internal contacts should now be separated and the reading on the ohmmeter infinity. If not, repeat the procedure in paragraph 7.
9   Remove the feeler blade.
10 Check the full throttle operation by connecting an ohmmeter between terminals 18 and 2, then fully opening the throttle so that dimension X (Fig. 3.14) is 4.0 mm (0.158 in). The internal contacts should close and the ohmmeter reading be zero.
11 If the switch does not operate correctly it should be renewed.

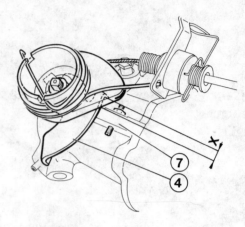

Fig. 3.14 Full throttle dimension X (Sec 22)

4   Throttle lever $X = 4.0$ mm (0.158 in)
7   Throttle housing

22.1 Removing the throttle switch connector

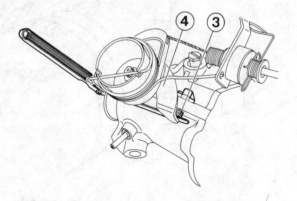

Fig. 3.13 Adjusting the throttle switch (Sec 22)

3   Idle speed adjustment screw   4   Throttle lever

23 Air intake system – checking for leaks

1   For the correct operation of the airflow sensor there must be no air entering the system upstream of the sensor.
2   Check that there is no leakage at the points arrowed in Fig. 3.15 or at the inlet manifold gasket.
3   If an air line is available, disconnect the airflow sensor inlet hose and use an adaptor to blow air through the intake system while fully opening the throttle, blocking the exhaust pipe and pinching the crankcase breather hose. If the points indicated in paragraph 2 are then brushed with soapy water any bad seals will be immediately evident.

24 Fuel pump – removal and refitting

1   Open the tailgate and remove the floor covering from the luggage area.
2   Prise up the right-hand plastic cover then disconnect the wiring, and the fuel supply and return pipes, noting their location (photo).
3   Unscrew the retaining screws and lift the fuel pump housing from the fuel tank.
4   Release the filter from the bottom of the housing, followed by the collar.
5   Disconnect the wiring and release the fuel pump from the upper collar.
6   Refitting is a reversal of removal, but fit new collars and make sure that the wiring terminals are positioned away from the pump terminals. Always fit a new gasket between the pump housing and fuel tank.

25 Supplementary air device (cold start) – removal and refitting

1   Remove the battery (Chapter 12).
2   Disconnect the air hoses then unbolt the airflow sensor and bracket. Disconnect the wiring.
3   Unscrew the supplementary air device bracket nuts and disconnect the wiring.
4   Tilt the assembly and coolant outlet housing (without disconnecting the coolant hoses) and remove the concealed mounting bolt.
5   Disconnect the air hoses, then remove the remaining mounting bolt and withdraw the unit.
6   Refitting is a reversal of removal.

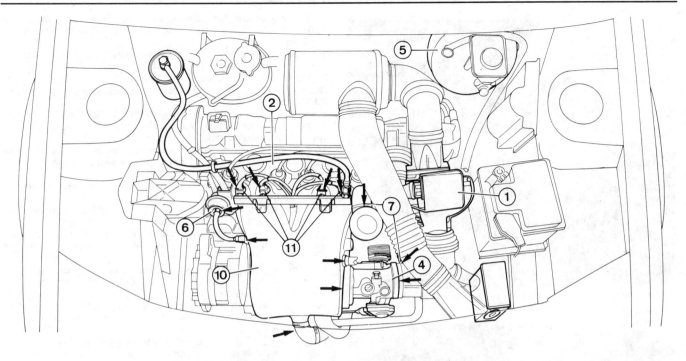

Fig. 3.15 Areas (arrowed) for checking air intake leakage (Sec 23)

1	Airflow sensor	4	Throttle housing	6	Fuel pressure regulator	10	Air distribution manifold
2	Cylinder head	5	Brake vacuum servo	7	Crankcase breather hose	11	Injectors

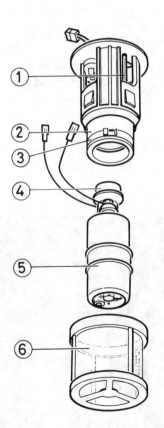

Fig. 3.16 Fuel pump components (Sec 24)

1	Bleed tube	4	Collar
2	Bracket	5	Fuel pump
3	Collar	6	Filter

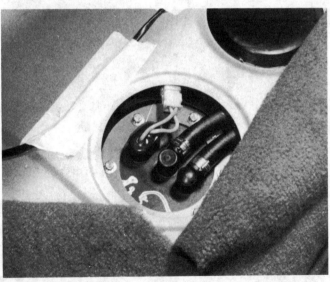

24.2 Fuel pump location and connections

26 Fuel injection system – complete test

1   Pull the connector from the airflow sensor and connect a voltmeter between wire 18A and earth (photos).

2   Disconnect the ignition control unit then operate the starter motor and check that a minimum of 9 volts is obtained.

3   Disconnect the battery negative lead.

4   Connect an ohmmeter between wire M18 and earth and check that the reading is less than 1 ohm.

5   Disconnect the airflow sensor inlet hose (photo) and use a screwdriver to open and close the sensor flap. The movement should be free. Clean the interior of the sensor if necessary.

26.1A Removing the connector from the airflow sensor

26.1B Showing terminals 18A (1) and M18 (2) on the airflow sensor connector

26.5 Disconnecting the airflow sensor inlet hose

6   Connect an ohmmeter between terminals 5 and 8 on the airflow sensor (Fig. 3.17) and check that a reading of 340 to 450 ohms is obtained.

7   Connect the ohmmeter between terminals 9 and 8 and check that the reading is now between 160 and 300 ohms.

8   Connect the ohmmeter between terminals 5 and 7, then move the flap with a screwdriver. The resistance should vary between 60 and 1000 ohms.

9   Connect the ohmmeter between the terminal on the engine temperature sensor (above the supplementary air device) and earth (photo). The reading should be less than 1 ohm.

10 Pull off the temperature sensor connector and connect the ohmmeter across the two terminals on the sensor. If the reading is infinity, renew the sensor.

11 Connect a voltmeter between wire 48 on the supplementary air device connector and earth.

12 Disconnect the ignition control unit then operate the starter motor and check that the reading is at least 9 volts.

13 With the battery disconnected, connect an ohmmeter between wire M24 on the connector and earth. The reading should be less than 1 ohm.

14 Remove the supplementary air device (Section 25) and check that, at an ambient temperature of 20°C (68°F), the opening in the diaphragm is visible through the end of the unit.

15 Connect an ohmmeter across the terminals of the unit and check that a reading of 45 to 55 ohms is obtained at an ambient temperature of 20°C (68°F).

16 Connect a 12 volt supply to the terminals of the unit. After five minutes the diaphragm must completely block the airflow aperture.

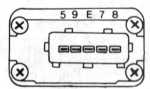

Fig. 3.17 Airflow sensor terminals (Sec 26)

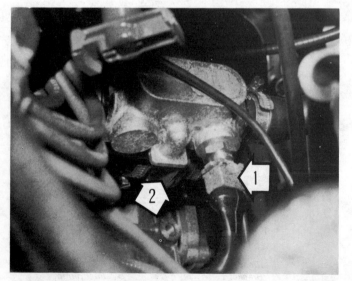

26.9 Engine temperature sensor (1) and supplementary air device (2)

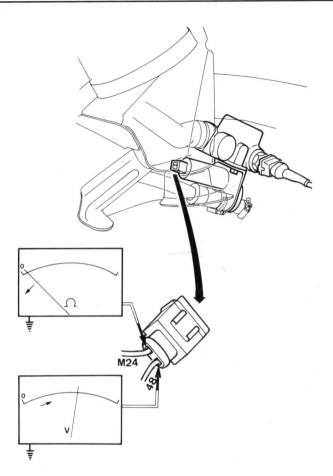

Fig. 3.18 Checking the supplementary air device wiring (Sec 26)

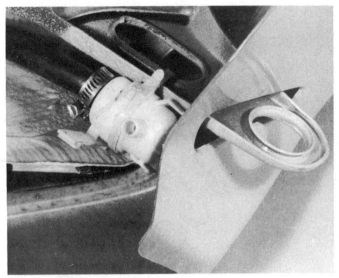

28.1 Fuel tank vent valve

29.1 Throttle cable adjustment ferrule (arrowed)

27 Fuel level transmitter – removal and refitting

Refer to Section 7.

28 Fuel tank – removal, repair and refitting

Refer to Section 8. Note that there is an additional vent valve located near the rear towing eye (photo).

29 Throttle cable – removal and refitting

The procedure is similar to that described in Section 14, but the adjustment ferrule is located beneath the inlet manifold (photo).

30 Manifolds and exhaust system – general

1   The inlet manifold is combined with an air distribution chamber. A single gasket seals the assembly to the cylinder head.
2   The exhaust manifold is similar in design to that described in Section 16.
3   The exhaust system is in three main sections with flexible rubber mountings.
4   Since removal is easy it is recommended that the complete system is removed even when renewing a single section.
5   When fitting the exhaust system observe the procedure for tightening the flange nuts given in Section 16 (photo).

30.5 Exhaust system flange nuts

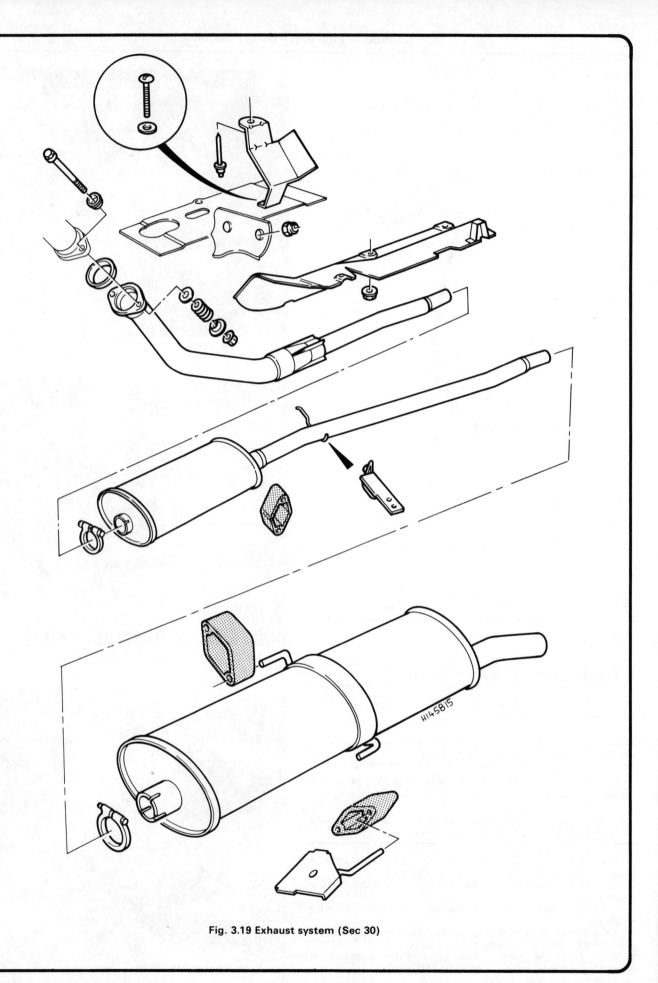

Fig. 3.19 Exhaust system (Sec 30)

PART D: FAULT DIAGNOSIS

31 Fault diagnosis – fuel and exhaust systems

Symptom	Reason(s)
Difficult starting from cold	Choke control inoperative (carburettor) Fuel pump fault Blocked fuel line or filter Needle valve sticking (carburettor) Supplementary air device fault (fuel injection) Temperature sensor faulty or disconnected (fuel injection)
Difficult starting when hot	Choked air filter Choke control sticking (carburettor) Fuel pump faulty
Excessive fuel consumption	Mixture setting incorrect Excessive fuel pressure (fuel injection) Temperature sensor faulty (fuel injection) Airflow sensor faulty (fuel injection)
Uneven idling	Mixture setting incorrect Air leak in intake system Throttle switch out of adjustment (fuel injection) Loose electronic control unit connector (fuel injection)

Chapter 4 Ignition system

For modifications, and information applicable to later models, see Supplement at end of manual

Contents

Specifications

System type .... Electronic (breakerless)

Distributor

Rotor rotation .... Anti-clockwise
Firing order .... 1 – 3 – 4 – 2 (No 1 at clutch end)
Pulse generator resistance .... 990 to 1210 ohms

Ignition timing (vacuum hose disconnected)

XV8 and XW7 engines .... 6° BTDC at 650 rpm
XY7 engine .... 8° BTDC at 650 rpm
XY8 engine:
    Early with M152E curve .... 0° BTDC at 950 rpm
    Later with M159E curve .... 8° BTDC at 850 to 950 rpm
XU5J engine .... 30° BTDC at 3500 rpm or 6° BTDC at 700 rpm

Spark plugs

Type:
    XV8, XW7, and XY7 engines .... Champion S281YC or BN9Y
    Bosch H7DC or H6DO
    PRO (Peugeot) CC10
    XY8 and XU5J engines .... Champion S279YC or BN79Y
    Bosch H6DC or H5DO
    PRO (Peugeot) CC8
Electrode gap .... 0.6 mm (0.024 in)

Ignition coil

Primary resistance .... 0.85 ohm
Secondary resistance .... 6000 ohms

Torque wrench settings

	Nm	lbf ft
Spark plugs	17.5	13
Timing plug (non-GTI models)	27.5	20
Timing plate bolt (non GTI models)	7.0	5

1 General description

The ignition system is of electronic breakerless type incorporating a control module (located near the ignition coil), pulse generator (located in the distributor), ignition coil and distributor. The spark plugs have taper seats without sealing washers.

In order that the engine may run correctly it is necessary for an electrical spark to ignite the fuel/air mixture in the combustion chamber at exactly the right moment in relation to engine speed and load.

Basically the ignition system functions as follows. Low tension voltage from the battery is fed to the ignition coil, where it is converted into high tension voltage. The high tension voltage is powerful enough to jump the spark plug gap in the cylinder many times a second under high compression pressure, providing that the ignition system is in good working order.

The ignition system consists of two individual circuits known as the low tension (LT) circuit and high tension (HT) circuit.

The low tension circuit (sometimes known as the primary circuit) comprises the ignition switch, primary ignition coil windings, and control module. The high tension circuit (sometimes known as the secondary circuit) comprises the secondary ignition coil windings, distributor cap, rotor arm, spark plugs and HT leads.

The primary circuit is initially switched on by the control module and a magnetic field is formed within the ignition coil. At the precise point of ignition the pulse generator causes the control module to switch off the primary circuit, and high tension voltage is then induced in the secondary circuit and fed to the spark plug via the distributor cap and rotor arm.

The ignition is advanced and retarded automatically by centrifugal weights and a vacuum capsule to ensure that the spark occurs at the correct instant in relation to engine speed and load.

Note: When working on the ignition system remember that the high tension voltage can be considerably higher than on a conventional system and in certain circumstances could prove fatal.

2 Routine maintenance

Carry out the following procedures at the intervals given in Routine Maintenance at the beginning of the manual.
1 Remove the spark plugs and renew them, with reference to Section 10. Do not forget to set the electrode gaps on the new plugs.
2 Check and, if necessary, adjust the ignition timing, as described in Section 7.

3 Distributor – removal and refitting

1 On GTI models, remove the air cleaner and inlet duct, as described in Chapter 3.
2 Identify the HT leads for position then disconnect them from the spark plugs.
3 Slide off the ignition coil cover and disconnect the HT lead from the coil.
4 Pull back the plastic cover then unclip and remove the distributor cap (photo).
5 Disconnect the wiring at the connector, where necessary pulling out the spring clip first.
6 Pull the hose from the vacuum advance unit.
7 Mark the distributor mounting flange in relation to the cylinder head (non-GTI models) or thermostat housing (GTI models).
8 Unscrew the mounting nuts, remove the small plates, and withdraw the distributor (photos).
9 Check the condition of the O-ring on the mounting flange and renew it if necessary.
10 Refitting is a reversal of removal, but turn the rotor arm as required to align the lugs with the offset slot in the camshaft (photo). If the old distributor is being refitted, align the previously made marks before tightening the mounting nuts. If fitting a new distributor, initially set the distributor in the middle of the slotted holes or follow the procedure given in Section 7, then finally adjust the ignition timing (Section 7).

4 Distributor – overhaul

1 Clean the exterior of the distributor.
2 Pull off the rotor arm and remove the plastic cover, where fitted.

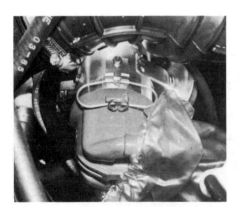

3.4 The distributor cap on a GTI model

3.8A Unscrew the mounting nuts ...

3.8B ... and remove the distributor (non-GTI models)

3.8C Removing the distributor on a GTI model

3.10 The offset slot in the end of the camshaft

Ducellier

3 Extract the screw and remove the clamp and wiring plug (photo).
4 Extract the three body screws. The lugs are offset so the body sections cannot be misaligned when reassembled. Separate the body sections (photo).
5 Invert the body upper section, pull out the plastic ring and lift out the magnetic coil (photo).
6 From the body upper section, extract the circlip and the thrust washer (photo).
7 Extract the vacuum unit screw and then lift out the baseplate at the same time unhooking the vacuum link (photos).
8 Extract the circlip and shim from the body lower section (photo).
9 Lift out the counterweight assembly.
10 The drive dog is secured to the shaft by a pin.
11 Reassembly is a reversal of dismantling, but note that one baseplate hole is marked by engagement of the vacuum unit link rod (photo).

Bosch

12 The procedure is similar to that for the Ducellier distributor but the body is in one piece. Refer to Fig. 4.2 (photos).

4.3 Clamp and wiring plug (Ducellier)

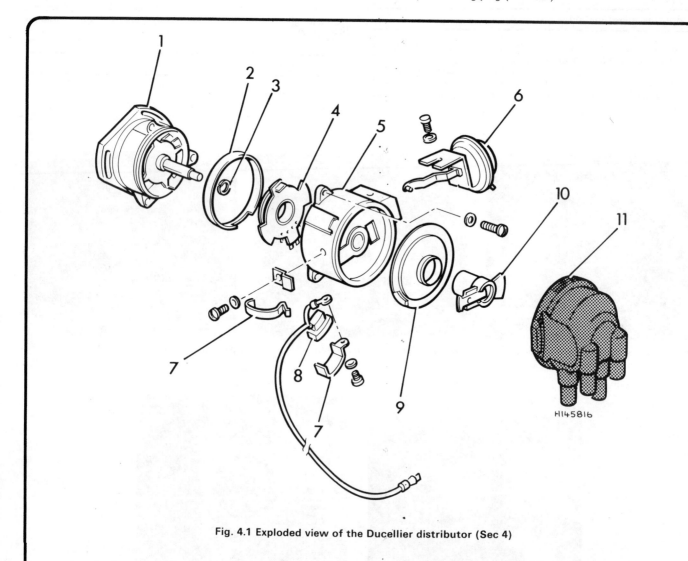

Fig. 4.1 Exploded view of the Ducellier distributor (Sec 4)

1 Lower body	4 Magnetic coil	7 Clips	10 Rotor arm
2 Plastic ring	5 Upper body	8 Wiring plug	11 Distributor cap
3 Circlip	6 Vacuum unit	9 Cover	

4.4 Separating body sections (Ducellier)

4.5A Remove the plastic ring (Ducellier)

4.5B ... and magnetic coil (Ducellier)

4.6 Removing the circlip and thrust washer (Ducellier)

4.7A Vacuum unit and screw (Ducellier)

4.7B Removing the baseplate (Ducellier)

4.8 View of reluctor, centrifugal weights and securing circlip – arrowed (Ducellier)

4.11 Hole marked for engagement of vacuum unit link (Ducellier)

4.12A Removing the clamp (Bosch) ...

4.12B ... and wiring connector (Bosch)

4.12C View of the bearing plate (Bosch)

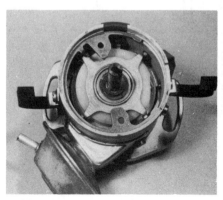

4.12D View of reluctor with bearing plate removed (Bosch)

Fig. 4.2 Exploded view of the Bosch distributor (Sec 4)

1 Wiring plug
2 Connector
3 Clip
4 Body
5 Vacuum unit
6 Distributor cap
7 Rotor arm
8 Cover
9 Bearing plate
10 Ring
11 Circlip
12 Reluctor
13 Magnetic coil
14 Stator
15 Baseplate
16 Clip
17 Shaft assembly

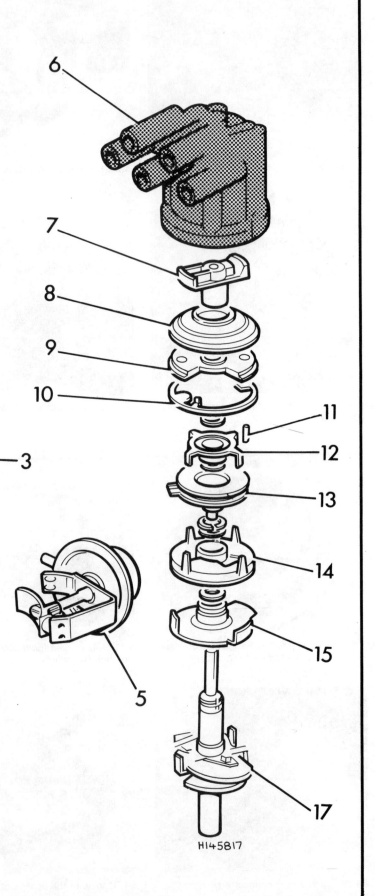

H145817

Measuring plug gap. A feeler gauge of the correct size (see ignition system specifications) should have a slight 'drag' when slid between the electrodes. Adjust gap if necessary

Adjusting plug gap. The plug gap is adjusted by bending the earth electrode inwards, or outwards, as necessary until the correct clearance is obtained. Note the use of the correct tool

Normal. Grey-brown deposits, lightly coated core nose. Gap increasing by around 0.001 in (0.025 mm) per 1000 miles (1600 km). Plugs ideally suited to engine, and engine in good condition

Carbon fouling. Dry, black, sooty deposits. Will cause weak spark and eventually misfire. Fault: over-rich fuel mixture. Check: carburettor mixture settings, float level and jet sizes; choke operation and cleanliness of air filter. Plugs can be re-used after cleaning

Oil fouling. Wet, oily deposits. Will cause weak spark and eventually misfire. Fault: worn bores/piston rings or valve guides; sometimes occurs (temporarily) during running-in period. Plugs can be re-used after thorough cleaning

Overheating. Electrodes have glazed appearance, core nose very white – few deposits. Fault: plug overheating. Check: plug value, ignition timing, fuel octane rating (too low) and fuel mixture (too weak). Discard plugs and cure fault immediately

Electrode damage. Electrodes burned away; core nose has burned, glazed appearance. Fault: pre-ignition. Check: as for 'Overheating' but may be more severe. Discard plugs and remedy fault before piston or valve damage occurs

Split core nose (may appear initially as a crack). Damage is self-evident, but cracks will only show after cleaning. Fault: pre-ignition or wrong gap-setting technique. Check: ignition timing, cooling system, fuel octane rating (too low) and fuel mixture (too weak). Discard plugs, rectify fault immediately

5   Ignition module – removal and refitting

1   Slide the cover off the ignition coil and module (photo).
2   Disconnect the battery negative lead.
3   Disconnect the wiring harness.
4   Remove the screws and withdraw the module from the mounting plate.
5   Refitting is a reversal of removal.

5.1 Removing the coil and module cover

6   Timing plate (non-GTI models) – setting

1   The timing plate which is located in the aperture under the plastic cover at the top of the flywheel housing can be moved within the limits of its elongated slot.
2   The plate is set during production and should not be disturbed

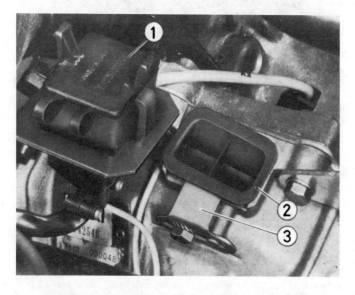

Fig. 4.3 Timing components on non-GTI models (Sec 6)

1   Diagnostic socket   *3   Timing plate*
2   Cover

unless a new flywheel, flywheel housing or other associated components have been fitted.
3   To set the timing plate, carry out the following operations.
4   Remove the plastic cover.
5   Using the crankshaft pulley nut, turn the crankshaft until the mark on the flywheel is at the start of the timing plate.
6   Remove the plug from behind the crankshaft pulley using an Allen key. Note that if the hole in the pulley is not over the plug, the crankshaft should be turned exactly half a turn. This is because there are two diametrically opposite timing marks on the flywheel, and the mark corresponding to TDC on No 2 and 3 cylinders must be used to bring the slot in the crankshaft counterbalance in line with the plug hole.
7   Insert the special tool 80133 into the plug hole and turn the crankshaft until the tool is felt to drop into the cut-out in the counterbalance weight of the crankshaft.
8   If the special tool is not available, use a rod 8.00 mm diameter x 100.0 mm long (photo).
9   The pistons 2 and 3 are now located at TDC.
10   Release the timing plate bolt and move the plate to align the flywheel, and 0 (TDC) mark on the plate. Tighten the bolt to the specified torque. Apply a blob of paint on the edge of the bolt so that any subsequent movement can be recognised.
11   Withdraw the pin, fit a new sealing ring to the plug and tighten to the specified torque.

6.8 Substitute rod for setting crankshaft position on non-GTI models

7   Ignition timing – checking and adjustment

Note: *The ignition timing may be checked and adjusted using the engine diagnosis socket, but the special Peugeot instrument necessary will not normally be available to the home mechanic.*

Non-GTI models (XV8, XW7, XY7 and XY8 engines)

1   To set the ignition timing statically so that the engine can be started first remove No 2 spark plug and turn the engine in the normal rotational direction until pressure is felt – indicating that the piston is commencing the compression stroke. The pressure can be felt using a suitable wooden rod or a piece of cork placed over the spark plug hole.
2   Remove the plastic cover from the timing aperture then continue turning the crankshaft until the mark on the flywheel is opposite the BTDC mark on the timing plate (photo).
3   Check that the distributor rotor arm is facing the No 2 HT lead segment position in the distributor cap. To do this, remove the cap and mark the outside in line with the segment, then put it back on the distributor noting which way the rotor arm is facing.

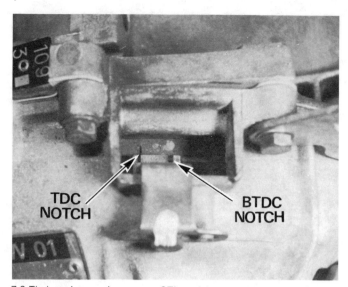

7.2 Timing plate marks on non-GTI models

4 If necessary, loosen the mounting nuts and turn the distributor body to bring the segment and rotor arm in line, then tighten the nuts. Refit No 2 spark plug.

5 Run the engine to normal operating temperature then stop it and connect a tachometer and stroboscopic timing light to it. If the HT pick-up lead of the timing light is connected to the HT lead on the ignition coil it is possible to detect any discrepancy between the firing of Nos 1 and 4 and Nos 2 and 3 cylinders since there are two diametrically opposite timing marks on the flywheel. However, the pick-up lead may be connected to any one of the spark plug HT leads, in which case only one of the flywheel timing marks will be used.

6 Disconnect and plug the vacuum pipe at the distributor vacuum advance unit.

7 Run the engine at the specified speed and point the timing light into the timing aperture. The single mark on the flywheel should be aligned with the BTDC mark on the timing plate. If the ignition coil HT lead has been used (see paragraph 5), and there is wear in the distributor, there will be two marks visible on the flywheel close to each other. In this case the mid-point between the two marks should be aligned with the BTDC mark on the timing plate.

8 If adjustment is necessary, loosen the distributor mounting nuts and rotate the distributor body as required. Tighten the nuts on completion.

9 The operation of the centrifugal advance weights in the distributor can be checked by increasing the engine speed with the timing light pointing in the timing aperture and observing that the mark on the flywheel advances from its initial position.

10 To check the vacuum advance unit, run the engine at a fast idle speed and reconnect the vacuum pipe. The flywheel mark should again advance.

11 Stop the engine, disconnect the tachometer and timing light and reconnect the vacuum pipe. Refit the timing aperture cover.

GTI models (XU5J engine)

12 To set the ignition timing statically so that the engine can be started, first remove No 1 spark plug (nearest clutch) and turn the engine in the normal rotational direction until pressure is felt – indicating that the piston is commencing the compression stroke. The pressure can be felt using a suitable wooden rod or piece of cork placed over the spark plug hole.

13 While looking into the timing aperture in the clutch housing/gearbox casing, continue turning the crankshaft until the single mark on the flywheel is opposite the BTDC mark on the timing plate.

14 Check that the distributor rotor arm is facing the No 1 HT lead segment position in the distributor cap. To do this, remove the cap and mark the outside in line with the segment, then put it back on the distributor noting which way the rotor arm is facing.

15 If necessary, loosen the mounting nuts and turn the distributor body to bring the segment and rotor arm in line, then tighten the nuts. Refit No 1 spark plug.

16 Run the engine to normal operating temperature then stop it and connect a tachometer to it.

17 Disconnect and plug the vacuum pipe at the distributor vacuum advance unit.

18 Disconnect and remove the air cleaner inlet duct then connect a stroboscipic timing light to the engine using the HT pick-up lead connected to No 1 spark plug HT lead.

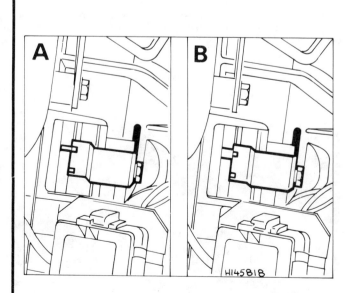

Fig. 4.4 Ignition timing adjustment on non-GTI models
(Sec 7)

A   Using spark plug HT lead   B   Using ignition coil HT lead

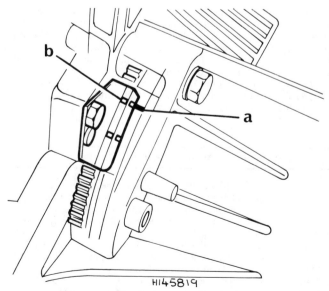

Fig. 4.5 Initial static ignition timing on GTI models (Sec 7)

a   Single flywheel mark   b   BTDC mark on timing plate

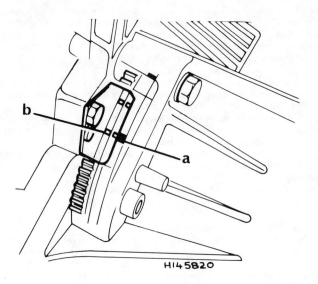

9.1 TDC sensor on non-GTI models

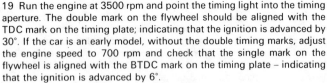

Fig. 4.6 Dynamic ignition timing on GTI models (Sec 7)

a Double flywheel mark   b TDC mark on timing plate

19 Run the engine at 3500 rpm and point the timing light into the timing aperture. The double mark on the flywheel should be aligned with the TDC mark on the timing plate; indicating that the ignition is advanced by 30°. If the car is an early model, without the double timing marks, adjust the engine speed to 700 rpm and check that the single mark on the flywheel is aligned with the BTDC mark on the timing plate – indicating that the ignition is advanced by 6°.
20 If adjustment is necessary, loosen the distributor mounting nuts and rotate the distributor body as required. Tighten the nuts on completion.
21 Check the centrifugal and vacuum advance characteristics of the distributor, as described in paragraphs 9 and 10.
22 Stop the engine, disconnect the tachometer and timing light then reconnect the vacuum pipe and air cleaner inlet duct.

8 Ignition coil – general

1 The maintenance of the coil is minimal and is limited to periodically wiping its surfaces clean and dry and ensuring that the lead connectors are secure. High voltages generated by the coil can easily leak to earth over its surface and prevent the spark plugs from receiving the electrical pulses. Water repellent sprays are now available to prevent dampness causing this type of malfunction.
2 Wipe clean and spray the HT leads and distributor cap also.
3 Special equipment is required to test a coil and is best left to an auto-electrician. Substitution of another coil is an alternative method of fault tracing.

9 TDC sensor – removal and refitting

1 The TDC sensor (photo) is for use with the diagnostic socket located on the clutch housing. As a special instrument and adaptor are required it will normally be used only by a Peugeot garage.
2 To remove the sensor, unscrew the mounting screw (non-GTI models) or release the clamp (GTI models).
3 The sensor forms part of the diagnostic socket assembly so, if it is to be completely removed, the socket must be unclipped from its bracket and the remaining wiring and earth leads disconnected.
4 Refitting is a reversal of removal, but the adjustment procedure for new and used sensors differs. New sensors have three extensions on the inner face and the unit should be inserted through the clamp until the extensions just touch the flywheel. The clamp screw is then tightened and clearance is provided as the flywheel rotates and wears the ends of the extensions. This method should not be used when refitting a used sensor. In this case, cut off the extensions completely

then temporarily insert the sensor until it touches the flywheel, remove it and reposition it in the clamp 1.0 mm (0.04 in) further out.

10 Spark plugs, HT leads and distributor cap – general

1 The correct functioning of the spark plugs is vital for the correct running and efficiency of the engine, and it is therefore important to keep them clean and correctly gapped in accordance with the information given in Section 2.
2 To remove the plugs, first open the bonnet and pull the HT leads from them. Grip the rubber end fitting not the lead otherwise the lead connection may be fractured. Also remove the extensions.
3 The spark plugs are deeply recessed in the cylinder head and it is recommended that dirt is removed from the recesses using a vacuum cleaner or compressed air, before removing the plugs, to prevent dirt dropping into the cylinders.
4 Unscrew the plugs using the special box wrench supplied with the car and located in the front left-hand corner of the engine compartment by the washer bottle (photo).

10.4 Removing a spark plug with the special box spanner

5   Examination of the spark plugs will give a good indication of the condition of the engine. If the insulator nose of the spark plug is clean and white, with no deposits, this is indicative of a weak mixture, or too hot a plug (a hot plug transfers heat away from the electrode slowly, a cold plug transfers heat away quickly). The plugs fitted as standard are specified at the beginning of this Chapter.

6   If the top and insulator nose are covered with hard black-looking deposits, then this is indicative that the mixture is too rich. Should the plug be black and oily, then it is likely that the engine is fairly worn, as well as the mixture being too rich.

7   If the insulator nose is covered with light tan to greyish brown deposits, then the mixture is correct and it is likely that the engine is in good condition.

8   If there are any traces of long brown tapering stains on the outside of the white portion of the plug, then the plug will have to be renewed, as this shows that there is a faulty joint between the plug body and the insulator, and compression is being allowed to leak away.

9   Before cleaning a spark plug, wash it in petrol to remove oily deposits.

10   Although a wire brush can be used to clean the electrode end of the spark plug this method can cause metal conductance paths across the nose of the insulator. It is therefore to be preferred that an abrasive powder cleaning machine is used. Such machines are available quite cheaply from motor accessory stores or you may prefer to take the plugs to your dealer who will not only be able to clean them, but also to check the sparking efficiency of each plug under compression.

11   The spark plug gap is of considerable importance as, if it is too large or too small, the size of the spark and its efficiency will be seriously impaired. For the best results the spark plug gap should be set in accordance with the Specifications at the beginning of this Chapter.

12   To set it, measure the gap with a feeler gauge, and then bend open, or close, the outer plug electrode until the correct gap is achieved. The centre electrode should never be bent, as this may crack the insulation and cause plug failure, if nothing worse.

13   Special spark plug electrode gap adjusting tools are available from most motor accessory shops.

14   Before refitting the spark plugs check that the threaded connector sleeves are tight and that the plug exterior surfaces and threads are clean.

15   Screw in the spark plugs by hand where possible, then tighten them to the specified torque. Take extra care to enter the plug threads correctly as the cylinder head is of aluminium.

16   Refit the extensions followed by the HT leads, making sure that the latter are in their correct order of 1–3–4–2 (No 1 nearest the clutch end of engine) in relation to the anti-clockwise direction of the rotor arm.

17   The HT leads and their connections should always be kept clean and dry and arranged neatly in the special holder. If any lead shows signs of cracking or chafing of the insulation it should be renewed.

18   Check the distributor cap whenever it is removed. If there are any very thin black lines running between the electrodes this indicates tracking and a new cap should be fitted. Check the rotor arm in a similar way. Where applicable check that the spring-tensioned carbon brush in the centre of the cap is free to move and is not worn excessively.

11 Fault diagnosis – ignition system

1   If the engine fails to start and the car was running normally when it was last used, first check that there is fuel in the fuel tank. If the engine turns over normally on the starter motor and the battery is evidently well charged first check the HT (high tension) circuit.

2   A common reason for bad starting is wet or damp spark plug leads and distributor cap. Check both items and wipe dry, if necessary.

3   If the engine still fails to start, disconnect an HT lead from any spark plug and, using a nail inserted into the end fitting, hold the lead approximately 5.0 mm (0.2 in) away from the cylinder head with well-insulated pliers. While an assistant spins the engine on the starter motor, check that a regular blue spark occurs. If so the spark plugs are probably the cause of the engine's not starting and they should therefore be cleaned and regapped.

4   If no spark occurs, disconnect the main feed HT lead from the distributor cap and check for a spark as in paragraph 3. If sparks now occur, check the distributor cap, rotor arm, and HT leads, as described in Section 10, and renew them as necessary.

5   Check the security of the wiring to the ignition coil, distributor and electronic module.

6   Using an ohmmeter, check the resistance of the distributor pulse generator coil and the ignition coil windings. Renew them if the readings are not as given in the Specifications.

7   If necessary, dismantle the distributor and check that the gaps between the reluctor arms and the stator posts are all equal.

8   Using a voltmeter, check that there is battery voltage at the ignition coil low tension positive terminal with the ignition switched on. Connect the voltmeter across the coil LT terminals and check that the reading is zero. If it is not zero the module may be defective or the coil-to-module wire earthed.

Chapter 5 Clutch

For modifications, and information applicable to later models, see Supplement at end of manual

Contents

Specifications

General

Type	Diaphragm spring, single dry plate, cable operation
Driven plate diameter:	
All models except GTI	180.0 mm
GTI	200.0 mm
Release bearing	Sealed ball-bearing
Clutch pedal stroke	140.0 mm

Torque wrench settings

	Nm	lbf ft
Clutch cover	10	7
Clutch housing	12	9

1 General description

The clutch is of diaphragm spring, single dry plate type with cable actuation.

The clutch pedal pivots in a bracket mounted under the facia and operates a cable to the clutch release arm (or fork). The release lever operates a thrust bearing (clutch release bearing) which bears on the diaphragm spring of the pressure plate, and releases the clutch driven plate from the flywheel. The driven plate (or disc) is splined to a shaft which transmits the drive to the gearbox. On non-GTI models with the BH 3 gearbox the shaft is part of the transfer gear assembly, but on GTI models with the side-mounted BE 1 gearbox the shaft is the gearbox input shaft.

The clutch release mechanism consists of a fork and bearing which are in permanent contact with release fingers on the pressure plate assembly. The fork pushes the release bearing forwards to bear against the release fingers, so moving the centre of the diaphragm spring inwards. The spring is sandwiched between two rings which act as fulcrum points. As the centre of the spring is pushed in, the outside of the spring is pushed out, so moving the pressure plate backwards and disengaging it from the clutch driven plate.

When the clutch pedal is released, the diaphragm spring forces the pressure plate into contact with the friction linings on the driven plate and at the same time pushes the driven plate a fraction of an inch forwards on its splines so engaging it with the flywheel. The driven plate is now firmly sandwiched between the pressure plate and the flywheel, so the drive is taken up.

As wear takes place on the driven plate friction linings the diaphragm fingers move outwards and the pedal stroke decreases; the cable mechanism incorporates an adjustment to compensate for this wear.

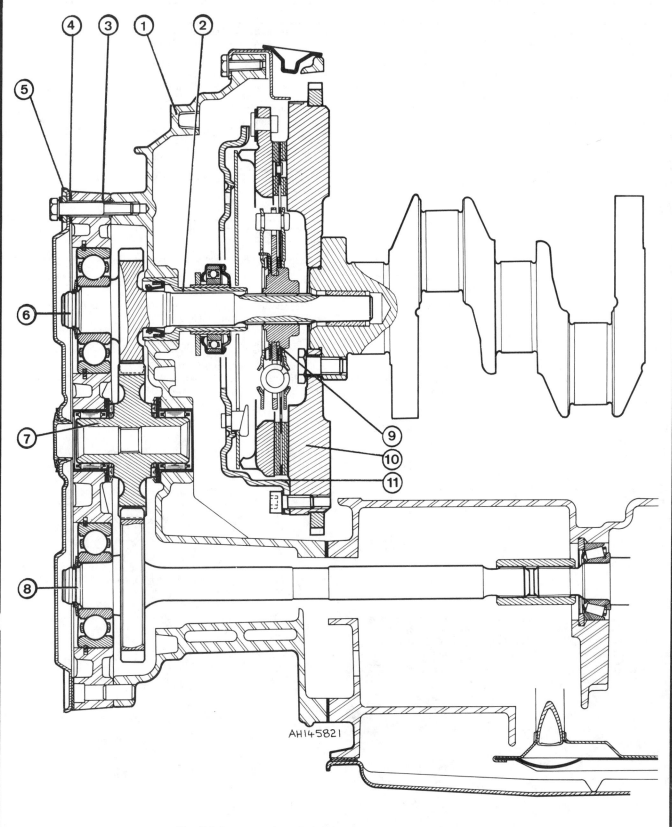

Fig. 5.1 Cross-section of the clutch and transfer gears (Sec 1)

1 Clutch housing
2 Guide sleeve
3 Intermediate plate
4 Gasket
5 Cover plate
6 Output (clutch) shaft
7 Intermediate gear
8 Input shaft
9 Driven plate
10 Flywheel
11 Pressure plate assembly

AH145821

2 Routine maintenance

Carry out the following procedures at the intervals given in Routine Maintenance at the beginning of the manual.

1 Depress the clutch pedal fully three times then, using a rule, measure the total stroke of the pedal pad.
2 If the stroke is not as given in the Specifications it will be necessary to adjust the pushrod bolt on the intermediate lever on non-GTI models or adjust the cable on GTI models.
3 On non-GTI models, loosen the locknut, then the pushrod bolt in the lever as required, then retighten the locknut (photo).
4 On GTI models, loosen the locknut at the gearbox end of the cable, turn the adjusting nut as required, then retighten the locknut.
5 Before checking the adjustment, fully operate the clutch pedal three times.

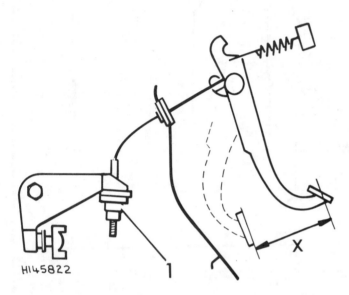

Fig. 5.2 Clutch pedal stroke (X) adjustment diagram for GTI models (Sec 2)

1   Adjustment nut and locknut

2.3 Clutch intermediate lever and adjustment bolt (arrowed) on non-GTI models

3 Clutch cable – removal and refitting

1 Working in the engine compartment, loosen the locknut and slacken the cable adjustment.
2 Release the cable end fitting from the intermediate lever. Recover the pushrod on non-GTI models.
3 Working inside the car, remove the lower facia panel from the steering column.
4 Pull off the spring clip and remove the clevis pin from the top of the pedal to disconnect the cable end.
5 Release the cable from the bulkhead and withdraw it into the engine compartment.
6 Refitting is a reversal of removal, but finally adjust the pedal stroke, as described in Section 2.

4 Clutch pedal – removal and refitting

1 Working in the engine compartment, loosen the locknut and slacken the cable adjustment.
2 Working inside the car, remove the lower facia panel from the steering column.
3 Pull off the spring clip and remove the clevis pin from the top of the pedal to disconnect the cable end.
4 Unhook the cable tension spring from the pedal.
5 Unscrew the nut from the pivot bolt, pull out the bolt and lower the clutch pedal from the bracket.
6 Examine the pedal bushes for wear and renew them if necessary.
7 Refitting is a reversal of removal, but lightly grease the bushes and clevis pin; finally adjust the pedal stroke, as described in Section 2.

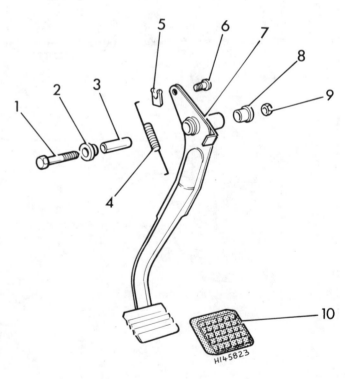

Fig. 5.3 Clutch pedal components (Sec 4)

1	Pivot bolt	6	Clevis pin
2	Bush	7	Pedal
3	Spacer	8	Bush
4	Tension spring (circular type on some models)	9	Nut
5	Clip	10	Pad

5 Clutch – removal

Non-GTI models with BH 3 gearbox

1 Remove the battery and starter motor, as described in Chapter 12.
2 Jack up the front of the car and drain the oil from the gearbox/engine assembly. Also disconnect the gear selector rod with reference to Chapter 6. Use stands to support the car and apply the handbrake.
3 Disconnect the bonnet stay from the right-hand suspension tower and use suitable U-brackets in the bonnet hinge holes to hold the bonnet in a vertical position.
4 Remove the complete air cleaner and brackets, as described in Chapter 3.
5 Disconnect the vacuum advance pipe from the distributor to prevent damage to it.
6 Disconnect the clutch cable at the gearbox end with reference to Section 3.

7 Working through the hole in the battery tray, unscrew and remove the top nut from the left-hand engine mounting. If necessary remove the splash guard from the wheel housing (photos).
8 Using a trolley jack and block of wood, support the left-hand side of the engine beneath the gearbox.
9 Unscrew the two nuts securing the left-hand engine mounting to the bottom of the battery tray (photo). Remove the mounting.
10 Lower the engine and gearbox until the left-hand driveshaft rests on the subframe.
11 Unclip the starter motor wiring from the clutch housing (photo).
12 Unscrew the bolts securing the clutch housing to the gearbox and engine noting the location of the lifting eye and earth cable. Do not forget to remove the bolt located in the bottom recess of the housing (photos).
13 If necessary for additional working room, unbolt and remove the battery tray (photo).

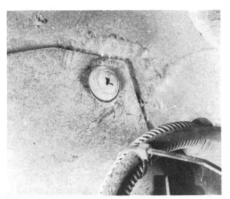
5.7A Splash guard screw in left-hand wheel housing

5.7B View of transfer gear housing with splash guard removed

5.9 Bottom view of left-hand engine mounting

5.11 Starter motor wiring clip (arrowed)

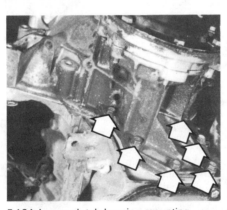
5.12A Lower clutch housing mounting bolts (arrowed)

5.12B Engine lifting eye

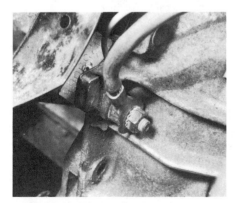
5.12C Earth cable location

5.12D Mounting bolt located in the clutch housing recess (arrowed)

5.13 Unbolting the battery tray

5.14A Remove the clutch housing and
transfer gear assembly ...

5.14B ... and the gasket

5.17 Removing the clutch pressure plate
assembly and driven plate

14 Withdraw the clutch housing and transfer gear assembly from the
engine and gearbox. Remove the gasket (photos).

GTI models with BE 1 gearbox
15 Remove the gearbox from the engine, as described in Chapter 6.

All models
16 Mark the clutch pressure plate in relation to the flywheel then
progressively loosen the bolts. If necessary hold the flywheel stationary
using a screwdriver engaged with the starter ring gear.
17 With all the bolts removed lift the pressure plate assembly from the
location dowels followed by the driven plate (photo).

6 Clutch – inspection and renovation

1   The clutch driven plate should be inspected for wear and for
contamination by oil. Wear is gauged by the depth of the rivet
heads below the surface of the friction material. If this is less than 0.6 mm
(0.024 in) the linings are worn enough to justify renewal.
2   Examine the friction faces of the flywheel and clutch pressure plate.
These should be bright and smooth. If the linings have worn too much
it is possible that the metal surfaces may have been scored by the rivet
heads. Dust and grit can have the same effect. If the scoring is very
severe it could mean that even with a new clutch driven plate, slip and
juddering and other malfunctions will recur. Deep scoring on the
flywheel face is serious because the flywheel will have to be removed
and machined by a specialist, or renewed. If the pressure plate is worn
excessively it must be renewed. If the driven plate friction linings are
contaminated with oil, the plate must be renewed and the source of the
oil traced and rectified.
3   If the reason for removal of the clutch has been because of slip and
the slip has been allowed to go on for any length of time, it is possible
that the heat generated will have adversely affected the diaphragm
spring in the cover with the result that the pressure is now uneven
and/or insufficient to prevent slip, even with a new driven plate. Where
this occurs, the friction surfaces on the flywheel and pressure plate will
often show a blue discolouration necessitating the renewal of the
pressure plate.
4   With the clutch removed, the release bearing should be checked for
excessive wear and noise, and renewed if necessary. Also check the
spigot bush in the crankshaft rear flange for wear and, if necessary,
renew it, as described in Chapter 1.

7 Clutch – refitting

1   Locate the driven plate on the flywheel with the cushioning spring
hub facing outwards (see Fig. 5.1), then place the pressure plate
assembly over it with the dowels and holes correctly aligned and fit the
bolts finger tight.
2   It is now necessary to align the centre of the driven plate with that

of the flywheel. To do this, use a special alignment tool located in the
flywheel spigot bearing, or alternatively a suitable diameter bar or
wooden dowel can be used. If the transfer gears have been removed
(non-GTI models) or the gearbox dismantled (GTI models) the
relevant shaft can be used (photo).
3   With the driven plate centralized, the cover bolts should be
tightened diagonally and evenly to the specified torque. Ideally new
spring washers should be used each time a replacement clutch is fitted.
When the bolts are tight remove the centralizing tool.

7.2 Using the transfer gear shaft to centralise the clutch driven plate

GTI models with BE 1 gearbox
4   Refit the gearbox, as described in Chapter 6.

Non-GTI models with BH 3 gearbox
5   Clean the mating surfaces, then locate a new gasket on the dowels
on the cylinder block.
6   Refit the clutch housing and transfer gear assembly to the engine and
gearbox. If the splines on the shafts do not line up correctly move the
flywheel fractionally. Make sure that the clutch cable intermediate lever
is in its working position.
7   Insert the bolts, together with the lifting eye and earth cable, and
tighten them progressively to the specified torque.
8   If removed, refit the battery tray and tighten the bolts.
9   Clip the starter motor wiring to the clutch housing.
10 Using a trolley jack and block of wood, raise the engine and gearbox,

locate the left-hand mounting and tighten the two nuts on the bottom of the battery tray.

11 Refit and tighten the mounting top nut.

12 Refer to Section 3 and reconnect the clutch cable. Also adjust the pedal stroke, as described in Section 2.

13 Reconnect the vacuum advance pipe.

14 Refit the air cleaner, with reference to Chapter 3, and refit the bonnet stay.

15 Reconnect the gear selector rod and lower the car to the ground.

16 Refit the starter motor and battery, with reference to Chapter 12.

17 Refill the gearbox/engine assembly with oil.

8 Clutch release mechanism – overhaul

Non-GTI models with BH 3 gearbox

1 Remove the clutch housing and transfer gear assembly, as described in Section 5.

2 Release the spring clips and slide the bearing from the guide sleeve (photos).

3 Remove the foam ring (photo).

4 Withdraw the release fork from the ball-stud (photo).

8.3 Foam cushion ring located behind the release bearing on non-GTI models

8.2A The release bearing and spring clips

8.4 Release fork disconnected from the ball-stud on non-GTI models

8.2B Reverse side of release bearing and fork

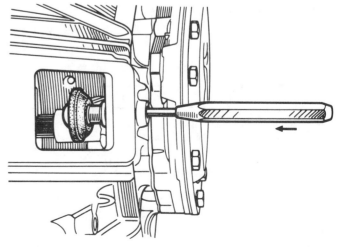

Fig. 5.4 Removing clutch release fork ball-stud (Sec 8)

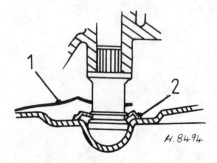

Fig. 5.5 Clutch release fork spring blade (1) and rubber cup (2) (Sec 8)

5   Do not clean the bearing with solvent as it will harm the bearing. Wipe it clean and check for excessive wear or play. Always renew if in doubt.

6   Inspect the fork retaining ball-stud and, if obviously distorted or worn, renew it. Drift the ball-stud from the housing using a suitable diameter drift. Fit the new one, together with a new rubber cup, by driving it carefully into position using a soft-faced hammer. Support the housing during this operation to prevent it from being damaged.

7   Before reassembly, check the output (clutch) shaft oil seal. If it is leaking then the complete guide sleeve/seal assembly must be renewed as the seal is not supplied separately.

8   Press the guide sleeve out of the clutch housing.

9   Press the new sleeve/seal assembly fully into its recess so that it seats firmly.

10 Any wear in the spigot bush which is located in the centre of the crankshaft rear flange (flywheel mounting) and supports the output shaft can be rectified by renewal of the bush, as described in Chapter 1.

11 Refit the components using a reversal of the removal procedure. Lubricate the ball-stud and guide sleeve with suitable high melting-point grease. When fitting the release fork, locate the spring blade **under** the rubber cap.

GTI models with BE 1 gearbox

12 Remove the gearbox, as described in Chapter 6.

13 Release the spring clips and slide the bearing from the guide sleeve.

14 Withdraw the release fork from the ball-stud.

15 Where applicable, the pivot bush may be removed as follows. First drill out the rivets which secure the old bush. Remove the bush and discard it. Position the new bush on the fork and pass its rivets through the holes. Heat the rivets with a cigarette lighter or a low powered blowlamp, then peen over their heads while they are still hot.

16 Lightly coat the bush with grease, then refit the release fork. Press it onto the ball-stud until it snaps home.

17 If the ball-stud requires renewal, remove it with a slide hammer having a suitable claw. Support the casing and drive in the new stud using a soft metal drift.

18 Refit the remaining components using a reversal of the removal procedure.

---

9   Transfer gears (non-GTI models) – removal and refitting

1   The transfer gears are located under a cover plate at the end of the clutch/flywheel housing. Their purpose is to transmit power from the engine crankshaft and clutch to the transmission input shaft which lies below the engine.

2   Remove the clutch housing and transfer gear assembly, as described in Section 5.

3   Unbolt the cover plate then unbolt and remove the transfer gear intermediate plate. The plate will probably require tapping off with a plastic-faced hammer. Take care that the intermediate gear does not drop out as the plate is removed.

4   Remove the intermediate gear.

5   Clean away all old gasket material and obtain a new one.

6   Examine the gearteeth for wear or damage, and the bearings for wear or 'shake'.

7   If a ball-bearing is to be renewed, use a pair of circlips pliers to fully expand the circlip before pressing the shaft out of the bearing or the shaft/bearing out of the intermediate plate.

8   When reassembling, remember that the shorter shaft is located at the narrower end of the intermediate plate. Always use new circlips and support the plate adequately during the pressing operation.

9   Always use a new Belleville washer under the circlip so that its concave face is towards the bearing.

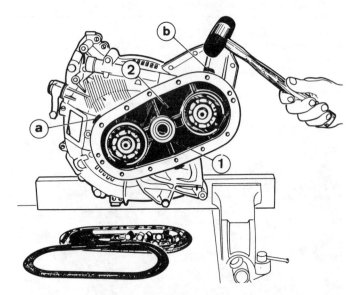

Fig. 5.6 Removing the intermediate plate (Sec 9)

| 1 | Intermediate plate | a | Casting boss (impact point) |
| 2 | Intermediate gear | b | Casting boss (impact point) |

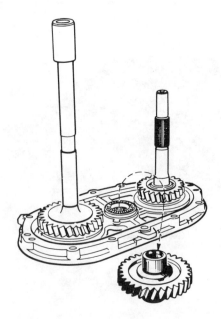

Fig. 5.7 Intermediate plate and gear removed (Sec 9)

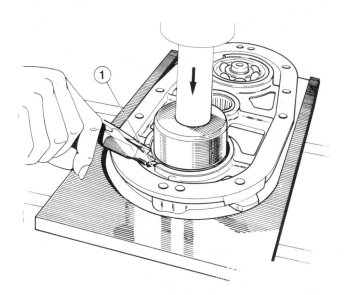

Fig. 5.8 Expanding circlip (1) and pressing out ball-bearing from intermediate plate (Sec 9)

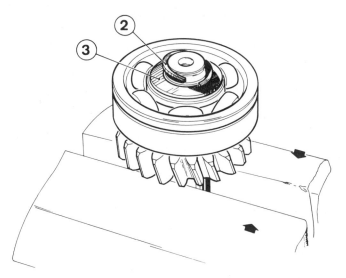

Fig. 5.9 Bearing circlip (2) and Belleville washer (3) (Sec 9)

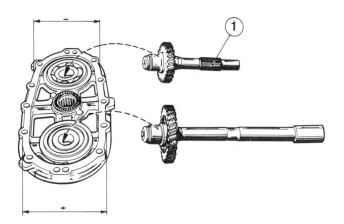

Fig. 5.10 Shaft identification (Sec 9)

1   Output (clutch) shaft

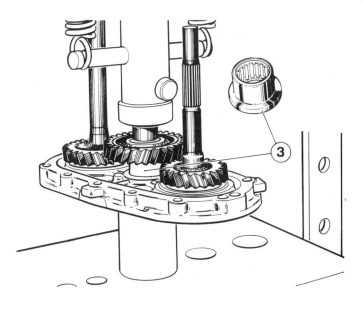

Fig. 5.11 Using intermediate shaft to press needle roller bearing (3) into intermediate plate (Sec 9)

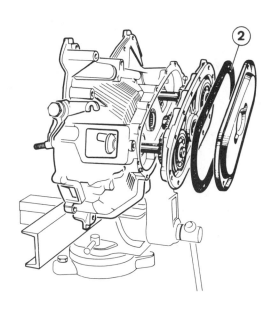

Fig. 5.12 Assembling transfer gears and cover plate (Sec 9)

2   Gasket

10 If the intermediate gear needle race if to be renewed in the intermediate plate, press the old one out and use the intermediate gear as an installation tool, but make sure that the gearteeth do not lock with those of the other gears during the pressing operation.
11 Lubricate the bearings and fit the intermediate gear.
12 Offer the transfer gears with intermediate plate to the clutch housing. No gasket is used (photo).
13 Locate the cover plate and its gasket (photo).
14 Fit the cover plate bolts and tighten to the specified torque setting.
15 Refit the clutch housing and transfer gear assembly, as described in Section 7.

10 Fault diagnosis – clutch

Symptom	Reason(s)
Judder when taking up drive	Loose engine/gearbox mountings Badly worn friction linings or contaminated with oil Worn splines on transfer/input shaft or driven plate hub Worn spigot bush in crankshaft flange
Clutch drag (failure to disengage so that gears cannot be meshed)	Incorrect cable adjustment Rust on splines (may occur after vehicle standing idle for long periods) Damaged or misaligned pressure plate assembly Cable stretched or broken
Clutch slip (increase in engine speed does not result in increase in vehicle road speed – particularly on gradients)	Incorrect cable adjustment Friction linings worn out or oil contaminated
Noise evident on depressing clutch pedal	Dry, worn or damaged release bearing Excessive play between drive plate hub splines and shaft splines
Noise evident as clutch pedal released	Distorted driven plate Broken or weak driven plate cushion coil springs Release bearing loose on retainer hub

Chapter 6 Transmission

For modifications, and information applicable to later models, see Supplement at end of manual

Contents

Specifications

BH 3/4 and BH 3/5 gearboxes
Type .... Four (BH 3/4) or five (BH 3/5) forward speeds all with synchromesh, and one reverse

Gear ratios
1st	3.882:1
2nd:	
XV8 and XW7 engines	2.074:1
XY7 and XY8 engines	2.296:1
3rd:	
XV8 and XW7 engines	1.377:1
XY7 and XY8 engines	1.502:1
4th:	
XV8 and XW7 engines	0.944:1
XY7 and XY8 engines	1.124:1
5th (XY7 and XY8 engines)	0.904:1
Reverse	3.568:1
Final drive:	
XV8 engine	3.563:1
XW7 engine	3.354:1
XY7 engine	3.177:1
XY8 engine	3.501:1

Lubrication .... Common supply with engine

Torque wrench settings

	Nm	lbf ft
Primary shaft nut	45	33
Secondary shaft nut:		
4-speed	23	17
5-speed	95	70
Crownwheel bolt	65	48
Reverse lockplate (5-speed)	10	7
Detent ball plug	12	9
Oil filter screen bolt	10	7
Sump plate bolts	12	9
Drain plug	27	20
Reverse lamp switch	27	20
Selector lever bolt	13	10
Half casing bolts (refer to Section 10)		
Primary shaft bearing preload on 4-speed transmission (refer to Section 10)		

BE 1/5 gearbox
Type .... Five forward speeds all with synchromesh, and one reverse

Gear ratios

1st	3.308:1
2nd	1.882:1
3rd	1.360:1 or 1.280:1 (close ratio)
4th	1.069:1 or 0.969:1 (close ratio)
5th	0.865:1 or 0.757:1 (close ratio)
Reverse	3.333:1 or 4.063:1 (close ratio)
Final drive	4.063:1

Lubrication

Oil capacity	2.0 litres (3.5 pints)
Oil type/specification (pre-1988 models)	Multigrade engine oil, viscosity SAE 10W/40 or 15W/40 (Duckhams QXR, Hypergrade, or 10W/40 Motor Oil)

Torque wrench settings

	Nm	lbf ft
Rear cover bolts (use thread locking compound)	12	9
Input and output shaft nuts	54	40
Rear bearing retainer bolts	15	11
Selector rod backplate bolt	15	11
End casing-to-main casing bolts	12	9
Reverse idle spindle bolt	20	15
Selector shaft spring bracket	15	11
Reverse selector spindle nut	20	15
Breather	15	11
Reversing lamp switch	24	18
Drain plug (gearbox)	10	7
Drain plug (final drive)	30	22
Speedometer pinion adaptor	12	9
Final drive extension housing bolts	15	11
Crownwheel securing bolts	65	48
Final drive half housing bolts, 10 mm	41	30
Final drive half housing bolts, 7 mm	12	9
Clutch release bearing guide tube bolts	12	9
Mounting stud nut	34	25

PART A: GENERAL DESCRIPTION AND ROUTINE MAINTENANCE

1 General description

BH 3/4 and BH 3/5 gearboxes
The transmission is mounted transversely directly under and to the rear of the engine with which it shares a common lubrication system.

The transmission casing is constructed in light alloy and incorporates the final drive and differential.

Power from the engine crankshaft is transmitted through the output shaft then the transfer gears to the transmission input shaft.

Drive to the front roadwheels is transmitted through open driveshafts from the differential side gears.

The transmission may be of four or five-speed type, depending upon the vehicle model. Both types are similar except for the 5th gear located on the ends of the primary and secondary shafts.

The transmission is of conventional two shaft constant-mesh layout. There are four pairs of gears, one for each forward speed. The gears on the primary shaft are fixed to the shaft, while those on the secondary or pinion shaft float, each being locked to the shaft when engaged by the synchromesh unit. The reverse idler gear is on a third shaft.

On five-speed units, the 5th gears are of fixed type with an extra synchromesh assembly.

The gear selector forks engage in the synchromesh unit; these slide axially along the shaft to engage the appropriate gear. The forks are mounted on selector shafts which are located in the base of the gearbox.

The helical gear on the end of the pinion shaft drives directly onto the crownwheel mounted on the differential unit. The latter differs from normal practice in that it runs in shell bearings and the end thrust is taken up by thrust washers in a similar manner to the engine crankshaft.

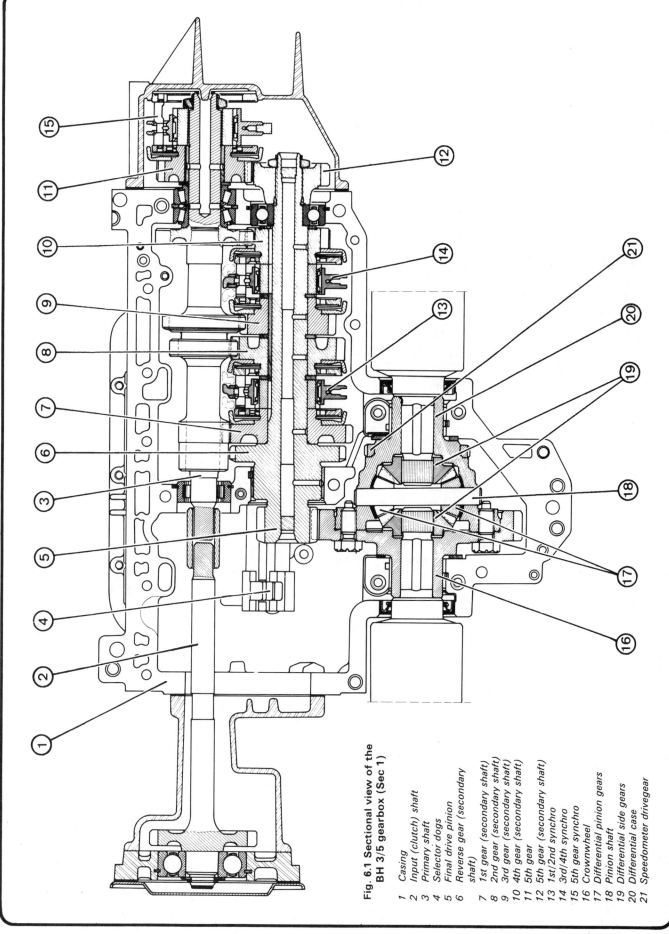

Fig. 6.1 Sectional view of the BH 3/5 gearbox (Sec 1)

1 Casing
2 Input (clutch) shaft
3 Primary shaft
4 Selector dogs
5 Final drive pinion
6 Reverse gear (secondary shaft)
7 1st gear (secondary shaft)
8 2nd gear (secondary shaft)
9 3rd gear (secondary shaft)
10 4th gear (secondary shaft)
11 5th gear
12 5th gear (secondary shaft)
13 1st/2nd synchro
14 3rd/4th synchro
15 5th gear synchro
16 Crownwheel
17 Differential pinion gears
18 Pinion shaft
19 Differential side gears
20 Differential case
21 Speedometer drivegear

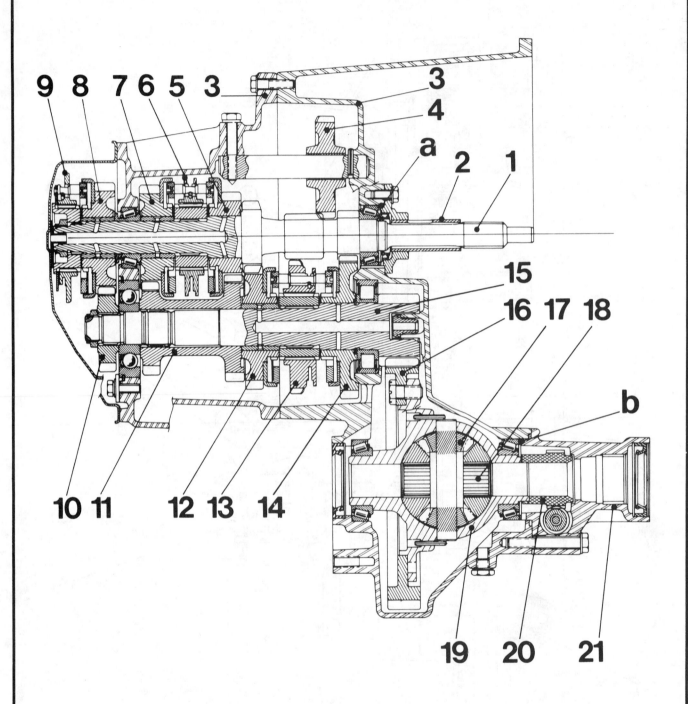

Fig. 6.2 Sectional view of the BE 1/5 gearbox (Sec 1)

1	Input shaft	8	5th gear (driving)	14	1st gear (driven)	20	Speedo driving gear
2	Release bearing guide tube	9	5th synchro	15	Output shaft	21	Extension housing
3	Casings	10	5th gear (driven)	16	Crownwheel	a	Selective shim – input shaft
4	Reverse idler gear	11	3rd/4th gears (driven)	17	Differential gear		bearing preload
5	3rd gear (driving)	12	2nd gear (driven)	18	Side gear	b	Selective shim – differential
6	3rd/4th synchro	13	1st/2nd synchro	19	Differential carrier		bearing preload
7	4th gear (driving)						

BE 1/5 gearbox

The transmission is mounted on the left-hand side of the engine and may be removed separately leaving the engine in the car.

The gearbox has five forward gears, all with synchromesh, and one reverse. As is common practice in five-speed units, the 5th gear components are on the far side of an intermediate plate which carries one pair of shaft bearings.

The differential (final drive) unit is contained in its own housing which is bolted to the gearbox casing. The gearbox and differential share the same lubricant.

2 Routine maintenance

Carry out the following procedures at the intervals given in Routine Maintenance at the beginning of the manual.

1 Using a suitable container beneath the transmission, remove the drain plug and drain the oil. On BH 3/4 and BH 3/5 gearboxes the engine uses the same oil, but on the BE 1/5 gearbox the oil is separate and two drain plugs are provided: one for the main gearbox, the other for the differential.

2 Clean the drain plug(s) then refit and tighten.

3 Refill the transmission with the correct quantity and grade of oil. On BH 3/4 and BH 3/5 gearboxes the level can be checked using the engine oil dipstick, but on the BE 1/5 gearbox there is no provision for checking the oil level so the correct quantity must be measured out before pouring into the top filler plug aperture. On the latter gearbox it is therefore important to completely drain the old oil. Refit and tighten the filler plug on completion.

4 There is no routine maintenance interval for checking and topping-up the transmission oil level on the BE 1/5 gearbox. The BH 3/4 and BH 3/5 gearboxes are automatically checked when checking the engine oil level.

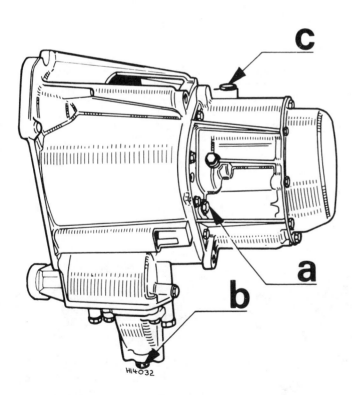

Fig. 6.3 Drain and filler plug locations on the BE 1/5 gearbox (Sec 2)

a Gearbox drain plug	c Filler plug
b Final drive drain plug	

PART B: BH 3/4 AND BH 3/5 GEARBOXES

3 Gearchange linkage – adjustment

1 The gearchange linkage does not normally require adjustment. If new parts have been fitted, however, set the balljointed link rods in accordance with the following dimensions:

Rod 1 (between centres of ball sockets) 73.0 to 87.0 mm (2.87 to 3.42 in)
Rod 2 (between centres of ball sockets) 171.0 to 173.0 mm (6.73 to 6.82 in) (photo)

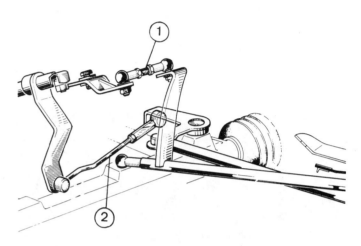

Fig. 6.4 Gearchange link rods (Sec 3)

1 Upper rod	2 Lower rod

3.1 Bottom view of gearchange linkage rod 2 (arrowed)

2 If the linkage is not already fitted with a tension spring, fit one as shown (Fig. 6.5).

3 The gear lever can be removed after withdrawal of the centre console (photos).

3.3A View of a link rod attached to the bottom of the gear lever

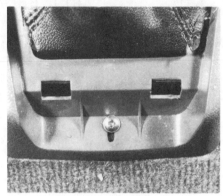

3.3B Centre console rear screw

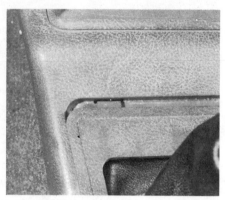

3.3C Removing the gear lever surround

Fig. 6.5 Location of gearchange link rod tension spring (2) (Sec 3)

4 Transmission overhaul – general

1   No work can be carried out to the transmission until the engine/transmission has been removed from the car, as described in Chapter 1, and cleaned externally.
2   Remove the clutch/flywheel housing and transfer gears, as described in Chapters 1 and 5. Drain the lubricating oil.
3   Unbolt and remove the timing chain cover and the flywheel, as described in Chapter 1.
4   Unscrew and remove all the engine-to-transmission connecting bolts, making sure that the two bolts and one nut are removed from the flange joint adjacent to the flywheel mounting flange on the end of the crankshaft.
5   Prise the transmission from the engine using a length of wood as a lever.

5 Transmission – dismantling into major units

1   With the transmission on the bench unbolt and remove the protective plate and sump cover (bolts).
2   Unbolt and remove the oil pick-up screen (photo).
3   Remove the speedometer drivegear (photo).
4   Unscrew and remove the reverse lamp switch (photo).
5   Release, but do not remove, the nineteen bolts which hold the two transmission half casing sections together.

Four-speed unit
6   Unscrew and remove the primary shaft bearing ring nut by engaging a suitable tool in the nut cut-outs (photo).

5.1A Sump protective plate

5.1B Sump cover and gasket

5.2 Oil pick-up screen

5.3 Speedometer drivegear

5.4 Reverse lamp switch

5.6 Primary shaft bearing ring nut cut-outs – arrowed (four-speed)

5.7 Removing primary shaft (five-speed)

5.8 Removing secondary shaft

5.10 Transmission shaft bearing shells

All units

7   Remove the casing bolts, separate the casing sections and lift out the primary shaft (photo).

8   Lift out the secondary shaft (photo).

9   Lift out the final drive/differential.

10   Remove the bearing shells, identifying them in respect of location if they are used again (photo).

11   Examine all components for wear or damage and carry out further dismantling as necessary and as described in the following Sections.

12   If it is intended to renew the casing sections then they must both be renewed at the same time as a pair.

13   Clean old gasket material from the original casings without scoring the metal and clean out the oilways.

6   Primary shaft – overhaul

1   Only the bearings can be renewed as the gears cannot be removed from the shaft.

Four-speed unit

2   Either support the bearing and press the shaft from it or draw the bearing form the shaft using a two legged puller (photo).

3   When fitting the bearing, apply pressure to the inner track only.

Five-speed unit

4   Mark the position of the 5th gear synchro sleeve in relation to the hub.

5   Grip the shaft in a vice fitted, with jaw protectors.

6   Unscrew the nut (photo).

7   Withdraw 5th gear synchro sleeve from the shaft (photo).

8   Support the gear and press the shaft out of the synchro-hub. Alternatively use a suitable puller (photo).

9   Remove 5th gear, bush and washer (photos).

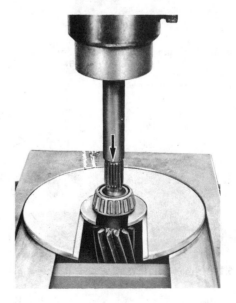

Fig. 6.6 Pressing primary shaft out of bearing (four-speed) (Sec 6)

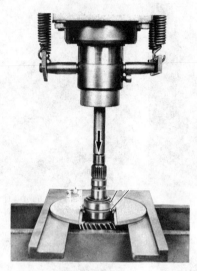

Fig. 6.7 Pressing primary shaft out of bearing (five-speed) (Sec 6)

Fig. 6.8 Primary shaft nut (3) (five-speed) (Sec 6)

Fig. 6.9 Pressing primary shaft from synchro-hub (five-speed) (Sec 6)

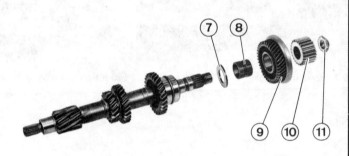

Fig. 6.10 5th gear primary shaft components (Sec 6)

7	Washer	10	Synchro-hub
8	Bush	11	Nut
9	5th gear		

Fig. 6.11 Primary shaft (five-speed) double taper bearing (Sec 6)

| 3 | Bearing | 5 | Washer |
| 4 | Bush | 6 | Bearing |

Fig. 6.12 Primary shaft (five-speed) single taper roller bearing (Sec 6)

6.2 Primary shaft bearing and circlip

6.6 Primary shaft nut (five-speed)

6.7 Primary 5th gear synchro sleeve

6.8 Removing 5th gear synchro-hub

6.9A 5th gear

6.9B 5th gear bush

6.9C 5th gear thrust washer

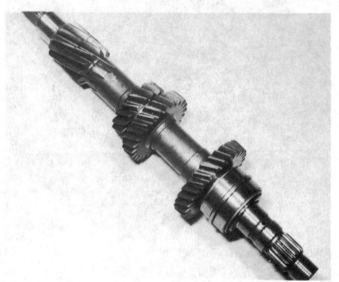

6.10 Primary shaft (five-speed)

10 Press the shaft out of the bearings or draw off the bearings using a suitable puller. Remove the washer (photo).
11 When refitting the bearings, apply pressure to the centre track only.
12 The bearings at the opposite end of the shaft are of single roller type.
13 When refitting the synchro-hub use a new nut, tighten to the specified torque and stake the nut into the shaft groove to lock it.

Four and five-speed units
14 Never re-use a bearing which has been removed from a shaft.
15 Do not mix the components of one new bearing set with another and do not attempt to remove the new bearing grease.

7 Secondary shaft – overhaul

1 Secure the shaft in a vice fitted with jaw protectors and unscrew the nut.

2 Using a press or a suitable puller remove the bearing (four-speed) or bearing and 5th gear (five-speed) (photo).
3 Remove the spacer and 4th gear.
4 Mark the relationship of the hub to the sleeve of the 3rd/4th synchro unit and then remove the synchro unit.
5 Remove the key (7) and spacer (8), Fig. 6.17.
6 Take off 3rd gear (9), Fig. 6.18.
7 Take off the spacer (10).
8 Remove 2nd gear (11) and the spacer (14).
9 Mark the relationship of the hub to the sleeve of the 1st/2nd synchro unit and then take off the synchro unit (13).
10 Remove 1st gear (15).

7.2 Removing secondary shaft bearing with 5th gear

Fig. 6.13 Secondary shaft (five-speed) (Sec 7)

1   Nut

Fig. 6.14 Removing secondary shaft 5th gear and bearing (Sec 7)

Fig. 6.15 Five-speed secondary shaft spacer (3) and 4th gear (4) (Sec 7)

Fig. 6.16 Five-speed secondary shaft synchro-hub (5) and sleeve (6) (Sec 7)

a   Alignment marks

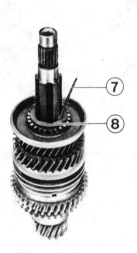

Fig. 6.17 Five-speed secondary shaft key (7) and spacer (8) (Sec 7)

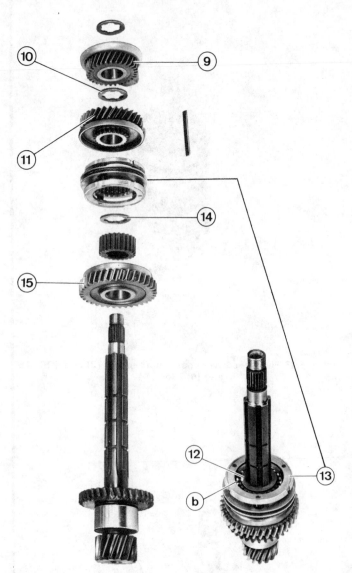

7.12 Fitting 1st gear to the secondary shaft

7.13 Fitting 1st/2nd synchro-hub to the secondary shaft

Fig. 6.18 Five-speed secondary shaft components (Sec 7)

9 3rd gear	13 Synchro sleeve
10 Spacer	14 Spacer
11 2nd gear	15 1st gear
12 Synchro-hub	b Alignment marks

Reassembly

11 As work progresses, dip each component in clean engine oil.

12 To the shaft fit 1st gear (photo).

13 Fit the 1st/2nd synchro-hub (photo).

14 Fit the spacer and align its splines so that the key can be fitted (photo).

15 Fit the 1st/2nd synchro sleeve so that its mark made at dismantling aligns with the one on the hub. The lines on the spacer pins are towards 1st gear (photos).

16 Fit 2nd gear (photo).

17 Fit the spacer and align the splines so that the key can be fitted (photo).

18 Fit 3rd gear (photo).

19 Fit the spacer, once more aligning the splines so that the key can be fitted (photo).

7.14 Fitting first spacer to the secondary shaft

7.15A Fitting 1st/2nd synchro sleeve to the secondary shaft

7.15B Lines on synchro spacer pins (arrowed)

7.16 Fitting 2nd gear to the secondary shaft

7.17 Fitting second spacer to the secondary shaft

7.18 Fitting 3rd gear to secondary shaft

7.19 Fitting third spacer to the secondary shaft

20 Push the key into the widest shaft groove so that the chamfered edge on the key is at the bottom of the groove. Push the key until it is flush with the spacer (photo).

21 Fit the 3rd/4th synchro-hub (photo).

22 Fit the 3rd/4th synchro sleeve so that its mark made at dismantling aligns with the one on the hub. The line on the spacer pin must be towards 3rd gear (photo).

23 Fit 4th gear (photo).

24 Fit the spacer (photo).

25 Press the bearing (four-speed) or the bearing and 5th gear (five-speed) onto the shaft (photos).

26 Engage a new circlip in the bearing outer track groove.

27 Screw on a new shaft nut to the specified torque and stake the nut into the groove in the shaft (photo).

8 Selector mechanism and reverse idler – dismantling and reassembly

1 Unscrew and remove the three threaded detent plugs and extract the coil springs and balls. If the plugs are very tight, tap their end-face hard using a rod and hammer.

Four-speed unit

2 Drive out the reverse fork roll pin.

Five-speed unit

3 Knock out the roll pin and unscrew the bolt and remove the reverse fork ball lock plate. Extract the two balls (4), Fig. 6.20. Move the position of the selector shaft slightly to release the second ball.

7.20 Pushing key into shaft groove

7.21 3rd/4th synchro-hub on the secondary shaft

7.22 Fitting 3rd/4th synchro sleeve to the secondary shaft

7.23 Fitting 4th gear to the secondary shaft

7.24 Fitting 4th gear spacer

7.25A Fitting secondary shaft bearing

7.25B Fitting 5th gear to the secondary shaft

7.27 Secondary shaft nut

Fig. 6.19 Driving out reverse fork roll pin (four-speed) (Sec 8)

Fig. 6.21 Interlock disc (5) (five-speed) (Sec 8)

Fig. 6.20 Detent ball retaining plate (3) and detent balls (4)
(Sec 8)

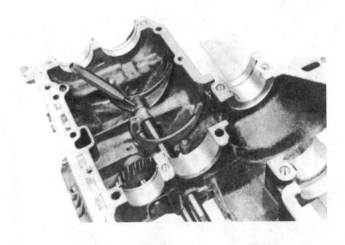

Fig. 6.22 Driving out 3rd/4th selector fork roll pin (Sec 8)

4   Slide the 5th/reverse selector shaft so that the dog contracts the housing web then drive out the roll pin which secures the dog.

All units
5   Withdraw the reverse selector shaft and retrieve the interlock disc (5), Fig. 6.21.
6   Drive out the roll pin which secures the 3rd/4th fork to the selector shaft. Remove the fork from the shaft.
7   Drive out the roll pin which secures the fork to the 1st/2nd selector shaft.

Five-speed unit
8   Drive out the roll pin which secures the dog to the 1st/2nd selector shaft. Before doing this, slide the shaft so that the dog is in contact with the housing web.

All units
9   Withdraw the 1st/2nd selector shaft.
10 Withdraw the 3rd/4th selector shaft.
11 Remove the 1st/2nd and reverse selector forks.
12 Drive out the reverse idler shaft roll pin (1), Fig. 6.25.

Fig. 6.23 Selector components (Sec 8)

1 1st/2nd selector shaft	3 1st/2nd selector fork
2 3rd/4th selector shaft	4 Reverse fork

Fig. 6.24 Removing 1st/2nd selector dog roll pin (Sec 8)

a   Casing web

Fig. 6.26 Selector lever (4) and pivot bolt (Sec 8)

Fig. 6.25 Reverse idler components (Sec 8)

1   Roll pin   3   Stop
2   Idler shaft

Fig. 6.27 Selector finger (6) and roll pins (5) (Sec 8)

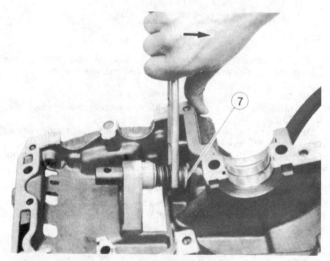

13 Remove reverse idler shaft (2) the stop (3) and reverse idler gear.
14 Remove the pivot bolt and withdraw the selector shaft lever (4), Fig. 6.26.
15 Drive out the dual roll pins (5) at the selector finger (6) and remove the finger, Fig. 6.27.
16 Compress the coil spring using an open-ended spanner or forked tool and remove the cups (7), Fig. 6.28.
17 Remove the remote control rod (8) and extract the oil seal (9), Fig. 6.29.

Reassembly
18 Lubricate all components with clean engine oil as work proceeds. Renew all roll pins and the remote control rod O-ring.
19 Fit the O-ring into its recess in the remote control rod housing.
20 Fit the remote control rod, together with spacer, spring and stop.

Fig. 6.28 Compressing selector finger coil spring to remove cup (7) (Sec 8)

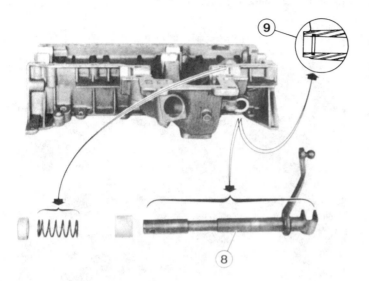

Fig. 6.29 Remote control rod (8) and casing oil seal (9)
(Sec 8)

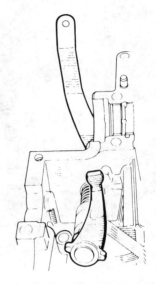

Fig. 6.31 Alignment of selector finger and lever bellcrank
(Sec 8)

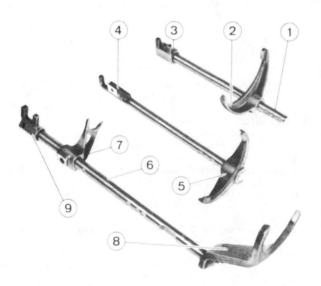

Fig. 6.30 Selector identification (Sec 8)

1 1st/2nd selector shaft
2 1st/2nd selector fork
3 1st/2nd selector dog
4 3rd/4th selector shaft
5 3rd/4th selector fork

6 Reverse (4-speed)
   Reverse/5th (5-speed)
   selector shaft
7 Reverse selector fork
8 5th gear selector shaft
9 5th/reverse selector dog

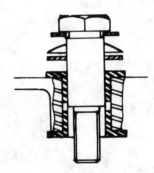

Fig. 6.32 Gearchange rod bellcrank pivot arrangement (Sec 8)

21 Compress the coil spring and fit the half cups.
22 Fit the selector finger, check for correct alignment and drive in the dual roll pins.
23 Using the pivot bolt, fit the gearchange rod lever. Tighten the pivot bolt to the specified torque.
24 Fit reverse idler gear, the stop and the idler shaft. Drive in the shaft roll pin (photos).
25 Place reverse fork in position and then fit the 1st/2nd selector shaft with its fork. The shaft will pass through the reverse fork cut-out (photos).

8.24A Reverse idler gear stop and shaft

8.24B Reverse idler shaft roll pin

8.25A 1st/2nd selector shaft with reverse fork viewed from oil pick-up screen side

8.25B 1st/2nd selector shaft with reverse fork viewed from inner side

Four-speed unit
26 Pin the fork to the 1st/2nd selector shaft.

Five-speed unit
27 Pin the dog to the 1st/2nd selector shaft (photo).

8.27 1st/2nd selector shaft dog and roll pin

All units
28 Fit the 3rd/4th selector shaft with its fork and drive in the securing pin.

Five-speed unit
29 Secure the fork to the 1st/2nd selector shaft by driving in the roll pin.

All units
30 Insert the reverse interlock disc so that it engages positively in the slots in the selector shafts (photo).
31 Slide the reverse selector shaft without disturbing the interlock disc.

Four-speed unit
32 Secure the reverse fork to the selector shaft with a roll pin (photo).

Five-speed unit
33 Fit 5th/reverse dog to its selector shaft and secure it with a roll pin (photos).
34 Place one detent ball in the reverse fork then fit the plate with the second ball (photos).
35 Tighten the plate fixing bolt to the specified torque.

All units
36 Fit the three detent balls and their springs. Apply thread locking fluid to clean threads of the detent plugs and tighten the plugs to the specified torque (photos). Do not apply too much fluid or it will run down and cause the balls to seize.

9 Final drive/differential – dismantling and reassembly

1 Unscrew the fixing bolts and remove the crownwheel from the differential case.
2 Remove the pinion shaft, pinion gears with friction washers and side gears with thrust washers.
3 Clean all components and examine for worn or chipped gearteeth. Renew components as necessary.
4 Commence reassembly by fitting the differential side gears and thrust washers. The grooved side of the washer must be towards the gear.

8.30 Interlock disc

8.32 Reverse fork roll pin (four-speed)

8.33A 5th/reverse selector dog roll pin

8.33B Selector shaft locations

8.34A Fitting first ball to reverse fork

8.34B Reverse fork second ball

8.34C Reverse fork lockplate

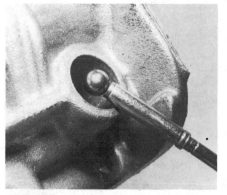

8.36A Using a pencil magnet to locate detent ball

8.36B Detent spring and plug

8.36C Location of remaining two detent springs and plugs

8.36D Allen key used to tighten detent plug

Fig. 6.33 Exploded view of final drive/differential (Sec 9)

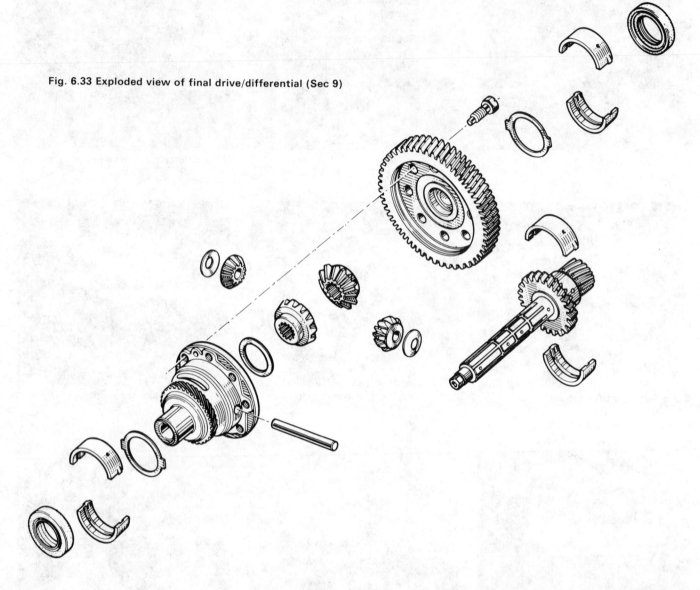

5   Fit the friction washers, pinion gears and push the pinion shaft into position.
6   Locate the crownwheel with the differential case, insert the connecting bolts and tighten to the specified torque. Make sure that the pinion shaft is retained by two of the crownwheel bolts.

10 Transmission – reassembly

1   Renew all gaskets and oil seals, also the shaft nuts. As reassembly proceeds, apply clean engine oil to all components.
2   Check that the housing half casing positioning dowels are in place.
3   Make sure that new bearing shells are in their recesses in the casings. If the original shells are being used, check that they are returned to their original locations and their recesses and the shell backs are perfectly clean and free from grit.
4   The selector mechanism will already have been fitted, as described in Section 8.
5   Fit the final drive/differential, together with the thrust washers, into the selector shaft half-casing. Make sure that the copper side of the thrust washer is towards the crownwheel and the tabs offset upwards (photo).
6   Fit the secondary shaft geartrain into the half-casing, making sure that the selector forks engage in the synchro sleeve grooves and the bearing circlip fits into its casing groove.

10.5 Differential thrust washer with tabs offset

7 Fit the primary shaft geartrain, remembering that on four-speed units the shaft must be fitted with bearing outer tracks and thrust washer. On five-speed units, the 5th/reverse synchro assembly must be positioned on the shaft with the longer spacer pins towards the end of the shaft (photo).

8 Make sure that the casing locating dowels are in position and then apply jointing compound to the mating face of the half casings (photo).

9 Fit the casings together, making sure that the selector finger engages in the selector shaft dog cut-outs.

10 Use new lock washers and screw in the connecting bolts finger tight. Note the location of the various bolt sizes and lengths, Fig. 6.34.

11 On four-speed transmissions, the primary shaft bearing preload must now be adjusted. Screw in the bearing ring nut finger tight and then tighten the casing internal bolts accessible through the sump plate aperture and upper casing.

12 Engage any gear and turn the nut on the end of the secondary shaft to settle the bearings.

13 Tighten the ring nut to 20 Nm (15 lbf ft) then loosen it and retighten to 9 Nm (7 lbf ft).

14 Finally stake the nut into the shaft groove. In order to be able to turn the ring nut, make up an adaptor (to engage in the nut cut-outs) to which a torque wrench can be connected.

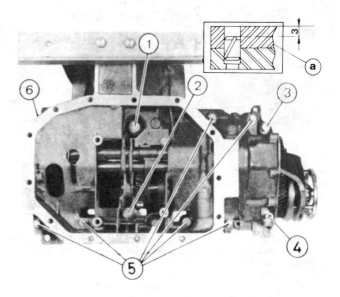

10.7 Geartrains and final drive (five-speed)

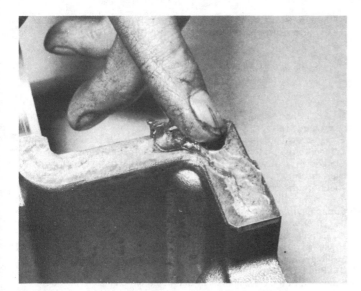

10.8 Applying jointing compound to casing flanges

Fig. 6.34 Transmission casing connecting bolt locations (Sec 10)

1	M10 x 1.50 x 75	7	M10 x 1.50 x 90
2	M8 x 1.25 x 55	8	M10 x 1.50 x 65
3	M8 x 1.25 x 55	9	M8 x 1.25 x 55
4	M8 x 1.25 x 55	10	M7 x 1.00 x 30
5	M7 x 1.00 x 75	a	Dowel protrusion.
6	M7 x 1.00 x 30		Measurement in mm

All units

15 Refer to Fig. 6.34 and tighten the bolts in the following order.

Stage 1	Torque
Bolts 2, 3, 4, 9	9 Nm (7 lbf ft)
Bolts 5, 6, 10	12 Nm (9 lbf ft)
Bolts 1, 7, 8	20 Nm (15 lbf ft)
Stage 2	
Bolts 2, 3, 4, 9	17 Nm (13 lbf ft)
Bolts 1, 7, 8	45 Nm (33 lbf ft)

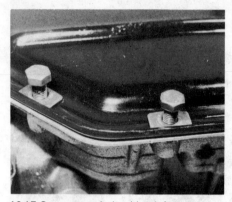

10.17 Sump cover bolt with reinforcement washer

10.18 Oil drain plug showing magnet

10.21 Driveshaft oil seal at transmission

16 Fit the oil pick-up filter, tightening the bolts to the specified torque.
17 Refit the sump cover plate with a new gasket. Tighten the bolts to the specified torque. Fit the protective plate (photo).
18 Fit and tighten the drain plug (photo).
19 Refit the speedometer drive pinion with a new O-ring.
20 Screw in the reverse lamp switch.
21 If new driveshaft oil seals have not already been fitted drive them squarely into position now and fill their lips with grease (photo).

Fig. 6.35 Ring nut adaptor tool (Sec 10)

11 Differential/driveshaft oil seals – renewal

1 The differential oil seals can be removed and refitted with the engine/transmission unit in position in the car, but the driveshafts will obviously have to be removed. This operation is covered in Chapter 7.
2 With the driveshafts withdrawn, the old oil seals can be extracted from the differential housing using a suitable screwdriver.
3 Clean out the seating before fitting a new seal. Lubricate the seal to assist assembly and drift carefully into position, with the lip facing inwards. Fill the seal lips with grease.
4 Always take care not to damage the oil seals when removing or refitting the driveshafts.

PART C: BE 1/5 GEARBOX

12 Transmission – removal and refitting

1 The BE 1 gearbox can be removed independently of the engine using the following procedure.
2 Disconnect the bonnet stay from the right-hand suspension tower and use suitable U-brackets in the bonnet hinge holes to hold the bonnet in a vertical position.
3 Remove the starter, as described in Chapter 12, but it is not necessary to disconnect the wiring as the unit may be placed to one side.
4 Remove the airflow sensor and associated hoses, as described in Chapter 3.
5 Remove the battery, as described in Chapter 12.
6 Disconnect the clutch cable and remove the pushrod and intermediate lever, as described in Chapter 5.

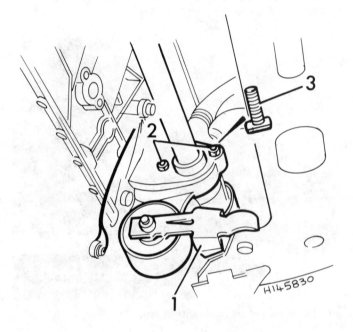

Fig. 6.36 Right-hand driveshaft intermediate bearing bracket and right-hand rear engine mounting link (Sec 12)

1 Link
2 Intermediate bearing nuts

3 Intermediate bearing bolts with special heads

7 Jack up the car and support on axle stands. Apply the handbrake.
8 Drain the transmission oil by removing the gearbox and final drive drain plugs (photo). Clean and refit the plugs on completion.
9 Unscrew and remove both front clamp bolts securing the hub carriers to the bottom of the front suspension struts.
10 Loosen the two nuts retaining the right-hand driveshaft intermediate bearing in the bracket bolted to the rear of the cylinder block, then turn the bolts so that their heads move through 90°.
11 Unbolt the right-hand rear engine mounting link from the subframe, loosen the front bolt, and let the link hang free.
12 Disconnect all three gearchange control rods (photos).
13 Turn the steering to full right-hand lock then pull the left-hand lower suspension arm down from the hub carrier and unbolt the balljoint guard plate.
14 Pull the hub carrier outwards, and at the same time withdraw the inner end of the driveshaft from the final drive unit. Refer to Chapter 7 and fit a suitable tool to the differential side gear in order to prevent it from falling into the final drive housing.

12.8 Final drive drain plug (arrowed)

12.12A Gearchange lower control rod

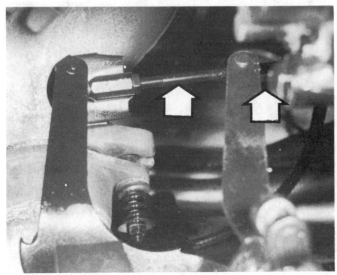

12.12B Gearchange upper control rods (arrowed)

15 Withdraw the right-hand driveshaft from the final drive unit using the procedure described in paragraphs 13 and 14 with the steering on full left-hand lock.
16 Disconnect the wiring from the reverse lamp switch and tie it to one side.
17 Disconnect the speedometer cable, as described in Chapter 12.
18 Using a hoist, take the weight of the engine then unscrew and remove the top nut from the left-hand engine mounting.
19 Unbolt and remove the battery tray.
20 Lower the engine until the timing cover touches the body at the same time pulling the unit forwards to prevent the final drive housing fouling the subframe.
21 Temporarily reconnect the right-hand rear engine mounting link to the subframe.
22 Support the gearbox with a trolley jack then remove the clutch housing-to-engine mounting bolts and remove the cover plate.
23 Withdraw the gearbox from the engine until the input shaft is clear of the clutch, then lower it through the engine compartment and remove from under the car.
24 Refitting is a reversal of removal, but note the following points:

(a) *It is recommended that the driveshaft oil seals in the final drive housing are renewed, as described in Chapter 7*
(b) *Tighten all nuts and bolts to the specified torque*
(c) *Refill the transmission with the correct quantity of oil (photo).*
(d) *Adjust the clutch cable, with reference to Chapter 5*
(c) *Check the operation of the gearchange linkage and adjust it if necessary*

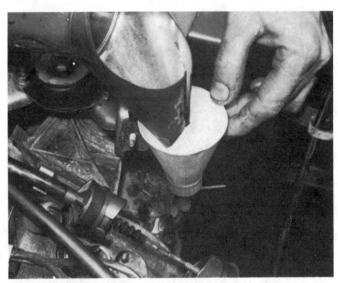

12.24 Filling the transmission with oil

13 Gearchange linkage – adjustment

1 Place the gear lever in neutral, then move it gently to the left until the commencement of resistance is felt.
2 Position a ruler against the gear knob with the zero marking aligned with the 1/2 mark on the knob.
3 Push the gear lever as far as possible to the left without moving the ruler and note the distance travelled by the knob. Repeat the operation two or three times. The desired travel is 36 to 40 mm.
4 If adjustment is necessary, unclip the gaiter from the surround and pull it up the gear lever.
5 If fitted, remove and discard the O-ring from the bottom of the gear lever.
6 Extract the spring clip and lift the plastic cam off its splines (photo), then reposition the cam on the splines to give the correct lever movement described in paragraphs 1 to 3. Refit the spring clip on completion.

13.6 Gear lever cam and stop

14.2 Removing the gearbox end cover

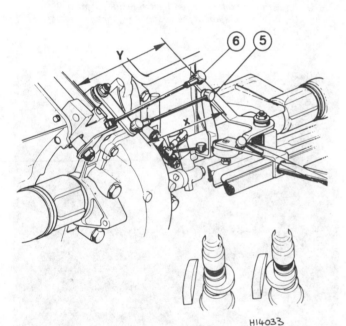

Fig. 6.37 Gearchange linkage adjustment (Sec 13)

6   Engagement rod Y = 284 mm   5   Selection rod X = 122 mm

7   If the correct adjustment cannot be achieved due to the cam's being at its minimum or maximum position, the selection rod (Fig. 6.37) should be lengthened by 6.0 mm (0.24 in) to provide extra movement or shortened by 6.0 mm (0.24 in) to provide less movement. The normal initial length of the selection rod is given in Fig. 6.37. Adjust the cam position again after altering the selection rod length.

8   Check that the length of the engagement rod is as given in Fig. 6.37 and adjust if necessary.

9   Apply a little grease to the gear lever stop, and refit the gear lever gaiter.

14 Transmission – dismantling into major assemblies

1   With the unit removed from the car, clean all exterior surfaces and wipe dry.

2   Remove the eight bolts and washers which secure the end cover. Remove the cover (photo).

3   Make alignment marks between the 5th gear synchro-hub and its sliding sleeve.

4   Engage 5th gear, then drive out the roll pin which secures 5th gear selector fork to the selector rod (photo).

5   Hold 5th gear selector fork in the engaged position and return the gear selector to neutral so that the selector rod moves through the fork.

6   Engage any other gear to lock up the shafts, then unscrew and remove the 28 mm nut from the end of the input shaft. If the nut is staked in position it may be necessary to relieve the staking (photo).

7   Remove 5th gear synchro-hub, sliding sleeve and selector fork from the input shaft. Be prepared for the ejection of the detent ball from the selector fork.

8   Refit the 5th gear sliding sleeve and hub and engage 5th gear again. Relieve the staking from the output shaft nut and remove the nut (photo). Remove the sliding sleeve and hub again.

9   Remove from the input shaft the 5th gear, its bush and the spacer.

10 Remove the two bolts and washers which secure the output shaft rear bearing.

11 Remove the circlip from the output shaft rear bearing by prising up

14.4 5th gear selector fork showing roll pin (arrowed)

14.6 Unscrewing the input shaft nut

14.8 Unscrewing the output shaft nut

14.12 Selector rod lockplate bolt

its ends. The circlip should be renewed anyway, so do not be afraid of breaking it. Raise the output shaft if the circlip is jammed in its groove.
12 Extract its securing bolt and remove the selector rod lockplate (photo).
13 Remove the bolt which retains the reverse idler gear spindle.
14 Remove the thirteen bolts and washers which secure the end casing to the main casing. Withdraw the end casing: it is located by dowels, and may need striking with a wooden or plastic mallet to free it. Do not use a metal hammer, nor lever in between the joint faces. Note the location of the clutch cable bracket.
15 Remove the selector arm and spring from the gear selector shaft. Remove the circlip and washer, push the shaft in and recover the O-ring (photo).
16 Drive out the roll pins which secure the selector finger and the interlock bracket to the selector shaft.

17 Inspect the cover which protects the end of the selector shaft. If it is tapered, proceed to the next paragraph. If it is cylindrical, use pliers or a self-gripping wrench to extract it, then press the gear selector shaft towards the cover so that the circlip and washer can be extracted from the end of the shaft (photos). These components are not fitted to earlier models; there are associated changes in the shaft itself, the main casing and 5th gear selector fork.
18 Pull the selector shaft out of the gearbox. From inside the gearbox recover, as they are freed from the shaft, the selector finger, the interlock bracket, the spring and its cup washers. Notice which way round the washers are fitted.
19 Screw the reverse idler spindle retaining bolt back into the spindle and use it as a lever to extract the spindle. Remove the reverse idler gear itself (photo).
20 Remove the swarf-collecting magnet from the casing (photo).

14.15 Gear selector shaft is secured by a circlip

14.17A Cylindrical cover must be removed ...

14.17B ... to extract the circlip

14.19 Removing the reverse idler spindle

14.20 The swarf-collecting magnet

21 Carefully lift out the two geartrains with their shafts, the selector forks and the selector rods.
22 Remove the spring support bracket from inside the main casing.
23 If not already removed, drive out the selector shaft end cover, using a drift of diameter no greater than 14 mm.
24 Extract the lubrication jet, using a wire hook.
25 Unscrew and remove the reversing lamp switch.
26 Remove the nut and washer which secure the reverse selector fork spindle. Remove the spindle and the selector fork. Recover the detent plunger and spring (photos).
27 Unscrew and remove the breather from the main casing (photo).
28 Turning to the clutch housing, remove the clutch release bearing (if not already done). Pull off the release fork.
29 Unbolt and remove the release bearing guide tube.
30 From behind the tube remove the preload shim and the outer track of the input shaft front bearing.
31 To remove the final drive unit, first unbolt and remove the speedometer pinion and its adaptor (photo).
32 Unbolt and remove the extension housing (photo). Recover the speedometer driving gear and the bearing preload shim (photo).

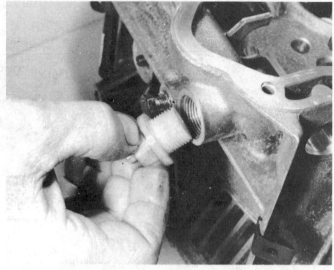

14.27 Removing the breather

14.26A Reverse selector fork

14.31 Removing the speedometer pinion

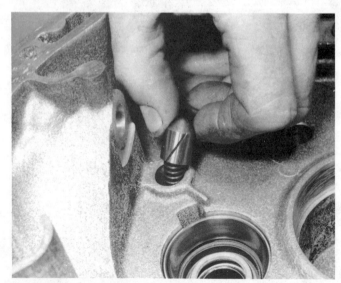

14.26B Reverse detent plunger and spring

14.32A Removing the final drive extension housing

14.32B Removing the speedometer driving gear

16.1A Input shaft bearing ...

33 Unbolt the final drive half housing. Remove the half housing and final drive unit. Note the location of the gearchange pivot bracket.
34 Identify the final drive bearing outer tracks: if they are to be re-used they must be refitted on the same sides.
35 Remove the selector lever from the main casing. It is retained by a circlip and a washer.
36 If it is wished to remove the clutch release lever balljoint, do so with a slide hammer having a suitable claw. (A new gearbox will not necessarily be fitted with a balljoint).
37 The gearbox is now dismantled into its major assemblies.

15 Transmission – examination and renovation

1 Clean all components and examine them thoroughly for wear and damage.
2 Circlips, roll pins, gaskets, oil seals and locking devices should all be renewed as a matter of course. Prise out the old oil seal from the clutch release bearing guide tube, but do not fit the new seal until so instructed during reassembly. Renew the input and output shaft nuts.
3 If new input shaft or differential bearings are to be fitted, a selection of preload shims will be required. Read through the relevant procedures before starting work.

16 Input shaft – dismantling and reassembly

1 Remove the 3rd and 4th gear components from the input shaft by supporting the assembly under the 3rd gear and pressing or driving the shaft through. Protect the end of the shaft. Once the rear bearing is free, the other components can be removed from the shaft in order: 4th gear and its bush, 3rd/4th synchro sleeve and hub and 3rd gear (photos).
2 Mark the synchro sleeve and hub relative to each other and to show which side faces 4th gear.
3 Remove the front bearing from the shaft, preferably with a press or a bearing puller. As a last resort it may be possible to support the bearing and drive the shaft through: be sure to protect the end of the shaft if this is done.
4 Once the input shaft bearings have been removed, they must be renewed. Press the rear bearing outer track from the end casing and press in the new track, making sure it enters squarely.
5 Before commencing reassembly, make sure that the input shaft is free from burrs and wear marks. Lubricate all parts as they are fitted.
6 Fit a new front bearing to the shaft, using a suitable tube to press or drive it home.

16.1B ... 4th gear ...

16.1C ... 4th gear bush ...

16.1D ... 3rd/4th synchro sleeve ...

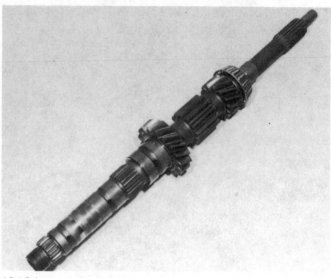

16.1G Input shaft with all components removed except the front bearing

16.1E ... synchro-hub ...

7   Fit 3rd gear, 3rd/4th synchro-hub and sleeve, 4th gear and its bush. Take care not to get 3rd and 4th gears mixed up, they are similar in appearance (4th gear has more teeth). If the original synchro components are being refitted, observe the mating marks made during dismantling.
8   Fit a new rear bearing to the shaft, again using a piece of tube.
9   The input shaft is not reassembled.

17 Output shaft – dismantling and reassembly

1   Remove 5th gear and the rear bearing from the output shaft. Use a puller or bearing extractor if they are a tight fit on the shaft (photo).
2   Remove 3rd/4th gear assembly, 2nd gear and its bush (photos).
3   Make alignment marks between the 1st/2nd synchro-hub and sleeve, then remove them from the shaft (photos).
4   Remove 1st gear and the half washers (early models) or needle thrust bearing and circlip (later models) (photos).

16.1F ... and 3rd gear

17.1 Output shaft rear bearing

17.2A 3rd/4th gear assembly ...

17.2B ... 2nd gear ...

17.2C ... and 2nd gear bush

17.3A 1st/2nd synchro sleeve ...

17.3B ... and hub

17.4A Remove 1st gear ...

17.4B ... the needle thrust bearing ...

17.4C ... and the bearing circlip

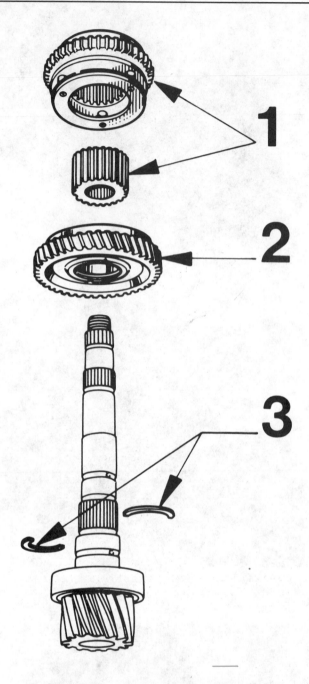

Fig. 6.38 Detail of early type output shaft (Sec 17)

1   1st/2nd synchro   3   Half washers
2   1st driven gear

5   Press or drive the shaft out of the pinion end bearing, protecting the end of the shaft.
6   Before commencing reassembly, make sure that the shaft is free from burrs or wear marks. Lubricate all parts as they are fitted.
7   Fit the pinion end bearing to the shaft, using a piece of tube to drive or press it home. On later models, fit a new circlip.
8   Fit the half washers above the bearing, using a smear of grease to hold them in position. On later models, fit the needle thrust bearing instead.
9   Refit 1st gear, taking care not to dislodge the half washers (when fitted).
10 Refit the 1st/2nd synchro unit, observing the mating marks made when dismantling. The chamfer on the external teeth must face towards 1st gear.
11 Fit 2nd gear and its bush.
12 Fit the 3rd/4th gear assembly, making sure it is the right way round.
13 Fit the rear bearing, with the circlip groove nearest the tail of the shaft.
14 Fit the 5th gear with its boss towards the bearing.

15 Fit a new nut to the output shaft but do not tighten it yet. Assembly of the output shaft is now complete.

18 Selector mechanism – dismantling and reassembly

1   One of the unusual features of this gearbox is that the detent springs and balls are located in the forks (photo). If a spring is weak, the whole fork must be renewed. (This does not apply to 5th gear fork).
2   Rotate the 1st/2nd and 3rd/4th selector rod to disengage the detent slots from the balls, the remove the rod from the forks.

18.1 Gear selector fork showing captive detent ball and spring (arrowed)

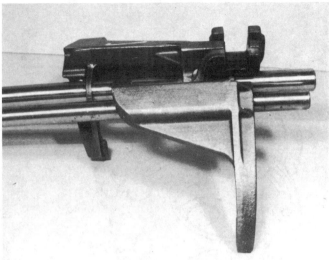

18.7 Selector forks and rods in neutral

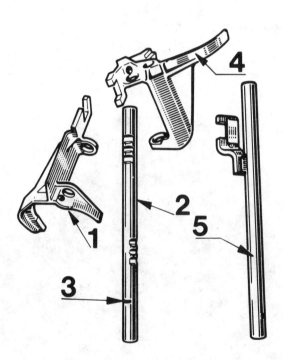

Fig. 6.39 Selector forks and rods (Sec 18)

1   3rd/4th fork
2   1st/2nd and 3rd/4th rod
3   Locking slot
4   1st/2nd fork
5   5th rod

3   Remove the 5th gear selector rod from the 1st/2nd fork.
4   Examine the forks and rods for wear and damage and renew as necessary.
5   Commence reassembly by inserting 5th gear selector rod into the 1st/2nd fork.
6   Offer the 3rd/4th fork to the 1st/2nd fork so that their holes and selector fingers align.
7   Insert the 1st/2nd and 3rd/4th selector rod, positioning the locking slot as shown (Fig. 6.40). Bring all the selector finger slots into line to position the selectors in neutral (photo).

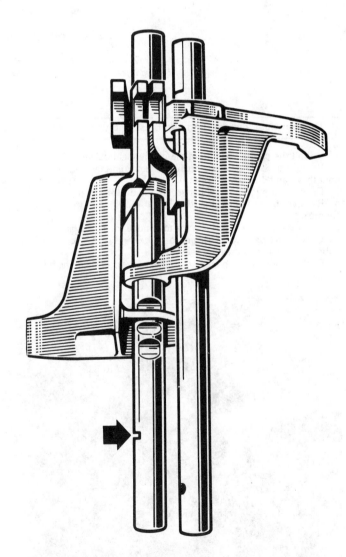

Fig. 6.40 Correct position of locking slot (arrowed) with forks and rods assembled (Sec 18)

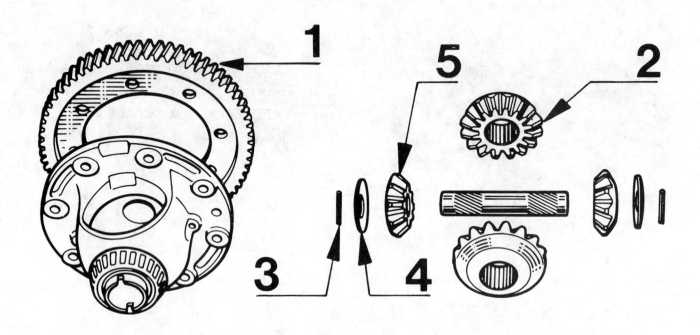

Fig. 6.41 Differential components (Sec 19)

1 Crownwheel	3 Roll pin	5 Differential gear
2 Side gear	4 Washer	

19 Differential – dismantling and reassembly

1   Unbolt the crownwheel from the differential housing.
2   Remove the side gears by pushing them round inside the housing until they can be removed (photo).
3   Drive out the roll pins which secure the differential gear spindle.
4   Remove the spindle, the differential gears and their washers (photo).
5   Use a press or bearing extractor to remove the bearings.
6   Examine all parts for wear and damage, and renew as necessary. Lubricate all parts as they are assembled.
7   Fit the bearings, using a piece of tube to press or drive them home.

19.4 Removing the differential spindle, gears and washers

19.2 Removing a differential side gear

8   Fit the spindle with the differential gears and washers. Secure the spindle with new roll pins, which should be driven in until they are centrally located in their holes (photo).
9   Fit the side gears, one at a time, and work them into their proper positions. Retain them in this position using tool 80317 M or equivalent (see Section 12, paragraph 14), inserted from the crownwheel side (photo).
10 Fit the crownwheel with its chamfer towards the differential housing. Secure with the bolts, tightening them in diagonal sequence to the specified torque.

19.8 Roll pin correctly located

20.2 Differential unit in position – note locating dowel

19.9 Side gear retaining tool in position

20.6A Measure from the joint face to the bearing outer track ...

20 Transmission – reassembly

1 Commence reassembly by fitting the selector lever into the main casing. Make sure that the locating dowel is in position in the final drive housing mating face.

2 Apply jointing compound to the mating face, then fit the differential assembly with its bearing tracks (photo).

3 Fit the final drive half housing and the extension housing, but only tighten their securing bolts finger tight at this stage.

4 Fit a new oil seal, lips well greased, to the other side of the final drive housing from the extension.

5 Remove the extension housing, fit a preload shim 2.2 mm thick to the bearing outer track and refit the extension housing (without its O-ring). Rotate the crownwheel while tightening the extension housing bolts until the crownwheel *just* starts to drag. This operation seats the bearings.

6 Remove the extension housing and the preload shim. With an accurate depth gauge, measure the distance from the final drive housing joint face to the bearing outer track. Call this dimension A.

20.6B ... and measure the spigot protrusion

Similarly measure the protrusion of the spigot on the extension housing above the joint face. Call this dimension B (photos).

7 The thickness S of preload shim required is determined by the formula:

$$S = (A - B) + 0.10 \text{ mm}$$

The extra 0.10 mm is the preload factor for the bearings. Shims are available in thicknesses of 1.1 to 2.2 mm in steps of 0.1 mm.

8 Tighten the final drive half housing securing bolts to the specified torque.

9 Fit the preload shim just determined, the speedometer driving gear and the extension housing with a new O-ring. Tighten the securing bolts to the specified torque (photo). Make sure that the crownwheel is still free to rotate.

10 Fit and secure the speedometer pinion and its adaptor.

11 Fit a new oil seal, lips well greased, into the extension housing.

12 Fit a new gear selector shaft oil seal in the main casing.

13 From the clutch housing side, fit the clutch release bearing guide tube. Do not use a gasket under the guide tube flange, and only tighten the bolts finger tight. Invert the casing and fit a preload spacer (any size) and the input shaft bearing outer track (photos).

14 Fit the gear selector shaft spring bracket and tighten its securing bolts to the specified torque. If removed, fit the two locating dowels in the main casing mating face.

15 Fit and tighten the breather.

16 Refit the lubrication jet (photo).

20.13B ... and front bearing outer track

20.9 Fitting the preload shim

20.16 Fitting the lubrication jet

20.13A Input shaft preload shim ...

17 Fit the reverse detent spring and plunger. Depress the plunger and fit the reverse selector fork and its spindle. Tighten the spindle securing nut to the specified torque.

18 Fit the reversing lamp switch using a new copper washer. Tighten it to the specified torque (photo).

19 Assemble the geartrains and the selector forks and rods. Offer the whole assembly to the gearcase (photo).

20 Fit the reverse idler spindle and gear, with the chamfer towards the rear of the gearbox. Make sure the pin in the shaft is correctly located.

21 Refit the swarf-collecting magnet.

22 Insert the spring and washers into the bracket (photo).

23 Enter the selector shaft into the casing, passing it through the compressed spring and washers inside the casing (photo). Also engage the shaft wth the selector finger and the interlock bracket. It may be helpful to keep the finger and the bracket together with a short length of rod (maximum diameter 14 mm) which can be withdrawn as the selector shaft enters.

24 Make sure that the flat on the shaft and the roll pin hole are correctly orientated (Fig. 6.42). Secure the selector finger and the interlock bracket with two new roll pins (photo). The slots in the roll pins should be 180° away from each other and in line with the longitudinal axis of the shaft.

20.18 The reversing lamp switch

20.19 Fitting the geartrains and selector mechanism

20.22 Spring and washers in the bracket

20.23 Fitting the selector shaft

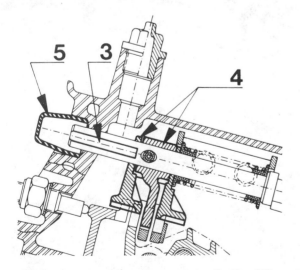

Fig. 6.42 Selector shaft fitting details (Sec 20)

3 Flat on shaft
4 Selector finger and interlock bracket
5 Cover (early type)

20.24 Selector finger/interlock bracket roll pins

25 On later models, fit the washer and a new circlip to the cover end of the shaft.

26 On all models, refit the selector shaft cover if it was removed.

27 To the lever end of the selector shaft fit a new O-ring, a washer and a new circlip.

28 Apply jointing compound to the main casing/end casing mating face. Fit the end casing, making sure that the input and output shafts and the selector rod pass through their respective holes. Fit the thirteen securing bolts and tighten them progressively to the specified torque; remember to fit the clutch cable bracket (photo).

29 Fit the reverse idler spindle bolt, using a new washer. Tighten the bolt to the specified torque.

30 Fit the drain plugs, using new washers, and tighten them to the specified torque.

31 Fit the selector rod lockplate. Secure it with its bolt and washer, tightening the bolt to the specified torque.

32 Fit the output shaft bearing circlip, making sure it is properly located in the groove.

33 Fit the output shaft rear bearing retaining washers and bolts. Tighten the bolts to the specified torque.

34 Fit the spacer (shoulder towards the bearing), 5th gear bush and 5th gear to the input shaft. Also fit the sliding sleeve and hub, but not the selector fork (photos).

35 Lock up the geartrains by engaging 5th gear with the sliding sleeve and any other gear with the selector shaft. Fit the output shaft nut and tighten it to the specified torque, then lock it by staking its skirt into the groove.

36 Remove the 5th gear sliding sleeve and hub, then refit them with the selector fork. If the original components are being refitting, observe the mating marks made when dismantling. As the fork is being lowered into position, insert the detent ball into its hole. Alternatively, extract the roll pin and insert the detent ball and spring from the other end (photos).

37 Engage two gears again, then fit the input shaft nut and tighten it

to the specified torque. Lock the nut by staking.

38 Secure 5th gear selector fork to its rod with a new roll pin.

39 Coat the mating faces with jointing compound, then refit the rear cover. Use thread locking compound on the securing bolts and tighten them to the specified torque.

40 Turn the clutch housing and remove the release bearing guide tube. If a new release lever balljoint is to be fitted, do so now: put thread locking compound on its splines and drive it in.

41 Refit the clutch release bearing guide tube with a preload spacer 2.4 thick and without a gasket. Insert the retaining bolts and tighten them progressively, at the same time rotating the input shaft. Stop tightening when the shaft *just* starts to drag: the bearings are then correctly seated.

42 Remove the guide tube and the shim. Using a depth gauge, accurately measure the distance from the bearing outer track to the joint face on the casing. Call this dimension C. Similarly measure the protrusion of the spigot on the guide tube flange above the joint face. Call this dimension D (photos).

43 The thickness T of preload shim required is given by the formula:

$$T = (C - D) + 0.15 \text{ mm}$$

The extra 0.15 mm is to provide bearing preload, and allows for the thickness of the gasket which will be fitted. Shims are available in thicknesses from 0.7 to 2.4 mm in steps of 0.1 mm.

44 Fit a new oil seal, lips well greased, to the guide tube.

45 Fit the preload shim (of calculated thickness), a new gasket and the guide tube. Secure with the bolts and tighten them to the specified torque (photo).

46 Refit the clutch release fork and release bearing (see Chapter 5).

47 If not already done, refit the gearchange levers, making sure that they are in the correct position. Also refit the gearchange pivot bracket (photos).

48 Reassembly of the transmission is now complete. Do not refill it with oil until the driveshafts have been engaged.

20.28 Clutch cable bracket is secured by two of the casing bolts

20.34A 5th gear spacer ...

20.34B ... 5th gear bush ...

20.34C ... and input shaft 5th gear

20.36A Insert the detent ball and spring ...

20.36B ... and secure with the roll pin

20.42A Measure the distance from the joint face to the bearing outer track

20.42B Measure the spigot protrusion

20.45 Input shaft preload shim

20.47A Remember to fit the spring under the gearchange lever

20.47B Fitting the gearchange pivot bracket – note spring washers

PART D: FAULT DIAGNOSIS

21 Fault diagnosis – transmission

Symptom	Reason(s)
Weak or ineffective synchromesh	Synchromesh units worn, or damaged
Jumps out of gear	Gearchange mechanism worn Synchromesh units badly worn Selector fork badly worn
Excessive noise	Incorrect grade of oil or oil level too low Gearteeth excessively worn or damaged Intermediate gear thrust washers worn allowing excessive end play Worn bearings
Difficulty in engaging gears	Clutch pedal adjustment incorrect Worn selector components Worn synchromesh units

Chapter 7 Driveshafts

For modifications, and information applicable to later models, see Supplement at end of manual

Contents

Specifications

Type	Open, with constant velocity joint at each end; solid or tubular, according to model

Driveshaft CV joint lubricant type .... Special lubricant supplied in repair kit

Torque wrench settings

	Nm	lbf ft
Hub carrier to strut clamp bolt	58	43
Hub nut:		
Non-GTI models	250	185
GTI models	260	192
Front suspension lower balljoint (GTI models)	35	26
Intermediate bearing bolt	18	13

1 General description

Drive to the front wheels is transmitted from the final drive unit to the front hubs by two driveshafts. The driveshafts incorporate inner and outer joints to accommodate suspension and steering angular movement.

The inner ends of the driveshafts are splined to the final drive/differential side gears, and the outer ends are splined to the front hubs.

2 Routine maintenance

Carry out the following procedures at the intervals given in Routine Maintenance at the beginning of the manual.

1 Jack up the front of the car and support on axle stands. Apply the handbrake.

2 Thoroughly examine the rubber bellows at each end of the driveshafts for splitting, damage and grease leakage (photo). If evident renew the bellows.

3 On GTI models, check the right-hand driveshaft intermediate housing for excessive wear by attempting to move the driveshaft up and down. Also turn the right-hand wheel and listen for excessive

2.2 Driveshaft outboard joint and bellows

noise which would indicate pitted tracks or balls. Renew the bearing if necessary.

4 If the driveshaft joints are excessively noisy, perhaps more noticeable when turning corners, renew the driveshaft or obtain an exchange unit.

3 Driveshaft (non-GTI models) – removal and refitting

1 Place a container beneath the engine and transmission unit and drain the coil. Clean the drain plug then refit and tighten it.

2 It is now necessary to prevent the front suspension coil spring expanding in subsequent operations. Peugeot garages use two special cables inserted through the holes at the top of the front suspension tower and engaged with further holes in the bottom coil spring seat. If available use these, otherwise fit coil spring compressors. **Do not** attempt to use any makeshift tool as considerable damage could occur if the spring breaks free. To fit either type of tool it will be necessary to turn the front wheel to full lock in alternate directions.

3 Loosen, but do not remove, the three top strut mounting nuts. This will allow the strut to be moved sideways later.

4 Fully apply the handbrake then, where possible, remove the front wheel centre trim and loosen the hub nut. On models without a centre trim the hub nut must be loosened after removing the front wheel. **Do not** apply the footbrake when loosening the nut as damage can occur to the brake disc retaining screws.

5 Jack up the front of the car and support on axle stands. Remove the wheel.

6 If the hub nut has yet to be loosened, use two wheel bolts and a length of bar to hold the hub.

7 Unscrew the clamp bolt securing the hub carrier to the bottom of the strut.

8 Release the front brake flexible and rigid pipes from the body bracket by pulling out the retaining plate (see Chapter 8).

9 Drive a suitable wedge into the slot in the hub carrier and slide the carrier from the bottom of the strut. If available, use the special Peugeot

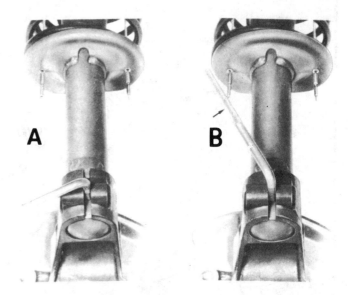

Fig. 7.2 Method of expanding the hub carrier to release the strut (Sec 3)

A   Special tool inserted   B   Tool turned through 90°

Fig. 7.3 Disconnecting the driveshaft from the hub (Sec 3)

tool which consists of a cranked rod inserted in the slot and turned through 90°.

10 Move the top of the hub carrier outwards and at the same time withdraw the outer end of the driveshaft from the hub.

11 Withdraw the inner end of the driveshaft from the gearbox.

12 With the driveshaft removed, the opportunity should be taken to renew the oil seal in the gearbox. To do this, prise out the old seal and wipe clean the recess. Fill the space between the new oil seal lips with grease then use a suitable block of wood to tap it into the casing. When fully fitted it should be slightly recessed.

13 Refitting is a reversal of removal, but make sure that the hub carrier is located fully onto the strut by using a trolley jack. Renew all self-locking nuts and tighten the nuts and bolts to the specified torque. After tightening the hub nut lock it by staking the shoulder into the two grooves on the end of the driveshaft.

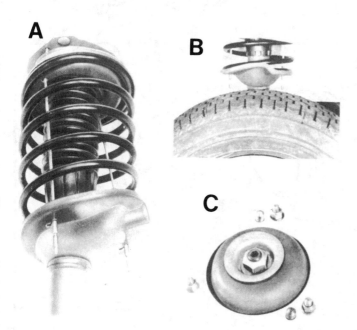

Fig. 7.1 Method of retaining front coil spring using Peugeot cables (Sec 3)

A   Cables fitted to strut
B   Side view of cables located in bottom coil spring seat
C   Strut top mounting with cables in position

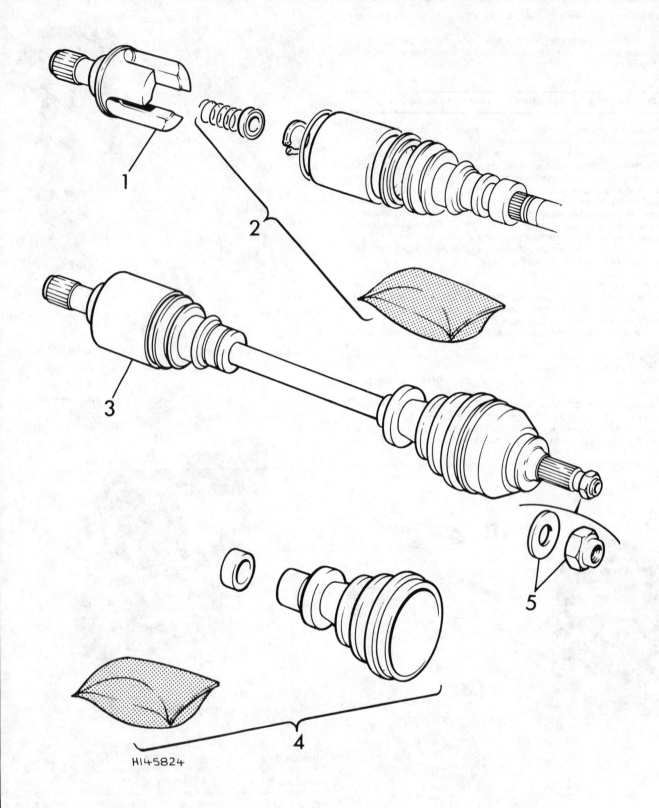

H145824

Fig. 7.4 Driveshaft fitted to non-GTI models (Sec 3)

1 Tulip
2 Inner joint kit
3 Driveshaft assembly
4 Outer joint kit
5 Hub nut and washer

4 Driveshaft (GTI models) – removal and refitting

1 Place a container beneath the gearbox and final drive casing then remove the two drain plugs and drain the oil. Clean the drain plugs then refit and tighten them.

2 Fully apply the handbrake then, where possible, remove the front wheel centre trim and loosen the hub nut. On models without a centre trim the hub nut must be loosened after removing the front wheel. **Do not** apply the footbrake when loosening the nut as damage can occur to the brake disc retaining screws.

3 Jack up the front of the car and support on axle stands. Remove the wheel.

4 If the hub nut has yet to be loosened use two wheel bolts and a length of bar to hold the hub.

5 Unscrew the clamp bolt securing the front suspension lower balljoint to the bottom of the hub carrier then pull the lower suspension arms down from the carrier.

6 Recover the balljoint guard plate.

Left-hand driveshaft

7 Turn the front wheels to full right-hand lock, and remove the hub nut.

8 Pull the hub carrier outwards and at the same time withdraw the outer end of the driveshaft from the hub.

9 Withdraw the inner end of the driveshaft from the final drive unit.

10 Note that the design of the differential unit is such that if both driveshafts are removed the differential side gears will fall down into the final drive housing. It is therefore important to retain the side gears using Peugeot tool 80317 (M and N), or alternatively re-insert the inner end of one driveshaft before removing the other. Another possibility is to improvise using a length of wooden dowel 1 inch in diameter, ground down slightly at one end to enter the splines in the side gear.

11 Note also that the weight of the car **must not** be taken by the front wheels with the driveshaft(s) removed otherwise damage may occur to the hub bearings.

Right-hand driveshaft

12 Loosen the two nuts retaining the intermediate bearing in the bracket bolted to the rear of the cylinder block, then turn the bolts so that their heads move through 90°.

13 Turn the front wheels to full left-hand lock, and remove the hub nut.

14 Pull the hub carrier outwards and at the same time withdraw the outer end of the driveshaft from the hub.

15 Withdraw the inner end of the driveshaft from the final drive unit and guide it through the intermediate bearing bracket.

16 Note the cautions given in paragraphs 10 and 11.

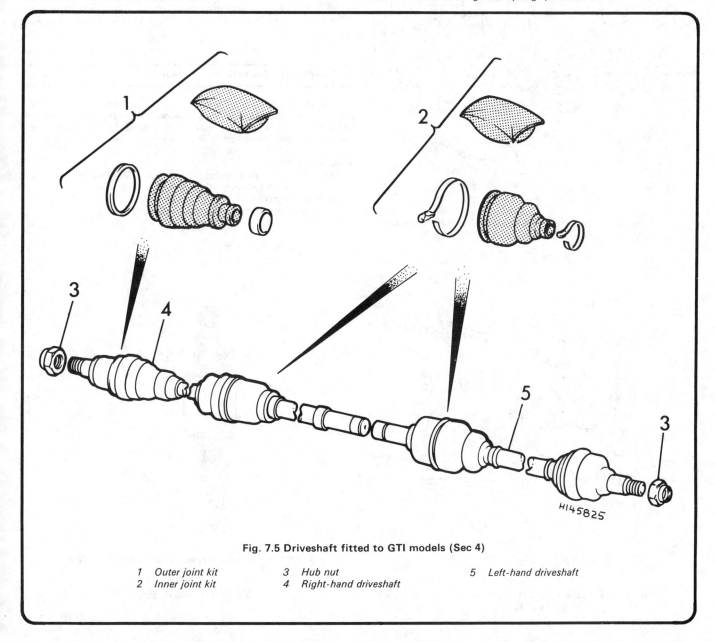

H145825

Fig. 7.5 Driveshaft fitted to GTI models (Sec 4)

1	Outer joint kit	3	Hub nut	5	Left-hand driveshaft
2	Inner joint kit	4	Right-hand driveshaft		

Both driveshafts
17 With the driveshafts removed, the opportunity should be taken to renew the oil seal in the final drive housing. To do this, prise out the old seal and wipe clean the recess. Fill the space between the new oil seal lips with grease then use a suitable block of wood to tap it into the housing. The right-hand oil seal should be flush with the housing, but the left-hand oil seal recessed. Fit the special protector to the right-hand oil seal.
18 Refitting is a reversal of removal, but tighten all nuts and bolts to the specified torque. When refitting the right-hand driveshaft make sure that the lugs on the intermediate bearing bolt heads are located over the bearing outer track, and after tightening the nuts remove the special protector from the oil seal. After tightening the hub nut lock it by staking the shoulder into the two grooves on the end of the driveshaft. Refill the gearbox with oil.

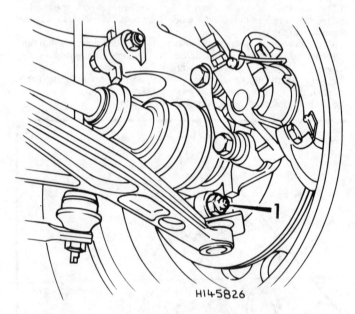

Fig. 7.6 Disconnecting the front suspension lower balljoint on GTI models (Sec 4)

1   Clamp bolt

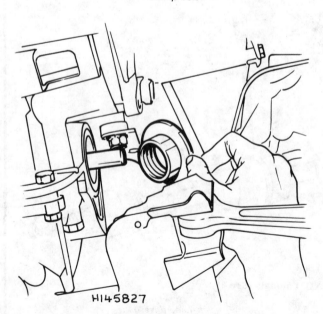

Fig. 7.7 Using the Peugeot tool to retain the differential side gears (Sec 4)

Fig. 7.8 Special oil seal protector for use when renewing the final drive housing right-hand oil seal on GTI models (Sec 4)

---

5   Driveshaft joint bellows – renewal

It is not practicable for the home mechanic to renew the driveshaft joint bellows on GTI models as special tools are required, therefore on these models the driveshaft should be removed and taken to a Peugeot garage. This Section describes the procedure for non-GTI models.

Inboard joint
1   With the driveshaft removed from the car, prise back the lip of the cover and then tap the cover off to expose the tulip yoke.
2   Remove the tulip yoke, spring and thrust cup.
3   Wipe away as much of the original grease as possible.

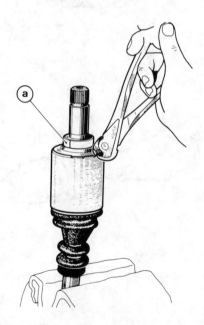

Fig. 7.9 Prising back driveshaft joint cover lip (Sec 5)

a   *Oil seal rubbing surface*

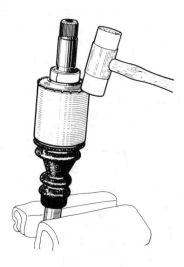

Fig. 7.10 Tapping off driveshaft joint cover (Sec 5)

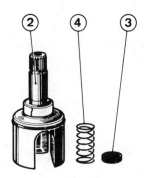

Fig. 7.11 Driveshaft inboard joint components (Sec 5)

2   Tulip   4   Spring
3   Thrust cap

H145878

Fig. 7.12 Suitable tool for fitting a new bellows (Sec 5)

4   If retaining circlips are not fitted, wind adhesive tape around the spider bearings to retain their needle rollers.

5   If it is now possible, borrow or make up a guide tool similar to the one shown (Fig. 7.12). The defective bellows can be cut off and the new ones slid up the tool (well greased) so that they will expand sufficiently to ride over the joint and locate on the shaft.

6   Where such a tool cannot be obtained, proceed in the following way.

7   Mark the relative position of the spider to the shaft.

8   Remove the spider retaining circlip.

9   Either support the spider and press the shaft from it, or use a suitable puller to draw it from the shaft.

10 Remove the bellows/cover and the small rubber retaining ring.

11 Commence reassembly by smearing the inside of the cover with grease, fit the spacer to the new bellows which are supplied as a repair kit complete with grease sachet.

12 Insert the spacer/gaiter into the cover.

13 Slide the small rubber ring onto the shaft followed by the bellows/cover assembly.

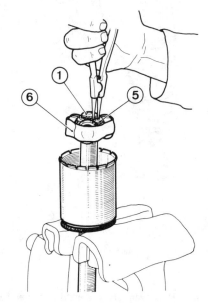

Fig. 7.13 Extracting spider circlip (Sec 5)

1   Shaft   6   Taped needle rollers
5   Needle roller cage

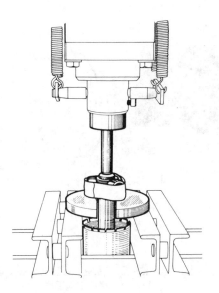

Fig. 7.14 Pressing shaft out of spider (Sec 5)

14 Using a piece of tubing as a drift, align the marks made before dismantling and drive the spider onto the shaft. Note that the chamfered side of the spider should go onto the shaft first.

15 Fit a new spider retaining circlip.

16 Remove the bearing retaining tape.

17 Draw the cover over the spider and apply grease from the sachet to all components. Refit the tulip yoke with spring and thrust cap. Use a new O-ring seal.

18 Peen the rim of the cover evenly all around the yoke.

19 Engage the rubber retaining ring over the narrow end of the bellows.

20 Carefully insert a thin rod under the narrow end of the bellows and released trapped air.

21 Set the dimension as shown in the diagram by sliding the bellows or cover (Fig. 7.19).

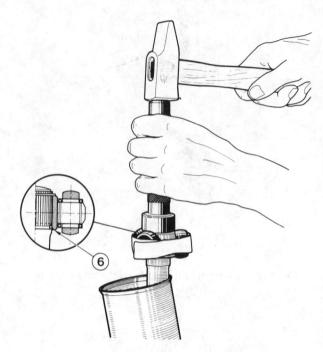

Fig. 7.17 Driving spider onto shaft (Sec 5)

6   Chamfered side

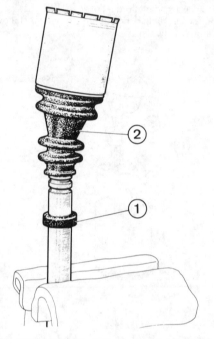

Fig. 7.15 Driveshaft inboard joint (Sec 5)

1   Rubber ring   2   Bellows

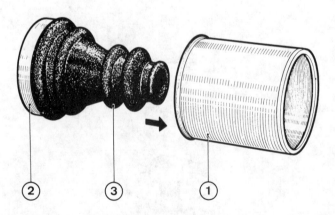

Fig. 7.16 Driveshaft inboard joint cover (1), spacer (2) and bellows (3) (Sec 5)

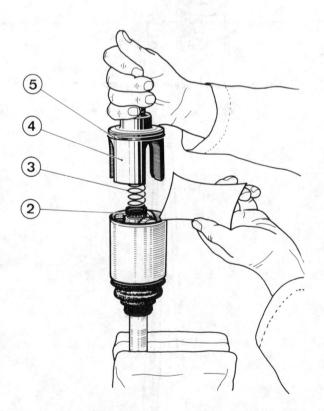

Fig. 7.18 Assembling inboard joint (Sec 5)

2   Thrust cap   4   Tulip
3   Spring   5   O-ring

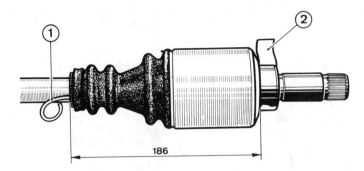

Fig. 7.19 Inboard joint bellows setting diagram (Sec 5)

1   Rod for air release

2   Protective tape

Measurement in mm

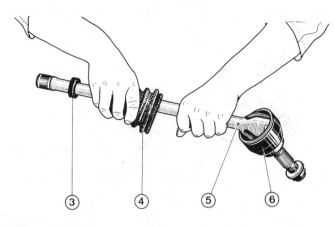

Fig. 7.21 Removing the outer bellows (Sec 5)

3   Rubber ring   5   Shaft
4   Bellows   6   Outboard joint

Outboard joint

22 If the guide tool mentioned in paragraph 5 is available, it is possible to cut the defective bellows from the shaft and fit the new bellows without dismantling the shaft. Where such a tool is not available, proceed in the following way.
23 With the driveshaft removed from the car and the inboard joint dismantled, as previously described, take off the spring clip which retains the larger diameter end of the bellows.
24 Prise off the rubber ring from the smaller diameter end of the bellows and slide the bellows down the shaft.
25 Wipe away as much grease as possible from the joint and discard the defective bellows.
26 Apply the grease supplied with the repair kit evenly between the bellows and joint.
27 Locate the new bellows, clip and rubber ring.
28 Insert a thin rod under the narrow end of the bellows to release any trapped air.
29 Refit the inboard joint, as previously described.

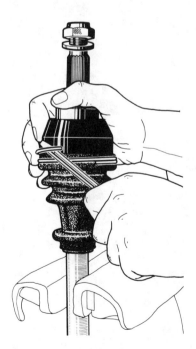

Fig. 7.20 Removing bellows clip from driveshaft outboard joint (Sec 5)

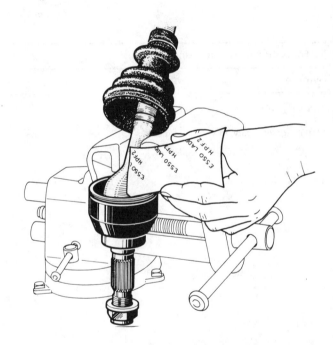

Fig. 7.22 Greasing the outboard joint (Sec 5)

6 Driveshaft intermediate housing (GTI models) – renewal

1   Remove the right-hand driveshaft, as described in Section 4.
2   Place the bearing and driveshaft in a vice with the inner track resting on the vice, then use a soft-faced mallet to drive out the driveshaft. Remove the end cover and oil seal from the driveshaft and intermediate bearing bracket. If the bearing has remained in the bracket when the driveshaft was removed use a metal tube on the inner track to drift it out.
3   Clean the bearing recess in the bracket.
4   Locate a new end cover on the driveshaft then use a metal tube on the inner track to drive the new bearing onto the special shoulder.
5   Press a new oil seal into the intermediate bearing bracket.
6   Refit the driveshaft, as described in Section 4.

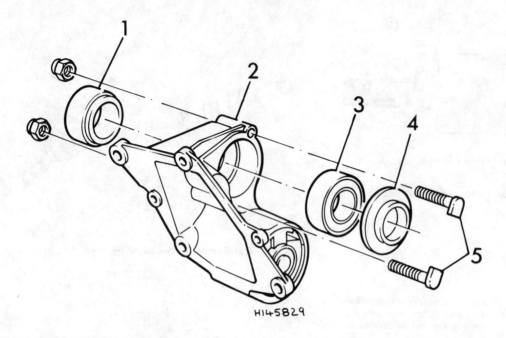

Fig. 7.23 Driveshaft intermediate bearing components fitted to GTI models (Sec 6)

1   Oil seal
2   Bracket/engine mounting
3   Bearing
4   End cover
5   Bolts

HI45829

7   Fault diagnosis – driveshafts

Symptom	Reason(s)
Knocking noise, particularly on full lock	Worn driveshaft joints
Metallic grating varying with roadspeed	Worn intermediate bearing on right-hand driveshaft

Chapter 8 Braking system

For modifications, and information applicable to later models, see Supplement at end of manual

Contents

Specifications

Type		Front disc brakes, rear drum brakes (self-adjusting). Servo assistance on all non-basic models. Rear brake compensator (inertia type on GTI). Cable-operated handbrake on rear wheels

Brake fluid type/specification ..... Hydraulic fluid to SAE J1703 or DOT 3 (Duckhams Universal Brake and Clutch Fluid)

Disc brakes

Disc diameter	247 mm
Disc thickness (new):	
Except GTI (non-ventilated)	10.0 mm
GTI (ventilated)	20.4 mm
Disc thickness (minimum after resurfacing):	
Except GTI (non-ventilated)	8.5 mm
GTI (ventilated)	18.9 mm
Disc run-out (maximum) measured 22.0 mm from rim	0.07 mm
Disc pad minimum lining thickness	2.0 mm

Drum brakes

Drum internal diameter (new)	180.0 mm
Drum internal diameter (maximum after resurfacing)	181.0 mm
Drum out-of-round (maximum)	0.10 mm
Shoe minimum lining thickness	1.0 mm

Vacuum servo unit

Type:	
Except GTI	Isovac 178 mm
GTI (RHD)	Isovac 178 mm
GTI (LHD)	Isovac 229 mm

Torque wrench settings

	Nm	lbf ft
Caliper mounting bolts:		
Girling	97	72
DBA Bendix	120	89
Rear backplate	37	27
Rear hub nut	215	159

1 General description

The braking system is of hydraulic type with discs on the front and drums on the rear. The handbrake is cable-operated on the rear wheels.

The hydraulic circuit is of two independent sections so that, in the event of the failure of one section, the remaining section is still functional. On non-GTI models the circuit is split diagonally, but on GTI models it is split front and rear.

A compensating valve (or valves) reduces the hydraulic pressure to the rear brakes under heavy applications of the brake pedal in order to prevent rear wheel lock-up.

A vacuum servo unit is fitted to all non-basic models.

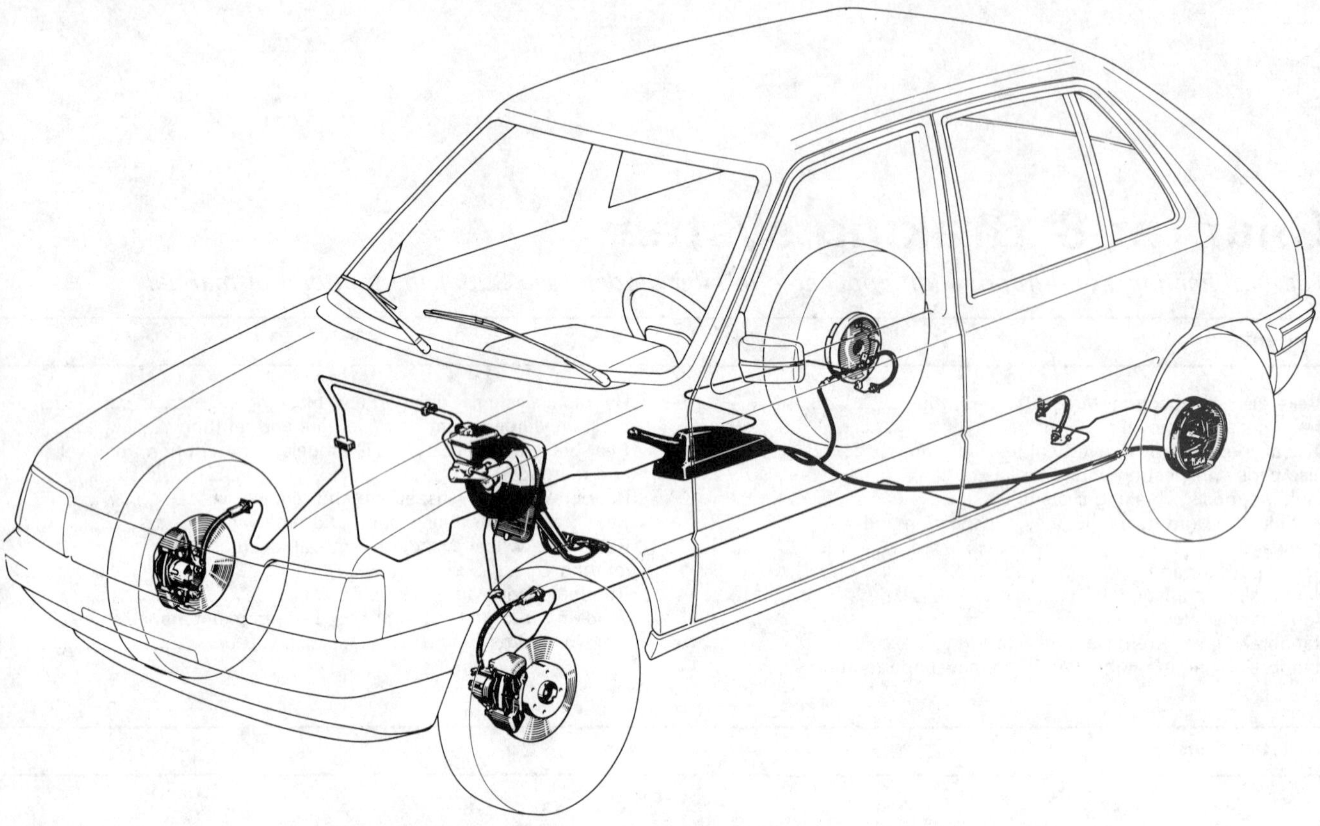

Fig. 8.1 Braking system layout for non-GTI models (Sec 1)

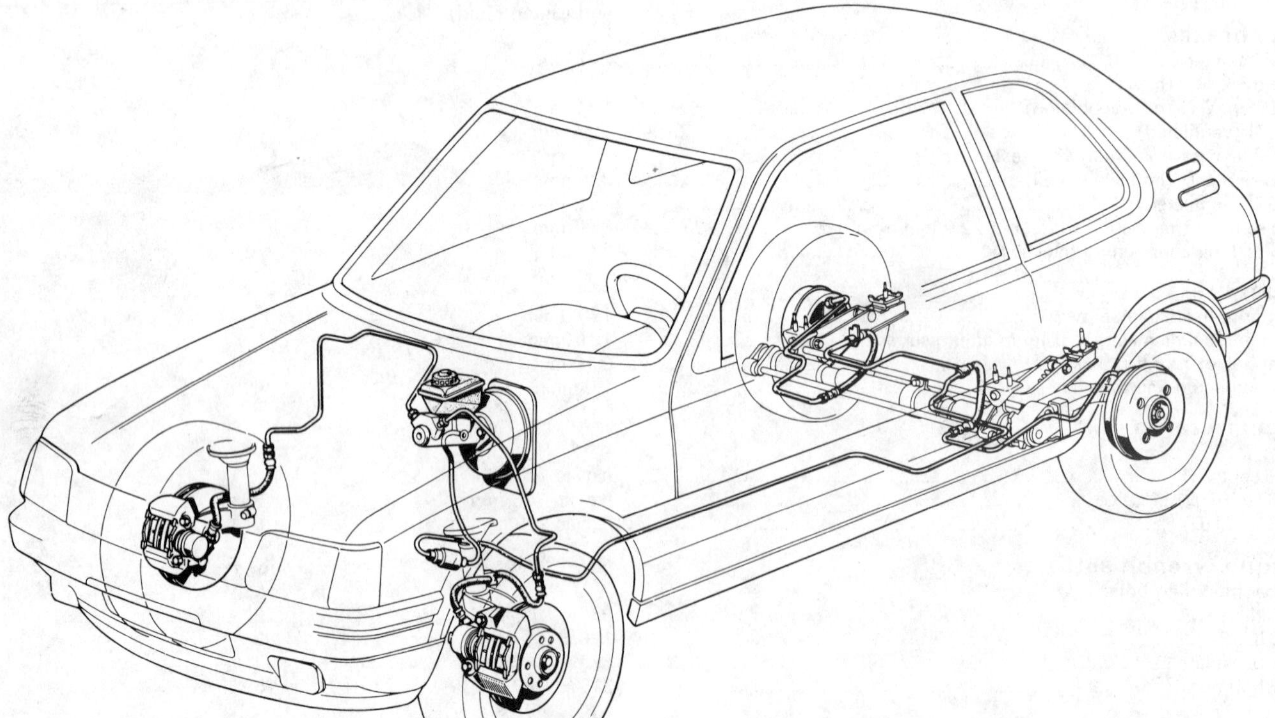

Fig. 8.2 Braking system layout for GTI models (Sec 1)

2 Routine maintenance

Carry out the following procedures at the intervals given in Routine Maintenance.

1   Check that the brake fluid level is near the top of the reservoir located on the master cylinder (photo). A slight fall in level is normal as the front disc pads wear, but a considerable drop will need investigating. If necessary top up the level after removing the filler cap.

2   Examine the hydraulic circuit lines and hoses for damage and deterioration, and for any signs of leakage. There is no need to retighten union nuts as this may distort the sealing faces.

3   Apply the handbrake and check that both rear wheels are locked.

4   To renew the hydraulic fluid, remove the filler cap from the reservoir and use a syringe to remove the fluid from both compartments. Fill the reservoir with new hydraulic fluid and proceed to bleed the system, as described in Section 12. Allow 5 or 6 depressions of the brake pedal to clear old fluid.

3.3A Pad sliding key clip – arrowed (DBA Bendix type)

2.1 Topping-up the brake fluid level

3 Disc pads – inspection and renewal

1   Jack up the front of the car and support on axle stands. Apply the handbrake and remove the roadwheels.

2   If the friction material has worn down to 2.0 mm (0.079 in) (this is indicated if the groove in the pad has disappeared) then the pads must be renewed as an axle set. The removal and refitting operations will vary according to the type of caliper, but first reduce the fluid level in the reservoir.

DBA Bendix disc caliper

3   Remove the clip from the end of the upper sliding key (photo). Disconnect the pad wear wiring as necessary (photo).

4   Pull out the upper sliding key (photo).

5   Using a lever against the front suspension strut, push the cylinder towards the brake disc so that the outer pad can be withdrawn from the caliper (photo).

6   Push back the caliper and withdraw the inner pad (photo).

7   Clean away all dust and dirt from the caliper. **Do not** inhale the dust, as it may be injurious to health. Check for brake fluid leakage around the piston dust seal and, if evident, overhaul the caliper, as described later in the Chapter. Check the brake disc for wear and also check that the rubber bellows on the cylinder sliding rods are in good condition.

8   Clean the backs of the disc pads and apply a little anti-squeal brake grease. Also apply the grease to the lower pad locating lip of the caliper (photo).

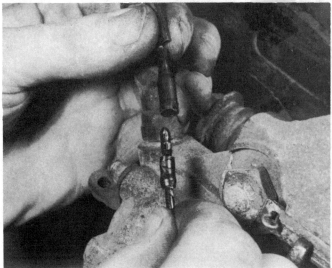

3.3B Disconnecting the pad wear wiring

3.4 Removing the pad sliding key (DBA Bendix type)

3.5 Removing the outer pad

3.6 Removing the inner pad

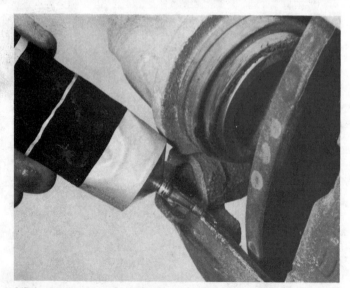

3.8 Applying anti-squeal brake grease to the pad locating lip on the caliper

9   With the caliper pushed inwards, insert the inner pad then push the caliper outwards and insert the outer pad.
10 Check that the pads are correctly located on the caliper lip (photo) then tap in the upper sliding key to lock them. Fit the sliding key clip.

Girling disc caliper
11 Extract the spring clips and tap out the pad retaining pins. Disconnect the pad wear wiring as necessary.
12 Lever the cylinder outwards and withdraw the outer pad then push in the caliper and withdraw the inner pad.
13 Clean and check the caliper, as described in paragraph 7, then clean the backs of the disc pads and apply a little anti-squeal brake grease. Note that, as from early 1985, a special spring is fitted to the inner pads to prevent pad knock within the caliper. The spring (obtainable from a

3.10 The correct location of the anti-rattle clips on the disc pads (DBA Bendix type)

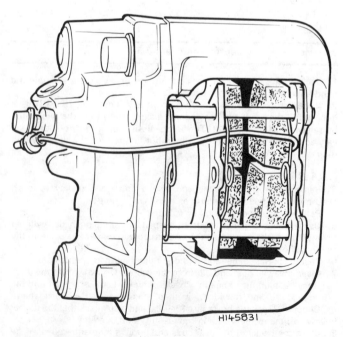

H145831

Fig. 8.3 Girling disc caliper and pads – without disc (Sec 3)

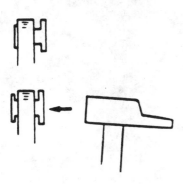

**Fig. 8.4 Method of fitting anti-knock spring to
Girling inner disc pad (Sec 3)**

1 Loop for rivet
2 Loop for lower retaining pin
3 Anti-knock spring

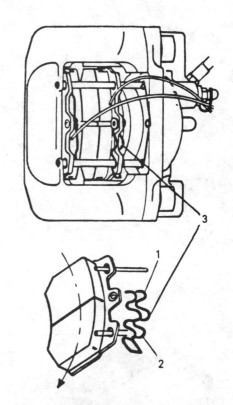

Peugeot parts store) may be fitted to earlier models by tapping the inner
pad control rivet through the backing plate so that the clip may be
located on both sides (Fig. 8.4).
14 With the caliper pushed inwards, insert the inner pad then push the
caliper outwards and insert the outer pad.
15 Tap in the pad retaining pins and fit the spring clips.
16 Where fitted, hook the anti-knock spring on the lower pad retaining
pin.

DBA Bendix and Girling disc calipers
17 Repeat the operations on the opposite disc caliper.
18 Apply the footbrake several times to position the pads against the
discs.
19 Top up the master cylinder reservoir to its correct level.
20 Refit the roadwheels and lower the car to the ground.

4 Rear brake shoes – inspection and renewal

1 Jack up the rear of the car and support it on axle stands. Chock the
front wheels and release the handbrake.
2 The lining thickness may be checked without removing the
drums/hubs. Pull out the rubber plugs from the backplates by the
handbrake cables and use a torch, if necessary, to check the lining
thickness (photo). If it is at or near the specified mimimum remove the
drums and make a more thorough inspection.
3 Remove the rear roadwheels.
4 Tap off the grease cap, taking care not to damage its outer lip, the
unscrew the staked nut from the end of the stub axle and remove the
washer (photos). Should the stub axle rotate within the trailing arm,
hold it stationary with a 12 mm Allen key on the inner end (photo).
5 Withdraw the hub/drum from the stub axle. If difficulty is
experienced, due to the shoes wearing grooves in the drum, insert a
screwdriver through one of the wheel bolt holes and depress the
handbrake lever on the rear brake shoe so that it slides back behind the
shoe (photo). This will retract the shoes and allow the hub/drum to be
removed.
6 Brush the dust and dirt from the shoes, backplate and drum. **Do
not** inhale it, as it may be injurious to health.

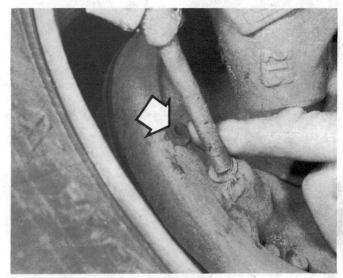

4.2 Remove the rubber plug (arrowed) from the rear brake
backplate and use a torch in the hole to check the lining thickness

7 It is now possible to inspect both shoe linings for wear. If either is
worn down the specified minimum amount, renew them both.
8 Note the position of each shoe and the location of the return and
steady springs (photo).
9 Unhook and remove the upper return spring (photo).
10 Remove the steady springs using pliers to depress the outer cups
and turn them through 90° (photo). Remove the pins from the
backplate.
11 Move the serrated automatic adjuster lever quadrant against spring
tension (photo), move the lever forwards and release the strut from the
top of the shoes (DBA Bendix type only).

4.4A Remove the grease cap ...

4.4B ... then unscrew the staked nut ...

4.4C ... and remove the washer

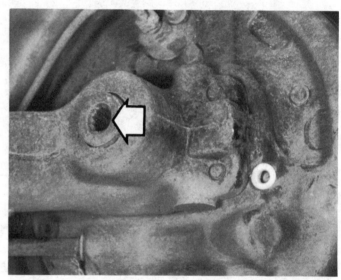

4.4D Inner end of rear stub axle (arrowed) which can be held with an Allen key

4.5A If the drum is difficult to remove, insert a screwdriver through a wheel bolt hole ...

4.5B ... and push the handbrake lever behind the shoe

4.8 Rear brake assembly

4.11 Automatic adjuster lever (arrowed) and bottom return spring location

4.9 Upper return spring location

12 Expand the shoes over the wheel cylinder then release them from the bottom anchor.

13 Unhook the lever return spring and the handbrake cable.

14 If necessary, position a rubber band over the wheel cylinder to prevent the pistons coming out. Should there be evidence of brake fluid leakage from the wheel cylinder, renew it or overhaul it, as described in Section 7.

15 Transfer the handbrake and automatic adjuster levers to the new shoes as required. Note that the levers and strut on each rear wheel are different, and that the leading and trailing shoes are fitted with different grade linings.

16 Place the shoes on the bench in their correct location and fit the lower return spring.

4.10 Shoe steady spring (arrowed)

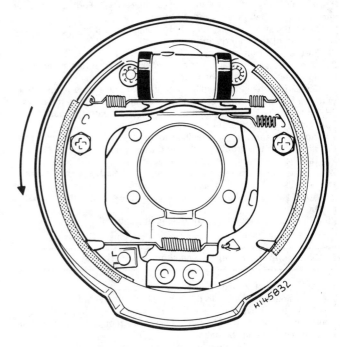

Fig. 8.5 Diagram of DBA Bendix type rear brake (Sec 4)

Arrow indicates wheel rotation

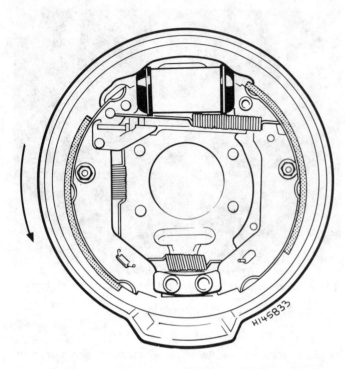

Fig. 8.6 Diagram of Girling type rear brake (Sec 4)

Arrow indicates wheel rotation

4.24A Tighten the rear hub nut ...

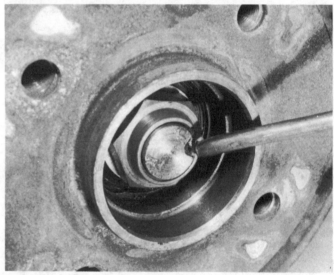

4.24B ... then stake it to the stub axle

17 Apply brake grease sparingly to the metal contact points of the shoes, then position them on the backplate and reconnect the handbrake cable. Locate the shoe ends on the bottom anchor.
18 Engage the strut with the slots at the top of the shoes, making sure it is located correctly on the automatic adjuster lever. Engage the upper shoe ends on the wheel cylinder pistons.
19 Insert the steady spring pins in the backplate and through the shoe webs, then fit the springs and outer cups.
20 Fit the upper return spring.
21 Move the serrated automatic adjuster lever quadrant against the spring tension to set the shoes at their minimum diameter.
22 Check that the handbrake lever on the rear brake shoe is positioned with the lug on the edge of the shoe web and not behind the shoe.
23 Fit the hub/drum on the stub axle and retain with the washer and nut. Always renew the nut.
24 Tighten the nut to the specified torque then lock it by staking the nut flange into the groove on the stub axle (photos).
25 Tap the grease cap into the hub/drum.
26 Repeat all the operations on the opposite rear brake then refit the roadwheels and lower the car to the ground.
27 Apply the footbrake several times to set the shoes in their adjusted position.
28 Adjust the handbrake, as described in Section 14.

5 Disc caliper – removal, overhaul and refitting

1 Remove the disc pads, as described in Section 3.
2 Fit a brake hose clamp to the flexible hose connected to the caliper. Alternatively remove the brake fluid reservoir filler cap and tighten it down onto a piece of polythene sheeting to reduce the loss of fluid when disconnecting the caliper.
3 Loosen the flexible hose union connection at the caliper.
4 Unscrew the two mounting bolts (photo), withdraw the caliper from the disc then unscrew the caliper from the flexible hose. Plug the hose to prevent loss of fluid.
5 Clean the exterior of the caliper.

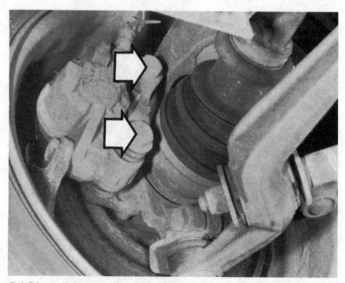

5.4 Disc caliper mounting bolts (arrowed)

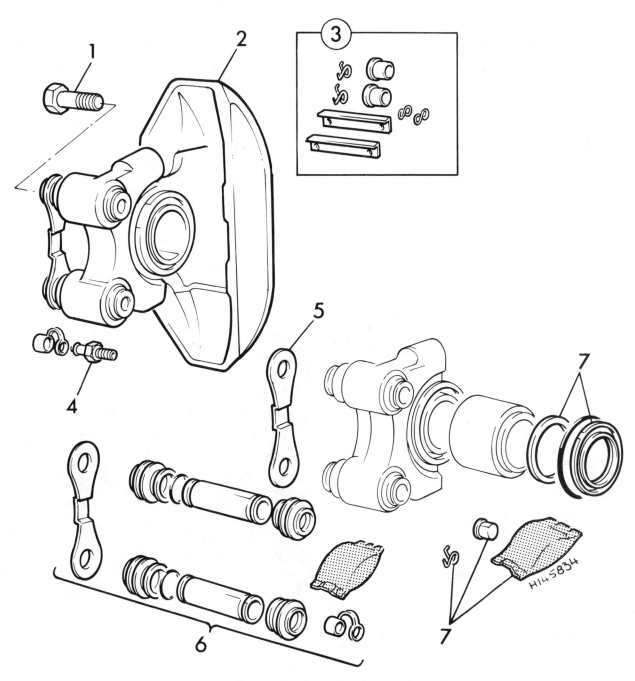

Fig. 8.7 Bendix type disc caliper components (Sec 5)

1	Mounting bolt	3	Sliding key kit	5	Retaining plate
2	Caliper assembly	4	Bleed screw	6	Sliding guide kit with grease

7   Repair kit with grease

6   On the Bendix type, unbolt the caliper frame from the cylinder.

7   Prise the dust cover and ring from the end of the piston.

8   Withdraw the piston from the cylinder. If necessary use air pressure from a foot pump in the fluid inlet to force the piston out.

9   Prise the seal from inside the cylinder, taking care not to damage the cylinder wall.

10 If required, dismantle the sliding guides. On the Bendix type unbolt the endplate from the guides and remove the rubber dust covers. Keep the guides identified for location.

11 Clean all the components using methylated spirit or clean brake fluid then examine them for wear and damage. Check the piston and cylinder surfaces for scoring, excessive wear and corrosion, and if evedent renew the complete caliper assembly. Similarly check the sliding guides. If the components are in good condition obtain a repair kit which will contain all the necessary rubber seals and other renewable items.

12 Dip the new seal in fresh brake fluid then locate it in the cylinder groove using the fingers only to manipulate it.

13 Dip the piston in brake fluid and insert it in the cylinder, twisting it as necessary to locate it in the seal.

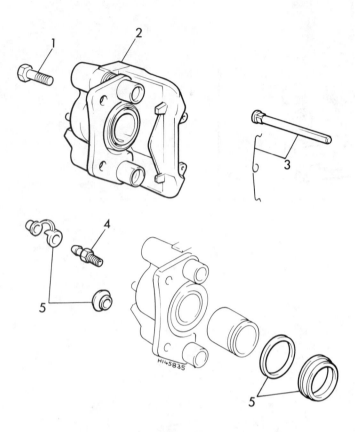

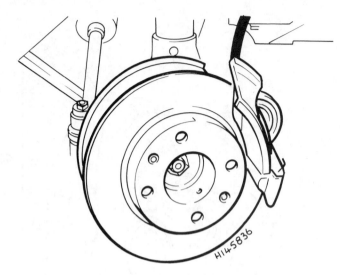

Fig. 8.9 Removing a brake disc (Sec 6)

Fig. 8.8 Girling type disc caliper components (Sec 5)

1   Mounting bolt   4   Bleed screw
2   Caliper assembly   5   Repair kit
3   Pad retaining pin and spring

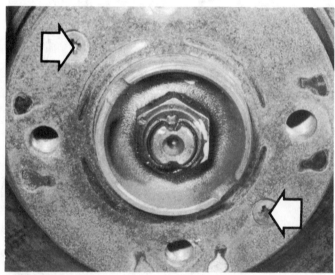

6.3 Disc retaining screws (arrowed)

14 Fit the dust cover and ring over the end of the piston and cylinder.
15 Lubricate the sliding guides with the grease supplied and refit them, together with the new seals. On the Bendix type refit the endplate and tighten the bolts.
16 On the Bendix type, refit the caliper frame and tighten the bolts.
17 To refit the caliper, first screw it onto the flexible hose and locate it over the brake disc so that the hose is not twisted.
18 Clean the mounting bolt threads and apply locking fluid. Insert the mounting bolts and tighten them to the specified torque.
19 Tighten the flexible hose union on the caliper. Check that the hose is clear of the strut and surrounding components and, if necessary, loosen the rigid pipe union on the body bracket, reposition the hose and retighten the union.
20 Refit the disc pads, as described in Secion 3.
21 Remove the brake hose clamp or polythene sheeting and bleed the hydraulic system, as described in Section 12. On GTI models it is only necessary to bleed the front circuit.

6   Brake disc – inspection, removal and refitting

1   Remove the disc pads, as described in Section 3.
2   Using a dial gauge or feelers and a fixed block, check that the disc run-out is within the specified limit. Do not confuse wheel bearing endfloat with disc wear. Also check the condition of the disc for scoring. Light scoring is normal, but if excessive either renew the disc or have it ground to within the specified limit.
3   To remove the disc, unscrew the two cross-head screws (where fitted) and withdraw the disc at an angle from the caliper and hub (photo).

4   Refitting is a reversal of removal, but make sure that the disc-to-hub mating surfaces are clean and that the cross-head screws are tightened fully. Refer to Section 3 when refitting the disc pads.

7   Rear brake wheel cylinder – removal, overhaul and refitting

1   Jack up the rear of the car and support on axle stands. Chock the front wheels and remove the relevant rear wheel.
2   Remove the hub/drum, as described in Section 4.
3   Note the location of the brake shoe upper return spring then unhook and remove it.
4   Pull the handbrake lever on the rear shoe fully forwards so that the upper ends of the shoes are clear of the wheel cylinder. Wedge the lever in this position using a block of wood.
5   Fit a brake hose clamp to the flexible hose supplying the rear

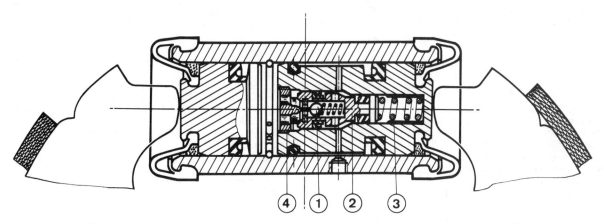

Fig. 8.10 Cross-section of a rear wheel cylinder incorporating a compensator (Sec 7)

1	Ball valve	2	Piston	3	Spring	4	Tappets

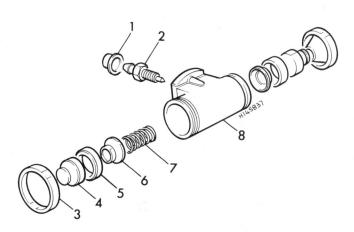

Fig. 8.11 Exploded view of a rear wheel cylinder (Sec 7)

1	Cap	5	Seal
2	Bleed screw	6	Spring seat
3	Dust excluder	7	Spring
4	Piston	8	Body

brakes. Alternatively remove the brake fluid reservoir filler cap and tighten it down onto a piece of polythene sheeting to reduce the loss of fluid when disconnecting the wheel cylinder.

6   Unscrew the hydraulic pipe union nut from the rear of the wheel cylinder.

7   Unscrew the two mounting bolts and withdraw the wheel cylinder from the backplate (photo). Take care not to spill any brake fluid on the brake shoe linings.

8   Clean the exterior of the wheel cylinder. Note that on all non-GTI models with a diagonally split hydraulic circuit the rear wheel cylinders incorporate compensators which **must not** be dismantled.

9   Pull off the dust excluders.

10 Extract the pistons, seals and return spring; keeping each component identified for location.

11 Check the surfaces of the cylinder bore and pistons for scoring and corrosion and, if evident, renew the complete wheel cylinder. If the components are in good condition discard the seals and obtain a repair kit which will contain all the necessary renewable components.

12 Clean the pistons and cylinder with methylated spirit or clean brake fluid then dip each component in fresh brake fluid and reassemble in

reverse order; making sure that the lips of the seats face into the cylinder. When completed, wipe clean the outer surfaces of the dust excluders.

13 Clean the backplate and refit the wheel cylinder using a reversal of the removal procedure. Refer to Section 4 when refitting the hub/drum

14 Make sure that the brake hose clamp or polythene sheeting is removed then bleed the hydraulic system, as described in Section 12. On GTI models it is only necessary to bleed the rear circuit.

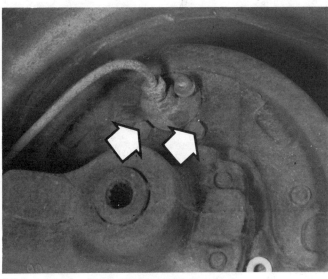

7.7 Rear wheel cylinder mounting bolts (arrowed)

8 Rear brake drum – inspection and renovation

1   Whenever the hub/brake drum is removed to check the linings, take the opportunity to inspect the interior of the drum.

2   If the drum is grooved, owing to failure to renew worn linings or after a very high mileage has been covered, then it may be possible to regrind it, provided the maximum internal diameter is not exceeded.

3   Even if only one drum is in need of grinding both drums must be reground to the same size in order to maintain even braking characteristics.

4   Judder or a springy pedal felt when the brakes are applied can be caused by a distorted (out-of-round) drum. Here again it may be possible to regrind the drums, otherwise a new drum will be required.

9 Master cylinder – removal, overhaul and refitting

1   Unscrew the filler cap from the brake fluid reservoir and draw out the fluid using a syringe.
2   Prise the reservoir from the master cylinder and remove the seals.
3   Unscrew the union nuts securing the rigid brake lines to the master cylinder and pull out the lines. Cap the pipe ends to prevent loss of fluid.
4   Unscrew the mounting nuts and withdraw the master cylinder from the bulkhead or servo unit, as applicable. Remove the gasket on non-servo models.
5   Clean the exterior of the master cylinder. It is not possible to overhaul the master cylinder fitted to non-servo models, therefore if it is known to be leaking or damaged the complete master cylinder must be renewed. On servo models proceed as follows.
6   Using circlip pliers, extract the circlip from the mouth of the cylinder.
7   Remove the primary and secondary piston components noting their locations. If necessary tap the cylinder on a block of wood.
8   Clean all the components in methylated spirit. Check the surfaces of the cylinder bore and pistons for scoring and corrosion, and if evident renew the complete master cylinder. If the components are in good condition remove and discard the seals and obtain a repair kit which will contain all the necessary renewable components.
9   Dip the new seals in fresh brake fluid and fit them to the pistons using the fingers only to manipulate them.
10 Reassemble the master cylinder in reverse order to dismantling and make sure that the circlip is fully engaged with the groove in the mouth of the cylinder.
11 On non-servo models check that the foot pedal pushrod protrudes from the bulkhead between 9.0 and 9.6 mm (0.355 and 0.378 in). If not, loosen the locknuts and adjust the position of the stop lamp switch inside the car on the pedal bracket.
12 Refitting is a reversal of removal, but fit a new gasket on non-servo models. Finally bleed the complete hydraulic system, as described in Section 12.

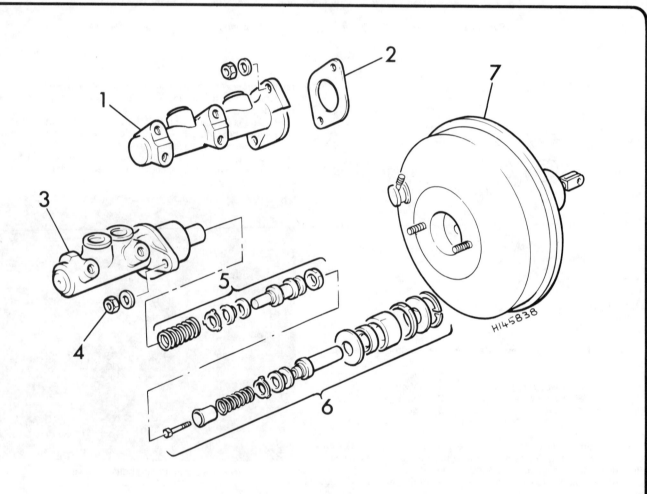

Fig. 8.12 Master cylinder components (Sec 9)

1	Body for non-servo models	3	Body for servo models	5	Secondary piston components
2	Gasket	4	Mounting nut	6	Primary piston components
				7	Servo unit

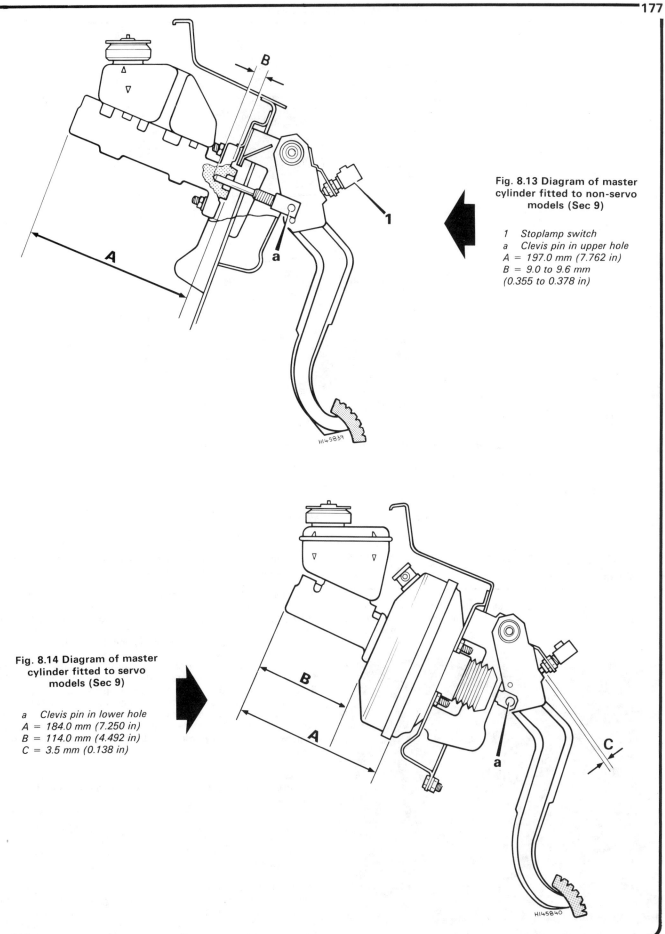

Fig. 8.13 Diagram of master
cylinder fitted to non-servo
models (Sec 9)

1   Stoplamp switch
a   Clevis pin in upper hole
A = 197.0 mm (7.762 in)
B = 9.0 to 9.6 mm
(0.355 to 0.378 in)

Fig. 8.14 Diagram of master
cylinder fitted to servo
models (Sec 9)

a   Clevis pin in lower hole
A = 184.0 mm (7.250 in)
B = 114.0 mm (4.492 in)
C = 3.5 mm (0.138 in)

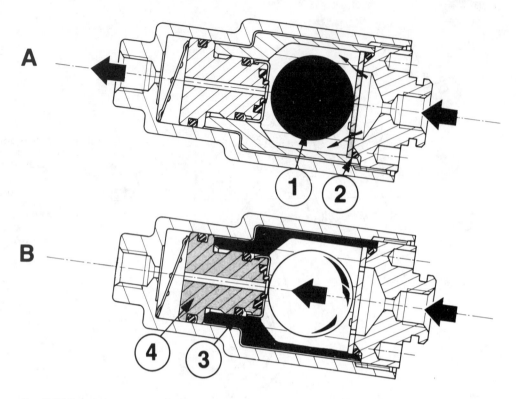

Fig. 8.15 Operation of the inertia type rear brake compensator fitted to GTI models (Sec 10)

A Rest position	B Cut-off position
1 Steel ball	3 Ramp
2 Diffuser	4 Piston

Movement of the ball seals the piston drilling

10 Rear brake compensator (GTI models) – description, removal and refitting

1   On GTI models the brake hydraulic circuit is split front and rear, and an inertia type compensator is incorporated in the rear brake circuit to prevent rear wheel lock-up during hard braking. The compensator is located in the engine compartment on the lower left-hand side panel (photo), and incorporates a steel ball which stops fluid entry to the rear circuit at a preset deceleration.

2   To remove the compensator, first remove the brake fluid reservoir filler cap and tighten it down onto a piece of polythene sheeting in order to reduce the loss of fluid when disconnecting the hydraulic pipes.

3   Jack up the front of the car and support on axle stands. Apply the handbrake and remove the relevant front wheel.

4   Unscrew the union nuts and disconnect the rigid hydraulic lines from each end of the unit while holding the unit on the flats provided.

5   Unbolt the clamp and withdraw the compensator.

6   Refitting is a reversal of removal, but note that the nose of the unit must face forwards and be inclined upwards at an angle of 22° to the horizontal. Provided that the mounting bracket is undamaged, this angle will automatically be achieved. Finally bleed the rear hydraulic circuit, as described in Section 12.

11 Flexible and rigid hydraulic lines – inspection and renewal

1   Examine all the unions for signs of leaks. Then look at the flexible hoses for signs of fraying and chafing (as well as for leaks). This is only a preliminary inspection of the flexible hoses as exterior condition does not necessarily indicate interior condition which will be considered later.

2   The steel pipes must be examined equally carefully. They must be thoroughly cleaned and examined for signs of dents or other percussive damage, rust and corrosion. Rust and corrosion should be scraped off and, if the depth of pitting in the pipes is significant, they will need renewal. This is most likely in those areas underneath the

10.1 Rear brake compensator fitted to GTI models

chassis and along the rear suspension arms where the pipes are exposed to the full force of road and weather conditions.

3 Rigid pipe removal is usually quite straightforward. The unions at each end are undone and the pipe drawn out of the connection. The clips which may hold it to the car body are bent back and it is then removed. Underneath the car exposed unions can be particularly stubborn, defying the efforts of an open-ended spanner. As few people will have the special split ring spanner required, a self-grip wrench is the only answer. If the pipe is being renewed, new unions will be provided. If not then one will have to put up with the possibility of burring over the flats on the union and use a self-grip wrench for replacement also.

4 Flexible hoses are always fitted to a rigid support bracket where they join a rigid pipe, the bracket being fixed to the chassis or rear suspension arm (photos). The rigid pipe unions must first be removed from the flexible union, then the retaining plate must be pulled out and the flexible hose and fitting released from the bracket.

5 Depending upon the make of the particular caliper, the flexible hose may be connected simply by screwing it into its tapped hole or by using a hollow bolt with banjo end fitting. Use a new copper sealing washer on each side of the banjo union.

6 Once the flexible hose is removed examine the internal bore. If clear of fluid it should be possible to see through it. Any specks of rubber which come out, or signs of restriction in the bore, mean that the inner lining is breaking up and the hose must be renewed.

7 Rigid pipes which need replacement can usually be purchased at any local garage where they have the pipe, unions and special tools to make them up. They will need to know the pipe length required and the type of flare used at the ends of the pipe. These may be different at each end of the same pipe.

8 Installation of the pipes is a reversal of the removal procedure. The pipe profile must be pre-set before fitting. Any acute bends must be put in by the garage on a bending machine, otherwise there is the possibility of kinking them and restricting the fluid flow.

9 All hose and pipe threads and unions are to metric standards. Screw in new components by hand initially to ensure that the threads are compatible.

10 Remember that a metric hose end fitting seals at the tip of its threaded section and will leave a gap between the hexagon of the end fitting and the surface of the component. Do not attempt to overtighten the hose end fitting in order to eliminate the gap.

11 The hydraulic system must be bled on completion of hose or rigid pipe renewal.

---

12 Hydraulic system – draining and bleeding

1 If the hydraulic system is to be drained follow the procedure given in Section 2. If the master cylinder or connecting pipes have been removed, the complete hydraulic system must be bled, but if only a caliper or wheel cylinder has been removed then only that particular circuit need be bled.

2 If the complete system is being bled, the sequence of bleeding should be as follows:

Non-GTI models (ie diagonally split system)
> *RH rear wheel*
> *LH front wheel*
> *LH rear wheel*
> *RH front wheel*

GTI models (ie front and rear split system)
> *LH rear wheel and inertia compensator*
> *RH rear wheel*
> *LH front wheel*
> *RH front wheel*

3 Unless the pressure bleeding method is being used, do not forget to keep the fluid level in the master cylinder reservoir topped up to prevent air from being drawn into the system which would make any work done worthless. Before commencing operations, check that all system hoses and pipes are in good condition with unions tight and free from leaks.

4 Take great care not to allow hydraulic fluid to come into contact with the vehicle paintwork as it is an effective paint stripper. Wash off any spilled fluid immediately with cold water.

5 On models with a vacuum servo destroy the vacuum by giving several applications of the brake pedal in quick succession.

Bleeding – two man method
6 Gather together a clean jar and a length of rubber or plastic tubing which will be a tight fit on the brake bleed screws.

7 Engage the help of an assistant.

8 Push one end of the bleed tube onto the first bleed screw (photo) and immerse the other end in the jar which should contain enough hydraulic fluid to cover the end of the tube.

9 Open the bleed screw one half a turn and have your assistant depress the brake pedal fully then slowly release it. Tighten the bleed screw at the end of each pedal downstroke to obviate any chance of air or fluid being drawn back into the system.

10 Repeat this operation until clean hydraulic fluid, free from air bubbles, can be seen coming through into the jar.

11 On GTI models only it is now important to dislodge air trapped in the inertia compensator. To do this, open the bleed screw again and have your assistant fully depress and release the brake pedal rapidly 4 or 5 times, finally keeping the pedal depressed before tightening the bleed screw.

12 With the bleed screw tightened, remove the bleed tube and proceed to the next wheel.

Bleeding – using one-way valve kits
13 There are a number of one-man, one-way brake bleeding kits available from motor accessory shops. It is recommended that one of these kits is used wherever possible as it will greatly simpliy the bleeding operation and also reduce the risk of air or fluid being drawn back into the system, quite apart from being able to do the work without the help of an assistant. To use the kit, connect the tube to the bleed screw and open the screw one half a turn.

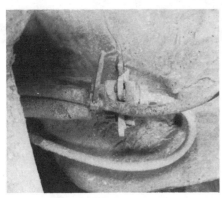

11.4A Front brake pipe bracket behind the suspension strut

11.4B Rear brake pipe bracket on the suspension arm

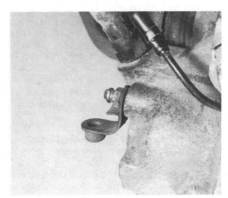

12.8 The bleed screw on the front disc caliper

14 Depress the brake pedal fully then slowly release it. The one-way valve in the kit will prevent expelled air from returning at the end of each pedal downstroke. Repeat the operation several times to be sure of ejecting all the air from the system. Some kits include a translucent container which can be positioned so that the air bubbles can actually be seen being ejected from the system.

15 Tighten the bleed screw, remove the tube and repeat the operations on the remaining brakes, on GTI models first carry out the procedure described in paragraph 11.

16 On completion, depress the brake pedal. If it still feels spongy, repeat the bleeding operations as air must still be trapped in the system.

Bleeding – using a pressure bleeding kit

17 These kits are available from motor accessory shops and are usually operated by air pressure from the spare tyre.

18 By connecting a pressurised container to the master cylinder fluid reservoir, bleeding is then carried out simply by opening each bleed screw in sequence and allowing the fluid to run out, rather like turning on a tap, until no air is visible in the expelled fluid.

19 By using this method, the large reserve of hydraulic fluid provides a safeguard against air being drawn into the master cylinder during bleeding which may occur if the fluid level in the reservoir is allowed to fall too low.

20 Pressure bleeding is particularly useful when bleeding the complete system at time of routine fluid renewal.

All methods

21 When bleeding is completed, check and top up the fluid level in the master cylinder reservoir.

22 Check the feel of the brake pedal. If it feels at all spongy, air must still be present in the system and the need for further bleeding is indicated. Failure to bleed satisfactorily after a reasonable repetition of the bleeding operations may be due to worn master cylinder seals.

23 Always discard brake fluid which has been bled from the system. It is almost certain to be contaminated with moisture, air and dirt, making it unsuitable for further use.

24 Clean fluid should always be stored in an airtight container as it absorbs moisture readily which lowers its boiling point and could affect braking performance under severe conditions.

13 Vacuum servo unit – description, testing, maintenance, removal and refitting

Description

1 The vacuum servo unit is fitted into the brake hydraulic circuit in series with the master cylinder to provide power assistance to the driver when the brake pedal is depressed.

2 The unit operates by vacuum obtained from the engine induction manifold and consists of, basically, a booster diaphragm and non-return valve.

3 The servo unit and the master cylinder are connected so that the servo piston rod acts as the master cylinder pushrod.

4 The driver's braking effort is transmitted from the brake pedal to the servo unit piston and its integral control system.

5 The forward chamber of the servo unit is held under vacuum at all times whilst the rear chamber is held under vacuum conditions only when the brake pedal is in the released position. When the pedal is depressed, the rear chamber opens to atmospheric pressure which causes the servo piston to move forward and so operate the master cylinder pushrod.

6 It is emphasised that a servo unit provides assistance only and, should a fault occur, the normal hydraulic braking system is unaffected except that the need for higher pedal pressure will be noticed.

Testing

7 With the engine switched off, depress the brake pedal several times. The distance by which the pedal moves should now alter over all applications.

8 Depress the brake pedal fully and hold it down then start the engine. The pedal should be felt to move downward slightly.

9 Hold the pedal depressed with the engine running, switch off the ignition and continue to hold the pedal depressed for 30 seconds during which period the pedal should neither rise or drop.

10 Start the engine whilst the brake pedal is released, run it for a minute

and switch off. Give several applications of the brake pedal. The pedal travel should decrease with each application.

11 Failure of the brake pedal to act in the way described will indicate a fault in the servo unit.

12 The servo unit should not be serviced or overhauled beyond the operations described in this Section and in the event of a fault developing, renew the servo complete.

13 Periodically check the condition of the vacuum hose and security of the clips.

14 Renew the hose if necessary.

15 If the servo hose right-angled non-return valve is loose in its sealing grommet, or if the grommet shows evidence of cracking or perishing, renew it. Apply some hydraulic fluid to the rubber to facilitate fitting.

Air filter – renewal

16 Although not a specified operation, the air filter through which the pushrod passes at the rear of the servo can become clogged after a high mileage. Disconnect the rod from the pedal, cut the filter diagonally having slipped the dust excluder off the rod. Fit the new filter.

Removal and refitting

17 Remove the master cylinder, as described in Section 9. Disconnect the servo vacuum hose.

18 Working inside the car, disconnect the pushrod from the brake pedal; noting that it is on the lower hole.

19 Unscrew the mounting nuts behind the pedal bracket then withdraw the servo unit into the engine compartment. Remove the gasket.

20 Before fitting a servo unit, check the pushrod dimensions shown in Fig. 8.16 and adjust where possible.

21 Refitting is a reversal of removal, but fit a new gasket and fully tighten the mounting nuts. Refer to Section 9 when refitting the master cylinder. Finally, with the brake pedal released, check that the clearance between the stop-lamp switch threaded shank and pedal is 3.5 mm (0.138 in). If necessary loosen the locknuts, adjust the switch and tighten the locknuts (photo).

13.21 Stoplamp switch (arrowed)

14 Handbrake – adjustment

1 The handbrake is normally kept adjusted by the action of the automatic adjusters on the rear brake shoes. However, in due course, the cables will stretch and will have to be adjusted in order to fully apply the handbrake.

2 To adjust, first place the handbrake lever onto the fifth notch.

3 Jack up the rear of the car and support on axle stands. Chock the front wheels.

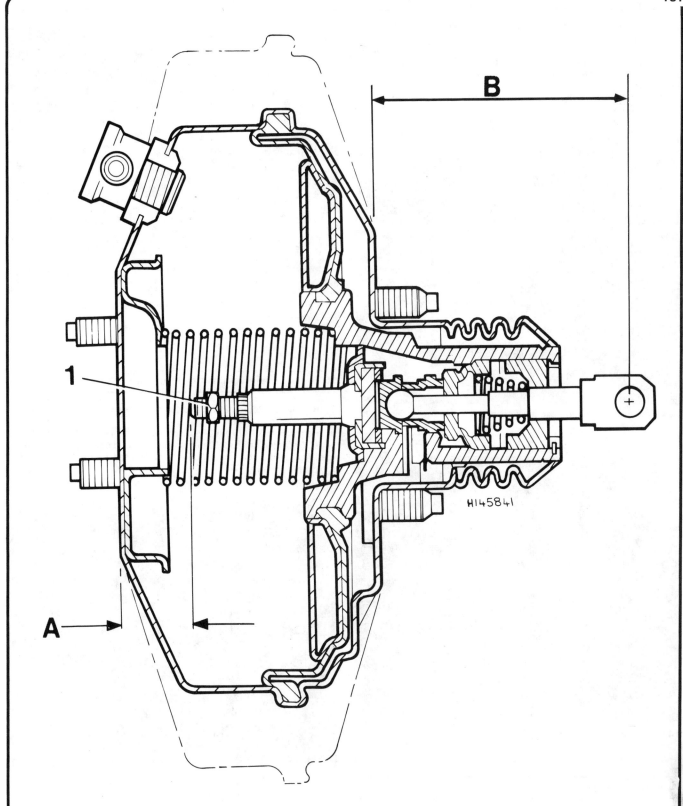

Fig. 8.16 Cross-section of the vacuum servo unit showing pushrod adjustment dimensions (Sec 13)

1   Adjustment screw

A = 22.2 to 22.4 mm (0.875 to 0.883 in)   B = 86.5 to 89.5 mm (3.408 to 3.526 in)

4 Working inside the car, remove the screw and lift the cover from the handbrake lever (photo).
5 Turn the adjustment nut on the rear of the cable compensator so that both rear wheels are just binding on the brake shoes (photo).
6 Fully apply the handbrake lever and check that both rear wheels are locked.
7 Fit the cover over the handbrake lever and lower the car to the ground.

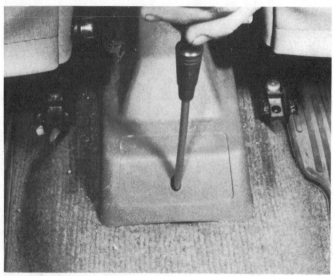

14.4 Removing the handbrake lever cover

14.5 Handbrake adjustment and locking nuts (arrowed)

15 Handbrake cables – renewal

1 Remove the rear brake shoes, as described in Section 4.
2 Working inside the car, remove the screw and lift the cover from the handbrake lever.
3 Unhook the cable(s) from the compensator.
4 Release the cable(s) from the retaining clips, the floor, the fuel tank, and the rear brake backplate(s) and withdraw from under the car (photo).
5 Fit the new cable(s) using a reversal of the removal procedure with reference also to Section 4. Finally adjust the cable(s) as described in Section 14.

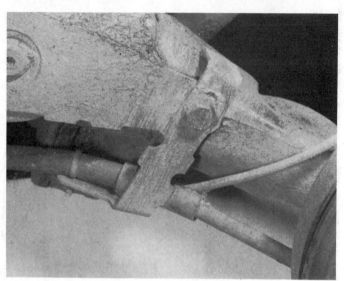

15.4 Handbrake cable clip and bracket located on the rear suspension arm

16 Brake pedal – removal and refitting

1 Remove the lower facia panel from the steering column in order to gain access to the pedal bracket.
2 Remove the clevis pin and disconnect the pushrod from the brake pedal. Note that on models with a vacuum servo unit the pushrod is on the lower hole, whereas the upper hole is used for models without a servo unit (photo).

16.2 Pushrod-to-brake pedal clevis pin – arrowed (note location in lower hole for models with vacuum servo)

3 Unscrew the self-locking nut from the pivot bolt, pull out the bolt and lower the brake pedal. Note that on non-servo models a return spring is also fitted to the pedal.
4 Examine the pedal bushes for wear and renew them if necessary.
5 Refitting is a reversal of removal, but lightly grease the bushes and clevis pin and renew the self-locking nut.

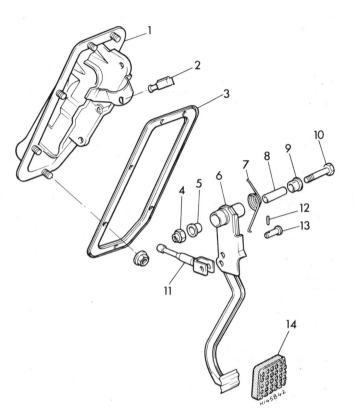

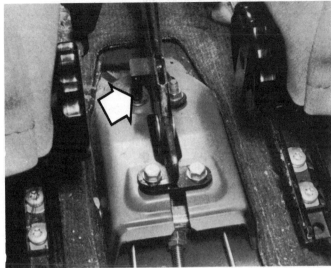

17.2 Handbrake warning light switch (arrowed)

2 Fully release the handbrake then unscrew the adjustment nut on the rear of the cable compensator until both cables can be unhooked.
3 Unbolt and remove the handbrake lever assembly from the floor (photo).
4 Refitting is a reversal of removal, but adjust the handbrake, as described in Section 14.

Fig. 8.17 Brake pedal components fitted to non-servo models (Sec 16)

1	Bracket	8	Spacer
2	Stop-lamp	9	Bush
3	Plate	10	Pivot bolt
4	Nut	11	Pushrod
5	Bush	12	Retainer
6	Pedal	13	Clevis pin
7	Return spring	14	Pad

17 Handbrake warning light switch – removal and refitting

1 Move the front seats fully forward then remove the screw and lift the cover from the handbrake lever.
2 With the handbrake applied, remove the mounting screw, withdraw the switch and disconnect the wiring (photo).
3 Refitting is a reversal of removal.

18 Handbrake lever – removal and refitting

1 Move the front seats fully forward then remove the screw and lift the cover from the handbrake lever.

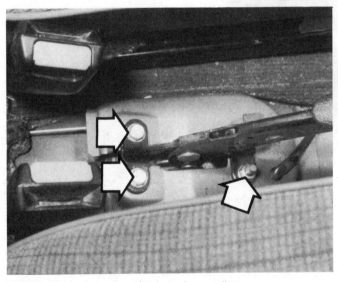

18.3 Handbrake lever mounting bolts (arrowed)

19 Fault diagnosis – braking system

Before diagnosing faults from the following chart, check that any braking irregularities are not caused by:
  (a) *Uneven and incorrect tyre pressures*
  (b) *Incorrect mix of radial and crossply tyres*
  (c) *Wear in the steering mechanism*
  (d) *Misalignment of the chassis geometry*

Symptom	Reason(s)
Pedal travels a long way before the brakes operate	Brake shoes set too far from the drums due to faulty self-adjusting mechanism
Stopping ability poor, even though pedal pressure is firm	Linings/pads and/or drums/disc badly worn or scored One or more wheel hydraulic cylinders or caliper pistons seized resulting in some brake shoes/pads not pressing against the drums/discs Brake linings/pads contaminated with oil Wrong type of linings/pads fitted (too hard) Brake shoes/pads wrongly assembled Faulty servo unit (where fitted)
Car veers to one side when the brakes are applied	Brake linings/pads on one side are contaminated with oil Hydraulic wheel cylinder/caliper on one side partially or fully seized A mixture of lining materials fitted between sides Unequal wear between sides caused by partially seized wheel cylinders/pistons
Pedal feels spongy	Air in the hydraulic system
Pedal feels springy when the brakes are applied	Brake linings/pads not bedded into the drums/discs (after fitting new ones) Master cylinder or brake backplate mounting bolts loose Out-of-round drums or discs with excessive run-out
Pedal travels right down with little or no resistance and brakes are virtually non-operative	Leak in hydraulic system resulting in lack of pressure for operating wheel cylinders/caliper pistons If no signs of leakage are apparent the master cylinder internals seals are failing to sustain pressure
Binding, juddering, overheating	One or a combination of causes given in the foregoing sections Handbrake over-adjusted Handbrake cable(s) seized
Lack of servo assistance	Vacuum hose leaking Non-return valve defective or leaking grommet Servo internal fault

Chapter 9 Suspension, hubs, wheels and tyres

For modifications, and information applicable to later models, see Supplement at end of manual

Contents

Specifications

Front suspension

Type	Independent, McPherson struts, coil springs, anti-roll bar
Coil spring free length:	
Models with engines XV8, XW7 and XY7	492.0 mm
Models with engine XY8	360.7 mm
Models with engine XU5J	335.0 mm
Hub bearings	Double row ball-bearings
Hub bearing lubricant type/specification	Multi-purpose lithium-based grease (Duckhams LB 10)

Rear suspension

Type	Independent, cross-tube with trailing arms, torsion bars, inclined shock absorbers, anti-roll bar
Ride height:	
Except GTI	420 to 434 mm
GTI	403 to 417 mm
Hub bearings	Taper roller (non-adjustable)

Roadwheels

Type:	
Non-GTI	Pressed steel
GTI	Light alloy
Size:	
Non-GTI	4.5 B (or J) 13 FH 4.35 or 5 B 13 FH 4.28
GTI	5.5 J 14 FH H 4.24

Tyres

Size:		
Non-GTI	135 SR 13, 145 SR 13 or 165/70 SR 13	
GTI	185/60 HR 14	
Pressures – bar (lbf/in²):	**Front**	**Rear**
135 SR 13	2.0 (29)	2.1 (30)
145 SR 13	1.9 (28)	2.1 (30)
165/70 SR 13	1.7 (25)	1.9 (28)
185/60 HR 14	2.0 (29)	2.0 (29)

Torque wrench settings
Front suspension

	Nm	lbf ft
Top mounting	12	9
Shock absorber piston rod:		
Self-locking	45	33
Crimped	70	52
Strut clamp bolt	58	43
Anti-roll bar clamp	35	26
Anti-roll bar end (non-GTI)	75	55
Bottom balljoint	35	26
Anti-roll bar guide bar	30	22
Lower suspension arm pivot bolt	35	26
Anti-roll bar end (GTI)	58	43
Lower suspension arm rear pivot bolt (GTI)	78	58

Rear suspension	Nm	lbf ft
Shock absorber upper mounting	75	55
Shock absorber lower mounting	118	87
Anti-roll bar arm	35	26
Torsion bar plug	20	15
Suspension top mountings	45	33
Suspension front mounting pivot bolt	80	59

Roadwheels		
Bolt for pressed steel type	80	59
Bolt for light alloy type	90	66

1   General description

The front suspension is of independent type; incorporating McPherson struts with coil springs and integral shock absorbers. On non-GTI models the lower suspension arm movement is controlled by the anti-roll bar, but on GTI models the arm has two inner pivot points and the anti-roll bar operates separately on the struts.

The rear suspension is also of independent type; incorporating a cross-tube with trailing arms set in each end and supported on needle or plain bearings. Torsion bars are fitted to the trailing arms and, on certain models, an anti-roll bar located inside the cross-tube stabilizes the car when cornering. The telescopic shock absorbers are inclined with their top mountings attached to the suspension side-members. A rubber cone bump stop is provided on each side for times of excessive movement of the trailing arms (photo).

2   Routine maintenance

Carry out the following procedures at the intervals given in Routine Maintenance at the beginning of the manual.

1   Check and adjust the tyre pressures and make sure that the caps are securely fitted to the valves.

2   Thoroughly examine the tyres for wear, damage and deterioration. If necessary, use a trolley jack to raise each wheel clear of the ground so that a complete check can be made.

3   Jack up each wheel in turn, then grip the top and bottom and attempt to rock the wheel. Any excessive play indicates wear in the hub bearings although, on the front wheels, check that the movement is not due to a worn lower suspension balljoint.

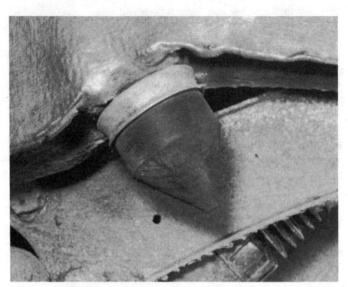

1.2 Rear suspension bump stop

4   Place the car on ramps or jack it up and support on axle stands, then check the front and rear shock absorbers for leakage of fluid. If evident, renew the shock absorber or strut as necessary. The efficiency of the shock absorbers can be checked as described later in this Chapter.

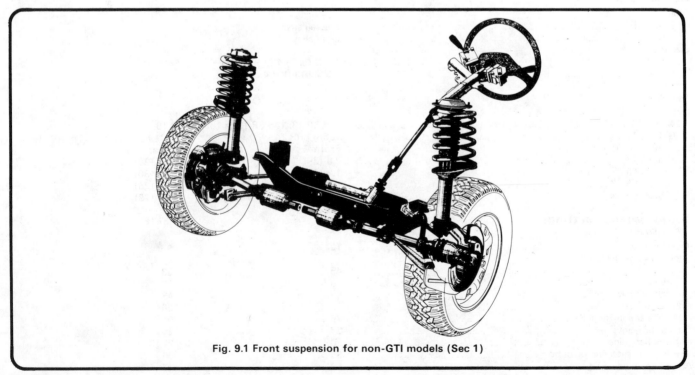

Fig. 9.1 Front suspension for non-GTI models (Sec 1)

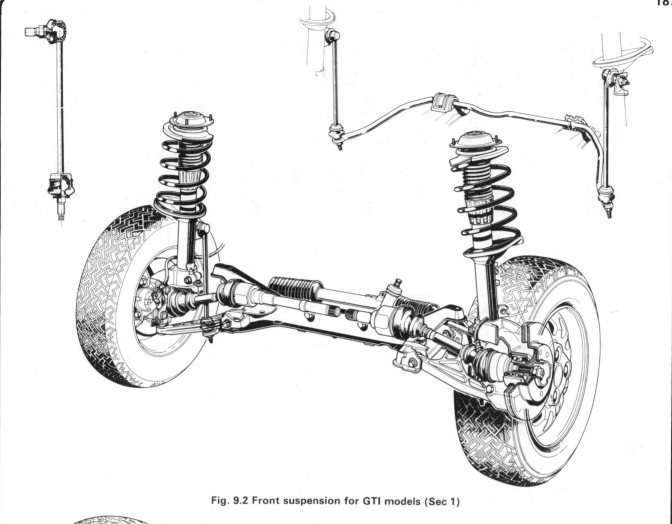

Fig. 9.2 Front suspension for GTI models (Sec 1)

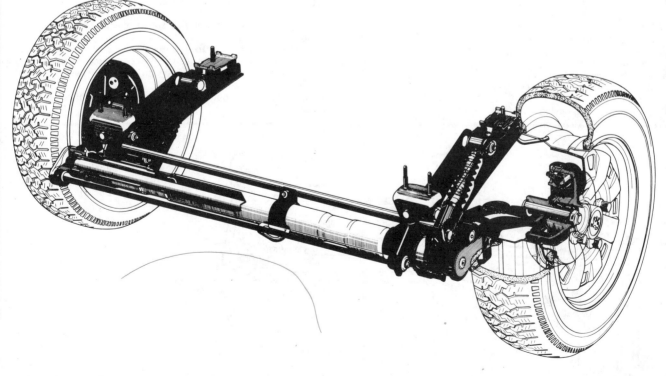

Fig. 9.3 Rear suspension for all models (Sec 1)

3.2 Anti-roll bar mounting in the lower
suspension arm on non-GTI models

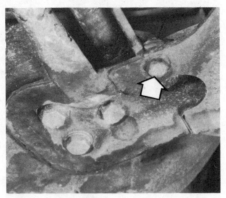

3.3 Anti-roll bar guide bar bolt (arrowed)
on non-GTI models

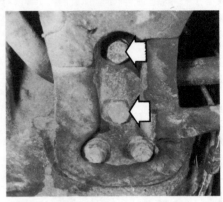

3.4 Anti-roll bar mounting clamp bolts
(arrowed)

3 Front anti-roll bar – removal and refitting

Non-GTI models

1   Remove the lower suspension arm from one side, as described in
Section 5.
2   Unscrew the nut securing the remaining end of the anti-roll bar to the
other suspension arm and recover the washer (photo).
3   Unbolt the guide bar from the subframe (photo).
4   Unscrew the mounting clamp bolts (photo) and withdraw the
anti-roll bar over the subframe.
5   Examine the rubber bearings for damage and deterioration, and
renew them if necessary. The bearings in the suspension arms can be
prised or driven out.
6   Refitting is a reversal of removal, but delay fully tightening the clamp
bolts until the full weight of the car is on the suspension. The guide bar
bolts should also remained loosened until after the bearing clamp bolts
have been tightened and its length should be suitably adjusted (see Fig.
9.4).

GTI models

7   Jack up the front of the car and support on axle stands. Apply the
handbrake and remove both front roadwheels.
8   Unscrew the self-locking nuts from the bottom of the link arms
(photo) and if necessary use a separator tool to release the joints.
9   Unscrew the bearing clamp bolts and withdraw the anti-roll bar over
the subframe.
10 Unscrew the self-locking nuts from the tops of the link arms and

remove the arms from the suspension struts, again using a separator tool
if required.
11 Examine the rubber bearings for damage and deterioration and
renew them if necessary. Check the balljoints on the link arms for
excessive wear, and the rubber boots for any damage. The balljoints
cannot be renewed separately, so if any damage is evident the complete
link arm must be renewed.
12 The left-hand side anti-roll bar bearing incorporates a location ring
and therefore the bearings must always be fitted to their correct sides.
The left-hand bearing is colour-coded in grey or red and the right-hand
bearing in yellow or white.
13 Refitting is a reversal of removal, but delay fully tightening the
mountings until the weight of the car is on the suspension.

4 Front suspension strut – removal, overhaul and refitting

1   Before raising the car it is recommended that a retaining tool is
fitted to the coil spring to enable easier removal of the strut. Peugeot
garages use two special cables inserted through the holes at the top of
the front suspension tower and engaged with further holes in the
bottom coil spring seat. If available use these, otherwise fit universal
coil spring compressors. **Do not** attempt to use any makeshift tool, as
considerable damage could occur if the spring breaks free. To fit either
type of tool it will be necessary to turn the front wheel to full lock in
alternate directions.
2   Loosen, but do not remove, the three top strut mounting nuts
(photo).

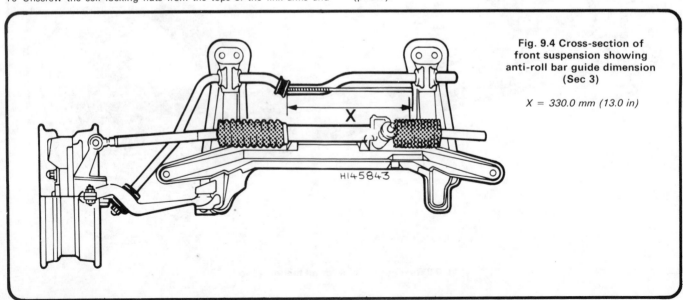

**Fig. 9.4 Cross-section of
front suspension showing
anti-roll bar guide dimension
(Sec 3)**

X = 330.0 mm (13.0 in)

H145843

3.8 Anti-roll bar link arm bottom joint on GTI models

4.4 Hub carrier-to-strut clamp bolt removal

4.2 Front suspension top mounting nuts (arrowed)

refitting to the strut. If the spring is to be renewed, release the compressors very gently and evenly until they can be removed and fitted to the new spring.

13 If necessary, remove the gaiter and bump stop from the piston rod. Note the location of each component to ensure correct refitting.

14 Check the strut for signs of fluid seepage at the piston rod seal. Temporarily refit the upper mounting to the piston rod and, with the bottom of the strut gripped in a vice, fully extend and retract the piston rod. If the resistance is not firm and even in both directions, or if there are signs of leakage or damage, the strut must be renewed.

15 Refitting is a reversal of removal, but note that the bump stop must be fitted with the largest diameter uppermost. Renew the piston rod nut and tighten it to the specified torque. Make sure that the strut fully enters the hub carrier; if there is any doubt about this loosen the clamp bolts with the full weight of the car on the suspension and the strut will be forced fully home. Retighten the bolt to the specified torque.

3   Jack up the front of the car and support on axle stands. Apply the handbrake and remove the roadwheel on the relevant side.

4   Unscrew the clamp bolt securing the hub carrier to the bottom of the strut (photo).

5   On GTI models, unscrew the nut and disconnect the anti-roll bar link from the strut.

6   In order to prevent any damage to the driveshaft joints, fit a length of wire from the top of the hub carrier to the subframe.

7   Drive a suitable wedge into the slot on the hub carrier and slide the carrier from the bottom of the strut. If available, use the special Peugeot tool which consists of a cranked rod inserted in the slot and turned through 90° (see Chapter 7).

8   Support the strut then unscrew the top mounting nuts and withdraw it from under the wing. Recover the washers.

9   Clean away all external dirt from the strut and coil spring.

10 Fit spring compressors to the coil spring (if applicable) and tighten them evenly until the spring is released from the upper mounting. If applicable, remove the Peugeot cables.

11 Unscrew the piston rod nut, if necessary using a 7 mm Allen key to hold the rod stationary.

12 Remove the washer and upper mounting, followed by the coil spring. The spring may remain in the compressed state ready for

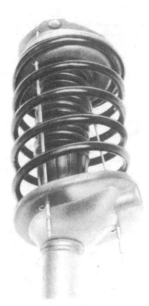

Fig. 9.5 Coil spring retaining cables fitted to the front suspension (Sec 4)

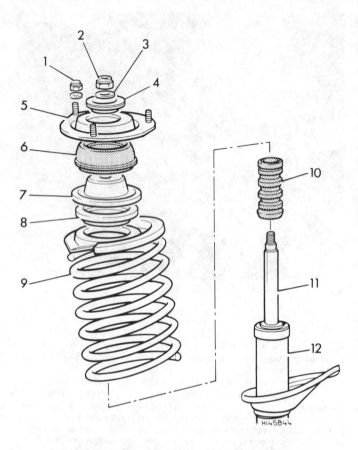

Fig. 9.6 Front suspension strut components (Sec 4)

1	Top mounting nut	7	Cap
2	Piston rod nut	8	Stop
3	Washer	9	Coil spring
4	Spacer	10	Bump stop
5	Top mounting	11	Piston rod
6	Pad	12	Strut

5.2 Front lower suspension arm inner pivot bolt (arrowed) on non-GTI models

5 Front lower suspension arm – removal, overhaul and refitting

1   Jack up the front of the car and support on axle stands. Apply the handbrake and remove the front roadwheel.
2   Unscrew and remove the inner pivot bolt(s), noting the fitting direction (photo).
3   On non-GTI models, unscrew the nut securing the anti-roll bar to the suspension arm and remove the washer.
4   Unscrew the clamp bolt securing the lower balljoint to the hub carrier, then drive a suitable wedge into the slot and release the lower suspension arm. Remove the balljoint protector where fitted.
5   On non-GTI models, lever down the anti-roll bar and withdraw the arm.
6   Check the inner pivot bushes for wear and deterioration. Check the lower balljoint on the outer end of the arm for excessive wear indicated by up and down movement of the ball in the socket. Check the arm for damage or deterioration. The bushes may be renewed using a simple puller consisting of a metal tube and washers, together with a long bolt and nut. It is not possible to renew the balljoint separately.
7   Refitting is a reversal of removal, but delay tightening the inner pivot bolt until the full weight of the car is on the suspension.

6 Front suspension hub carrier – removal and refitting

1   Refer to Chapter 7 and disconnect the outer end of the driveshaft

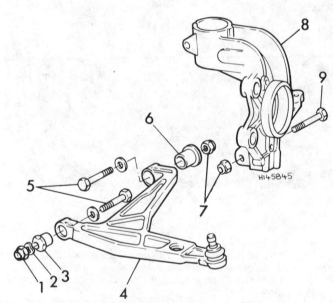

Fig. 9.7 Front lower suspension arm components on GTI models (Sec 5)

1	Nut	6	Bush
2	Washer	7	Nuts
3	Bush	8	Hub carrier
4	Suspension arm	9	Clamp bolt
5	Bolts		

from the hub. Note that it is not necessary to drain the oil from the engine/transmission unit.
2   Unbolt the brake disc caliper from the hub carrier and either place it on a stand or tie it to one side.
3   Remove the two screws and withdraw the brake disc.
4   Unscrew the nut and use a balljoint removal tool to separate the track rod arm from the steering arm.
5   On non-GTI models, unscrew the lower suspension balljoint clamp

bolt, then drive a suitable wedge into the slot and lift the hub carrier from the lower suspension arm.

6 On GTI models, unscrew the clamp bolt then drive a suitable wedge into the slot on the hub carrier and slide the carrier from the bottom of the strut. If available, use the special Peugeot tool described in Chapter 7 instead of the wedge.

7 Where applicable, unbolt the balljoint protector.

8 Refitting is a reversal of removal, but refer to Chapters 7 and 8 respectively when refitting the driveshaft and brake disc caliper.

7 Front hub and bearing – renewal

1 Remove the hub carrier, as described in Section 6. Note that the hub and bearing can be renewed with the hub carrier attached to the track rod and lower suspension arm (non-GTI models) or strut (GTI models).

2 Clean away all external dirt with a wire brush.

3 Using circlip pliers, extract the bearing retaining circlip from the inner side of the hub carrier.

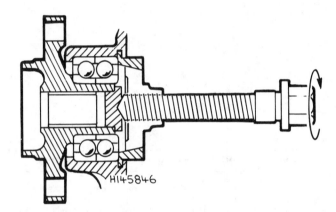

Fig. 9.8 Using Peugeot tool 80613B to remove the front hub (Sec 7)

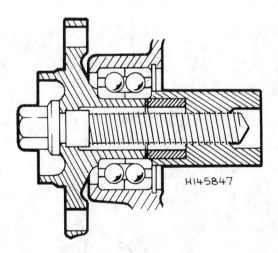

Fig. 9.9 Using Peugeot tool 80613B to refit the front hub (Sec 7)

4 The hub must now be pressed or driven from the bearing using force from the inner side of the hub carrier. If available, use Peugeot tool 80613 B which locates in the circlip groove, otherwise use a suitable soft metal drift. Note that the bearing becomes unsuitable for further use after removal of the hub.

5 Using a puller, remove the bearing inner track half from the hub and refit it to the outside of the bearing.

6 Press or drive the bearing from the hub carrier.

7 Clean the hub and bearing recess in the carrier. Do not attempt to remove the seals or plastic ring from the new bearing.

8 Smear a little grease on the bearing recess in the carrier.

9 Press or drive the new bearing into the hub carrier using force on the outer track only, then refit the circlip in the groove.

10 Press the hub into the bearing inner tracks using the special Peugeot tool shown in Fig. 9.9 or a similar tool made from metal tubing, washers, a long bolt and nut. Note that the tube must locate on the inner track and there must be a space provided to receive the plastic ring which is pushed out by the hub.

11 Refit the hub carrier with reference to Section 6.

8 Rear anti-roll bar – removal and refitting

1 Jack up the rear of the car and support on axle stands. Chock the front wheels and remove the rear wheels.

2 Working on the right-hand side, unscrew the bolt securing the anti-roll bar lever and bracket to the trailing arm. Move the bracket down, leaving it still attached to the handbrake cable.

3 Unscrew the plug from the end of the anti-roll bar then insert a well oiled bolt into the lever and tighten it until the lever is forced off. If available use the bolt included in the Peugeot tool kit 70908.

4 Working on the left-hand side, unscrew the bolt securing the anti-roll bar lever and bracket to the trailing arm, then move the bracket down leaving it still attached to the handbrake cable.

5 Withdraw the anti-roll bar to the left.

6 Mount the anti-roll bar in a vice with the lever uppermost then remove the lever using the procedure described in paragraph 3.

7 Before refitting the anti-roll bar, clean the splines both on the bar and levers and coat them with Esso Norva 275 grease.

8 Mount the anti-roll bar in the vice with its left-hand end uppermost. Note that the left-hand end has an additional shoulder, as shown in Fig. 9.11.

9 Fit a new sealing ring to the left-hand lever. The left-hand lever has a single identification line on its inner face. Locate the ring with the curved end facing inwards and apply some Kluber Proba grease to its outer surface.

10 Slide the lever on the bar with the identification line aligned with the line on the bar shoulder.

11 Press the lever fully onto the splines using Peugeot tool 70908 or a suitable nut, bolt and washer. If the lever is particularly tight it is permissible to drive it on with a length of metal tube.

12 Remove the tool and fit a temporary bolt in the bar to ensure the lever does not move in subsequent work.

13 Where the lever incorporates a 2 mm recess, fit a new seal; otherwise apply some sealant to the lever shoulder.

14 Insert the anti-roll bar into the left-hand side of the suspension tube then position the handbrake lever bracket, insert the bolt and tighten it to the specified torque.

15 Fit a new sealing ring to the right-hand lever. The right-hand lever has three identification lines at 120° intervals on its inner face. Locate the ring with the curved end facing inwards and apply some Kluber Proba grease to its outer surface.

16 Slide the lever on the bar so that the bolt holes in the lever and trailing arm are aligned.

17 Locate a 1.0 mm (0.039 in) spacer between the lever and trailing arm, as shown in Fig. 9.12, then press on the lever using the method described in paragraph 11. If a metal tube is used, the left-hand lever must be suitably supported.

18 Remove the tool and spacer, then position the handbrake lever bracket, insert the bolt, and tighten it to the specified torque.

19 Remove the temporary bolt fitted in paragraph 12.

20 Apply sealing compound to the threads and collars of the end plugs and screw them into the levers.

21 Refit the rear wheels then lower the car to the ground.

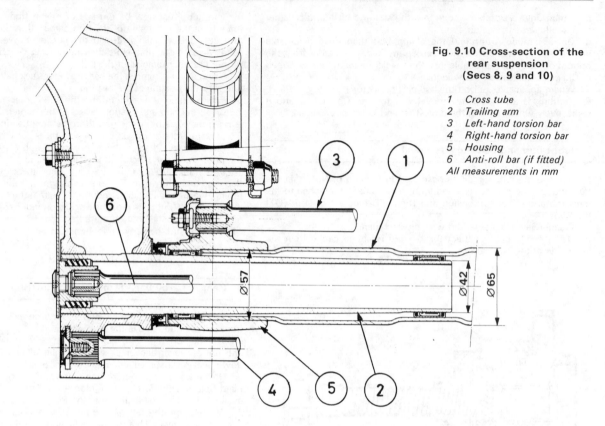

Fig. 9.10 Cross-section of the rear suspension (Secs 8, 9 and 10)

1   Cross tube
2   Trailing arm
3   Left-hand torsion bar
4   Right-hand torsion bar
5   Housing
6   Anti-roll bar (if fitted)
All measurements in mm

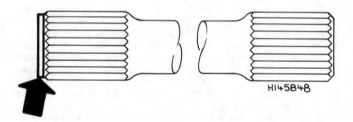

Fig. 9.11 The shoulder at the left-hand end of the rear anti-roll bar – arrowed (Sec 8)

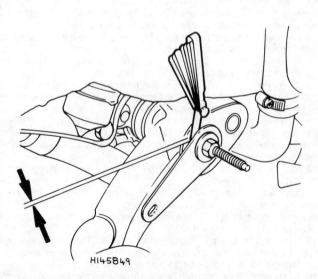

Fig. 9.12 Using feeler blades to check the rear anti-roll bar end gap (Sec 8)

9   Rear shock absorber – testing, removal and refitting

1   The efficiency of a rear shock absorber can be checked by depressing the rear corner of the car then releasing it quickly. If the body rises then stabilises, the shock absorber is good, but if there are several oscillations it should be renewed.

2   Position the rear of the car on ramps or alternatively jack it up and support it beneath the wheels. Apply the handbrake.

3   Unscrew the shock absorber bottom mounting nut and tap the bolt outwards until it clears the shock absorber (photo). If the bolt head fouls the handbrake cable bracket, loosen the bracket bolt on the side of the trailing arm and lift the bracket as required. Do not forget to tighten the bolt after refitting the shock absorber.

9.3 Rear shock absorber bottom mounting

4 Unscrew the upper mounting nut, remove the washer, and tap out the bolt.

5 Withdraw the shock absorber from under the car.

6 A more thorough check of the shock absorber may now be made by gripping the bottom mounting in a vice and attempting to extend and retract it. If the resistance is not firm and even in both directions, or if there are signs of leakage or damage, the shock absorber must be renewed.

7 Refitting is a reversal of removal, but renew the self-locking nuts. The nuts must be tightened when the distance between the mounting bolt centres is 288.0 mm (11.347 in). The Peugeot tool 80911 for this operation consists of a bar and adjustable bolt located beneath the lifting ramp and hooked on the suspension tube; however, loading the rear of the car by trial and error will produce the same result.

10 Rear torsion bar – removal and refitting

1 Jack up the rear of the car and support on axle stands under the body. Chock the front wheels and remove the rear wheels.

2 Remove the rear anti-roll bar, as described in Section 8 (where applicable).

3 Remove the shock absorber on the side being worked on, with reference to Section 9.

4 In order to retain the suspension ride height it is necessary to hold the trailing arm stationary with the torsion bar relaxed. Note that the arm itself must be slightly raised to eliminate the effect of its own weight. If available use Peugeot tool 70908 fitted in place of the shock absorber, otherwise firmly support the trailing arm and record the distance between the shock absorber mounting bolt centres.

5 Unscrew and remove the nut and washer from the torsion bar end fitted to the suspension tube.

6 Unscrew the bolt and remove the seal and thrust washer from the torsion bar end fitted to the trailing arm.

7 Using a centre punch, mark the torsion bar and trailing arm in relation to each other.

8 Support the trailing arm then extract the torsion bar using a slide hammer and adaptor screwed into the end of the bar. When removing the left-hand side torsion bar take care not to damage the hydraulic brake line.

9 Unscrew the shouldered stud from the end of the bar.

10 Note that the right and left-hand torsion bars are different – the right one is identified by one painted ring whereas the left one has two painted rings.

11 If the original torsion bar is being refitted and the ride height is correct, check that the dimension recorded in paragraph 4 is still correct. If the ride height is being adjusted refer to Section 11 and set

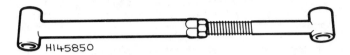

Fig. 9.13 Peugeot tool 70908 for use on a dummy rear shock absorber (Sec 10)

the dimension accordingly. If a new torsion bar is being fitted, set the dimension by raising or lowering the trailing arm to the following table:

Models with engines XV, XW and XY7	340.0 mm (13.396 in)
Models with engine XY8	336.0 mm (13.238 in)
Models with engine XU5J	330.5 mm (13.022 in)

12 Screw in the shouldered stud fully into the 22.5 mm (0.887 in) diameter end of the torsion bar.

13 Coat the torsion bar splines with Esso Norva 275 grease, then insert the small end through the arm and engage it with the splines on the suspension tube bracket. It will be necessary to try the bar in several positions if the original is not being refitted, and the bar will initially only enter by approximately 10.0 mm (0.4 in) as the splines at each end are not in the same plane. When the correct splines are engaged, drive the bar fully into position using the slide hammer and adaptor or a suitable drift.

14 Pack the recess in the arm with grease then fit the thrust washer, a new seal and the bolt. Tighten the bolt to the specified torque.

15 Using a feeler gauge, check that the gap between the trailing arm and suspension tube is 0.05 mm (0.002 in). If it is greater strike the outer surface of the arm with a wooden mallet.

16 Unscrew the shouldered stud at the opposite end of the bar until it just contacts the cup. Recheck the gap, as in paragraph 15, then fit the washer and nut and tighten the nut. To prevent the stud moving hold it with a screwdriver while tightening the nut.

17 Refit the shock absorber (Section 9) and anti-roll bar (Section 8).

18 Refit the rear wheels and lower the car to the ground.

11 Rear suspension ride height – adjustment

1 The rear suspension ride height must be checked with the car on a level surface with the correct tyre pressures and unladen, but with a full

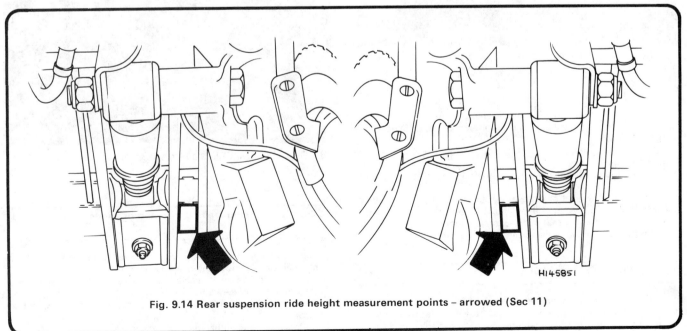

Fig. 9.14 Rear suspension ride height measurement points – arrowed (Sec 11)

fuel tank. The height dimension is given in the Specifications and is taken from the points indicated in Fig. 9.14. The difference between the dimension on each side must not exceed 10.0 mm (0.4 in).

2   It is recommended that the rear of the car is bounced before taking a measurement, and that the average of three successive measurements be taken as the final reading.

3   Note that an adjustment on one side will slightly alter the ride height on the opposite side.

4   To adjust the ride height the torsion bar must be removed and repositioned after setting the trailing arm. A change in the dimension between the shock absorber mounting bolt centres of 2.0 mm (0.08 in) is equivalent to a change in ride height of 3.0 mm (0.12 in). Therefore it is essential to record the existing shock absorber and ride height dimensions before making an adjustment. The torsion bar removal and refitting procedure is given in Section 10.

12 Rear suspension assembly – removal and refitting

1   Remove the handbrake cables, with reference to Chapter 8.

2   Remove the complete exhaust system, with reference to Chapter 3.

3   Disconnect the flexible brake hoses from the rear suspension assembly, with reference to Chapter 8.

4   Unscrew the left-hand rear mounting nut, remove the exhaust bracket then temporarily refit the nut.

5   Unbolt and remove the front clamp and bracket (photo), but do not unscrew the seat belt anchorage.

12.5 Rear suspension cross-tube front clamp and seat belt anchorage

6   Adjust the position of the car on the stands so that the rear wheels are just touching the ground, then place additional stands beneath the suspension tube.

7   Working in the luggage compartment unscrew the front and rear mounting nuts.

8   Jack up the rear of the car and withdraw the assembly from under the car.

9   Refitting is a reversal of removal, but tighten all nuts and bolts to the specified torque. When tightening the front clamp make sure that the ring is centred in the seat belt anchorage bracket. Refer to Chapter 3 and 8 as required and finally bleed the brake hydraulic system.

13 Rear hub/drum – servicing

1   The removal and refitting of the rear hub/drum is described in Chapter 8, together with the inspection of the drum for wear.

2   It is not possible to obtain replacement hub bearings from Peugeot

although they do in fact supply a bearing retaining circlip separately (photo). If the bearings are worn excessively it will therefore be necessary to renew the complete hub/drum unless non-genuine bearings become available.

3   If the hub/drum oil seal is worn or damaged it can be renewed by prising it out with a screwdriver and pressing in the new one with a metal tube (photo). Clean and grease the seal contact surface on the trailing arm before refitting the hub/drum.

13.2 Rear hub bearing retaining circlip (arrowed)

13.3 Oil seal (arrowed) in the rear hub/drum

14 Rear suspension trailing arm and bearings – removal and refitting

1   Jack up the rear of the car and support on axle stands. Chock the front wheels and remove the rear wheels.

2   Remove the handbrake cable and brake shoes on the side being worked on, with reference to Chapter 8.

3   Remove the anti-roll bar, as described in Section 8 (where applicable).

4   Remove the torsion bar, as described in Section 10.

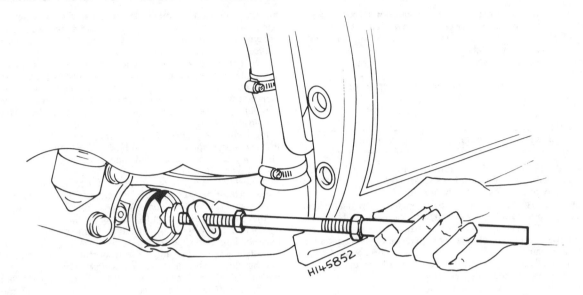

Fig. 9.15 Peugeot tool 70526 for removing the rear suspension trailing arm bearings (Sec 14)

5   Disconnect the hydraulic brake pipes from the wheel cylinder, with reference to Chapter 8.
6   Slide the trailing arm from the suspension tube.
7   Prise the oil seal from the end of the tube and remove the seal sleeve.
8   An extractor is required to remove both the inner and outer bearings and it is recommended that Peugeot tool 70526 is used. The tool comprises a rod and tilting washer which locates behind the bearing – the outer bearing is removed using a slide hammer attachment and the inner bearing is removed using a threaded rod, spacer and nut. If the inner bearing is very tight, a length of rod can be inserted from the opposite end of the tube to release it. Note that the inner bearing may be either of plain or needle roller type.
9   If necessary the shaft may be removed from the trailing arm using a press, but first note the fitted position of the shaft, as on some models it is recessed by 2.0 mm (0.08 in) from the outer surface, on others it is flush. Always refit the shaft in its original position.
10 To fit the bearings, first pack them with multi-purpose grease then use the special tool to pull or drive them into position. When fitting the needle bearings the side with the manufacturer's name on it must face towards the relevant open end of the tube.
11 Drive the seal sleeve into the end of the tube.
12 Locate the new seal over the trailing arm shaft, having first filled the spacers between the lips with grease.
13 Insert the trailing arm in the tube until the seal contacts the sleeve, then position a 0.05 mm (0.002 in) feeler gauge between the arm and tube and use a wooden mallet to drive the arm into position.
14 Refit the hydraulic brake pipe to the wheel cylinder and tighten the union.
15 Refit the torsion bar (Section 10) and anti-roll bar (Section 8) as applicable.
16 Refit the handbrake cable and brake shoes then bleed the brakes, as described in Chapter 8.
17 Refit the wheels and lower the car to the ground.

15 Rear suspension mountings and bushes – renewal

1   Remove the rear suspension assembly, as described in Section 12.
2   Unbolt the rear mountings from the side-members (photo).
3   Identify the front mounting brackets for position then unscrew the bolts and remove the brackets.
4   Saw off the ends of the front mounting bushes then drive them out with a metal bar.
5   Dip the new bushes in soapy water and press them into position

15.2 Rear suspension rear mounting and retaining nut (arrowed)

Fig. 9.16 The notch in the rear suspension mounting bushes (arrowed) must be fitted in the vertical plane (Sec 15)

using a long bolt, nut and spacers. Note that the notch in the flange must be in the vertical plane (ie facing up or down when fitted).

6   Refit the front mounting bracket, insert the bolts from the rear and tighten the nuts with the brackets horizontal.

7   Fit the new rear mountings with the studs towards the wheel side and tighten the nuts.

8   Refit the suspension assembly, with reference to Section 12.

16 Wheels and tyres – general care and maintenance

Wheels and tyres should give no problems in use provided that a close eye is kept on them with regard to excessive wear or damage. To this end, the following points should be noted.

Ensure that tyre pressures are checked regularly and maintained correctly. Checking should be carried out with the tyres cold and not immediately after the vehicle has been in use. If the pressures are checked with the tyres hot, an apparently high reading will be obtained owing to heat expansion. Under no circumstances should an attempt to made to reduce the pressures to the quoted cold reading in this instance, or effective underinflation will result.

Underinflation will cause overheating of the tyre owing to excessive flexing of the casing, and the tread will not sit correctly on the road surface. This will cause a consequent loss of adhesion and excessive wear, not to mention the danger of sudden tyre failure due to heat build-up.

Overinflation will cause rapid wear of the centre part of the tyre tread coupled with reduced adhesion, harsher ride, and the danger of shock damage occurring in the tyre casing.

Regularly check the tyres for damage in the form of cuts or bulges, especially in the sidewalls. Remove any nails or stones embedded in the tread before they penetrate the tyre to cause deflation. If removal of a nail *does* reveal that the tyre has been punctured, refit the nail so that its point of penetration is marked. Then immediately change the wheel and have the tyre repaired by a tyre dealer. Do *not* drive on a tyre in such a condition. In many cases a puncture can be simply repaired by the use of an inner tube of the correct size and type. If in any doubt as to the possible consequences of any damage found, consult your local tyre dealer for advice.

Periodically remove the wheels and clean any dirt or mud from the inside and outside surfaces. Examine the wheels rims for signs of rusting, corrosion or other damage. Light alloy wheels are easily damaged by 'kerbing' whilst parking, and similarly steel wheels may become dented or buckled. Renewal of the wheel is very often the only course of remedial action possible.

The balance of each wheel and tyre assembly should be maintained to avoid excessive wear, not only to the tyres but also to the steering and suspension components. Wheel imbalance is normally signified by vibration through the vehicle's bodyshell, although in many cases it is particularly noticeable through the steering wheel. Conversely, it should be noted that wear or damage in suspension or steering components may cause excessive tyre wear. Out-of-round or out-of-true tyres, damaged wheels and wheel bearing wear/maladjustment also fall into this category. Balancing will not usually cure vibration caused by such wear.

Wheel balancing may be carried out with the wheel either on or off the vehicle. If balanced on the vehicle, ensure that the wheel-to-hub relationship is marked in some way prior to subsequent wheel removal so that it may be refitted in its original position.

General tyre wear is influenced to a large degree by driving style – harsh braking and acceleration or fast cornering will all produce more rapid tyre wear. Interchanging of tyres may result in more even wear, but this should only be carried out where there is no mix of tyre types on the vehicle. However, it is worth bearing in mind that if this is completely effective, the added expense of replacing a complete set of tyres simultaneously is incurred, which may prove financially restrictive for many owners.

Front tyres may wear unevenly as a result of wheel misalignment. The front wheels should always be correctly aligned according to the settings specified by the vehicle manufacturer.

Legal restrictions apply to the mixing of tyre types on a vehicle. Basically this means that a vehicle must not have tyres of differing construction on the same axle. Although it is not recommended to mix tyre types between front axle and rear axle, the only legally permissible combination is crossply at the front and radial at the rear. When mixing radial ply tyres, textile braced radials must always go on the front axle, with steel braced radials at the rear. An obvious disadvantage of such mixing is the necessity to carry two spare tyres to avoid contravening the law in the event of a puncture.

In the UK, the Motor Vehicle Constructions and Use Regulations apply to many aspects of tyre fitting and usage. It is suggested that a copy of these regulations is obtained from your local police if in doubt as to the current legal requirements with regard to tyre condition, minimum tread depth, etc.

17 Fault diagnosis – suspension, hubs, wheels and tyres

Symptom	Reason(s)
Car pulls to one side	Worn front suspension lower balljoint
	Incorrect tyre pressures
Excessive pitching or rolling	Worn shock absorbers
Wheel wobble or vibration	Unbalanced wheels
	Damaged wheels
	Worn wheel bearings
	Worn shock absorbers
Excessive tyre wear	Incorrect tyre pressures
	Worn front suspension lower balljoint
	Unbalanced wheels

Chapter 10 Steering system

For modifications, and information applicable to later models, see Supplement at end of manual

Contents

Specifications

General

Type	Rack and pinion, steering column with universal joint
Steering wheels turns, lock to lock	3.8
Turning circle (between kerbs)	9.95 m (32.6 ft)
Steering rack lubricant type/specification	Lithium-based molybdenum disulphide grease (Duckhams LBM 10)

Front wheel alignment

Toe-in:
    Non-GTI models .... 2.5 to 4.5 mm
    GTI models .... 1.0 to 3.0 mm

Castor:
    Non-GTI models .... 1°15′ to 2°15′
    GTI models .... 1°20′ to 2°20′

Camber:
    Non-GTI models .... 0° to 1°
    GTI models .... −30° to 30′

Steering axis inclination:
    Non-GTI models .... 8°15′ to 9°15′
    GTI models .... 9° to 10°·

Torque wrench settings

	Nm	lbf ft
Steering gear	35	26
Column-to-pinion clamp bolt	15	11
Track rod balljoint nut	35	26
Track rod inner joint	50	37
Steering wheel nut	30	22

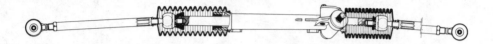

Fig. 10.1 Cutaway diagram of the steering gear (Sec 1)

1 General description

The steering system is of rack and pinion type with side track rods connected to the hub carriers by balljoints. Further balljoints on the inner ends of the track rods are screwed into the rack.

The steering column incorporates a single universal joint at its lower end connected to an intermediate shaft which also incorporates a universal joint at its connection to the pinions on the steering gear. The steering column is angled to prevent direct movement into the passenger compartment in the event of a front end impact.

2 Routine maintenance

Carry out the following procedures at the intervals given in Routine Maintenance at the beginning of the manual.
1   Jack up the front of the car and support on axle stands. Apply the handbrake. Thoroughly examine the bellows at each end of the steering gear for splitting and deterioration, and renew if necessary.
2   Check the track rod ends for excessive wear by attempting to move them up and down. If there is more than the very slightest movement the track rod end should be renewed. Similarly check the track rod inner joints by gripping the track rod through the bellows and attempting to move them up and down. Track rod ends should also be renewed if the rubber boots are split or damaged.

3 Steering wheel – removal and refitting

1   Set the front wheels in the straight-ahead position.
2   Prise out the centre pad, then use a socket to unscrew the retaining nut (photo).
3   Mark the hub in relation to the inner column then pull off the steering wheel. If it is tight a rocking action may release it from the splines.

3.2 Steering wheel retaining nut

4   Refitting is a reversal of removal, but check that the steering wheel is correctly centred with the front wheels straight ahead. Tighten the nut while holding the steering wheel rim.

4 Steering column and lock – removal and refitting

1   Remove the steering wheel, as described in Section 3.
2   Remove the lower trim panel from under the steering column (photo).
3   Mark the column lower universal joint in relation to the intermediate shaft then unscrew and remove the clamp bolt (photo).
4   Remove the combination switches, as described in Chapter 12.
5   Disconnect the ignition switch wiring multi-plugs.
6   Unscrew the mounting nuts and bolts, disconnect the inner column from the intermediate shaft, and withdraw the steering column from the car. Where shear bolts are fitted they must be drilled to remove the heads, then unscrewed after removing the column.
7   If necessary, the intermediate shaft can be removed after prising out the grommet and unscrewing the bottom clamp bolt (photos).
8   To remove the steering lock, unscrew the retaining bolt then, with the ignition key aligned with the small arrow between the 'A' and 'M' positions, depress the plunger in the housing and withdraw the lock.
9   Refitting is a reversal of removal.

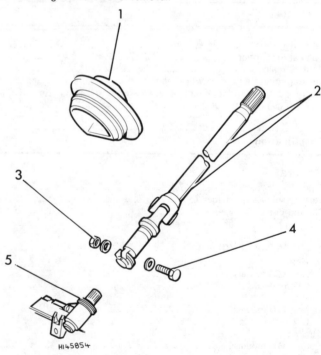

Fig. 10.2 Steering column intermediate shaft components (Sec 4)

1 Grommet	4 Bolt
2 Intermediate shaft	5 Steering gear
3 Nut	

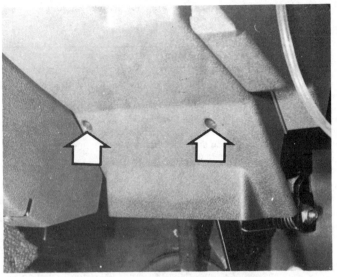

4.2 Steering column lower trim panel screws (arrowed)

4.7B Steering column intermediate shaft (arrowed)

4.3 Steering column lower universal joint and clamp bolt (arrowed)

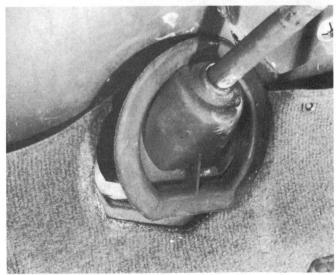

4.7A Removing the intermediate shaft grommet

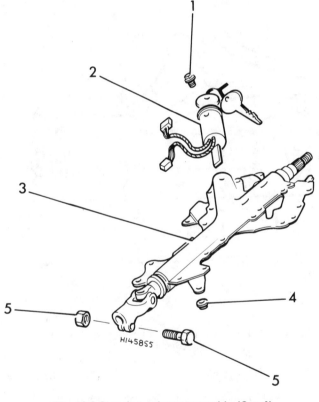

H1458SS

Fig. 10.3 Steering column assembly (Sec 4)

1	Bolt	3	Steering column
2	Steering lock and ignition switch	4	Mounting nut
		5	Clamp bolt and nut

---

5   Steering gear – removal and refitting

1   Jack up the front of the car and support on axle stands. Apply the handbrake and remove the front wheels.

2   Unscrew the track rod end nuts then use a separator tool to detach the track rod end balljoints from the hub carriers (photo).

5.2 Separating the track rod end from the hub carrier

**Fig. 10.4 Steering gear mounting bolt locations – arrowed
(Sec 5)**

3 Mark the lower column in relation to the pinion on the steering gear.
4 Unscrew and remove the column-to-pinion clamp bolt.
5 Unscrew and remove the two mounting bolts and withdraw the steering gear from one side of the subframe.
6 Refitting is a reversal of removal, but tighten all nuts and bolts to the specified torque and check the front wheel alignment on completion.

6 Steering gear – overhaul

The steering gear has a very long life before any wear becomes evident; always provided that the bellows are kept in order to maintain adequate lubrication.

In view of the special tools and gauges required to overhaul the steering gear it is recommended that, when the need for this arises, the assembly should be changed for a new or factory reconditioned one rather than dismantle the worn unit.

7 Track rod end – removal and refitting

1 Jack up the front of the car and support on axle stands. Apply the handbrake and remove the relevant roadwheel.
2 Loosen the locknut on the track rod.
3 Unscrew the balljoint nut and use an extractor tool to separate the taper from the hub carrier.
4 Unscrew the track rod end from the track rod, noting the number of turns necessary to remove it.
5 Screw the new track rod end the same number of turns on the track rod.
6 Clean the taper surfaces then fit the balljoint to the hub carrier and tighten the nut to the specified torque. **Note:** *If difficulty is experienced in loosening or tightening a balljoint taper pin nut due to the taper pin turning in the eye, apply pressure with a jack or long lever to the balljoint socket to force the taper pin into its conical seat.*
7 Tighten the locknut on the track rod end.
8 Refit the roadwheel and lower the car to the ground.
9 Check and if necessary adjust the front wheel toe-in setting, as described in Section 10.

8 Steering rack bellows – renewal

1 Remove the relevant track rod end, as described in Section 7.
2 Release the clips from each end of the bellows then ease the bellows from the steering gear and pull it from the track rod.
3 Clean the track rod and bellows location on the steering gear. If necessary, add grease to the steering gear.
4 Slide the new bellows onto the track rod and steering gear, check that it is not twisted, then fit the clips.
5 Refit the track rod end with reference to Section 7.

9 Track rod – renewal

1 Remove the steering rack bellows, as described in Section 8.
2 Using open-ended spanners, hold the rack and loosen the track rod joint socket. Unscrew the socket and withdraw the track rod.

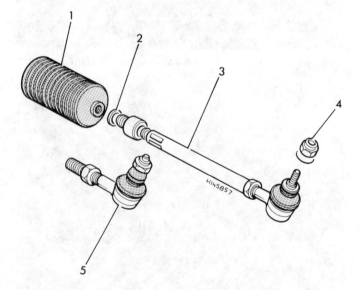

Fig. 10.5 Track rod components (Sec 9)

1 *Bellows*   4 *Self-locking nut*
2 *Lock washer*   5 *Track rod end*
3 *Track rod*

3   Fit the new track rod using a reversal of the removal procedure, but fit a new lock washer and tighten the joint socket to the specified torque.

10 Steering angles and front wheel alignment

1   Accurate front wheel alignment is essential to provide good steering and roadholding characteristics and to ensure slow and even tyre wear. Before considering the steering angles, check that the tyres are correctly inflated, that the front wheels are not buckled, the hub bearings are not worn and that the steering linkage is in good order, without slackness or wear at the joints.

2   Wheel alignment consists of four factors:
Camber is the angle at which the roadwheels are set from the vertical when viewed from the front or rear of the vehicle. Positive camber is the angle (in degrees) that the wheels are tilted outwards at the top from the vertical.
Castor is the angle between the steering axis and a vertical line when viewed from each side of the vehicle. Positive castor is indicated when the steering axis is inclined towards the rear of the vehicle at its upper end.
Steering axis inclination is the angle when viewed from the front or rear of the vehicle between vertical and an imaginary line drawn between the upper and lower strut mountings.

Camber, castor and steering axis inclination are set during production of the car and any deviation from specified tolerance must therefore be due to gross wear in the suspension mountings or collision damage.
Toe is the amount by which the distance between the front inside edges of the roadwheel rims differs from that between the rear inside edges. If the distance between the front edges is less than that at the rear, the wheels are said to toe-in. If the distance between the front inside edges is greater than that at the rear, the wheels toe-out.

3   To check the front wheel alignment, first make sure that the lengths of both track-rods are equal when the steering is in the straight-ahead position.

4   The length of each track rod should be as shown in Fig. 10.6 or very near this dimension. If it is necessary to check the dimension, release the bellows from the steering gear and double it back over the track rod. Refit the bellows after making the check.

5   Obtain a tracking gauge. These are available in various forms from accessory stores or one can be fabricated from a length of steel tubing suitably cranked to clear the sump and bellhousing and having a setscrew and locknut at one end.

6   With the gauge, measure the distance between the two wheel inner rims (at hub height) at the rear of the wheel. Push the vehicle forward to rotate the wheels through 180° (half a turn) and measure the distance between the wheel inner rims, again at hub height, at the front of the wheel. This last measurement should differ from the first by the appropriate toe-in according to specification (see Specifications Section).

7   Where the toe-in is found to be incorrect, release the track rod end locknuts and turn the track-rods equally. Only turn them a quarter of a turn at a time before rechecking the alignment, and release the bellows outer clips to prevent the bellows from twisting.

8   On completion tighten the track rod end locknuts, and refit the bellows clips.

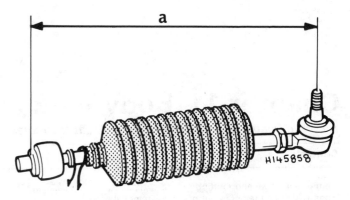

Fig. 10.6 Track rod initial setting dimension (Sec 10)

a = 356.0 mm (14.03 in)

11 Fault diagnosis – steering system

Symptom	Reason(s)
Stiff action	Lack of rack lubrication Seized track rod end balljoint Seized track rod inner balljoint
Excessive movement at steering wheel	Worn track rod end balljoints Worn rack and pinion
Tyre squeal when cornering and excessive tyre wear	Incorrect wheel alignment

Chapter 11 Bodywork and fittings

For modifications, and information applicable to later models, see Supplement at end of manual

Contents

1 General description

The body shell is of one-piece design and safety cell construction, whereby the outer members yield progressively and in a controlled direction in the event of impact, giving maximum protection to the passenger compartment. The body panels are of lightweight high strength steel.

The front wings are bolted to the main body for ease of removal. The complete body is given an extensive anti-corrosion treatment during manufacture; including stone chip protection and wax injection. Peugeot guarantee the body against perforation as a result of corrosion for a period of six years provided the car is given periodic inspections by a Peugeot garage.

2 Maintenance – bodywork and underframe

The general condition of a vehicle's bodywork is the one thing that significantly affects its value. Maintenance is easy but needs to be regular. Neglect, particularly after minor damage, can lead quickly to further deterioration and costly repair bills. It is important also to keep watch on those parts of the vehicle not immediately visible, for instance the underside, inside all the wheel arches and the lower part of the engine compartment.

The basic maintenance routine for the bodywork is washing – preferably with a lot of water, from a hose. This will remove all the loose solids which may have stuck to the vehicle. It is important to flush these off in such a way as to prevent grit from scratching the finish. The wheel arches and underframe need washing in the same way to remove any accumulated mud which will retain moisture and tend to encourage rust. Paradoxically enough, the best time to clean the underframe and wheel arches is in wet weather when the mud is thoroughly wet and soft. In very wet weather the underframe is usually cleaned of large accumulations automatically and this is a good time for inspection.

Periodically, except on vehicles with a wax-based underbody protective coat, it is a good idea to have the whole of the underframe of the vehicle steam cleaned, engine compartment included, so that a thorough inspection can be carried out to see what minor repairs and renovations are necessary. Steam cleaning is available at many garages and is necessary for removal of the accumulation of oily grime which sometimes is allowed to become thick in certain areas. If steam cleaning facilities are not available, there are one or two excellent grease solvents available which can be brush applied. The dirt can then be simply hosed off. Note that these methods should not be used on vehicles with wax-based underbody protective coating or the coating will be removed. Such vehicles should be inspected annually, preferably just prior to winter, when the underbody should be washed down and any damage to the wax coating repaired. Ideally, a completely fresh coat should be applied. As the car ages, it would also be worth considering the reapplication of wax-based protection into door panels, sills, box sections, etc, as a continued safeguard against rust damage.

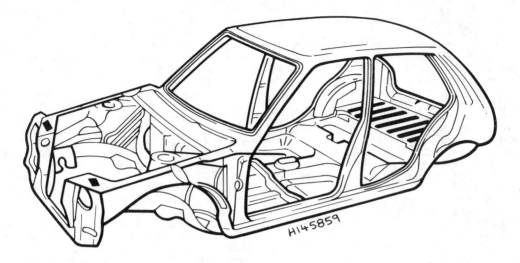

Fig. 11.1 Peugeot 205 one-piece body shell (Sec 1)

After washing paintwork, wipe off with a chamois leather to give an unspotted clear finish. A coat of clear protective wax polish will give added protection against chemical pollutants in the air. If the paintwork sheen has dulled or oxidised, use a cleaner/polisher combination to restore the brilliance of the shine. This requires a little effort, but such dulling is usually caused because regular washing has been neglected. Care needs to be taken with metallic paintwork, as special non-abrasive cleaner/polisher is required to avoid damage to the finish always check that the door and ventilator opening drain holes and pipes are completely clear so that water can be drained out (photos). Bright work should be treated in the same way as paintwork. Windscreens and windows can be kept clear of the smeary film which often appears, by adding a little ammonia to the water. If they are scratched, a good rub with a proprietary metal polish will often clear them. Never use any form of wax or other body or chromium polish on glass.

2.4A Checking a sill drain hole for blockage

3   Maintenance – upholstery and carpets

Mats and carpets should be brushed or vacuum cleaned regularly to keep them free of grit. If they are badly stained remove them from the vehicle for scrubbing or sponging and make quite sure they are dry before refitting. Seats and interior trim panels can be kept clean by wiping with a damp cloth. If they do become stained (which can be more apparent on light coloured upholstery) use a little liquid detergent and a soft nail brush to scour the grime out of the grain of the material. Do not forget to keep the headlining clean in the same way as the upholstery. When using liquid cleaners inside the vehicle do not over-wet the surfaces being cleaned. Excessive damp could get into the seams and padded interior causing stains, offensive odours or even rot. If the inside of the vehicle gets wet accidentally it is worthwhile taking some trouble to dry it out properly, particularly where carpets are involved. *Do not leave oil or electric heaters inside the vehicle for this purpose.*

4   Minor body damage – repair

The photographic sequences on pages 206 and 207 illustrate the operations detailed in the following sub-sections.

Note: *For more detailed information about bodywork repair, the Haynes Publishing Group publish a book by Lindsay Porter called* The Car Bodywork Repair Manual. *This incorporates information on such aspects as rust treatment, painting and glass fibre repairs, as well as details on more ambitious repairs involving welding and panel beating.*

Repair of minor scratches in bodywork

If the scratch is very superficial, and does not penetrate to the metal of the bodywork, repair is very simple. Lightly rub the area of the scratch

2.4B Checking a door drain hole for blockage

with a paintwork renovator, or a very fine cutting paste, to remove loose paint from the scratch and to clear the surrounding bodywork of wax polish. Rinse the area with clean water.

Apply touch-up paint to the scratch using a fine paint brush; continue to apply fine layers of paint until the surface of the paint in the scratch is level with the surrounding paintwork. Allow the new paint at least two weeks to harden: then blend it into the surrounding paintwork by rubbing the scratch area with a paintwork renovator or a very fine cutting paste. Finally, apply wax polish.

Where the scratch has penetrated right through to the metal of the bodywork, causing the metal to rust, a different repair technique is required. Remove any loose rust from the bottom of the scratch with a penknife, then apply rust inhibiting paint to prevent the formation of rust in the future. Using a rubber or nylon applicator fill the scratch with bodystopper paste. If required, this paste can be mixed with cellulose thinners to provide a very thin paste which is ideal for filling narrow scratches. Before the stopper-paste in the scratch hardens, wrap a piece of smooth cotton rag around the top of a finger. Dip the finger in cellulose thinners and then quickly sweep it across the surface of the stopper-paste in the scratch; this will ensure that the surface of the stopper-paste is slightly hollowed. The scratch can now be painted over as described earlier in this Section.

Repair of dents in bodywork

When deep denting of the vehicle's bodywork has taken place, the first task is to pull the dent out, until the affected bodywork almost attains its original shape. There is little point in trying to restore the original shape completely, as the metal in the damaged area will have stretched on impact and cannot be reshaped fully to its original contour. It is better to bring the level of the dent up to a point which is about 1/8 in (3 mm) below the level of the surrounding bodywork. In cases where the dent is very shallow anyway, it is not worth trying to pull it out at all. If the underside of the dent is accessible, it can be hammered out gently from behind, using a mallet with a wooden or plastic head. Whilst doing this, hold a suitable block of wood firmly against the outside of the panel to absorb the impact from the hammer blows and thus prevent a large area of the bodywork from being 'belled-out'.

Should the dent be in a section of the bodywork which has a double skin or some other factor making it inaccessible from behind, a different technique is called for. Drill several small holes through the metal inside the area – particularly in the deeper section. Then screw long self-tapping screws into the holes just sufficiently for them to gain a good purchase in the metal. Now the dent can be pulled out by pulling on the protruding heads of the screws with a pair of pliers.

The next stage of the repair is the removal of the paint from the damaged area, and from an inch or so of the surrounding 'sound' bodywork. This is accomplished most easily by using a wire brush or abrasive pad on a power drill, although it can be done just as effectively by hand using sheets of abrasive paper. To complete the preparation for filling, score the surface of the bare metal with a screwdriver or the tang of a file, or alternatively, drill small holes in the affected area. This will provide a really good 'key' for the filler paste.

To complete the repair see the Section on filling and re-spraying.

Repair of rust holes or gashes in bodywork

Remove all paint from the affected area and from an inch or so of the surrounding 'sound' bodywork, using an abrasive pad or a wire brush on a power drill. If these are not available a few sheets of abrasive paper will do the job just as effectively. With the paint removed you will be able to gauge the severity of the corrosion and therefore decide whether to renew the whole panel (if this is possible) or to repair the affected area. New body panels are not as expensive as most people think and it is often quicker and more satisfactory to fit a new panel than to attempt to repair large areas of corrosion.

Remove all fittings from the affected area except those which will act as a guide to the original shape of the damaged bodywork (eg headlamp shells etc). Then, using tin snips or a hacksaw blade, remove all loose metal and any other metal badly affected by corrosion. Hammer the edges of the hole inwards in order to create a slight depression for the filler paste.

Wire brush the affected area to remove the powdery rust from the surface of the remaining metal. Paint the affected area with rust inhibiting paint; if the back of the rusted area is accessible treat this also.

Before filling can take place it will be necessary to block the hole in

some way. This can be achieved by the use of aluminium or plastic mesh, or aluminium tape.

Aluminium or plastic mesh is probably the best material to use for a large hole. Cut a piece to the approximate size and shape of the hole to be filled, then position it in the hole so that its edges are below the level of the surrounding bodywork. It can be retained in position by several blobs of filler paste around its periphery.

Aluminium tape should be used for small or very narrow holes. Pull a piece off the roll and trim it to the approximate size and shape required, then pull off the backing paper (if used) and stick the tape over the hole; it can be overlapped if the thickness of one piece is insufficient. Burnish down the edges of the tape with the handle of a screwdriver or similar, to ensure that the tape is securely attached to the metal underneath.

Bodywork repairs – filling and re-spraying

Before using this Section, see the Sections on dent, deep scratch, rust holes and gash repairs.

Many types of bodyfiller are available, but generally speaking those proprietary kits which contain a tin of filler paste and a tube of resin hardener are best for this type of repair. A wide, flexible plastic or nylon applicator will be found invaluable for imparting a smooth and well contoured finish to the surface of the filler.

Mix up a little filler on a clean piece of card or board – measure the hardener carefully (follow the maker's instructions on the pack) otherwise the filler will set too rapidly or too slowly. Using the applicator apply the filler paste to the prepared area; draw the applicator across the surface of the filler to achieve the correct contour and to level the filler surface. As soon as a contour that approximates to the correct one is achieved, stop working the paste – if you carry on too long the paste will become sticky and begin to 'pick up' on the applicator. Continue to add thin layers of filler paste at twenty-minute intervals until the level of the filler is just proud of the surrounding bodywork.

Once the filler has hardened, excess can be removed using a metal plane or file. From then on, progressively finer grades of abrasive paper should be used, starting with a 40 grade production paper and finishing with 400 grade wet-and-dry paper. Always wrap the abrasive paper around a flat rubber, cork, or wooden block – otherwise the surface of the filler will not be completely flat. During the smoothing of the filler surface the wet-and-dry paper should be periodically rinsed in water. This will ensure that a very smooth finish is imparted to the filler at the final stage.

At this stage the 'dent' should be surrounded by a ring of bare metal, which in turn should be encircled by the finely 'feathered' edge of the good paintwork. Rinse the repair area with clean water, until all of the dust produced by the rubbing-down operation has gone.

Spray the whole repair area with a light coat of primer – this will show up any imperfections in the surface of the filler. Repair these imperfections with fresh filler paste or bodystopper, and once more smooth the surface with abrasive paper. If bodystopper is used, it can be mixed with cellulose thinners to form a really thin paste which is ideal for filling small holes. Repeat this spray and repair procedure until you are satisfied that the surface of the filler, and the feathered edge of the paintwork are perfect. Clean the repair area with clean water and allow to dry fully.

The repair area is now ready for final spraying. Paint spraying must be carried out in a warm, dry, windless and dust free atmosphere. This condition can be created artificially if you have access to a large indoor working area, but if you are forced to work in the open, you will have to pick your day very carefully. If you are working indoors, dousing the floor in the work area with water will help to settle the dust which would otherwise be in the atmosphere. If the repair area is confined to one body panel, mask off the surrounding panels; this will help to minimise the effects of a slight mis-match in paint colours. Bodywork fittings (eg chrome strips, door handles etc) will also need to be masked off. Use genuine masking tape and several thicknesses of newspaper for the masking operations.

Before commencing to spray, agitate the aerosol can thoroughly, then spray a test area (an old tin, or similar) until the technique is mastered. Cover the repair area with a thick coat of primer; the thickness should be built up using several thin layers of paint rather than one thick one. Using 400 grade wet-and-dry paper, rub down the surface of the primer until it is really smooth. While doing this, the work area should be thoroughly doused with water, and the wet-and-dry paper periodically rinsed in water. Allow to dry before spraying on more paint.

Spray on the top coat, again building up the thickness by using several thin layers of paint. Start spraying in the centre of the repair area and then, using a circular motion, work outwards until the whole repair area and about 2 inches of the surrounding original paintwork is covered. Remove all masking material 10 to 15 minutes after spraying on the final coat of paint.

Allow the new paint at least two weeks to harden, then, using a paintwork renovator or a very fine cutting paste, blend the edges of the paint into the existing paintwork. Finally, apply wax polish.

5 Major body damage – repair

The construction of the body is such that great care must be taken when making cuts, or when renewing major members, to preserve the basic safety characteristics of the structure. In addition, the heating of certain areas is not advisable.

In view of the specialised knowledge necessary for this work, and the alignment jigs and special tools frequently required, the owner is advised to consult a specialist body repairer or Peugeot dealer.

6 Bonnet – removal and refitting

1 Open the bonnet and support with the stay.
2 Using a pencil, mark the position of the hinges on the bonnet (photo).

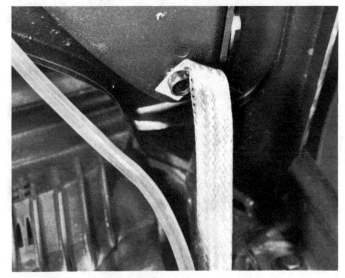
6.3 Braided lead fitted to the bonnet

6.2 Bonnet hinge

7.2A Top view of the bonnet lock

3 Unbolt the braided lead and disconnect the windscreen washer tubing (photo).
4 While an assistant supports the bonnet, unscrew the nut and remove the bottom of the stay from the right-hand suspension tower.
5 Place some cloth beneath the rear corners of the bonnet, unscrew the hinge bolts and withdraw it from the car.
6 Refitting is a reversal of removal, but check that the bonnet is central within its aperture and flush with the front wings. If necessary loosen the hinge bolts and move it within the elongated holes to reposition it, then adjust the bonnet lock and striker, as described in Section 7.

7 Bonnet lock and remote control cable – removal, refitting and adjustment

1 Remove the front grille, as described in Section 8.
2 Unbolt the lock from the crossmember and disconnect the control cable (photos).

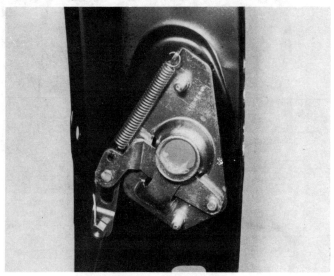
7.2B Bottom view of the bonnet lock

This sequence of photographs deals with the repair of the dent and paintwork damage shown in this photo. The procedure will be similar for the repair of a hole. It should be noted that the procedures given here are simplified — more explicit instructions will be found in the text

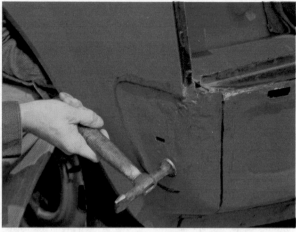

In the case of a dent the first job — after removing surrounding trim — is to hammer out the dent where access is possible. This will minimise filling. Here, the large dent having been hammered out, the damaged area is being made slightly concave

Now all paint must be removed from the damaged area, by rubbing with coarse abrasive paper. Alternatively, a wire brush or abrasive pad can be used in a power drill. Where the repair area meets good paintwork, the edge of the paintwork should be 'feathered', using a finer grade of abrasive paper

In the case of a hole caused by rusting, all damaged sheet-metal should be cut away before proceeding to this stage. Here, the damaged area is being treated with rust remover and inhibitor before being filled

Mix the body filler according to its manufacturer's instructions. In the case of corrosion damage, it will be necessary to block off any large holes before filling — this can be done with aluminium or plastic mesh, or aluminium tape. Make sure the area is absolutely clean before ...

... applying the filler. Filler should be applied with a flexible applicator, as shown, for best results; the wooden spatula being used for confined areas. Apply thin layers of filler at 20-minute intervals, until the surface of the filler is slightly proud of the surrounding bodywork

Initial shaping can be done with a Surform plane or Dreadnought file. Then, using progressively finer grades of wet-and-dry paper, wrapped around a sanding block, and copious amounts of clean water, rub down the filler until really smooth and flat. Again, feather the edges of adjoining paintwork

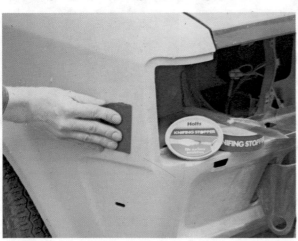

Again, using plenty of water, rub down the primer with a fine grade wet-and-dry paper (400 grade is probably best) until it is really smooth and well blended into the surrounding paintwork. Any remaining imperfections can now be filled by carefully applied knifing stopper paste

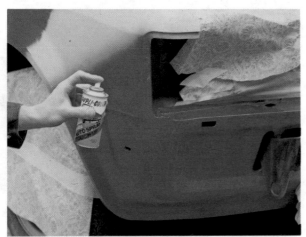

The top coat can now be applied. When working out of doors, pick a dry, warm and wind-free day. Ensure surrounding areas are protected from over-spray. Agitate the aerosol thoroughly, then spray the centre of the repair area, working outwards with a circular motion. Apply the paint as several thin coats

The whole repair area can now be sprayed or brush-painted with primer. If spraying, ensure adjoining areas are protected from over-spray. Note that at least one inch of the surrounding sound paintwork should be coated with primer. Primer has a 'thick' consistency, so will find small imperfections

When the stopper has hardened, rub down the repair area again before applying the final coat of primer. Before rubbing down this last coat of primer, ensure the repair area is blemish-free — use more stopper if necessary. To ensure that the surface of the primer is really smooth use some finishing compound

After a period of about two weeks, which the paint needs to harden fully, the surface of the repaired area can be 'cut' with a mild cutting compound prior to wax polishing. When carrying out bodywork repairs, remember that the quality of the finished job is proportional to the time and effort expended

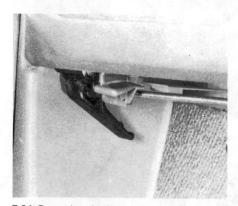

7.3A Removing the bonnet release lever screws (facia panel in position)

7.3B View of the bonnet release lever (facia panel removed)

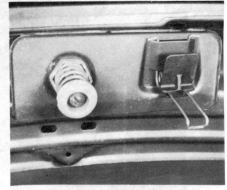

7.5 Bonnet striker and safety spring

8.2A Remove the screws ...

8.2B ... and lift the front grille from the outer ...

8.2C ... and inner mounting holes

3　Working inside the car, remove the cross-head screws from the cable release lever located below the left-hand end of the facia (photos).
4　Unclip the cable and withdraw it from inside the car.
5　If necessary the bonnet striker may be unscrewed from the bonnet and the safety spring unclipped (photo).
6　Refitting is a reversal of removal, but check that the striker enters the lock centrally and holds the front of the bonnet level with the front wings. If necessary loosen the lock bolts and move the lock within the elongated holes. Adjust the bonnet height by screwing the striker pin in or out. Adjust the rubber buffers to support the front corners of the bonnet.

8　Front grille – removal and refitting

1　Open the bonnet and support with the stay.
2　Remove the screws from the top of the grille then lift it upwards from the lower mounting holes (photos).
3　Refitting is a reversal of removal.

9　Front wing – removal and refitting

1　Remove the front indicator lamp, as described in Chapter 12. Support the bonnet in its open position.
2　Remove the front bumper, as described in Section 10.
3　Unscrew the mounting bolts located on the top flange, rear flange and inner rear lower edge of the wheel arch (photo). Access to the rear flange is gained by opening the front door.
4　Prise the wing from the mastic bead and remove it from the car.

5　Refitting is a reversal of removal, but apply mastic to the inner surface of the flanges. If a new wing is being fitted, paint the inside surfaces and apply an anti-corrosion sealant.

9.3 A front wing mounting bolt

10 Bumpers – removal and refitting

Front

1   Unscrew the two front mounting nuts at the brackets.
2   On non-GTI models, unscrew the side mounting nuts beneath the front wheel arches and withdraw the bumper from the car, together with the side mounting rubbers (photo).
3   On GTI models, remove the driving lamps (Chapter 12) then loosen only the side mounting bolts beneath the front wheel arches and withdraw the bumper forwards over the special guides. If applicable, remove the hoses from the washer jets.
4   The brackets may be removed separately if required.
5   Refitting is a reversal of removal.

Rear

6   Unscrew the rear, side and bottom mounting nuts and withdraw the bumper rearwards.
7   The brackets may be removed separately if required.
8   Refitting is a reversal of removal.

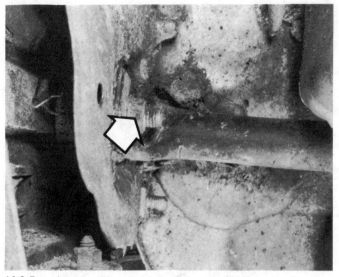

10.2 Front bumper side mounting nut (arrowed)

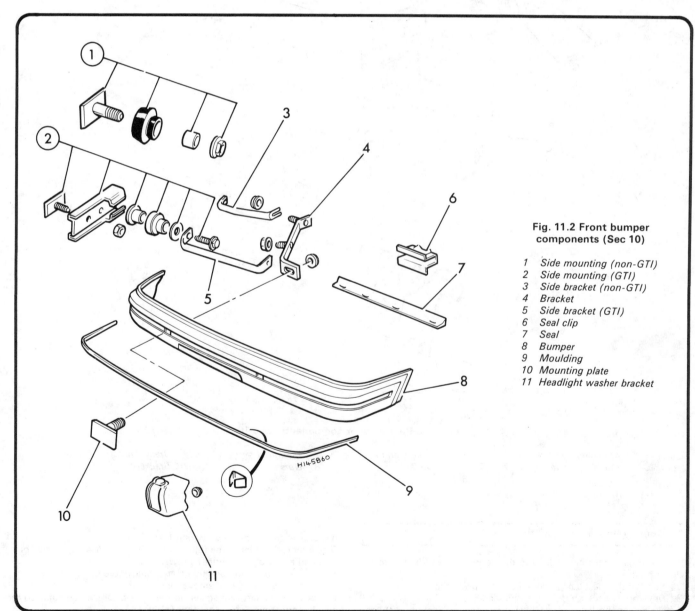

Fig. 11.2 Front bumper components (Sec 10)

1   Side mounting (non-GTI)
2   Side mounting (GTI)
3   Side bracket (non-GTI)
4   Bracket
5   Side bracket (GTI)
6   Seal clip
7   Seal
8   Bumper
9   Moulding
10 Mounting plate
11 Headlight washer bracket

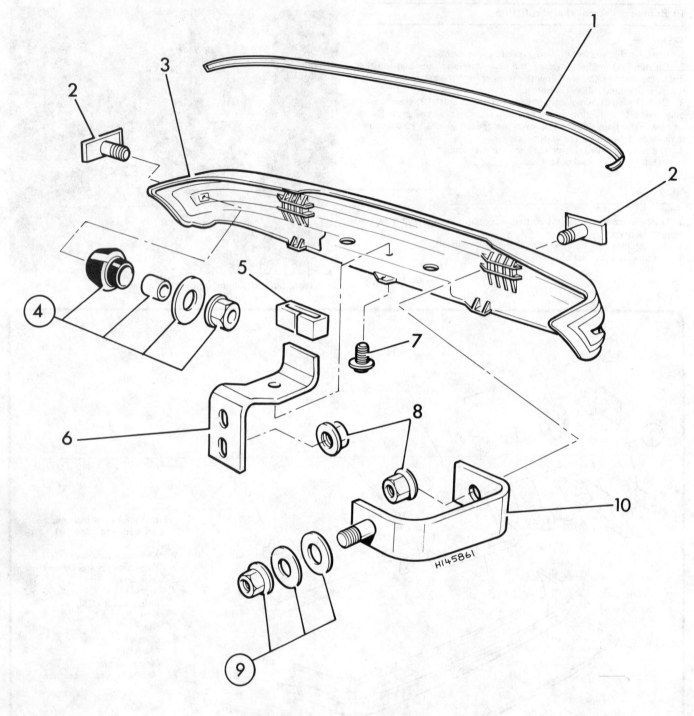

Fig. 11.3 Rear bumper components (Sec 10)

1 Moulding	4 Side mounting and nut	7 Mounting bolt	9 Bracket nut and washers
2 Mounting plates	5 Rubber buffer	8 Nuts	10 Bracket
3 Bumper	6 Bracket		

11 Door – removal and refitting

1   The door hinges are welded to the body pillar and bolted to the door (photo).
2   Remove the plastic caps from the hinge pivot pins.
3   Drive out the roll pin from the door check strap.
4   Where applicable, remove the trim panel (Section 12) and

disconnect the loudspeaker wiring from the door.
5   Support the door in the fully open position by placing blocks, or a jack and a pad of rag, under its lower edge.
6   Drive out the hinge pivot pins and remove the door.
7   Refit by reversing the removal operations.
8   Where necessary, the striker on the body pillar may be adjusted to ensure correct closure of the door (photo).

11.1 Door hinge

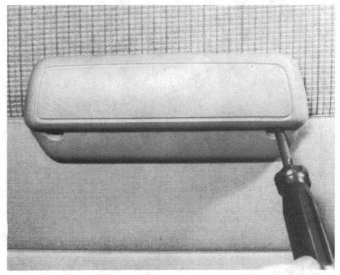

12.1 Removing the armrest

11.8 Front door striker

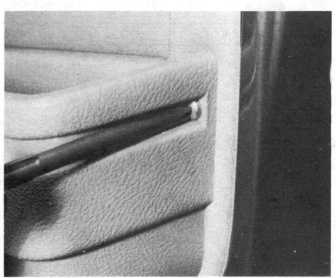

12.2 Removing the side pocket

12 Door trim panel – removal and refitting

Front doors

1   Remove the two screws and withdraw the armrest (photo).
2   Remove the screws and withdraw the side pocket (photo).
3   Fully close the window and note the position of the window regulator handle, then pull the handle from the spindle (photo).
4   Prise out the interior door handle surround (photo).
5   Using a wide-bladed screwdriver, or similar tool, prise the trim panel from the door – working progressively from the bottom upwards and inserting the screwdriver adjacent to each clip.
6   Refitting is a reversal of removal, but first make sure that the clips are correctly located in the panel.

Rear doors

7   The procedure is as given for the front doors, but there are slight trim differences.

Models with electric windows

8   The procedure is basically the same as given previously, but there will be no regulator handle to remove. Be sure to disconnect the battery before releasing the motor switch wiring.

12.3 Removing the window regulator handle

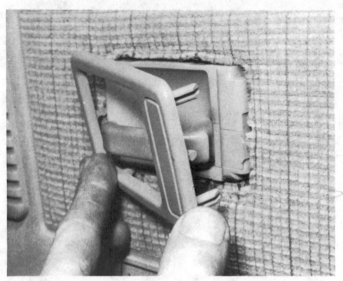

12.4 Removing the interior door handle surround

13.2B The window regulator lifting arms and window glass channel

13 Door – dismantling and reassembly

1   Remove the trim panel, as described in Section 12.

Window regulator

2   To remove the window regulator, unscrew the mounting nuts, slide the two lifting arms from the channels, and withdraw the regulator through the access aperture (photos). Support the glass during this operation.

Door lock

3   To remove the door lock and inner remote handle, disconnect the link rods as necessary and, unscrew the Torx screws retaining the lock (photos).

Exterior handle

4   To remove the exterior handle, disconnect the link rod and unscrew the bolts. The private lock is removed by disconnecting the link rod and pulling out the retaining clip (photo).

13.3A Door lock and mounting screws

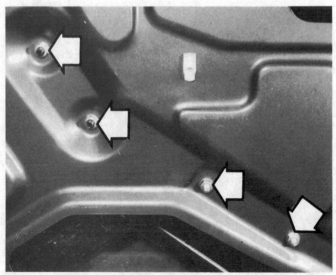

13.2A Window regulator mounting nuts (arrowed)

13.3B Door inner remote handle

13.4 View of the private lock from inside the door

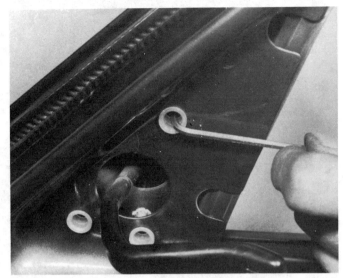

13.6B ... and remove the exterior mirror mounting screws

Door glass
5   To remove the door glass, first remove the window regulator then unbolt the glass side channels, tilt the glass and withdraw it upwards.

Exterior mirror
6   To remove the exterior mirror, prise off the inner cover and use an Allen key to remove the mounting screws (photos).

General reassembly
7   Reassembly of the door is a reversal of the dismantling procedure. However, when refitting the door glass, adjust the position of the side channels so that the glass moves smoothly without excessive play.

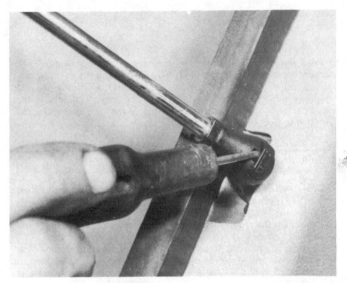

14 Tailgate – removal and refitting

1   Open the tailgate and have an assistant support it.
2   Disconnect the struts from the body by prising out the plastic clips and pulling off the sockets (photos).
3   Disconnect the wiring for the heated rear window and tailgate wiper motor. Also disconnect the washer tube.

14.2A Prise out the plastic clips ...

13.6A Remove the inner cover ...

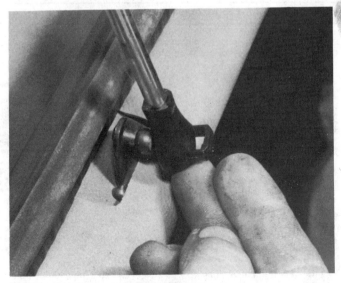

14.2B ... and disconnect the tailgate struts

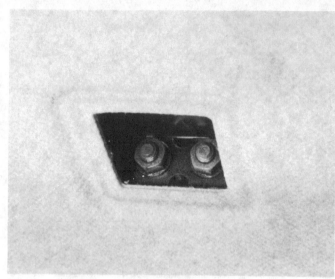

14.4 Tailgate mounting nuts behind the headlining

event of breakage. Special equipment and adhesive are required for removal of the old glass and fitting of the new, which may not be readily available to the home mechanic.

17 Rear quarter glass (GTI models) – removal and refitting

1   Open the quarter window and remove the screw securing the glass to the latch. Remove the special nut from the glass.
2   Open the window further then support it and remove the screws securing the glass to the front hinges. Remove the special nuts.
3   Refitting is a reversal of removal.

18 Seats – removal and refitting

Front
1   Move the seat fully forward and remove the rear inner mounting bolts (photo).
2   Remove the remaining mounting bolts from under the car and from the brackets, then remove the seat from the car (photo).
3   Refitting is a reversal of removal.

Rear
4   Fold the cushion forwards and unbolt it from the hinges (photo).
5   Fold the backrest down, unscrew the nuts from the outer pivot bracket(s) (photo) and withdraw the backrest from the inner pivot (where applicable).
6   Refitting is a reversal of removal.

4   Prise the blanking plates from the rear of the headlining, then unscrew the mounting nuts and lift the tailgate from the car (photo).
5   Refitting is a reversal of removal, but before fully tightening the mounting nuts check that the tailgate is positioned centrally in the body aperture and make any adjustments to the lock and striker, as described in Section 15.

15 Tailgate lock – removal and refitting

1   Open the tailgate and prise off the trim panel using a wide-bladed screwdriver (photo).
2   Unbolt the latch and disconnect the operating rod.
3   Slide out the spring clip and withdraw the lock barrel and escutcheon (photo).
4   Refitting is a reversal of removal. Check that the latch engages the striker correctly and, if necessary, adjust the striker position within the elongated bolt holes. Adjust the rubber stops so that the tailgate is supported firmly at the corners when shut (photo).

16 Windscreen and tailgate glass – general

Both the windscreen and tailgate glass are bonded in position and therefore it is recommended that a professional filter is employed in the

19 Grab handles – removal and refitting

1   Prise up the cover plates for access to the screws (photo).
2   Remove the screws and the grab handles.
3   Refitting is a reversal of removal.

20 Sunroof – general

1   The sunroof fitted to some models incorporates an outer glass and inner cover. The control handle operates lock latches located at the rear of the sunroof. The handle also operates a vacuum seal system which holds and seals the sunroof in any desired position (photo).
2   The vacuum seal is operated by engine vacuum. With the handle shut, the vacuum valve is closed and the seal exerts pressure under the periphery of the glass. When the handle is opened, the vacuum valve opens and causes the seal to collapse, enabling the glass to be moved.
3   It is recommended that removal and refitting of the sunroof be entrusted to a Peugeot dealer.

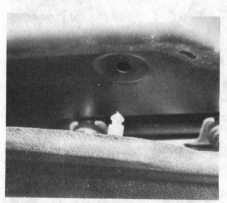

15.1 Tailgate trim panel clip

15.3 Tailgate lock and lock barrel

15.4 Tailgate rubber stop

18.1 Front seat rear inner mounting bolts

18.2 The front seat rear outer mounting on a GTI model

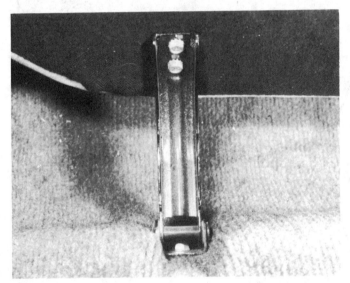

18.4 Rear seat cushion hinge

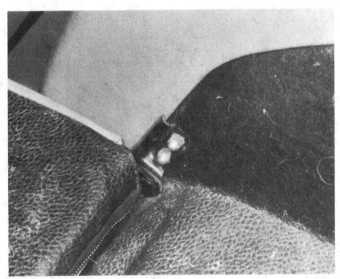

18.5 Rear seat backrest outer pivot bracket

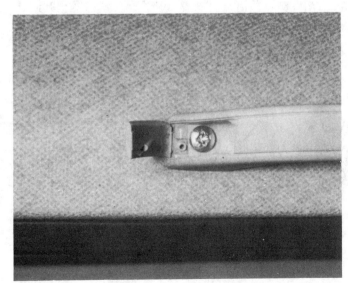

19.1 Grab handle mounting screw location

20.1 Sunroof handle in open position

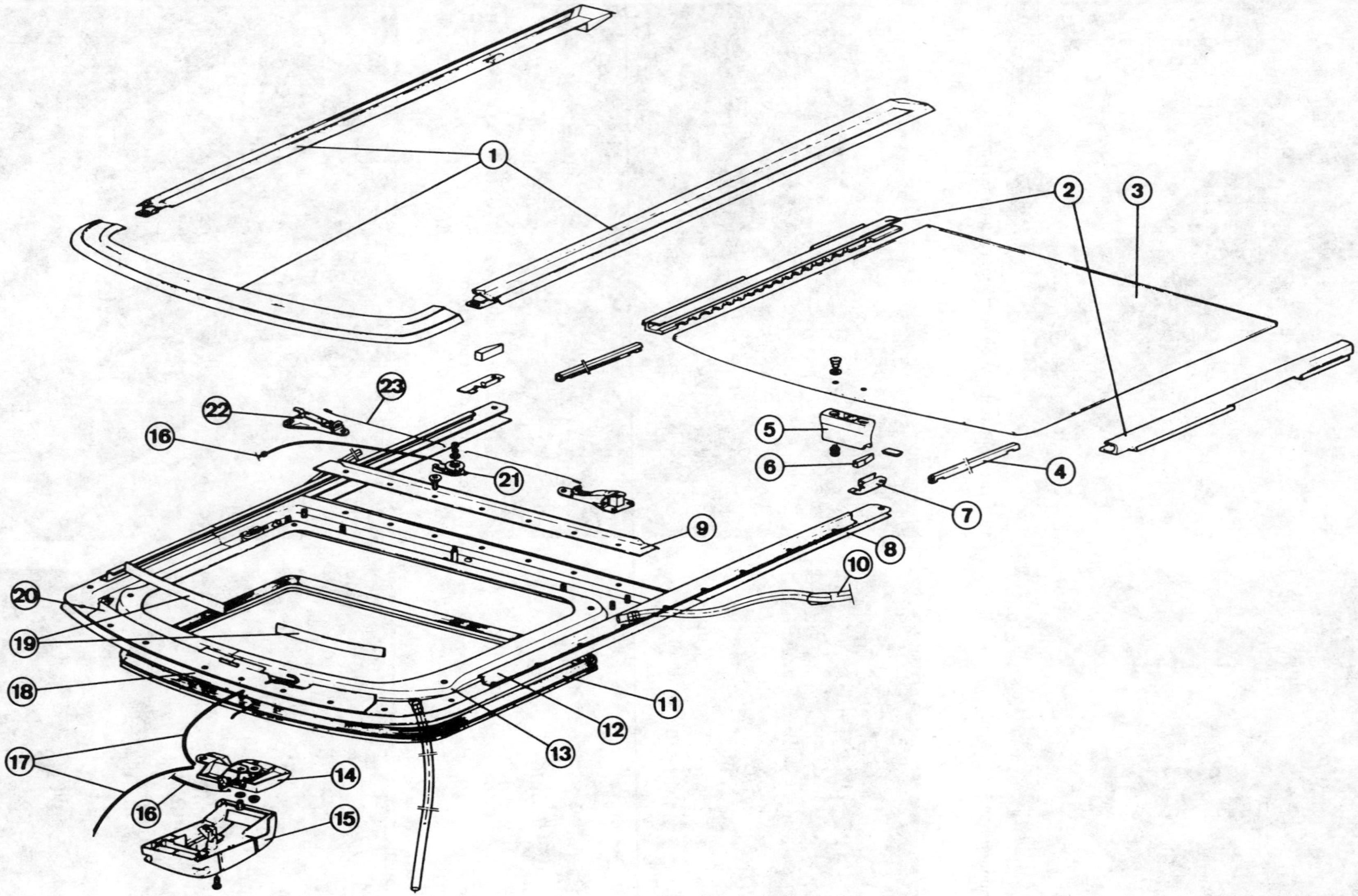

Fig. 11.4 Sunroof components (Sec 20)

1 Cover and slide
2 Glass channel
3 Glass
4 Support
5 Latch

6 Rear stop
7 Support
8 Rear seal
9 Glass seal
10 Water drain pipes

11 Vacuum seal
12 Slide
13 Frame
14 Handle
15 Console

16 Control cable
17 Vacuum pipe
18 Front seal
19 Stop

20 Support
21 Swivel
22 Latch
23 Control rod

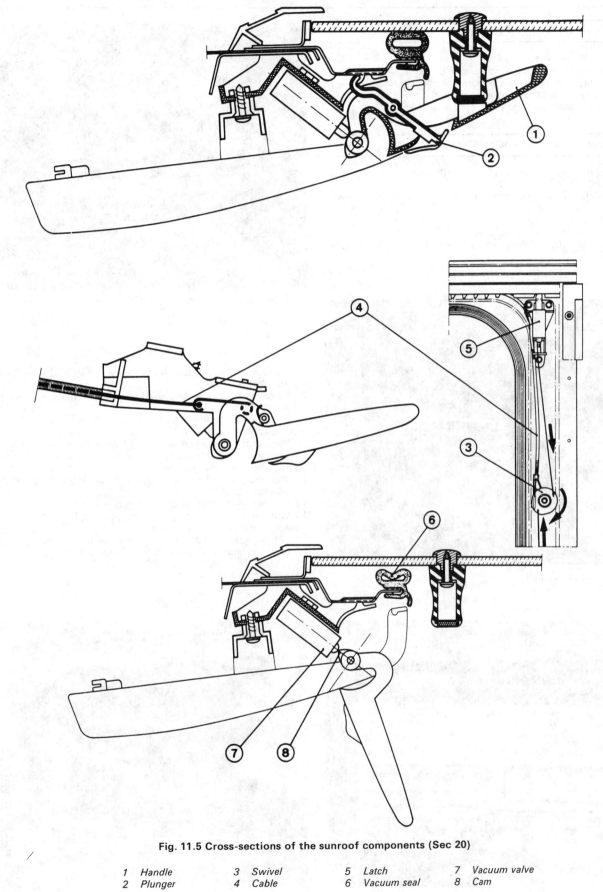

Fig. 11.5 Cross-sections of the sunroof components (Sec 20)

1 Handle	3 Swivel	5 Latch	7 Vacuum valve
2 Plunger	4 Cable	6 Vacuum seal	8 Cam

21 Glovebox – removal and refitting

1   Open the glovebox.
2   Remove the pivot retainers from under the facia, disconnect the pivots from the hinge plates and withdraw the glovebox.
3   If necessary the striker can be unbolted and removed.
4   Refitting is a reversal of removal.

22 Facia panel – removal and refitting

1   Remove the steering wheel (Chapter 10) and instrument panel (Chapter 12).
2   Remove the screws and withdraw the steering column lower shroud.
3   Remove the ashtray (photo).
4   Prise out the central air vents (photo).
5   Prise out the digital clock which is retained by plastic barbs (photo).

22.5 Digital clock and retaining barbs (arrowed)

22.3 Removing the ashtray

6   Using a hooked instrument, withdraw the rear of the oddments recess (photo).
7   Remove the radio, as described in Chapter 12, or prise out the blank (as required).
8   Remove the handbrake lever surround and centre console, noting that the console is held at the stop by plastic clips (photo).
9   Remove the screw from inside the ashtray recess (photo).
10 Unscrew the facia bottom mounting bolts including the one on the bonnet release handle (photo).
11 With the glovebox open, remove the mounting screw located near the glovebox lamp (photo).
12 Remove the central lower panels (photo).
13 With the bonnet open, remove the plastic grille and unscrew the front facia mounting nuts (photo).
14 Withdraw the facia panel at the same time disconnecting the relevant switches and cigar lighter. Reconnect the switch wiring immediately to ensure correct refitting.
15 Refitting is a reversal of removal.

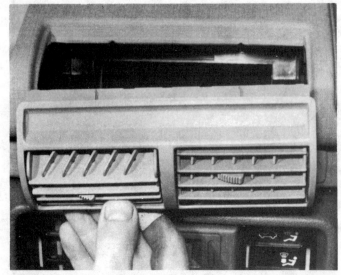

22.4 Removing the central air vents

22.6 Removing the rear of the oddments tray

22.8 Centre console upper clip (arrowed)

22.9 Facia mounting screw located in the ashtray recess (arrowed)

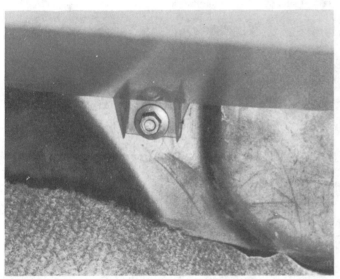

22.10 A facia bottom mounting bolt

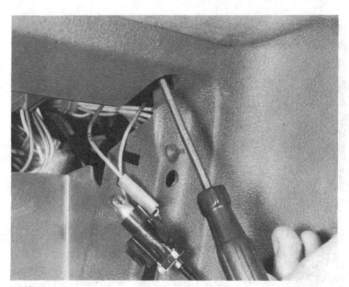

22.11 Removing a facia mounting screw

22.12 Facia central lower panels and bracket

22.13 Facia front mounting nut

23 Heater assembly – removal, dismantling and refitting

1   Remove the facia panel, as described in Section 22.
2   Disconnect the lower air vents (photo).
3   Note the position of the wiring loom and switches then remove the clips and withdraw the wiring to the left (photo). Lower the fuse board with reference to Chapter 12, Section 11.
4   Drain the cooling system, with reference to Chapter 2, and disconnect the heater hoses located on the bulkhead in the engine compartment.
5   Unscrew the five heater assembly mounting nuts and withdraw it from the car (photos).
6   To remove the matrix, disconnect the pipe clip and unscrew the mounting screws then slide the matrix from the casing. If necessary the pipes can be removed by unscrewing the flange screws (photo). Use water from a hose to clean both the inside and outside of accumulated debris.
7   To remove the heater blower, unscrew the mounting screws and lift the unit from the casing (photos).
8   If necessary remove the heater control panel and cable (photos).
9   Refitting is a reversal of removal, but fill the cooling system with reference to Chapter 2.

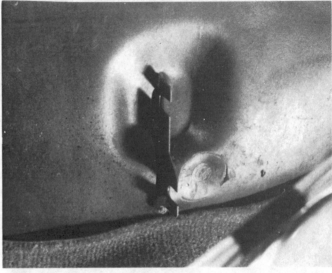

23.5A Heater lower mounting bracket

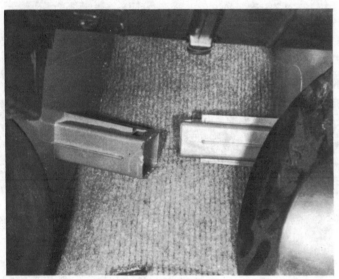

23.2 Disconnecting the lower air vents

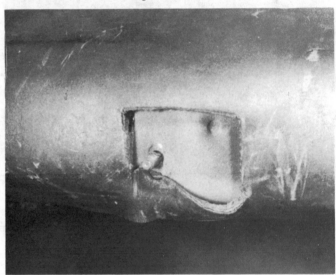

23.5B Left-hand heater mounting

23.3 Wiring loom with facia removed

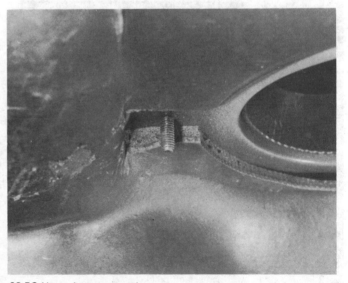

23.5C Upper heater mounting

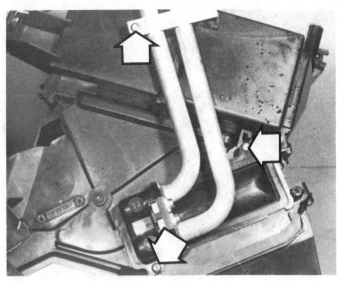

23.6A Heater matrix mounting screws (arrowed)

23.6B Removing the heater matrix

23.6C Heater matrix pipes and flanges

23.7A Remove the mounting screws ...

23.7B ... and lift out the heater blower unit

23.8A Heater control panel

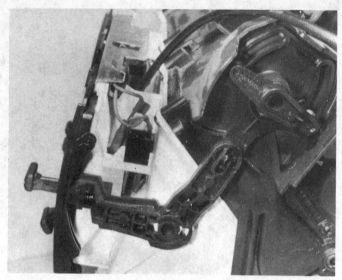

23.8B Heater air inlet control levers

23.8C Heater fresh air control levers and cable

23.8D Heater temperature control levers

Chapter 12 Electrical system

For modifications, and information applicable to later models, see Supplement at end of manual

Contents

Specifications

System type .... 12 volt negative earth, battery, alternator, and pre-engaged starter motor

Battery

XV8 and XW7 engines	150 amp; 25 amp/hour
XY7 and XY8 engines	175 amp; 29 amp/hour
XU5J engine	175 amp; 29 amp/hour or 200 amp; 33 amp/hour

Alternator

Rating	750 watt
Drivebelt tension:	
XV8, XW7, XY7 and XY8 engines	Deflection: 12.5 mm
XU5J engine:	
Without tensioner	Deflection: approx 6.0 mm
Using Krikit tensioner	60 kg/span (new belt) or 40 kg/span (used belt)

Starter motor

Type	Pre-engaged
Minimum brush length	12.7 mm
Starter drive pinion-to-stop clearance with solenoid energised	1.5 mm

Fuses

No	Circuit protected	Rating (amp)
1	Reverse lamp, cooling fan relay, tachometer (GTI)	10
2	Accessories, indicators, fuel gauge, warning lights, heater blower motor	25
3	Ignition switch, wash/wipe system, stop-lamps, tachometer (non-GTI option), radio, heated rear window, electric window relay (option), clock illumination (GTI)	25

No	Circuit protected	Rating (amp)
4	Central door locking (option)	10
5	Cooling fan	25
6	Hazard warning switch	10
7	Spare	–
8	Cigarette lighter, clock, interior lamps, glovebox illumination, radio	20
9	Electric front windows	25
10	Heated rear window, horns	20
11	Rear foglamp	5
12	Side/tail lamps/warning light, instrument panel illumination, number plate lamps	5
13	(In-line) fuel pump (GTI)	25

Bulbs

	Wattage
Headlamps:	
Non-GTI	45/40
GTI	H4 (55)
Front parking lamps	5
Direction indicator lamps	21
Front driving lamp (GTI)	H3 (55)
Tail/stop-lamps	5/21
Reverse lamp	21
Rear foglamps	21
Interior lamp	5

Torque wrench settings

	Nm	lbf ft
Alternator mounting bolt (non-GTI)	45	33
Alternator adjuster link bolt (non-GTI)	17	13
Starter motor mounting bolts (non-GTI)	12	9
Alternator pivot bolt (GTI)	39	29
Alternator strap bolt (GTI)	20	15
Starter motor bolts (GTI)	34	25

1 General description

The electrical system is of the 12 volt negative earth type and the major components consist of a battery, of which the negative terminal is earthed, an alternator which is belt-driven from the crankshaft pulley, and a starter motor.

The battery supplies a steady amount of current for the ignition, lighting and other electrical circuits and provides a reserve of electricity when the current consumed by the electrical equipment exceeds that being produced by the alternator.

The alternator is controlled by a regulator which ensures a high output if the battery is in a low state of charge or the demand from the electrical equipment is high, and a low output if the battery is fully charged and there is little demand for the electrical equipment.

When fitting electrical accessories it is important, if they contain silicone diodes or transistors, that they are connected correctly, otherwise serious damage may result to the components concerned. Items such as radios, tape recorders, electronic ignition systems, electronic tachometer, automatic dipping etc, should all be checked for correct polarity.

It is important that both battery leads are always disconnected if the battery is to be boost charged; also, if body repairs are to be carried out using electric arc welding equipment, the alternator must be disconnected, otherwise serious damage can be caused to the more delicate instruments. Whenever the battery has to be disconnected it must always be reconnected with the negative terminal earthed.

2 Routine maintenance

Carry out the following procedures at the intervals given in Routine Maintenance at the beginning of the manual

1 Remove the battery cell covers and check the electrolyte level, as described in Section 3. Top up if necessary. Note that topping-up is not usually necessary for the standard low maintenance battery used under normal conditions.

2 Check and, if necessary, adjust the alternator drivebelt, as follows. Firmly depress the drivebelt midway between the pulleys (water pump and alternator on non-GTI models) and check that it deflects by the amount given in the Specifications (photo). If not, loosen the pivot

and adjustment bolts, reposition the alternator then retighten the bolts. On non-GTI models lever the alternator, but on GTI models turn the special adjustment screw as required (photo).

3 Battery – maintenance and inspection

1 The battery fitted as original equipment is of low maintenance type; however, on some models, it incorporates the standard cell covers for checking the electrolyte level (photo). Under normal conditions it is not necessary to check the level, but if the battery is subject to severe conditions such as taxi work or extreme temperatures, the level should be checked every 10 000 miles (15 000 km).

2 When topping-up is required use only distilled water and cover the battery plates to a depth of 10.0 mm (0.40 in).

3 Acid should never be required if the battery has been correctly filled from new, unless spillage has occurred.

4 Inspect the battery terminals and mounting tray for corrosion. This is the white fluffy deposit which grows at these areas. If evident, clean it away and neutralise it with ammonia or baking soda. Apply petroleum jelly to the terminals and paint the battery tray with a suitable anti-corrosion preparation.

5 Keep the top surface of the battery casing dry.

6 An indication of the state of charge of a battery can be obtained by checking the electrolyte in each cell using a hydrometer. The specific gravity of the electrolyte for fully charged and fully discharged conditions at the electrolyte temperature indicated, is listed below.

Fully discharged	Electrolyte temperature	Fully charged
1.098	38°C (100°F)	1.268
1.102	32°C (90°F)	1.272
1.106	27°C (80°F)	1.276
1.110	21°C (70°F)	1.280
1.114	16°C (60°F)	1.284
1.118	10°C (50°F)	1.288
1.122	4°C (40°F)	1.292
1.126	–1.5°C (30°F)	1.296

7 There should be very little variation in the readings between the different cells, but if a difference is found in excess of 0.025 then it will probably be due to an internal fault indicating impending battery

2.2A Checking the alternator drivebelt tension

2.2B Adjusting the alternator drivebelt tension on GTI models

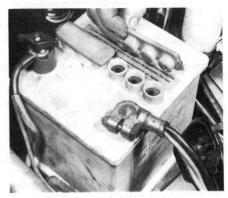

3.1 Checking the battery electrolyte level

failure. This assumes that electrolyte has not been spilled at some time and the deficiency made up with water only.

8 If electrolyte is accidentally spilled at any time, mop up and neutralise the spillage at once. Electrolyte attacks and corrodes metal rapidly; it will also burn holes in clothing and skin. Leave the addition of acid to a battery cell to your dealer or service station as the mixing of acid with distilled water can be dangerous.

9 Never smoke or allow naked lights near the battery; the hydrogen gas which it gives off is explosive.

10 With normal motoring, the battery should be kept in a good state of charge by the alternator and never need charging from a mains charger.

11 However, if the daily mileage is low, with much use of starter and electrical accessories, it is possible for the battery to become discharged owing to the fact that the alternator is not in use long enough to replace the current consumed.

12 Also, as the battery ages, it may not be able to hold its charge and some supplementary charging may be needed. Before connecting the charger, disconnect the battery terminals or, better still, remove the battery from the vehicle.

13 Specially rapid 'boost' charges which are claimed to restore the power of the battery in 1 to 2 hours are most dangerous as they can cause serious damage to the battery plates through overheating.

14 While charging the battery note that the temperature of the electrolyte should never exceed 38°C (100°F).

15 When charging a low maintenance battery **do not** remove the cell covers; however, on other types of battery, the cell covers should be removed.

4 Battery – removal and refitting

1 The battery is located in the front left-hand corner of the engine compartment.

2 Disconnect the battery leads. on non-GTI models the negative lead has a wing type terminal nut which, if unscrewed two or three turns, will isolate the battery without the need for complete removal. This is a useful facility when undertaking routine electrical jobs on the car.

3 Release the battery clamp and lift the battery carefully from the engine compartment.

4 Refitting is a reversal of removal, but smear the terminals with petroleum jelly on completion.

5 Alternator – general description and maintenance

1 All models covered by this manual are fitted with alternators. The alternator generates alternating current (AC) which is rectified by diodes into direct current (DC) which is the current needed for charging the battery.

2 The main advantage of the alternator lies in its ability to provide a high charge at low revolutions. Driving slowly in heavy traffic with a dynamo invariably means no charge is reaching the battery. In similar conditions, even with the heater, wiper, lights and perhaps radio switched on, the alternator will ensure a charge reaches the battery.

3 The alternator is of the rotating field ventilated design and comprises principally a laminated stator, on which is wound the output winding, a rotor carrying the field winding and a diode rectifier.

4 The rotor is belt-driven from the engine through a pulley keyed to the rotor shaft. A fan adjacent to the pulley draws air through the unit. Rotation is clockwise when viewed from the drive end.

5 The voltage regulator is mounted externally on the rear cover of the alternator.

6 The equipment has been designed for the minimum amount of maintenance in service, the only items subject to wear being the brushes and bearings.

7 Brushes should be examined after about 80 000 miles (120 000 km) and renewed if necessary. The bearings are pre-packed with grease for life, and should not require further attention.

8 Regularly check the drivebelt tension, as described in Section 2.

6 Alternator – removal and refitting

1 Disconnect the battery negative lead.

2 Loosen the pivot and adjustment bolts, swivel the alternator towards the engine then remove the drivebelt.

3 On non-GTI models, move the air cleaner to one side (Chapter 2).

4 Disconnect the wiring from the alternator (photo).

5 Unscrew the pivot and adjustment bolts and lift the alternator from the engine. On GTI models note that the alternator front bracket is slotted to allow the pivot bolt to remain in the bracket on the engine.

6 Refitting is a reversal of removal, but tension the drivebelt, as described in Section 2.

6.4 The alternator wiring connections

7 Alternator – brush renewal

1   Remove the alternator (Section 6) then remove the rear shield (where fitted).
2   Remove the regulator/brush holder mounting screws and withdraw the assembly. Disconnect the regulator lead, where necessary.
3   With the brush holder removed, check the condition of the slip rings. If they are blackened, clean them with a fuel-moistened rag. If they are deeply scored or grooved then it will probably indicate that the alternator is coming to the end of its life.
4   Unsolder the old brushes and solder in the new ones. Have this done professionally if you lack skill in soldering.
5   Refit the regulator/brush holder and tighten the mounting screws. Reconnect the regulator lead, where necessary.
6   Refit the rear shield (where fitted) then refit the alternator, with reference to Section 6.

8 Starter motor – description and testing

1   The starter motor is mounted on the front of the engine and is of the pre-engaged type, where the drive pinion is brought into mesh with the starter ring gear on the flywheel before the main current is applied.
2   When the starter switch is operated, current flows from the battery to the solenoid which is mounted on the top of the starter motor body. The plunger in the solenoid moves inwards, so causing a centrally pivoted lever to push the drive pinion into mesh with the starter ring gear. When the solenoid plunger reaches the end of its travel, it closes an internal contact and full starting current flows to the starter field coils. The armature is then able to rotate the crankshaft, so starting the engine.
3   A special freewheel clutch is fitted to the starter drive pinion so that as soon as the engine fires and starts to operate on its own it does not drive the starter motor.
4   When the starter switch is released, the solenoid is de-energised

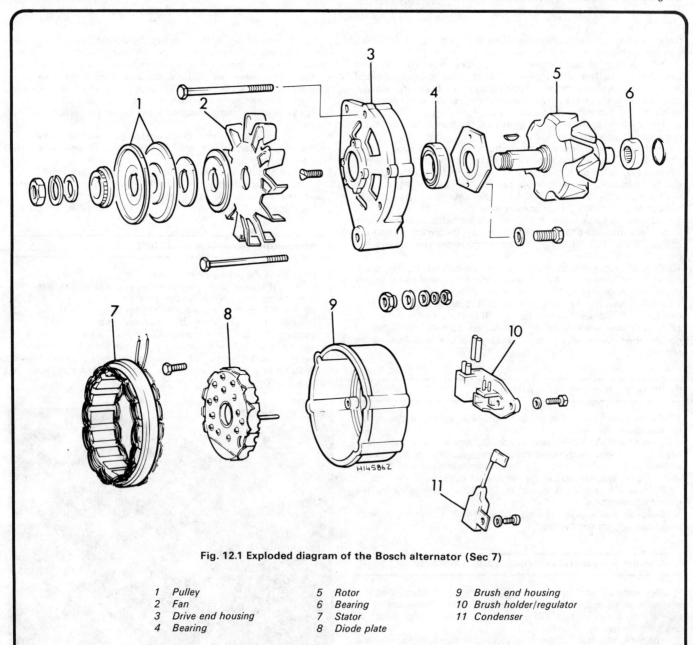

Fig. 12.1 Exploded diagram of the Bosch alternator (Sec 7)

1 Pulley	5 Rotor	9 Brush end housing
2 Fan	6 Bearing	10 Brush holder/regulator
3 Drive end housing	7 Stator	11 Condenser
4 Bearing	8 Diode plate	

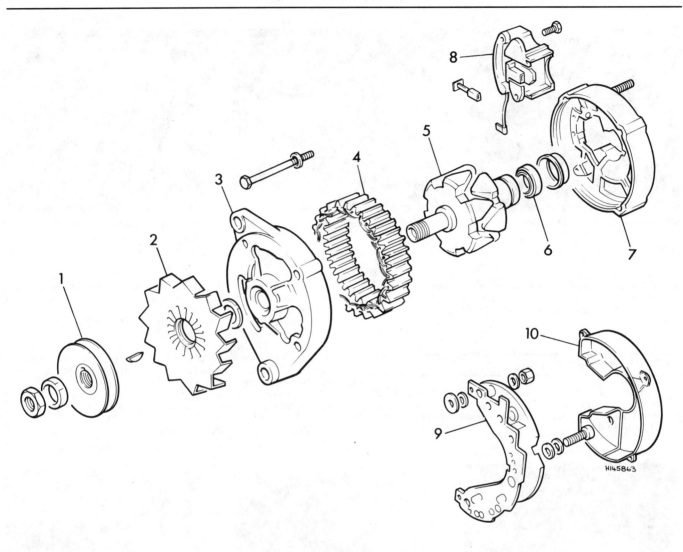

Fig. 12.2 Exploded diagram of the Paris-Rhône alternator (Sec 7)

1 Pulley	5 Rotor	8 Brush holder/regulator
2 Fan	6 Bearing	9 Diode plate
3 Drive end housing	7 Brush end housing	10 Cover
4 Stator		

and a spring moves the plunger back to its rest position. This operates the pivoted lever to withdraw the drive pinion from engagement with the starter ring.

5   If the starter motor fails to turn the engine when the switch is operated there are four possible reasons why:

(a) *The battery is discharged or faulty*
(b) *The electrical connections between switch, solenoid, battery and starter motor are somewhere failing to pass the necessary current from the battery, through the starter to earth*
(c) *The solenoid has an internal fault*
(d) *The starter motor is electrically defective*

6   To check the battery, switch on the headlights. If they go dim after a few seconds the battery is discharged. If the lamp glows brightly, next operate the ignition/starter switch and see what happens to the lights. If they do dim it is indicative that power is reaching the starter motor but failing to turn it. If the starter should turn very slowly go on to the next check.

7   If, when the ignition/starter switch is operated, the lights stay bright then the power is not reaching the starter motor. Check all connections from the battery to solenoid for cleanliness and tightness. With a good battery fitted this is the most usual cause of starter motor problems. Check that the earth cable between the engine and body is

also intact and cleanly connected. This can sometimes be overlooked when the engine is taken out.

8   If no results have yet been achieved turn off the headlights, otherwise the battery will soon be discharged. It may be possible that a clicking noise was heard each time the ignition/starter switch was operated. This is the solenoid switch operating but it does not necessarily follow that the main contact is closing properly. (If no clicking has been heard from the solenoid it is certainly defective.) The solenoid contact can be checked by putting a voltmeter or bulb between the main cable connection on the starter side of the solenoid and earth. When the switch is operated there should be a reading or a lighted bulb. If not, the switch has a fault.

9   Starter motor – removal and refitting

1   Disconnect the battery negative lead.
2   On non-GTI models, remove the air cleaner. On GTI models, remove the inlet manifold, with reference to Chapter 3.
3   Disconnect the wiring from the solenoid (photo).
4   Unscrew the bolts securing the brush end bracket to the engine (photo).
5   Unscrew the mounting bolts at the flywheel end (photo).

9.3 Starter motor solenoid wiring

9.4 Starter motor brush end bracket (non-GTI models)

9.5 Removing starter motor mounting bolts (non-GTI models)

6   Withdraw the starter motor from the engine (photo).
7   Refitting is a reversal of removal, but first insert all mounting bolts finger tight, then tighten the flywheel end bolts followed by the brush end bolts.

10 Starter motor – overhaul

1   The starter motor may be of Paris-Rhône, Bosch or Ducellier make. The following paragraphs describe the overhaul of a Paris-Rhône starter motor, but overhaul of the other makes is similar if reference is made to Figs. 12.3 to 12.6.

2   With the starter removed from the car, disconnect the solenoid leads (photo), then unscrew the nuts and remove the brush end bracket (photo).
3   Unscrew the three nuts and remove the solenoid (photos).
4   Prise the plastic cap from the endplate (photo).
5   Unscrew the two tie-rod nuts.
6   Mark the set position of the head of the engagement lever pivot pin. The pin is of eccentric type and its rotation and final setting control the end stop clearance.
7   Tap out the pivot pin (photo).
8   Withdraw the drive end housing complete with tie-bolts. Note the internal shaft shim (photos).
9   Lift off the engagement fork (photo).

9.6 Removing the starter motor (non-GTI models)

10.2A Starter field coil-to-solenoid lead

10.2B Removing brush end bracket

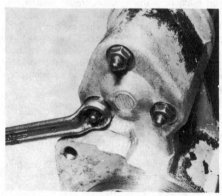

10.3A Starter solenoid nuts

10.3B Withdrawing starter solenoid

10.4 Removing cap from starter endplate

10.7 Starter engagement lever pivot pin

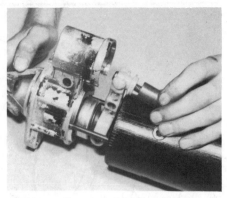

10.8 Removing starter drive end housing

10.9 Starter engagement fork

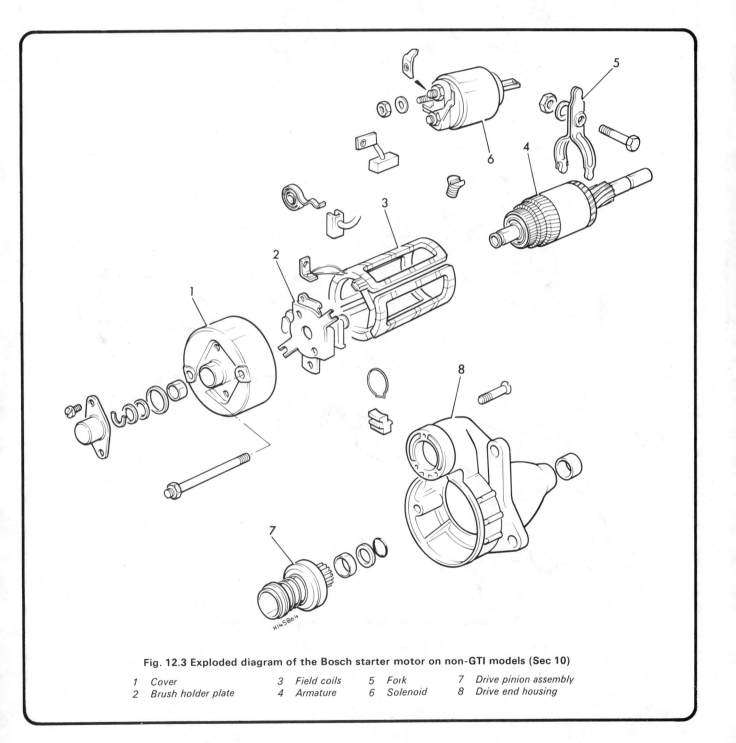

Fig. 12.3 Exploded diagram of the Bosch starter motor on non-GTI models (Sec 10)

1	Cover	3	Field coils	5	Fork	7 Drive pinion assembly
2	Brush holder plate	4	Armature	6	Solenoid	8 Drive end housing

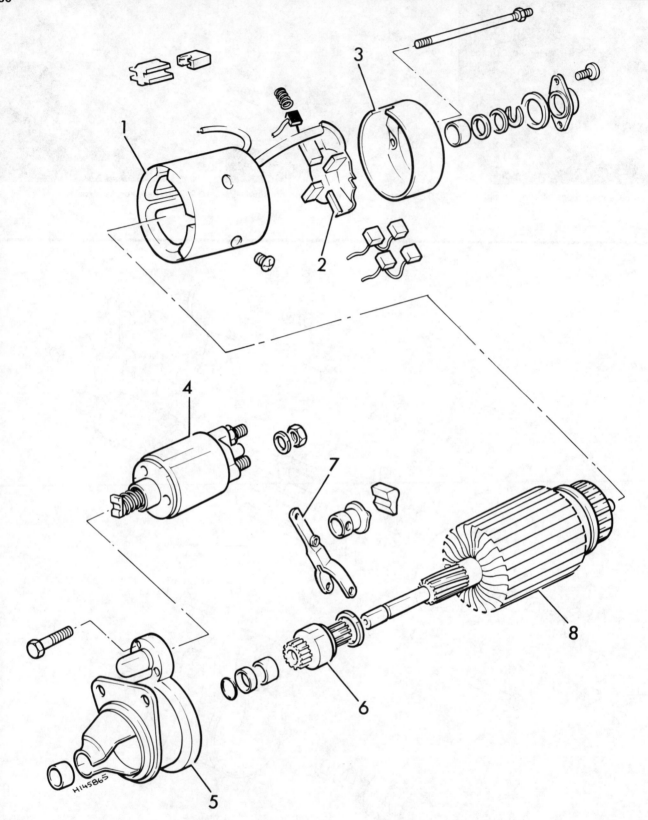

Fig. 12.4 Exploded diagram of the Bosch starter motor on GTI models (Sec 10)

1	Yoke	3	Cover	5	Drive end housing	7	Fork
2	Brush holder plate	4	Solenoid	6	Drive pinion assembly	8	Armature

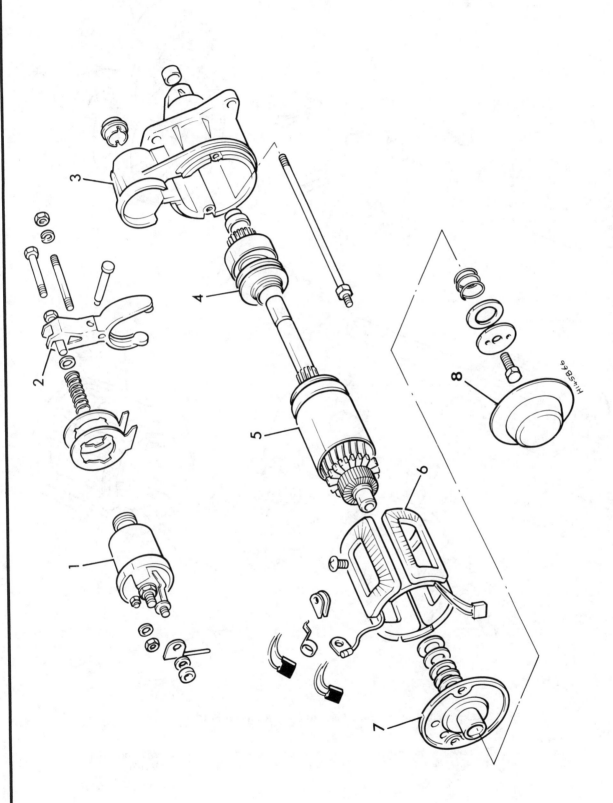

Fig. 12.5 Exploded diagram of the Ducellier starter motor (Sec 10)

1	Solenoid	5	Armature
2	Fork	6	Field coils
3	Drive end housing	7	Bearing assembly
4	Drive pinion assembly	8	Cover

H14586

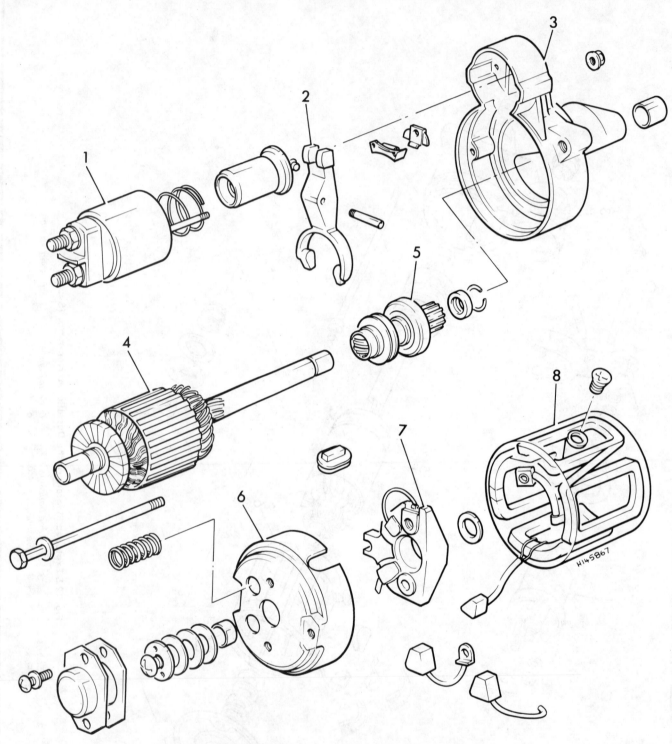

Fig. 12.6 Exploded diagram of the Paris-Rhône starter motor (Sec 10)

1 *Solenoid*	3 *Drive end housing*	5 *Drive pinion assembly*	7 *Brush holder plate*
2 *Fork*	4 *Armature*	6 *Brush end housing*	8 *Field coils*

10 Depress and then unscrew the armature endplate bolt. Note the wave and plain washers (photo).
11 Remove the endplate, noting that located under it are a wave washer, two plain washers and a fibre washer (photo).
12 Withdraw the armature, noting the shim, wave washer, shim and

fibre washer (in that order) located against the commutator end face (photo).
13 If the brushes are worn down they can be renewed (photo). The brush lead from the field coil must be cut and the new one soldered on. Take care not to allow heat to damage the field coils nor to allow solder to run down the lead or their flexibility will be ruined.

10.10 Starter armature endplate bolt

10.11 Removing starter endplate

10.12 Starter armature

10.13 Starter motor brushes

10.18 Starter drive jump ring

10.19 Drawing jump ring cover sleeve over jump ring

14 Undercut the separators of the commutator using an old hacksaw blade to a depth of about 0.5 to 0.8 mm (0.02 to 0.03 in). The commutator may be further surface cleaned using a strip of very fine glass paper. Do not use emery cloth for this purpose as the carborundum particles will become embedded in the copper surfaces.

15 Testing of the armature is best left to an auto-electrician, but if an ohmmeter is available it can be done by placing one probe on the armature shaft and the other on each of the commutator segments in turn. If there is a reading indicated at any time during the test, then the armature is defective and must be renewed.

16 The field coil can also be tested using an ohmmeter. Connect one probe to the field coil positive terminal and the other to the positive brush holder. If there is no indication of a reading then the field coil circuit has a break in it.

17 Connect one lead of the meter to the field coil positive lead and the other one to the yoke. If there is a low resistance then the field coil is earthed due to a breakdown in the insulation. If this proves to be the case the field coils must be renewed. As field coil replacement requires special tools and equipment it is a job that should be entrusted to your auto-electrician. In fact it will probably prove more economical and beneficial to exchange the starter motor for a reconditioned unit.

18 If the starter drive is faulty, it can be removed if the sleeve is tapped up the shaft, using a piece of tubing, to expose the jump ring. Remove the jump ring and starter drive (photo).

19 Once the starter drive has been refitted with its jump ring, draw the covering sleeve over it using a small puller of claw type (photo).

20 Reassembly is a reversal of dismantling, but observe the following points.

21 Apply high melting-point grease to the armature shaft bearings.

22 Note the locating pip on the yoke which aligns with the notch in the rim of the endplate (photo).

23 If the setting of the engagement lever pivot pin was not marked at dismantling, energise the starter solenoid and check that the clearance between the end face of the pinion shaft and the stop button within the drive end housing is 1.5 mm (0.059 in). If not, withdraw the eccentric type pivot pin from the engagement lever and rotate it a few splines then recheck the clearance.

10.22 Yoke/endplate alignment 'pip' and notch (arrowed)

11 Fuses – general

1   The fuse board is located above the glovebox on the left-hand side of the facia. Access to it is gained by opening the glovebox then depressing the spring clip and lowering the fuse board.
2   Blade type fuses are used and symbols by the fuses denote the circuit protected (photo).
3   On GTI models an in-line fuse for the fuel pump is located near the rear of the fuse board. The fuse board also incorporates a connector which can be adjusted to supply the radio with negative or positive current according to the polarity of the radio fitted.
4   Should a fuse blow, replace it only with one of identical rating and if the new one blows again immediately, trace and rectify the cause; usually due to a bare wire touching the bodywork due to the insulation having chafed.
5   The fuse board is retained at the rear by two plastic ball and socket joints which can be snapped apart to remove the assembly (photo).

12 Direction indicator/hazard warning flasher unit – general

1   The unit is located on the fuse board and controls both the direction indicator and hazard warning functions.

11.2 Removing a fuse

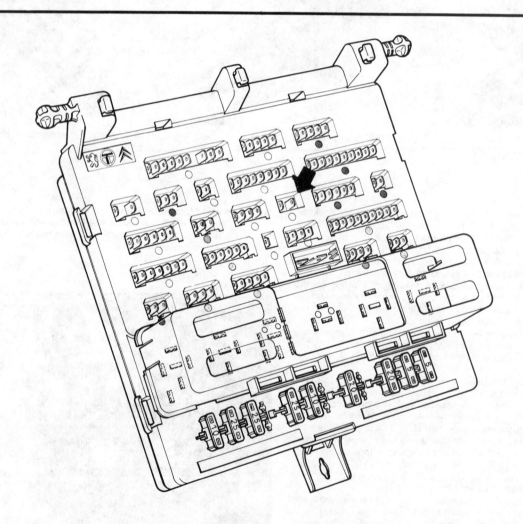

Fig. 12.7 Diagram of fuse board showing connector terminals (arrowed) for setting polarity supply to radio (Sec 11)

11.5 Fuse board ball and socket (arrowed)

6 Make sure that the lamp casing or bulb earth connection is making a good contact.

13 Steering column combination switches – removal and refitting

1 Disconnect the battery negative lead.
2 Remove the steering wheel and column shrouds, with reference to Chapter 10 (photo).
3 Disconnect the wiring harness plug.
4 Remove the relevant screws and withdraw the switch from the column platform (photo).
5 Refitting is a reversal of removal.

14 Facia-mounted switches – removal and refitting

1 Carefully prise out the switch against the tension of the plastic retaining tabs (photos).
2 Disconnect the wiring or multi-plug, noting the fitted location, and remove the switch.
3 Refitting is a reversal of removal.

15 Courtesy lamp switch – removal and refitting

1 The switch is secured to the door pillar by a self-tapping screw. Extract the screw and withdraw the switch and leads (photo).
2 If the leads are disconnected, tape them to the pillar to prevent them from slipping inside the pillar cavity.
3 It is recommended that the metal contacts of the switch are smeared with petroleum jelly as a precaution against corrosion.
4 Refit by reversing the removal operation.

2 In the event of either system not operating, or one lamp flashing very quickly, carry out the following checks before renewing the flasher unit itself.
3 Inspect the circuit fuse and renew it if it is blown.
4 Check the condition of all wiring and the security of the connections.
5 Check the lamp which is malfunctioning for a broken bulb.

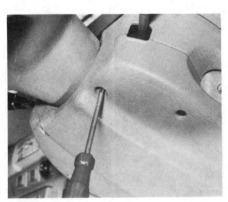

13.2 Removing the steering column shrouds

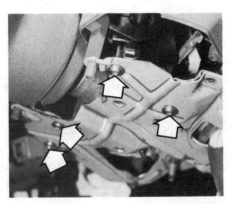

13.4 Combination switch screws (arrowed)

14.1A Instrument illumination rheostat

14.1B Heated rear window switch and cigar lighter removed from facia

15.1 Removing a courtesy lamp switch

16 Glovebox illumination switch – removal and refitting

1   Disconnect the battery negative lead.
2   Open the glovebox then reach up and release the switch from the inside of the facia (photo).
3   Disconnect the wiring.
4   Refitting is a reversal of removal.

17 Instrument panel – removal and refitting

1   Disconnect the battery negative lead.
2   Using an Allen key, unscrew the two upper retaining screws at each end of the panel surround (photo).

3   Unscrew the two lower surround retaining screws located either side of the steering column shroud (photo).
4   Withdraw the surround from the facia.
5   Pull out the instrument panel while depressing the lower spring supports, then disconnect the multi-plugs and speedometer cable (photos).
6   If necessary, the individual components can be removed for repair or renewal – with reference to Figs. 12.8 and 12.9 (photos).
7   Refitting is a reversal of removal.

18 Speedometer cable – renewal

1   Disconnect the speedometer cable from the transmission by removing the retaining bolt or rubber plug (photo).

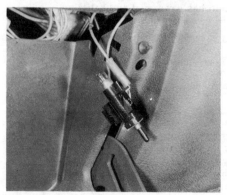

16.2 Glovebox illumination switch

17.2 Removing the instrument panel upper ...

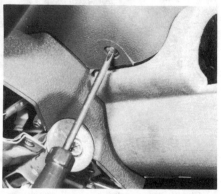

17.3 ... and lower retaining screws

17.5A Instrument panel spring support

17.5B Instrument panel right-hand upper multi-plug

17.5C Instrument panel left-hand upper multi-plugs

17.6A View of instrument panel face

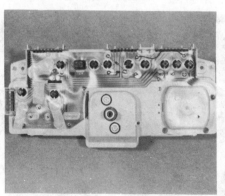

17.6B View of instrument panel rear

18.1 Removing the speedometer cable from the transmission (non-GTI models)

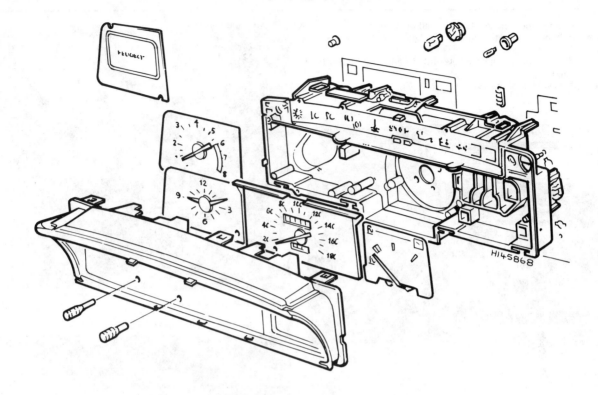

Fig. 12.8 Exploded diagram of non-GTI instrument panel (Sec 17)

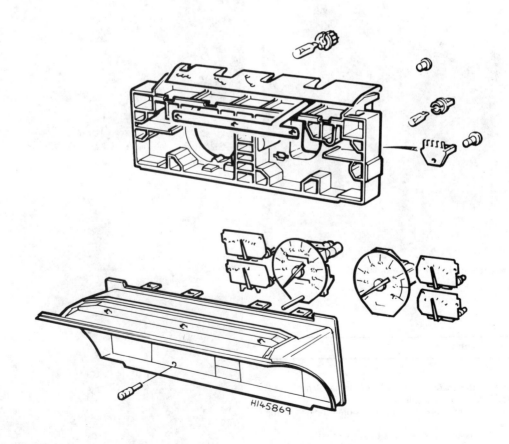

Fig. 12.9 Exploded diagram of GTI instrument panel (Sec 17)

2   Remove the instrument panel, as described in Section 17.
3   Prise the rubber grommet from the bulkhead beneath the facia (photos).
4   Remove the retaining clips, where fitted, and withdraw the speedometer cable.
5   Refitting is a reversal of removal.

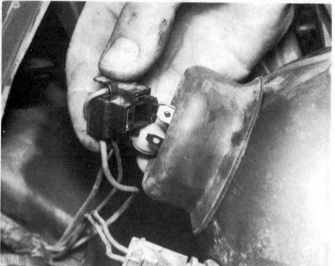

19.2 Pull off the connector ...

18.3A Speedometer cable end with instrument panel removed

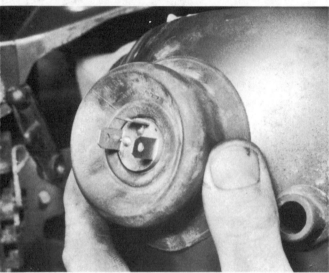

19.3 ... remove the rubber cover ...

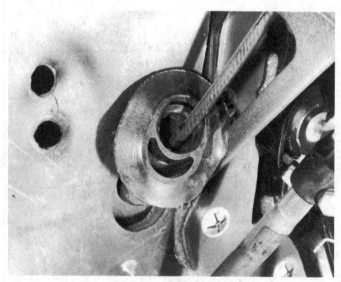

18.3B Speedometer cable grommet on the bulkhead

19 Bulbs (exterior) – renewal

Headlamps

1   Where fitted, remove the cover from the rear of the headlamp.
2   Pull the connector from the bulb (photo).
3   Remove the rubber cover, noting that the water drain hole is at the bottom (photo).
4   Release the spring clips and withdraw the bulb (photos).
5   Fit the new bulb with the locating tab uppermost. **Do not** touch the glass as this can shorten the bulb's life. If necessary, clean with methylated spirit before fitting.

19.4A ... release the spring clips ...

19.4B ... and withdraw the headlamp bulb

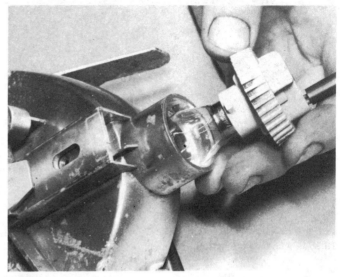

19.7 Remove the front direction indicator lamp bulbholder ...

Front parking lamps

6   Pull the bulbholder from the rear of the headlamp then depress and twist the bulb to remove it (photo).

Front direction indicator lamps

7   Turn the bulbholder anti-clockwise and withdraw it from the rear of the lamp (photo).
8   Depress and twist the bulb to remove it (photo).

Front driving lamps (GTI models)

9   Remove the two lens surround retaining screws and withdraw the surround, lens and reflector (photos).
10 Release the spring clips and place the lens assembly to one side (photo).
11 Detach the bulb feed wire at the connector.

Rear lamp cluster

12 Remove the lens upper retaining screws then tilt the lens back and release it from the lower tabs (photos).
13 Depress and twist the bulb to remove it (photo).

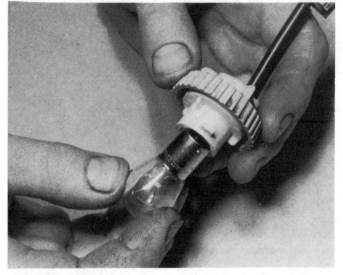

19.8 ... and extract the bulb

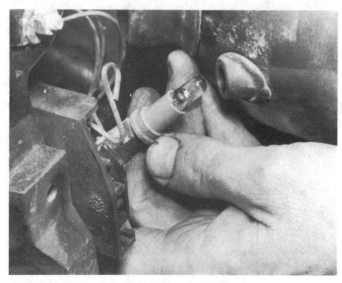

19.6 Removing the front parking lamp bulbholder

19.9A Remove the screws from the front driving lamp ...

19.9B ... withdraw the reflector assembly ...

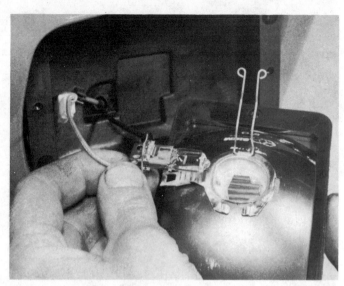

19.10 ... and remove the bulb

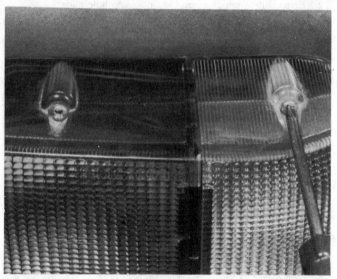

19.12A Remove the rear lamp cluster screws ...

19.12B ... and release the lens from the tabs

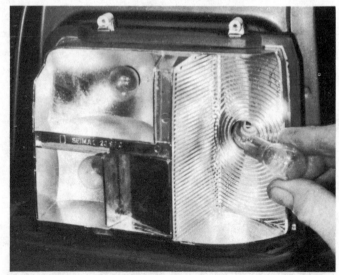

19.13 Removing a rear lamp cluster bulb

19.14 Remove the rear foglamp lens ...

Rear foglamp
14 Remove the screws and withdraw the lens (photo).
15 Depress and twist the bulb to remove it (photo).

Rear number plate lamp
16 Twist off the lens (photo).
17 Depress and twist the bulb to remove it (photo).

All bulbs
18 Refitting is a reversal of removal.

20 Bulbs (interior) – renewal

Interior lamp
1   Prise the lamp from the console (photo).
2   Extract the festoon type bulb (photo).

Map reading lamp
3   Prise the lamp from the console and extract the festoon type bulb (photo).

19.17 ... and extract the bulb

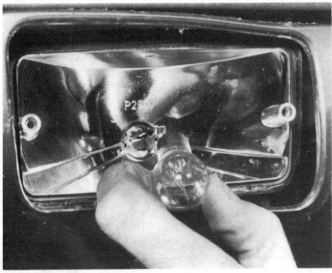

19.15 ... and extract the bulb

20.1 Prise out the interior lamp ...

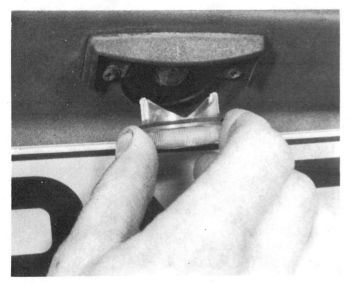

19.16 Remove the rear number plate lamp lens ...

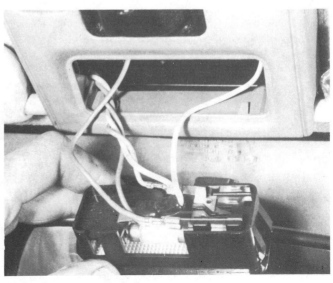

20.2 ... for access to the bulb

20.3 Removing the map reading lamp

Glovebox lamp

6   Remove the switch, with reference to Section 16.
7   Depress and twist the bulb to remove it.

Digital clock illumination lamp

8   Prise the clock from the facia.
9   Twist the bulbholder from the rear of the clock (photo).

Heater control panel illumination lamps

10 Remove the facia centre air vents, with reference to Chapter 11.
11 Pull the bulbholder from the rear of the panel and extract the bulb (photo).

All bulbs

12 Refitting is a reversal of removal.

21 Headlamp – removal and refitting

1   Remove the headlamp and front parking lamp bulbs, as described in Section 19.
2   Remove the radiator front grille (Chapter 11)
3   Release the spring clips from the pivot pins on each side of the headlamp (photo).
4   Press the load level adjustment arm from the lever ball (photo).
5   Withdraw the headlamp
6   Refitting is a reversal of removal.

22 Headlamp – beam adjustment

1   It is recommended that the adjustment of the headlamp beams is left to a service station having suitable equipment.

Instrument panel lamps

4   Remove the instrument panel, as described in Section 17.
5   Two types of bulb are fitted. Pull out the square type bulbholder and remove the wedge type holder (photo). Twist the round type bulbholder through 90° to remove it, but on this type the bulb cannot be separated from the holder (photo).

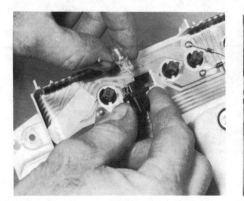

20.5A Removing square type instrument panel bulbholder

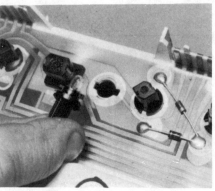

20.5B Removing round type instrument panel bulbholder

20.9 Removing digital clock illumination lamp bulb

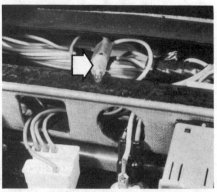

20.11 Heater control panel illumination lamp bulb (arrowed)

21.3 Releasing the headlamp spring clips

21.4 Disconnecting the headlamp load level adjustment arm

23.3A Remove the mounting screw ...

2   Each headlamp incorporates a manual adjustment to compensate for different leads (photo). If this fails to provide the correct beam, emergency adjustment is possible by turning the screw in the top of the manual adjustment for vertical movement and the knob at the rear of the headlamp for horizontal movement.

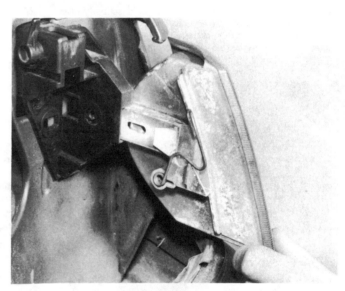

23.3B ... and withdraw the front direction indicator lamp

22.2 Headlamp manual adjustment lever

23 Front direction indicator lamp – removal and refitting

1   Remove the headlamp, as described in Section 21.
2   Remove the indicator bulb (Section 19).
3   Remove the screw securing the lamp to the headlamp adjustment assembly and withdraw the lamps (photos).
4   Refitting is a reversal of removal.

24 Windscreen wiper blades and arms – removal and refitting

1   Whenever the wiper blades fail to clean the screen, the blades or their rubber inserts should be renewed.
2   To remove a blade, pull the arm from the glass, swivel the blade, pinch the two sides of the U-shaped plastic block together and slide the assembly out of the hook of the arm (photo).
3   When refitting, note the pivot pin in the blade is offset to allow the blade to swivel fully against the glass. Make sure, therefore, that the blade is fitted the right way round so the the 'pip' on the plastic block locates in the cut-out in the hook of the wiper arm.
4   Before removing a wiper arm, stick some masking tape along the edge of the blade so that its position on the glass can be restored when the arm is being refitted to its spindle splines.
5   Flip up the plastic cover, unscrew the nut and pull the arm from the spindle (photo).
6   Refitting is a reversal of removal.

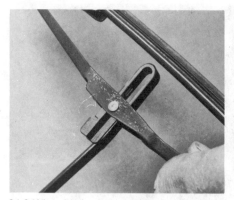

24.2 Wiper blade attachment

24.5A Unscrew the nut ...

24.5B ... and remove the wiper arm

25 Windscreen wiper motor and linkage – removal and refitting

1   Remove the wiper blades and arms, as described in Section 24.
2   Disconnect the battery negative lead.
3   Open the bonnet then remove the air intake grille by removing the screws and easing the grille from the windscreen weatherstrip (photo).
4   Unscrew the nuts from the wiper spindle bodies (photo).
5   Disconnect the wiper motor multi-plug (photo).
6   Unscrew the mounting bolt and disengage the wiper motor from the upper location pins.
7   The motor can be separated from the linkage by removing the nut securing the crank to the spindle.

8   Refitting is a reversal of removal, but use a screwdriver to lift the weatherstrip as the grille is inserted (photo).

26 Tailgate wiper motor – removal and refitting

1   Remove the wiper arm and blade, as described for the windscreen in Section 24.
2   Remove the tailgate trim, with reference to Chapter 11.
3   Disconnect the battery negative lead.
4   Disconnect the wiring and the relay multi-plug (photos).
5   Unscrew the spindle nut and remove the spacer and washer.
6   Unscrew the mounting bolts and withdraw the motor assembly, noting the location of the washers and earth wires (photo).

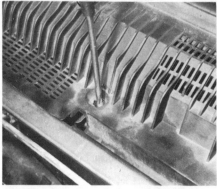

25.3 Removing the air intake grille screws

25.4 Wiper spindle body

25.5 Windscreen wiper motor and multi-plug

25.8 Inserting the intake grille beneath the weatherstrip

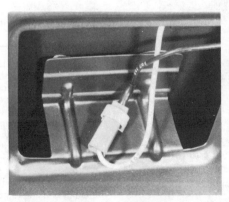

26.4A Tailgate wiper motor wiring connection

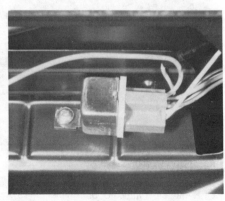

26.4B Tailgate wiper motor relay

26.6 Tailgate wiper motor and mounting bolts

27.1A Upper view of washer fluid reservoir

7　The relay can be removed by removing the mounting screw.
8　Refitting is a reversal of removal.

27 Washer system – general

1　The washer fluid reservoir is located in the left-hand front corner of the engine compartment with the bulk of the unit below the wheel arch (photos). The reservoir supplies both the windscreen and tailgate jets. On some models a headlight washer system is installed with the reservoir in the right-hand front corner of the engine compartment.
2　The washer jets are adjustable by inserting a pin into their nozzles and moving them to give an acceptable pattern on the glass.
3　The use of a good quality screen wash product is recommended. In winter add some methylated spirit to the fluid to prevent freezing. **Never** use cooling system anti-freeze as it will damage the paintwork.

28 Tailgate heated window – general

1　Take great care not to scratch the heater elements with carelessly stacked luggage or rings on the fingers.

2　Avoid sticking labels over the elements, and clean the glass interior surface with warm water and a little detergent, wiping in the same direction as the elements run.
3　Should an element be scratched, so that the current is interrupted, it can be repaired using one of the silver paint products now available for the purposse.

29 Electrically-operated front windows – general

1　Operation of the front door windows on some models is by electric motors controlled by two switches on the driver's door and a single switch on the passenger door.
2　Access to the motors is gained by dismantling the doors, as described in Chapter 11.

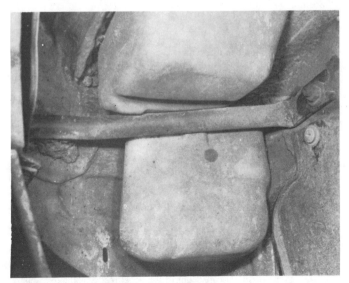

27.1B Lower view of washer fluid reservoir

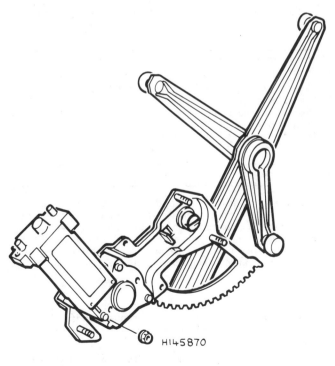

H145870

Fig. 12.10 Window regulator with electric motor (Sec 29)

30 Central door locking system – general

1   On models fitted with the central door locking system it is possible to lock all doors, including the tailgate, simply by locking the driver's door.

2   The system uses electric actuators to move the door lock mechanisms. The actuators can be removed by dismantling the doors, as described in Chapter 11.

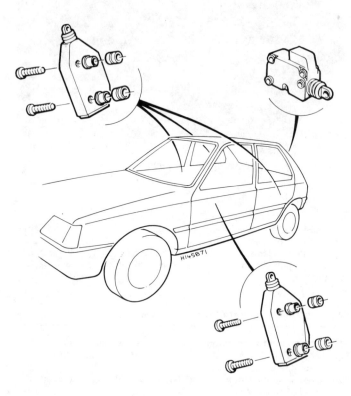

Fig. 12.11 Electric actuators fitted on models with central door locking (Sec 30)

31 Horn – removal and refitting

1   Remove the relevant headlamp, as described in Section 21.
2   Disconnect the battery negative lead.
3   Unscrew the mounting nut, remove the horn and disconnect the wiring (photo).
4   Refitting is a reversal of removal.

32 Radio – general

1   A standard radio aperture is provided in the centre console.
2   To remove the radio, pull off the control knobs and unscrew the mounting nuts. The surround can then be withdrawn and the radio removed after disconnecting the aerial and wiring (photo).
3   An in-line fuse is normally fitted to the feed wire behind the radio.
4   Loudspeakers are fitted in the doors and/or rear quarter panels (see next Section).

33   Mobile radio equipment – interference-free installation

Aerials – selection and fitting

The choice of aerials is now very wide. It should be realised that the quality has a profound effect on radio performance, and a poor, inefficient aerial can make suppression difficult.

31.3 Horn and mounting nut

32.2 Removing the radio

A wing-mounted aerial is regarded as probably the most efficient for signal collection, but a roof aerial is usually better for suppression purposes because it is away from most interference fields. Variants which are not fitted with a roof aerial as standard are still equipped with the relevant aerial wiring, and also have the roof cut to accept the Peugeot fitment. Therefore it is obviously worthwhile to approach your dealer for the parts which will bolt straight on. Stick-on wire aerials are available for attachment to the inside of the windscreen, but are not always free from the interference field of the engine and some accessories.

Motorised automatic aerials rise when the equipment is switched on and retract at switch-off. They require more fitting space and supply leads, and can be a source of trouble.

There is no merit in choosing a very long aerial as, for example, the type about three metres in length which hooks or clips on to the rear of the car, since part of this aerial will inevitably be located in an interference field. For VHF/FM radios the best length of aerial is about one metre. Active aerials have a transistor amplifier mounted at the base and this serves to boost the received signal. The aerial rod is sometimes rather shorter than normal passive types.

A large loss of signal can occur in the aerial feeder cable, especially over the Very High Frequency (VHF) bands. The design of feeder cable is invariably in the co-axial form, ie a centre conductor surrounded by a flexible copper braid forming the outer (earth) conductor. Between the inner and outer conductors is an insulator material which can be in solid or stranded form. Apart from insulation, its purpose is to maintain the correct spacing and concentricity. Loss of signal occurs in this insulator, the loss usually being greater in a poor quality cable. The quality of cable used is reflected in the price of the aerial with the attached feeder cable.

The capacitance of the feeder should be within the range 65 to 75 picofarads (pF) approximately (95 to 100 pF for Japanese and American equipment), otherwise the adjustment of the car radio aerial trimmer may not be possible. An extension cable is necessary for a long run between aerial and receiver. If this adds capacitance in excess of the above limits, a connector containing a series capacitor will be required, or an extension which is labelled as 'capacity-compensated'.

Fitting an alternative to the roof aerial will normally involve making a ⅞ in (22 mm) diameter hole in the bodywork, but read the instructions that come with the aerial kit. Once the hole position has been selected, use a centre punch to guide the drill. Use sticky masking tape around the area for this helps with marking out and drill location, and gives protection to the paintwork should the drill slip. Three methods of making the hole are in use:

(a) Use a hole saw in the electric drill. This is, in effect, a circular hacksaw blade wrapped round a former with a centre pilot drill.
(b) Use a tank cutter which also has cutting teeth, but is made to shear the metal by tightening with an Allen key.
(c) The hard way of drilling out the circle is using a small drill, say ⅛ in (3 mm), so that the holes overlap. The centre metal drops out and the hole is finished with round and half-round files.

Whichever method is used, the burr is removed from the body metal and paint removed from the underside. The aerial is fitted tightly ensuring that the earth fixing, usually a serrated washer, ring or clamp, is making a solid connection. *This earth connection is important in reducing interference.* Cover any bare metal with primer paint and topcoat, and follow by underseal if desired.

Aerial feeder cable routing should avoid the engine compartment and areas where stress might occur, eg under the carpet where feet will be located.

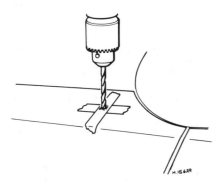

Fig. 12.12 Drilling the bodywork for aerial mounting (Sec 33)

Loudspeakers

Speakers should be matched to the output stage of the equipment, particularly as regards the recommended impedance. Power transistors used for driving speakers are sensitive to the loading placed on them.

Models which do not have speakers already fitted are partially prepared to accept them behind the ready-fitted grilles in the front doors and rear quarter panels. Some models have the speaker electrical leads in position, but others do not and will require the installation of suitable cable. If it is necessary to drill holes for speaker cables fit grommets in the holes to stop chafing.

Before choosing loudspeakers, check that they will fit and not obstruct the glass or winder mechanism. Do not omit a waterproofing cover, usually supplied with door speakers. If the speaker has to be fixed to metal, use self-tapping screws.

On some models it will be necessary to remove the grille from the door trim and cut a suitable hole in the trim and waterproofing sheet so

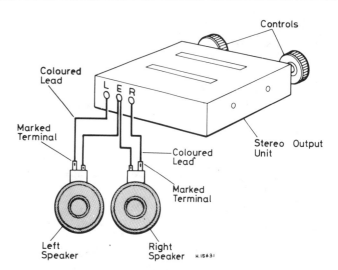

Fig. 12.13 Speaker connections must be correctly made as shown (Sec 33)

as not to obstruct the speakers. Removal of the rear quarter panel trim is straightforward; once again it may be necessary to cut suitable apertures.

When connecting up speakers, ensure the polarity is correct.

Unit installation

Many vehicles have a dash panel aperture to take a radio/audio unit, a recognised international standard being 189.5 mm x 60 mm. Alternatively a console may be a feature of the car interior design and this, mounted below the dashboard, gives more room. If neither facility is available a unit may be mounted on the underside of the parcel shelf; these are frequently non-metallic and an earth wire from the case to a good earth point is necessary. A three-sided cover in the form of a cradle is obtainable from car radio dealers and this gives a professional appearance to the installation; in this case choose a position where the controls can be reached by a driver with his seat belt on.

Installation of the radio/audio unit is basically the same in all cases, and consists of offering it into the aperture after removal of the knobs *(not* push buttons) and the trim plate. In some cases a special mounting plate is required to which the unit is attached. It is worthwhile supporting the rear end in cases where sag or strain may occur, and it is usually possible to use a length of perforated metal strip attached between the unit and a good support point nearby. In general it is recommended that tape equipment should be installed at or nearly horizontal.

Connections to the aerial socket are simply by the standard plug terminating the aerial downlead or its extension cable. Speakers for a stereo system must be matched and correctly connected, as outlined previously.

Note: *While all work is carried out on the power side, it is wise to disconnect the battery earth lead.* Before connection is made to the vehicle electrical system, check that the polarity of the unit is correct. Most vehicles use a negative earth system, but radio/audio units often have a reversible plug to convert the set to either + or – earth. *Incorrect connection may cause serious damage.*

The power lead is often permanently connected inside the unit and terminates with one half of an in-line fuse carrier. The other half is fitted with a suitable fuse (3 or 5 amperes) and a wire which should go to a power point in the electrical system. This may be the accessory terminal on the ignition switch, giving the advantage of power feed with ignition or with the ignition key at the 'accessory' position. Power to the unit stops when the ignition key is removed. Alternatively, the lead may be taken to a live point at the fusebox with the consequence of having to remember to switch off at the unit before leaving the vehicle.

Before switching on for initial test, be sure that the speaker connections have been made, for running without load can damage the output transistors. Switch on next and tune through the bands to ensure that all sections are working, and check the tape unit if applicable. The aerial trimmer should be adjusted to give the strongest reception on a weak signal in the medium wave band, at say 200 metres.

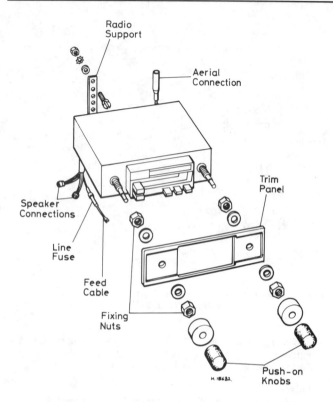

Fig. 12.14 Mounting component details for radio/cassette unit (Sec 33)

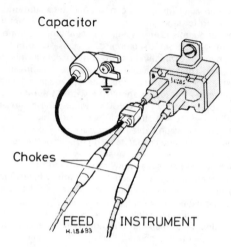

Fig. 12.15 Voltage stabiliser interference suppression (Sec 33)

Interference

In general, when electric current changes abruptly, unwanted electrical noise is produced. The motor vehicle is filled with electrical devices which change electric current rapidly, the most obvious being the contact breaker.

When the spark plugs operate, the sudden pulse of spark current causes the associated wiring to radiate. Since early radio transmitters used sparks as a basis of operation, it is not surprising that the car radio will pick up ignition spark noise unless steps are taken to reduce it to acceptable levels.

Interference reaches the car radio in two ways:

(a) by conduction through the wiring.
(b) by radiation to the receiving aerial.

Initial checks presuppose that the bonnet is down and fastened, the radio unit has a good earth connection (not through the aerial download outer), no fluorescent tubes are working near the car, the aerial trimmer has been adjusted, and the vehicle is in a position to receive radio signals, ie not in a metal-clad building.

Switch on the radio and tune it to the middle of the medium wave (MW) band off-station with the volume (gain) control set fairly high. Switch on the ignition (but do not start the engine) and wait to see if irregular clicks or hash noise occurs. Tapping the facia panel may also produce the effects. If so, this will be due to the voltage stabiliser, which is an on-off thermal switch to control instrument voltage. It is located usually on the back of the instrument panel, often attached to the speedometer. Correction is by attachment of a capacitor and, if still troublesome, chokes in the supply wires.

Switch on the engine and listen for interference on the MW band. Depending on the type of interference, the indications are as follows.

A harsh crackle that drops out abruptly at low engine speed or when the headlights are switched on is probably due to a voltage regulator.

A whine varying with engine speed is due to the dynamo or alternator. Try temporarily taking off the fan belt – if the noise goes this is confirmation.

Regular ticking or crackle that varies in rate with the engine speed is due to the ignition system. With this trouble in particular and others in general, check to see if the noise is entering the receiver from the wiring or by radiation. To do this, pull out the aerial plug, (preferably shorting out the input socket or connecting a 62 pF capacitor across it). If the noise disappears it is coming in through the aerial and is radiation noise. If the noise persists it is reaching the receiver through the wiring and is said to be line-borne.

Interference from wipers, washers, heater blowers, turn-indicators, stop lamps, etc is usually taken to the receiver by wiring, and simple treatment using capacitors and possibly chokes will solve the problem. Switch on each one in turn (wet the screen first for running wipers!) and listen for possible interference with the aerial plug in place and again when removed.

Electric petrol pumps are now finding application again and give rise to an irregular clicking, often giving a burst of clicks when the ignition is on but the engine has not yet been started. It is also possible to receive whining or crackling from the pump.

Note that if most of the vehicle accessories are found to be creating interference all together, the probability is that poor aerial earthing is to blame.

Component terminal markings

Throughout the following sub-sections reference will be found to various terminal markings. These will vary depending on the manufacturer of the relevant component. If terminal markings differ from those mentioned, reference should be made to the following table, where the most commonly encountered variations are listed.

Alternator	Alternator terminal (thick lead)	Exciting winding terminal
DIN/Bosch	B+	DF
Delco Remy	+	EXC
Ducellier	+	EXC
Ford (US)	+	DF
Lucas	+	F
Marelli	+B	F

Ignition coil	Ignition switch terminal	Contact breaker terminal
DIN/Bosch	15	1
Delco Remy	+	–
Ducellier	BAT	RUP
Ford (US)	B/+	CB/–
Lucas	SW/+	–
Marelli	BAT/+B	D

Voltage regulator	Voltage input terminal	Exciting winding terminal
DIN/Bosch	B+/D+	DF
Delco Remy	BAT/+	EXC
Ducellier	BOB/BAT	EXC
Ford (US)	BAT	DF
Lucas	+/A	F
Marelli		F

Suppression methods – ignition

Suppressed HT cables are supplied as original equipment by manufacturers and will meet regulations as far as interference to neighbouring equipment is concerned. It is illegal to remove such suppression unless an alternative is provided, and this may take the form of resistive spark plug caps in conjunction with plain copper HT cable. For VHF purposes, these and 'in-line' resistors may not be effective, and resistive HT cable is preferred. Check that suppressed cables are actually fitted by observing cable identity lettering, or measuring with an ohmmeter – the value of each plug lead should be 5000 to 10 000 ohms.

A 1 microfarad capacitor connected from the LT supply side of the ignition coil to a good nearby earth point will complete basic ignition interference treatment. *NEVER fit a capacitor to the coil terminal to the contact breaker – the result would be burnt out points in a short time.*

If ignition noise persists despite the treatment above, the following sequence should be followed:

(a) Check the earthing of the ignition coil; remove paint from fixing clamp.

(b) If this does not work, lift the bonnet. Should there be no change in interference level, this may indicate that the bonnet is not electrically connected to the car body. Use a proprietary braided strap across a bonnet hinge ensuring a first class electrical connection. If, however, lifting the bonnet increases the interference, then fit resistive HT cables of a higher ohms-per-metre value.

(c) If all these measures fail, it is probable that re-radiation from metallic components is taking place. Using a braided strap between metallic points, go round the vehicle systematically – try the following: engine to body, exhaust system to body, front suspension to engine and to body, steering column to body (especially French and Italian cars), gear lever to engine and to body (again especially French and Italian cars), Bowden cable to body, metal parcel shelf to body. When an offending component is located it should be bonded with the strap permanently.

(d) As a next step, the fitting of distributor suppressors to each lead at the distributor end may help.

(e) Beyond this point is involved the possible screening of the distributor and fitting resistive spark plugs, but such advanced treatment is not usually required for vehicles with entertainment equipment.

Electronic ignition systems have built-in suppression components, but this does not relieve the need for using suppressed HT leads. In some cases it is permitted to connect a capacitor on the low tension supply side of the ignition coil, but not in every case. Makers' instructions should be followed carefully, otherwise damage to the ignition semiconductors may result.

Suppression methods – generators

For older vehicles with dynamos a 1 microfarad capacitor from the D (larger) terminal to earth will usually cure dynamo whine. Alternators

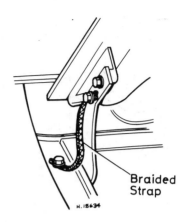

Fig. 12.16 Braided earth strap between bonnet and body (Sec 33)

should be fitted with a 3 microfarad capacitor from the B + main output terminal (thick cable) to earth. Additional suppression may be obtained by the use of a filter in the supply line to the radio receiver.

It is most important that:

(a) *Capacitors are never connected to the field terminals of either a dynamo or alternator.*

(b) *Alternators must not be run without connection to the battery.*

Suppression methods – voltage regulators

Voltage regulators used with DC dynamos should be suppressed by connecting a 1 microfarad capacitor from the control box D terminal to earth.

Alternator regulators come in three types:

(a) *Vibrating contact regulators separate from the alternator. Used extensively on continental vehicles.*

(b) *Electronic regulators separate from the alternator.*

(c) *Electronic regulators built-in to the alternator.*

In case (a) interference may be generated on the AM and FM (VHF) bands. For some cars a replacement suppressed regulator is available. Filter boxes may be used with non-suppressed regulators. But if not available, then for AM equipment a 2 microfarad or 3 microfarad capacitor may be mounted at the voltage terminal marked D+ or B+ of the regulator. FM bands may be treated by a feed-through capacitor of 2 or 3 microfarad.

Electronic voltage regulators are not always troublesome, but where

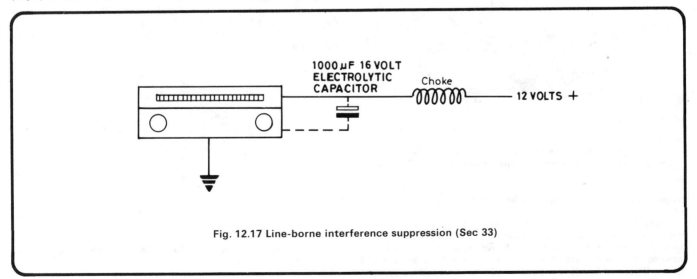

Fig. 12.17 Line-borne interference suppression (Sec 33)

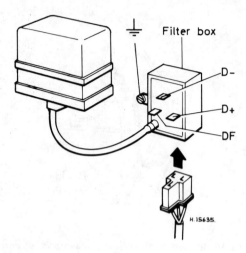

Fig. 12.18 Typical filter box for vibrating contact voltage regulator (alternator equipment) (Sec 33)

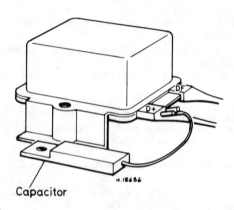

Fig. 12.19 Suppression of AM interference by vibrating contact voltage regulator (alternator equipment) (Sec 33)

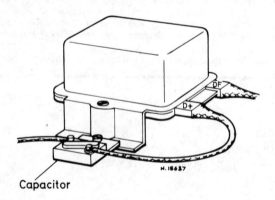

Fig. 12.20 Suppression of FM interference by vibrating contact voltage regulator (alternator equipment) (Sec 33)

necessary, a 1 microfarad capacitor from the regulator + terminal will help.

Integral electronic voltage regulators do not normally generate much interference, but when encountered this is in combination with alternator noise. A 1 microfarad or 2 microfarad capacitor from the warning lamp (IND) terminal to earth for Lucas ACR alternators and Femsa, Delco and Bosch equivalents should cure the problem.

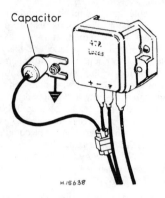

Fig. 12.21 Electronic voltage regulator suppression (Sec 33)

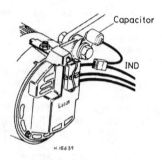

Fig. 12.22 Suppression of interference from electronic voltage regulator when integral with alternator (Sec 33)

Suppression methods – other equipment

Wiper motors – Connect the wiper body to earth with a bonding strap. For all motors use a 7 ampere choke assembly inserted in the leads to the motor.

Heater motors – Fit 7 ampere line chokes in both leads, assisted if necessary by a 1 microfarad capacitor to earth from both leads.

Electronic tachometer – The tachometer is a possible source of ignition noise – check by disconnecting at the ignition coil CB terminal. It usually feeds from ignition coil LT pulses at the contact breaker terminal. A 3 ampere line choke should be fitted in the tachometer lead at the coil CB terminal.

Horn – A capacitor and choke combination is effective if the horn is directly connected to the 12 volt supply. The use of a relay is an alternative remedy, as this will reduce the length of the interference-carrying leads.

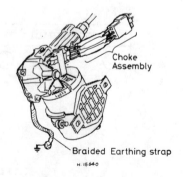

Fig. 12.23 Wiper motor suppression (Sec 33)

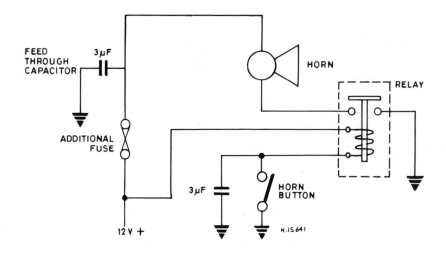

Fig. 12.24 Use of relay to reduce horn interference (Sec 33)

Electrostatic noise – Characteristics are erratic crackling at the receiver, with disappearance of symptoms in wet weather. Often shocks may be given when touching bodywork. Part of the problem is the build-up of static electricity in non-driven wheels and the acquisition of charge on the body shell. It is possible to fit spring-loaded contacts at the wheels to give good conduction between the rotary wheel parts and the vehicle frame. Changing a tyre sometimes helps – because of tyres' varying resistances. In difficult cases a trailing flex which touches the ground will cure the problem. If this is not acceptable it is worth trying conductive paint on the tyre walls.

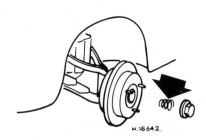

Fig. 12.25 Use of spring contacts at wheels (Sec 33)

Fuel pump – Suppression requires a 1 microfarad capacitor between the supply wire to the pump and a nearby earth point. If this is insufficient a 7 ampere line choke connected in the supply wire near the pump is required.

Fluorescent tubes – Vehicles used for camping/caravanning frequently have fluorescent tube lighting. These tubes require a relatively high voltage for operation and this is provided by an inverter (a form of oscillator) which steps up the vehicle supply voltage. This can give rise to serious interference to radio reception, and the tubes themselves can contribute to this interference by the pulsating nature of the lamp discharge. In such situations it is important to mount the aerial as far away from a fluorescent tube as possible. The interference problem may be alleviated by screening the tube with fine wire turns spaced an inch (25 mm) apart and earthed to the chassis. Suitable chokes should be fitted in both supply wires close to the inverter.

Radio/cassette case breakthrough

Magnetic radiation from dashboard wiring may be sufficiently intense to break through the metal case of the radio/cassette player. Often this is due to a particular cable routed too close and shows up as

ignition interference on AM and cassette play and/or alternator whine on cassette play.

The first point to check is that the clips and/or screws are fixing all parts of the radio/cassette case together properly. Assuming good earthing of the case, see if it is possible to re-route the offending cable – the chances of this are not good, however, in most cars.

Next release the radio/cassette player and locate it in different positions with temporary leads. If a point of low interference is found, then if possible fix the equipment in that area. This also confirms that local radiation is causing the trouble. If re-location is not feasible, fit the radio/cassette player back in the original position.

Alternator interference on cassette play is now caused by radiation from the main charging cable which goes from the battery to the output terminal of the alternator, usually via the + terminal of the starter motor relay. In some vehicles this cable is routed under the dashboard, so the solution is to provide a direct cable route. Detach the original cable from the alternator output terminal and make up a new cable of at least 6 mm² cross-sectional area to go from alternator to battery with the shortest possible route. *Remember – do not run the engine with the alternator disconnected from the battery.*

Ignition breakthrough on AM and/or cassette play can be a difficult problem. It is worth wrapping earthed foil round the offending cable run near the equipment, or making up a deflector plate well screwed down to a good earth. Another possibility is the use of a suitable relay to switch on the ignition coil. The relay should be mounted close to the ignition coil; with this arrangement the ignition coil primary current is not taken into the dashboard area and does not flow through the ignition switch. A suitable diode should be used since it is possible that at ignition

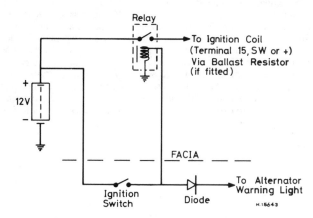

Fig. 12.26 Use of ignition coil relay to suppress case breakthrough (Sec 33)

switch-off the output from the warning lamp alternator terminal could hold the relay on.

Connectors for suppression components

Capacitors are usually supplied with tags on the end of the lead, while the capacitor body has a flange with a slot or hole to fit under a nut or screw with washer.

Connections to feed wires are best achieved by self-stripping connectors. These connectors employ a blade which, when squeezed down by pliers, cuts through cable insulation and makes connection to the copper conductors beneath.

Chokes sometimes come with bullet snap-in connectors fitted to the wires, and also with just bare copper wire. With connectors, suitable female cable connectors may be purchased from an auto-accessory shop together with any extra connectors required for the cable ends after being cut for the choke insertion. For chokes with bare wires, similar connectors may be employed together with insulation sleeving as required.

VHF/FM broadcasts

Reception of VHF/FM in an automobile is more prone to problems than the medium and long wavebands. Medium/long wave transmitters are capable of covering considerable distances, but VHF transmitters are restricted to line of sight, meaning ranges of 10 to 50 miles, depending upon the terrain, the effects of buildings and the transmitter power.

Because of the limited range it is necessary to retune on a long journey, and it may be better for those habitually travelling long distances or living in areas of poor provision of transmitters to use an AM radio working on medium/long wavebands.

When conditions are poor, interference can arise, and some of the suppression devices described previously fall off in performance at very high frequencies unless specifically designed for the VHF band. Available suppression devices include reactive HT cable, resistive distributor caps, screened plug caps, screened leads and resistive spark plugs.

For VHF/FM receiver installation the following points should be particularly noted:

(a) Earthing of the receiver chassis and the aerial mounting is important. Use a separate earthing wire at the radio, and scrape paint away at the aerial mounting.

(b) If possible, use a good quality roof aerial to obtain maximum height and distance from interference generating devices on the vehicle.

(c) Use of a high quality aerial downlead is important, since losses in cheap cable can be significant.

(d) The polarisation of FM transmissions may be horizontal, vertical, circular or slanted. Because of this the optimum mounting angle is at 45° to the vehicle roof.

Citizens' Band radio (CB)

In the UK, CB transmitter/receivers work within the 27 MHz and 934 MHz bands, using the FM mode. At present interest is concentrated on 27 MHz where the design and manufacture of equipment is less difficult. Maximum transmitted power is 4 watts, and 40 channels spaced 10 kHz apart within the range 27.60125 to 27.99125 MHz are available.

Aerials are the key to effective transmission and reception. Regulations limit the aerial length to 1.65 metres including the loading coil and any associated circuitry, so tuning the aerial is necessary to obtain optimum results. The choice of a CB aerial is dependent on whether it is to be permanently installed or removable, and the performance will hinge on correct tuning and the location point on the vehicle. Common practice is to clip the aerial to the roof gutter or to employ wing mounting

where the aerial can be rapidly unscrewed. An alternative is to use the boot rim to render the aerial theftproof, but a popular solution is to use the 'magmount' – a type of mounting having a strong magnetic base clamping to the vehicle at any point, usually the roof.

Aerial location determines the signal distribution for both transmission and reception, but it is wise to choose a point away from the engine compartment to minimise interference from vehicle electrical equipment.

The aerial is subject to considerable wind and acceleration forces. Cheaper units will whip backwards and forwards and in so doing will alter the relationship with the metal surface of the vehicle with which it forms a ground plane aerial system. The radiation pattern will change correspondingly, giving rise to break-up of both incoming and outgoing signals.

Interference problems on the vehicle carrying CB equipment fall into two categories:

(a) Interference to nearby TV and radio receivers when transmitting.

(b) Interference to CB set reception due to electrical equipment on the vehicle.

Problems of break-through to TV and radio are not frequent, but can be difficult to solve. Mostly trouble is not detected or reported because the vehicle is moving and the symptoms rapidly disappear at the TV/radio receiver, but when the CB set is used as a base station any trouble with nearby receivers will soon result in a complaint.

It must not be assumed by the CB operator that his equipment is faultless, for much depends upon the design. Harmonics (that is, multiples) of 27 MHz may be transmitted unknowingly and these can fall into other user's bands. Where trouble of this nature occurs, low pass filters in the aerial or supply leads can help, and should be fitted in base station aerials as a matter of course. In stubborn cases it may be necessary to call for assistance from the licensing authority, or, if possible, to have the equipment checked by the manufacturers.

Interference received on the CB set from the vehicle equipment is, fortunately, not usually a severe problem. The precautions outlined previously for radio/cassette units apply, but there are some extra points worth noting.

It is common practice to use a slide-mount on CB equipment enabling the set to be easily removed for use as a base station, for example. Care must be taken that the slide mount fittings are properly earthed and that first class connection occurs between the set and slide-mount.

Vehicle manufacturers in the UK are required to provide suppression of electrical equipment to cover 40 to 250 MHz to protect TV and VHF radio bands. Such suppression appears to be adequately effective at 27 MHz, but suppression of individual items such as alternators, clocks, stabilisers, flashers, wiper motors, etc, may still be necessary. The suppression capacitors and chokes available from auto-electrical suppliers for entertainment receivers will usually give the required results with CB equipment.

Other vehicle radio transmitters

Besides CB radio already mentioned, a considerable increase in the use of transceivers (ie combined transmitter and receiver units) has taken place in the last decade. Previously this type of equipment was fitted mainly to military, fire, ambulance and police vehicles, but a large business radio and radio telephone usage has developed.

Generally the suppression techniques described previously will suffice, with only a few difficult cases arising. Suppression is carried out to satisfy the 'receive mode', but care must be taken to use heavy duty chokes in the equipment supply cables since the loading on 'transmit' is relatively high.

34 Fault diagnosis – electrical system

Symptom	Reason(s)
Starter fails to turn engine	Battery discharged
	Battery defective internally
	Battery terminal leads loose or earth lead not securely attached to body
	Loose or broken connections in starter motor circuit
	Starter motor switch or solenoid faulty
	Starter brushes badly worn, sticking, or brush wires loose
	Commutator dirty, worn or burnt
	Starter motor armature faulty
	Field coils earthed
Starter turns engine very slowly	Battery in discharged condition
	Starter brushes badly worn, sticking or brush wires loose
	Loose wires in starter motor circuit
Starter motor noisy or excessively rough engagement	Pinion or flywheel gearteeth broken or worn
	Starter motor retaining bolts loose
Battery will not hold charge for more than a few days	Battery defective internally
	Electrolyte level too low or electrolyte too weak due to leakage
	Plate separators no longer fully effective
	Battery plates severely sulphated
	Drivebelt slipping
	Battery terminal connections loose or corroded
	Alternator not charging
	Short in lighting circuit continual battery drain
	Regulator unit not working correctly
Ignition light fails to go out, battery runs flat in a few days	Drivebelt loose and slipping or broken
	Alternator brushes worn, sticking, broken or dirty
	Alternator brush springs worn or broken
	Internal fault in alternator
	Regulator faulty

Failure of individual electrical equipment to function correctly is dealt with alphabetically, item-by-item, under the headings below

Horn

Horn operates all the time	Horn push either earthed or stuck down
	Horn cable to horn push earthed
Horn fails to operate	Cable or cable connection loose, broken or disconnected
	Horn has an internal fault
	Blown fuse
Horn emits intermittent or unsatisfactory noise	Cable connections loose

Lights

Lights do not come on	If engine not running, battery discharged
	Wire connections loose, disconnected or broken
	Light switch shorting or otherwise faulty
Lights come on but fade out	If engine not running, battery discharged
	Wire connections loose
	Light switch shorting or otherwise faulty

Wipers

Wiper motor fails to work	Blown fuse
	Wire connections loose, disconnected or broken
	Brushes badly worn
	Armature worn or faulty
Wiper motor works very slowly and takes excessive current	Commutator dirty, greasy or burnt
	Armature bearings dirty or unaligned
	Armature badly worn or faulty
Wiper motor works slowly and takes little current	Brushes badly worn
	Commutator dirty, greasy or burnt
	Armature badly worn or faulty

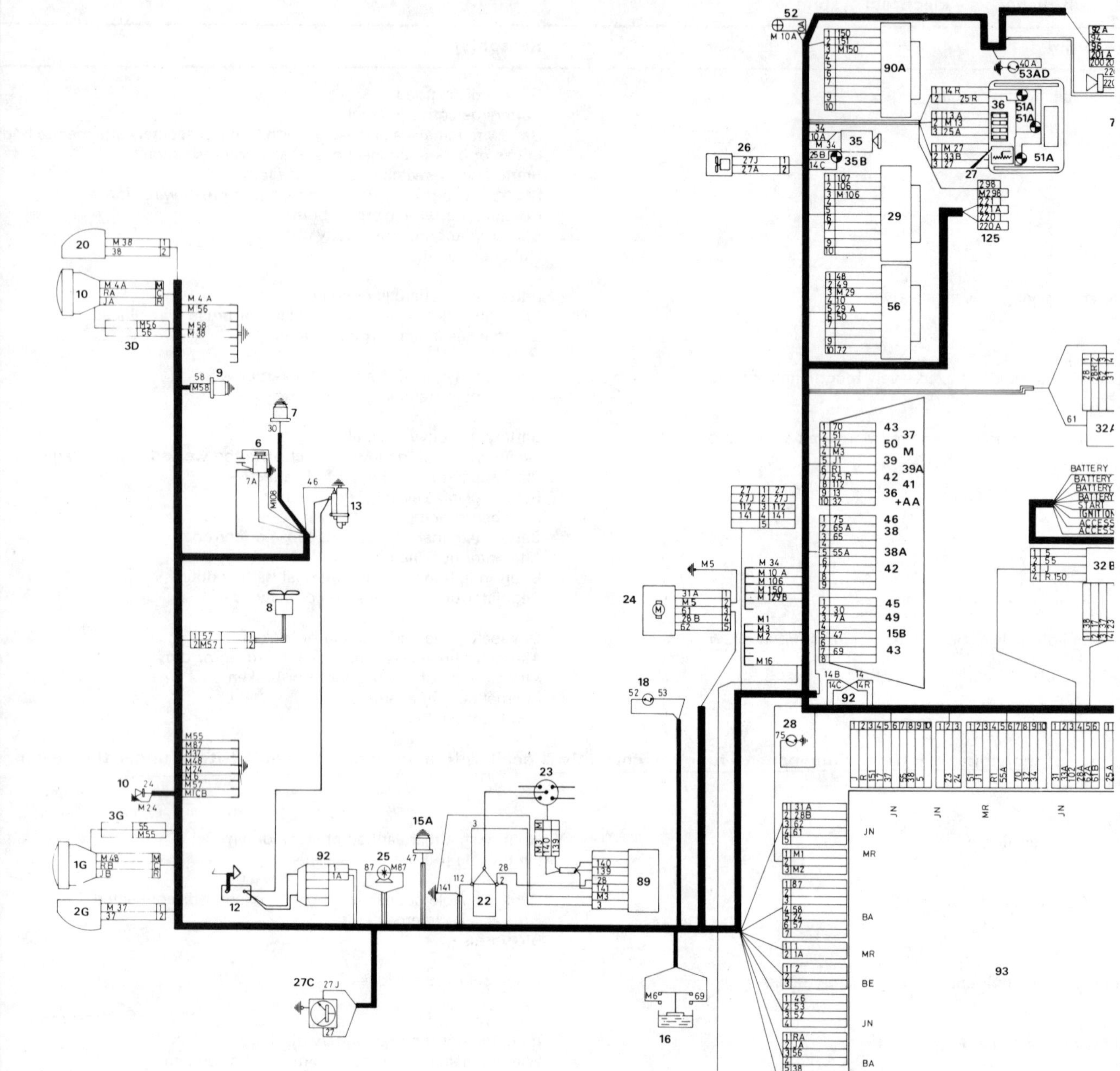

Fig. 12.27 Wiring diagram for non-GTI models – pre 1986 (key on page 258)

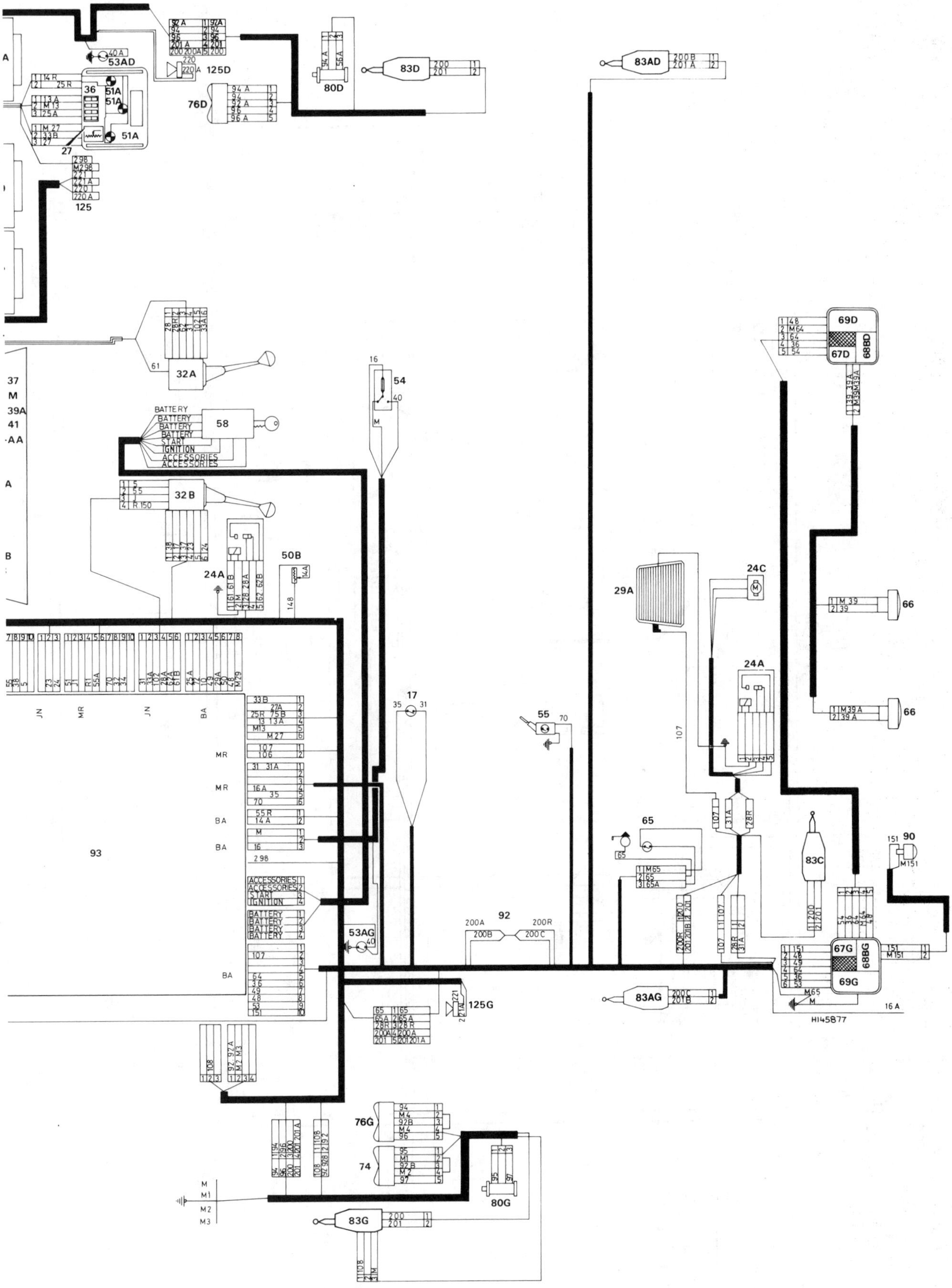

Fig. 12.27 Wiring diagram for non-GTI models – pre 1986 (continued) (key on page 258)

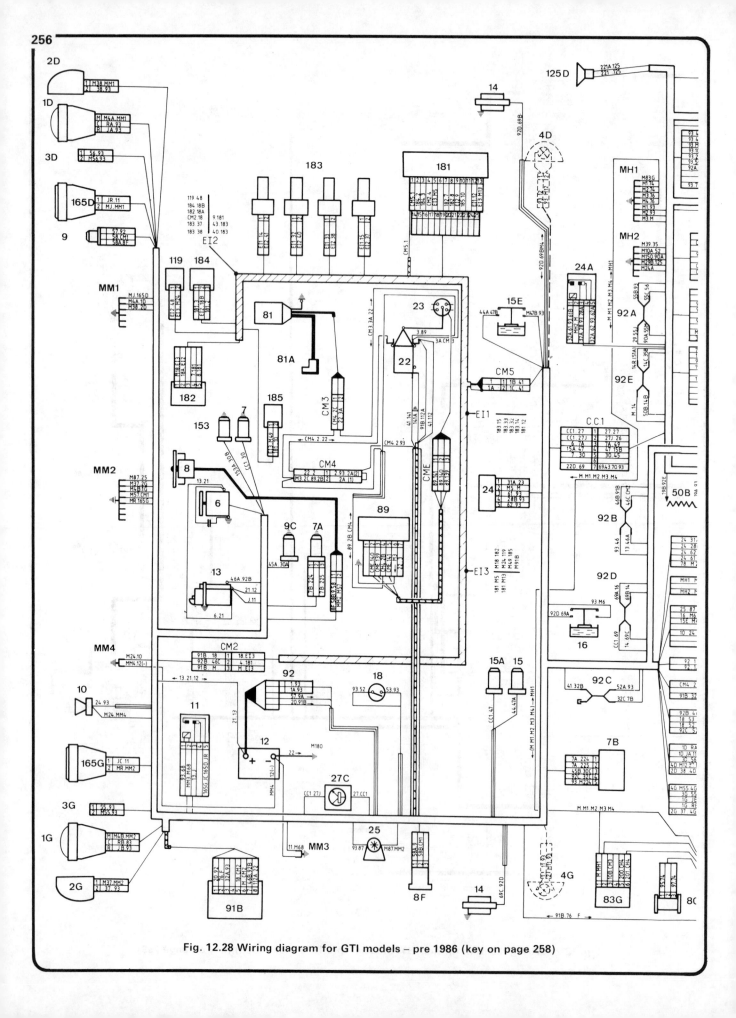

Fig. 12.28 Wiring diagram for GTI models – pre 1986 (key on page 258)

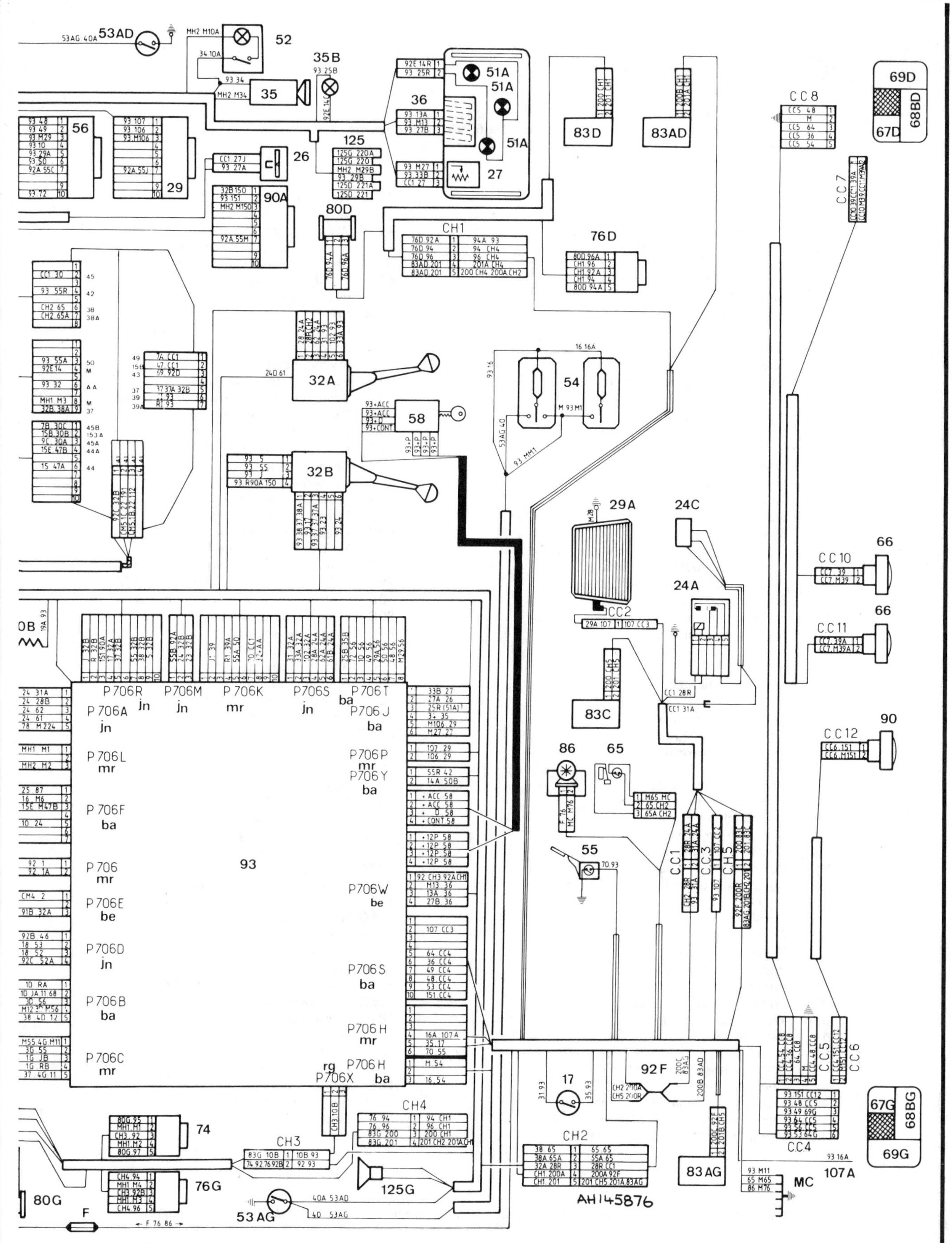

Fig. 12.28 Wiring diagram for GTI models – pre 1986 (continued) (key on page 258)

AH145876

Key to pre 1986 wiring diagrams

1D	Headlamp, RH		45B	Warning light, engine oil level
1G	Headlamp, LH		46	Warning light, brake control
2D	Direction indicator, front RH		49	Warning light, low battery charge
2G	Direction indicator, front LH		50	Illumination, instrument panel
3D	Sidelamp, RH		50B	Rheostat, panel illumination
3G	Sidelamp, LH		51A	Illumination, console
4D	Indicator repeater, RH		52	Illumination, glove box
4G	Indicator repeater, LH		53AD	Courtesy switch, RH front door
6	Alternator		53AG	Courtesy switch, LH front door
7	Sender unit, oil pressure		54	Interior lamp
7A	Sensor, engine oil level		55	Switch, handbrake
7B	Control unit, engine oil level		56	Switch, hazard warning
8	Motor, engine cooling fan		58	Switch, ignition/steering, lock/starter
8F	Resistor, cooling fan motor		65	Tank unit, fuel gauge
9	Temperature switch, fan motor		66	Illumination, number plate
9C	Sender unit, oil temperature		67D	Reverse lamp, RH
10	Horn		67G	Reverse lamp, LH
11	Relay, headlamps		68BD	Stop/tail lamp, RH
12	Battery		68BG	Stop/tail lamp, LH
13	Starter motor		69D	Direction indicator, rear, RH
14	Brake pads		69G	Direction indicator, rear LH
15	Sender unit, coolant temperature gauge		74	Switch, electric window, front LH
15A	Sender unit, coolant temperature		76D	Switch, RH electric window, front RH
15B	Warning light, coolant temperature		76G	Switch, LH electric window, front RH
15E	Sensor, coolant minimum level		80D	Motor, electric window, front, RH
16	Brake fluid reservoir		80G	Motor, electric window, front, LH
17	Switch, stop-lights		81	Diagnostic socket
18	Switch, reverse lamps		81A	TDC sensor, diagnostic socket
22	Ignition coil		83C	Actuator, tailgate lock
23	Ignition distributor		83D	Actuator, door lock, front, RH
24	Windscreen wiper		83G	Actuator, door lock, front, LH
24A	Relay, windscreen wiper		83AD	Actuator, door lock, rear, RH
24C	Wiper motor, tailgate		83AG	Actuator, door lock, rear, LH
25	Pump, screen wash		86	Fuel pump
26	Blower motor, heater		89	Control unit, ignition
27	Rheostat, blower motor		90	Foglamp, rear
27C	Control unit, heater blower		90A	Switch, rear foglamp
28	Switch, choke warning light		91B	Tachometric relay
29	Switch, heated rear window		92 to 92F	Multi-plug/connectors
29A	Heated rear window		93	Connector board
32A	Column switch; wash/wipe		107A	Socket, towing attachment
32B	Column switch; lighting, indicators and horn		119	Supplementary air device
35	Cigarette lighter		125	Connector, radio
35B	Illumination, cigarette lighter		125D	Radio speaker, front, RH
36	Clock		125G	Radio speaker, front, LH
37	Warning light, direction indicators		153	Sensor, oil pressure
38	Fuel contents gauge		153A	Oil pressure gauge
38A	Warning lamp, low fuel		165D	Long range driving lamp, RH
39	Warning lamp, main beam		165G	Long range driving lamp, LH
39A	Warning lamp, dipped beam		181	Control unit, fuel injection
41	Tachometer		182	Airflow sensor
42	Warning lamp, side/tail lamps		183	Injectors
43	Warning lamp, brake system		184	Housing, throttle switch
44	Coolant temperature gauge		185	Sensor, engine temperature
44A	Warning lamp, minimum coolant level		+AA	Supply to accessories
45	Warning light, low oil pressure		M	Earth
45A	Warning light, high oil temperature		F	Fuse

The wires are not colour-coded; just given identification numbers/letters to aid the tracing of circuits

Not all items are fitted to all models

Chapter 13 Supplement:
Revisions and information on later models

Contents

1 Introduction

This Supplement contains information which has become available between 1985 and 1988. It covers the Cabriolet and automatic transmission models introduced in April 1986, 1.6 and 1.9 GTI models, and the TU engine and MA gearbox introduced in 1988.

In order to use the Supplement to the best advantage, it is suggested that it is referred to before the main Chapters of the manual; this will ensure that any relevant information can be noted and incorporated within the procedures given in Chapters 1 to 12. Time and cost will therefore be saved, and the particular job will be completed correctly.

Project vehicles

The vehicles used in the preparation of this Supplement, and appearing in many of the photographic sequences, were a 1987 205 1.9 GTI and a 1988 205 XS.

2 Specifications

The specifications below are revisions of, or supplementary to, those at the beginning of the preceeding Chapters.

XV, XW and XY engines
Valve clearances (cold)
Early 1987 on, from engine number:
  XV8 28401
  XW7 42460
  XY7 877201
  XY8 877001
    Inlet .... 0.15 mm (0.006 in)
    Exhaust .... 0.30 mm (0.012 in)

All XU engines, early 1987 on
Cylinder liners
Protrusion from block (without seal) .... 0.03 to 0.10 mm (0.001 to 0.004 in)

Torque wrench settings
Cylinder head bolts (Torx type):

	Nm	lbf ft
Stage 1	60	44

Slacken, then immediately tighten to Stage 2	20	15
Stage 3	Tighten a further 300°	Tighten a further 300°

XU5JA engine
General
As XU5J engine except for the following:

Maximum power (DIN)	115 bhp at 6250 rpm
Maximum torque (DIN)	13.6 kgf m at 4000 rpm
Valve timing:	
Inlet opens	8° BTDC
Inlet closes	42° ATDC
Exhaust opens	40°30′ BBDC
Exhaust closes	2°30′ ATDC
Valve clearances (cold):	
Inlet	0.15 mm (0.006 in)
Exhaust	0.25 mm (0.010 in)

XU 51C engine
General
As XU5J engine except for the following:

Compression ratio	9.35:1
Maximum power (DIN)	80 bhp at 5600 rpm
Maximum torque (DIN)	13.5 kgf m at 2850 rpm
Valve timing:	
Inlet opens	10°16′ BTDC
Inlet closes	28°28′ ATDC
Exhaust opens	41°20′ BBDC
Exhaust closes	4°37′ ATDC
Valve clearances (cold):	
Inlet	0.15 mm (0.006 in)
Exhaust	0.25 mm (0.010 in)

XU9JA engine
General
As XU5J engine except for the following:

Displacement	1905 cc (116.2 cu in)
Bore x stroke	83 x 88 mm
Compression ratio	9.6 : 1
Maximum power (DIN)	130 bhp at 6000 rpm
Maximum torque (DIN)	16.8 kgf m at 4750 rpm

Valves

Head diameter:	
Inlet	41.2 mm
Exhaust	34.5 mm
Stem diameter:	
Inlet and exhaust	7.98 mm
Valve timing:	
Inlet opens	11° 30′ BTDC
Inlet closes	43° ATDC
Exhaust opens	46° BBDC
Exhaust closes	2° ATDC
Valve clearances (cold):	
Inlet	0.20 mm (0.008 in)
Exhaust	0.40 mm (0.016 in)

Crankshaft

Crankpin diameter	49.684 to 50.000 mm (1.9561 to 1.9685 in)

Torque wrench settings

	Nm	lbf ft
Sump spacer plate bolt	10	7
Oil cooler union nuts	20	15

TU engine
General ....
Four-cylinder, in-line, overhead camshaft. All alloy with wet cylinder liners. Mounted transversely and inclined 6° to the front. Transmission mounted on left-hand end of engine

Code and displacement:	
TU9	954 cc
TU1	1124 cc
TU3	1360 cc
Bore and stroke:	
TU9	70 x 62 mm
TU1	72 x 69 mm
TU3	75 x 77 mm

Compression ratio:
    TU9 and TU1 .... 9.4:1
    TU3 .... 9.3:1
Maximum power:
    TU9 .... 32.5 kW (42.3 bhp) at 5200 rpm
    TU1 .... 40.0 kW (52.0 bhp) at 5800 rpm
    TU3 .... 47.0 kW (61.1 bhp) at 5400 rpm
Maximum torque:
    TU9 .... 72.5 Nm (53 lbf ft) at 2400 rpm
    TU1 .... 87.5 Nm (64 lbf ft) at 3200 rpm
    TU3 .... 111 Nm (82 lbf ft) at 3000 rpm
Firing order .... 1-3-4-2 (No 1 at flywheel end)

Camshaft

Drive .... Toothed bolt
Friction .... Rocker arms

Crankshaft

Number of main bearings 5
Main journal diameter:
    New .... $49.981 \begin{smallmatrix} -\ 0 \\ -\ 0.016 \end{smallmatrix}$ mm

    Undersize .... $49.681 \begin{smallmatrix} -\ 0 \\ -\ 0.0016 \end{smallmatrix}$ mm

Crankpin diameter:

	TU9	**TU1 and TU3**
New	38.0 ± 0.008 mm	$45.0 \begin{smallmatrix} -\ 0.009 \\ -\ 0.025 \end{smallmatrix}$ mm
Undersize	37.7 ± 0.008 mm	$44.7 \begin{smallmatrix} -\ 0.009 \\ -\ 0.025 \end{smallmatrix}$ mm

Endfloat .... 0.052 to 0.452 mm (0.002 to 0.018 in)
Thrust washer thickness available .... 2.40, 2.50, 2.55 and 2.60 mm

Connecting rods

Maximum weight difference on any engine .... 3 grams

Cylinder liners

Type .... Wet, removable, cast iron, matched to piston
Protrusion from block (without seal) .... 0.03 to 0.10 mm (0.001 to 0.004 in)
Protrusion difference between liners .... 0.10 mm (0.004 in)

Pistons

Type .... Aluminium alloy, with two compression rings and one scraper, matched to piston

Gudgeon pins

Fit .... Clearance in piston, interference in connecting rod

Cylinder head

Material .... Aluminium alloy
Maximum distortion .... 0.05 mm (0.002 in)
Height .... 111.2 mm (4.378 in)
Number of camshaft bearings 5

Valves

Seat combined angle:
    Inlet .... 120°
    Exhaust .... 90°
Valve clearances (cold):
    Inlet .... 0.20 mm (0.008 in)
    Exhaust .... 0.40 mm (0.016 in)

Valve timing (at nominal clearance of 0.7 mm/0.028 in)

	TU9	**TU1**	**TU3**
Inlet opens BTDC	9°17′	5°19′	5°55′
Exhaust opens BBDC	31°21′	43°50′	44°26′
Inlet closes ABDC	11°10′	32°58′	32°22′
Exhaust closes ATDC	6°55′	0°6′	0°42′

Cylinder block

Material .... Aluminium alloy
Height:
    TU9 and TU1 .... 187.48 ± 0.05 mm (7.381 ± 0.002 in)
    TU3 .... 206.98 ± 0.05 mm (8.149 ± 0.002 in)

Lubrication system

Oil pump type .... Two-gear, chain driven from crankshaft

Filter type	Full-flow with internal pressure relief valve, disposable
Sump capacity:	
With filter	3.5 litres (6.2 pints)
Without filter	3.2 litres (5.6 pints)
Difference between minimum and maximum marks on dipstick	1.4 litres (2.5 pints)
Minimum oil pressure at 90°C (194°F):	
650 rpm	1.5 bar (21.8 lbf/in²)
4000 rpm	4.0 bar (58.0 lbf/in²)
Oil pressure warning light operates at	0.8 bar (11.6 lbf/in²)
Lubricant type/specification	Multigrade engine oil, viscosity SAE 10W/40 or 15W/40 (Duckhams QXR, Hypergrade, or 10W/40 Motor Oil)

Torque wrench settings

	Nm	lbf ft
Crankshaft pulley	100	74
Camshaft sprocket	80	59
Big-end bearing cap	37.5	28
Flywheel	65	48
Distributor/fuel pump housing	8	6
Camshaft thrust fork	17	13
Thermostat housing	8	6
Main bearing cap casting main bearing bolts:		
Stage 1	20	15
Stage 2	Tighten a further 45°	Tighten a further 45°
Oil pump	8	6
Sump	8	6
Main bearing cap casting to block	8	6
Water pump housing:		
8 mm bolts	30	22
6 mm bolts	50	37
Cylinder head bolts:		
Stage 1	20	15
Stage 2	Tighten a further 240°	Tighten a further 240°
Timing belt tensioner	20	15
Timing cover	6	4
Valve cover	5	4
Dipstick tube	15	11
Oil pressure switch	28	21
Oil filter	15	11

Cooling system
General

System capacity:	
XU51C engine (automatic)	6.7 litres (11.8 pints)
TU9 and TU3 engines	5.8 litres (10.2 pints)
TU1 engine	7.0 litres (12.3 pints)
Pressure cap setting (all models from April 1987)	1 bar (14.5 lbf/in²)
Warning lamp switch operating temperature (all models from April 1987)	110°C (230°F)
Electric cooling fan operating temperatures (all models from April 1987):	
Cut-in – 1st speed	97°C (207°F)
Cut-in – 2nd speed (where applicable)	101°C (214°F)
Cut-out – 1st speed	92°C (198°F)
Cut-out – 2nd speed (where applicable)	96°C (205°F)
Thermostat (TU engine):	
Starts to open:	
TU9 and TU3 engines	88°C (190°F)
TU1 engine	83°C (181°F)
Fully open:	
TU9 and TU3 engines	102°C (216°F)
TU1 engine	96°C (205°F)

Torque wrench settings (TU engine models)

	Nm	lbf ft
Water pump upper stud	16	12
Water pump lower bolt	8	6
Housing inlet elbow	8	6
Housing to block:		
8 mm bolts	30	22
10 mm bolts	50	37

Fuel and exhaust systems
Carburettor

Type	Fixed jet, downdraught
Application:	
XY8 (1360 cc) from early 1985	Weber 35 IBSH
XU51C (1580 cc)	Weber 36 TLC

Calibration and settings:	XY8	XU51C
Venturi	26 mm	28 mm
Main jet	130 ± 5	$140 \pm \frac{2}{3}$
Air correction jet	165 ± 15	150 ± 10
Emulsion tube	F104	F80
Accelerator pump injector	45 ± 5	40
Needle valve	150	150
Idling fuel jet	45 ± 5	$47 \pm \frac{2}{0}$
Idling speed	975 ± 25 rpm	900 rpm
CO%	2.0 ± 0.5	1.0 ± 0.5
Float level	9.0 mm (0.354 in)	28.0 mm (1.102 in)
Choke opening	3.25 mm (0.128 in)	

Type – TU9, TU1 and TU3 engines .... Single barrel fixed jet downdraught
Type – TU3S engine .... Double barrel progressive, fixed jet downdraught

Application:
TU9 engine .... Weber 32 IBSH 16 or Solex 32 PBISA 16
TU1 engine .... Solex 32 PBISA 16
TU3 engine .... Weber 34 TLP 3
TU3S engine .... Solex 32-34 Z2

Calibration and settings:	TU9	TU1	TU3	TU3S
Venturi	25	25	26	24/27
Main jet	Weber: 122 Solex: 127.5	127.5	132	117/130
Air correction jet	Weber: 135 Solex: 155	175	145	145/170
Emulsion tube	Weber: F112 Solex: 31	EM	F80	27/AZ
Enrichener	Weber: 30	35	40	–
Idling jet	Weber: 45 Solex: 47	45	43	43-45 GFZ/80
Idling air jet	Weber: 150 Solex: 135	165	140	190/150
Accelerator pump	40	40	40	35/35
Needle valve	Weber: 1.5 Solex: 1.6	1.6	1.5	1.8/-
Float level	Weber: 8 mm	–	28 mm	–
Idling speed	700 rpm	700 rpm	700 rpm	750 rpm
Maximum CO%	1.5	1.5	1.5	1.5

Fuel injection system

Idling speed	900 rpm
CO%	1.0
Rpm limiter cut-out speed from February 1985	6900 rpm

Ignition system
Distributor
Pulse generator resistance from early 1986:

Bosch	320 ± 30 ohms
Ducellier	190 ± 30 ohms
Magneti-Marelli	815 ± 55 ohms

Ignition timing (vacuum hose disconnected)

XU5J engine from VIN 5520364 (early 1985)	$10° \pm 1°$ BTDC at 850 ± 50 rpm or $30° \pm 1°$ BTDC at 3000 ± 100 rpm
XU5JA engine	10° BTDC at 700 rpm or 30° BTDC at 3000 rpm
XU51C engine	10° BTDC at 900 rpm
XU9JA engine	5° BTDC at 700 rpm
TU9A, TU1, TU3 and TU3S engines	8° BTDC at 700 rpm

Spark plugs

XV8, XW7, and XY7 engines	Champion S9YC
XY8 engine	Champion S7YC
XU51C engine	Champion C9YC
XU5J, XU5JA and XU9JA engines	Champion C7YC
TU9A, TU1 and TU3 engines	Eyquem FC52LS
TU3S engine	Eyquem FC62LS

Electrode gap:

XV, XW and XY engines	0.6 mm (0.024 in)
XU and TU engines	0.8 mm (0.032 in)

Clutch
Driven plate
Diameter:

TU9A engine (954 cc)	160.0 mm
TU1 engine (1124 cc)	181.0 mm

TU3S engine (1360 cc) .... 181.5 mm

Manual transmission
BE 1/5 gearbox – general
Gear ratios (from approx January 1987 on):
  1st:
    Except 1.9 GTI .... 3.250 : 1
    1.9 GTI .... 2.923 : 1
  2nd .... 1.850 : 1
Oil capacity (drain and refill) .... 2.0 litres (3.5 pints)
Lubricant type/specification (1988-on models) .... Gear oil, viscosity SAE 75W/80 (Duckhams Hypoid PT 75W/80)

MA gearbox – general

	MA 4	MA 5
Type	Four or five forward speeds, all synchromesh, one reverse	
Gear ratios:		
1st	3.417 : 1	3.417 : 1
2nd	1.810 : 1	except XS and SR : 1.810 : 1
		XS and SP : 1.857 : 1
3rd	1.129 : 1	except XS and SR : 1.276 : 1
		XS and SR : 1.357 : 1
4th	0.814 : 1	except XS and SR : 0.975 : 1
		XS and SR : 1.054 : 1
5th	–	except XS and SR : 0.767 : 1
		XS and SR : 0.854 : 1
Reverse	3.583 : 1	3.583 : 1
Final drive	TU1 engine : 3.765 : 1	TU1 engine : 3.938 : 1
	TU3 engine : 3.938 : 1	TU3 engine : 2.765 : 1
	TU9 engine : 4.286 : 1	TU3S engine : 4.286 : 1
Oil capacity (drain and refill)	2.0 litres (3.5 pints)	
Lubricant type/specification	Gear oil, viscosity SAE 75W/80 (Duckhams Hypoid PT 75W/80)	

Torque wrench settings (MA gearbox)

	Nm	lbf ft
Gearbox housing to clutch/final drive housing	18	13
Intermediate plate to clutch/final drive housing	50	37
Pressed-steel housing	18	13
Bearing half-rings	18	13
Output shaft nut (MA 5)	140	103
Drain and filler plugs	25	19
Gearbox to engine	45	33

Automatic transmission
General
Make .... ZF
Type 4 HP14
Number of speeds .... Four forward and one reverse
Ratios (overall) – pre May 1987:
  1st 8.83:1
  2nd 5.02:1
  3rd 3.66:1
  4th 2.71:1
  Reverse 10.36:1
Final drive ratio 3.17:1
Ratios (overall) – May 1987 on:
  1st 9.61:1
  2nd 5.45:1
  3rd 3.98:1
  4th 2.94:1
  Reverse 11.26:1
Final drive 3.82:1

Lubrication
Lubricant type/specification .... Dexron II type ATF (Duckhams D-Matic)
Lubricant capacity:
  From dry .... 6.2 litres (10.9 pints)
  Drain and refill .... 2.4 litres (4.25 pints)
Note: *Final drive uses transmission fluid although it is drained separately*

Torque wrench settings

	Nm	lbf ft
Inhibitor switch	41	30
Fluid cooler	50	37
Dipstick tube nut	45	33
Selector cable bracket	30	22
Torque converter to driveplate	35	26
Transmission to engine	45	33

LH mounting to transmission	35	26
LH mounting to body	18	13

Driveshafts (1988-on models)
Torque wrench settings

	Nm	lbf ft
Hub nut	265	196
Front suspension lower balljoint	45	33

Braking system (1.9 GTI)
Type .... Front and rear disc brakes, servo-assisted rear brake compensators, cable-operated handbrake on rear wheels

Disc brakes – general

	Front	Rear
Disc diameter	247 mm	247 mm
Disc thickness (new)	20.4 mm	8.0 mm
Disc thickness (minimum after resurfacing)	18.5 mm	7.0 mm
Disc run-out (maximum)	0.07 mm	0.07 mm
Disc pad minimum lining thickness	2.0 mm	2.0 mm
Vacuum servo unit type (RHD only)	Isovac 204 mm	

Torque wrench settings

	Nm	lbf ft
Front disc caliper (1.9 GTI)	100	74
Rear disc caliper (1.9 GTI)	120	88
Caliper guide bolt (1.9 GTI)	35	26

Suspension and roadwheels
Rear wheel alignment

Camber:
All models except GTI, Automatic and Cabriolet	−0°30′ ± 30′
GTI, Automatic and Cabriolet	−0°50′ ± 30′

Toe-in:
All models except GTI, Automatic and Cabriolet, and models with TU Engine	0.5 ± 1 mm (0.02 ± 0.04 in)
GTI (1.6)	1.5 ± 1 mm (0.06 ± 0.04 in)
GTI (1.9)	1.0 ± 1 mm (0.04 ± 0.04 in)
Automatic and Cabriolet	1.0 ± 1 mm (0.04 ± 0.04 in)
All models with TU engine	1.0 ± 2 mm (0.04 ± 0.08 in)

Roadwheels

Type:
CTI	Light alloy
1.9 GTI	Pressed steel or light alloy

Size:
CTI	5.5J 14 FH H 4.24
1.9 GTI	6.5J 15 CH 4.19

Tyres

Size:
	Front	Rear
CTI	185/60 HR 14	
1.9 GTI	185/55 VR 15	
Pressures – bar (lbf/in²):		
145 SR 13 (Van)	1.9 (28)	2.3 (33) unladen
		2.6 (38) laden
165/70 SR 13 (Automatic)	2.0 (29)	2.0 (29)
185/60 HR 14 (CTI)	2.0 (29)	2.1 (30)
185/55 VR 15 (1.9 GTI)	2.0 (29)	2.0 (29)

Torque wrench setting

	Nm	lbf ft
Roadwheels (revised setting for all steel and alloy wheels)	85	62

Steering system
General

Turning circle (between kerbs):
CTI	10.30 m (33 ft 9 in)
1.9 GTI	11.20 m (36 ft 9 in)

Front wheel alignment

Toe-in:
CTI	3.0 ± 1.0 mm (0.118 ± 0.04 in)
1.9 GTI	2.0 ± 1.0 mm (0.08 ± 0.04 in)

Castor:
CTI	1°35′ ± 30′
1.9 GTI	2° ± 30′

Camber:
    CTI .... 0°15' ± 30'
    1.6 GTI .... 0° ± 30'
    1.9 GTI .... 0°10' ± 30'
Steering axis inclination:
    CTI .... 9° 20' ± 30'
    1.9 GTI .... 9° 30' ± 30'

Electrical system
Battery
XU5JA and XU51C engine .... 29 amp/hour or 33 amp/hour

Alternator
Rating (GTI and CTI from July 1986) .... 1130 watt
Drivebelt tension (TU engines) .... As XU engine

Fuses (1986 GTI and CTI)

No	Circuit protected	Rating (amp)
1	Reversing lamps, tachometer	10
2	Direction indicators, heater blower motor, oil pressure gauge, oil temperature gauge, heated seats, fuel gauge, coolant temperature gauge, low battery charge warning, oil pressure warning, brake system warning, coolant temperature warning, low coolant level warning	25
3	Windscreen wiper/washer, stop-lights, headlamp washer, radio accessories	25
4	Spare	–
5	Hazard warning	10
6	Spare	–
7	Cigarette lighter, clock, interior lights, boot lamp, central door locking, radio	25
8	Horns	25
9	Electrically-operated windows	20
10	Rear foglamp (LH)	5
11	Tail lamp (RH), number plate light	5
12	Tail lamp (LH)	5
13	Instrument panel illumination, parking lights	5
14	Fuel pump	15

Fuses (1988-on models)

No	Circuit protected	Rating (amp)
1	Reversing lamps	10
2	Direction indicators, heater motor, ignition warning light	25
3	Fuel gauge, stop-lamps, front and rear wash/wipe, tachometer, headlamp wash, radio, storage tray light, warning lights (coolant temperature, oil pressure, coolant level, handbrake, choke)	25
4	Spare	–
5	Hazard warning	10
6	Spare	–
7	Cigarette lighter, clock, interior lamps, boot lamp, central door locking, radio	25
8	Horns, heated rear windows	25
9	Electrically operated windows	20
10	Rear foglamp	5
11	Tail lamp, number plate lamp	5
12	Spare	–
13	Instrument panel, sidelights	5

Bulbs   ## Wattage
Number plate lamp 5

Torque wrench settings
    CTI .... As for GTI

---

3 Routine maintenance

        As from 1988 model year, the manual gearboxes types MA and BE 1 are filled with a special gearbox oil which does not require draining at the previously stated intervals. However, it is necessary to carry out an oil level check every 36 000 miles (60 000 km) and, should topping-up be required, it is important to use only the identical oil as given in 'Recommended lubricants and fluids'.

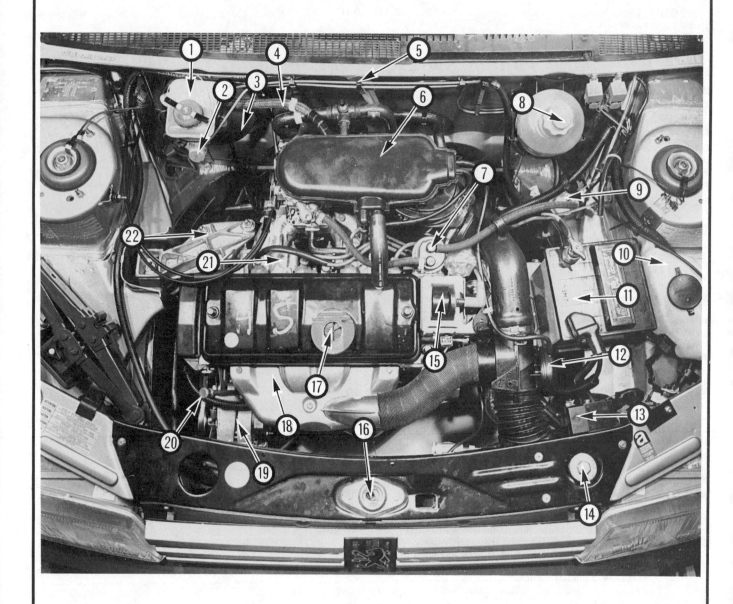

Under-bonnet view of TU3S engine

1 Brake fluid reservoir filler
   cap
2 Brake master cylinder
3 Brake vacuum servo unit
4 Servo vacuum hose
5 Cooling system bleed screw
6 Air cleaner cover

7 Fuel pump
8 Cooling system expansion
   bottle
9 Fuel filter
10 Washer fluid reservoir
11 Battery
12 Air temperature control unit

13 Auxiliary fusebox
14 Radiator filler cap
15 Ignition coil
16 Bonnet lock
17 Engine oil filler cap
18 Exhaust manifold hot air
   shroud

19 Alternator
20 Engine oil level dipstick
21 Inlet manifold
22 Right-hand engine
   mounting

View of front underside of TU3S engine model

1 Gearbox (type MA)	8 Hydraulic brake lines	15 Front towing eye
2 Disc caliper	9 Intermediate exhaust pipe	16 Bottom hose
3 LH driveshaft	10 Gearchange rod	17 Alternator
4 Anti-roll bar	11 Subframe	18 Engine sump drain plug
5 Track rod	12 Rear lower engine mounting	19 Oil filter
6 Guide bar	13 Lower suspension arm	20 Exhaust front downpipe
7 Fuel supply pipe	14 RH driveshaft	21 Radiator

4 Engine (except TU)

Main bearing shells – modification

1   As from early 1986 the locating tabs of the main bearing shells on XV, XW and XY engines are offset as shown in Fig. 13.1. It is not possible to fit the earlier type of main bearing shell to later models with this modification.

Cylinder head – modifications

2   As from early 1986 on XV, XW and XY engines, the two cylinder head-to-block locating dowels are reduced in diameter from 16.0 mm to 14.0 mm. A new cylinder head gasket with reduced diameter holes is also fitted.
3   From the same date three additional locating dowels are fitted to the rocker shaft pedestals, and the bolt holes in the camshaft cover are increased in diameter.
4   If necessary it is possible to mate the cylinder head to a non-compatible block by using stepped locating dowels, together with the later type head gasket.

Valve clearances (XV, XW and XY engines) – adjustment

5   As from January 1987 XV, XW and XY engines are fitted with bi-metal rockers consisting of an aluminium arm and steel pad. This modification has resulted in revised valve clearances as given in the Specifications. Note also that the valve timing is revised.

XU5JA engine – description

6   As from February 1986 GTI models may be fitted with the XU5JA engine. The CTI model has been fitted with this engine since its introduction in April 1986. This engine is an uprated version of the XU5J engine described in Chapter 1, and the main differences are described in the following paragraphs.
7   The recommended plain and grooved bearing arrangement for the XU5JA engine is as follows (Chapter 1, Section 36):

Bearing No	1	2	3	4	5
Top (block)	G	G	G	G	G
Bottom (cap)	G	P	P	P	P

8   The XU5JA engine is also fitted with improved liners, connecting rods and valve springs. Larger valves are fitted, together with modified combustion chambers and inlet/exhaust ports. A modified camshaft is fitted with a lift of 11.5 mm (0.453 in).

XU51C engine – description

9   The XU51C engine is fitted to automatic transmission models. It is identical to the XU5J engine described in Chapter 1, but it is fitted with a carburettor instead of fuel injection equipment. All procedures are basically as given in Chapter 1 but references to the fuel injection components should be ignored, and where necessary carburettor removal and refitting substituted.

Engine (automatic transmission models) – removal and refitting

10   Due to the additional weight involved, it is recommended that the automatic transmission is removed independently as described in Section 12 of this Supplement before removing the engine. Refer to Chapter 1, Section 28 for the removal of the engine, and Section 38 for refitting.

XU9JA engine – description

11   The XU9JA engine is fitted to the 1.9 GTI, and its general construction is identical to that of the XU5JA as fitted to the 1.6 GTI and 1.6 CTI.
12   Apart from the differences given in the Specifications, the main changes concern the camshaft, sump, pistons, and the addition of an oil cooler. The camshaft endfloat is controlled by machined shoulders on the No 1 bearing instead of a thrust plate. The height of the sump is reduced to accommodate a spacer plate, which acts as a stiffener. The pistons have special dished crowns. The oil cooler is mounted in front of the radiator on the right-hand side.
13   Work procedures are as for the XU5JA engine except for the differences described in paragraphs 12 and 14 to 21.

← FRONT

Fig. 13.1 Main bearing shell tab offset – 1986-on XV, XW and XY engines (Sec 4)

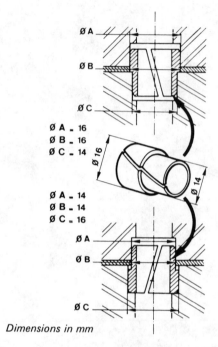

Ø A = 16
Ø B = 16
Ø C = 14

Ø A = 14
Ø B = 14
Ø C = 16

Dimensions in mm

Fig. 13.2 Stepped locating dowels available for matching the cylinder head to the block on XV, XW and XY engines (Sec 4)

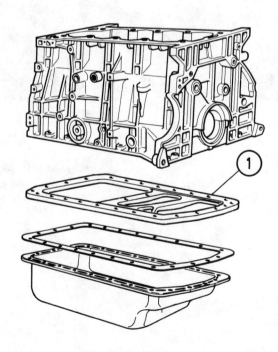

Fig. 13.3 Spacer plate (1) fitted to the sump on the XU9JA engine (Sec 4)

Oil cooler (1.9 GTI) – removal and refitting

14 Remove the radiator grille and front bumper as described in Chapter 11 and Section 16 of this Chapter.

15 Unbolt the engine compartment front crossmember and position it to one side, leaving the bonnet release cable still attached.

16 Remove the air inlet hose (photo).

17 Remove the stone guard from the front cowling (photos).

18 Unscrew the retaining bolts, then release the clips and move the front cowling forwards for access to the oil cooler (photos).

19 Place rags or a container beneath the oil cooler to collect any spilled oil. Unscrew the union nuts while holding the connection stubs stationary (photo). Plug the stubs, or tie them to one side.

20 Unscrew the nuts, release the oil cooler from the front cowling and remove it from the car (photos).

21 Refitting is a reversal of removal, but tighten the union nuts carefully to the specified torque while holding the connection stubs stationary.

Sump spacer plate (1.9 GTI) – removal and refitting

22 Remove the sump and gasket.

23 Unscrew the two bolts from the diagonally opposite corners and remove the spacer plate from the cylinder block. If it is stuck, use a thin knife to cut into the jointing compound.

24 Thoroughly clean the surfaces of the block, spacer plate and sump.

25 Apply silicone jointing compound to the upper mating surface of the spacer plate, position the plate on the block, then insert and tighten the two bolts to the specified torque.

26 Refit the sump together with a new gasket. Insert and tighten the bolts to the specified torque.

Right-hand engine mounting (XU engines) – modification

27 As from March 1987 (chassis number 5737675) the adjustment shims have been deleted from the right-hand engine mounting, and the rubber buffers are increased in thickness by 5.5 mm (0.217 in). On vehicles with this modification, the adjustment procedure given in Chapter 1, Section 38 is not applicable.

28 To prevent scuffing noises from the buffers, it is recommended that the inner surfaces which contact the engine bracket are lubricated with rubber grease.

Cylinder head bolts and cylinder liners (XU engines) – modifications

29 As from early 1987, the cylinder head bolts are of No 55 Torx type, and 8mm (0.315 in) thick washers are fitted instead of the previous 3 mm (0.118 in) thick washers fitted to the hexagon head bolts. The spacer fitted to the bolt at the timing belt end is now 25 mm (0.984 in) thick, (previously 23 mm), and is identified by a groove around its perimeter.

30 A Torx extension will be required to loosen and tighten the head bolts, and this should be obtained from an auto accessory store or tool suppliers.

31 At the same time, the cylinder liners were reduced in height by 0.05 mm (0.002 in), and consequently the protrusion dimensions are reduced by the same amount, as given in the Specifications. A modified cylinder head gasket was also fitted, so it is important to quote the engine number accurately when obtaining a new one.

32 The tightening procedure for the Torx cylinder head bolts is different as given in the Specifications, and this method must never be used on hexagonal cylinder head bolts. It is **not** necessary to re-tighten the bolts after initial running.

33 When fitting the Torx cylinder head bolts, apply a little molybdebum disulphide grease to their threads and to the contact surface of their heads.

Electronic oil level sensor – description

34 Some 1985 models have an oil level sensor fitted to the engine sump, together with a warning lamp on the instrument panel. The system was only fitted in the 1985 model year and has been deleted from later models.

35 The sensor incorporates a high resistance wire which varies in conductivity depending on whether it is immersed in or above the oil. An electronic control unit mounted under the right-hand side of the facia monitors the conductivity and operates the warning lamp when necessary.

36 It should be noted that the system only functions accurately if the car is on a level surface. When the ignition is initially switched on the

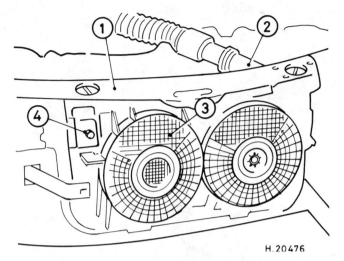

Fig. 13.4 Oil cooler removal (Sec 4)

1 *Front crossmember*   3 *Stone guard*
2 *Air inlet hose*   4 *Cowling retaining bolt*

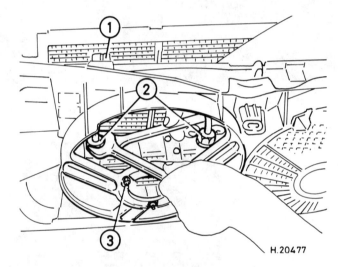

Fig. 13.5 Oil cooler removal (Sec 4)

1 *Cowling clip*   3 *Oil cooler mounting nuts*
2 *Oil cooler connection stubs*

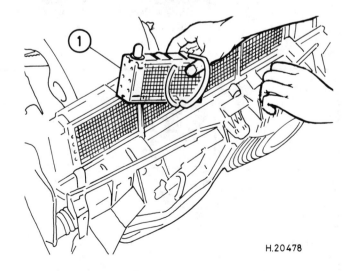

Fig. 13.6 Removing the oil cooler (1) (Sec 4)

4.16 Air inlet hose (arrowed)

4.17A Stone guard outer clips (arrowed) ...

4.17B ... and inner clips (arrowed)

4.18A Radiator clip on the front cowling

4.18B Separating the radiator and front cowling

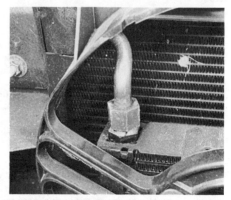

4.19 Oil cooler union nut

4.20A Oil cooler mounting nuts

4.20B Oil cooler pipe bracket nut (arrowed)

Fig. 13.7 Torx type cylinder head bolt (Sec 4)

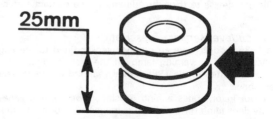

Fig. 13.8 The 25 mm (0.984 in) spacer is identified by a groove (Sec 4)

warning lamp should light for two seconds. If the oil level is correct the lamp will then go out, but if it starts to flash the oil level is low.

37 To prevent the system functioning unnecessarily after the engine has started, the control unit is earthed through the oil pressure switch. The level check is made before starting the engine. Some early models are not earthed through the oil pressure switch and on these, the warning lamp may flash if for instance the engine is temporarily stalled and the oil has not returned to the sump. It is possible to modify the existing wiring; however this work is best entrusted to a Peugeot dealer.

Crankcase ventilation hoses – maintenance

38 Periodically, and particularly at high mileages, the crankcase ventilation hoses should be removed and cleaned. Check the interior of the hoses for collapsed linings or other restrictions.

39 Blockage of a crankcase ventilation hose can cause the engine oil filler cap to blow off, or the oil separators to fill with oil.

---

5 Engine (TU)

Engine – general description

1 The TU engine is a lighter but more powerful version of the XU5J engine described in Chapter 1. The most significant difference is that the TU engine is inclined forward by 6°, with the exhaust manifold mounted on the front of the cylinder head and the inlet manifold and carburettor mounted on the rear.

Operations possible without removing the engine from the car

2 The following components can be removed and refitted with the engine in the car:

  (a) Cylinder head
  (b) Timing belt and camshaft
  (c) Sump and oil pump
  (d) Clutch and flywheel (after removal of transmission)

3 Since the sump and cylinder head can be removed *in situ*, it is possible to renew the pistons, liners and big-end bearings without removing the engine. However, this work is not recommended, since it can be performed more easily with the engine on the bench.

Engine – removal and refitting

4 The engine and transmission assembly is removed by lifting upwards from the engine compartment. The transmission is separated from the engine on the bench.

5 Remove the bonnet (Chapter 11) or alternatively disconnect the bonnet stay, fully raise the bonnet, and retain by inserting two suitable U-bolts in the special holes in the hinges.

6 Remove the battery (Chapter 12) and unbolt the tray bracket (photos).

7 Jack up the front of the car and support on axle stands. Alternatively position the front of the car on ramps or over an inspection pit.

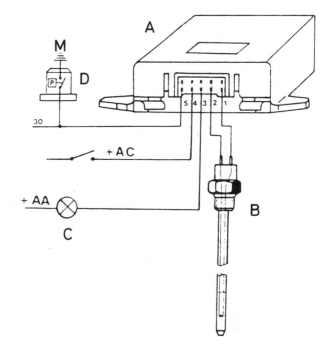

Fig. 13.9 Electronic oil level sensor wiring diagram (Sec 4)

A Electronic control unit	M Earth
B Sensor	+AC Ignition
C Warning lamp	ACC Accessory supply
D Oil pressure switch	

8 Drain the cooling system (Section 6).

9 Drain the engine oil (photo) and gearbox oil.

10 Disconnect the choke and accelerator cables and unbolt the bracket.

11 Remove the air cleaner (Section 7).

12 Disconnect the fuel supply hose from the fuel pump.

13 Remove the radiator (Section 6).

14 Unscrew the two bolts from the lower rear engine mounting and remove the yoke (photo).

15 Remove both driveshafts by referring to Chapter 7 and Section 13 of this Chapter.

16 Unbolt the exhaust front pipe from the exhaust manifold and remove the metal gasket.

17 Unbolt the front pipe bracket from the gearbox, unbolt the flange from the rear exhaust system, and remove the front pipe.

18 Pull out the rubber cotter and disconnect the speedometer cable from the gearbox (photo).

19 Disconnect the gearchange control rods (photo).

5.6A Battery clamp bolt (arrowed)

5.6B Removing the battery tray bracket

5.9 Engine oil drain plug

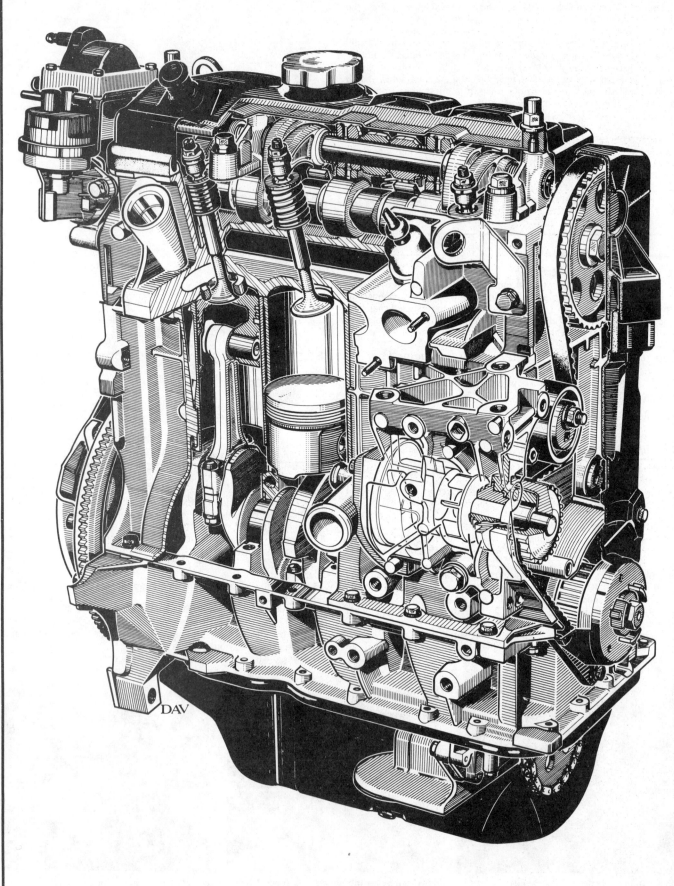

Fig. 13.10 Cutaway view of the TU engine (Sec 5)

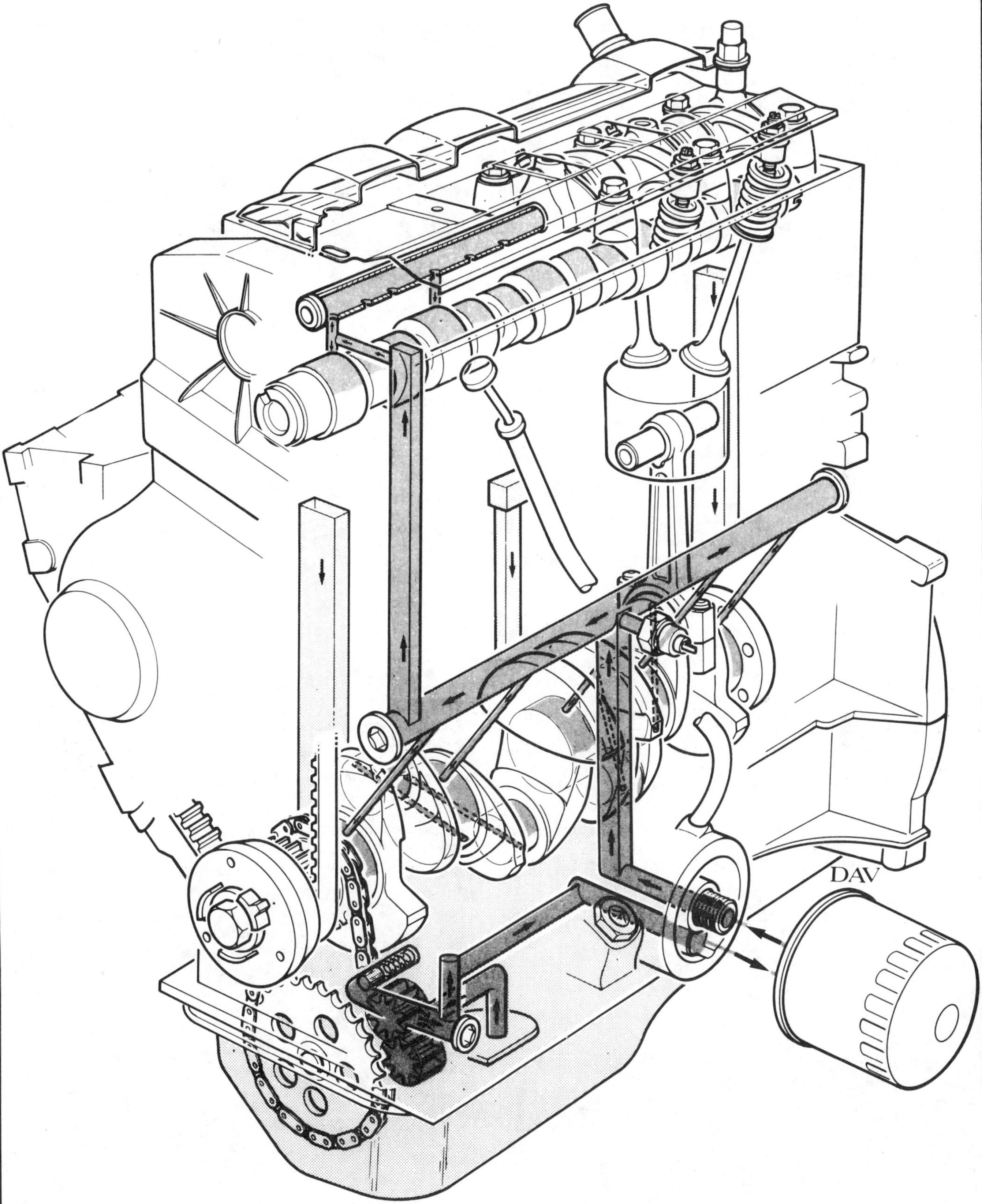

Fig. 13.11 Lubrication system on the TU engine (Sec 5)

5.14 Lower rear engine mounting yoke

5.18 Removing the speedometer cable (arrowed)

5.19 Gearchange control rods – arrowed (engine removed for clarity)

20 Unbolt the right-hand driveshaft bearing bracket from the cylinder block.
21 Disconnect the clutch cable (Chapter 5).
22 Disconnect the heater hoses and bottom hose from the engine (photo).
23 Unscrew the nut and remove the earth cable from the gearbox (photo).
24 Disconnect the brake servo vacuum hose.
25 Note the location of the engine wiring harness, then disconnect it from the various components (photos). Also unscrew the nut and disconnect the pink battery lead from the fusebox.
26 Connect a hoist to the two engine lifting eyes, and support the weight of the engine and gearbox.
27 Unscrew the left-hand mounting nuts, including the nut on the centre stud and remove the mounting (photo).
28 Unscrew the right-hand mounting centre nut. If necessary, unscrew the nuts and remove the bracket completely (photo).
29 Lower the engine and gearbox so that the left-hand mounting stud cleans the mounting bracket, turn the assembly so that it is positioned diagonally in the engine compartment, then slowly lift the assembly while guiding it clear of the components in the engine compartment (photos).
30 When clear of the front panel, move it forwards and lower to the ground.
31 Refitting is a reversal of removal, but note the following additional points:

   (a) Use a plastic protector (see Section 13) when refitting the right-hand driveshaft
   (b) Adjust the clutch cable with reference to Chapter 5

   (c) Adjust the choke and accelerator cables with reference to Chapter 3
   (d) Fill the engine and gearbox with oil
   (e) Fill the cooling system as described in Section 6
   (f) Tension the alternatior drivebelt with reference to Chapter 12

Engine – separation from transmission
32 Unbolt and remove the starter motor together with the air cleaner bracket (photos).
33 Unscrew and remove the gearbox-to-engine bolts (photo).
34 Support the engine and lift the gearbox away from it. Recover any loose dowels.

Engine dismantling – general
35 Refer to Chapter 1, Section 10.

Engine – complete dismantling
36 Disconnect the HT leads from the spark plugs, unbolt the lead support (photo), disconnect the HT lead from the coil, and remove the distributor cap.
37 Remove the spark plugs.
38 Disconnect the vacuum hose between the distributor and carburettor.
39 Disconnect the hoses between the fuel pump and carburettor, and water pump and thermostat housing (photo).
40 Unscrew the nuts and remove the inlet manifold complete with carburettor from the studs on the cylinder head (photo). Note that there is no gasket.
41 Unbolt and remove the fuel pump and remove the gasket.

5.22 Bottom hose connection to water pump housing

5.23 Earth cable attachment (arrowed)

5.25A Wiring to starter motor

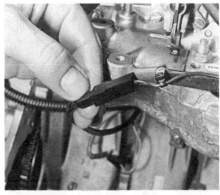

5.25B Carburettor stop solenoid wiring connector

5.25C Wiring harness clip on cylinder block

5.25D Wiring harness clips on timing cover

5.25E Water temperature sender and wiring

5.27 Left-hand engine mounting

5.28 Right-hand engine mounting bracket

5.29A Removing the engine and gearbox assembly

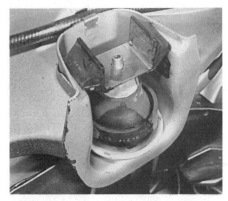

5.29B Right-hand engine mounting (engine removed)

5.32A Unscrew the bolts ...

5.32B ... and remove the starter motor

5.33 Gearbox-to-engine bolt (arrowed)

5.36 Removing the HT lead support

5.39 Hose from water pump to thermostat housing

5.40 Removing the inlet manifold complete with carburettor

42 Loosen the alternator pivot and adjustment bolts, then unscrew the tension bolt and slip the drivebelt from the pulleys. Remove the pivot and adjustment bolts and remove the alternator (photos).
43 Unbolt the pulley from the front of the crankshaft (photo).
44 Unbolt and remove the coil, after unclipping the TDC connector (photo).
45 Unbolt the exhaust manifold hot air shroud.
46 Unscrew the brass nuts, remove the washers, and remove the exhaust manifold from the studs on the cylinder head. Remove the gaskets.
47 Remove the distributor with reference to Chapter 4.
48 Remove the thermostat with reference to Section 6.
49 Unbolt the thermostat housing from the cylinder head (photo).
50 Unbolt the distributor mounting flange from the cylinder head (photo).
51 Unbolt the TDC sensor from the flywheel end of the cylinder block, and unclip the lead from the timing plate (photos).
52 Unbolt and remove the timing plate (photo).
53 Unscrew and remove the oil filter, using a removal strap if

necessary (photo).
54 Unscrew and remove the oil pressure switch (photo).
55 Unscrew the mounting bolt and pull the engine oil dipstick holder from the main bearing cap casting. Remove the dipstick from the holder (photos).
56 Unscrew the nuts and remove the valve cover. Remove the rubber gasket from the cover (photos).
57 Remove the two spacers and baffle plate from the studs (photos).
58 Unbolt the upper timing cover, followed by the intermediate cover and lower cover (photos).
59 Turn the engine clockwise, using a socket on the crankshaft pulley bolt, until the small hole in the camshaft sprocket is aligned with the corresponding hole in the cylinder head. Insert the shank of a close-fitting twist drill (eg a 10 mm drill) into the holes (photo).
60 Align the TDC holes in the flywheel and cylinder block rear flange and insert a further twist drill or long bolt (photo).
61 Loosen the timing belt tensioner roller nut (photo), turn the tensioner clockwise using a screwdriver or square drive in the special hole, then re-tighten the nut.

5.42A Alternator pivot (A), adjustment (B) and tension (C) bolts

5.42B Removing alternator pivot bolt

5.43 Unbolting the crankshaft pulley

5.44A TDC connector on the coil (arrowed)

5.44B Coil location over the distributor

5.49 Removing the thermostat housing

5.50 Distributor mounting flange

5.51A TDC sensor wiring clip ...

5.51B .. and mounting bolt (arrowed)

5.52 Timing plate (arrowed)

5.53 Removing the oil filter

5.54 Oil pressure switch

5.55A Dipstick holder upper mounting

5.55B Dipstick holder removal from main bearing cap casting

5.56A Removing the valve cover nuts

5.56B Removing the valve cover gasket

5.57A Remove the spacers (arrowed) ...

5.57B ... and baffle plate

5.58A Unscrew the bolts ...

5.58B ... and remove the upper timing cover ...

5.58C ... intermediate cover ...

5.58D ... and lower cover

5.59 Camshaft sprocket set to TDC

5.60 Using a long bolt through the cylinder block rear flange into the flywheel TDC hole

62 Mark the normal direction of rotation on the timing belt, then remove it from the camshaft, water pump, and crankshaft sprockets.

63 Unscrew the tensioner nut and remove the tensioner roller.

64 Progressively loosen the cylinder head bolts using the reverse sequence to that shown in Fig. 13.13 then remove all the bolts.

65 Lift off the rocker arm assembly (photo).

66 Rock the cylinder head to free it from the block, then it from the location dowels (photo). Two angled metal rods, shown in Fig. 13.12, may be used for this purpose.

67 Remove the cylinder head gasket from the block.

68 Fit liner clamps (see Chapter 1, Section 24) if it is not proposed to remove the pistons and liners.

69 Progressively loosen the clutch pressure plate bolts and remove the pressure plate and friction disc from the flywheel (photo).

70 Unbolt the water pump housing from the side of the block and prise out the O-ring.

71 Have an assistant hold the flywheel stationary with a wide-bladed screwdriver inserted between the starter ring gear teeth, then unscrew the crankshaft pulley bolt and remove the hub/sprocket and oil seal flange (photos).

72 Using a screwdriver, prise the front oil seal from the block and main bearing casting (photo).

73 Hold the flywheel stationary as described in paragraph 71 and unscrew the flywheel bolts. Lift the flywheel from the dowel on the crankshaft rear flange.

74 Prise out the crankshaft rear oil seal using a screwdriver.

75 Invert the engine and support on blocks of wood.

76 Unscrew the nuts and bolts securing the sump to the main bearing casting, and remove it by carefully prising it free of the jointing compound (photos).

77 Unbolt the oil pump and tilt it to release the drive sprocket from the chain (photos).

78 Support the block on its flywheel end.

79 Mark the liners for position, starting with No 1 (at the flywheel end). Similarly mark the big-end bearing caps.

80 Temporarily refit the crankshaft pulley bolt and turn the crankshaft so that Nos 1 and 4 pistons (No 1 at flywheel end) are at bottom dead centre (BDC).

81 Unscrew the nuts and remove the big-end bearing caps (photo). Remove the lower big-end shells, keeping them identified for position.

82 Remove the clamps and withdraw the liners, complete with

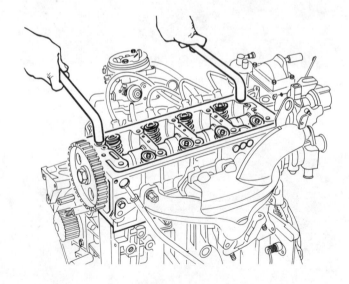

13.12 Using two angled metal rods to free the cylinder head from the block (Sec 5)

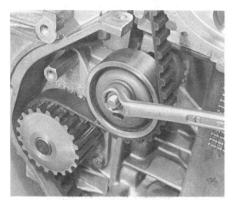

5.61 Loosening the timing belt tensioner roller nut

5.65 Removing the rocker arm assembly

5.66 Lifting the cylinder head from the block

5.69 Clutch pressure plate and friction disc removal

5.71A Unscrew the crankshaft pulley bolt ...

5.71B .. and remove the hub/sprocket ...

5.71C ... and oil seal flange

5.72 Prising out the crankshaft front oil seal

5.76A Unscrew the nuts and bolts ...

5.76B ... and remove the sump

5.77A Unscrew the bolts ...

5.77B ... and remove the oil pump from the chain

5.81 Removing a big-end bearing cap

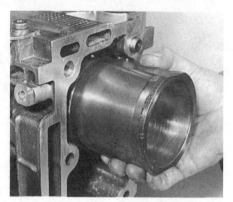

5.82 Removing a liner and piston assembly

5.83 Liner bottom O-ring (arrowed)

pistons, from the block (photo).
83 Remove the liner bottom O-rings (photo).
84 Repeat the procedure for Nos 2 and 3 pistons and liners.
85 Invert the engine again, and unscrew the bolts securing the main bearing cap casting to the block (photos).
86 Progressively unscrew the main bearing bolts, and lift the main bearing cap casting from the block. Gently tap it with a wooden or soft-headed mallet to release it. Prise out the main bearing shells, keeping them identified for location.
87 Remove the oil pump sprocket and chain from the crankshaft (photo).
88 Lift the crankshaft from the block and remove the main bearing shells, keeping them identified for location. Also remove the endfloat rings from No 2 main bearing location (photos).

Cylinder head – dismantling, decarbonising and reassembly

89 Remove the twistdrill from the camshaft sprocket, then hold the sprocket stationary using an oil filter stop wrench or tool as shown in photo 5.96. Unscrew the bolt and remove the sprocket (photos).
90 Unbolt and remove the camshaft thrust fork (photo).
91 Prise out the oil seal and carefully withdraw the camshaft from the cylinder head (photos).
92 Remove the valves and springs, clean and check the cylinder head, and refit the valves and springs with reference to Chapter 1, Section 32 (photos).
93 Oil the camshaft bearings and insert the camshaft into the cylinder head.
94 Refit the camshaft thrust fork and tighten the bolt (photo).
95 Dip the new oil seal in oil, and press it into the cylinder head until flush, using a metal tube or large socket and hammer (photo).
96 Refit the camshaft sprocket so that the location peg enters the cut-out. Insert and tighten the bolt while holding the sprocket stationary using either method described in paragraph 89 (photo).

Engine components – examination and renovation (general)

97 Refer to Chapter 1, Section 13.

Examination and renovation of dismantled components

98 Refer to Chapter 1, Section 34, but note that there is no camshaft lubrication manifold, as the camshaft runs in an oil bath. Also note that although the timing belt should be renewed when the engine is overhauled or if it is contaminated with oil, there is no specified replacement mileage. When handling the timing belt, do not bend it as this may damage the internal fibres.

Engine reassembly – general

99 Refer to Chapter 1, Sections 16 and 17.

Engine – complete reassembly

Note: *For details of modified pistons fitted to TU9 engines, refer to the end of this Section*
100 With the block upside-down on the bench, press the main bearing upper shells into position. Note that the grooved bearings are fitted to positions No 2 and 4.
101 Smear a little grease on the endfloat rings and locate them each side of No 2 bearing with their grooves facing outwards.

102 Oil the bearings and lower the crankshaft into position (photo).
103 Check that the crankshaft endfloat is as given in the Specifications, using a feeler blade between an endfloat ring and the crankshaft web. The rings are available in four thicknesses.
104 Fit the oil pump sprocket and chain to the front of the crankshaft, locating the sprocket on the Woodruff key.
105 Press the main bearing lower shells into position in the main bearing cap casting, noting that the grooved bearings are fitted to positions No 2 and 4.
106 Apply jointing compound to the mating face, then lower the main bearing cap casting into position over the crankshaft. At the same time, feed the oil pump chain through the aperture (photos).
107 Insert the main bearing bolts dry, then tighten them evenly to the initial torque wrench setting. Angle-tighten the bolts by a further 45° (photos).
108 Refit the bolts securing the main bearing cap casting to the block and tighten them to the specified torque.
109 Support the block on its flywheel end.
110 Check that the lower big-end bearing shells are fitted to the big-end caps and the upper shells to the connecting rods.
111 Oil the liner bores and piston rings.
112 Position the piston ring end gaps at 120° from each other so that neither is in line with another.
113 Fit a piston ring compressor to each piston in turn, and push the pistons in their respective liners using a hammer handle (photos). Make sure that the arrows on the piston crowns face the front (timing belt end) of the liners.
114 Fit the bottom O-rings to the liners, taking care not to twist them.
115 Check that the crankshaft rotates freely, then position Nos 1 and 4 crankpins at bottom dead centre (BDC). Oil the crankpins.
116 Insert No 1 liner/piston into the block, and guide the connecting rod big-end onto the crankpin. Refit the big-end bearing cap and tighten the nuts evenly to the specified torque (photo).
117 Check that the crankshaft rotates freely, while holding the liner in position with a clamp. Temporarily refit the crankshaft pulley bolt to turn the crankshaft.
118 Repeat the procedure to fit the remaining pistons and liners.
119 Support the block upside-down on the bench.
120 Check that the oil pump location pin is fitted to the main bearing casting, then refit the oil pump while tilting it to engage the drive sprocket with the chain. Insert and tighten the bolts.
121 Apply jointing compound to the mating faces of the sump and main bearing casting. Refit the sump, insert the bolts and tighten them to the specified torque.
122 Dip the new crankshaft rear oil seal in oil and locate it over the rear of the crankshaft (photo).
123 Peugeot garages use their special tool (0132 U) to fit the oil seal, however it may be fitted by using the flywheel. Temporarily locate the flywheel on the crankshaft using four bolts, then tighten the bolts evenly until the flywheel contacts the rear flange (photo). Remove the flywheel and use a metal tube or block of wood to drive the oil seal fully into position.
124 Apply locking fluid to the threads of the flywheel bolts, locate the flywheel on the crankshaft dowel, then insert the bolts and tighten them to the specified torque while holding the flywheel as described in paragraph 71 (photos).
125 Support the engine upright on the bench.

5.85A Unscrew the main bearing cap casting front bolts ...

5.85B ... and side bolts (arrowed)

5.87 Oil pump sprocket and chain removal

5.88A Removing the crankshaft ...

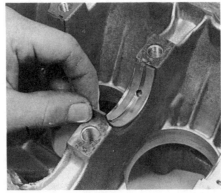

5.88B ... main bearing shells ...

5.88C ... and endfloat rings

5.89A Unscrew the bolt ...

5.89B ... and remove the camshaft sprocket – note location peg and cut-out (arrowed)

5.90 Camshaft thrust fork (arrowed)

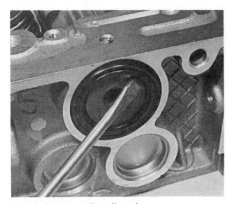

5.91A Prise out the oil seal ...

5.91B .. and withdraw the camshaft

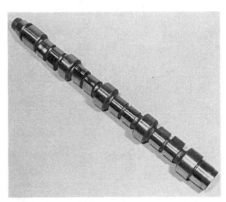

5.91C Camshaft removed from the cylinder head

5.92A Compress the valve spring and remove the collets ...

5.92B ... retainer ...

5.92C ... spring ...

5.92D .. spring seat ...

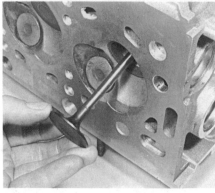

5.92E ... and valve

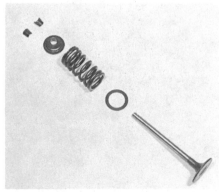

5.92F Valve components removed from the cylinder head

5.94 Refitting the camshaft thrust fork

5.95 Refitting the camshaft oil seal

5.96 Using a home-made tool to hold the camshaft sprocket while tightening the bolt

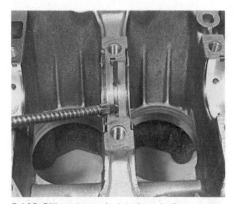

5.102 Oiling the main bearing shells

5.106A Apply jointing compound to the mating faces ...

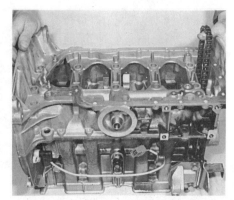

5.106B ... then lower the main bearing cap casting into position

5.107A Torque-tighten the main bearing bolts ...

5.107B ... then angle-tighten a further 45°

5.113A Piston assembly

5.113B Fit the compressor and lower the piston in the liner

5.113C Use a hammer handle to push the piston into the liner

5.116 Tightening the big-end bearing cap nuts

5.122 Refitting the crankshaft rear oil seal

5.123 Using the flywheel and four bolts to fit the crankshaft rear oil seal

5.124A Apply locking fluid to the flywheel bolts ...

5.124B ... and tighten to the specified torque

5.126 Refitting the crankshaft front oil seal

5.127 Tightening the crankshaft pulley bolt

126 Dip the crankshaft front oil seal in oil, locate it over the front of the crankshaft, and drive it in flush with the front of the block using a metal tube or socket (photo). There is no seating, so take care not to drive it in too far.

127 Fit the oil seal flange, followed by the hub/sprocket. Insert the pulley bolt and spacer, and tighten the bolt to the specified torque while holding the flywheel stationary (photo).

128 Refit the water pump housing together with a new O-ring, and tighten the bolts to the specified torque.

129 Locate the clutch friction disc and pressure plate on the flywheel with the dowels engaged. Insert the bolts finger-tight.

130 Centralise the friction disc using a universal tool, or by making a wooden adaptor to the dimensions shown in Fig. 13.38 (photo).

131 Tighten the pressure plate bolts evenly to the specified torque (photo).

132 Clean the cylinder head and block joint faces thoroughly. Also clean the cylinder head bolt holes.

133 Locate the new cylinder head gasket on the block dowels with the manufacturer's name uppermost (photo).

134 Align the TDC holes in the flywheel and block rear flange, and insert a twist drill or long bolt.

135 Align the small hole in the camshaft sprocket with the hole in the cylinder head and insert a twist drill or bolt (photo).

136 Lower the cylinder head onto the block so that it engages the two dowels.

137 Refit the rocker arm assembly.

138 Lubricate the cylinder head bolt threads and heads with molybdenum disulphide grease. Insert them and tighten to the initial torque using the sequence given in Fig. 13.13 (photo).

139 Using the same sequence, angle-tighten the bolts by 240° (photo).

140 Refit the timing belt tensioner roller, turn it clockwise, and tighten the nut.

141 Engage the timing belt with the crankshaft sprocket then, keeping it taut, feed it onto the camshaft sprocket, around the tensioner pulley, and onto the water pump sprocket.

142 Loosen the nut and turn the tensioner roller anti-clockwise by hand. Tighten the nut.

143 Peugeot garages use the special tool shown in Fig. 13.14 to tension the timing belt. A similar tool may be fabricated using an 8.0 cm (3.2 in) long arm and a 1.5 kg (3.3 lb) weight. The torque applied to the roller will approximate 12 kgf cm (10.5 lbf in). Pre-tension the timing belt with the tool and tighten the nut, then remove the timing pins and rotate the crankshaft through two complete turns. Loosen the nut and allow the roller to re-position itself. Tighten the nut.

144 If the special tool is not available, an approximate setting may be achieved by turning the roller hub anti-clockwise, until it is just possible to turn the timing belt through 90° by finger and thumb midway between the crankshaft and camshaft sprockets. The square in the roller hub should then be directly below the adjustment nut, and the deflection of the belt in the midway position should be approximately 6.0 mm (0.24 in). If using this method, the tension should be re-checked by a Peugeot garage at the earliest opportunity.

145 Refit the lower, intermediate, and upper timing covers and tighten the bolts (photo).

146 Adjust the valve clearances as described in paragraphs 176 to 185.

147 Refit the baffle plate with its edges pointing downwards, followed by the two spacers.

148 Fit the rubber gasket to the valve cover, locate the cover in position and tighten the nuts.

149 Apply a little sealant to the end of the engine oil dipstick holder, and insert it in the main bearing cap casting. Insert and tighten the mounting bolt.

150 Insert and tighten the oil pressure switch.

151 Smear a little oil on the sealing ring, and tighten the oil filter into position by hand only.

152 Refit the timing plate and tighten the bolts.

153 Refit the TDC sensor and tighten the bolt. Fix the lead in the plastic clip on the timing plate. Note that the main body of the TDC sensor should be 1.0 mm (0.04 in) from the flywheel.

154 Apply jointing compound to the distributor mounting flange, then refit it to the cylinder head, and tighten the bolts.

155 Apply jointing compound to the thermostat housing, then refit it to the cylinder head, and tighten the bolts.

156 Refit the thermostat with reference to Section 6.

157 Refit the distributor with reference to Chapter 4.

158 Refit the exhaust manifold together with new gaskets. Refit the nuts and washers and tighten the nuts.

159 Refit the exhaust manifold hot air shroud and tighten the bolts.

160 Locate the coil and bracket over the distributor and tighten the bolts.

161 Position the pulley on the front of the crankshaft. Insert and tighten the bolts.

162 Refit the alternator and insert the pivot and adjustment bolts. Slip the drivebelt onto the pulleys and tighten the tension bolt until the deflection of the belt midway between the pulleys is approximately 6.0 mm (0.24 in) under firm thumb pressure. Tighten the pivot and adjustment bolts.

163 Refit the fuel pump together with a new gasket and tighten the bolts.

164 Thoroughly clean the mating faces of the inlet manifold and cylinder head, and apply jointing compound.

165 Refit the inlet manifold complete with carburettor and tighten the nuts.

166 Reconnect the hose between the fuel pump and carburettor, and tighten the clips.

167 Reconnect the vacuum hose between the distributor and carburettor.

168 Refit and tighten the spark plugs.

169 Refit the HT leads and distributor cap.

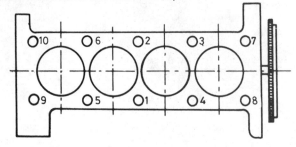

Fig. 13.13 Cylinder head bolt tightening sequence (Sec 5)

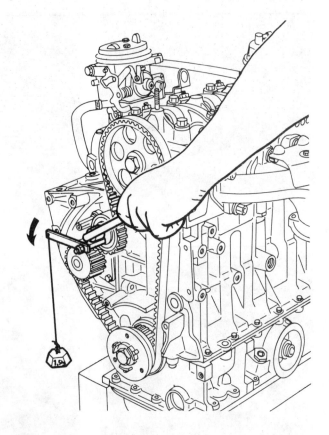

Fig. 13.14 Using Peugeot tool 0132 X to tension the timing belt (Sec 5)

Engine – reconnection to transmission
170 Check that the clutch release bearing is correctly fitted to the release fork. To prevent the bearing being disconnected while fitting the gearbox to the engine, tie the external release arm in the released position.
171 Lubricate the input shaft splines, clutch release bearing sleeve and fork fingers with molybdenum disulphide grease.
172 Refit any location dowels removed, then offer the gearbox to the engine so that the input shaft enters the clutch friction disc and engages the splines.
173 Push the gearbox fully onto the engine location dowels.
174 Insert and tighten the gearbox-to-engine bolts, noting that the hose bracket with the two cable ties locates on the top right-hand bolt (viewed from gearbox end).
175 Refit the starter motor, together with the air cleaner bracket, and tighten the bolts.

Valve clearances – checking and adjustment (engine cold)
176 Disconnect the crankcase ventilation hose from the valve cover.
177 Unscrew the nuts and remove the valve cover.
178 Remove the two spacers and baffle plate from the studs.
179 Prepare to rotate the crankshaft, either by jacking up one front wheel and turning the wheel with 4th or 5th gear engaged, or by using a spanner on the crankshaft pulley bolt. Rotation will be easier if the spark plugs are first removed.
180 Rotate the crankshaft until No 1 exhaust valve (flywheel end) is fully open. No 3 inlet valve and No 4 exhaust valve clearances may now be checked and adjusted.
181 Insert a feeler blade of the correct thickness between the rocker arm and valve stem. It should be a firm sliding fit if the clearance is correct. If adjustment is necessary, loosen the adjuster nut with a ring spanner, turn the adjuster as required with a screwdriver, then retighten the nut (photo).

5.130 Using a universal clutch centralising tool

5.131 Tightening the pressure plate bolts

5.133 Cylinder head gasket located on the block

5.135 Camshaft sprocket set at TDC

5.138 Tightening the cylinder head bolts to initial torque

5.139 Angle tightening the cylinder head bolts by 240°

5.145 Timing covers refitted

5.181 Adjusting the valve clearances

182 Adjust the valve clearances in the following sequence:

Valve fully open	Adjust valve
No 1 Exhaust	No 3 Inlet and No 4 Exhaust
No 3 Exhaust	No 4 Inlet and No 2 Exhaust
No 4 Exhaust	No 2 Inlet and No 1 Exhaust
No 2 Exhaust	No 1 Inlet and No 3 Exhaust

183 When all the valve clearances have been adjusted, refit the baffle plate with its edges pointing downwards, followed by the two spacers.
184 Check that the rubber gasket is re-usable, then refit the valve cover and tighten the nuts.
185 Reconnect the crankcase ventilation hose.

Engine – initial start-up after overhaul
186 Refer to Chapter 1, Section 22, paragraphs 1 to 5.
187 The cylinder head bolts **do not** require re-tightening on the TU engine, and the timing belt does not require re-tensioning.
188 If new bearings and/or pistons have been fitted, treat the engine as new, and run it in at reduced speeds. Also change the engine oil at 1000 miles (1500 km).

Engine (TU9) – fitment of modified pistons
189 From the beginning of January 1988 (engine no 155776), the TU9 engine was fitted with modified pistons, which can be identified by flanges on both sides, perpendicular to the piston centre-line.

6   Cooling system

Cooling system (XV, XW and XY engines) – purging of air
1   Air locks in the cooling system can cause fluctuations of the coolant level, and intermittent illumination of the system warning light when the level appears to be correct. Where this occurs it is recommended that the following procedure is carried out.
2   With the engine cold, remove the expansion bottle cap, then tie the bottle as high as possible as shown in Chapter 2.
3   Remove the filler plug from the top left-hand side of the radiator. Fill the radiator until it overflows, then refit and tighten the filler plug.
4   Carefully open the two bleed screws, Chapter 2, Section 3, and slowly pour water into the expansion bottle until air no longer emerges from them. Tighten the bleed screws.
5   Fill the expansion bottle to 30 mm (1.18 in) above the maximum level.
6   Start the engine, leaving the cap off the bottle, and run it at 2000 rpm for one minute. During this time, squeeze the top and bottom radiator hoses several times to cause any trapped air to rise.
7   Slacken, and then retighten the bleed screws to allow any air which has risen to escape.
8   Repeat paragraphs 6 and 7.
9   Refit the expansion bottle cap, and then start the engine and run at 2000 rpm until the cooling fan cuts in. Allow the engine to idle until the fan stops. Stop the engine and squeeze the top and bottom hoses as described in paragraph 6.
10 Repeat paragraph 7.
11 Allow the engine to cool for at least 15 minutes.

12 Check that the coolant is at the maximum level on the expansion bottle. If it has risen to within 30.0 mm (1.18 in) of the top of the bottle, there is still some air trapped in the system.
13 When satisfied that no further bleeding is necessary, refit the expansion bottle in its correct position and allow the engine to cool for 2 hours. Top up the coolant to the maximum level if necessary.
14 Note that the bleed screws should not be opened with the expansion bottle in its normal position otherwise air may be drawn into the system. As bleeding depressurises the system, the engine should always be allowed to cool for at least one hour before normal use.

Cooling system (XU51C engine) – description
15 The XU51C engine is fitted to automatic transmission models. The transmission incorporates a fluid cooler which is connected to the cooling system by a hose from the cylinder head outlet and a further hose to the heater matrix inlet. Because of this additional circuit the system capacity is increased (see Specifications).

Cooling system (TU engine) – description
16 The cooling system on the TU engine is similar to the system on GTI models, described in Chapter 2.

Cooling system (TU engine) – draining, flushing and refilling
17 With the engine cold, unscrew the filler caps from the expansion bottle and radiator (photo).
18 Place a suitable container beneath the left-hand side of the radiator, then unscrew the drain plug and drain the coolant.
19 Drain the cylinder block by removing the plug located on the front left-hand side of the block.
20 To flush the radiator, disconnect the top and bottom hoses and insert a garden hose in the top inlet. Flush with cold water until there are no traces of sediment.
21 With the system clean, refit the hoses and tighten the drain plugs.
22 Release the rubber ring and tie the expansion bottle to the bonnet as high as possible.
23 Loosen the bleed screws on the thermostat housing and heater hose (photo).
24 Fill the radiator with coolant (photo). Tighten the thermostat housing bleed screw when the water flows free of air bubbles.
25 Fill the radiator to overflowing, then refit and tighten the radiator filler cap.
26 Fill the expansion bottle to the maximum level mark, then tighten the heater hose bleed screw when the water flows free of air bubbles.
27 Add more coolant to the expansion bottle until the level is about 30.0 mm (1.2 in) above the maximum mark. Refit and tighten the filler cap.
28 Start the engine and run it at 1500 rpm until the electric cooling fan starts.
29 Let the engine idle, then when the cooling fan stops, unscrew the expansion bottle filler cap (using a thick cloth as a precaution against scalding).
30 Slowly loosen the radiator filler cap until coolant flows, then re-tighten it. Similarly purge any air from the bleed screws on the thermostat housing and heater hose.

6.17 Radiator filler cap

6.23 Air bleed screw on heater hose

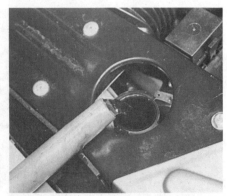
6.24 Filling the radiator with coolant

6.32 Topping-up the expansion bottle

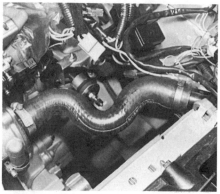

6.33A Radiator top hose

6.33B Radiator bottom hose

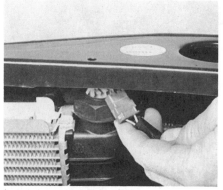

6.33C Low level sensor and wiring

6.33D Cooling fan relay (arrowed)

6.33E Radiator vent hose

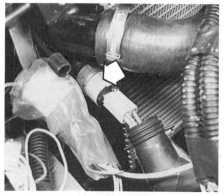

6.33F Radiator thermo-switch (arrowed)

6.33G Removing the radiator

6.43A Bypass hose connection to water pump housing (arrowed)

6.43B Water pump housing and bolts

6.43C Water pump housing O-ring seal

6.44A Removing the water pump from the housing

31 Top up the expansion bottle to 30.0 mm (1.2 in) above the maximum mark and refit the filler cap. The high level is necessary at this stage because the coolant is hot.

32 Refit the expansion bottle in its normal position and secure with the rubber ring. Top up when cold (photo).

Radiator (TU engine) – removal and refitting

33 The procedure is as described in Chapter 2, Section 6. However, additionally, the cooling fan relay must be removed from the clip on the top of the radiator (photos).

Water pump (TU engine) – removal and refitting

34 Drain the cooling system as previously described.

35 Unbolt and remove the upper and intermediate timing covers, leaving the lower cover in position.

36 Turn the engine clockwise using a socket on the crankshaft pulley bolt until the small hole in the camshaft sprocket is aligned with the corresponding hole in the cylinder head. Insert a close-fitting twist drill or bolt into the holes.

37 Align the TDC holes in the flywheel and cylinder block rear flange and insert a further twist drill or long bolt.

38 Loosen the timing belt tensioner roller nut, turn the tensioner clockwise using a screwdriver or square drive in the special hole, then re-tighten the nut.

39 Release the timing belt from the water pump sprocket.

40 Unscrew the nut from the right-hand engine mounting.

41 Using a trolley jack and block of wood, lift the right-hand side of the engine as far as possible.

42 Unscrew the nuts and remove the mounting bracket from the water pump housing.

43 Disconnect the hoses from the housing, then unbolt the housing from the block. Remove the O-ring seal (photos).

44 Unbolt the water pump from the housing and remove the O-ring (photos). If necessary, similarly remove the inlet elbow.

45 Refitting is a reversal of removal, but note the following points:

   (a) Renew the O-rings
   (b) Make sure that the housing-to-block location dowels are in position
   (c) Tighten all nuts and bolts to the specified torque
   (d) Refit and tension the timing belt with reference to Section 5 paragraphs 141 to 144

6.44B Water pump O-ring (arrowed)

   (e) Refill the cooling system as previously described

Cooling fan thermo-switch – testing

46 With the thermo-switch removed, connect an ohmmeter between the terminals.

47 Suspend the thermo-switch in a container of water which is being heated. Check the temperature of the water with a thermometer. With the unit cold, there should be no continuity, but when the cut-in temperature range is reached, the internal contacts should close and the ohmmeter should register nil resistance.

48 Allow the water to cool, and check that the switch cuts out within the specified temperature range.

Thermostat (TU engine) – removal, testing and refitting

49 The procedure is as given in Chapter 2, Section 5, but note the different housing on the TU engine (photos).

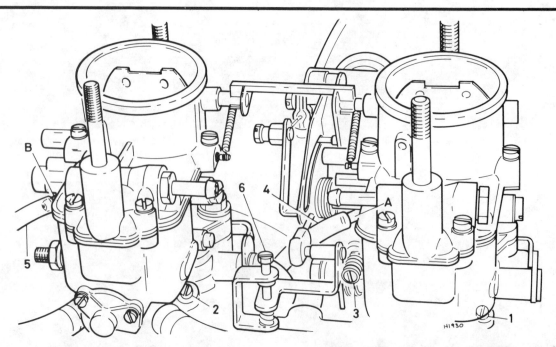

Fig. 13.15 Adjustment screw locations on the Weber 35 IBSH carburettors (Sec 7)

  1 Mixture screw (control   2 Mixture screw (controlled   3 Combined idle speed screw   6 Throttle synchroniser
      carburettor)   carburettor)   4 and 5 Vacuum pipes   adjustment screw
                                                                                        A and B Vacuum connections*

7 Fuel and exhaust systems

Weber 35 IBSH carburettor – description

1   As from early 1985 some XYB (1360 cc) engines may be fitted with Weber 35 IBSH carburettors instead of the Solex type. The Weber carburettors are of single barrel downdraught type, and two linked units are fitted to the XY8 engine. The choke is manually operated, but a vacuum controlled opening device is fitted.

Weber 35 IBSH carburettors – idle speed and mixture adjustment

2   The procedure is as described in Chapter 3 for the Solex 35 PBISA 8 carburettors, but refer to Fig. 13.15.

Weber 35 IBSH carburettor – overhaul

3   The dismantling and reassembly procedure is straightforward, but refer to Fig. 13.16. Carry out the adjustments given in the following paragraphs during reassembly.

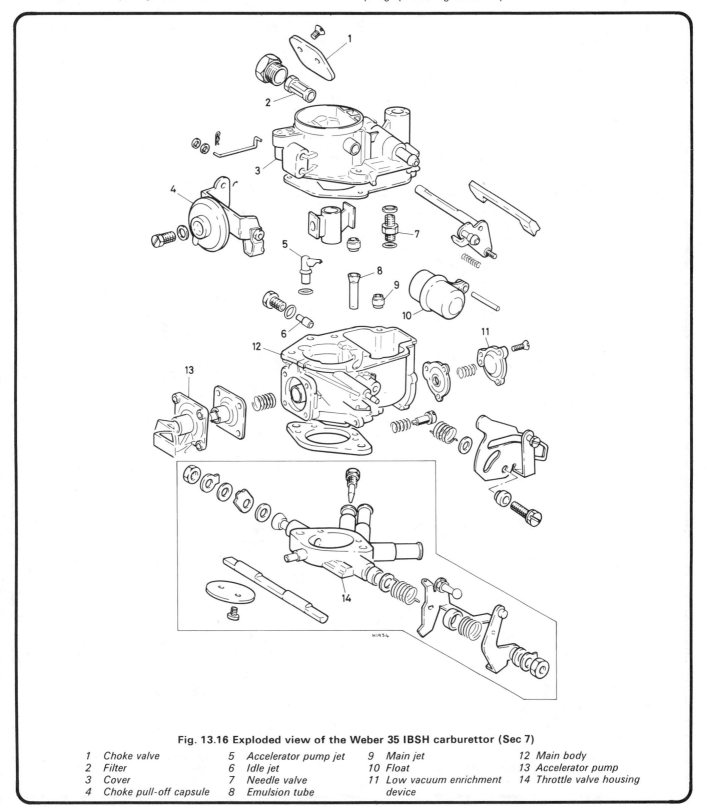

Fig. 13.16 Exploded view of the Weber 35 IBSH carburettor (Sec 7)

1 Choke valve	5 Accelerator pump jet	9 Main jet	12 Main body
2 Filter	6 Idle jet	10 Float	13 Accelerator pump
3 Cover	7 Needle valve	11 Low vacuum enrichment	14 Throttle valve housing
4 Choke pull-off capsule	8 Emulsion tube	device	

Float level

4   Hold the cover vertical with the float arm touching, but not depressing, the spring tensioned ball on the needle valve.

5   Using vernier calipers measure the dimension between the float and the fitted gasket (Fig. 13.17). If it is not 9.0 mm (0.354 in), bend the tongue on the arm as necessary.

Throttle normal idling position

6   This adjustment is made after overhauling the carburettors, and is necessary to enable the engine to be started and to prevent the throttle valve sticking in the closed position. The idle speed screw must be adjusted to set the throttle valve 6° open, however, a special angle gauge is necessary to measure the movement of the valve. If unavailable, the setting can be made by inserting a piece of card which has been cut to the correct angle.

Fast idle setting

7   With the choke fully closed the throttle valve should be open by 14°. Use a piece of card as described in paragraph 6 if an angle gauge is not available, and where necessary adjust the fast idle screw on the throttle lever.

Choke opening setting

8   This adjustment can be made with the carburettor removed using a vacuum pump, or with the carburettor fitted and the engine running.

9   Turn the choke lever so that the choke is fully closed.

10 With the engine running or vacuum applied, check that the gap between the lower edge of the choke valve and the barrel is 3.25 mm (0.128 in). Use a twist drill to make the check and if adjustment is

necessary, turn the screw located in the end of the vacuum capsule.

Weber 36 TLC carburettor – description

11 The Weber 36 TLC carburettor is fitted to the XU51C (1580 cc) engine on automatic transmission models. It is of single barrel downdraught type, incorporating an automatic choke, and a temperature-controlled air cleaner is fitted.

Weber 36 TLC carburettor – idle speed and mixture adjustment

12 Where fitted remove the tamperproof cap from the mixture screw (Fig. 13.20).

13 Select the Park (P) position with the transmittion selector lever, then run the engine to normally operating temperature. Do not remove the air cleaner.

14 Connect a tachometer to the engine.

Without an exhaust gas analyser

15 With the engine idling, adjust the idle speed screw (Fig. 13.21) so that the engine speed is 950 rpm.

16 Adjust the mixture screw (Fig. 13.20) to obtain the highest engine speed.

17 Repeat the procedure given in paragraphs 15 and 16 until the highest engine speed is 950 rpm.

18 Screw in the **mixture** screw until the engine idling speed is 900 rpm.

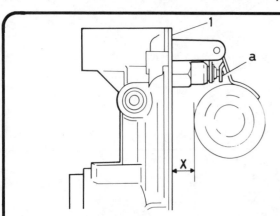

Fig. 13.17 Checking the float level dimension 'X' on the Weber 35 IBSH carburettor (Sec 7)
1   Gasket   a   Adjustment tongue

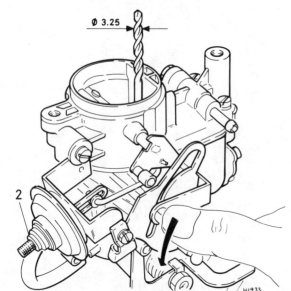

Fig. 13.19 Checking the choke opening setting on the Weber 35 IBSH carburettor (Sec 7)
2   Choke valve adjustment screw

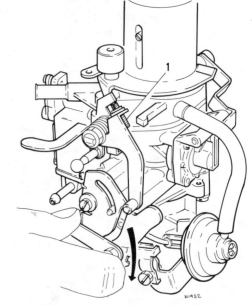

Fig. 13.18 Fast idle adjustment on the Weber 35 IBSH carburettor using an angle gauge (Sec 7)
1   Fast idle screw

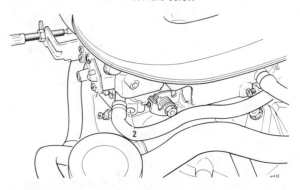

Fig. 13.20 Mixture screw location (2) on the Weber 36 TLC carburettor (Sec 7)

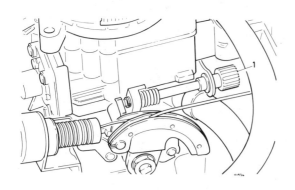

Fig. 13.21 Idle speed screw (1) on the Weber 36 TLC carburettor (Sec 7)

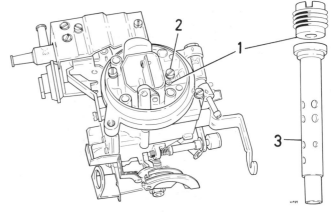

Fig. 13.22 Upper view of the Weber 36 TLC carburettor (Sec 7)

1 Air correction jet   3 Emulsion tube
2 Idling jet

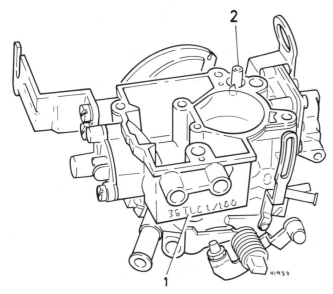

Fig. 13.23 Weber 36 TLC carburettor with cover removed (Sec 7)

1 Type number   2 Accelerator pump injector

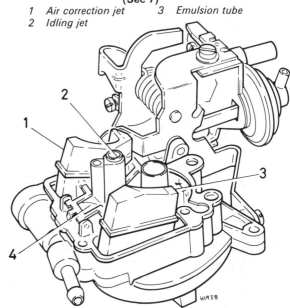

Fig. 13.24 Inverted cover of the Weber 36 TLC carburettor (Sec 7)

1 Float   3 Secondary venturi
2 Main jet   4 Needle valve

With an exhaust gas analyser
19 With the engine idling adjust the idle speed screw (Fig. 13.21) until the engine speed is 900 rpm.
20 Adjust the mixture screw (Fig. 13.20) to obtain a CO reading of 1.0 ± 0.5%.
21 Repeat the procedure given in paragraphs 19 and 20 as necessary.

Weber 36 TLC carburettor – overhaul
22 The procedure is straightforward, but refer to Figs. 13.22 to 13.24 for the positions of the various jets.
23 To check the float level, hold the cover vertically with the gasket in place. Check that the dimension shown in Fig. 13.25 is as specified, and if necessary bend the tongue on the float arm to correct it.
24 To adjust the cold start device choke opening after starting (COAS), the engine must be hot and idling, the air cleaner hose removed, and the cold start device cover removed. Peugeot tool 0.145 G is essential to make this adjustment.
25 Refer to Fig. 13.27 and fit the tool as shown, then turn screw (4) until the cam (5) contacts the tool peg (6). Using a 9.5 mm drill, check that the choke flap has opened by 9.5 mm – if not adjust screw (1) (Fig. 13.28).
26 Disconnect and plug the hose (1) shown in Fig. 13.29, and check now that the choke flap is open by 5.5 mm – if not, loosen screw (1) (Fig. 13.30), hold the roller (1) (Fig. 13.31) against the top of the cam, and adjust lever (2). Retighten the screw and reconnect the hose afterwards.

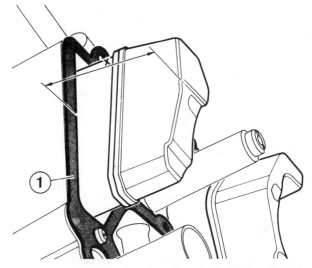

Fig. 13.25 Float level setting on the Weber 36 TLC carburettor (Sec 7)

1 Gasket   X = 28.0 mm (1.1 in)

Fig. 13.26 Peugeot tool 0145 G (Sec 7)

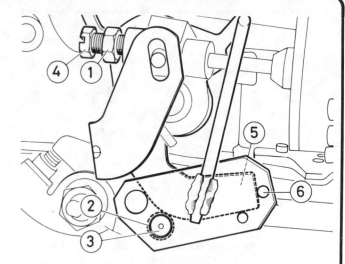

Fig. 13.27 COAS adjustment on the Weber 36 TLC
carburettor (Sec 7)

1	Locknut	4	Adjusting screw
2	Hole	5	Cam
3	Roller	6	Peg on tool

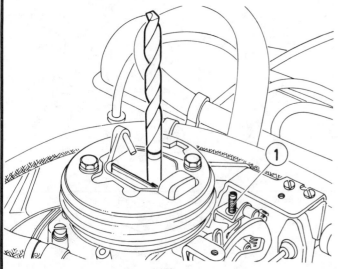

Fig. 13.28 COAS adjusting screw (1) on the Weber 36
TLC carburettor (Sec 7)

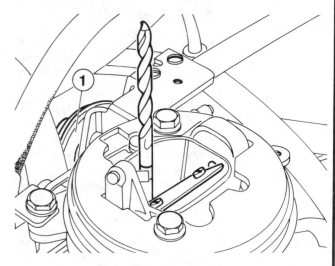

Fig. 13.29 COAS adjustment on the Weber 36 TLC
carburettor (Sec 7)
1   Hose

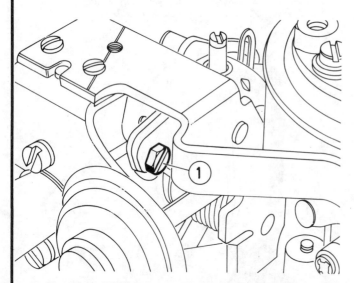

Fig. 13.30 COAS adjustment on the Weber 36 TLC
carburettor (Sec 7)
1   Screw

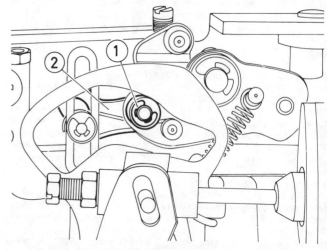

Fig. 13.31 COAS adjustment on the Weber 36 TLC
carburettor (Sec 7)
1   Roller   2   Lever

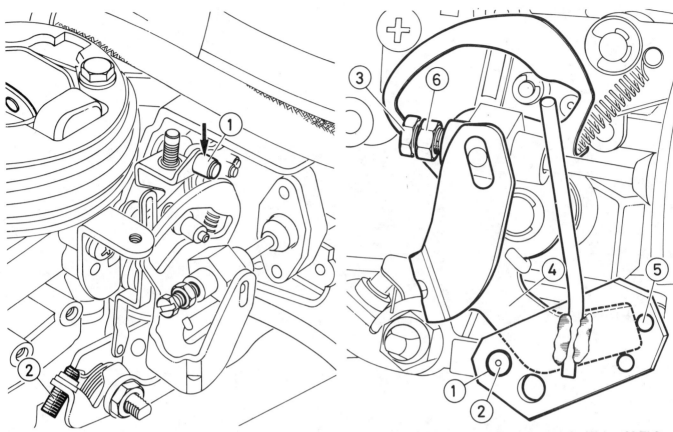

Fig. 13.32 PTO adjustment on the Weber 36 TLC carburettor (Sec 7)

1 Roller 2 Adjusting screw

Fig. 13.33 Choke cam adjustment on the Weber 36 TLC carburettor (Sec 7)

1 Hole	*4 Cam*
2 Roller	*5 Peg on tool*
3 Adjusting screw	*6 Locknut*

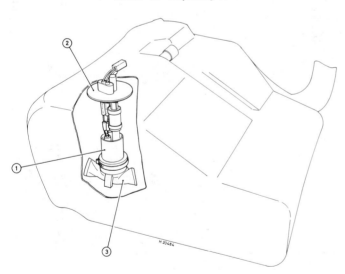

Fig. 13.34 Fuel pump fitted to later automatic models (Sec 7)

1 Electric fuel pump 3 Fuel filter
2 Cover

27 To adjust the positive throttle opening (PTO), press the roller to open the choke flap and check that the engine speed is 2000 rpm with the electric fan stopped. If necessary, adjust screw (2) (Fig. 13.32).
28 To adjust the choke cam, fit the tool 0145 G as shown in Fig. 13.33 and adjust screw (3) until the cam (4) contacts peg (5). Tighten the locknut (6).
29 Stop the engine and refit the cold start device cover and air cleaner hose.

Fuel pump (automatic models) – description
30 On automatic models manufactured from November 1986, an electric fuel pump submerged in the fuel tank is fitted instead of the previous mechanical type. A filter is incorporated in the pump. The two relays which supply the pump are located on the side of the heater. One relay incorporates a safety feature, in that its primary windings are short-circuited to earth via the engine oil pressure switch. When the engine is stationary, this relay will not operate the fuel pump, but as soon as the engine is running it will supply current to the pump. The other relay operates in conjunction with the starter motor to operate the starter motor for starting.

Air cleaner and element (TU engine) – removal and refitting
31 Loosen the screw and release the air cleaner ducting from the carburettor (photo).
32 Disconnect the crankcase ventilation hoses (photos) from the valve cover and carburettor.
33 Release the spring clips and lift the element and ducting from the body (photos).
34 Disconnect the fuel pump inlet hose and release it from the clip on the ducting (photo).
35 Disconnect the hose from the vacuum motor (photo).
36 Disconnect the inlet and warm air hoses (photo).
37 Remove the special clip (photo), then lift the air cleaner and

ducting from the mounting on the starter motor.
38 Refitting is a reversal of removal.

Fuel pump (TU engine) – removal and refitting
39 Remove the air cleaner body as previously described.
40 Disconnect the inlet and outlet hoses (photo).
41 Unscrew the bolts and remove the fuel pump and gasket (photos).
42 Refitting is a reversal of removal.

Carburettors (TU engine) – description
43 The TU9 engine is fitted with a Weber 32 IBSH 16 or Solex 32 PBISA 16 carburettor, the TU1 engine has a Solex 32 PBISA 16 carburettor, the TU3 engine a Weber 34 TLP 3 carburettor, and the TU3S engine a Solex 32-34 Z2 carburettor.
44 The adjustment and overhaul procedures are as given for similar carburettors in Chapter 3, unless described specifically in the following paragaphs.

7.31 Removing the air cleaner ducting

7.32A Crankcase ventilation hose from the valve cover ...

7.32B ... and inlet manifold

7.33A Release the spring clips ...

7.33B ... and remove the air cleaner element

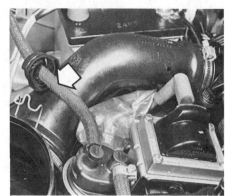

7.34 Fuel pump inlet hose (arrowed)

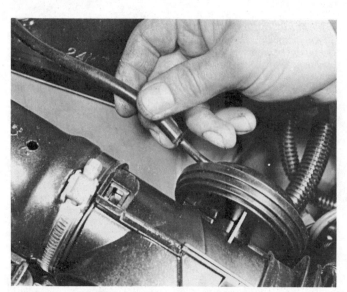

7.35 Disconnecting the hose from the vacuum motor

7.36A Disconnecting the inlet hose

7.36B Warm air hose

7.37 Special clip securing air cleaner ducting to the ignition coil bracket

7.40 The fuel pump inlet hose disconnected

7.41A Unbolting the fuel pump

7.41B Fuel pump gasket

Weber 32 IBSH 16 and 34 TLP 3 carburettors – idling adjustments

45 With the engine hot and idling, adjust the idle speed screw to obtain 750 rpm.

46 Adjust the mixture screw to obtain the specified CO reading or, if an exhaust gas analyser is not available, adjust the mixture screw to obtain the highest engine speed, then screw it in to lower the speed by 50 rpm.

47 Adjust the idling speed screw to obtain 700 rpm.

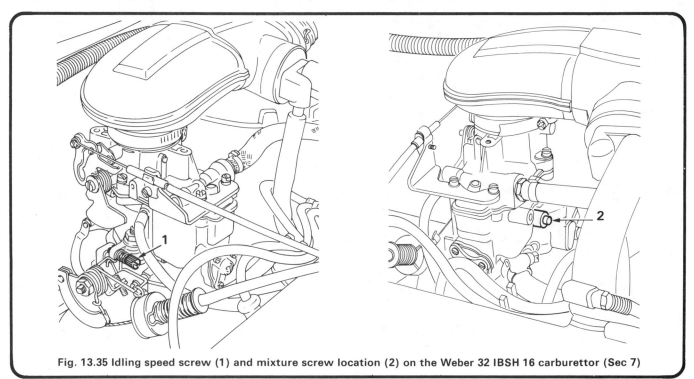
Fig. 13.35 Idling speed screw (1) and mixture screw location (2) on the Weber 32 IBSH 16 carburettor (Sec 7)

Weber 32 IBSH 16 and 34 TLP 3 carburettors – fast idle setting
48 With the carburettor removed, invert it then pull the choke lever fully on.
49 Using a twist drill, check that the gap between the throttle valve and barrel is 0.8 mm. If not, turn the adjustment screw (Fig. 13.36).

Solex 32 PBISA 16 carburettor – idling adjustments
50 Refer to Chapter 3, Section 10, but adjust the idling speed to 700 rpm.

Solex 32 PBISA 16 carburettor – choke opening after starting adjustment
51 Close the choke flap, then fully operate the pneumatic opener either manually or by vacuum.
52 Using a twist drill, check that the gap between the choke flap and barrel is 3.0 mm. If not, turn the adjusting screw in the end of the opener.

Solex 32 PBISA 16 carburettor – fast idle setting
53 The procedure is as described in paragraphs 48 and 49, although the adjustment screw is different.

Solex 32-34 Z2 carburettor cover – removal and refitting
54 Remove the air cleaner as previously described.
55 Disconnect the fuel inlet hose (photo).
56 Disconnect the choke inner cable from the choke lever (photo).
57 Remove the screws and lift the cover from the main body (photos).
58 If necessary, extract the pivot pin and remove the float, needle valve, and gasket (photo).
59 Clean the main body (photo), then refit the cover using a reversal of the removal procedure. Renew the gasket if necessary.

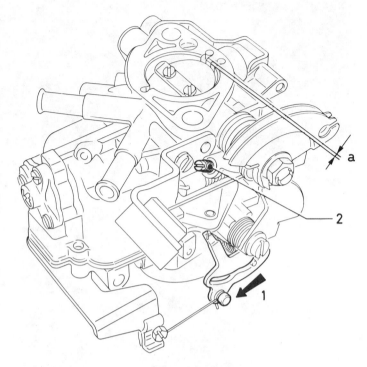

Fig. 13.36 Fast idle adjustment on the Weber 32 IBSH 16 carburettor (Sec 7)
1   Choke lever fully on   a   = 0.8 mm
2   Adjustment screw

7.55 Disconnecting the carburettor fuel inlet hose

7.56 Choke inner cable (arrowed)

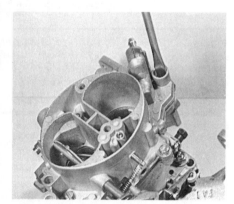

7.57A Remove the screws ...

7.57B ... and lift off the cover

7.58 Carburettor cover and gasket

7.59 Carburettor main body with cover removed

Inlet manifold (TU engine) – removal and refitting

60 Remove the air cleaner and carburettor.
61 Disconnect the brake servo vacuum hose (photo).
62 Drain the cooling system, then disconnect the hose from the bottom of the inlet manifold.
63 Unscrew the nuts and withdraw the inlet manifold from the studs on the cylinder head (photo). There is no gasket.
64 When refitting, thoroughly clean the mating surfaces and apply a thin coat of jointing compound.
65 Refitting is a reversal of removal.

Exhaust manifold (TU engine) – removal and refitting

66 Disconnect the hot air hose from the exhaust manifold shroud.
67 Unbolt the shroud from the exhaust manifold (photo).
68 Unscrew the nuts securing the front downpipe to the exhaust manifold, and remove the metal gasket (photo).
69 Unscrew the nuts and withdraw the exhaust manifold from the studs on the cylinder head. Remove the gaskets (photos).

Exhaust system (TU engine) – general

70 The exhaust system is in three sections; the front downpipe, intermediate pipe and silencer, and tail pipe and silencer.
71 A ball-and-socket type joint is provided between the front and intermediate pipes to allow for engine movement (photo).
72 The front pipe is supported by a bracket attached to the gearbox (photo). However, the rest of the exhaust system is supported by conventional rubber mountings.

Exhaust system (XY and XW engines) – general

73 On later XY8, XY7 and XW7 engines the exhaust front downpipe is of 'siamesed' type instead of twin-pipe type, and is attached to the manifold by a single spherical joint.
74 On automatic transmission models the front exhaust pipe incorporates a special silencer.

Idle speed and mixture (fuel injection engine) – adjustment

75 The procedure is as given in Chapter 3, Section 21, with the following amendments:

   (a) In paragraph 3 adjust the idling speed to 600 rpm
   (b) In paragraph 5 unscrew the air screw to set the idling speed to 900 rpm
   (c) In paragraph 6 check that the CO reading is 1%

Throttle switch (fuel injection engine) – checking and adjustment

76 The procedure is as given in Chapter 3, Section 22 with the following amendment:

   The feeler blade described in paragraph 5 is not used. Fig. 3.13 therefore only applies to the 0.70 mm (0.028 in) feeler blade described in paragraph 8. The procedure given in paragraphs 6 and 7 is still applicable.

Tachymetric relay (fuel injection engine) – revised location

77 From chassis no 7 900 001, the tachymetric relay has been relocated on the facia, near the injection control unit.

Fault diagnosis – fuel injection engine

78 Should the engine cut out intermittently or be difficult to start when hot, check that the fuel pump fuse is correctly fitted in its holder and that the terminals are clean.
79 Fouling of the injector nozzles can cause misfiring and stalling. Where this occurs on an engine which is in good mechanical condition and tuned correctly, the injectors can be cleaned by adding a special cleaning mixture to the fuel tank. The mixture is obtainable from Peugeot dealers under part number 9733.05.

7.61 Disconnecting the brake servo vacuum hose

7.63 Removing the inlet manifold mounting nuts

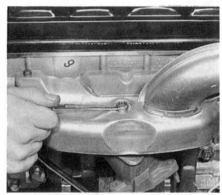
7.67 Removing the exhaust manifold shroud

7.68 Exhaust manifold-to-downpipe flange

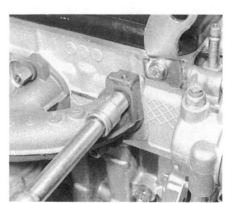
7.69A Unscrew the nuts ...

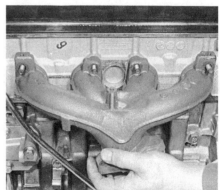
7.69B ... and remove the exhaust manifold ...

7.69C ... and gaskets

7.71 Flexible joint between exhaust front and intermediate pipes

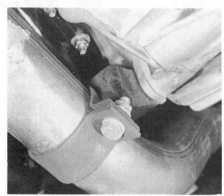

7.72 Exhaust front pipe support bracket

8 Ignition system

Ducellier distributor cap – modification
1   As from mid-1986, Ducellier distributor caps are retained by two screws instead of spring clips (photo). On some 1124 cc engines, this modification applies from *early* 1986.

Ignition timing (GTI/CTI models) – checking and adjustment
2   As from VIN 5520364 (early 1985 XU5J engine CTI models are fitted with a new distributor. The ignition timing procedure is as described in Chapter 4, Section 7 except that the advance is as given in the Specifications at the beginning of this Chapter.
3   The revised timing is also shown on a label attached to the airflow sensor.
4   Later GTI (post February 1986) and CTI models, with the XU5JA engine also have different ignition timing – see Specifications.

Fault diagnosis – ignition system
5   If the HT lead from the ignition coil is routed too close to the distributor LT wiring or electronic control unit, misfiring may result under certain conditions. Where this occurs reposition the HT lead as shown in Fig. 13.37.

Ignition coil (TU engine) – removal and refitting
6   Remove the air cleaner inlet ducting.
7   Disconnect the HT cable from the coil.
8   Disconnect the LT wiring (photo).
9   Unhook the TDC connector from the coil bracket.
10   Unbolt the mounting bracket and remove the coil.
11   Refitting is a reversal of removal.

Distributor (TU engine) – removal and refitting
12   Remove the ignition coil as previously described.

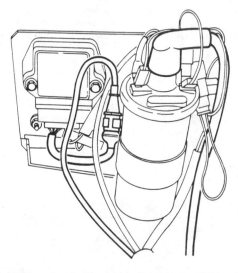

Fig. 13.37 Showing improved rating of the HT lead from the ignition coil (Sec 8)

13   Identify the HT leads for position, then disconnect them from the spark plugs (photo).
14   Unbolt the HT lead support from the cylinder head.
15   Pull back the plastic cover, then extract the screws and remove the distributor cap (photo).
16   Disconnect the wiring at the connector (photo).
17   Pull the hose from the vacuum advance unit (photo).
18   Mark the distributor mounting flange in relation to the distributor/fuel pump housing (photo).

8.1 Later distributor caps are retained by screws

8.8 Disconnecting the LT wiring (arrowed) from the coil

8.13 Disconnecting the HT leads from the spark plugs

8.15 Removing the distributor cap

8.16 Disconnecting the wiring (arrowed) from the distributor

8.17 Distributor vacuum advance unit and hose

8.18 Mark the distributor and housing before ...

8.19 ... removing the distributor

8.23 Ignition module removal

19 Unscrew the mounting nuts, remove the small plates, and withdraw the distributor (photo).
20 Check the condition of the O-ring on the mounting flange, and renew it if necessary.
21 Refitting is a reversal of removal, but turn the rotor arm as required to align the lugs with the offset slot in the camshaft. If the old distributor is being refitted, align the previously-made marks before tightening the mounting nuts. If fitting a new distributor, initially set the distributor in the middle of the slotted holes, or follow the procedure given in Chapter 4, Section 7, then finally adjust the ignition timing.

Ignition module (TU engine) – removal and refitting
22 The module is attached to the side of the distributor. First disconnect the wiring at the connector.
23 Remove the two screws and withdraw the module from the distributor, taking care not to bend the terminals (photo).
24 Do not wipe away the special heat-conductive grease, as this protects the semiconductor components within the module. If necessary obtain new grease from a Peugeot dealer.
25 Refitting is a reversal of removal, but make sure that the special grease is spread evenly over the mating surfaces.

---

9 Clutch

Clutch (all models) – removal and refitting
1 Whenever the clutch is removed, the clutch shaft splines, release bearing guide tube and the release fork ball-stud and fingers should be cleaned and lubricated with a molybdenum disulphide based grease. This will prevent clutch judder or drag which would otherwise result in difficult engagement of gears. Do not, however, apply an excessive amount of grease, which could find its way onto the clutch driven plate linings or flywheel.

Transfer gears (with BH 3 gearbox) – modification
2 As from December 1984, the transfer idler gear bearings are increased in diameter from 33.0 mm (1.299 in) to 38.0 mm (1.496 in). The intermediate plate is also modified to accommodate the new bearings.
3 It is not possible to interchange components between the early and later types.

Clutch (TU engine) – refitting
4 When refitting the clutch, a centralising tool made to the dimensions shown in Fig. 13.38 should be used to centralise the driven plate. The tool may be made out of wood.

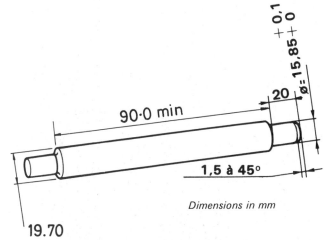

Dimensions in mm

Fig. 13.38 Clutch centralising tool dimensions for the TU engine (Sec 9)

10　Manual transmission (BE 1/5)

Gearchange linkage – modification

1　As from mid-1985 the reverse gear stop is actuated by a cable on the gearbox, instead of an eccentric cam at the base of the gear lever. Reverse gear is still selected by lifting the sleeve on the gear lever.
2　When selecting reverse the cable releases a detent from the selector rod, but for selection of all other gears the detent prevents accidental engagement of reverse.
3　Where the cable is fitted, all references to the cam and stop in Part C of Chapter 6 may be ignored. The cable requires no adjustment.

Transmission – removal and refitting

4　On models fitted with the reverse stop cable described in paragraphs 1 to 3, it will be necessary to unscrew the nut and release the cable in addition to the procedure described in Part C of Chapter 6.

Differential – modifications

5　As from early 1985 the differential side gears are positively located within the carrier instead of being located only by insertion of the driveshafts. A location ring is now fitted as shown in Fig. 13.40 with corresponding cut-outs machined in the side gears and carrier. Shouldered thrust washers are now fitted over the location rings instead of the earlier plain types.
6　Due to these modifications it is not possible to dismantle and reassemble the differential in the order described in Chapter 6, Section 19. When dismantling, the spindle and gears must be removed first before removal of the side gears. Reassemble the components in reverse order.
7　As from early 1986 some units are fitted with a special differential extension housing which eliminates the need for bearing preload adjustment. The housing can be identified by measuring the length of the shoulder shown in Fig. 13.42. If the shoulder length is 10.0 mm (0.394 in) no preload shims must be fitted, but if it is 8.65 mm (0.341 in) the preload must be adjusted as described in Chapter 6, Section 20.
8　When fitting the modified housing (ie without preload adjustment) the bolts should be tightened progressively while turning the differential unit to seat the bearings. The torque setting remains the same as for the earlier type.

Selector forks – modifications

9　As from early 1986, the selector forks are modified to improve gear engagement, as shown in Fig. 13.43. The removal and refitting procedures remain the same as described in Part C of Chapter 6. Modified selection and engagement parts are used in conjunction with the forks. Some models may have a combination of the later selector and engagement parts with the earlier forks. If any parts are renewed, the new parts should be the same as that originally fitted, ie early and later parts are not interchangeable.

3rd/4th speed driven gears – modifications

10　To allow fitting of the modified selector forks described in paragraph 9, the diameter between the 3rd and 4th speed driven gears is reduced to 38 mm instead of 43 mm (Fig. 13.44). The later type of gears replace the earlier ones.

Transmission – reassembly

11　In Chapter 6, Section 20, paragraph 43 a formula is given for calculation of the input shaft bearing preload. The manufacturers have now revised this to provide an endfloat and the formula should now read:

$$T = (C - D) + 0.03 \text{ mm}$$

Allowance is included for the thickness of the gasket.

Transmission – oil capacity

12　The oil capacity of the BE 1/5 gearbox is increased from 1.4 litres (2.5 pints) to 2.0 litres (2.5 pints) as given in the Specifications. This applies to all BE 1/5 gearboxes (regardless of age).

Transmission – draining and oil level checking

13　In early 1986, the gearbox drain plug and the gearbox/final drive level plug were deleted. Draining of the gearbox final drive from this time is through the final drive drain plug only ('b' on Fig. 6.3, Chapter 6). However, in October 1986 the level plug was reinstated, but in a different location on the gearbox end cover (Fig. 13.45). The plug is fitted with a copper washer, which should be cleaned and checked for condition before refitting.
14　All 1988 models (chassis number 7 900 001 on) have a special gearbox oil which does not require changing at the routine maintenance intervals, and in addition the oil level check intervals have been extended. It is important on these models to use only the specified oil for topping-up purposes.

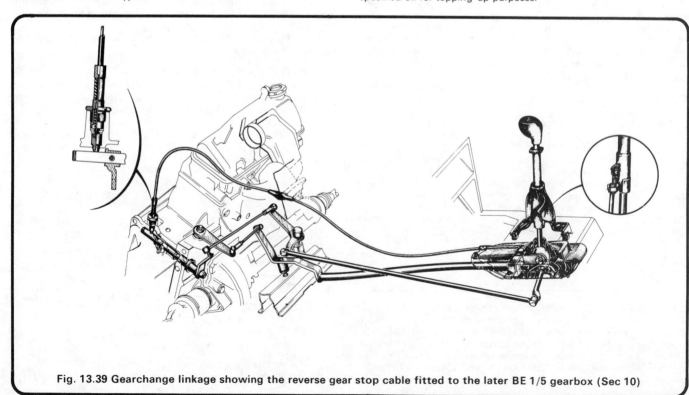

Fig. 13.39 Gearchange linkage showing the reverse gear stop cable fitted to the later BE 1/5 gearbox (Sec 10)

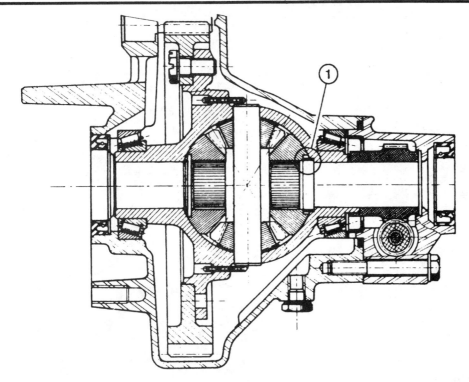

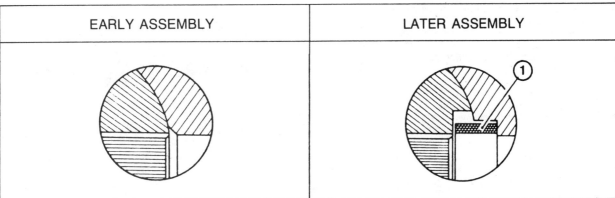

EARLY ASSEMBLY	LATER ASSEMBLY

Fig. 13.40 Showing positive location side gears on the later BE 1/5 differential (Sec 10)

1   Location ring

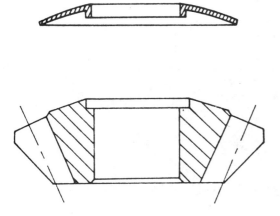

Fig. 13.41 Shouldered thrust washer fitted to the later BE 1/5 differential (Sec 10)

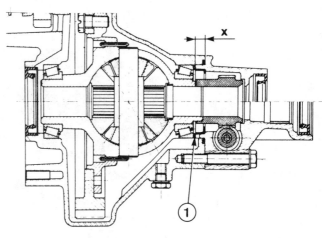

Fig. 13.42 Comparison of early (lower section) and later (upper section) differential extension housing (Sec 10)

X = 10.0 mm (0.394 in)   1   Bearing preload shim

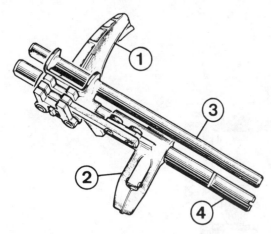

Fig. 13.43 Later type selector forks on the BE 1/5 gearbox (Sec 10)

1	1st/2nd selector fork	3	5th selector fork and rod
2	3rd/4th selector fork	4	Fixed selector rod

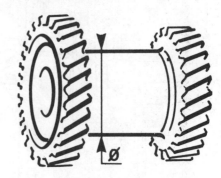

Fig. 13.44 Later type 3rd/4th speed driven gears for the BE 1/5 gearbox (Sec 10)

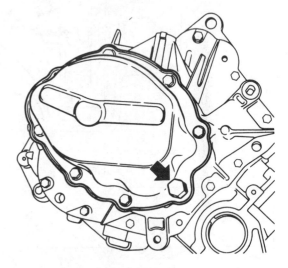

Fig. 13.45 Location of the level plug on the BE 1/5 gearbox from October 1986 (Sec 10)

11 Manual transmission (MA)

Transmission – general description

1   The MA gearbox is mounted on the left-hand side of the engine, and may be removed separately, leaving the engine in the car. It has either four or five forward gears depending on the model, all with synchromesh, and one reverse gear. All the synchromesh units are located on the output shaft, and the differential unit is located in the main gearbox casing.

Transmission – routine maintenance

2   There are no oil change requirements for the MA gearbox, however oil level checks should be carried out every 36 000 miles (60 000 km). Make sure that all topping-up is made using only the specified grade of oil.

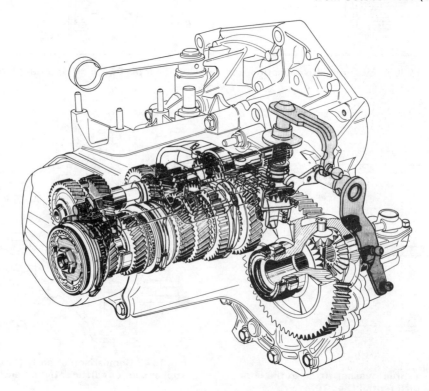

Fig. 13.46 Internal components of the MA 5-speed gearbox (Sec 11)

MA.5

MA.4

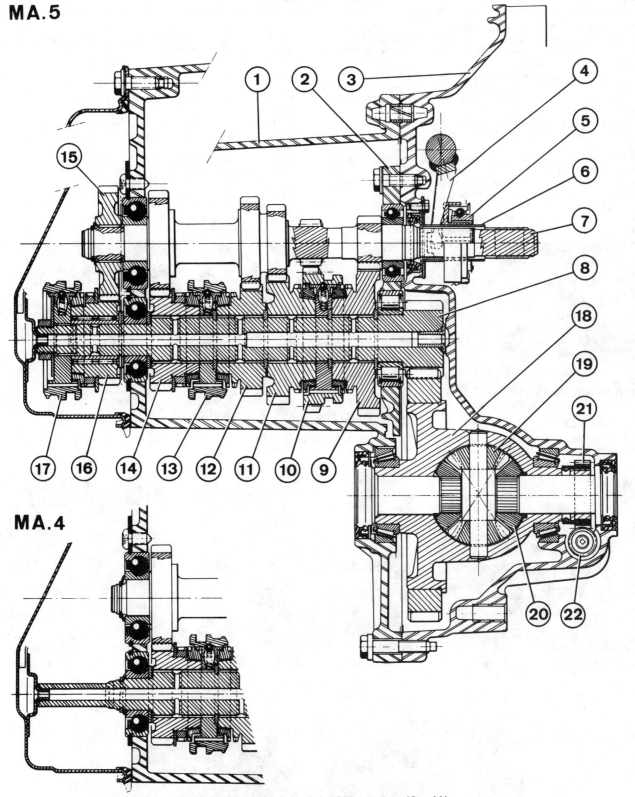

Fig. 13.47 Cross-section of the MA gearbox (Sec 11)

1 Gearbox housing	9 1st speed driven gear	16 5th speed driven gear
2 Intermediate plate	10 1st/2nd speed synchroniser	17 5th speed synchroniser
3 Clutch and final drive	(and reverse driven gear)	18 Differential housing
housing	11 2nd speed driven gear	19 Differential pinions
4 Clutch fork (on shaft)	12 3rd speed driven gear	20 Differential gears
5 Release bearing	13 3rd/4th speed synchroniser	21 Speedometer drive worm
6 Release bearing guide	14 4th speed driven gear	22 Speedometer drive pinion
7 Input shaft	15 5th speed drive gear	Insert shows 4-speed gearbox
8 Output shaft		

Transmission – removal and refitting

3   Disconnect the bonnet stay from the right-hand suspension tower, and use suitable U-brackets in the bonnet hinge holes to hold the bonnet in a vertical position.

4   Remove the battery as described in Chapter 12.

5   Remove the air cleaner as described in Section 7 of this Chapter.

6   Unscrew the nut and detach the battery negative cable from the gearbox.

7   Disconnect the wiring from the reversing lamp switch.

8   Pull out the rubber cotter and remove the speedometer cable from the gearbox.

9   Prise the two gearchange control rods from the gearbox levers. A small open-ended spanner may be used to good effect.

10   Disconnect the clutch cable and position it to one side (photo).

11   Release the heater hose from the clips.

12   Unbolt the starter motor and air cleaner bracket and support them to one side. There is no need to disconnect the wiring.

13   Apply the handbrake, then jack up the front of the car and support on axle stands.

14   Unscrew the drain and filler plugs, and drain the gearbox oil into a suitable container (photos).

15   Remove both driveshafts with reference to Chapter 7 and Section 13 of this Chapter.

16   Unscrew and remove the lower rear bolt securing the gearbox to the engine, noting that the exhaust front pipe bracket is located on the bolt.

17   Support the left-hand side of the engine, using a hoist on the left-hand lifting eye, or a trolley jack and block of wood beneath the sump.

18   Unscrew the left-hand mounting nuts, including the nut on the centre stud, and remove the mounting.

19   Unbolt the battery tray.

20   Unscrew the nuts and remove the left-hand mounting bracket from the gearbox.

21   Lower the engine until the exhaust front pipe contacts the front suspension .crossmember.

11.10 Disconnecting the clutch cable

11.14A Gearbox drain plug (arrowed)

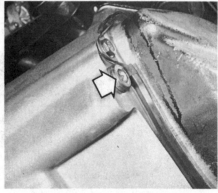

11.14B Gearbox filler plug (arrowed)

11.26 Removing the clutch release bearing

11.28A Unscrew the bolt ...

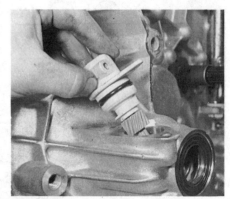

11.28B ... and remove the speedometer drive pinion

11.29A Unscrew the bolt ...

11.29B ... and remove the pressed-steel housing

22 Unscrew the remaining bolts securing the gearbox to the engine.
23 Support the gearbox with a trolley jack or suitable sling, then withdraw it from the engine until clear of the clutch, and lower it to the ground.
24 Refitting is a reversal of removal, but note the following points:

    (a) *It is recommended that the driveshaft oil seals and filler/drain plug washers are renewed*
    (b) *Tighten all nuts and bolts to the specified torque*
    (c) *Lubricate the input shaft splines, clutch release bearing sleeve and fork fingers with molybdenum disulphide grease*
    (d) *Refill the gearbox with the correct grade and quantity of oil*
    (e) *Adjust the clutch cable with reference to Chapter 5*
    (f) *The gearchange control rods cannot be adjusted*

Transmission – dismantling into major assemblies
25 With the unit removed from the car, clean all exterior surfaces and wipe dry.
26 Pull the clutch release bearing from the guide sleeve, and release the spring clips from the fork ends (photo).
27 Position the gearbox with the clutch end downwards.
28 Unbolt and remove the speedometer drive pinion (photos).
29 Unbolt the pressed-steel housing. Remove the rubber gasket (photos).
5-speed gearbox only
30 Drive the pin from the 5th speed selector fork.
31 Engage both reverse and 5th gears with reference to Fig. 13.48, then loosen the nut on the end of the output shaft. Return the gears to neutral.
32 Remove the nut and lockwasher (photos).
33 Remove the 5th synchro unit together with its selector fork, making sure that the sleeve remains central on the hub to avoid loss of the internal balls and springs (photo).
34 Remove from the output shaft the 5th synchro ring, followed by the 5th speed driven gear, needle bearing, sleeve, and thrust washer (photos).
35 Extract the circlip from the end of the input shaft, followed by the special washer, noting that the convex side is uppermost.
36 Using a suitable puller if necessary, pull the 5th speed drive gear from the splines on the input shaft (photo).
4 and 5-speed gearboxes
37 Unscrew the Torx screws and extract the half-rings from the grooves in the shaft bearings, noting their locations (photos).
38 Unscrew the bolts securing the gearbox housing to the clutch/final drive housing, noting the location of the bolts (photo).
39 Lift the gearbox housing from the clutch/final drive housing (photo), at the same time guiding the selector fork shafts through the housing. Do not prise the housings apart with a screwdriver, but use a wooden or hide mallet to release them from the sealant.
40 Remove the plastic ring from the reverse idler gear shaft, then remove the shaft from the clutch/final drive housing and remove the idler gear (photos).
41 Press down on the reverse selector arm directly over the shaft, and at the same time extract the shaft from the intermediate plate. Remove the reverse selector arm (photos).

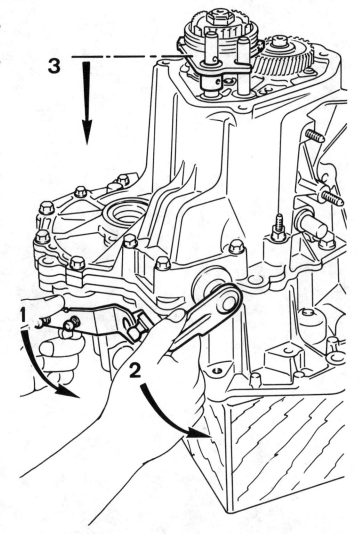

Fig. 13.48 Sequence for selecting reverse and 5th gears (Sec 11)

11.32A Remove the 5th synchro nut ...

11.32B ... and lockwasher

11.33 Removing the 5th synchro unit and selector fork

11.34A Removing the 5th synchro ring ...

11.34B ... 5th speed driven gear ...

11.34C ... needle bearing ...

11.34D ... sleeve ...

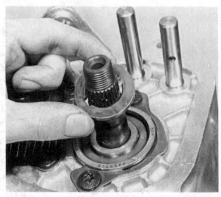

11.34E ... and thrust washer

11.35 Removal of the special washer from the input shaft

11.36 Removing the 5th speed drive gear

11.37A Unscrew the Torx screws ...

11.37B ... and extract the bearing half-rings

11.38 Unbolting the gearbox housing

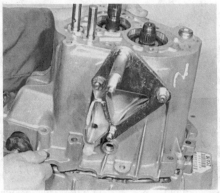

11.39 Lifting the gearbox housing from the clutch/final drive housing

11.40A Removing the plastic ring ...

11.40B ... reverse idler gear shaft ...

11.40C ... and reverse idler gear

11.41A Removing the reverse selector shaft ...

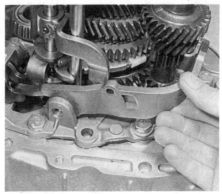
11.41B ... and arm

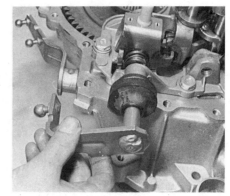
11.44 Selector shaft removal

11.45 Removing the neutral return spring and plastic cups

11.46A Interlocking key and selector finger assembly

11.46B Interlocking key and selector finger separated

42 Lift the gate lever to the 1st/2nd position and support with a block of wood.
43 Using a suitable pin punch, drive out the pin securing the selector finger to the selector shaft. Recover the pin and return the gate lever to neutral.
44 Pull out the selector shaft and remove the rubber boot from it (photo).
45 Prise out the neutral return spring together with the two plastic cups (photo).
46 Lift the gate lever, and at the same time remove the interlocking key and selector finger (photos).
47 Tie the two selector fork shafts together as an aid to reassembly.
48 Using both hands, lift the input and output shafts, together with the selector fork shafts, directly from the clutch/final drive housing (photo). Separate the input shaft from the output shaft, and disengage

the selector forks from the synchro units on the output shaft.
49 Unscrew the bolts and remove the intermediate plate from the clutch/final drive housing (photo). Adhesive is used on assembly, so some difficulty may be experienced, however do not lever directly on the mating faces.
50 Remove the reverse locking plunger and spring, using a magnet if available (photos).
51 Lift out the differential unit (photo).
52 The gearbox is now dismantled into its major assemblies.

Transmission – examination and renovation
53 Clean all components and examine them thoroughly for wear and damage. Circlips, locking pins, gaskets and oil seals should all be renewed as a matter of course. Read through the reassembly sub-section and obtain the necessary adhesive and sealants required.

11.48 Lifting input and output shafts with selector fork shafts from the clutch/final drive housing

11.49 Intermediate plate removal

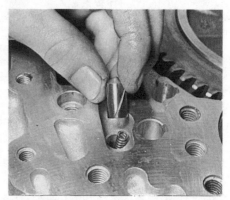

11.50A Removing the reverse locking plunger ...

11.50B ... and spring

11.51 Removing the differential unit

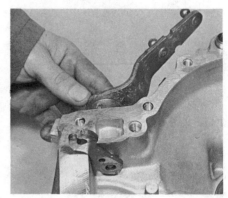

11.54 Gate lever removal

11.56A Prising out the driveshaft oil seal ...

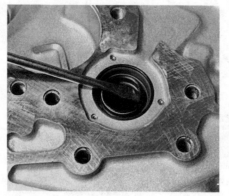

11.56B ... and input shaft oil seal

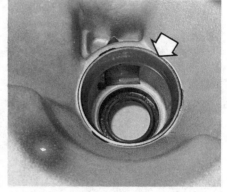

11.58 Right-hand final drive bearing outer track (arrowed)

Clutch/final drive housing – overhaul

54 Using a suitable punch, drive out the locking pin and remove the gate lever from the shaft (photo).

55 Withdraw the shaft and prise the oil seal from the housing.

56 Prise out the driveshaft and input shaft oil seals (photos).

57 If necessary drive out the location dowels.

58 If necessary drive out the right-hand final drive bearing outer track, using a punch through the cut-outs provided (photo).

59 Unbolt the clutch release bearing guide sleeve (photo).

60 Clean all the components.

61 Commence reassembly by refitting the clutch release bearing guide sleeve, together with a new input shaft seal. Apply jointing compound to the threads, then insert and tighten the bolts. Smear a little oil on the seal.

62 Using a metal tube, drive the right-hand final drive bearing outer track fully into the housing.

63 Drive in the location dowels.

64 Oil the new driveshaft oil seal, and drive it into the housing using a block of wood.

65 Oil the new gate lever shaft oil seal and drive it into the housing. Oil the shaft and refit it.

66 Locate the gate lever on the shaft towards the final drive, align the holes and drive in the new locking pin.

Gearbox housing – overhaul

67 Prise out the driveshaft oil seal.

68 If necessary, drive out the left-hand final drive bearing outer track using a punch through the cut-outs provided (photo).

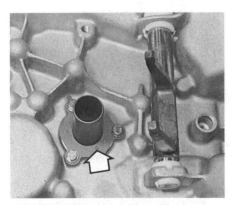

11.59 Clutch release bearing guide sleeve (arrowed)

11.68 Left-hand final drive bearing outer track

11.73 Input shaft and bearings

11.76 Output shaft bearing removal

11.77A Removing the thrust washer ...

11.77B ... 4th gear ...

11.77C ... 4th synchro ring ...

11.77D ... 3rd/4th synchro unit ...

11.77E ... and the 3rd synchro ring

69 Using a metal tube, drive the new outer track fully into the housing.
70 Oil the new driveshaft oil seal and drive it into the housing using a block of wood.

Input shaft – dismantling and reassembly

71 On the 4-speed gearbox, extract the circlip with circlip pliers and remove the washer.
72 On 4 and 5-speed gearboxes, pull the bearing from the 4th speed end of the input shaft using a suitable puller. Similarly pull the bearing from the 1st speed end. Note that the re-use of removed bearings is not recommended.
73 To reassemble, drive the bearing on the 1st speed end of the shaft using a length of metal tube on the inner track. Similarly drive the bearing on the 4th speed end, but note that the groove in the outer

track must be towards the end of the shaft (photo).
74 Locate the washer over the end of the shaft on the 4-speed gearbox. Rest the circlip on the tapered end of the shaft, and use a socket to drive it into the groove. Check that the circlip is seated correctly by squeezing it with pliers.

Output shaft – dismantling and reassembly

75 On the 4-speed gearbox, extract the circlip with circlip pliers and remove the washer.
76 On 4 and 5-speed gearboxes, pull the bearing from the shaft using a suitable puller if necessary (photo).
77 Remove the thrust washer, followed by 4th gear, the 4th synchro ring, the 3rd/4th synchro unit, and the 3rd synchro ring (photos). Keep the synchro unit sleeve central on the hub.

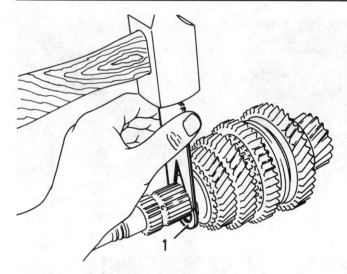

Fig. 13.49 Forked tool for removing C-clips (1) from the output shaft (Sec 11)

78 Tap out the C-clip using a screwdriver or a forked tool made with reference to Fig. 13.49 (photo).
79 Remove the 3rd gear, the C-clip, the 2nd gear, 2nd synchro ring, 1st/2nd synchro unit, 1st synchro ring, the C-clip, 1st gear, and the final C-clip (photos). Keep the synchro unit sleeve central on the hub.
80 Remove the final bearing using a suitable puller, or by supporting the bearing in a vice and driving the output shaft through it. Note that the re-use of removed bearings is not recommended.

81 To reassemble, drive the bearing onto the output shaft using a length of metal tube on the inner track. Do not support the shaft on the plastic lubrication disc.
82 Press the C-clip into its groove, followed by 1st gear and the next C-clip (photo).
83 Fit the 1st synchro ring, then lower the 1st/2nd synchro unit onto the splines with the selector groove downwards, at the same time aligning the projections on the 1st synchro ring with the rockers on the synchro unit.
84 Fit the 2nd synchro ring, aligning the projections as described in paragraph 83.
85 Fit the 2nd gear, the C-clip, 3rd gear, and the C-clip.
86 Fit the 3rd synchro ring, 3rd/4th synchro unit, and the 4th synchro ring as described in paragraph 83.
87 Fit the 4th gear and thrust washer.
88 Locate the bearing on the shaft, with the groove towards the end of the shaft. Drive the bearing onto the shaft using a length of metal tube on the inner track (photo). Do not support the shaft on the plastic lubrication disc.
89 On the 4-speed gearbox, locate the washer on the end of the shaft. Rest the circlip on the tapered end of the shaft, and use a socket to drive it into the groove. Check that the circlip is seated correctly by squeezing it with pliers.

Differential bearings – renewal
90 Lever off the speedometer drive worm (photo).
91 Pull the bearings from both sides of the differential unit using a suitable puller. Identify them for location if they are to be re-used.
92 Drive the new bearings into position using a length of metal tube on their inner tracks.
93 Press the speedometer drive worm into position.

Selector fork shafts – dismantling and reassembly
94 Support the 3rd/4th selector fork shaft in a soft-jawed vice, then drive out the roll pin using a suitable punch. Slide off the selector fork,

11.78 Remove the C-clip ...

11.79A ... 3rd gear ...

11.79B ... C-clip ...

11.79C ... 2nd gear ...

11.79D ... 2nd synchro ring ...

11.79E ... 1st/2nd synchro unit ...

11.79F ... 1st synchro ring ...

11.79G ... C-clip ...

11.79H ... 1st gear ...

11.79I ... and the final C-clip (arrowed)

11.82 Inserting a C-clip

11.88 Driving the bearing onto the output shaft

11.90 Speedometer drive worm (arrowed)

noting which way round it is fitted.

95 Similarly drive out the roll pin, and remove the 1st/2nd selector fork and the reverse control relay from the other shaft.

96 Reassembly is a reversal of dismantling, but use new roll pins.

Synchro units – dismantling and reassembly

97 Mark the hub and the outer sleeve in relation to each other to ensure correct reassembly.

98 Wrap the unit in a cloth, then slide the sleeve from the hub. Recover the three balls, three springs, and three rockers.

99 To reassemble the units, first insert the hub in the sleeve. The rocker slots in the hub and sleeve must be in alignment.

100 Pull out the hub until the rockers, springs and balls can be inserted, then press in the balls and push the hub fully into the sleeve. A large worm drive clip, piston ring compressor, or three narrow strips of metal may be used to press in the balls.

Transmission – reassembly

101 With the clutch/final drive housing on the bench, lower the differential unit into position.

102 Insert the reverse locking spring and plunger.

103 Apply Loctite Autoform 549 adhesive to the contact area on the intermediate plate, then lower the plate onto the clutch/final drive housing, at the same time guiding the gate lever through the hole provided (photo).

104 Apply locking fluid to the bolt threads. Insert the bolts and progressively tighten them to the specified torque (photo). Clean the excess adhesive from the bearing locations.

105 Tie the two selector fork shaft assemblies together (photo).

106 Engage the selector forks in the synchro unit grooves, and mesh the input and output shaft assemblies together. Using both hands, lower the complete assembly into the clutch/final drive housing (photo).

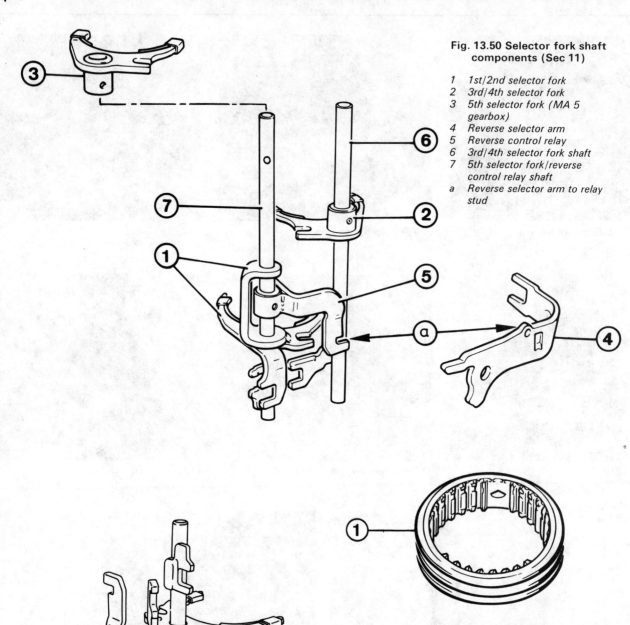

Fig. 13.50 Selector fork shaft
components (Sec 11)

1 1st/2nd selector fork
2 3rd/4th selector fork
3 5th selector fork (MA 5
   gearbox)
4 Reverse selector arm
5 Reverse control relay
6 3rd/4th selector fork shaft
7 5th selector fork/reverse
   control relay shaft
a Reverse selector arm to relay
   stud

Fig. 13.51 Driving out the roll pin from the reverse
control relay (Sec 11)

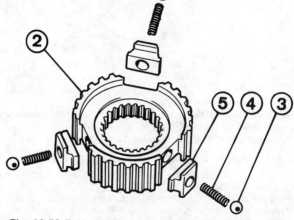

Fig. 13.52 Exploded view of a synchro unit (Sec 11)

1 Sleeve   4 Spring
2 Hub   5 Rocker
3 Ball

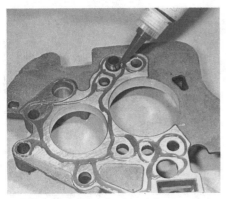

11.103A Applying adhesive to the intermediate plate

11.103B Guiding the gate lever through the intermediate plate

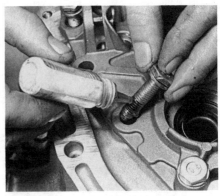

11.104A Apply locking fluid to the bolt threads ...

11.104B ... and tighten them to the specified torque

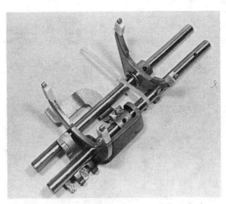

11.105 Selector fork shaft assemblies tied together with a plastic strap

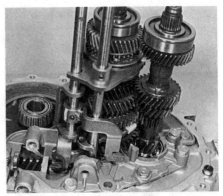

11.106 Shafts and selector forks assembled in the clutch/final drive housing

107 Locate the selector finger within the interlocking key, then lift the gate lever and insert the key assembly in the clutch/final drive housing. Make sure that the selector finger engages the fork gates, and that the gate lever engages the outer plate of the interlocking key.

108 Engage the plastic cups with the neutral return spring, and insert them between the interlocking key and intermediate plate (photos).

109 Fit the rubber boot on the selector shaft. Insert the shaft through the intermediate plate, interlocking key and selector finger, align the holes and drive in the locking pin (photo).

110 Insert the reverse selector arm in the intermediate plate, press down on it to depress the plunger, and insert the shaft. Make sure that the stud on the arm enters the cut-out on the control relay.

111 Engage the reverse idler gear with the selector arm, with the projecting shoulder uppermost, and insert the shaft, cut-out end downwards. Turn the shaft until the cut-out drops in the recess.

112 Fit the plastic ring on the shaft.

113 Apply a thin, even, coat of a silicone-based jointing compound to the mating face of the clutch/final drive housing (photo).

114 Lower the gearbox housing onto the clutch/final drive housing, at the same time guiding the input and output shaft bearings and selector fork shafts through their holes.

115 Insert the bolts in their previously-noted locations, and tighten them evenly to the specified torque.

116 Fit the retaining half-rings in the bearing grooves with the chamfers uppermost, then insert and tighten the bolts.

5-speed gearbox only

117 Locate the 5th speed drive gear on the input shaft splines, support the opposite end of the shaft on a block of wood and fully drive the gear on the splines using a metal tube.

118 Fit the washer on the input shaft with its convex side uppermost.

119 Fit the circlip using a suitable socket and hammer. Check that it is fully entered in the groove by squeezing with pliers (photo).

120 Fit the thrust washer to the output shaft (oil groove uppermost) followed by the sleeve, needle bearing, 5th speed driven gear and the 5th synchro ring.

121 Engage the selector fork with the 5th synchro unit, then lower

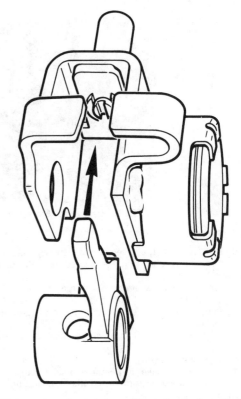

Fig. 13.53 Locating the selector finger in the interlocking key (Sec 11)

11.108A Fitted neutral return spring and plastic cups (arrowed)

11.108B Fitted neutral return spring showing gate lever (arrowed) engaged with interlocking key

11.109A Insert the locking pin ...

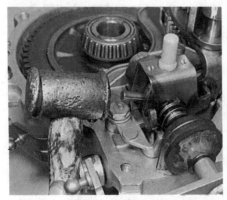

11.109B ... and drive it through the selector shaft

11.113 Applying jointing compound to the clutch/final drive housing

11.119 Squeezing the circlip into the groove in the input shaft

11.123 Tightening the 5th synchro nut

11.124 Driving in the 5th selector fork locking pin

them onto the output shaft and selector fork shafts. Make sure that the projections on the synchro ring are aligned with the rockers in the synchro unit.

122 Fit the special lockwasher and nut (finger-tight).

123 Engage both reverse and 5th speed gears with reference to Fig. 13.48. Tighten the nut to the specified torque, then return the gears to neutral (photo).

124 Align the holes in the 5th speed selector fork and shaft, and drive in the locking pin (photo).

4 and 5-speed gearboxes

125 Fit the dry rubber gasket to the pressed steel housing. Locate the housing on the gearbox housing, insert the bolts and tighten them to the specified torque.

126 Refit the speedometer drive pinion. Insert and tighten the bolt.

127 Apply a little grease to the guide sleeve, then refit the clutch release bearing and engage the spring clips with the fork ends.

12 Automatic transmission

General description

1   The automatic transmission was introduced in April 1986 and incorporates four forward speeds and one reverse.

2   In the interests of fuel economy the torque converter is completely bypassed in top (4th) gear and partially bypassed in 3rd; this reduces losses due to torque converter slip.

3   Gearchange is automatic in use, the transmission responding to changes in speed and load. The usual kickdown facility is provided for enhanced acceleration when the throttle is depressed fully.

4   Instead of the customary oil cooler mounted in the radiator, cooling is by means of a coolant/oil heat exchanger mounted on the side of the transmission.

Safety precautions

5 The following safety precautions must be adhered to where an automatic transmission is fitted. Whenever the vehicle is parked, or is being serviced or repaired, ensure that the handbrake is fully applied and the selector lever is in P.

6 If it is necessary to tow a vehicle with automatic transmission, the towing speed must be restricted to 30 mph and the distance to 30 miles. If these conditions cannot be met, or if transmission damage is the reason for seeking a tow, the vehicle must be transported on a trailer.

Fluid level – checking

7 This check should be made directly after the vehicle has been used so that the transmission oil is at its normal operating temperature.

8 With the vehicle parked on level ground and the engine running,

move the selector lever through all positions a number of times then finally leave it in P. The handbrake must be fully applied throughout the check procedure.

9 With the engine still running, remove the transmission fluid dipstick, wipe it clean, reinsert it fully then withdraw it again and check the fluid level. The fluid level must be between Min and Max levels.

10 If required, top up the fluid level (but do not overfill) through the dipstick guide tube.

11 Stop the engine and refit the dipstick on completion.

Fluid – draining and refilling

12 Position a suitable container with a minimum capacity of three litres under the transmission (hot). There are two drain plugs to be removed, these being shown in Fig. 13.54. Remove the plugs and drain the fluid, then refit the plugs.

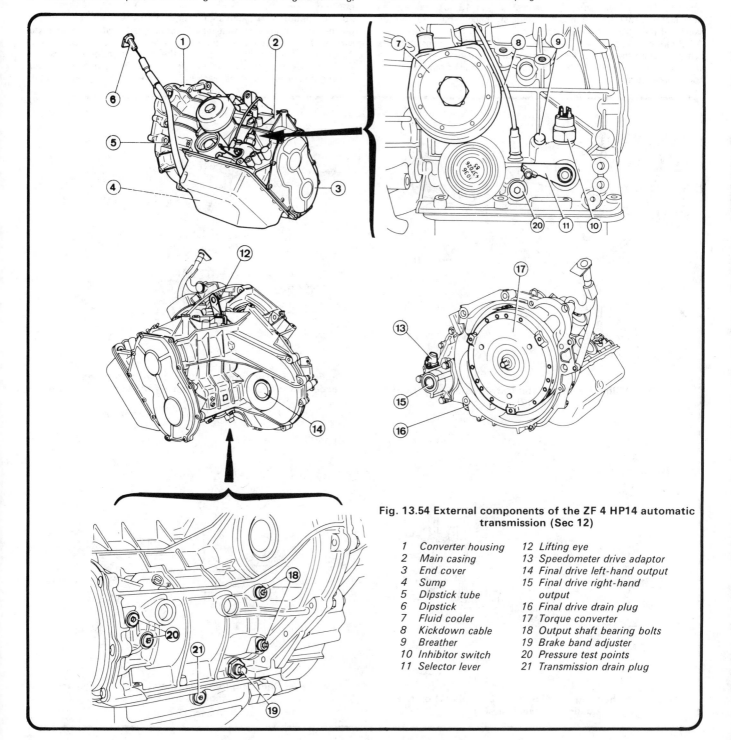

Fig. 13.54 External components of the ZF 4 HP14 automatic transmission (Sec 12)

1 Converter housing	12 Lifting eye
2 Main casing	13 Speedometer drive adaptor
3 End cover	14 Final drive left-hand output
4 Sump	15 Final drive right-hand
5 Dipstick tube	output
6 Dipstick	16 Final drive drain plug
7 Fluid cooler	17 Torque converter
8 Kickdown cable	18 Output shaft bearing bolts
9 Breather	19 Brake band adjuster
10 Inhibitor switch	20 Pressure test points
11 Selector lever	21 Transmission drain plug

13 Refill, using 2.4 litres of the recommended fluid, through the dipstick guide tube.

14 Recheck the fluid level after a nominal mileage has been covered and, if necessary, top up the fluid, as described in paragraphs 7 to 11 inclusive.

Kickdown cable – checking and adjustment

15 The kickdown cable checks and adjustments must be made with the engine at normal operating temperature, the electric cooling fan having cut in, then off.

16 Check and if necessary adjust the engine idle speed, as described in Section 5 of this Supplement.

17 With the engine switched off, first check the accelerator cable for correct adjustment. Detach the kickdown cable from the cam on the carburettor. Pull the accelerator cable sheath stop pin out and reposition it to allow a small clearance at 'a' (Fig. 13.56). Depress the accelerator pedal fully and simultaneously check that the throttle valves of the carburettor are fully opened.

18 Pull the kickdown cable as shown in Fig. 13.57 until resistance is felt, indicating the start of kickdown. At this point the stop nipple on the cable must be distance 'x' (39.0 mm or 1.535 in) from the end of the cable adjuster.

19 Reconnect the kickdown cable to the cam and fit the clip.

20 In the idle position, check that there is a small clearance between the stop nipple and the end of the cable adjuster (Fig. 13.58) up to a maximum of 0.5 mm (0.020 in). If necessary reposition the adjuster by loosening the nuts, then re-tighten the nuts.

21 Kickdown cable renewal is best left to your Peugeot dealer, as it involves removal of the valve block.

Selector control – adjustment

22 Remove the air cleaner, then using a spanner as shown in Fig. 13.59 disconnect the control rod balljoint from the lever on the transmission.

23 Move the lever on the transmission fully forwards to the 'P' position.

24 Inside the car, move the selector lever fully forwards to the 'P' position.

25 The control rod balljoint should align exactly with the coupling ball on the selector lever so that when reconnected, neither the selector lever within the vehicle nor the selector lever on the gearbox move. Adjust the position of the balljoint on the connecting rod if necessary.

26 If the selector control was adjusted, check the setting by starting the engine and, when it has reached its normal operating temperature,

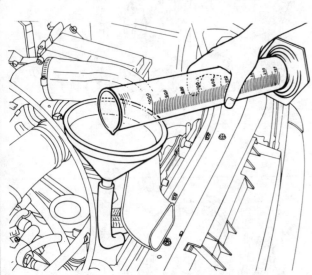

Fig. 13.55 Filling the automatic transmission with fluid (Sec 12)

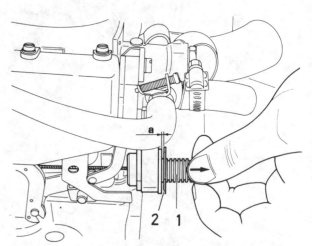

Fig. 13.56 There must be a clearance at (a) on the accelerator cable before adjusting the kickdown cable (Sec 12)

1 Adjustment ferrule   2 Stop pin

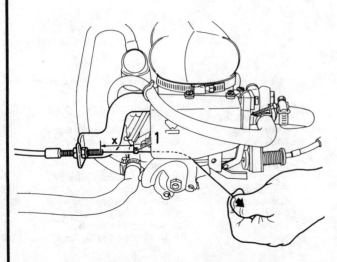

Fig. 13.57 Checking position of stop nipple (1) on the kickdown cable (Sec 12)

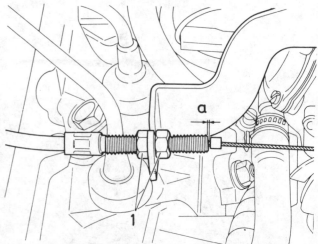

Fig. 13.58 Checking idle clearance (a) on the kickdown cable (Sec 12)

1 Adjustment nuts

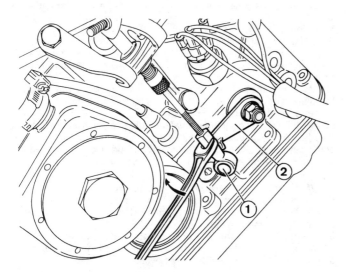

Fig. 13.59 Disconnecting the selector control rod balljoint
(1) from the transmission lever (2) (Sec 12)

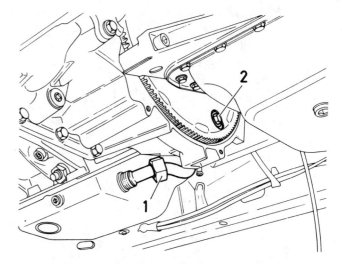

Fig. 13.60 Unscrew the dipstick tube nut (1) and torque
converter bolts (2) (Sec 12)

move the selector lever within the vehicle to P. The vehicle should be
stationary and the gearbox parking pawl fully engaged.
27 Now move the lever to R with the handbrake off. The vehicle
should move rearwards, the pawl having been released.
28 If either of the checks in paragraphs 26 and 27 is unsatisfactory,
unscrew the control rod balljoint one complete turn and repeat the
checks until satisfactory.
29 Refit the air cleaner.

Automatic transmission – removal and refitting
30 Remove the bonnet (Chapter 12).
31 Apply the handbrake and loosen the front wheel nuts, then jack up
the front of the car and support on axle stands.
32 Remove both front roadwheels.
33 Drain the transmission fluid as previously described.
34 Remove both driveshafts as described in Chapter 7. The driveshafts
are the same as fitted to GTI models.
35 Unscrew the dipstick tube nut from the transmission sump.
36 Unbolt the driveplate cover, then unscrew the torque converter
bolts while holding the crankshaft pulley bolt with a bar and socket.
The pulley may have a plastic cover on it which must first be removed.
The three torque converter bolts are spaced equally around the
driveplate.
37 Remove the air cleaner (Chapter 3) and the battery and battery tray
(Chapter 12).
38 Disconnect the selector control rod balljoint from the lever on the
transmission, then unbolt the cable bracket.
39 Disconnect the fluid hoses from the cooler and plug them.
40 Unbolt the earth cables.
41 Disconnect the wiring from the inhibitor switch.
42 Disconnect the kickdown cable at the carburettor end, wind it into
a loose coil and attach it to the transmission.
43 Unbolt and remove the dipstick tube and bracket.
44 Disconnect the speedometer cable and unbolt the TDC sensor.
45 Support the weight of the engine. Peugeot recommend the use of a
bar as shown in Fig. 13.61; however, a hoist may be used or
alternatively a trolley jack and suitable cradle from below.
46 Unbolt the left-hand mounting, then lower the engine sufficiently
to allow for removal of the transmission.
47 Support the weight of the transmission. A hoist may be used as
shown in Fig. 13.62 or a trolley jack and suitable cradle from below.
48 Unscrew the three hexagon and single socket head bolts securing
the transmission to the engine.
49 Separate the transmission from the engine while making sure that
the torque converter remains engaged with the transmission. When
clear of the engine, fit a bracket as shown in Fig. 13.63 to hold the
torque convertor in place.

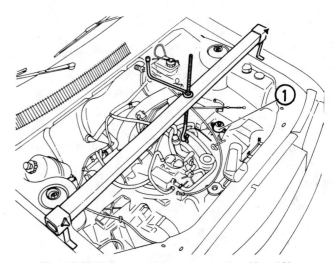

Fig. 13.61 Using an engine support bar (Sec 12)
1   Left-hand mounting

Fig. 13.62 Support the weight of the transmission then
unscrew the bolts (1) (Sec 12)

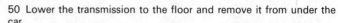

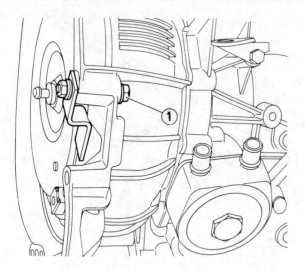

Fig. 13.63 Bracket and bolt (1) for holding torque converter in transmission (Sec 12)

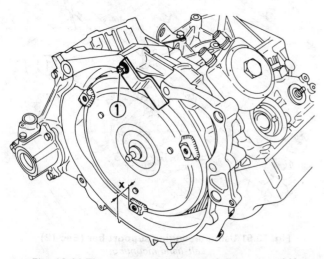

Fig. 13.64 The torque converter is fully engaged if dimension 'x' is more than 7.0 mm (0.28 in) (Sec 12)

1   *Retaining bracket and bolt*

50 Lower the transmission to the floor and remove it from under the car.

51 Before refitting the transmission, check the condition of the spigot bush in the rear of the crankshaft, and apply a little grease to aid entry of the torque convertor. Also check that the two locating dowels are in place on the engine. Apply a little grease to the differential/driveshaft seals.

52 Make sure that the torque convertor is fully engaged by checking the dimension shown in Fig. 13.64. If necessary rotate the torque convertor until it is correctly engaged.

53 Refitting is a reversal of removal but tighten all nuts and bolts to the specified torque, and adjust the kickdown cable and selector control as previously described. Fill the transmission as previously described and bleed the cooling system with reference to Section 4.

Fault diagnosis – automatic transmission

54 Faults not due to incorrect fluid level or adjustment of the selector and kickdown cables must be diagnosed by a Peugeot dealer or automatic transmission specialist.

55 Do not remove the transmission for specialist repair without allowing the specialist to test it *in situ*. Some faults cannot be diagnosed with the transmission removed.

Modifications

56 As from May 1987, the gear ratios have been changed to provide improved performance (see Specifications).

---

13 Driveshafts

Driveshafts (automatic transmission) – description

1   The driveshafts fitted to automatic transmission models are the same as those fitted to GTI models, as described in Chapter 7, and the following sub-section.

Driveshafts – removal and refitting

2   On 1988 and later models, the procedure for driveshaft removal and refitting is basically as described in Section 4 of Chapter 7 (photos). Note, however, that paragraph 10 no longer applies for any model produced after early 1985.

3   Always use a plastic protector when refitting the right-hand driveshaft (photo).

4   On later models, a multi-position lockwasher and spring clip is fitted to the hub nut instead of the locking shoulder type of hub nut (photo).

5   After tightening the hub nut to the specified torque, locate the lockwasher over the nut so that the cut-outs in the shoulder are aligned with the hole in the driveshaft stub, then insert the spring clip (photo).

Driveshafts (1.9 GTI) – identification

6   The driveshafts on 1.9 GTI models are strengthened, and are identified by two grooves on the open shaft between the inner and outer joints. There are no grooves on the driveshafts for other models.

13.2A Remove the bolt (arrowed) ...

13.2B ... and withdraw the front suspension lower balljoint for driveshaft removal

13.3 Inserting the right-hand driveshaft – protector arrowed

13.4 Staking a locking shoulder type hub nut

13.5 Spring clip on later type hub nut inserted

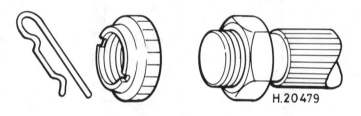

H.20479

Fig. 13.65 Multi-position lockwasher and spring clip for locking the hub nut on later models (Sec 13)

14 Braking system

Braking system (CTI models) – description
1   The braking system on CTI models is the same as that described for GTI models in Chapter 8.

Abrasive disc pads – description
2   As from late 1985, genuine Peugeot disc pads have a thin coating of abrasive material, which cleans the disc during the initial applications of the brakes. This coating also removes any disc imperfections which would cause steering vibration.
3   After fitting these pads the brakes must be applied lightly and intermittently for the first 3 miles (5 km), then 'bedded-in' for 120 miles (200 km), avoiding heavy or prolonged braking.
4   Note that non-genuine disc pads may not have the abrasive coating.

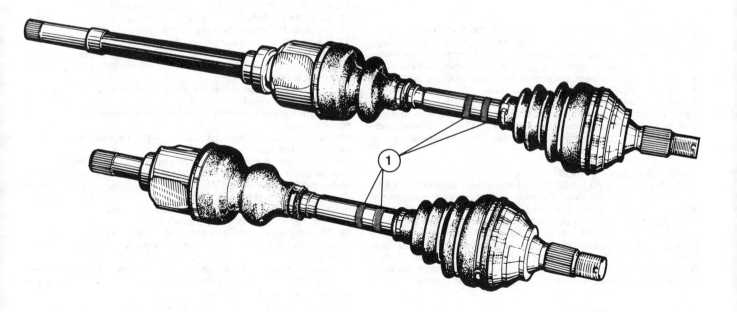

Fig. 13.66 Identification grooves (1) on the 1.9 GTI driveshafts (Sec 13)

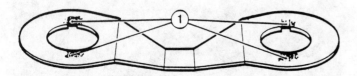

Fig. 13.67 On DBA Bendix disc calipers, the lugs (1) may be ground away from the guide retaining plates (Sec 14)

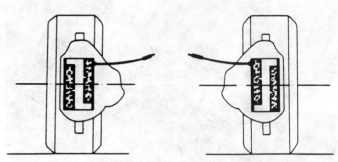

Fig. 13.68 Front view of DBA Bendix disc calipers fitted with offset disc pads (Sec 14)

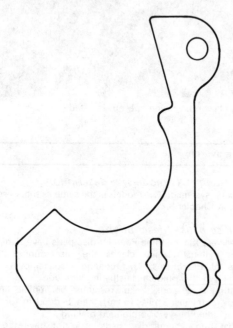

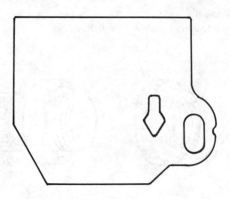

Fig. 13.70 Anti-squeal shim fitted to later Girling disc pads (Sec 14)

Fig. 13.69 Anti-squeal shim fitted to early Girling disc pads (Sec 4)

DBA Bendix disc calipers and pads – modifications

5   On early models fitted with the DBA Bendix disc calipers, the lugs on the guide retaining plates can cause misalignment of the guide sleeves, resulting in the outer disc pads wearing quicker than the inner pads. The lugs have been discontinued on later retaining plates and may be ground off the earlier type if necessary.

6   As from September 1987, offset front disc pads may be fitted to some models to reduce squeal and whistle. It is important to fit these pads in the correct positions as shown in Fig. 13.68. The inner pads with pad wear wires must be located at the top of the caliper.

Girling disc pads – modifications

7   As from chassis no 5 600 000, an anti-squeal shim (Fig. 13.69) was fitted between the inner disc pads and the caliper pistons, being located on both upper and lower pad retaining pins. However, as from chassis no 5 957 000, the shim was modified to the shape shown in Fig. 13.70, being located only on the lower pad retaining pin.

8   When fitting the anti-squeal shims, the arrow cut-out must face downwards (ie in the forward rotational direction of the disc).

9   If problems of brake squeal are experienced on models fitted with the early type of shim, the later type should be fitted instead.

Braking system (1.9 GTI) – description

10 The 1.9 GTI braking system differs from the system fitted to the 1.6 GTI in that the hydraulic circuit is split diagonally, the Girling front disc caliper is modified, DBA rear disc calipers are fitted, and two rear brake compensators are fitted in the two rear hydraulic circuits.

Front disc pads (1.9 GTI) – inspection and renewal

11 Apply the handbrake, then jack up the front of the car and support on axle stands. Remove the front roadwheels.

12 Viewing through the hole in the caliper, check if the friction material has worn down to 2.0 mm (0.079 in) or less. This is indicated by the central groove in the pads, which will not be visible when the wear limit is reached.

13 To remove the pads, first disconnect the wire for the pad wear warning light (photo).

14 Hold the lower guide stationary with one spanner, then unscrew the bolt (photo).

15 Swivel the caliper upwards, then withdraw the two disc pads from the bracket (photos).

16 Clean away all dust and dirt, however do not inhale the dust as it may be injurious to health. Check for brake fluid leakage around the piston dust seal and, if evident, overhaul the caliper with reference to Chapter 8. Check the brake disc for wear, and also check that the rubber bellows on the guides are in good condition.

17 Push the piston fully into the cylinder.

18 Clean the backs of the disc pads and apply a little anti-squeal brake grease. Refit the inner pad (with the pad wear warning wire), then the outer pad.

19 Lower the caliper. Apply locking fluid to the lower guide bolt, insert it, and tighten to the specified torque while holding the guide stationary with another spanner.

20 Reconnect the pad wear warning light wire.

21 Fully depress the brake pedal several times to set the disc pads in their normal position.

22 Check the fluid level in the reservoir and top up if necessary.

23 Repeat the operations on the opposite disc caliper.

24 Refit the roadwheels and lower the car to the ground.

14.13 Pad wear warning light wire and connector

14.14 Unscrewing the lower guide bolt

14.15A Swivel the caliper upwards ...

14.15B ... and withdraw the disc pads

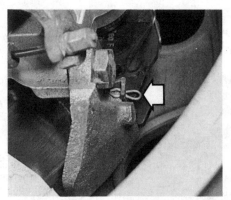

14.28 Spring clip (arrowed) retaining locking key

14.29A Removing the rear disc pads

14.29B Rear disc pad

14.31 Turning the rear caliper piston with a screwdriver

Rear disc pads (1.9 GTI) – inspection and renewal

25 Chock the front wheels, then jack up the rear of the car and support on axle stands. Remove the rear wheels.

26 Release the handbrake.

27 Check the disc pads for wear as described in paragraph 12.

28 To remove the pads, extract the spring clip (photo) and slide out the locking key retaining the bottom of the pads.

29 Withdraw the disc pads using pliers, while pressing down on the upper locating ears (photos).

30 Clean away all dust and dirt, taking care not to inhale it as it may be injurious to health. Check for brake fluid leakage around the piston dust seal, and if evident overhaul the caliper using the basic procedure described in Chapter 8. Check the brake disc for wear, and also check that the rubber bellows on the guides are in good condition.

31 The automatic handbrake adjustment must now be retracted in order to accommodate the new disc pads. To do this, turn the piston using a screwdriver in the grooves (photo), at the same time using a second screwdriver to apply an outward force to the caliper. Do not damage the brake disc while carrying out this procedure.

32 Set the piston so that the mark (Fig. 13.72) is horizontal, and either above or below the piston groove.

33 Apply a little anti-squeal brake grease to the pad contact areas on the caliper.

34 Locate the two disc pads in the caliper, pressing the upper ears fully into position.

35 Slide the locking key into the caliper and secure with the spring clip.

36 Fully depress the brake pedal several times to set the automatic adjuster and position the disc pads in their normal position.

37 Check the fluid level in the reservoir and top up if necessary.

38 Repeat the operations on the opposite disc caliper.

39 Refit the roadwheels and lower the car to the ground.

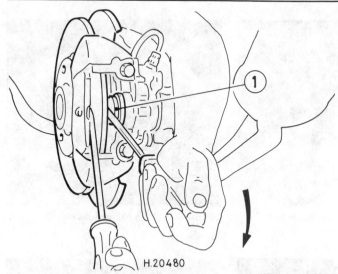

**Fig. 13.71 Retracting the automatic handbrake adjustment
on the 1.9 GTI (Sec 14)**
1   Piston

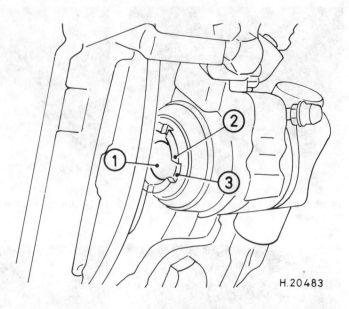

H.20483

**Fig. 13.72 Correct final position of piston on the 1.9 GTI
rear caliper (Sec 14)**
*1   Piston   3   Groove
2   Mark*

Rear disc caliper (1.9 GTI) – removal and refitting
40 Remove the disc pads as previously described.
41 Fit a brake hose clamp to the flexible hose connected to the caliper.
Alternatively, where possible, remove the filler cap from the brake fluid
reservoir, then tighten it down onto a piece of polythene sheeting.
42 Loosen the brake hose union at the caliper (photo).
43 Unhook the handbrake cable from the lever on the caliper, and
withdraw the outer cable (photo).
44 Unscrew the two mounting bolts, withdraw the caliper from the
disc, then unscrew the caliper from the brake hose. Plug the hose to
prevent loss of fluid.
45 To refit the caliper, first screw it onto the brake hose and locate it
over the brake disc, so that the hose is not twisted.
46 Clean the mounting bolt threads and apply a little locking fluid.
Insert the bolts together with the anti-rotation plate and tighten them
to the specified torque.
47 Tighten the brake hose union.
48 Insert the handbrake outer cable and re-connect the inner cable to
the lever.

14.42 Rear caliper brake hose and union

14.43 Handbrake cable at the rear caliper

14.52 Rear brake disc retaining screw (arrowed)

49 Refit the disc pads as previously described.
50 Remove the brake hose clamp or polythene sheeting, and bleed the hydraulic system with reference to paragraph 56.
51 Check and if necessary adjust the handbrake as described in paragraphs 57 to 64.

Brake discs (1.9 GTI) – removal and refitting
52 The procedure is as given in Chapter 8, Section 6 (photo). However, before removing the front disc the caliper must be unbolted and tied to one side. There is no need to disconnect the hydraulic hose.
53 Refer to Chapter 8, Section 5 when refitting the caliper.

Rear brake compensators (1.9 GTI) – general
54 Two compensators are fitted, since the hydraulic system is split diagonally. Each compensator is located in the rear circuit near the rear wheel (photo). They are of fixed calibration and not load-sensitive.
55 Removal and refitting procedures are basically as given in Chapter 8, Section 10.

Hydraulic system (1.9 GTI) – draining and bleeding
56 Refer to Chapter 8, Section 12, and proceed as for the diagonally split system.

Handbrake (1.9 GTI) – adjustment
57 Chock the wheels and fully release the handbrake.
58 Apply the brake pedal hard several times.
59 Working inside the car, remove the screw and lift the cover from the handbrake lever.
60 Working beneath the rear of the car, measure the distance between the operating levers on the calipers and the end stops on the inner cables.

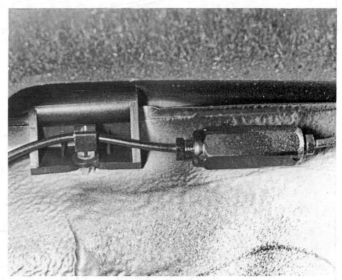
14.54 Rear brake compensator

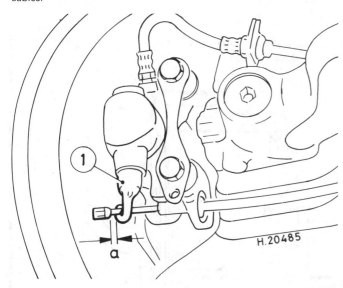

Fig. 13.73 Handbrake adjustment on the 1.9 GTI (Sec 14)

1   Handbrake operating lever on the caliper
a   Clearance of 5.0 mm (0.197

in) for checking amount of operating lever

61 Inside the car, loosen the nut on the handbrake lever until the distance measured in paragraph 60 is 5.0 mm (0.197 in) on both sides.
62 Check that the operating levers on both calipers move freely and return positively to their stops.
63 Now tighten the nut on the handbrake lever so that the handbrake is fully applied between 7 and 9 notches.
64 Refit the cover over the handbrake lever.

Handbrake cables (1.9 GTI) – renewal
65 Working inside the car, remove the screw and lift the cover from the handbrake lever.
66 Unhook the cable from the compensator.
67 Chock the front wheels, then jack up the rear of the car and support on axle stands.

14.71 Stop-lamp switch and wiring (arrowed)

68 Release the cable(s) from the retaining clips, the floor, the fuel tank, the bracket(s), and the caliper lever(s), and withdraw from under the car.
69 Fit the new cable(s) using a reversal of the removal procedure. Finally adjust the handbrake as described previously.

Stop-lamp switch – removal and refitting
70 Remove the lower facia panel from the steering column.
71 Disconnect the two wires (photo).
72 Unscrew the locknut nearest the pedal, and withdraw the switch from the bracket.
73 Refitting is a reversal of removal, but adjust the locknuts so that the distance between the end of the switch threaded body and the pedal (fully released) is 3.5 mm (0.138 in).

15 Suspension and hubs

Front anti-roll bar (non-GTI models) – general
1   On non-GTI models, the front anti-roll bar is located laterally by a guide bar. It is possible for the bar to become dislocated or bent following an impact to a front wheel, resulting in the vehicle pulling to the left or right.

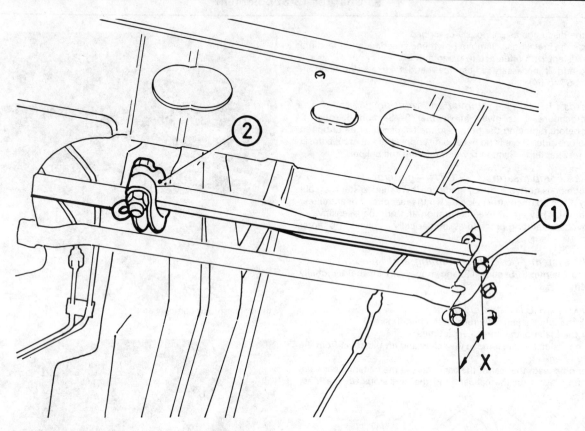

Fig. 13.74 7.0 mm diameter front anti-roll bar guide bar and split clamp (Sec 15)

1 Mounting bolt   X = 101.0 mm (3.98 in)
2 Split clamp

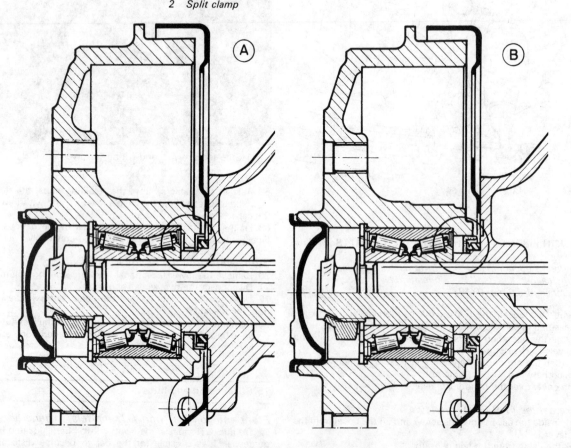

Fig. 13.75 Early (A) and later (B) rear hub oil seal location (Sec 15)

2   The guide bar length must be adjusted as described in Chapter 9, Section 3. Note that a full-circle clamp is fitted to early models with a 6.0 mm diameter bar, whereas a split clamp is fitted to later models with a 7.0 mm diameter bar. On the later type, position the clamp centrally on the turned-back end of the bar before tightening the bolts.

Rear suspension assembly (five-door models) – modification
3   On five-door models manufactured from mid-September 1986 onwards, the seat belt anchorage as shown in photo 12.5, Chapter 9 is no longer fitted. However, the anchorage must always be fitted to earlier five-door models and all three-door models.

Rear hub/drum assembly – modifications
4   Models manufactured from early 1986 are fitted with modified rear hub/drum assemblies which allow the rear hub bearings to be renewed, this not previously being possible. Reference to Fig. 13.75 shows that the oil seal shoulder is removed on the later hub/drum assemblies in order to allow the use of a special bearing removal tool (Peugeot tool No. 7.052X).
5   Bearing renewal requires the use of a press in conjunction with the special tool to remove the old bearing, and this is best entrusted to your Peugeot dealer (once removed, a bearing is rendered unserviceable).
6   When renewing the oil seal, Peugeot recommend the use of special tool No. 7.052Y to seat the new seal. If unavailable, make a careful note of the position of the original seal before removing it.

16   Bodywork and fittings

Minor body damage – repair
Plastic components
1   With the use of more and more plastic body components by the vehicle manufacturers (eg bumpers, spoilers, and in some cases major body panels), rectification of damage to such items has become a matter of either entrusting repair work to a specialist in this field, or renewing complete components. Repair by the DIY owner is not really feasible owing to the cost of the equipment and materials required for effecting such repairs. The basic technique involves making a groove along the line of the crack in the plastic, using a rotary burr in a power drill. The damaged part is then welded back together by using a hot air gun to heat up and fuse a plastic filler rod into the groove. Any excess plastic is then removed and the area rubbed down to a smooth finish. It is important that a filler rod of the correct plastic is used, as body components can be made of a variety of different types (eg polycarbonate, ABS, polypropylene).
2   If the owner is renewing a complete component himself, he will be left with the problem of finding a suitable paint for finishing which is compatible with the type of plastic used. At one time the use of a universal paint was not possible owing to the complex range of plastics encountered in body component applications. Standard paints, generally speaking, will not bond to plastic or rubber satisfactorily. However, is it now possible to obtain a plastic body parts finishing kit which consists of a pre-primer treatment, a primer and coloured top coat. Full instructions are normally supplied with a kit, but basically the method of use is to first apply the pre-primer to the component concerned and allow it to dry for up to 30 minutes. Then the primer is applied and left to dry for about an hour before finally applying the special coloured top coat. The result is a correctly coloured component where the paint will flex with the plastic or rubber, a property that standard paint does not normally possess.

Door trim panel – removal and refitting
3   On certain later models the radio speakers are located in the doors, and it is therefore necessary to disconnect the speaker wiring during removal of the door trim panel.

Door (Cabriolet) – dismantling and reassembly
4   Remove the trim panel.
5   Disconnect the wiring from the regulator motor.
6   Unscrew the nuts and withdraw the regulator from the door.
7   Detach the weatherstrips from the top edge of the door.
8   Raise the door glass and lift it from the door.
9   Unscrew the mounting nuts and remove the fixed quarter-light glass through the sliding glass location.

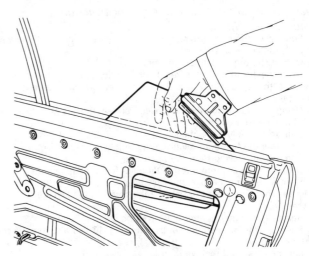

Fig. 13.76 Removing the fixed quarter-light glass on Cabriolet models (Sec 16)

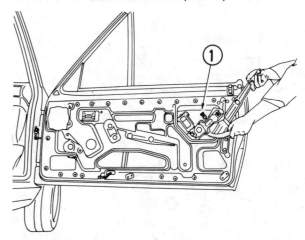

Fig. 13.77 Door glass height adjustment screw (1) shown during removal of regulator assembly (Sec 16)

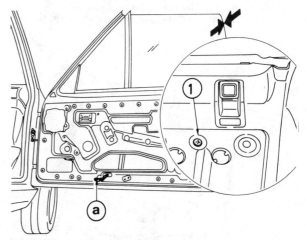

Fig. 13.78 Door glass rear edge adjustment screw (1) on Cabriolet models (Sec 16)
a   Switch wiring

10   Reassembly is a reversal of dismantling but carry out the following adjustments. With the regulator wiring reconnected, close the window, then if necessary adjust the height by reaching through the speaker aperture and turning the screw shown in Fig. 13.77. Close the door and check that the rear edge of the door glass seals correctly with the hood. If not, remove the cap and turn the screw shown in Fig. 13.78.

Rear quarter-light glass and regulator (Cabriolet) – removal and refiting

11 Fold down the front and rear seats, then open the hood a little way.

12 Fully close the quarter-light.

13 Unbolt the outer seal belt anchor.

14 Note the position of the regulator handle, then remove it using pliers of the type shown in Fig. 13.79 or an alternative similar instrument.

15 Using a wide-bladed screwdriver, release the plastic clips and withdraw the trim panel.

16 Pull off the polythene sheet.

17 Unscrew the five bolts securing the regulator mechanism.

18 Remove the casing from the hood hinge.

19 Remove the pad from the quarter glass lower channel.

20 Push in the mechanism then tilt it and withdraw it through the aperture, complete with the cable. Take care not to damage the seat belt reel.

21 Remove the inner quarter glass weatherstrip and clips.

22 Push out the plastic rivet centre pins (Fig. 13.81) and remove the stretcher support.

23 Lift the glass and remove it.

24 Refitting is a reversal of removal. If a new glass is being fitted, position the lower channel as shown in Fig. 13.83. Remove the guide

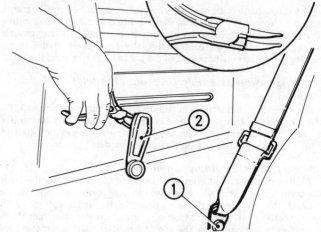

Fig. 13.79 Using special pliers to remove the rear quarter-light glass regulator handle on Cabriolet models (Sec 16)

1   Outer seat bolt anchor   2   Regulator handle

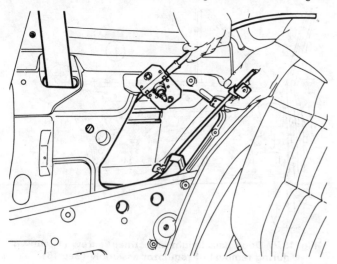

Fig. 13.80 Removing the rear quarter-light glass regulator mechanism on Cabriolet models (Sec 16)

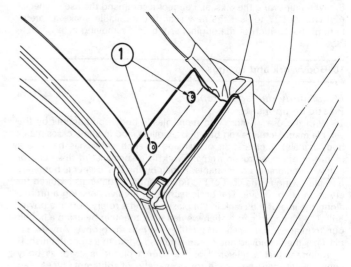

Fig. 13.81 Plastic rivets (1) securing the stretcher support (Sec 16)

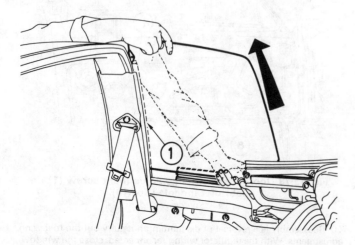

Fig. 13.82 Removing the rear quarter-light glass on Cabriolet models (Sec 16)

1   Guide channel

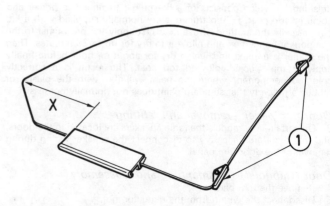

Fig. 13.83 Channel position on the rear quarter-light glass (Sec 16)

X   = 145.0 mm (5.71 in)   1   Guide pads

pads from the old glass by drilling out the rivet heads. Fit them to the new glass using the special sleeves and screws obtainable from a Peugeot dealer. Apply a little locking fluid to the screw threads before inserting and tightening them. Unlike the door glass there are no adjustment points.

Hood and rear window (Cabriolet) – removal and refitting

25 Open the hood to the point shown in Fig. 13.85.
26 Prise out the caps and unscrew the hinge cover screws.
27 Unbolt the front corner brackets and the lower edge trim supports.
28 Fold down the rear seats and remove the panel shelf.
29 Slide off the mouldings and release the side clips.
30 Prise off the rear trim strip and remove the crossmember screws.
31 Unzip and remove the rear window.
32 Unclip the tensioners, then unscrew the remaining mounting bolts and lift the hood from the car.
33 Refitting is a reversal of removal, but the main mounting bolts should be left loose until the hood is correctly tensioned. To do this fix the front of the hood, then position the mounting brackets to eliminate any wrinkles and tighten the bolts. If necessary adjust the front locking hooks so that the front of the hood is held firmly in position. With the hood folded down, check that the stop brackets are in contact with the stop bolts and if necessary adjust the bolts.

Sunroof glass – removal and refitting

34 Working inside the car remove the roof console.
35 Remove the screws from the handle and latch.
36 From outside the car remove the front cover and the corner screws.

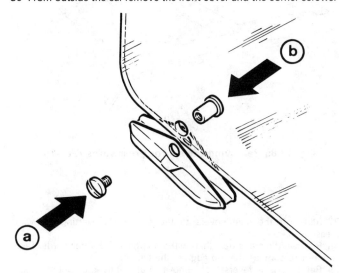

Fig. 13.84 Screw (a) and sleeve (b) for fitting the guide pads to the rear quarter-light glass on Cabriolet models (Sec 16)

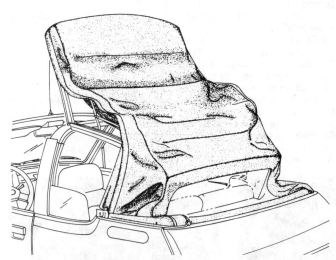

Fig. 13.85 Hood opening balance point (Sec 16)

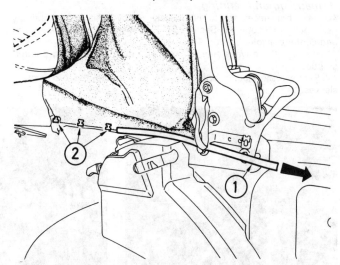

Fig. 13.86 Slide off the moulding (1) and release the clips (2) (Sec 16)

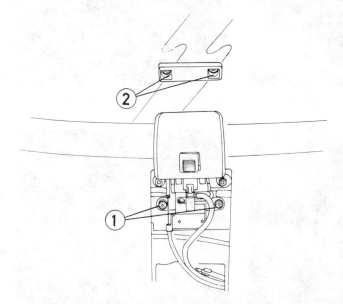

Fig. 13.87 Sunroof handle screws (1) and latch screws (2) Sec 16)

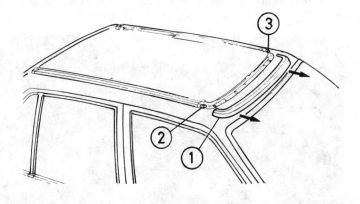

Fig. 13.88 Remove the front cover (1) and corner screws (2 and 3) (Sec 16)

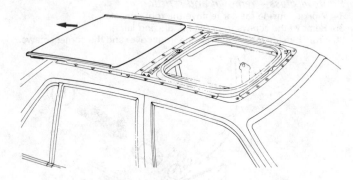

Fig. 13.89 Removing the sunroof rearwards (Sec 16)

37 Slide off the side covers to the rear while exerting outward pressure.
38 Remove the rear stops, then withdraw the sunroof rearwards. Take care not to damage the top edge of the tailgate.
39 Refitting is a reversal of removal, but lightly grease the guide channels.

Heater assembly (1986/87 models) – removal, dismantling and refitting

40 It is not necessary to completely remove the facia panel as described in Chapter 11, Section 23. First remove the gear lever trim and centre console.
41 Remove the driver's side parcel shelf and lower steering column shroud.
42 Remove the heater side trims by uncoupling the box-section sleeves.

43 Unscrew the heater panel screws, but do not remove the panel at this stage.
44 Clamp the heater hoses inside the engine compartment.
45 Inside the car, protect the carpet from water spillage with a polythene sheet, then remove the heater pipes.
46 Remove the glovebox together with the heater panel.
47 Unscrew the mounting bolts, disconnect the wiring, and withdraw the heater assembly from the car.
48 The dismantling procedure is as given in Chapter 11.
49 Refitting is a reversal of removal, but top up the cooling system if necessary.

Facia panel (1988 models) – removal and refitting

50 Disconnect the battery negative lead.
51 Remove the screws and withdraw the right-hand lower facia panel (photo).
52 Prise out the instrument panel rheostat and disconnect the wires.
53 Remove the screws and withdraw the lower steering column shroud (photo).
54 Prise out the coin box and the triangular cover (photos).
55 Pull off the heater control knobs (photo).
56 Remove the screws and withdraw the heater control surround (photos).
57 Remove the screws and withdraw the central vent assembly (photos).
58 Remove the radio (Section 17) or oddments compartment as applicable.
59 Remove the screws and withdraw the trim quadrants from each side of the facia (photo).
60 Remove the ashtray and disconnect the wiring from the cigar lighter (photos). Identify the wiring.
61 Unclip the clock surround (photo).
62 Insert lengths of welding rod, or similar, into the holes at the top of the switch surround to release the upper clips, then undo the lower screws and remove the surround (photos).
63 Prise the steering column grommet from the floorpan (photo).
64 Unscrew the mounting nuts and lower the steering column to the floor (photo).

16.51 Right-hand lower facia panel removal

16.53 Lower steering column shroud removal

16.54A Removal of the coin box ...

16.54B ... and triangular cover

16.55 Removing the heater control knobs

16.56A Remove the screws ...

16.56B ... and withdraw the heater control surround

16.57A Removing the central vent assembly upper ...

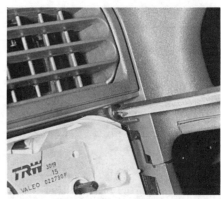

16.57B ... and lower screws

16.59 Trim quadrant and screw

16.60A Remove the ashtray ...

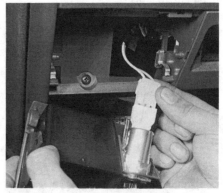

16.60B ... and disconnect the cigar lighter wiring

16.61 Clock surround removal

16.62A Method of releasing the switch surround upper clips

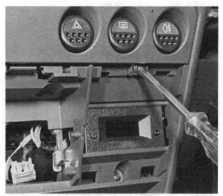

16.62B Remove the lower screws ...

16.62C ... and withdraw the switch surround

16.63 Steering column grommet

16.64 Steering column mounting nuts (arrowed)

16.65 Prise out the vent ...

16.66 ... and remove the screw

16.67 Removing the centre console tray

16.68A Remove the screws ...

16.68B ... and slide the surround up the gearstick

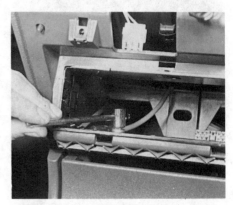

16.69A Removing the centre console upper nuts ...

16.69B ... and lower nut

16.71A Front facia panel screws (arrowed)

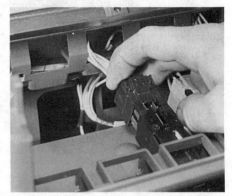

16.71B Disconnecting the switch wiring

65 Prise the small vents from each side of the centre console (photo).
66 Pull back the carpet and remove the screws (photo).
67 Prise the small tray from the centre console (photo).
68 Remove the screws and slide the surround up the gearstick (photos).
69 Remove the upper and lower nuts and withdraw the centre console (photos).
70 Unclip the felt cover from under the facia.
71 Remove the screws and withdraw the front facia panel. Disconnect the wiring from the switches (photos).
72 Remove the heater control panel retaining screws (photos).
73 If necessary, remove the side vents (photo).
74 Remove the instrument panel (Section 17) and choke cable (Section 7).

75 Remove the left lower facia mounting screw (photo).
76 Unclip the glovebox and remove the lighting switch (photo). Also remove the light.
77 Remove the remaining mounting screws and nuts, and withdraw the facia sufficiently to disconnect the wiring. Access to the front mounting nuts is gained by removing the plastic guard from the plenum chamber in the engine compartment (photos). Identify each wire for location.
78 Unclip the fuse and relay panel, and withdraw the facia panel from the car.
79 With the facia removed, access is gained to the heater and heater control panel (photos).
80 Refitting is a reversal of removal, but on completion check the operation of all electrical components.

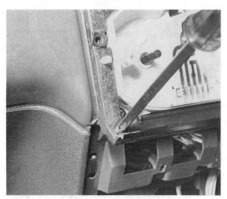

16.72A Removing the heater control panel support screws

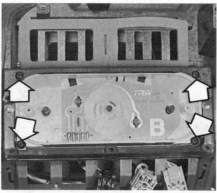

16.72B Heater control panel mounting screws (arrowed)

16.73 Side vent removal

16.75 Left lower facia mounting screw removal

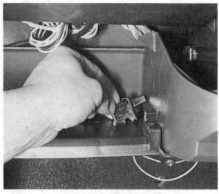

16.76 Glovebox light switch removal

16.77A Removing the facia lower left screw ...

16.77B ... left mounting nut ...

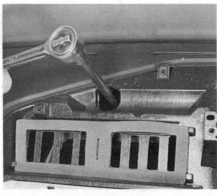

16.77C ... centre mounting nut ...

16.77D ... and front mounting nuts (arrowed)

16.77E Wiring connectors

16.79A Heater motor assembly

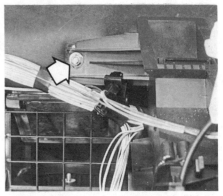

16.79B Heater mounting nut (arrowed)

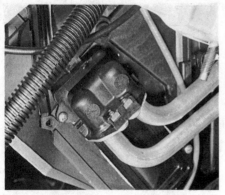
16.79C Heater matrix and supply tubes

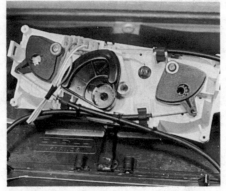
16.79D Heater control panel

16.79E Heater control cable and flap lever

16.81 Removing the trim cover

16.82A Remove the mounting screws ...

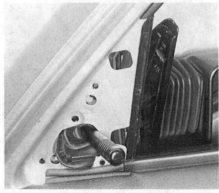
16.82B ... and withdraw the exterior mirror

16.84 Lubricating a door safety strap

16.85 Lubricating the bonnet lock

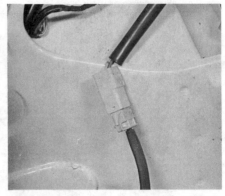
16.86A Front foglight wiring connector

16.86B Front bumper mounting bracket

16.86C Front bumper side bracket nut removal

16.86D Front wing trim retaining clip

16.86E Using a socket to remove the front bumper centre bolts

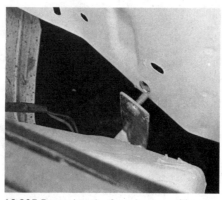

16.86F Removing the front bumper side mounting bracket

16.86G Front bumper mounting socket

17.5 Starter motor cable from the solenoid (arrowed)

17.6 Removing the solenoid from the drive end bracket

17.7A Unscrew the bolt ...

Exterior mirror (1988 models) – removal and refitting
81 Carefully prise the trim cover from the interior mirror control lever (photo).
82 Remove the mounting screws, then feed the rubber grommet through the hole and withdraw the mirror from outside (photos).
83 Refitting is a reversal of removal.

Bodywork – maintenance
84 Door hinges and safety straps should be lubricated with multi-purpose oil (photos).
85 The bonnet lock should be lubricated with a lithium-based grease (photo).

Front bumper (1.9 GTI) – removal and refitting
86 The procedure is basically as given in Section 10 of Chapter 11, but note the additional details shown (photos).

17 Electrical system

Alternator (Paris-Rhone) – regulator renewal
1 There are two types of regulator fitted to Paris-Rhone alternators, one having the part number 5761 67 and the other 5761 56. The two regulators differ in that they supply the current to the rotor windings in opposite directions. Due to residual magnetism in the rotor pole pieces, the alternator may not 'self-excite' after replacing one type of regulator with the other. Where this occurs, the following procedure will be necessary.
2 Disconnect the ignition warning lamp wire from the single terminal on the regulator (terminal L).
3 Connect a wire to the battery positive terminal, then touch the free end of the wire on the regulator terminal for approximately three seconds.
4 Disconnect the wire from the battery and re-connect the ignition warning lamp wire.

Starter motor (Valeo) – dismantling and reassembly
5 Unscrew the nut and disconnect the motor cable from the solenoid (photo).
6 Unscrew the through-bolts and remove the solenoid from the drive end bracket, at the same time unhooking the solenoid core from the lever (photo).
7 Unscrew the bolt and remove the washers from the commutator end (photo).
8 Unscrew the nuts from the through-bolts and withdraw the end cover, at the same time extracting the field brush (photos).
9 Remove the thrust washers from the armature (photo).
10 Mark the yoke and end bracket in relation to each other, then remove the yoke (photo).
11 Prise out the rubber bearing and withdraw the armature from the drive end bracket (photo).
12 Remove the rubber bearing from the lever (photo).
13 Remove the core and spring from the solenoid (photo).
14 Reassembly is a reversal of dismantling.

Fuses
15 The fuse circuits for later models are changed as shown in the Specifications at the beginning of this Chapter.

Facia switches (1988 models) – removal and refitting
16 Disconnect the battery negative lead.
17 Open the ashtray.
18 Unclip the bottom of the clock surround (where fitted) and remove it.
19 Remove the screws from the bottom of the switch panel, then insert lengths of welding rod, or similar into the special holes and remove the switch panel.
20 The individual switches may now be removed by inserting two small screwdrivers in the slots on each side of the switch, extracting the switch, and disconnecting the wiring.
21 Refitting is a reversal of removal.

17.7B ... and remove the washers

17.8A Unscrew the through-bolt nuts (arrowed) ...

17.8B ... and withdraw the end cover

17.9 Removing the armature thrust washers

17.10 Removing the yoke

17.11 Withdrawing the armature from the drive end bracket

17.12 Armature and lever (rubber bearing removed)

17.13 Solenoid with core and spring

Clock (1988 models) – removal and refitting

22 Disconnect the battery negative lead.
23 Remove the trapezium-shaped coin compartment or cover from the top of the facia by lifting the bottom edge.
24 Pull off the heater control knobs using card or thick cloth and pliers on the central bars.
25 Remove the screws beneath the control knobs and withdraw the upper front panel surround.
26 Open and remove the ashtray.
27 Unclip the bottom of the clock surround and remove it.
28 Remove the oddments tray, or if fitted, the radio, as described later in this Section.
29 Remove the screws and withdraw the lower front panel surround by releasing the bottom edge first.
30 Disconnect the wiring plug from the rear of the clock, then release the clock from the lower front panel surround.
31 Refitting is a reversal of removal.

Instrument panel (1988 models) – removal and refitting

32 Disconnect the battery negative lead.
33 Remove the trapezium-shaped coin compartment or cover from the top of the facia by lifting the bottom edge.
34 Pull off the heater control knobs using card or thick cloth and pliers on the central bars.
35 Remove the screws beneath the control knobs and withdraw the upper front panel surround.
36 Remove the screws and withdraw the visor from the instrument panel.
37 Remove the screws and withdraw the centre vents.
38 Using a screwdriver through the steering column lower shroud, unscrew the visor locating studs.
39 Remove the side screw then lift away the visor.
40 Remove the mounting screws from each side of the instrument panel (photo).
41 Tilt the instrument panel and disconnect the wiring plugs, noting

17.40 Instrument panel mounting screw removal

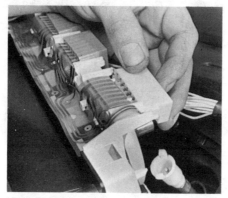

17.41 Disconnecting the wiring plugs

17.42A Disconnecting the speedometer cable (arrowed)

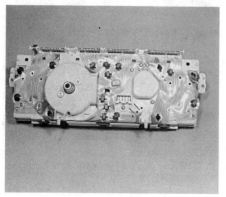

17.42B Rear view of the instrument panel

17.44A Removing later type side repeater light

17.44B Side repeater light components

their locations (photo).
42 Disconnect the speedometer cable by squeezing the end fitting. Remove the instrument panel (photos).
43 Refitting is a reversal of removal.

Side repeater light and bulb – removal and refitting

44 On early models, reach up behind the front wing, squeeze the plastic tabs together and push out the lamp. On later models, turn the lamp anti-clockwise and withdraw it from the front wing (photos).
45 Disconnect the wiring, remove the end cap, and extract the bulb.
46 Refitting is a reversal of removal, but on the early type, position the lamp so that the location peg enters the hole in the front wing.

Dim-dip lighting – description

47 All models manufactured from late 1986 are fitted with a dim-dip lighting system, which essentially prevents the vehicle from being driven with the sidelights alone switched on.
48 When the ignition is switched on with the sidelights also switched on, the relay is energised, closing the internal contacts and supplying current to the dipped beam circuit via the resistor. This causes the dip filaments in the headlamps to be illuminated at one-sixth dipped beam brightness. The relay winding is earthed through the headlamp main beam filaments so that the relay is de-energised when the main beam is switched on.

Radio (later models) – removal and refitting

49 Disconnect the battery negative lead.
50 Remove the radio side trims (photo), and insert lengths of welding rod on metal dowel into the exposed holes to release the clips.
51 Withdraw the radio from the facia and disconnect the aerial and wiring (photo).
52 Refitting is a reversal of removal.

Instrument panel rheostat – removal and refitting

53 Prise the rheostat from the steering column lower shroud and

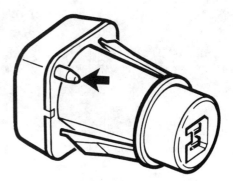

Fig. 13.90 Location peg on early type side repeater light (Sec 17)

disconnect the wiring (photo).
54 Refitting is a reversal of removal.

Reversing light switch – removal and refitting

55 Disconnect the wiring and unscrew the switch from the top of the gearbox (photo). Remove the washer.
56 Refitting is a reversal of removal, but renew the washer if necessary.

Clock illumination bulb (1988 models) – renewal

57 Remove the clock as previously described.
58 Twist the bulbholder to remove it, then extract the bulb (photo).

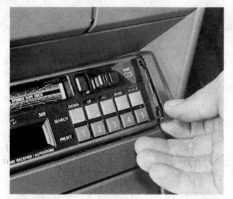

17.50 Removing the radio side trims

17.51 Disconnecting the radio wiring

17.53 Removing the instrument panel rheostat

17.55 Removing the reversing light switch

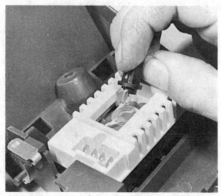

17.58 Removing the clock illumination bulb

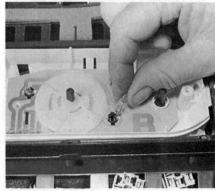

17.60 Removing the heater control panel illumination bulb

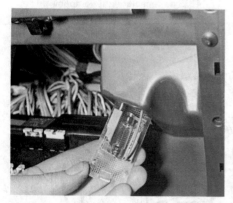

17.61 Glovebox illumination bulb and lamp

17.65 Air compressor (A) and horn (B) (1.9 GTI)

17.67A Fusebox by radiator

17.67B Relays on bulkhead

17.67C Relay near horn (1.9 GTI)

Heater control panel illumination bulb (1988 models) – renewal

59 Follow the procedure given in paragraphs 22 to 25.
60 Pull the bulb from the control panel (photos).

Glovebox illumination bulb (1988 models) – renewal

61 Open the glovebox and prise out the lamp (photo).
62 Remove the festoon type bulb from the terminals.

Air compressor and horn (1.9 GTI) – removal and refitting

63 Remove the front grille and front bumper, as described in Chapter 11 and Section 16 of this Chapter.
64 Disconnect the air hose and supply wire.
65 Unbolt and remove the compressor or horn as required (photo).
66 Refitting is a reversal of removal.

Fuses and relays (1988 models) – general

67 In addition to the fuses and relays above the glovebox, fuses are located behind the left-hand side of the radiator, on the left-hand side of the bulkhead, and near the horn on 1.9 GTI models (photos).

Use of wiring diagrams – general

68 The components are numbered from 1 to 999, and the vehicle is divided into four sections for the purpose of component location. Each section is identified by a letter, which precedes the component number, as given below.

M = Engine compartment
P = Fascia
H = Passenger compartment
C = Luggage area

Wiring diagrams overleaf

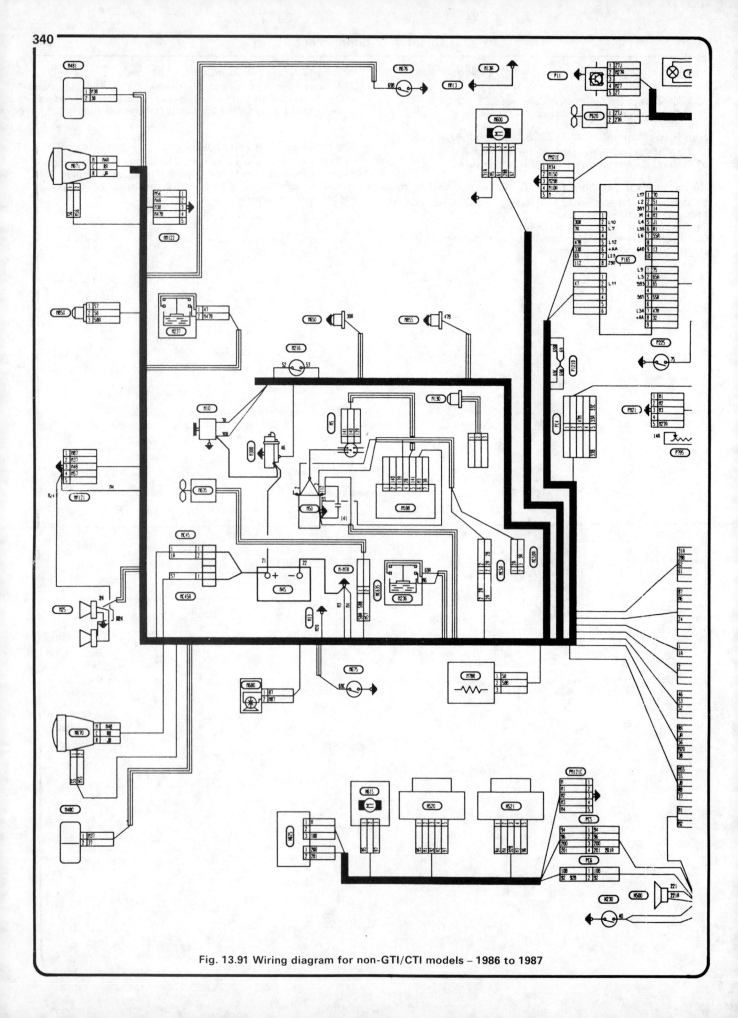

Fig. 13.91 Wiring diagram for non-GTI/CTI models – 1986 to 1987

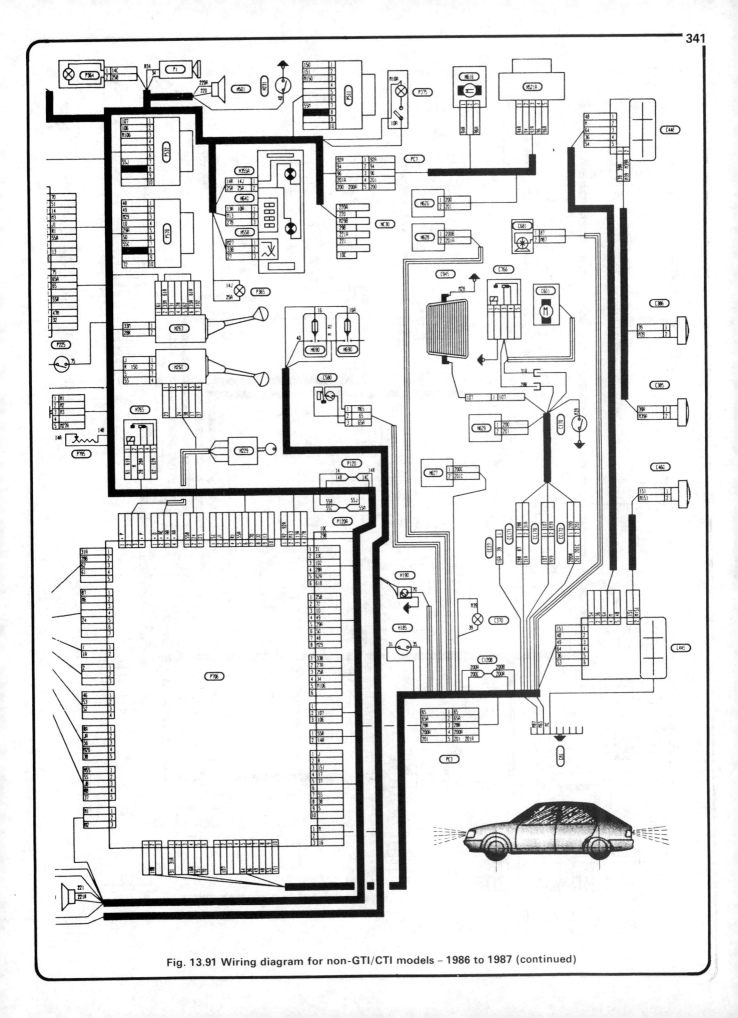

Fig. 13.91 Wiring diagram for non-GTI/CTI models – 1986 to 1987 (continued)

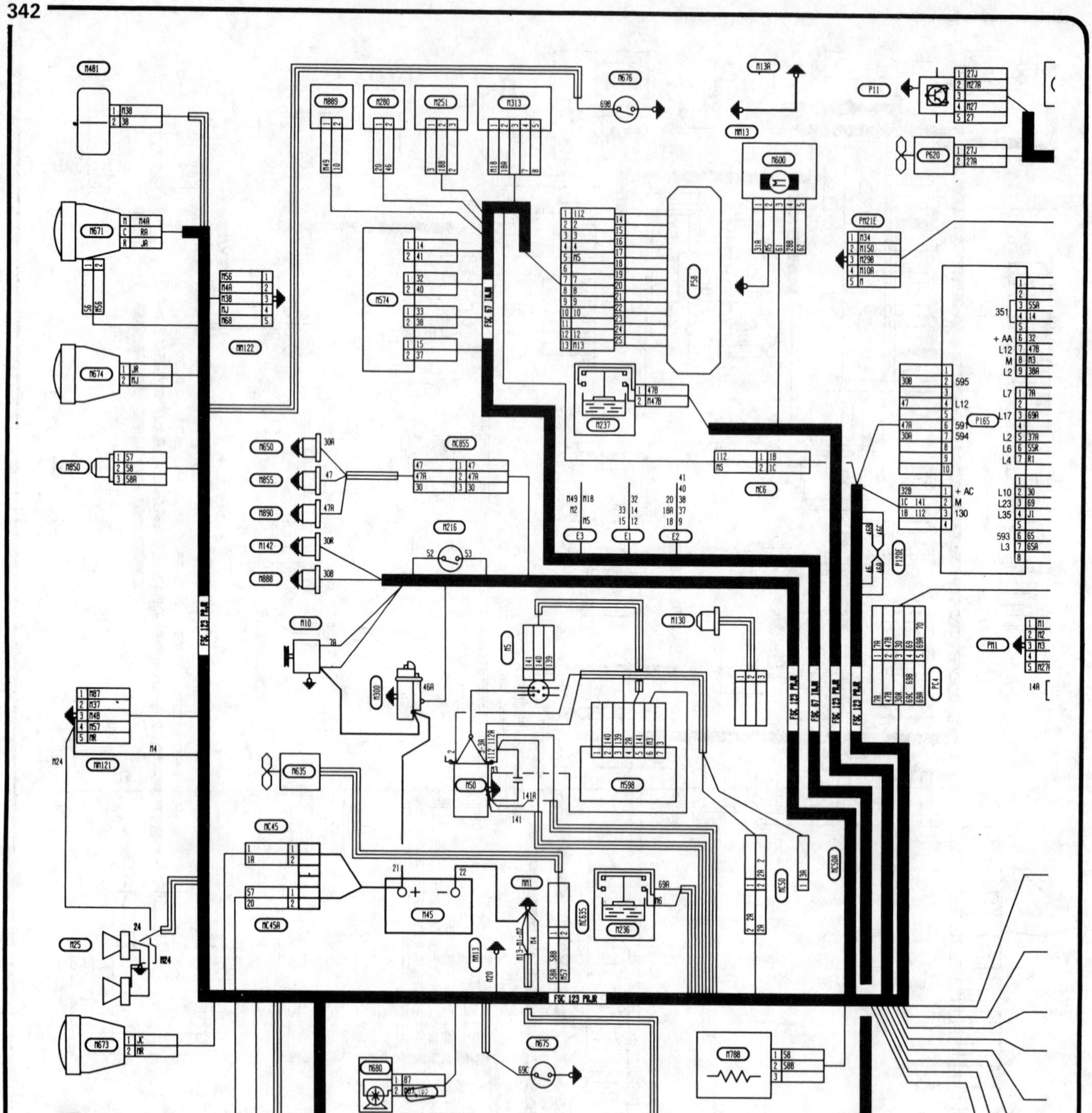

Fig. 13.92 Wiring diagram for GTI/CTI models – 1986 on

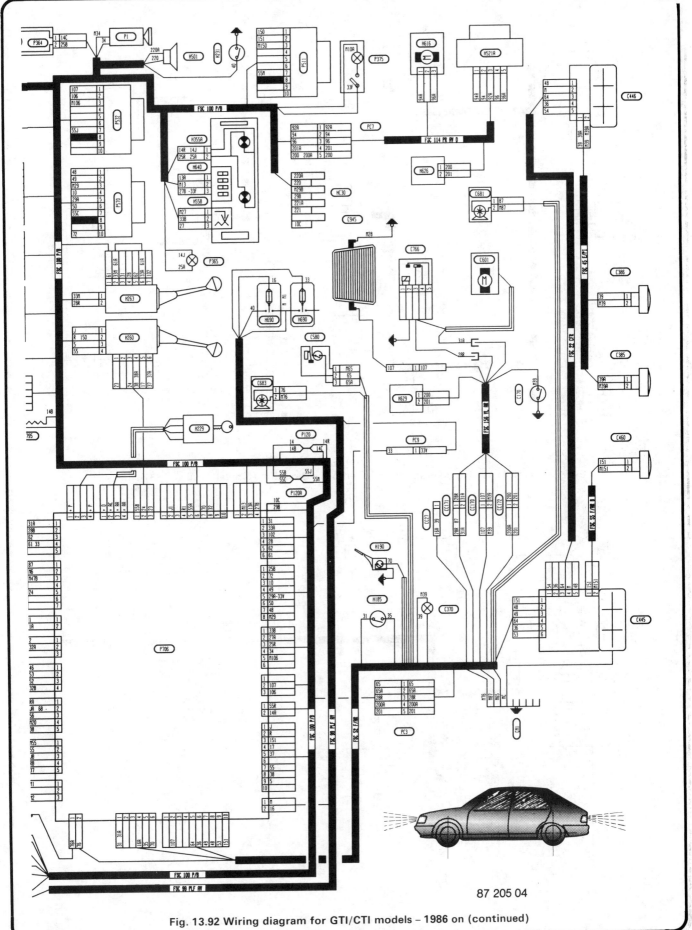

Fig. 13.92 Wiring diagram for GTI/CTI models – 1986 on (continued)

87 205 04

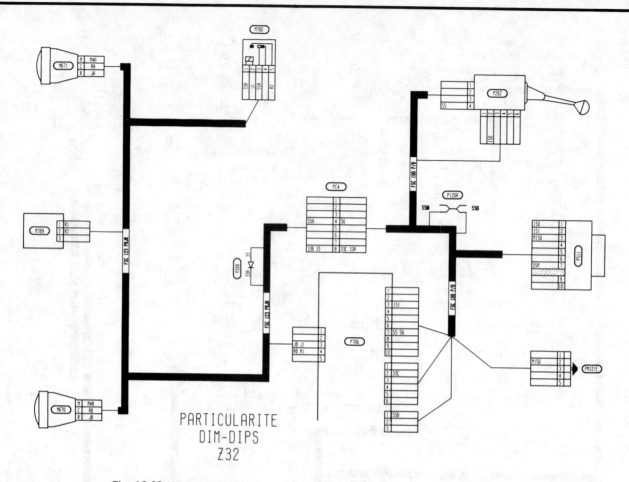

Fig. 13.93 Wiring diagram for automatic transmission (typical) – up to 1987

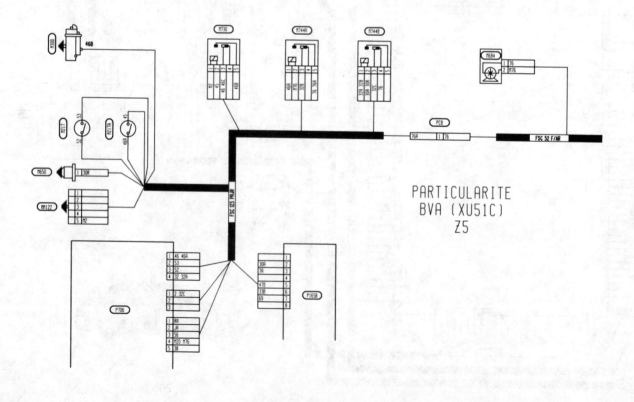

Fig. 13.94 Wiring diagram for dim-dip lighting (typical) – up to 1987

Key to wiring diagrams – 1986 on

1	Cigar lighter, front
3	Cigar lighter, rear
5	Distributor, ignition
10	Alternator
11	Transistor, heater blower control (power transistor)
13	Strut (earth connection)
14	Ammeter (battery charge)
20	Radio aerial, electric
25	Horn
25A	Horn, low note
25B	Horn, high note
27	Connector, towing attachment
28	Dimmer, dipped beams
30	Radio
35	Actuator, fuel output (VP15)
40	Radio balance control, front
41	Radio balance control, front/rear
45	Battery
50	Ignition coil
53	Control box, exhaust emission, for pilot carburettor
54	Emission control unit (ignition advance modulator)
55	Emission control unit (idle retard)
56	Control unit, automatic transmission (idle speed)
57	Alarm unit, theft protection
58	Control unit, injection
60	Control unit, air conditioning
65	Control unit, screenwiper
66	Control box, power steering
75	Control unit, ignition, or pick-up amplifier module
76	Detector unit, bulb failure
80	Cruise control unit
85	Indicator unit, oil level
86	Indicator unit, coolant level
90	Control unit, central door locking
95	Infra red signal receiver (PLIP)
96	Control unit, knock detector
97	Thermostat unit (passenger compartment)
110	Control unit, preheater
111	Control unit, fuel cut-off on overrun
112	Control unit, fuel flow (trip computer)
113	Electronic control unit, advance (Diesel)
114	Control box, coolant temperature, air conditioning
115	Preheater plug
120	Terminal connector
121	Buzzer (P4, warning, coolant temperature, oil pressure, charge warning light)
122	Buzzer, direction indicator (P4)
125	Audible warning, seat belt
126	Audible warning (key in the ignition/steering lock with the driver's door open)
127	Audible warning, excessive speed
128	Audible warning, (lights on, door open or 'STOP' warning lamp on)
130	TDC sensor
131	Altitude sensor
132	Knock detector
133	Sensor, engine speed
134	Sensor, absolute pressure (Diesel)
135	Sensor, potentiometer (econoscope vacuum)
136	Sensor, demisting the rear glass
140	Speed sensor, drive shaft
141	Speed sensor, trip computer
142	Sensor, oil pressure
143	Sensor, No 1 cylinder
144	Sensor, diesel injector needle lifted
145	Direction indicator flasher unit
150	Air temperature sensor (air conditioning)
151	Load sensor (Diesel)
155	Pilot carburettor
160	Battery isolator
165	Instrument panel
167	Connector, emission control setting
169	Switch, starter/preheater
170	Switch, luggage compartment lamp
171	Switch, enrichment (LPG)
175	Switch, door lock
176	Switch, vacuum (LPG)
177	Switch, LH front lock (door open detector)
178	Switch, RH front lock (door open detector)
179	Switch, LH rear lock (door open detector)
180	Switch, RH rear lock (door open detector)
181	Switch, luggage compartment lock (lid open detector)
182	Switch, bonnet lock (bonnet open detector)
185	Switch, stop lamps
186	Switch, brake pedal travel

190	Switch, handbrake
195	Switch, low pressure (Freon)
196	Switch, mean pressure (Freon)
200	Thermal switch (Freon)
205	Switch, glove box lamp
210	Switch, seat belt
211	Switch, display (trip computer)
215	Switch, starter inhibitor
216	Switch, reverse lamps
217	Switch, reverse lamp/starter inhibitor
220	Switch, heating/ventilation fan
221	Switch, heating/ventilation fan (rear)
225	Switch, choke warning light
229	Switch, ignition/steering lock
230	Door switch, LH front
231	Door switch, RH front
232	Door switch, LH rear
233	Door switch, RH rear
234	Control switch, audible warning (ignition key 'in')
235	Switch, brake fluid pressure drop
236	Switch, brake fluid level
237	Switch, coolant level
238	Switch, water sensing, fuel system
239	Switch, washer bottle level
240	Limit switch, sun roof
241	Switch on accelerator pedal (idle speed)
242	Switch, idle speed
243	Switch, power take-off (P4)
247	Switch, rear differential lock
248	Switch, front differential lock
249	Switch, windscreen wiper lockout (P4)
250	Disengaging switch, cruise control (brake)
250A	Disengaging switch, cruise control (clutch)
251	Throttle switch (idling + full load)
260	Control, lighting/direction indicators/horn
261	Control, lighting/screen wiper/screen wash
262	Control, lighting/screen wiper/direction indicator/horn
263	Control, screen wiper/wash
264	Control, lighting/horn
265	Control, direction indicator/horn
266	Switch, cruise control
267	Switch, cruise control/direction indicator
268	Switch, flasher unit (P4)
269	Switch, lighting/blackout (P4)
270	Switch, windscreen wiper (P4)
275	Control, driver's seat position
276	Control, rear view mirror LH
277	Control, rear view mirror RH
280	Supplementary air device (cold start)
281	Corrector, fuel reheating
285	Capacitor, coil positive
286	Capacitor, direction indicator flasher unit
290	Tachometer
295	Compressor
296	Compressor, air horn
300	Starter motor
301	Vapour relief valve (LPG)
302	Diode, relay protection
303	Diode, rear fog lamps
304	Protection diode, electronic control unit
305	Checking diode, coolant temperature warning light
306	Checking diode, brake warning light
307	Diode, air conditioning control
308	Diode, lighting dimmer
309	Diode, electric fan
310	Diode, compressor
311	Diode, roof lamp
312	Diode, speech synthesizer
313	Flow sensor
329	Solenoid valve, cruise control deceleration
330	Solenoid valve, air conditioning
331	Solenoid valve, EGR (pilot carburettor)
332	Solenoid valve, opening the carburettor throttle valve
333	Solenoid valve, injection cut-off on over-run
334	Solenoid, emission control advance modulator
335	Solenoid, exhaust emission
336	Solenoid, carburettor breather
340	Solenoid, pump stop
344	Solenoid, turbine fan
345	Solenoid valve, fast idle stabiliser
346	Solenoid, canister
347	Solenoid, cruise control
348	Advance solenoid, diesel
349	Solenoid valve, temperature control
350	Switches, illumination

351	Illumination, instrument panel
355	Illumination, heating/ventilation control
360	Illumination, console
361	Courtesy lamp
364	Illumination, cigar lighter
365	Illumination, ashtray
370	Illumination, luggage compartment (or tailgate)
375	Illumination, glove box
380	Illumination, engine compartment
385	Illumination, number plate LH
386	Illumination, number plate RH
390	Illumination, ignition switch/steering lock
395	Floor illumination, driver's side
396	Floor illumination, passenger's side
397	Sill illumination, driver's side
398	Sill illumination, passenger side
400	Illumination, gear selector lever
410	Clutch, compressor
420	Idling cut-off, carburettor
425	Map reading lamp
440	Sidelamp LH
441	Sidelamp RH
445	Tail lamp cluster LH
446	Tail lamp cluster RH
452	Marker lamp, LH rear
453	Marker lamp, RH rear
455	Door marker lamp LH
456	Door marker lamp RH
460	Rear fog lamp LH
461	Rear fog lamp RH
462	Reverse lamp
463	Stop lamp
464	Reverse lamp + fog lamp (rear)
465	Suppression filter, tachometer
469	Fuse holder, LAMBDA sensor heater
470	Fuses (fuse box)
471	Fuse holder (radio)
472	Fuse holder (locks)
473	Fuse holder (dipped beams)
474	Fuse holder (speech synthesizer)
475	Fuse holder (carburettor heater)
476	Fuse holder (cruise control)
477	Fuse holder, supply pump
478	Flashing lamps, priority
480	Direction indicator lamp, LH front
481	Direction indicator lamp, RH front
482	Direction indicator lamp, LH rear
483	Direction indicator lamp, RH rear
484	Side lamp/direction indicator, LH front
485	Side lamp/direction indicator, RH front
486	Suppression filter, speech synthesizer
490	Impulse generator (speed)
491	Rotating lamp
500	Loudspeaker, LH front
501	Loudspeaker, RH front
502	Loudspeaker, LH rear
503	Loudspeaker, RH rear
505	Hour meter (P4)
510	Switch, front fog lamps
511	Switch, rear fog lamps
512	Switch, auxiliary driving lamp
513	Switch, siren
514	Switch, rotating lamp
515	Switch, rheostat, instrument panel illumination
516	Switch, parking lights
517	Switch, general (military P4)
518	Test switch, oil, coolant or charging fault (P4)
519	Switch, horn (P4)
520	Switch, window winder (driver's)
521	Switch, window winder (passengers')
521A	Switch, passenger's window winder
522	Switch, window winder, LH rear
523	Switch, window winder, RH rear
524	Switch, window winder, LH rear (in rear compartment)
525	Switch, window winder, RH rear (in rear compartment)
526	Child safety switch, rear window winders
527	Switch, main/dip beams (P4)
530	Switch, sun roof
532	Switch, heated rear window
535	Switch driver's seat heating
536	Switch, passenger's seat heating
540	Switch, preheater
545	Switch, central roof lamp
548	Test switch, brake wear warning light
549	Diagnostic switch, diesel
550	Switch, rear screen wiper
552	Switch, headlamp wiper
555	Switch, fuel supply warning light
556	Switch, police horn
557	Switch, rotating lamp
558	Switch, air fan
560	Switch, warning bell
565	Switch, pressure drop
566	Switch, air conditioning control
567	Switch, cruise control
570	Switch, hazard warning
571	Test switch
572	Switch, lamps (police)
574	Injectors
575	Cold start injector
576	Information display, injection control box
580	Fuel gauge
590	Map reading lamp
591	Indicator, coolant temperature
592	Gauge, turbocharger pressure
593	Fuel gauge
594	Gauge, engine oil temperature
595	Gauge, engine oil pressure
598	Electronic control unit, ignition
600	Motor, screen wiper
601	Motor, window wiper, rear
605	Wiper motor, headlamp LH
606	Wiper motor, headlamp RH
607	Motor, heater control flap
610	Motor, sun roof
615	Motor, LH front window winder
616	Motor, RH front window winder
617	Motor, LH rear window winder
618	Motor, RH rear window winder
620	Motor, heating/ventilation fan
625	Actuator, LH front door lock
626	Actuator, RH front door lock
627	Actuator, LH rear door lock
628	Actuator, RH rear door lock
629	Actuator, luggage compartment lock
630	Motor, fuel filler flap lock
635	Motor, engine cooling fan
636	Motor, air conditioning fan
640	Clock
645	Pressure switch, brake servo
646	Pressure switch, power steering
647	Pressure switch, air conditioning cut-out
650	Oil pressure switch
651	Vacuum-pressure switch
652	Pressure switch, turbocharger cut-out
660	Trip computer
660A	Keyboard, trip computer
660B	Display, trip computer
669	Potentiometer, throttle
669A	Potentiometer, accelerator pedal (Diesel)
670	Headlamp LH
671	Headlamp RH
672	Headlamp blackout (P4)
673	Driving lamp LH
674	Driving lamp RH
675	Brake pads, LH front
676	Brake pads, RH front
677	Brake pads, LH rear
678	Brake pads, RH rear
679	Vacuum pump, cruise control
680	Washer pump, front
681	Washer pump, rear
682	Washer pump, headlamp
683	Pump, fuel supply
684	Scavenge pump
685	Coolant pump, heater matrix
688	Interior lamp, front
689	Interior lamp, rear
690	Interior lamp, centre
691	Interior lamp, LH front
692	Interior lamp, RH front
693	Interior lamp, LH rear
694	Interior lamp, RH rear
697	PLIP
700	Pressure switch
705	Connector board
706	Services connector board
710	Battery supply socket
720	Diagnostic socket
721	Test socket (injection)

Key to wiring diagrams – 1986 on (continued)

723	Front foglamp LH
724	Front foglamp RH
729	Relay, emission control
730	Relay, starter motor
731	Relay, preheater
732	Relay, fan clutch
733	Relay, electric fan motor
734	Relay, hour meter (P4)
735	Relay, main beams
736	Relay, auxiliary driving lamps
737	Relay, dipped beams
738	Relay, heating/ventilation fan, fast speed
740	Relay, coil
741	Relay, coil resistance
742	Relay, cold start control
743	Relay, compressor
744	Tachymetric relay or pump control relay
745	Relay, air horn compressor
746	Tachymetric relay (cut-off on over-run)
747	Relay, CLT
748	Relay, ECU, exhaust emission
749	Relay, cold cut-off
750	Relay, front foglamps
751	Relay, rear foglamps
752	Relay, compressor cut-out (105°)
753	Relay, pump, brake anti-lock
754	Relay, power circuit, brake anti-lock
755	Relay, headlamp wiper
756	Relay, headlamp wiper timer
757	Relay, advance curve selection
760	Relay, heated rear window
761	Relay, rear electric window
762	Relay, front electric window
763	Relay, sunroof
764	Relay, sunroof tilt + central locking
765	Relay, front screen wiper
766	Relay, rear window wiper
767	Relay, bulb failure warning
770	Relay, accessories
771	Relay, visual warning
772	Relay, two-speed (mixture control)
773	Relay, carburettor heater
775	Relay, starter motor isolator
776	Relay, cruise control disengagement
777	Relay, pilot carburettor supply
778	Relay, scavenge pump
780	Relay, lighting dimmer
781	Relay, excessive speed
782	Relay, ignition supply
783	Relay, injection supply
784	Relay, trip computer/cruise control/speech synthesizer information
785	Relay, brake warning (Australia)
786	Resistor, coil
787	Resistor, heating/ventilation fan
788	Resistor, two-speed cooling fan
789	Resistor, lighting dimmer
790	Heater, diesel fuel
791	Heater, carburettor
793	Resistor, preheater (P4)
794	Resistor, injection matching
795	Rheostat, instrument illumination
800	Regulator, voltage
801	Regulator, control pressure
810	Side repeater flasher LH
811	Side repeater flasher RH
812	Rheostat, temperature display
814	Rear view mirror LH
815	Rear view mirror RH
817	Heated seat, front LH
818	Heated seat, front RH
820	Bell
829	Servo, power steering
830	Servo, cruise control
832	Sensor, evaporator
833	Sensor, blown air
834	Sensor, interior air temperature
835	Sensor, oil level
836	Sensor, fuel flow (trip computer)
837	Sensor, coolant level
838	Sensor, mixture regulator
840	Sensor, high temperature
841	Siren
845	Speech synthesizer
846	Sensor, body temperature (exhaust)

847	Sensor, passenger compartment temperature regulation
848	Lambda sensor
849	Sensor, external air temperature
850	Thermal switch, cooling fan (coolant)
852	Thermal switch, transmission oil
853	Thermal switch, 18°C (coolant temperature)
855	Thermal switch, coolant
861	Thermal switch, 40°C (coolant temperature)
862	Thermal switch, 60°C (coolant temperature)
865	Thermostat, electronic (air conditioning)
870	Thermal time switch (cold start opening)
880	Tachograph
885	Timer switch, seat belt
886	Timer switch, interior lamp
887	Timer switch, headlamp wash
888	Sender unit, oil temperature gauge
889	Temperature sender unit, injection
890	Sender unit, coolant temperature gauge
891	Temperature sender unit, electronic (heating/ventilation)
892	Sender unit, engine oil temperature
893	Timer switch, rear screen wiper
893A	Timer switch, windscreen wiper
894	Temperature sender unit, controlling cooling fan motors by ECU (liquid cooling)
895	Sender unit, exhaust emission
896	Thermal resistor, inlet air temperature
897	Tester, anti-lock
898	Sender unit, oil pressure
899	Test unit, variable power steering
929	Proportioning valve, cruise control
930	Fan, electromagnetic clutch
935	Fan, heating/ventilation
936	Fan, heating/ventilation, rear
945	Heated rear window
950	Fan
955	Ram, driver's seat
960	Fan, air conditioning
965	Cold start flap
970	Voltmeter
L1	Warning lamp, seat belt
L2	Warning lamps, direction indicator
L3	Warning lamp, low fuel level
L4	Warning lamp, main beams
L5	Warning lamp, hazard warning
L6	Warning lamp, side/tail lamps 'on'
L7	Warning lamp, no battery charge
L8	Warning lamp, preheater
L9	Warning lamp, choke control
L10	Warning lamp, oil pressure
L11	Warning lamp, oil and coolant
L12	Warning lamp, coolant temperature
L13	Warning lamp, brake safety
L14	Warning lamp, rear foglamps
L15	Warning lamp, fuel supply
L16	Warning lamp, stop
L17	Warning lamp, brake fluid/stop-lamps
L18	Warning lamp, sidelamp failure
L19	Warning lamp, tail lamp failure
L20	Warning lamp, screenwash level
L21	Warning lamp, coolant level
L22	Warning lamp, engine oil level
L23	Warning lamp, brake pad wear
L24	Manual test switch, instrument panel
L25	Warning lamp, oil temperature
L26	Warning lamp, 'door open'
L27	Warning lamp, tail lamp or rear foglamp failure
L30	Warning lamp, rear differential lock
L31	Warning lamp, front differential lock
L32	Warning lamp, knock detector
L33	Warning lamp, diagnosis
L34	Warning lamp, water in fuel
L35	Warning lamp, dipped beams
L36	Warning lamp, trailer direction indicator
L37	Warning light, power take-off (P4)
L38	Warning lamp, catalytic converter
L39	Warning lamp, brake anti-lock alert
+AA	Supply from accessories terminal
+P	Supply from battery
+D	Supply from starter motor
+AC	Supply from ignition switch
M	Earth connections
BL	Screened cable

The wires are not colour-coded; just given identification numbers/letters to aid the tracing of circuits

Not all items are fitted to all models

H706 – 205 all models – ⊢→ 5820 001
→⊦ 7330 000

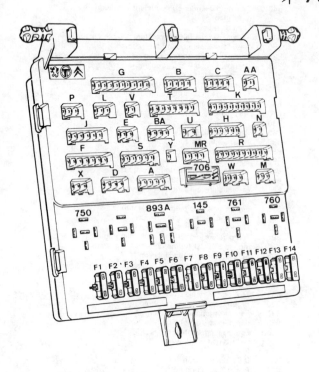

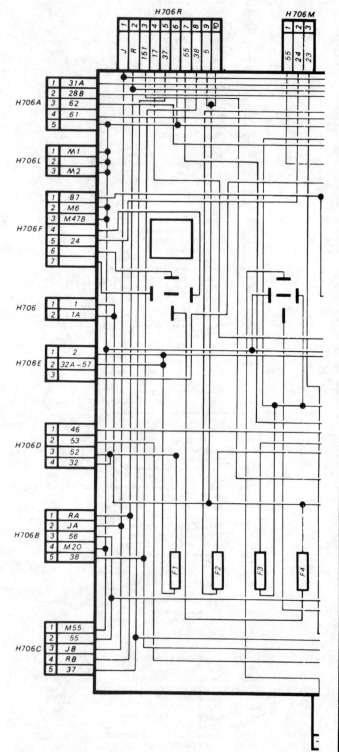

F1 – 10 A
F2 – 25 A
F3 – 25 A
F4 –
F5 – 10 A
F6 –
F7 – 25 A
F8 – 25 A
F9 – 20 A
F10 – 5 A
F11 – 5 A
F12 – 5 A
F13 – 5 A
F14 – 15 A

Fig. 13.95 Wiring diagram for fuse/relay/connector board – chassis no 5 820 001 to 7 330 000

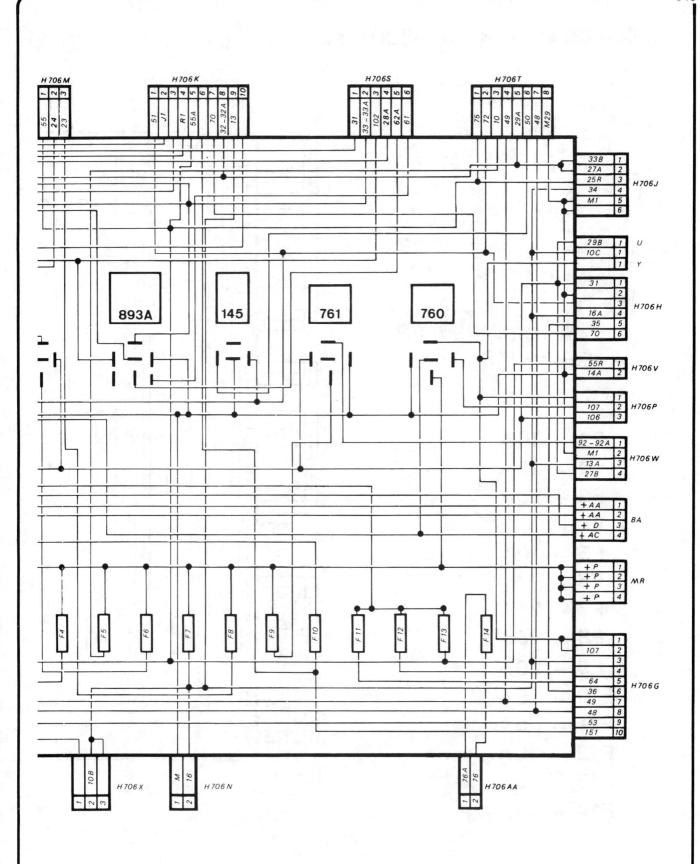

Fig. 13.95 Wiring diagram for fuse/relay/connector board – chassis no 5 820 001 to 7 330 000 (continued)

H706 – 205 all models - $\mapsto$ 7330 001

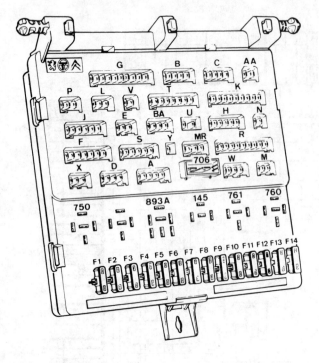

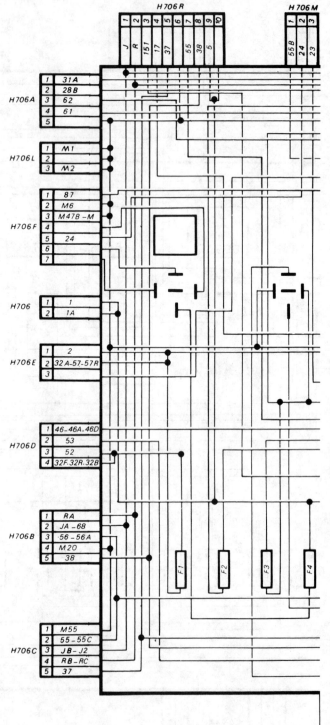

F1 – 10 A
F2 – 25 A
F3 – 25 A
F4 –
F5 – 10 A
F6 –
F7 – 25 A
F8 – 25 A
F9 – 20 A
F10 – 5 A
F11 – 5 A
F12 – 5 A
F13 – 5 A
F14 – 15 A

Fig. 13.96 Wiring diagram for fuse/relay/connector board – chassis no 7 330 001 on

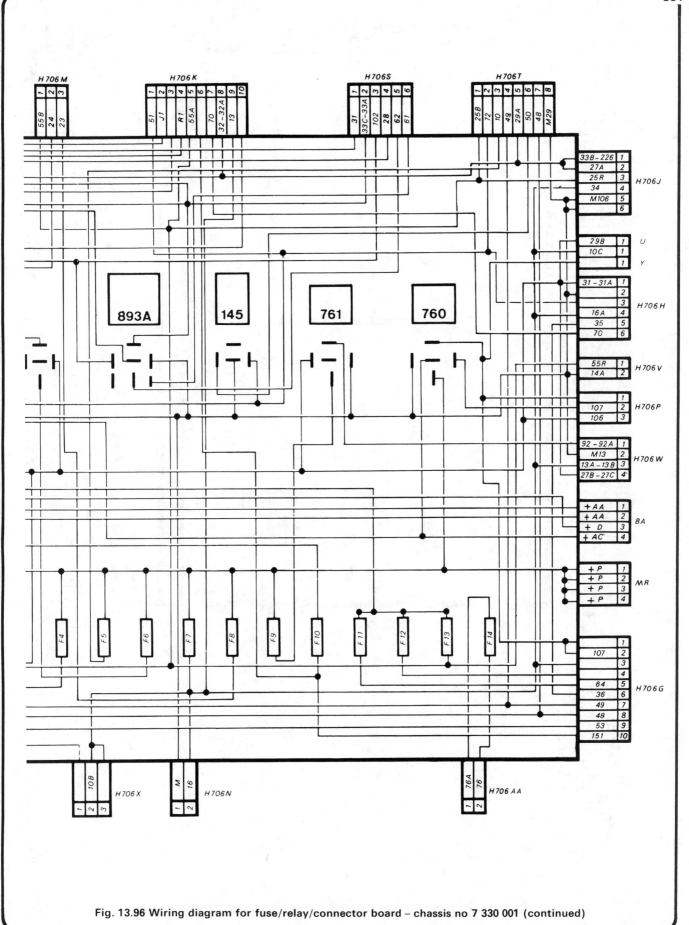

Fig. 13.96 Wiring diagram for fuse/relay/connector board – chassis no 7 330 001 (continued)

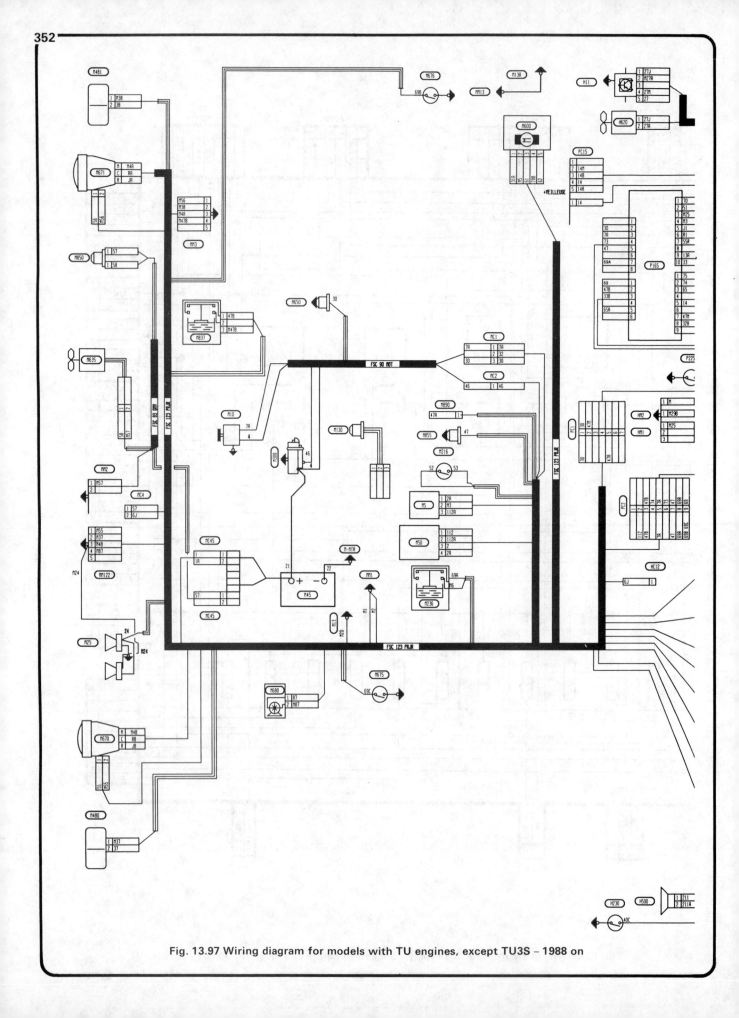

Fig. 13.97 Wiring diagram for models with TU engines, except TU3S – 1988 on

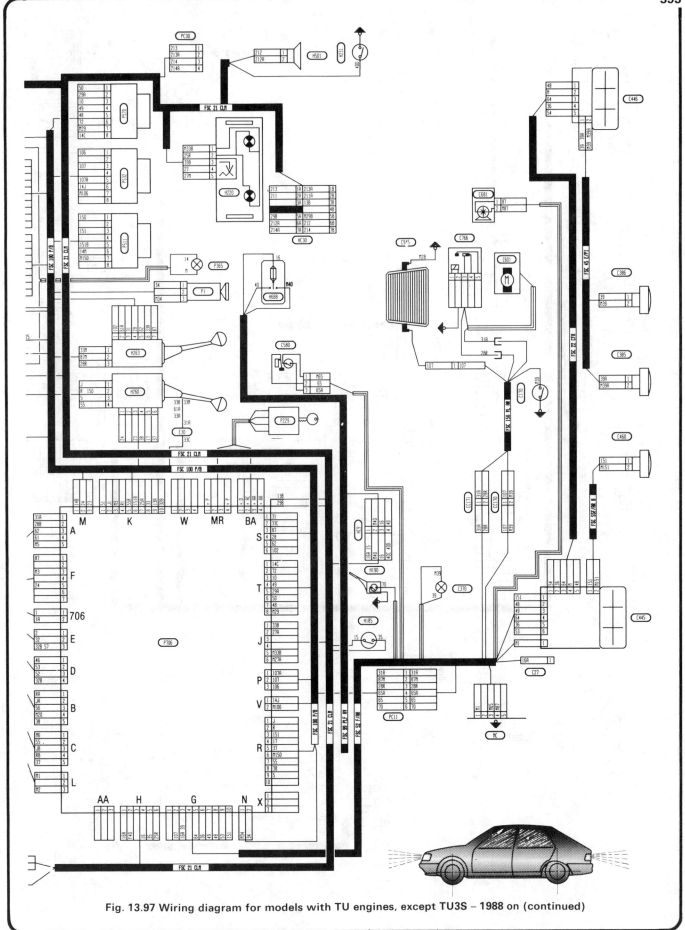

Fig. 13.97 Wiring diagram for models with TU engines, except TU3S – 1988 on (continued)

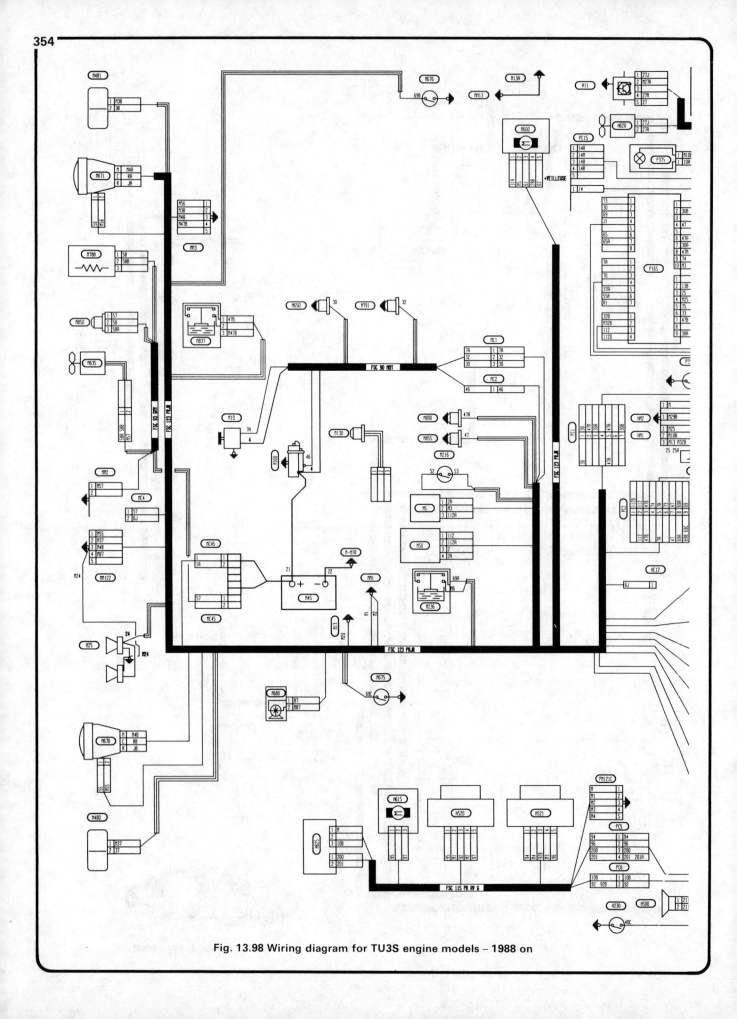

Fig. 13.98 Wiring diagram for TU3S engine models – 1988 on

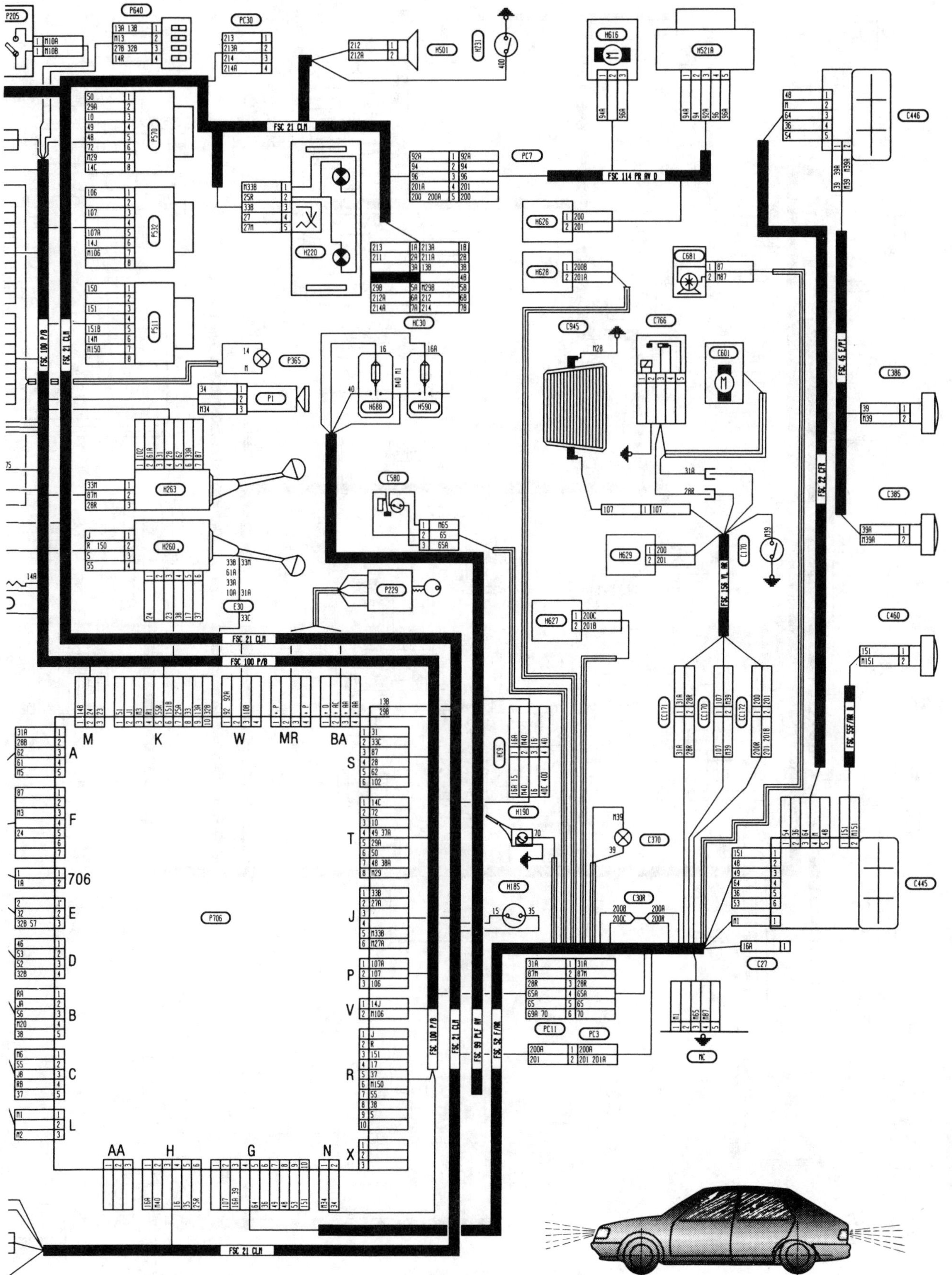

Fig. 13.98 Wiring diagram for TU3S engine models – 1988 on (continued)

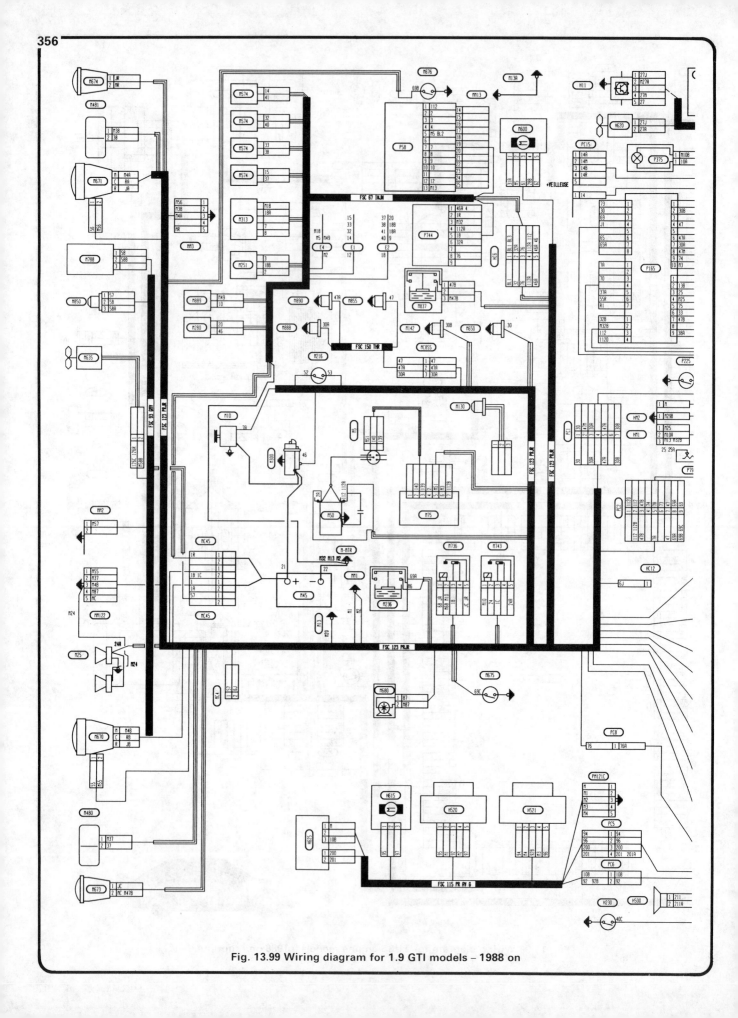

Fig. 13.99 Wiring diagram for 1.9 GTI models – 1988 on

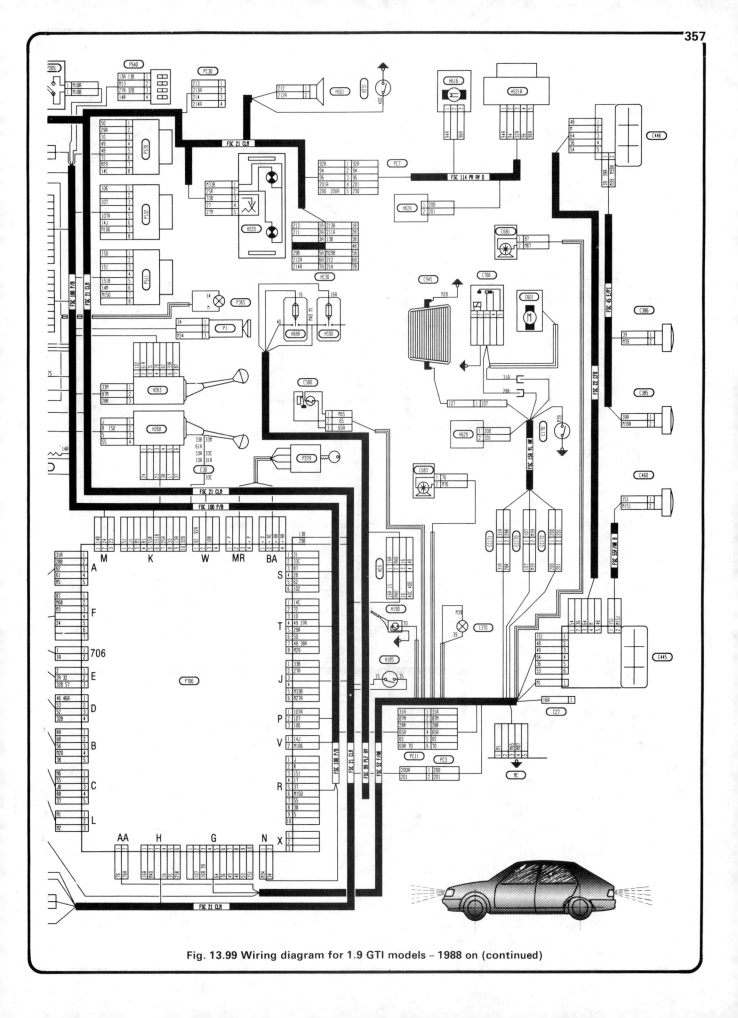

Fig. 13.99 Wiring diagram for 1.9 GTI models – 1988 on (continued)

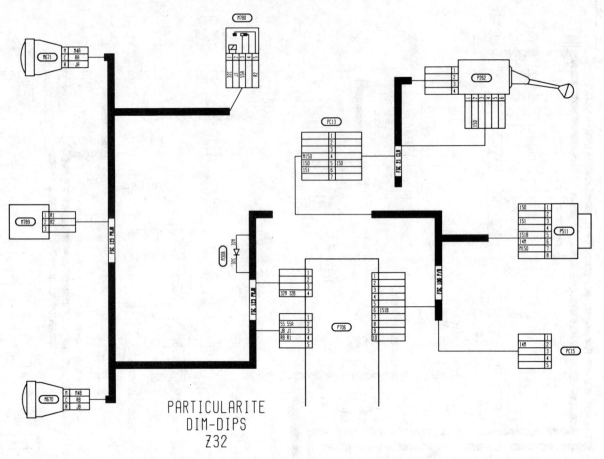

Fig. 13.100 Wiring diagram for dim-dip lighting – **1988 on**

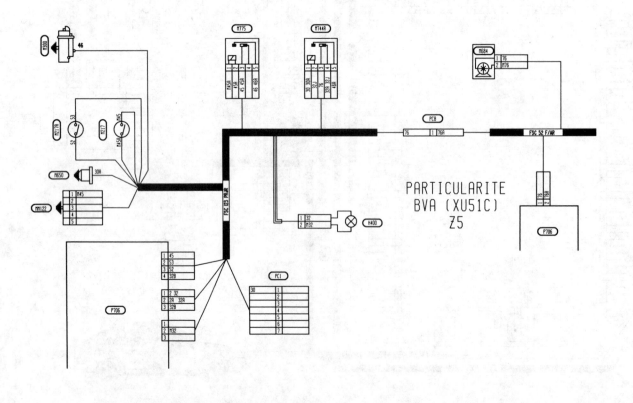

Fig. 13.101 Wiring diagram for automatic transmission – **1988 on**

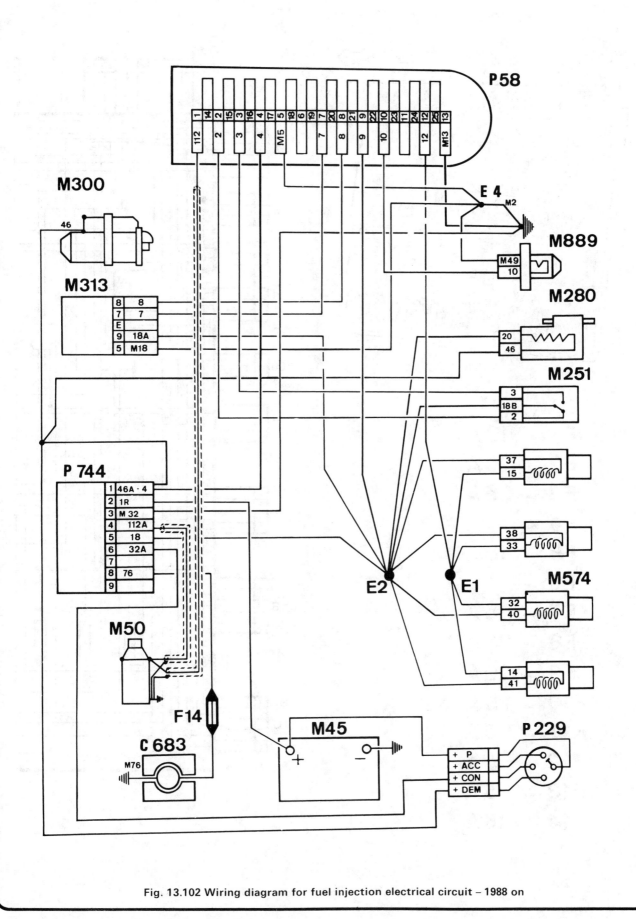

Fig. 13.102 Wiring diagram for fuel injection electrical circuit – 1988 on

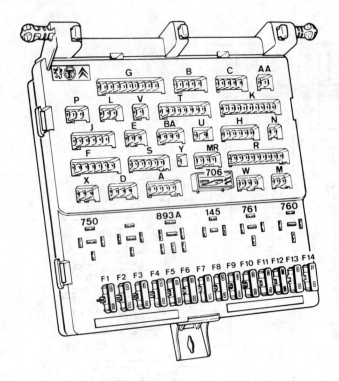

F1 – 10 A
F2 – 25 A
F3 – 25 A
F4 –
F5 – 10 A
F6 –
F7 – 25 A
F8 – 25 A
F9 – 20 A
F10 – 5 A
F11 – 5 A
F12 – 5 A
F13 – 5 A
F14 – 15 A

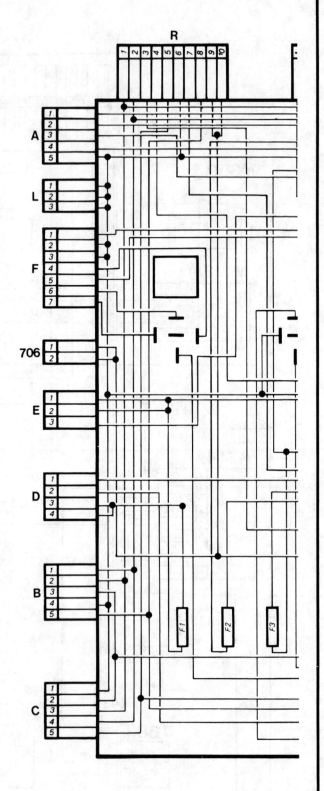

Fig. 13.103 Wiring diagram for fuse/relay/connector board – **1988 on**

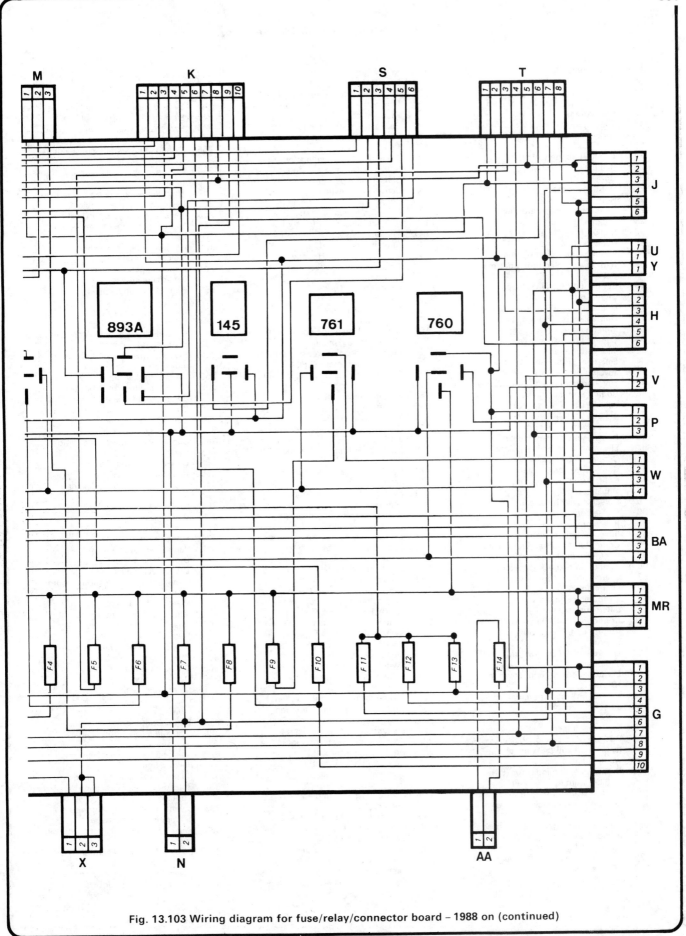

Fig. 13.103 Wiring diagram for fuse/relay/connector board – 1988 on (continued)

Key to wiring diagrams 1988 on

1	Cigar lighter, front	132	Knock sensor		speed)
3	Cigar lighter, rear	133	Sensor, engine speed	242	Switch, idle speed
5	Distributor, ignition	134	Sensor, absolute pressure (Diesel)	243	Switch, power take-off (P4)
5	Idling actuator (idling solenoid)	135	Sensor, potentiometer (econoscope	247	Switch, rear differential lock
10	Alternator		vacuum)	248	Switch, front differential lock
11	Transistor, heater blower control	136	Sensor, demisting the rear glass	249	Switch, windscreen wiper lockout
	(power transistor)	137	Pressure sensor, inlet manifold		(P4)
13	Strut (earth connection)	138	Pressure sensor	250	Disengaging switch, cruise control
14	Ammeter (battery charge)	140	Speed sensor, speedometer cable		(brake)
20	Radio aerial, electric	141	Speed sensor, trip computer	250A	Disengaging switch, cruise control
25	Horn	142	Sensor, oil pressure		(clutch)
25A	Horn, low note	143	Sensor, No.1 cylinder	251	Throttle switch (idling + full load)
25B	Horn, high note	144	Sensor, diesel injector needle lifted	252	Level switch, brake antilock
27	Connector, towing attachment	145	Direction indicator flasher unit.	253	Switch, driver's passive seat belt
28	Dimmer, dipped beams	146	Antilock sensor, LH front wheel	254	Switch, passenger's passive seat
30	Radio	147	Antilock sensor, RH front wheel		belt
35	Actuator, fuel output (VP15)	148	Antilock sensor, LH rear wheel	260	Control, lighting/direction
40	Radio balance control, front	149	Antilock sensor, RH rear wheel		indicators/horn
41	Radio balance control, front/rear	150	Air temperature sensor, (air	261	Control, lighting/screen
45	Battery		conditioning)		wiper/screen wash
46	Control unit, positive supply	151	Load sensor (Diesel)	262	Control, lighting/screen
47	Diodes unit	155	Pilot carburettor		wiper/direction indicator/horn
48	Unit, electric pump group (EPG)	160	Battery isolator	263	Control, screen wiper/wash
49	Unit, fuse board group (FBG)	165	Instrument panel	264	Control, lighting/horn
50	Ignition coil	167	Connector, emission control setting	265	Control, direction indicator/horn
53	Control box, exhaust emission, for	169	Switch, starter/preheater	266	Switch, cruise control
	pilot carburettor	170	Switch, luggage compartment lamp	267	Switch, cruise control/direction
54	Emission control unit (ignition	171	Switch, enrichment (LPG)		indicator
	advance modulator)	172	Switch, air filter clogging warning	268	Switch, flasher unit
55	Emission control unit (idle retard)		lamp	269	Switch, lighting/blackout (P4)
56	Control unit, automatic	173	Switch, number plate	270	Switch, windscreen wiper (P4)
	transmission (idle speed)	175	Switch, door lock	275	Control, driver's seat position
57	Alarm unit, theft protection	176	Switch, vacuum (LPG)	276	Control, rear view mirror LH
58	Control unit, injection	177	Switch, LH front lock (door open	277	Control, rear view mirror RH
60	Control unit, air conditioning		detector)	280	Supplementary air device (cold
61	Electronic unit, brake antilock	178	Switch, RH front lock (door open		start)
65	Control unit, screenwiper		detector)	281	Corrector, fuel reheating
66	Control box, power steering	179	Switch, LH rear lock (door open	285	Capacitor, coil positive
75	Control unit, ignition, or pick-up		detector)	286	Capacitor, direction indicator
	amplifier module	180	Switch, RH rear lock (door open		flasher unit
76	Detector unit, bulb failure		detector)	290	Tachometer
80	Cruise control unit	181	Switch, luggage compartment lock	295	Compressor
85	Indicator unit, oil level		(lid open detector)	296	Compressor, air horn
86	Indicator unit, coolant level	182	Switch, bonnet lock (bonnet open	300	Starter motor
90	Control unit, central door locking		detector)	301	Vapour relief valve (LPG)
95	Infra red signal receiver (PLIP)	185	Switch, stop lamps	302	Diode, relay protection
96	Control unit, knock detector	186	Switch, brake pedal travel	303	Diode, rear fog lamps
97	Thermostat unit (passenger	190	Switch, handbrake	304	Protection diode, electronic control
	compartment)	195	Switch, low pressure (Freon)		unit
98	Electronic control unit for	196	Switch, mean pressure (Freon)	305	Checking diode, coolant
	differential locking	200	Thermal switch (Freon)		temperature warning light
110	Control unit, preheater	205	Switch, glove box lamp	306	Checking diode, brake warning
111	Control unit, fuel cut-off on	210	Switch, seat belt		light
	overrun	211	Switch, display (trip computer)	307	Diode, air conditioning control
112	Control unit, fuel flow (trip	215	Switch, starter inhibitor	308	Diode, lighting dimmer
	computer)	216	Switch, reverse lamps	309	Diode, electric fan
113	Electronic control unit, advance	217	Switch, reverse lamp/starter	310	Diode, compressor
	(Diesel)		inhibitor	311	Diode, roof lamp
114	Control box, coolant temperature,	220	Switch, heating/ventilation fan	312	Diode, speech synthesizer
	air conditioning	221	Switch, heating/ventilation fan	313	Flow sensor
115	Preheater plug		(rear)	314	Diode, boot locking
120	Terminal connector	225	Switch, choke warning light	328	Solenoid valve, turbo-charge
121	Buzzer (P4, warning, coolant	229	Switch, ignition/steering lock		regulator
	temperature, oil pressure, charge	230	Door switch, LH front	329	Solenoid valve, cruise control
	warning light)	231	Door switch, RH front		deceleration
122	Buzzer, direction indicator (P4)	232	Door switch, LH rear	330	Solenoid valve, air conditioning
125	Audible warning, seat belt	233	Door switch, RH rear	331	Solenoid valve, EGR (pilot
126	Audible warning (key in the	234	Control switch, audible warning		carburettor)
	ignition/steering lock with the		(ignition key 'in')	332	Solenoid valve, opening the
	driver's door open)	235	Switch, brake fluid pressure drop		carburettor throttle valve
127	Audible warning, excessive speed	236	Switch, brake fluid level	333	Solenoid valve, injection cut-off on
128	Audible warning (lights on, door	237	Switch, coolant level		over-run
	open or 'STOP' warning lamp on)	238	Switch, water sensing, fuel system	334	Solenoid, emission control advance
129	Condenser, radio interference	239	Switch, washer bottle level		modulator
130	TDC sensor	240	Limit switch, sunroof	335	Solenoid, exhaust emission
131	Altitude sensor	241	Switch on accelerator pedal (idle	336	Solenoid, carburettor breather

Key to wiring diagrams 1988 on (continued)

337	Main solenoid, brake antilock
338	Control solenoid, brake antilock
340	Solenoid, pump stop
343	Solenoid valve, air intake
344	Solenoid, turbine fan
345	Solenoid valve, fast idle stabiliser
346	Solenoid, canister
347	Solenoid, cruise control
348	Advance solenoid, diesel
349	Solenoid valve, temperature control
350	Switches, illumination
351	Illumination, instrument panel
355	Illumination, heating/ventilation control
360	Illumination, console
361	Courtesy lamp
364	Illumination, cigar lighter
365	Illumination, ashtray
370	Illumination, luggage compartment (or tailgate)
375	Illumination, glove box
380	Illumination, engine compartment
385	Illumination, number plate LH
386	Illumination, number plate RH
390	Illumination, ignition switch/steering lock
395	Floor illumination, driver's side
396	Floor illumination, passenger's side
397	Sill illumination, driver's side
398	Sill illumination, passenger side
400	Illumination, gear selector lever
410	Clutch, compressor
420	Idling cut-off, carburettor
425	Map reading lamp
440	Sidelamp LH
441	Sidelamp RH
445	Tail lamp cluster LH
446	Tail lamp cluster RH
452	Marker lamp, LH rear
453	Marker lamp, RH rear
455	Door marker lamp LH
456	Door marker lamp RH
457	Front fog lamp RH
458	Front fog lamp LH
459	Fuse holder (front fog lamps)
460	Rear fog lamp LH
461	Rear fog lamp RH
462	Reverse lamp
463	Stop lamp
464	Reverse lamp + fog lamp (rear)
465	Suppresion filter, tachometer
466	Fuse holder (+ accessories, brake antilock)
467	Fuse holder (for warning light, brake antilock)
468	Fuse holder (power circuit, brake antilock)
469	Fuse holder, LAMBDA sensor heater
470	Fuses (fuse box)
471	Fuse holder (radio)
472	Fuse holder (locks)
473	Fuse holder (dipped beams)
474	Fuse holder (speech synthesizer)
475	Fuse holder (carburettor heater)
476	Fuse holder (cruise control)
477	Fuse holder, supply pump
477A	Fuse holder (injection and ignition control unit supply)
478	Flashing lamps, priority
479	Fuse holder (pump, brake antilock)
480	Direction indicator lamp, LH front
481	Direction indicator lamp, RH front
482	Direction indicator lamp, LH rear
483	Direction indicator lamp, RH rear
484	Side lamp/direction indicator, LH

	front
485	Side lamp/direction indicator, RH front
486	Suppression filter, speech synthesizer
487	Fuse holder (control unit, fuel output VP15)
488	Fuse holder (control unit, advance regulator VP15)
489	Fuse holder, cooling fan group (CFG)
490	Impulse generator (speed)
491	Rotating lamp
500	Loudspeaker, LH front
501	Loudspeaker, RH front
502	Loudspeaker, LH rear
503	Loudspeaker, RH rear
505	Hour meter (P4)
510	Switch, front fog lamps
511	Switch, rear fog lamps
512	Switch, auxiliary driving lamp
513	Switch, siren
514	Switch, rotating lamp
515	Switch, rheostat, instrument panel illumination
516	Switch, parking lights
517	Switch, general (military P4)
518	Test switch, oil, coolant or charging fault (P4)
519	Switch, horn (P4)
520	Switch, window winder (driver's)
521	Switch, window winder (passenger's)
521A	Switch, passenger's window winder
522	Switch, window winder, LH rear
523	Switch, window winder, RH rear
524	Switch, window winder, LH rear (in rear compartment)
525	Switch, window winder, RH rear (in rear compartment)
527	Switch, main/dip beams
530	Switch, sun roof
532	Switch, heated rear window
535	Switch, driver's seat heating
536	Switch, passenger's seat heating
540	Switch, preheater
545	Switch, central roof lamp
548	Test switch, brake wear warning light
549	Diagnostic switch, diesel
550	Switch, rear screen wiper
552	Switch, headlamp wiper
555	Switch, fuel supply warning light
556	Switch, police horn
557	Switch, rotating lamp
558	Switch, air fan
560	Switch, warning bell
565	Switch, pressure drop
566	Switch, air conditioning control
567	Switch, cruise control
570	Switch, hazard warning
571	Test switch
572	Switch, lamps (police)
574	Injectors
575	Cold start injector
576	Information display, injection control box
580	Fuel tank unit
590	Map reading lamp
591	Indicator, coolant temperature
592	Gauge, turbocharger pressure
593	Fuel gauge
594	Gauge, engine oil temperature
595	Gauge, engine oil pressure
598	Electronic control unit, ignition

600	Motor, screen wiper
601	Motor, window wiper, rear
605	Wiper motor, headlamp LH
606	Wiper motor, headlamp RH
607	Motor, heater control flap
610	Motor, sun roof
615	Motor, LH front window winder
616	Motor, RH front window winder
617	Motor, LH rear window winder
618	Motor, RH window winder
620	Motor, heating/ventilation fan
625	Actuator, LH front door lock
626	Actuator, RH front door lock
627	Actuator, LH rear door lock
628	Actuator, RH rear door lock
629	Actuator, luggage compartment lock
630	Motor, fuel filler flap lock
631	Motor, driver's passive seat belt
632	Motor, passenger's passive seat belt
635	Motor, engine cooling fan
636	Motor, air conditioning fan
640	Clock
645	Pressure switch, brake servo
646	Pressure switch, power steering
647	Pressure switch, air conditioning cut-out
650	Oil pressure switch
651	Vacuum-pressure switch
652	Pressure switch, turbocharger cut-out
653	Full throttle enrichment switch
654	Advance curve selection switch
660	Trip computer
660A	Keyboard, trip computer
660B	Display, trip computer
668	PTC (positive temperature coefficient resistance)
669	Potentiometer, throttle
669A	Potentiometer, accelerator pedal (Diesel)
670	Headlamp LH
671	Headlamp RH
672	Headlamp blackout (P4)
673	Driving lamp LH
674	Driving lamp RH
675	Brake pads, LH front
676	Brake pads, RH front
677	Brake pads, LH rear
678	Brake pads, RH rear
679	Vacuum pump, cruise control
680	Washer pump, front
681	Washer pump, rear
682	Washer pump, headlamp
683	Fuel supply pump
684	Scavenge pump
685	Coolant pump, heater matrix
686	Hydraulic pump, brake antilock
688	Interior lamp, front
689	Interior lamp, rear
690	Interior lamp, centre
691	Interior lamp, LH front
692	Interior lamp, RH front
693	Interior lamp, LH rear
694	Interior lamp, RH rear
697	PLIP
700	Pressure switch
705	Connector board
706	Services connector board
710	Battery supply socket
720	Diagnostic socket
721	Test socket (injection)
723	Front fog lamp LH
724	Front fog lamp RH
727	Lambda sensor heating relay
728	Relay, passive seat belt (non

Key to wiring diagrams 1988 on (continued)

	motorised)
729	Relay, emission control
730	Relay, starter motor
731	Relay, preheater
732	Relay, fan clutch
733	Relay, electric fan motor
734	Relay, hour meter (P4)
735	Relay, main beams
736	Relay, auxiliary driving lamps
737	Relay, dipped beams
738	Relay, heating/ventilation fan, fast speed
740	Relay, coil
741	Relay, coil resistance
742	Relay, cold start control
743	Relay, compressor
744	Tachymetric relay or pump control relay
745	Relay, air horn compressor
746	Tachymetric relay (cut-off on over-run)
747	Relay, CLT
748	Relay, ECU, exhaust emission
749	Relay, cold cut-off
750	Relay, front fog lamps
751	Relay, rear fog lamps
752	Relay, compressor cut-off (105°)
753	Relay, pump, brake antilock
754	Relay, power circuit, brake antilock
755	Relay, headlamp wiper
756	Relay, headlamp wiper timer
757	Relay, advance curve selection
758	Relay, brake warning lamp (anti-lock brake system)
760	Relay, heater rear window
761	Relay, rear electric window
762	Relay, front electric window
763	Relay, sun roof
764	Relay, sun roof tilt + central locking
765	Relay, front screen wiper
766	Relay, rear window wiper
767	Relay, warning light occultation (P4)
770	Relay, accessories
771	Relay, visual warning
772	Relay, two-speed (mixture control)
773	Relay, carburettor heater
775	Relay, starter motor isolator
776	Relay, cruise control disengagement
777	Relay, pilot carburettor supply
778	Relay, scavenge pump
779	PTC resistance control relay
780	Relay, lighting dimmer
781	Relay, excessive speed
82	Relay, ignition supply
783	Relay, injection supply
784	Relay, trip computer/cruise control/speech synthesizer information
785	Relay, brake warning (Australia)
786	Resistor, coil
787	Resistor, heating/ventilation fan
788	Resistor, two-speed cooling fan

789	Resistor, lighting dimmer
790	Heater, diesel fuel
791	Heater, carburettor
793	Resistor, preheater (P4)
794	Resistor, injection matching
795	Rheostat, instrument illumination
800	Regulator, voltage
801	Regulator, control pressure
810	Side repeater flasher LH
811	Side repeater flasher RH
812	Rheostat, temperature display
814	Rear view mirror LH
815	Rear view mirror RH
817	Heated seat, front LH
818	Heated seat, front RH
820	Bell
821	Diagnostic test socket
829	Servo, power steering
830	Servo, cruise control
832	Sensor, evaporator
833	Sensor, blown air
834	Sensor, interior air temperature
835	Sensor, oil level
836	Sensor, fuel flow (trip computer)
837	Sensor, coolant level
838	Sensor, mixture regulator
840	Sensor, high temperature
841	Siren
845	Speech synthesizer
846	Sensor, body temperature (exhaust)
847	Sensor, passenger compartment temperature regulation
848	Lambda sensor
849	Sensor, external air temperature
850	Thermal switch, cooling fan (coolant)
852	Thermal switch, transmission oil
853	Thermal switch, 18°C (coolant temperature)
855	Thermal switch, coolant
861	Thermal switch, 40°C (coolant temperature)
862	Thermal switch, 60°C (coolant temperature)
865	Thermostat, electronic (air conditioning)
870	Thermal time switch (cold start opening)
871	Temperature switch 15 degrees (air temperature)
880	Tachograph
885	Timer switch, seat belt
886	Timer switch, interior lamp
887	Timer switch, headlamp wash
888	Sender unit, oil temperature gauge
889	Temperature sender unit, injection
890	Sender unit, coolant temperature gauge
891	Temperature sender unit, electronic (heating/ventilation)
892	Sender unit, engine oil temperature
893	Timer switch, rear screen wiper
893A	Timer switch, windscreen wiper
894	Temperature sender unit, controlling cooling fan motors by

	ECU (liquid cooling)
895	Sender unit, exhaust emission
896	Thermal resistor, inlet air temperature
897	Tester, anti-lock
898	Sender unit, oil pressure
899	Test unit, variable power steering
929	Proportioning valve, cruise control
930	Fan, electromagnetic clutch
935	Fan, heating/ventilation
936	Fan, heating/ventilation, rear
945	Heated rear window
950	Fan
955	Ram, driver's seat
960	Fan, air conditioning
965	Cold start flap
970	Voltmeter
L1	Warning lamp, seat belt
L2	Warning lamps, direction indicator
L3	Warning lamp, low fuel level
L4	Warning lamp, main beams
L5	Warning lamp, hazard warning
L6	Warning lamp, side/tail lamps 'on'
L7	Warning lamp, no battery charge
L8	Warning lamp, preheater
L9	Warning lamp, choke control
L10	Warning lamp, oil pressure
L11	Warning lamp, oil and coolant
L12	Warning lamp, coolant temperature
L13	Warning lamp, brake safety
L14	Warning lamp, rear fog lamps
L15	Warning lamp, fuel supply
L16	Warning lamp, "stop"
L17	Warning lamp, brake fluid/stop lamps
L18	Warning lamp, sidelamp failure
L19	Warning lamp, tail lamp failure
L20	Warning lamp, screenwash level
L21	Warning lamp, coolant level
L22	Warning lamp, engine oil level
L23	Warning lamp, brake pad wear
L24	Manual test switch, instrument panel
L25	Warning lamp, oil temperature
L26	Warning lamp, 'door open'
L27	Warning lamp, tail lamp or rear fog lamp failure
L30	Warning lamp, rear differential lock
L31	Warning lamp, front differential lock
L32	Warning lamp, knock detector
L33	Warning lamp, diagnosis
L34	Warning lamp, water in fuel -
L35	Warning lamp, dipped beams
L36	Warning lamp, trailer direction indicator
L37	Warning light, power take-off (P4)
L38	Warning lamp, catalytic converter
L39	Warning lamp, brake antilock alert
+AA	Supply from accessories terminal
+P	Supply from battery
+D	Supply from starter motor
+AC	Supply from ignition switch
M	Earth connections
BL	Screened cable

Index